Banking and Financial
Services Regulation

Banking and Financial Services Regulation

Third edition

William Blair QC
Barrister, 3 Verulam Buildings, Gray's Inn

Austin Allison BA (Oxon), BCL, FCIArb
Barrister. Partner, TT International Investment Management

Guy Morton MA (Oxon)
Partner, Freshfields Bruckhaus Deringer

Peter Richards-Carpenter MA (Oxon)
Partner, Mayer, Brown, Rowe & Maw

George Walker LLB, DAES (Bruges), LLM (Lond), PhD (Lond)
Senior Fellow, Centre for Commercial Law Studies. Consultant, Farrer & Co

Nicholas Walmsley MA (Cantab)
Barrister. Solicitor. Director, Compliance, Dresdner Kleinwort Wasserstein

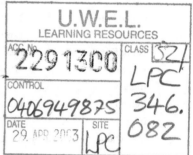

With contributions by:

Richard Alexander MA (Cantab), Dip Law
Research Officer in European and Financial Services Law, Institute of Advanced Legal Studies

Susan Brownlie BA, ACCA
Director, Financial Regulation, KPMG

Andrew Haynes BA (Hons) Law, PhD, Cert Ed, FSALS
Head, Institute of Finance Law, University of Wolverhampton

Owen Watkins MA, DPhil (Oxon)
Barrister. Member of the General Counsel's Division, Financial Services Authority

Consultant Editor:

Keith Palmer MBA, MSI, MCMI
Solicitor and former Global Head of Compliance, Dresdner Kleinwort Wasserstein

Butterworths
LexisNexis™

Members of the LexisNexis Group worldwide

United Kingdom	LexisNexis Butterworths Tolley, a Division of Reed Elsevier (UK) Ltd, Halsbury House, 35 Chancery Lane, LONDON, WC2A 1EL, and 4 Hill Street, EDINBURGH EH2 3JZ
Argentina	LexisNexis Argentina, BUENOS AIRES
Australia	LexisNexis Butterworths, CHATSWOOD, New South Wales
Austria	LexisNexis Verlag ARD Orac GmbH & Co KG, VIENNA
Canada	LexisNexis Butterworths, MARKHAM, Ontario
Chile	LexisNexis Chile Ltda, SANTIAGO DE CHILE
Czech Republic	Nakladatelství Orac sro, PRAGUE
France	Editions du Juris-Classeur SA, PARIS
Hong Kong	LexisNexis Butterworths, HONG KONG
Hungary	HVG-Orac, BUDAPEST
India	LexisNexis Butterworths, NEW DELHI
Ireland	Butterworths (Ireland) Ltd, DUBLIN
Italy	Giuffrè Editore, MILAN
Malaysia	Malayan Law Journal Sdn Bhd, KUALA LUMPUR
New Zealand	LexisNexis Butterworths, WELLINGTON
Poland	Wydawnictwo Prawnicze LexisNexis, WARSAW
Singapore	LexisNexis Butterworths, SINGAPORE
South Africa	Butterworths SA, DURBAN
Switzerland	Stämpfli Verlag AG, BERNE
USA	LexisNexis, DAYTON, Ohio

A CIP Catalogue record for this book is available from the British Library.

First edition 1993
Second edition 1998

ISBN 0 406 94987 5

Typeset by Kerrypress Ltd, Luton, Bedfordshire
Printed and bound by Bookcraft, Midsomer Norton, Bath

Visit Butterworths LexisNexis *direct* at www.butterworths.com

Preface

The third edition of *Banking and Financial Services Regulation* follows the now nearly complete implementation of the regulatory reforms first announced in 1997, and has been largely rewritten. There have also been some changes in the team of authors, to all of whom I am very grateful. Chapters 1, 10 and 20 were written by William Blair QC (with a contribution to Chapter 10 by Nicholas Walmsley), Chapters 2, 6, 15–18 and 21 by Dr George Walker, Chapters 3, 4 and 9 by Guy Morton, Chapter 5 by Nicholas Walmsley, Chapters 7, 13 and 14 by Austin Allison (with a contribution to Chapter 14 by Nicholas Walmsley), Chapter 8 by Austin Allison and Owen Watkins, Chapter 11 by Dr Andrew Haynes, Chapter 12 by Susan Brownlie and Chapter 19 by Richard Alexander and Peter Richards-Carpenter. I would also like to thank Keith Palmer for his encouragement and support, though he has not written for this edition.

We all thank Butterworths for the exceptional efforts made to publish this book efficiently and promptly. Needless to say any errors or infelicities are the authors' responsibility.

Bill Blair
October 2002

Foreword to the first edition

The authors have extensive practical experience in the banking and financial services field and are peculiarly qualified to write this important new book on banking and the Financial Services Act 1986. They consider the Act from the perspective of banks and their customers, and examine in practical terms the steps which banks must take to comply with its provisions. As the authors point out:

> 'The banking sector has a strong interest in the evolution of a system of regulation which achieves the right balance between a sufficient degree of investor protection on the one hand, and the avoidance of unnecessarily oppressive and formalistic regulation on the other.'

This work is timely because of the continuing debate about the structure of the regulatory regime, and the increasing impact of EC Directives (particularly the Second Banking Directive with effect from 1 January 1993). It provides a welcome contribution to a proper understanding of the many FSA issues that arise, and will be essential reading for all who are concerned with the conduct of investment business whether as bankers, legal advisers, compliance officers, investment practitioners or members of the investing public.

London   Peter Cresswell
April 1993

Preface to the second edition

This book began life as *Banking and the Financial Services Act*. At the time it was published, the regulatory system established under that Act was quite new. There has been much practical experience since then. The system is now in the process of further reform with the advent of the unified regulator. In the circumstances, it no longer made sense to treat the regulation of financial services separately; the second edition therefore now includes the regulation of banking, hence the change of title. The flux in the system inevitably means that some of the text will be subject to change fairly soon. On the other hand, since the system will not be fully operative until the year 2000, we believe that a new edition is of value now. A short description of the draft Financial Services and Markets Bill, released as this edition went to press, follows this preface.

The authors welcome the advent of the unified regulator as a bold and innovative step. The challenge it faces is to improve domestic retail supervision, whilst at the same time avoiding over-burdensome regulation of the wholesale sector. We are in no doubt that the successful balance which has been achieved in the past has been an important factor in the vitality and success of the financial sector in the UK.

We are grateful for the assistance we have received from many people, in particular Robert Elliott and Simon Firt, both partners at Linklaters, and Richard Alexander, Garretts research officer in European financial services law and co-ordinator of the International Training Unit at the Institute of Advanced Legal Studies.

Any inaccuracies which remain are our sole responsibility.

August 1998

WB
AA
KP
PR-C
GW

Contents

Contents

Contents

Table of statutes

Table of statutory instruments

Table of European legislation

Table of cases

Chapter 1

Banks and the regulatory regime

INTRODUCTION

1.1 Until 1979, there was little by way of formal regulatory law applying to the business of banking in the UK. The regulation of deposit-taking was first put on a statutory basis in that year. The regulation of investment business was put on a statutory basis in 1986. Thereafter, the two regulatory systems operated side-by-side. Meanwhile, the business of banking was changing rapidly. At the international level, the so-called 'big bang' transformed London's financial activities and brought about the large-scale acquisition of UK firms by non-UK institutions. London consolidated its position as a centre for international financial business. Domestically, retail banking business was being conducted by a much wider range of institutions. Overall, as boundaries between financial business became increasingly harder to demarcate, the division between banking and investment business appeared an artificial basis on which to conduct regulation.

1.2 In 1997, a radical reform of the regulatory system was set in motion. Its chief feature is a bringing of financial regulation under a single roof – a unified regulator in the form of the Financial Services Authority (FSA). The new system formally came into effect on 1 December 2001, though it had been implemented on an operational basis for some years before.

Despite the boldness of the reform, it is best viewed as part of an evolutionary process and as a logical response to changing market conditions. In any case, regulation (like banking) is now an international activity. Bodies such as the Basel Committee on Banking Supervision and the International Organisation of Securities Commissions (IOSCO) have been central in forging international standards. As a member of the European Union, banking and investment business in the UK is subject to European directives. Monetary

1

union in Europe is giving an added impetus to the harmonisation of the European regulatory system, though full regulatory integration is a long way off.

THE CHANGING STRUCTURE OF THE UK BANKING SECTOR

1.3   Traditionally, banks operating in the UK were placed in a number of main categories.[1] First, the clearing banks, with their network of branches inside the UK.[2] Building societies were largely mutual societies concentrating on savings and home mortgages and were regulated separately from banks under the Building Societies Acts.

Second, the 'merchant' or investment banks. The leading firms used to be known as 'Accepting Houses', because of the dominant role that they played in the finance of international trade by adding their 'acceptances' to trade bills of exchange. Their business included the provision of financial advice to companies and governments, and the issuance of securities. (According to Baron Schroder, whilst the acceptance was the merchant bank's bread and butter, the jam was security flotations.)[3]

Third, the non-UK banks, operating through branches, subsidiaries or representative offices, many of which concentrate on international banking, but some of which transact substantial UK banking businesses in their own right. In this category are some of the biggest names in international banking and financial services. Through the acquisition of local securities houses, these banks played a central role in bringing together banking and investment business within the same group. In any case the threefold categorisation has to a considerable extent broken down. At the retail level, the business of banks and building societies has become increasingly the same. At the wholesale level, the market is dominated by international banking groups providing a range of financial services.

1   See for example the classic analysis in Revell, *The British Financial System* (1973).
2   The structure in Scotland is different from that in England and Wales, but not materially so for regulatory purposes.
3   Quoted in Cameron and Bovykin, *International Banking 1870–1914* (1991), p 34.

1.4   In order to enable banking and investment businesses to merge, certain barriers had to be removed. The legal restraints were not in themselves substantial. Regulatory restraints against banks conducting securities business, which have had a structural effect on the development of the financial sector in a number of countries (particularly the US), did not exist in the UK, where there has never been a formal Glass-Steagall type separation of banking and securities activities. The separation of functions existed for more prosaic reasons. As Professor Dale put it, as a matter of practice, banks circumscribed their activities, and market segmentation was formalised by a Stock Exchange rulebook that prevented outsiders from taking a controlling interest in member firms.[1] Deregulation in the UK had more to do with market forces than with the removal of legal restrictions.

1   Richard Dale, *International Banking Deregulation* (1992), p 6.

DEVELOPMENT OF BANKING REGULATION

1.5   The supervision of the banking sector was historically the function of the Bank of England, which also performs central bank functions for the UK. It was founded in 1694 by Act of Parliament, and its first charter also dates to that year. Since 1946 it has been state-owned, in that its share capital is held by the Treasury. The prestige of the Bank of England was a vital ingredient in the UK supervisory process. Until comparatively recently, it had remarkably few formal supervisory powers:

'One of the most striking characteristics of the UK banking system was that until 1979, unlike most Western countries, supervision of the banking sector operated on a largely non-statutory basis. Self-regulation operated by the Bank of England relied upon personal knowledge of the banks which operated in the UK. Moral persuasion, a form of coercive persuasion, was very much the order of the day. Whenever the Bank wished to exercise its considerable authority, in the event of a suspected deviation from acceptable practice, the Governor of the Bank would simply send a polite letter to the appropriate institution indicating the way in which the Bank expected the institution to conduct its business. When it wished to enforce a policy of general application, it would send out formal letters of request requiring each bank to conform to new practice and new procedures which the bank deemed appropriate. Although such letters had no force of law, the Bank expected its views to be observed in the spirit as well as the letter, and it was often remarked that no banker in his right mind would buck the Bank of England.'[1]

1 Graham Penn, *Banking Supervision* (1988), p 3. For a detailed history of the Bank's supervisory role see C Hadjiemannuil, *Banking Regulation and the Bank of England* (1996).

1.6   Whereas a licence was required for moneylending, until recently no licence was required for deposit-taking. There were a number of express statutory powers (such as those contained in the Protection of Depositors Act 1963) but, as Lord Justice Bingham put it, these powers:

'did not provide an effective framework for the supervision either of banks properly so called or other deposit-taking institutions. But an important ingredient has to be added: the influence which the Bank was able to exercise by virtue of its role as "the arm of the government in the City" and the "banker's best friend", its power in the market, the respect in which its senior officials were held and the deference habitually paid to its opinions. To an extent unexplained by its very limited formal powers the Bank was able to exercise an effective tutelary role in relation to discount houses, accepting houses and aspirants to that status. But the Bank did not exercise prudential supervision over the clearing banks and branches of banks incorporated overseas. And its informal supervisory role, very largely dependent on mutual trust and co-operation, was harder to achieve (if it was achieved at all) in relation to the newer, less substantial, institutions which sprang up in the 1960s and 1970s: to these the grant of the less important statutory recognitions and exemptions . . . gave an aura of reliability which was not always justified.'[1]

1 Lord Justice Bingham, 'Inquiry into the Supervision of The Bank of Credit and Commerce International' (HMSO, 1992), para 1.8: the report contains an excellent summary of the history of banking supervision in the UK.

1.7   A number of factors combined to put an end to this state of affairs. Banking business increased greatly in complexity and volume. It was said that the 'homogeneity' of the City of London had disappeared with the influx of non-UK banks. Two matters in particular gave rise to the first UK Banking Act of 1979: first, in the aftermath of the secondary banking crisis of 1973–74, which was caused in large part by over-lending followed by plummeting property values, it became apparent that a large number of deposit-taking institutions operated outside the Bank's supervisory regime; and second, legislation was necessary to implement the first EEC Banking Directive of 1977, the object of which was amongst other things to harmonise the

3

authorisation of credit institutions throughout the Member States of the European Community.

1.8 Central bank independence is widely considered to have beneficial effects as regards inflation, in that the setting of interest rates is placed outside the political sphere. It was not until recently a feature of the UK system. By the Bank of England Act 1946, s 4(1), the Treasury was empowered from time to time give such directions to the Bank as, after consultation with the Governor of the Bank, it thought necessary in the public interest. There was in practice however considerable independence from the Government, and in particular the Bank conducted its supervisory functions virtually independently. The position changed in the reforms of May 1997. By Part II of the Bank of England Act 1998, operational responsibility for monetary policy has been given to the Bank. The Monetary Policy Committee of the Bank has responsibility within the Bank for formulating monetary policy. By the same Act, supervisory responsibility is shifted from the Bank to the FSA.

Definitions

1.9 One result of the historically informal nature of banking supervision in the UK is that there is still no formal list of permitted, or prohibited, activities that banks may carry on, as is found in the banking legislation of many countries. This is not to say that the concept of 'banking' as a distinct activity has no legal significance. The terms 'bank' and 'banker' appear in numerous statutes, and are relevant for some purposes at common law (for example, in connection with the banker's duty of confidentiality and right of set-off). The courts recognise that such terms may mean different things at different times.[1]

The most detailed judicial analysis in recent times was in 1966, when the Court of Appeal had to determine whether a company was carrying on the business of moneylending or the business of banking. The court sought to identify the core characteristics of banking as then understood. It considered that such characteristics were the taking of deposits from customers and the honouring of customers' payment orders through the medium of a current account.[2]

1 *Bank of Chettinad Ltd of Colombo v IT Comrs of Colombo* [1948] AC 378 at 383, PC.
2 *United Dominions Trust Ltd v Kirkwood* [1966] 2 QB 431 at 437, CA, Lord Denning MR.

1.10 Plainly, 'banking' business covers a much wider field than the taking of deposits and the honouring of customers' payment orders. Under the Banking Act 1979 (most of which is now repealed), the recognition of a deposit-taking institution as a bank depended in part on whether the institution provided a 'wide range of banking services'. These were defined to include sterling or foreign currency current or deposit account facilities; the acceptance of funds in the wholesale money markets; finance in the form of overdraft or loan facilities in sterling or foreign currency; the lending of funds in the wholesale money markets; foreign exchange services; foreign trade finance and documentation; financial advice or investment management services; and facilities for arranging the purchase and sale of securities.[1]

1 Banking Act 1979, Sch 2. The distinction between banks and other deposit-taking institutions was abolished by the Banking Act 1987.

1.11   In fact, there seems to be no international consensus as to what is to be considered as constituting 'banking' business.[1] However, for members of the European Community (EC), a benchmark has emerged in the EC legislation on credit institutions. Under the Credit Institutions Directive, a 'credit institution' is defined as an undertaking whose business is to receive deposits and other repayable funds from the public and to grant credits for its own account.[2] Focus is thus placed not only on the taking of deposits (as in the traditional English statutory and common law definitions in the Banking Acts and the *Kirkwood*[3] case) but also on the lending function. So far as the UK is concerned, the definition includes both banks and building societies.

Under the Credit Institutions Directive (which is a consolidating directive), a credit institution can freely undertake throughout the EC all the activities listed in Annex I either through a branch or by supplying services, provided that it is authorised to carry out those activities in its home Member State.[4] The activities listed in the Annex give probably the most helpful indication of what would generally be considered within the scope of 'banking business' today. They are:

(1)   acceptance of deposits and other repayable funds;
(2)   lending (including, *inter alia*, consumer credit, mortgage credit, factoring, with or without recourse, and the financing of commercial transactions (including forfaiting));
(3)   financial leasing;
(4)   money transmission services;
(5)   issuing and administering means of payment (eg credit cards, travellers' cheques and bankers' drafts);
(6)   guarantees and commitments;
(7)   trading for own or customers' account in:
  (a)   money market instruments (cheques, bills, certificates of deposit, etc);
  (b)   foreign exchange;
  (c)   financial futures and options;
  (d)   exchange and interest rate instruments;
  (e)   transferable securities;
(8)   participation in securities issues and the provisions of services related to such issues;
(9)   advice to undertakings on capital structure, industrial strategy and related questions and advice as well as services relating to mergers and the purchase of undertakings;
(10)   money broking;
(11)   portfolio management and advice;
(12)   credit reference services; and
(13)   safe custody services.

The list in the Annex can be compared to the list of activities set out in the Annex to the Investment Services Directive which contains similar 'single passport' provisions for investment firms. That Annex does not include deposit-taking or lending, but there is considerable overlap. This is a practical demonstration (were one needed) of the extent to which banking and investment business has become assimilated.

1   See *Prudential Supervision in Banking* (OECD, Paris, 1987), p 57.
2   Credit Institutions Directive, 2000/12/EC, art 1.
3   *United Dominions Trust Ltd v Kirkwood* [1966] 2 QB 431, CA.
4   Credit Institutions Directive, 2000/12/EC, art 18.

Change and deregulation: cause and effect

1.12   By the beginning of the 1980s, 'globalisation' was in full swing. Professor LCB Gower who was reviewing financial regulation in the UK wrote:

> 'Originally a stock-broker was just a broker of stocks and shares, an insurance broker a broker of insurance policies, a commodity broker a broker of commodities, a banker a provider of banking services and a unit trust manager a manager of unit trusts. And, by and large, each stuck to his last. Today all these roles, and others, may, and often will, be undertaken by the same firm or group. And groups offering a full range of financial services are tending to become multi-national with ultimate control of the British operations not necessarily being British.'[1]

These services were themselves becoming ever more sophisticated, with the development of new and esoteric financial instruments, which often required specialist departments to handle them.

1   LCB Gower, 'Review of Investor Protection: A Discussion Document' (HMSO, 1982), p 59.

1.13   Given London's importance as an international banking centre, it was inevitable that whatever barriers existed to the development of financial conglomerates would be swept away. As already mentioned, such barriers were not principally in the form of statutory limitations, but rather resulted from restrictions on participation in the London Stock Market. The so-called 'Big Bang' (which happened officially on 27 October 1986 when the major reforms finally took effect) was therefore in form primarily concerned with the reform of the London Stock Exchange. Three reforms were especially important:

(i)   the 'single capacity' system, which was unique to London,[1] under which 'jobbers' as wholesalers of stocks and shares (in other words, market-makers) operated quite separately from brokers acting as investors' agents, was phased out;

(ii)   at the same time, the remaining restrictions on the ownership of firms of jobbers and stockbrokers, and the unlimited personal liability of partners or directors, were removed; and

(iii)   a large number of these firms were bought by banks (both British and foreign) which thereby entered the business of stockbroking or making markets in securities, or both.

The trend towards the financial conglomerate was not in any way unique to the UK, but developments which elsewhere took place gradually over ten or more years, occurred in the UK in less than three.[2] Many banks are now contained within financial conglomerates, with the attendant risk of intragroup contagion. Banking business has expanded and blurred into securities, investment, and insurance-related businesses. The emergence of secondary debt-trading markets, asset securitisation, and credit derivatives have all provided increasing liquidity to bank balance sheets. International banks have assumed a role in both the exchange-traded and over-the-counter (OTC) derivatives markets. They possess enormous swaps and derivatives trading portfolios and have increasingly relied on proprietary trading to supplement profits, as spreads from traditional banking activities have narrowed. Finally, advances in technology have linked financial markets on an international basis and, at the same time, facilitated product innovation, the performance of which is sometimes untried.

1   Revell, *The British Financial System* (1973), p 62.
2   LCB Gower, 'Review of Investor Protection, Report: Part II' (HMSO, 1985), p 4.

1.14   These developments had important regulatory implications. The Banking Act of 1979 was concerned to regulate deposit-taking businesses. From 1979, deposit-taking businesses could not be conducted in the UK without a licence. But banks were now conducting whole new swathes of securities and other businesses which had nothing to do with deposit-taking and which did not fall inside this regulatory regime.

At about the same time as Big Bang, and in response to concerns about City fraud, the UK Government was conducting a complete reappraisal of the adequacy of the UK's system of investor protection. This process resulted in a new regulatory structure governing the conduct of investment business. In the event, banks in the UK found that their deposit-taking business fell under one regulatory regime, whereas their investment business fell under another. Besides producing duplication, this duality did not assist in resolving fundamental regulatory issues such as how to regulate a financial conglomerate effectively. As the Bank of Commerce and Credit International (BCCI) affair showed, the problem was even more acute in the case of a bank straddling international boundaries and outside the practical control of any one regulator. These were the considerations that led to the creation of a unified regulator in 1997. However, it has been more difficult to merge the content of regulation, because of the differences between deposit-taking and investment business, and different underlying policy considerations.

REGULATION OF UK DEPOSIT-TAKING BUSINESS

1.15   As noted, the first Banking Act of 1979 was precipitated by the 'secondary banking' crisis and the shortcomings that it uncovered. The Banking Act 1987 was passed after the Bank of England found itself obliged to rescue a small bank, namely Johnson Matthey Bankers Ltd. The Act gave the Bank of England significant new powers (though according to the Government the changes were not designed to make a fundamental break with the past).[1] Then came the Bank of England Act 1998,[2] the effect of which was to transfer the powers previously exercised by the Bank of England under the Banking Act 1987 (and related regulatory provisions) to the FSA.

The 1987 Act is no longer in force, the statutory provisions being contained in Financial Services and Markets Act (FSMA) 2000. This Act deals with the supervision of both deposit-taking and investment business. The provisions as regards deposit-taking are considered in detail in Chapter 6 below.

1   See generally, *Encyclopaedia of Banking Law*, Division A.
2   See generally, M Blair, R Cranston, C Ryan, M Taylor, *Blackstone's Guide to the Bank of England Act 1998*.

1.16   Although the 1987 Act is described as a 'Banking' Act, as was the case with its predecessor, it was only the carrying-on of a deposit-taking business in the UK that necessitated authorisation under the Act. The focus is on deposit-taking, because that is where the public is deemed to be at risk. The Bank set out its requirements in non-statutory 'notices'. It did not conduct regular examinations as is the practice in the United States. Also, under the 'single passport' provisions of the Second Banking Directive (now the Credit Institutions Directive, 2000/12/EC), primary regulatory responsibility for branches of banks incorporated in other EU Member States resides with the authorities in the home State. The *retail* banking sector was not subject to conduct of business regulation. This remains the case, though there is an important semi-voluntary code followed by banks and building societies in their relations with personal customers (the Banking Code). Another code is the Code of Mortgage Lending Practice.

1.17 Much of the framework survives in the new regime. There are prescribed minimum criteria for authorisation. These gave the Bank of England, and now the FSA, a wide discretion, though it is required to publish a statement of the principles on which it acts in interpreting the minimum criteria. The criteria include a requirement that directors, controllers and managers must be 'fit and proper persons'. The institution must conduct its business in a prudent manner and must maintain net assets and other financial resources commensurate with the nature and scale of its operations and sufficient to safeguard the interests of its depositors, adequate liquidity, adequate provision for depreciation or diminution in the value of assets and an adequate accounting system. There is also a minimum capital requirement conforming to international rules. In the case of a non-UK institution, the FSA may regard itself as satisfied that certain of the statutory minimum criteria are fulfilled if the relevant supervisory authority in that country informs it that it is satisfied with respect to the institution's prudent management and overall financial soundness. Provision is also made for the establishment of representative offices of non-UK banks. Some other features may be noted.

Control over UK banks

1.18 For many years, the Bank of England considered that prospective controlling shareholders should obtain the supervisor's prior consent before acquiring their holding, and, apparently in the vast majority of cases, this requirement was respected.[1] Under the 1987 Act, the requirement became mandatory. A vetting procedure was established for prospective shareholder controllers of UK-incorporated banks. Included in the definition of 'shareholder controller' are minority controllers (whose proposed holdings will be 10% or more), majority or principal controllers, a parent controller or an indirect controller of an authorised institution.

1 White Paper, Cmnd 9695, para 14.2.

Large exposures

1.19 The Bank of England's own review following the Johnson Matthey affair concluded that concentrations of lending to individual borrowers or economic sectors were the most important recent cause of difficulties in banks.[1] Broadly, a UK bank must report exposure to any one person in excess of 10% of its available capital resources. Exposure in excess of 25% must be reported before being incurred. The Credit Institutions Directive[2] imposes similar 10% and 25% limits on all EEA banks.

1 Report of the Leigh-Pemberton Committee, Cmnd 9550 (June 1985), Ch 5.
2 2000/12/EC.

Information

1.20 Any system of supervision depends heavily on the provision of regular prudential returns and relevant statistical and other information. According to the Bank, this information has always been supplied voluntarily, and the statutory powers to require the provision of information from and the production of documents by an authorised institution 'were enacted to cover the possibility that institutions not used to the customary style of supervision might be backward in giving the Bank the information it needed'.

Recent cases suggest that the courts will give full effect to the information-gathering powers, which are now vested in the FSA. In *A v B Bank (Bank of England intervening)*[1] the Commercial Court held that the Bank of England's statutory power to order an authorised deposit-taking institution to disclose documents which it reasonably required for the performance of its supervisory functions, overrode a court order restraining the institution from disclosing the documents to a third party (which the third party had obtained on the grounds that such disclosure would be a breach of the duty of confidence). In a similar vein, in *PriceWaterhouse v BCCI Holdings (Luxembourg) SA*[2] the accountants PriceWaterhouse (formerly BCCI's auditors) were held to be entitled to produce confidential banking information to the judicial inquiry into the BCCI collapse, on the ground that the public interest in confidentiality gave way to the public interest in disclosure when necessary for the purposes of inquiry into past performance by the Bank of England of its statutory functions.[3] Information once received is subject to the confidentiality provisions of s 82.[4]

1   [1993] QB 311, [1992] 1 All ER 778, Hirst J.
2   [1992] BCLC 583, Millett J.
3   See also *Bank of England v Riley* [1992] Ch 475, [1992] 1 All ER 769, CA, in which it was held that a defendant to proceedings brought under the 1987 Act was not entitled to rely on the privilege against self-incrimination as a reason for not disclosing documents when required.
4   See *BCCI v Price Waterhouse* [1998] Ch 84, [1997] 4 All ER 781.

Financial Services Compensation Scheme

1.21 The deposit protection scheme consisted of a Deposit Protection Board administering a Deposit Protection Fund. The object was to protect deposits made with the offices of UK authorised institutions against such institutions' insolvency. In calculating the amount of the protection, separate accounts in the same name are aggregated and joint accounts (other than partnership accounts) are divided equally between account-holders. Secured deposits, 'own funds' deposits, deposits made by authorised institutions and deposits made by related companies or individuals are not protected.[1]

The scheme has now been combined in a single Financial Services Compensation Scheme, and the limits raised. The compensation limits for the new Scheme are:

(a)   *deposits:* £31,700 (100% of £2,000 and 90% of £33,000);
(b)   *investments:* £48,000 (100% of £30,000 and 90% of next £20,000);
(c)   *long-term insurance:* at least 90% of the value of the policyholder's guaranteed fund at the date of default;
(d)   *general insurance:* compulsory, 100% of valid claim/unexpired premiums; non compulsory, 100% of the first £2,000 of valid claim/unexpired premiums and 90% of the remainder of the claim.

1   An assignee is not a 'depositor' for these purposes: *Deposit Protection Board v Dalia* [1994] 2 AC 367, [1994] 1 All ER 539, CA.

DEVELOPMENT OF REGULATION OF UK INVESTMENT BUSINESS

1.22   In some respects, the history of UK regulation of investment business is similar to that of the regulation of banking business, in that until recently there was little by way of statute law.[1] The main difference is that there was no body equivalent to the Bank of England conducting overall supervision on a non-statutory basis. A further difference is one of emphasis; the regulation of the banking sector has tended to focus on the capital adequacy of institutions as the best means of protecting the depositor. The regulation of investment businesses has been equally concerned to lay down detailed rules on conduct of business intended to promote investment protection. To some extent this remains true under the new regime.

1   Excellent accounts of the history of regulation appear in Rider, Abrams & Ashe, *Guide to Financial Services Regulation* (3rd edn), Chs 1 and 2; and in Pennington, *The Law of the Investment Markets* (1987), Ch 2.

1.23   There were, and still are, remedies under the general law available to an investor who has been the victim of malpractice (for example actions for misrepresentation and breach of fiduciary and other duties). On a wider level, a fiduciary relationship exists between a promoter and the company he brings into existence.[1] For many years statute law has regulated particular aspects of the financial services sector, as under the Companies Acts in relation to the issue of capital. Self-regulation on varying levels of formality also in practice played an important part.[2] The UK did not, however, experience anything comparable to the regulatory reforms instituted in the United States after the Wall Street Crash of 1929 and the ensuing depression. There was no regulatory body similar to the Securities and Exchange Commission (SEC).

1   *Erlanger v New Sombrero Phospate Co* (1878) 3 App Cas 1218, HL.
2   Rider, Abrams & Ashe, *Guide to Financial Services Regulation* (3rd edn), para 202.

1.24   The first serious attempt at general regulation came in the Prevention of Fraud (Investments) Act 1939, which was re-enacted with amendments in 1958. This Act prohibited a person from carrying on the business of dealing in securities except under the authority of a licence issued by the Board of Trade, subsequently the Department of Trade and Industry (DTI).

The word 'securities' was defined to include shares or debentures (s 26 of the 1958 Act), but the definition was considered unsatisfactory. For example, it was unclear whether a warrant, an option or a bearer certificate of deposit was within it.[1]

1   LCB Gower, 'Review of Investor Protection: A Discussion Document' (HMSO, 1982), p 62.

1.25   The DTI was given power under the Act to make rules regulating the conduct by licence holders of their business of dealing in securities. The last of such rules were the Licensed Dealers (Conduct of Business) Rules introduced in April 1983, which were much stricter than their predecessors, and can be seen as a statutory precursor of the rules made under the subsequent regulatory regime.

1.26   In practice the operation of the Act was limited by wide exemptions from the licensing requirement. In particular the DTI had power to declare any person to be an exempted dealer provided certain conditions were met (s 16 of the 1958 Act). Although the original intention was that exempted status would be granted sparingly, by 1982 there were some 400 exempted dealers, mainly merchant banks, licensed deposit-takers and insurance companies; apparently exemption had come to be regarded as a 'prized status symbol'.[1]

1   LCB Gower, 'Review of Investor Protection: A Discussion Document' (HMSO, 1982), p 15.

Moves to reform

1.27   In July 1981, Professor LCB Gower was appointed to review the existing statutory framework, and to make recommendations on the statutory protection and controls required by private and business investors.[1] He summarised the defects in the existing system as being: complication; uncertainty; irrationality; failure to treat like alike; inflexibility; excessive control in some areas and too little (or none) in others; the creation of an elite and a fringe; lax enforcement; delays; over-concentration on honesty rather than competence; undue diversity of regulations and regulators; and failure overall to achieve a proper balance between governmental regulation and self-regulation.[2]

1   For an entertaining account of the process by Professor Gower himself see 'Big Bang and City Regulation' 51 MLR 1 (1988).
2   LCB Gower, 'Review of Investor Protection: A Discussion Document' (HMSO, 1982), p 137.

1.28   As to what should replace it, Professor Gower found a consensus in favour of the basic principle of a comprehensive system of regulation within a statutory framework based, so far as possible, on self-regulation subject to governmental surveillance.[1]

To achieve that, he recommended that the 1958 Act should be replaced by a new Investor Protection Act providing a system whereby basic policy, overall surveillance and residual regulation of investment business would be undertaken by a governmental agency but day-to-day regulation, so far as possible, by self-regulatory agencies. He proposed that the new Act should make it an offence to carry on an investment business unless registered either directly with the governmental agency or through membership of a recognised self-regulatory agency.

In essence, this was the approach adopted by the Government in the White Paper[2] published in January 1985, which set out the proposals upon which the Financial Services Bill was later based.

1   LCB Gower 'Review of Investor Protection, Report: Part 1' Cmnd 9125 (January 1984), p 10.
2   'Financial Services in the United Kingdom: A new framework for investor protection' Cmnd 9432 (January 1985).

1.29   A key issue was the position of banks under the proposed new order. In particular, how was the new regulatory regime to apply to banks conducting increasing volumes of investment business, but which had always been subject to supervision by the Bank of England under powers now formalised in the 1979 Act?

Professor Gower was well aware of the significance of the emergence of the financial conglomerate. He recognised that under his proposals such conglomerates would fall within the new regime so far as they carried on investment business, though their deposit-taking business would continue to be regulated by the Bank of England under the Banking Act. But he concluded that banks conducting investment business should not be given special treatment:

> 'Banks, merchant or clearing, or their subsidiaries would, of course, be affected by any new securities legislation in so far as they carried on business as issuing houses, fund managers or investment advisers. An argument by the banks that they should be excluded from regulation under a Securities Act because they are regulated under the Banking Act could not, I think, be sustained, since the Bank of England does not purport to regulate their activities in respect of these activities other than by attempting to ensure that they maintain their overall solvency.[1] Nor, I think, an argument by the clearing banks that the only investment advice they give is through their central investment departments. It is widely recognised that the investment adviser most often turned to by the investor is his bank manager – and judicial decisions clearly establish that the bank will not escape liability if the manager negligently gives bad advice. Whether or not advice is paid for separately, it is part of the business service supplied by the banks to their customers.'[2]

1　For reasons already explained, Professor Gower may have understated the scope of the Bank of England's scrutiny, for example its ability to review all aspects of a bank's activities by application of the criteria of fitness and properness and prudent management.
2　LCB Gower, 'Review of Investor Protection: A Discussion Document' (HMSO, 1982), p 125.

Financial Services Act 1986

1.30　The statute which emerged from the Gower review was the Financial Services Act 1986. It was the product of intensive lobbying from the financial services industry, fearful of over-regulation and the emergence of a US-style SEC, and from consumer interests, concerned not to see the original aim of investor protection unduly watered-down.

The initial result was a regulatory system which was too complicated, both in terms of structure and in terms of the body of regulatory law itself. The system came into effect at about the time of the October 1987 stock market crash and the downturn in securities business that followed, with the result that the industry found itself having to implement expensive new procedures just at the time when its profit margins were coming under greatest pressure. There was a determined effort to simplify the system, and with some success. But the experience has shown just how difficult it is to devise a system that does not over-regulate the industry, but at the same time does not under-protect the investor.

1.31　The Financial Services Act 1986 contained a general prohibition on the carrying-on of investment business in the UK without authorisation. 'Investments' were defined to include stocks and shares, debentures, CDs (Certificates of Deposit), government securities, warrants, unit trusts, options, futures and the like.[1] A bank's deposit-taking and lending activities did not constitute investment business, and continued to be regulated under the Banking Act 1987. However its securities, underwriting, corporate finance and investment management businesses all came, to a greater or lesser degree, within the Financial Services Act regime. Other forms of authorisation might also be required, such as a licence to carry on a consumer credit business under the Consumer Credit Act 1974.

Thus the approach was along 'functional' rather than 'institutional' lines. The multiplicity of regulators was mitigated by lead regulation, the object of was to ensure that a firm was not subject to more than one set of financial rules.

1 Financial Services Act 1986, Sch 1.

Self-regulation

1.32 The Financial Services Act 1986 was based on the principle of 'self-regulation'. This contrasted with the position in the United States, where the emphasis is on policing by independent agencies. The approach adopted in the UK fitted with the political perspectives of the time, but underlying it was a more general concern that overly-formalistic regulation would damage the flourishing markets in the City of London, and a belief that regulation was best left in the hands of practitioners who understood the markets.

In retrospect, it is unclear whether self-regulation was a benefit or a bane. It undoubtedly contributed to the complexity of the structure of the regulatory regime, with its proliferation of responsible bodies. On the other hand, the industry was able to set many of its own rules, and in some respects succeeded in averting the demands of consumer pressure groups (as in commission disclosure and the like). However this in turn led to complaints that the conduct of regulation unduly favoured the industry at the expense of the public.

1.33 At the top of the regulatory structure was a new regulatory body, the Securities and Investments Board (SIB). This body was the direct predecessor of the modern FSA. SIB was conceived as the watchdog of the system, as opposed to the body which granted licences to individual investment businesses. Consistent with the principle of self-regulation, the licensing function was primarily assigned to a number of 'self-regulating organisations' (SROs).

The SROs were constituted as members' organisations recognised by SIB. They served two primary purposes in the regulatory structure. First, membership of an SRO was the primary route to authorisation under the 1986 Act (though under the 'appointed representatives' provisions of the Act tied agents did not require direct authorisation). Second, the SROs as the bodies charged with the supervisory function made their own rules by which their members were expected to abide. They also had important disciplinary and enforcement powers.

There were originally five, and latterly three, SROs, namely:

(i)   the Securities and Futures Authority (SFA, formed in 1991 by the merger of the Securities Association and the Association of Futures Brokers and Dealers);
(ii)   the Investment Management Regulatory Organisation (IMRO); and
(iii)   the Personal Investment Authority (PIA, formed by the merger of the Financial Intermediaries, Managers and Brokers Regulatory Association and the Life Assurance and Unit Trusts Regulatory Organisation).

The names of these organisations were broadly descriptive of the type of investment businesses which their members transacted. Most banks which carried on an investment business which required authorisation were members of the SFA, IMRO and/or PIA.

Until 1992 the government department responsible for the Financial Services Act 1986 was the Department of Trade and Industry (DTI). Because the Bank of England, then supervisor of deposit-taking institutions, is responsible to the Treasury, the result was a division of governmental responsibility for the supervision of financial conglomerates. To remedy this, the functions of the DTI were transferred to the Treasury in 1992.

1.34 Despite its title, the Financial Services Act 1986 did not regulate the entire UK financial services industry. One exemption important for banks related to London money markets. These were considered unsuitable for inclusion in a system that was concerned primarily with investor protection, and were in any event already regulated informally by the Bank of England. Under s 43 of the Act, banks and other institutions included on a list maintained by the Bank of England were exempted from the requirements of the Act in respect of transactions on these markets. The result is that the wholesale markets in sterling, foreign exchange and bullion were regulated on a non-statutory basis. These markets are primarily the short-term money markets in London. Institutions benefiting from the exemption included many banks which act as brokers or market-makers in one or more of the relevant money-market instruments. The Bank of England issued a 'London Code of Conduct' which set out the principles governing the conduct of those transacting business in the relevant markets to ensure that proper standards of integrity and fair dealing were observed, taking account of the fact that the participants were professionals. Though the statutory exemption has gone under FSMA 2000, the general approach has been maintained in the section of the FSA handbook dealing with inter-professional conduct.

1.35 Conduct of business rules were the province of the SIB and the SROs. The Financial Services Act 1986 did, however, contain marketing restrictions of general application. It placed restrictions on uninvited telephone calls and personal visits (so-called 'cold calling') as a means of marketing investments. Cold calling was, broadly speaking, prohibited, though the effect of the prohibition was in practice reduced by permissions in regulations issued by SIB (see s 56). Restrictions were also placed on the issue of investment advertisements in the UK, unless the advertisement was issued or approved by an authorised person (see s 57). These rules can be compared with the current FSMA rules on 'financial promotion'.

1.36 After it was set up, the SIB issued rules for the conduct of investment business. To qualify for recognition as an SRO, organisations had to offer investors protection which was 'at least equivalent' to that afforded by the SIB rules. The rulebooks that emerged from this process had few admirers, though the task of drawing them up was bound to be a difficult one, particularly given the view originally expressed by Professor Gower that the SROs should 'so far as possible promulgate precise Rules and Regulations and not seek to duck difficult issues by publishing, instead or in addition, more loosely drafted Codes of Conduct of doubtful status'.[1]

It was and still is difficult to get the balance right between rules which are sufficiently detailed to provide clear guidance without being unduly restrictive.

---

1 LCB Gower, 'Review of Investor Protection: A Discussion Document' (HMSO, 1982), p 135. He made it clear, incidentally, in Part I of his Report that this was not to be taken as a criticism of codes of conduct as such, and that he had no objection to codes supplementing rules or regulations (see p 183).

1.37   Responding to criticism, in 1989 the Financial Services Act 1986 was substantially amended by the Companies Act of that year to enable a 'new settlement' to be introduced. The SIB was empowered to issue statements of principle[1] and codes of practice,[2] and to designate rules and regulations which applied directly to members of SROs.[3] In place of the 'equivalence' test, the SRO rules had to be such as to afford an 'adequate' level of protection for investors.[4] Codes of practice and statements of principle continue to be a feature of the new regime.

1   S 47A.
2   S 63C.
3   S 63A.
4   Sch 2, as amended.

1.38   In what was at the time seen as an innovative provision intended to encourage compliance with the rules by the threat of legal proceedings brought by investors damaged by a breach, s 62 provided that a contravention of rules made under the Act was actionable at the suit of a person who suffered loss as a result of the contravention subject to the defences applying to actions for breach of statutory duty. There was considerable concern that this provision might expose firms to an avalanche of claims, but this did not happen. In 1989 the industry did, however, succeed in obtaining the amendment of s 62. Section 62A (inserted by the Companies Act 1989) restricted the rights of action under s 62 to the private investor. The provision did not in any event apply to breaches of statements of principle or codes of practice promulgated under the provisions described above. Section 62 was concerned to expand on investors' rights rather than to place restrictions on them. Thus, though it did not give an investor any right of rescission of a contract consequent on a breach of the rules (being in terms confined to an action for damages) such a right might arise under the general law.[1]

The current provisions which are similar are contained in FSMA 2000, s 150.

1   *Securities and Investments Board v Pantell SA (No 2)* [1993] Ch 256, [1992] 1 All ER 134, CA.

1.39   The establishment of a fund to compensate investors for the failure of investment businesses proved more controversial than the deposit protection scheme (described at para 1.21 above). There was a concern that solid financial institutions should not bear an undue burden in respect of the activities of riskier firms. Also, in practice most compensation claims arise from particular types of business, especially retail sales of packaged insurance products.

The Investors' Compensation Scheme began on 27 July 1988. Entitlement to claim under the scheme was limited to investors who suffered loss as the result of the collapse of an authorised investment business in respect of liabilities incurred on or after 18 December 1986 (the date on which the provisions in the Financial Services Act 1986 giving meaning to the words 'investment business' came into effect).[1] The scheme has now been replaced by the combined Financial Services Compensation Scheme (see para 1.21 above).

1   *Securities and Investments Board v Financial Intermediaries Managers and Brokers Regulatory Association Ltd* [1992] Ch 268, [1991] 4 All ER 398, Morritt J.

THE MOVE TO A SINGLE REGULATOR

1.40   On 6 May 1997, the Chancellor announced that responsibility for monetary policy was being transferred to the Bank of England. This would necessitate legislation, and on 20 May 1997 he announced that he was taking the opportunity to tackle the question of regulatory reform. He referred to the increasing blurring of different types of financial business and said:

> 'So there is a strong case in principle for bringing the regulation of banking, securities and insurance together under one roof. Firms organise and manage their businesses on a group-wide basis. Regulators need to look at them in a consistent way. This would bring the regulatory structure closer into line with the day's increasingly integrated financial markets. It would deliver more effective and more efficient supervision, giving both firms and customers better value for money.'

The SIB was requested to produce a plan to implement the proposal. So far as the UK was concerned, the debate as to the direction of financial regulation reform was now settled.[1]

1 For a detailed summary of the various arguments see Goodhart, Hartmann, Llewellyn, Rojas-Suarez and Weisbrod, *Financial Regulation: Why, How and Where Now?*, Monograph for the Central Bank Governors' Meeting at the Bank of England, 6 June 1997.

1.41 It rapidly became clear that the key features of the reforms were:

— a single financial regulator covering banking, financial services and insurance with responsibility both for prudential regulation and conduct of business;

— the Bank of England losing its supervisory responsibilities, but remaining charged with the overall integrity of the financial system; and

— the abandonment of the principle of self-regulation, in favour of an independent agency operating under statutory authority with a degree of practitioner involvement.

In all, nine regulatory bodies were subsumed, namely: (i) the Building Societies Commission; (ii) the Friendly Societies Commission; (iii) the Insurance Directorate of the DTI; (iv) the Investment Management Regulatory Organisation (IMRO); (v) the Personal Investment Authority (PIA); (vi) the Registry of Friendly Societies; (vii) the Securities and Futures Authority (SFA); (viii) the Securities and Investments Board (SIB); and (ix) the Supervision and Surveillance Division of the Bank of England.

1.42 The SIB reported to the Chancellor at the end of July 1997. It sketched out how the unified regulator would operate, and described an implementation strategy. In essence, the plan went forward operationally ahead of the completion of the legal framework.

The new regulator was launched by its incoming Chairman, Howard Davies, on 28 October 1997. Legally, it was the SIB renamed as the Financial Services Authority (FSA). Under fast-track plans for early integration, existing staff employed by the SROs were re-employed by the FSA on a subcontract basis (until the SROs' functions were formally transferred to the FSA). In the transition period, the FSA was in effect performing the SROs' supervisory duties. During 1998, the Bank of England supervisory staff and SRO staff transferred to the new regulator, and were integrated under one roof in Canary Wharf in London's Docklands. The Bank of England Act 1998 transferred banking supervision from the Bank to the FSA (this date was referred to as 'N1').

After the FSMA 2000 came into force on 1 December 2001, the FSA became the single regulator with direct responsibility for the regulation of deposit-taking, insurance and investment business. This date was referred to as

'N2', and from that time the new system was in effect in law as well as practice. The process continues with the vesting of responsibility in respect of certain aspects of mortgage regulation in the FSA (a date referred to as 'N3').

Structure of the legal provisions

1.43   Chapter 2 below describes the regime in detail.

The setting up of a new body implied that henceforth regulatory action would have to be grounded in ascertainable powers. An inevitable consequence was that the new regulatory settlement is, for want of a better description, 'rule-based'. It is important to understand the structure of the legal provisions that underlie it. The structure may be seen as a hierarchy:

—   At the top is the statute, the FSMA 2000. This provides for the establishment of the FSA and its powers and duties, and other matters consequent on the regulatory system.
—   Beneath that is a layer of regulation in the form of statutory instruments, such as the Regulated Activities Order.[1] This contains much key material that was formerly in statutory form.
—   Underneath that come the provisions that are promulgated by the FSA itself. These are contained in the FSA Handbook. A great deal of thought went into developing a coherent legal structure for the mass of material in the Handbook. It is classified according to the legal effect of the provisions. Part of it consists of rules made under the general rule-making power in FSMA 2000, s 138, or under specific rule-making powers. Part of it consists of guidance made pursuant to s 157. There are also 'evidential provisions' tending to establish a contravention of, or compliance with, another rule made under s 149. This is the main classification. In addition, there are the 'safe harbour' provisions in s 122(1) which have the effect of making binding certain provisions of the Code of Market Conduct as regards market abuse. In short, the Handbook contains a mixture of hard and soft law. The layout indicates the status of material by a letter in the margin.

1   Financial Services and Markets Act 2000 (Regulated Activities) Order 2001 (SI 2001/544).

1.44   Guidance is not, as such, legally binding. It is intended to be flexible and responsive, and to enable the FSA to deliver on a pledge not to rely on unpublished rules and standards. Guidance is only the expression of the FSA's views on the matter concerned, though in practice it may carry considerable weight. When the regulator sets something down in black and white, it acquires its own force, whether expressed as a rule or not. Compliance officers may not spend much time debating whether a given passage of the Handbook consists of rules or guidance. And if a firm complies, it will likely have an answer not only to any enforcement procedures but also to any claim that it has contravened the criminal perimeter, or an action for civil damages under s 150. If a firm decides it does *not* agree with the guidance, and agreement cannot be reached, the ultimate sanction open to the FSA is enforcement proceedings, but only if a breach of the rules has resulted.

1.45   The predecessors to the FSMA 2000 did not include 'regulatory objectives'. This is an innovation. The content of the objectives and the accompanying 'principles' were subject to intense scrutiny and debate in the course of the passage of the Bill. They provide a kind of regulatory blueprint, setting out what the new regulatory system is intended to achieve.

The core provisions in s 2 are a careful legislative balancing exercise. Section 2 provides that in discharging its *general* functions the FSA must 'act in a way which is *compatible* with the regulatory objectives', and 'which it considers most appropriate for the purpose of meeting' the objectives. The FSA's general functions are defined as: making rules; issuing codes and giving general guidance under the Act (considered as a whole); and determining the general policy and principles by reference to which it performs *particular* functions.

The four regulatory objectives are:

(i) market confidence;
(ii) public awareness;
(iii) the protection of consumers; and
(iv) the reduction of financial crime.

These objectives are briefly elaborated on in ss 3 to 6.

In discharging its general functions, the FSA 'must have regard to' the seven 'principles' set out in s 2(3), which may be summarised as:

(i) efficiency and economy;
(ii) responsibility of business managers;
(iii) proportionality;
(iv) facilitating innovation;
(v) maintaining the UK's competitive position internationally;
(vi) no unnecessary distortion of competition; and
(vii) the facilitation of competition.

1.46 What is the effect of these provisions legally? According to the Economic Secretary to the Treasury, the legislative intention was as follows:

> 'We want something that requires the FSA to give proper weight to the principles and to ensure that it takes them properly into account but, at the same time, does not expose the regulators to tactical litigation on individual regulatory decisions. Exploration of these issues has led to the conclusion that the current formulation strikes the right balance.'[1]

It is interesting to see the Joint Committee's view, which under Lord Burns took an independent and well-informed view of the legislation. It stated that the 'statutory objectives . . . do not apply directly to individual acts of rule-making, advice or guidance; and they apply only at the level of general policy and principles to the granting of authorisation, permission, approval and recognition, and to investigation, intervention and disciplinary action'.[2] The Joint Committee also stated that:

> 'We support the principle that the Bill should set statutory objectives and principles for the FSA to inform its behaviour as it seeks to ensure markets of integrity and to provide a yardstick for accountability. We agree that these should be set at a high level of generality, so as to be adaptable to changing circumstances. We agree that they should apply at the level of general policy and principles, rather than applying directly to every single act and decision of the FSA. We agree that they should not be ranked.'[3]

According to one author, because the first three functions are to be 'considered as a whole' and the fourth is 'general', the drafting suggests that the objectives 'cannot easily be used to challenge any *particular* ruling of the FSA'. He adds that it seems unlikely that any action of the FSA could be declared void 'just because it offended one of the principles'.[4] According the FSA, the Act applies the objectives and principles to specific activities, and 'in addition [the objectives and principles] form a more general foundation for our public accountability'.[5]

1   Vol 343 HC, 27 January 2000, cc 646 and 647.
2   First Report, para 18.
3   First Report, para 24.
4   Alcock, *The Financial Services and Markets Act 2000*, pp 34 and 39.
5   FSA, *A New Regulator for the New Millennium*, January 2000, p 5.

Chapter 2

The Financial Services Authority and the Financial Services and Markets Act 2000

INTRODUCTION

2.1   The new integrated regulatory regime within the UK is implemented and administered by the Financial Services Authority (FSA).[1] The FSA had been created as a reconstituted Securities and Investments Board (SIB) at its formal launch on 28 October 1997. Until then, it had simply been referred to as 'NewRO' (for New Regulatory Organisation).

Responsibility for the supervision of banks was transferred to the FSA under the Bank of England Act 1998 (which was referred to as 'N1').[2] While responsibility in respect of all other financial sectors was announced during the second half of 1997 and early 1998, formal authority in this regard only commenced with the coming into effect of the Financial Services and Markets Act (FSMA) 2000 on 1 December 2001 ('N2'). This process of regulatory assumption will now be completed early 2004 with the transfer of responsibility in respect of mortgage sales, advice and general insurance to the FSA ('N3').

1 See Chapter 1 and paras 2.4–2.8.
2 See paras 2.49–2.50.

2.2   Since N2, the FSA has been responsible for the supervision and regulation of all financial services and markets in the UK. This represents one of the most significant examples of institutional integration attempted in any country. The creation of a single regulator has been followed elsewhere, although not on this scale and not in a market of comparable complexity.

This institutional reform has also been accompanied by substantive integration with the production of the new Handbook of Rules and Guidance issued by the FSA under ss 138 and 157 of the FSMA 2000.[1] With this, the FSA has created a single set of regulatory provisions for all services and markets. While a substantial body of provision has already been issued with the Handbook, further post-N2 rules revision will follow at the same time as the FSA continues its work on the production of a fully integrated single prudential sourcebook for all sectors. Separate interim prudential sourcebooks have been included within the initial Handbook, which largely replicate the existing sector provisions dealing with solvency and other financial as well as general systems requirements. A single fully integrated final sourcebook is expected in due course based on a new risk-by-risk principle.[2]

1 See paras 2.51–2.82; and paras 2.83–2.146.
2 See Chapter 6, paras 6.84–6.100; and Chapter 15.

2.3   The purpose of this chapter is to consider the immediate background to the establishment of the FSA and the enactment of the FSMA 2000. The interim regulatory arrangements set up pre-N2 are referred to and the initial aims and regulatory approach of the FSA noted. The new statutory objectives and supporting regulatory principles adopted for the FSA are considered. The current operational structure of the FSA is then examined. The Memorandum of Understanding entered into between the FSA, the Treasury and the Bank of England and the general purpose and content of the Bank of England Act are referred to. The main provisions set out in the FSMA 2000 are then examined in further detail with the basic structure and content of the FSA Handbook of Rules and Guidance. Reference is also made to the scope of territorial application of the provisions of the Act.

FINANCIAL REFORM

2.4   The Chancellor of the Exchequer originally announced on 20 May 1997 that the structure of financial regulation would be revised in two stages.[1] It was considered that reform was long overdue in simplifying the delivery of financial services within the UK. Accordingly, work was to start immediately on the required legislation.[2] The Chancellor also announced that the opportunity would be taken to transfer responsibility for bank supervision from the Bank of England to a strengthened Securities and Investments Board (SIB – now the FSA). This would be included within the Bank of England Bill which was being drafted at that time. The SIB would then be assigned responsibility for the regulation of financial services under the Financial Services and Markets Bill which would be prepared separately.

1 See Chapter 1, paras 1.40–1.42.
2 See HM Treasury News Release 'The Chancellor's Statement to the House of Commons on Bank of England', 49/97, 20 May 1997, para 13.

2.5   The Chancellor wrote to the Chairman of the SIB on 20 May 1997 to ask the SIB to take this work forward and to manage the process of implementation with the self-regulating organisations (SROs) and the financial services industry generally. In connection with this, the SIB was asked to develop an implementation plan to cover both logistical and organisational issues as well as the final architecture of the legislation and the transitional arrangements required.[1] The SIB Report was subsequently presented to the Chancellor on 29 July 1997.[2]

1 See Letter from the Chancellor to Sir Andrew Large, 'Reform of Financial Regulation', 20 May 1997.
2 See SIB 'Report to the Chancellor on the Reform of the Financial Regulatory System', July 1997 ('the July 1997 Report').

2.6 Under the reforms announced, the Bank of England would be responsible for the operation of monetary policy and for ensuring overall financial stability, while the FSA would assume responsibility for the supervision of banks and securities firms, as well as the regulation of financial services and markets as a whole.

The former complex structure of financial regulation, under which a number of separate agencies were involved in controlling the activities of distinct financial institutions on a functional basis, would be replaced by a new unitary structure with a single authority responsible for all institutions. The Bank of England would manage systemic stability and provide liquidity assistance as required. This responsibility would be supported by the Memorandum of Understanding entered into between the FSA, the Treasury and the Bank of England on October 1998.[1]

1 See paras 2.40–2.47.

2.7 Special interim regulatory arrangements had to be entered into between N1 and N2 concerning the regulation of investment firms. The Bank of England's functions in respect of banking supervision under the Banking Act 1987, the Banking Coordination (Second Council Directive) Regulations 1992[1] and s 101(4) of the Building Societies Act 1986 were transferred to the FSA with effect from N1.[2] Responsibility for listed money market institutions under s 43 of the Financial Services Act 1986 and the Investment Services Regulations 1995 and in relation to the listing of persons providing settlement arrangements under s 171 of the Companies Act 1989 were also transferred at that stage.

There was, however, no assumption of responsibility for the regulation of investment business in the UK until N2 with the effect that banks and investment firms had to continue to apply to the former SROs. As all relevant personnel had been engaged under new contracts of employment with the FSA from N1, appropriate 'service level agreements' had to be entered into between the FSA and each SRO to provide for the secondment of staff back to the SRO until N2 when their former statutory functions became redundant.

1 SI 1992/3218.
2 Bank of England Act 1998, s 21. See paras 2.49–2.50.

2.8 While the basic nature of the new regulatory system to be established had been outlined in the Chancellor's Statement to the House of Commons in May 1997, the more detailed arrangements necessary to take the creation of a unitary structure forward were developed in a series of further papers and consultative documents including the July 1998 Report and the FSA's Launch Document on 28 October 1997.[1] The necessary statutory framework for the new regime was then set up under the FSMA 2000, which was enacted on 14 June 2000.[2]

All of the more detailed substantive requirements have then been developed by the FSA through an extended consultation and discussion process since N1. Much of this has since been included within the FSA's Handbook of Rules and Guidance[3] with all of the relevant consultation and supporting papers still being made available on the Handbook section of the FSA's website (www.fsa.gov.uk).

1 See FSA *Financial Services Authority: An Outline*, October 1997 ('FSA Launch Document'). See also the further consultative documents issued at the launch: *Consumer involvement, Practitioner involvement* and *Paying for banking supervision* (October 1997).
2 See paras 2.51–2.82.
3 See paras 2.83–2.146.

AIMS AND REGULATORY APPROACH

2.9   It had been determined at an early stage that a number of statutory objectives would be adopted for the FSA. This represented a significant departure from previous practice and was generally designed to improve the discharge of regulatory function within the UK by directing activity and resources at the same time as improve accountability. The possible content of the statutory objectives were discussed in the preparatory papers issued by the FSA[1] and then set out in s 2(2) of the FSMA 2000.[2] These are supplemented by a number of further principles included within s 2(3) that apply with regard to the FSA's conduct of financial supervision under the Act. In addition to considering the possible terms of these statutory objectives, the FSA had produced some more general statements of intent and practice at an early stage. These included, in particular, a general statement of aims and outline regulatory approach.

1 See FSA Launch Document, para 30; and FSA Launch Conference, speech by Mr Howard Davies, 28 October 1997. See Blair et al (2nd edn), paras 2.10–2.14.
2 See paras 2.16–2.21.

Statement of aims

2.10   The FSA issued a general statement of aims during the early stages of policy development after the decision had been taken to establish a single financial authority.[1] This would reflect the statutory objectives to be adopted subsequently. The high-level aims related, in particular, to the protection of the interests of consumers of financial services, the promotion of clean and orderly markets and maintenance of confidence in the financial system.[2]

1 See July 1997 Report, Section 1; and FSA Launch Document, Appendix 1, paras 1 and 2.
2 See Blair et al (2nd edn), paras 2.12–2.15.

Regulatory approach

2.11   The general approach that the FSA would follow in pursuing these aims was also set out in a number of guiding principles contained in its early papers.[1] Despite the application of these principles, it was stressed that regulation would not absolve consumers of responsibility for their own decisions or financial failures. The experience of the recipient of the financial service was, however, to be taken into account as their ability to assume risk would depend upon their level of knowledge and expertise. The general distinction between the professional and personal investor had already been enshrined in the Financial Services Act 1986 and the European Investment Services Directive.

In developing its regulatory approach, a number of specific guiding principles were set out by the FSA with regard to its style and process of regulation, external relationships and accountability and efficiency and effectiveness. Much of this has since been incorporated into the Handbook of Rules and Guidance[2] as well as the separate supervisory principles set out in the FSMA 2000 in addition to the core statutory objectives adopted.

1 See July 1997 Report, Section 2; and FSA Launch Document, Appendix 1, para 3.
2 See paras 2.105–2.168.

Style and process of regulation

2.12 With regard to the style and process of regulation to be adopted, five general guiding principles were created in relation to: risk-based supervision; senior management responsibility; a commitment to high standards; consistency in authorisation; and appropriate enforcement.

The FSA would, in particular, attempt to adopt a flexible but differentiated risk-based approach to financial supervision. It would look to the boards and senior management of regulated firms to ensure financial soundness and proper conduct of their business in accordance with regulatory requirements by acting with prudence and integrity, by developing and operating effective governance structures, systems and controls and by ensuring that staff were competent.

It would also seek to promote throughout regulated firms and markets recognition of and compliance with the standards expected of them. It would adopt a consistent and co-ordinated approach to the authorisation of firms and individuals across the range of business it regulated. Where expected standards were not met, it would use its intervention and enforcement powers to secure, as appropriate, remedial action and discipline.

External relationships and accountability

2.13 The two further guiding principles to be followed concerned: accountability and openness; and co-operation with other authorities.

The FSA would take into account the continuing need – especially having regard to its size and scope – to ensure that it was responsive to the concerns of those affected by its activity. While the precise arrangements for accountability were matters to be determined in the relevant legislation, the FSA would be formally accountable to the government and Parliament in respect of its exercise of its statutory powers and be subject to periodic external scrutiny.[1] According to the FSA, it recognised obligations to all those whose interest it existed to protect and would deal with them in an open and accessible manner.

1 See paras 2.69–2.79.

Efficiency and effectiveness

2.14 In terms of promoting efficiency and cost-effectiveness, five guiding principles were to be followed concerning: competition and innovation;

cost-effectiveness; involvement of practitioners and consumers; professionalism and judgment of staff; and effective use of information technology.

The FSA would operate in a way that recognised the benefits of competition and innovation to consumers, to the UK financial sector and to the economy as a whole and which supported competitive and innovative markets for financial products. According to the FSA, it was to be cost-effective both in terms of its own activities and of their effect on practitioners and consumers. It would attempt to ensure that industry practitioners were able to contribute their expertise and views to its policy formulation and decision-making.

Much of this has since been incorporated into the principles of good regulation incorporated in s 2(3) of the FSMA 2000,[1] in addition to the basic statutory objectives set out in s 2(2).[2]

1   See para 2.19.
2   See paras 2.16–2.18.

2.15 The more general new regulatory approach to be adopted by the FSA has been developed in a number of papers subsequently. This included its January 2000 paper on *A new regulator for the new millennium*[1] and later documents including the December 2000 and February 2002 *Progress Reports*.[2] These explain the manner in which the FSA interprets its statutory objectives and principles of good regulation and set out the FSA's provisional new operating framework which is generally based on a number of probability and impact factors.[3]

1   See FSA, *A new regulator for the new millennium* (January 2000).
2   See FSA, *Building the new regulator – Progress report 1* (December 2000); and *Building the new regulator – Progress report 2* (February 2002).
3   See paras 2.16–2.21 and Chapter 6, paras 6.84–6.100.

STATUTORY OBJECTIVES AND PRINCIPLES OF GOOD REGULATION

Statutory objectives

2.16 The statutory objectives of the FSA are set out in s 2(2) of the FSMA 2000. This states that the new objectives to be followed are:

(i)   market confidence;
(ii)   public awareness;
(iii) protection of consumers; and
(iv)   reduction of financial crime.

Each of these is developed further in ss 3 to 6.

2.17 *Market confidence* involves maintaining confidence in the financial system, which is defined to include the financial markets and exchanges, regulated activities and all other activities connected with financial markets and exchanges in the UK.[1]

Public awareness is promoting public understanding of the financial system which includes developing awareness of the benefits and risks associated with different kinds of investment or other financial dealing and the provision of appropriate information and advice.[2]

Consumer protection is concerned with securing the appropriate degree of protection for consumers.[3] In assessing this, the FSA is to have regard to the varying degrees of risk involved in different kinds of investments or other transactions, the different degrees of experience and expertise that consumers may possess, consumer needs for advice and accurate information and the general principle that consumers should take responsibility for their decisions.

Reduction of financial crime is concerned with reducing the extent to which it is possible for a business carried on by a regulated person or in breach of the general prohibition set out in the Act to be used for a purpose connected with financial crime.[4] In considering this objective, the FSA must, in particular, have regard to the desirability of regulated persons being aware that their businesses may be used for criminal purposes, the need for them to take appropriate measures to prevent financial crime, facilitate its detection and monitor its incidence especially with regard to administration and employment practices as well as conduct of transactions with adequate resources being maintained in this regard. Financial crime includes any offence relating to fraud or dishonesty, misconduct or misuse of information relating to a financial market or handling the proceeds of any crime. Offence includes any act or omission which would be an offence if it had taken place in the UK.

1   FSMA 2000, s 3.
2   FSMA 2000, s 4(1) and (2).
3   FSMA 2000, s 5(1).
4   FSMA 2000, s 6(1).

2.18   The FSMA 2000 accordingly sets out a specific set of core statutory objectives for the FSA to follow in carrying on its regulatory activities. 'Financial stability' outside the regulatory area is the responsibility of the Bank of England, while more general 'market stability' is governed by the terms of the Memorandum of Understanding entered into between the FSA, the Treasury and the Bank of England. The FSA has nevertheless indicated that, in practice, it will interpret market confidence as including market stability to the extent necessary. It may then be that the same result will be achieved as if the FSA had been given express and specific responsibility in this regard.

Principles of good regulation

2.19   In addition to its statutory objectives, the FSA is to have regard to seven further supervisory or regulatory principles.[1] These generally consist of:

(i)   efficient use of its resources;
(ii)   recognition of management responsibility;
(iii)   proportionality; and
(iv)   promotion of innovation;

and three further specific competition principles dealing with:

(v)   the competitive position of the UK;
(vi)   the need to minimise any adverse effects on competition; and
(vii) the desirability of promoting competition between regulated institutions.

These requirements have been generally referred to as principles of good governance or good regulation.

1   FSMA 2000, s 2(3).

2.20 Under the FSMA 2000, the FSA is to comply with the regulatory objectives in discharging its general functions under the Act.[1] These are defined to include its rule-making function,[2] preparing and issuing codes,[3] giving guidance[4] and determining the general policy and principles in accordance with which it performs any particular function. These general functions accordingly relate more to policy development and rule promulgation rather than specific regulatory actions or decisions taken in connection with particular institutions or individuals.

1　FSMA 2000, s 2(4).
2　FSMA 2000, s 138.
3　Such as under FSMA 2000, s 143.
4　FSMA 2000, s 157.

2.21 The main value of setting out four regulatory objectives and the seven further statutory principles is to direct FSA activity and to improve account-ability. This statutory statement of objectives and principles may, in practice, have little effect in restricting the scope of authority of the FSA and have no general effect on the validity of any decisions taken. The Act only requires that the FSA acts insofar as reasonably possible in a way that is compatible with the regulatory objectives and is considered to be most appropriate in meeting those objectives.[1] The FSA is also only to have regard to the further principles of good regulation in discharging its general functions.[2] The FSA accordingly has general discretion in determining whether its actions are compatible with the regulatory objectives and in balancing the possibly conflicting requirements of each objective. Only in the most extreme of situations where the FSA has acted in a manner that is clearly contrary to the objectives may challenge be possible. Explaining compliance with statutory objectives and principles of good regulation will nevertheless assist in assessing the propriety of any action taken and in enhancing the accountability of the FSA.[3]

1　FSMA 2000, s 2(1)(a) and (b).
2　FSMA 2000, s 2(3).
3　See paras 2.69–2.79.

OPERATIONAL STRUCTURE

2.22 In designing the organisational structure of the new authority, it was decided to adopt a model based on regulatory function rather than regulated group, type of business or in accordance with prudential supervision or conduct of business lines.[1] The initial core functions identified were policy formation and review, authorisation of firms and vetting and registration of individuals, investigations, enforcement and discipline, relations with consum-ers and the public and supervision of both the prudential and conduct of business aspects of firms' activities.[2] This was reflected in the original organisational structure set up although this has been revised subsequently as the FSA's operational policy and practice have developed.

1　See July 1997 Report, Section 4, paras 8 and 9. For earlier discussion see M Taylor, 'Twin Peaks: A Regulatory Structure for the New Century' CSFI, December 1995; M Taylor, 'Peak Practice: How to Reform the UK's Regulatory System' CSFI, October 1996; M Taylor, 'Regulatory Leviathan: Will Super-SIB Work?' October 1997; and M Hall, 'All Change at the Bank of England' (1997) 7 JIBFL 295. See also R Monro-Davies, 'Where Angels Fear to

Tread?' (1997) 6 JIBFL 241 and D Turing and M Sah, 'NEWRO: Getting it Right' (1997) 9 JIBFL 4.11.
2   See Blair et al (2nd edn), paras 2.20–38.

2.23   The current operational structure is made up of four Directorates consisting of:

(i)   Consumer, Investment & Insurance;
(ii)   Deposit Takers & Markets;
(iii)   Regulatory Processes & Risk; and
(iv)   Operations;

with a number of other separate functions reporting to the Chairman directly.

Each Directorate (originally called 'function') is divided into a number of divisions which are, in turn, made up of departments (and teams within departments).[1] The effect of the revised structure adopted is generally to divide financial supervision into investment and insurance business in one main section with banks (and building societies) and markets in another. Consumer issues have been separated from authorisation and enforcement under the revised organisational arrangements adopted and moved to the new Consumer, Investment & Insurance directorate.[2] A separate risk assessment section has been set up within Regulatory Processes & Risk.

Further changes have also been necessary as the FSA has continued to develop its operations or assumed new functions such as with regard to mortgages and retail insurance sales.

1   The current organisational structure is available on www.fsa.gov.uk. The original arrangements were discussed in Blair et al (2nd edn), paras 2.20–2.38 and supporting Tables.
2   See Blair et al (2nd edn), paras 2.30–2.38.

2.24   Supervision was originally managed by Michael Foot, formerly the Executive Director of the Bank of England responsible for banking supervision. Currently (at the time of writing) Michael Foot is responsible for Deposit Takers & Markets. Consumer, Investment & Insurance is headed by John Tiner and Regulatory Processes & Risk by Carol Sergeant.[1] The earlier Authorisation, Enforcement and Consumer Relations function was managed by Phillip Thorpe, formerly Chief Executive of the Investment Management Regulatory Organisation, although this has now been split between Consumer, Investment & Insurance and Regulatory Processes & Risk. The Chief Operating Officer is currently Paul Boyle. The original Operations function was headed by Richard Farrant, formerly Chief Executive of the Securities and Futures Authority.

In addition to these main divisions within the FSA, other central functions report directly to the Chairman. These originally included central policy, quality assurance, internal audit, General Counsel to the Board and communications and corporate affairs.[2] The revised functions consist of General Counsel to the Board, Quality Assurance & Internal Audit, International Policy Co-ordination & EU Affairs, the Regulatory Decisions Committee Secretariat and Company Secretary, Press Office & Events and Public Affairs & Accountability.[3]

1   See also FSA, *Introduction to the Financial Services Authority* (December 2001), Appendix 2; and FSA, *Annual Report 2000/2001* (2001), Appendix 6.
2   See Blair *et al* (2nd edn), paras 2.20–2.38 and supporting Tables.
3   See FSA, *Introduction to the Financial Services Authority*, Sections 3, 4, 5 and 6; and FSA, *Plan and Budget*, Section 4.

2.25 The FSA now employs a total of approximately 2,300 staff and is responsible for the supervision of around 10,000 regulated institutions operating within the UK. This includes 7,500 investment firms, over 660 banks, 70 building societies, 1,000 insurance companies and friendly societies as well as Lloyd's of London.[1] There are approximately 180,000 approved persons within regulated institutions and from 2002, the FSA has also become responsible for the supervision of a further 700 credit unions.[2]

1 See FSA, *Introduction to the Financial Services Authority*, Section 1.
2 FSA, *Introduction to the Financial Services Authority*, Section 1.

2.26 In carrying out its functions under the FSMA 2000, the FSA works with the Treasury and the Bank of England under the terms of the Memorandum of Understanding entered into between them. The FSA also co-operates with the DTI on company and insolvency matters; the Department for Work and Pensions on pensions policy; the Occupational Pensions Regulatory Authority (OPRA) on occupational schemes; the Office of Fair Trading on consumer credit, consumer protection and competition issues; and the Serious Fraud Office and National Criminal Intelligence Service on financial crime.

The general objective is to ensure that all relevant functions are carried out in as effective a manner as possible with full co-operation being secured with all other bodies concerned.

The internal organisation and operations of the FSA are considered in further detail in the following sections.

Deposit takers and markets

2.27 Financial supervision is conducted through two Directorates dealing with investment and insurance business (Consumer, Investment & Insurance) and with banks and building societies (Deposit Takers & Markets).[1] These are responsible for both prudential and conduct of business regulation.[2] The Deposit Takers & Markets Directorate also deals with Major Complex Groups, Markets & Exchanges, Listing and Prudential Standards more generally.

1 See FSA, *Introduction to the Financial Services Authority*, Section 3.
2 See FSA, *Introduction to the Financial Services Authority*, p 12.

Deposit takers

2.28 Bank supervision is managed through the Deposit Takers division within the Deposit Takers & Markets Directorate. This has separate departments dealing with Domestic Firms, International Firms and Risk and Operational Support. There is also a separate policy division on Prudential Standards.

The standards of banking supervision formerly adopted by the Bank of England have generally been maintained within FSA. This is essentially based on the collection and examination of regular prudential information, management visits, specialist reports, inspections and verification and supervisory enforcement.[1] Much of this has been re-applied within the new supervisory arrangements in place, although changes have been necessary to reflect the new statutory basis for all of the powers exercised as well as the need to give effect to the new statutory objectives and supporting principles imposed. This has also had to be adjusted to take effect within the new operating framework that the FSA is developing which is, in turn, based on its new regulatory approach.[2] Many of the pre-N2 changes to bank supervision that were developed by the Bank of England following the collapse of Barings have nevertheless been re-applied until now. This includes the new RATE (Risk Assessment, Tools of Supervision, Evaluation) framework developed for UK-incorporated banks and branches of non-EU overseas banks.[3] A revised Statement of Principles had been produced by the Bank of England under the Banking Act 1987 which was supplemented by a separate Guide to Supervisory Policy. This was re-issued by the FSA in 1998. The FSA Guide has since been revised and reissued as the interim prudential sourcebook for banks (IPRU (BANK)),[4] although this will be replaced during 2004 by a single integrated sourcebook for all regulated institutions.[5]

1   See Chapter 6, paras 6.2 and 6.15–6.19.
2   See Chapter 6, paras 6.84–6.100.
3   See Chapter 6, para 6.4.
4   See Chapter 6, para 6.5 and Chapter 15.
5   See Chapter 6, paras 6.85–6.88.

Complex groups

2.29   Complex Groups are supervised under the Major Financial Groups division within the Deposit Takers & Markets Directorate. This has further subdivisions or departments dealing with UK, Europe & Japan and America & Risk Management.

Although the original Complex Groups function only dealt with banking and securities entities, it also now includes insurance operations. The earlier lead supervisory arrangements that operated between the separate sector regulatory agencies in the UK in connection with the supervision of financial conglomerates were continued under the new regime.[1] The contact and co-operation systems that were previously in place have accordingly been maintained although now operate within the new single institutional structure set up with the FSA. A separate section was, however, established to supervise the largest financial groups on a unitary basis which is now dealt with under the Major Financial Groups division within Deposit Takers & Markets.

The objective of lead supervision is to allow the FSA to adopt a coherent and integrated approach with regard to the supervision of large financial groups based on co-operation and exchange of relevant information.[2] While this may still be appropriate in certain cases, the Major Financial Groups Division is attempting to develop a number of new techniques to improve the supervision of such operational structures which will, in particular, allow it to understand more fully all risks created across the group as well as apply common standards to senior management and internal systems and controls. This work continues.

1   See July 1997 Report, Section 4, paras 17–20; and FSA Launch Document, paras 55–59.
2   See FSA, *Introduction to the Financial Services Authority*, Section 3. See also FSA, *Lead Supervision: the FSA's new approach to the co-ordination of its supervision of groups* (June 1999), Consultation Guide. See Blair et al (2nd edn), para 2.27.

Markets and listing

2.30   The supervision of markets is managed through a separate division within the Deposit Takers & Markets Directorate on Markets & Exchanges. This includes sub-operations dealing with Market Infrastructure & Conduct, Market Infrastructure and Policy.

The FSA is responsible for the recognition of investment markets and clearing houses under Part XVIII of the FSMA 2000, although it is also concerned with the supervision of other market infrastructure providers and with market surveillance and transaction monitoring.[1] The FSA is also the UK Listing Authority with responsibility for official listing under Part VI of the Act.[2] This is managed through a dedicated division within Deposit Takers & Markets. The FSA is also responsible for monitoring CREST as an approved system for dematerialised settlement under the Uncertificated Securities Regulations 1995.[3]

1 See Chapter 18, paras 18.116–18.142.
2 See Chapter 18, paras 18.6–18.107.
3 SI 1995/3272.

Investments, insurance and consumers

Investment business

2.31 Responsibility for the oversight of investment firms is conducted by the Consumer, Investment & Insurance Directorate. This includes separate sections dealing with Investment Firms and with conduct of business (COB Standards).

Medium-sized securities firms are generally regulated through the Relationship Management departments within Investment Firms. The largest firms and any more complex operations are dealt with through Major Financial Groups within the Deposit Takers & Markets Directorate. The much larger number of smaller firms are then dealt with through the Regulatory Events department within the Investment Firms division. Any more particular cross-sector or important regulatory issues are managed under a Themes sub-unit within Investment Firms.

The larger Directorate also contains further divisions dealing with the Consumer, Pensions Review, Industry Training and Insurance Firms as well as new sections on Insurance Firms and on High Street Firms.[1] Mortgage and general insurance services are to become subject to FSA-control from 2004. This will be dealt with through the new High Street Firms division.

1 See FSA, *Introduction to the Financial Services Authority*, Section 3. See para 2.32.

Insurance and consumer relations

2.32 The Consumer, Investment & Insurance Directorate is responsible for insurance business and consumer relations. Insurance companies are generally dealt with under the Insurance Firms division which includes Life Insurers and Non-Life Insurers. Insurance Firms includes separate operations on Actuarial Support and Themes. The revision of insurance regulation more generally was originally managed through a separate division referred to as the Insurance Regulation Project which was conducted in response to the Baird Report in October 2001 into the collapse of Equitable Life.[1] A new High Street Firms division has been set up to prepare for the regulation of mortgage and general insurance in addition to the Pensions Review division. Consumer relations is now also dealt with under Consumer, Investment & Insurance which was transferred from the earlier Authorisation, Enforcement & Consumer Relations division. This work includes providing consumers with relevant information directly, the provision of consumer help and establishment of a Consumer Helpline, the promotion of personal finance education and the production of comparative tables to allow consumers to compare relevant products more effectively.[2] Consumer, Investment & Insurance also includes a separate division on Industry Training.

1 See Report by Ronnie Baird, Director of Internal Audit at the FSA, *The Regulation of Equitable Life – An Independent Report* (17 October 2001).
2 See FSA, *Introduction to the Financial Services Authority*, Section 3.

Authorisation, enforcement and risk assessment

2.33 Authorisation, enforcement and risk assessment are dealt with under Regulatory Processes & Risk.

Authorisation

2.34 Authorisation[1] is managed through a dedicated division within Regulatory Processes & Risk which includes separate departments dealing with Corporate Authorisation, Individual Vetting & Approval, Intelligence & Records, Authorisation Enquires, Notification, Reporting & Data Maintenance and Mutual Societies Registration.

One of the main objectives of the new regime has been to establish a single regulatory requirement for all financial activities under the general prohibition set out in s 19(1) of the FSMA 2000. This is supported by a single examination system. The purpose of the new single application procedure has been to rationalise all of the earlier systems and requirements in place insofar as possible and to create a single administrative process with differentiation only being maintained insofar as necessary to distinguish particular types of activity. All of the main provisions in this regard are now set out in the Authorisation manual which forms part of the Regulatory Processes Block 3 of the FSA Handbook.[2] Grandfathering arrangements were applied with regard to existing authorisations as well as relevant conditions and disciplinary and regulatory records, although FSA has retained power to require an individual firm or group to re-apply for authorisation where this is considered appropriate.[3]

All applications are now dealt with through a single set of integrated procedures which are designed to ensure, in particular, that all financial firms are honest, solvent and competent and that relevant staff have appropriate experience and training subject to any special sector or firm distinctions.

1 See Chapter 5.
2 See FSA, *Introduction to the Financial Services Authority*, Section 3; and see Chapter 5.
3 See FSA, *Countdown to N2: Grandfathering* (25 July 2001), Press release; and FSA, *FSA aims for smooth transfer of firms* (11 December 2000), Press release. See also FSA, *Grandfathering Concessions and Individual Guidance* (April 2001), Consultation Paper 89; FSA, *Instructions for the review of controlled functions draft lists* (October 2001); FSA, *RPB Firms Grandfathering – Opt-In Pack* (October 2001); *Grandfathering of firms, individuals and products* (January 2001).

Enforcement

2.35 Enforcement is managed through a separate division within Regulatory Processes & Risk. This deals with all aspects of investigation, enforcement and disciplinary work.[1] The intention was to bring all necessary skills and expertise together within a new unit that could work in close co-operation with the supervision function. Where appropriate, it will also work with criminal authorities in respect of unregulated firms and individuals. While a single division has been maintained for this purpose, it has since been divided into a number of subgroups including Retail Sales, Deposit Taking & Financial Stability, Market Integrity, Retail Stockbroking & Fund Management and Law, Policy & International Co-operation with a separate Leading FSA Advocate's office.[2]

1 See paras 2.64–2.68 and Chapter 14.
2 See FSA, *Introduction to the Financial Services Authority*, Section 3.

2.36 All of the main provisions with regard to investigations and discipline are set out in the Enforcement manual within the FSA Handbook.[1] This explains how the FSA exercises its enforcement powers under the FSMA 2000. This includes more general provisions with regard to information gathering and investigations[2] as well as disciplinary measures,[3] intervention in connection with incoming firms,[4] injunctions and restitution[5] and general offences.[6] The 2000 Act also provides for a number of other more specific offences such as with regard to breach of the general prohibition,[7] false claims as to authorisation or exemption,[8] breach of the financial promotions restrictions[9] and the new provisions on market abuse.[10]

It was always intended that the FSA would have all necessary powers at its disposal, at least, equivalent to those of its earlier constituent bodies as well as additional powers in certain respects including, for example, with regard to the civil disposal of cases of serious market misconduct.

1 See paras 2.64–2.68 and 2.125–2.126.
2 Part XI.
3 Part XIV.
4 Part XIII.
5 Part XXV.
6 Part XXVII.
7 FSMA 2000, s 23.
8 FSMA 2000, s 24.
9 FSMA 2000, s 25.
10 FSMA 2000, s 118.

Risk assessment

2.37 Regulatory Processes & Risk also includes a separate division on Risk Assessment which is further divided into a number of separate sub-units dealing with Regulatory Planning & Performance Measurement, Risk & Research and Risk Assessment Framework & Regulatory Processes.

Operations

2.38 The general work of the FSA is supported by the Operations Directorate. Its role is to enhance the operational effectiveness of the FSA by providing an integrated range of support services and ensure that resources are used in an efficient and economic manner. This is generally directed by a 'Resources Strategies' framework which attempts to balance the use of resources against more general regulatory objectives. The Directorate contains subdivisions on Premises, Human Resources (including Corporate Learning & Development), Information Systems (Strategy & Knowledge Management,

Programme Management, Customer Relationship and Information Support Services) and Finance & Business Planning (including Communications & Publications).

Central functions

2.39 A number of central functions are also carried out within FSA that report directly to the Chairman. The current organisational structure includes the General Counsel to the Board (with separate Chief Counsel Banking & General, Chief Counsel Investment Business, Chief Counsel Insurance & Friendly Societies and Chief Counsel Markets); Quality Assurance & Internal Audit; and International Policy Co-ordination & EU Affairs. The Regulatory Decisions Committee Secretariat also reports directly to the Chairman with the Company Secretary, Press Office & Events and Public Affairs & Accountability.

MEMORANDUM OF UNDERSTANDING

2.40 To ensure that its relationships with other agencies operate in a transparent and effective manner, the FSA has entered into various Memoranda of Understanding (MoUs). These govern its operations with certain other bodies and authorities both within the UK and elsewhere. Closer co-operation with other bodies has been secured through the transfer of former MoUs concerning supervisory matters to which the Bank of England was party to FSA before N1 and in respect of all of the other constituent organisations by N2.[1] This is in addition to its continued participation in various international banking, securities and insurance fora. Rather than relinquish its involvement with such work, the Bank of England has continued its participation and will often sit with the FSA at regular committee meetings such as those of the Basel Committee on Banking Supervision.[2]

1 See FSA Launch Document, paras 69–70.
2 See Chapter 21.

FSA, Treasury and Bank of England

2.41 As noted in Chapter 1, the most important external relationships of the FSA are with the Bank of England and the Treasury. In the light of this, an MoU was entered into in October 1997,[1] setting out how the three authorities work together towards the common objective of financial stability and how their respective responsibilities are to be discharged. The division of responsibilities is stated to be based on the four guiding principles of clear accountability; transparency; no duplication; and regular information exchange.

1 See FSA 'Memorandum of Understanding between FSA, Treasury and Bank of England', Press Release, 28 October 1997.

The Bank's responsibilities

2.42 Under para 2 of the MoU, the Bank is primarily responsible for the overall stability of the financial system including stability of the monetary system, financial system infrastructure and, in particular, the payments system at home and abroad. It should also carry out a broad overview of the system as a whole, undertake official financial operations in exceptional circumstances in accordance with the procedures set out in paras 11 to 13 of the MoU as well as monitor the efficiency and effectiveness of the financial sector especially with regard to the promotion of international competitiveness.

FSA's responsibilities

2.43　While the powers and responsibilities of FSA are incorporated legally in the FSMA 2000, under para 3 of the MoU the FSA is responsible for:

— the authorisation and prudential supervision of banks, building societies, investment firms, insurance companies and friendly societies;
— the supervision of financial markets and of clearing and settlement systems;
— the conduct of operations in response to problem cases affecting firms, markets and clearing and settlement systems within its responsibilities; and
— regulatory policy in these areas.

The Treasury's responsibilities

2.44　The Treasury is primarily responsible for the overall institutional structure of regulation and the legislation which governs it. It has no operational responsibility in respect of the activities of FSA or the Bank although the Treasury is to be informed of possible difficulties such as where a serious problem arises that could cause wider economic disruptions, a support operation may be necessary, diplomatic or foreign relations problems may arise, the law may have to be changed or questions may have to be referred to Ministers in Parliament.

Information exchange and gathering

2.45　While the FSA and the Bank will collect the data and information required to discharge their responsibilities, they will work to avoid separate collection through agreed information-gathering arrangements. Information-sharing arrangements were also established between the FSA and the Bank to ensure that all information was fully and freely shared, while close and regular contact is to be maintained between the two bodies especially through overlapping memberships and secondments.

　Information which is received under these arrangements must only be used for the purposes of discharging relevant responsibilities and must not be transmitted to third parties, except where permitted by law.

Standing Committee and support operations

2.46　A Standing Committee of representatives of the Treasury, the Bank and the FSA was established to discuss individual cases of significance and other developments relevant to financial stability on a monthly basis. Emergency meetings may also be convened at short notice.

　Under para 11 of the MoU, the Bank and the FSA should immediately inform and consult with each other in circumstances where exceptional support operations may be required. This would apply where the stability of the financial system may be threatened and the operation goes beyond the Bank's routine activity in the money market to implement its interest rate objectives. The particular response adopted is to be determined by the lead institution in such cases with the appointment being determined in accordance with the relevant responsibilities as set out in paras 2 and 3 of the MoU. The Bank and FSA are to work closely together in all cases and immediately to inform the Treasury to allow the Chancellor to refuse support action as required. Thereafter the Treasury must be kept fully informed about the developing situation.

The MoU also contains additional provisions with regard to consultation and policy changes, membership of committees, provision of services, litigation and records.

2.47 The MoU is important in determining the precise scope of the relationships between the three bodies concerned as well as the procedures in the event of some lender-of-last-resort support operation being required. The provision of lender-of-last-resort support to the financial markets has been one of the most important functions of the Bank of England historically. Despite the removal of its supervisory role, the Bank will continue to have to exercise a close monitoring role over the operation of the financial system to ensure that unnecessary difficulties do not occur and that in the event of a potential crisis arising proper support is made available. In practice, the terms of the MoU will only serve as a basic framework document with the action taken by each institution depending upon the particular circumstances.

SEC, CFTC, Bank of England and FSA

2.48 At the time of the FSA launch, a further MoU was entered into between the Securities and Exchange Commission (SEC), the Commodity Futures Trading Commission (CFTC), the Bank of England and the FSA with a view to enhancing the ability of the authorities to obtain information about the activities of US and UK internationally active firms, including information concerning their internal controls and risk management systems.[1]

Procedures for co-operation to deal with potentially significant market events experienced by US or UK securities or banking firms were also provided for. It was intended that the MoU will improve the effectiveness of financial supervision at a time of increased cross-border and cross-sectoral activities.

1 See FSA, 'Memorandum of Understanding between SEC, CFTC, Bank of England and FSA', Press Release, 28 October 1997.

BANK OF ENGLAND ACT 1998

2.49 The Bank of England Bill was originally published at FSA's launch on 28 October 1997. It received its Royal Assent on 23 April 1998 and came into effect on 1 June 1998 (N1).[1] The purpose of the Act was to introduce further statutory provision concerning the structure and operation of the Bank of England and to provide for the transfer of responsibility for banking supervision from the Bank to the FSA. Under the 1998 Act, the constitution and duties of the Court of Directors are revised with new provisions being enacted in relation to the funding, accounts and profits of the Bank. The Act confirms the establishment of the Monetary Policy Committee (MPC) within the Bank and provides a statutory basis for the Bank's operational responsibility in relation to monetary policy.[2]

1   See M Blair, R Cranston, C Ryan and M Taylor, *Guide to the Bank of England Act 1998* (1998).
2   See Blair et al (2nd edn), paras 2.62–2.76.

2.50   Part III of the 1998 Act provides for the transfer to the FSA of the Bank's functions under the Banking Act 1987, the Banking Coordination (Second Council Directive) Regulations 1992[1] and the Building Societies Act 1986, as well as its functions under s 43 of the Financial Services Act 1986, the Investment Services Regulations 1995 and under s 171 of the Companies Act 1989.

The transfer to the FSA of the Bank's functions in relation to the supervision of banks was, in particular, given effect to under s 21(a). The functions of the Bank in respect of listed money market institutions as well as in respect of its functions in relation to the listing of persons providing settlement arrangements under s 171 of the Companies Act 1989 were transferred under s 21(b) and (c). A number of supplementary provisions with regard to the transfer of functions were set out in Sch 4.[1]

1   SI 1992/3218.
2   See Blair et al (2nd edn), paras 2.67–2.73.

FINANCIAL SERVICES AND MARKETS ACT 2000

2.51   The FSMA 2000 received its Royal Assent on 14 June 2000. The Act comprises 433 sections and 22 Schedules. It followed an extended and often tortuous drafting and debate procedure. The draft Bill was produced by the Treasury in July 1998. This was accompanied by Explanatory Notes and a separate guidance paper. Lord Burns, the former Permanent Secretary to the Treasury, was asked to chair a joint committee of both the House of Commons and House of Lords to consider the most important issues that arose under the Bill in an independent and non-partisan manner. Evidence was taken from industry and consumer representatives and other Government and official witnesses. A First Report was produced on 29 April 1999 and a Second Report on 29 May 1999. The draft Bill was then introduced to the House of Commons on 17 June 1999 and went into Committee stage in July 1999. The Bill was (unusually) carried over into the next session of Parliament in October 1999. The Bill began its Report stage in January 2000. It was considered for a final time in the House of Lords on Monday 12 June and given Royal Assent on 14 June. By that stage, over 2,750 amendments had been considered with 1,500 having been adopted during 200 hours of Parliamentary debate.

2.52   The FSMA 2000 is complex and substantial, although it only creates the outline statutory framework for the new supervisory and regulatory regime set up in the UK. The Act generally provides for the creation of a dual authorisation and permission regime, the introduction of a new definition of regulated activities, revised restrictions on financial promotion, the establishment of an extended approved persons regime, the creation of the new offence of market abuse and conferral on the FSA of general authority to issue rules

and guidance concerning the more detailed day-to-day regulatory requirements to be imposed on regulated firms and individuals. Enhanced enforcement powers are assigned to the FSA with the Act also providing for the
establishment of a new integrated Ombudsman, Financial Services Compensation Scheme and Financial Services and Markets Tribunal. The Act contains
further provision with regard to Official Listing (following the appointment of
the FSA as the UK Listing Authority) and new provision concerning banking
and insurance business transfers. The Act contains only minimal regulatory
provision. The Act focuses on the creation of necessary offences and conferral
on the FSA of all appropriate power and authority to enforce these provisions.
The main body of substantive regulatory provision is now set out in the
Handbook of Rules and Guidance issued by the FSA under ss 138 and 157 of
the Act. This is considered further below.[1]

1 See paras 2.83–2.146.

2.53 The main elements of the new statutory framework created under the
FSMA 2000 are concerned with (i) the establishment of the new authorisation
and permission regimes, (ii) the issuance of rules and guidance, (iii)
enforcement, (iv) accountability and transparency and (v) integrated support
with the new integrated Ombudsman and Compensation arrangements. These
are considered in turn below.

Authorisation and permission

2.54 The system of statutory control set up under the FSMA 2000 is based
on three main provisions. These consist of the general prohibition, the
permission requirement and restriction on financial promotion.

Under the Act, no person may carry on a regulated activity in the UK (or
purport to do so) unless he is an authorised person or an exempt person.[1] This
is referred to as the 'general prohibition'. An authorised person is also required
to act only in accordance with the scope of any permission conferred under
Part IV or any other provision of the Act.[2]

Any person who contravenes the general prohibition commits an authorisation offence[3] and is liable for up to two years' imprisonment or a fine or both.[4]
Any agreement entered into is unenforceable and the other party is entitled to
recover any money or property paid or transferred and compensation for any
loss sustained.[5]

1 FSMA 2000, s 19(1).
2 FSMA 2000, s 20(1).
3 FSMA 2000, s 23(2).
4 FSMA 2000, s 23(1).
5 FSMA 2000, s 26(1) and (2).

2.55 While the general prohibition may be breached by anyone and
constitutes an offence with the transaction being unenforceable, breach of the
permission requirement only amounts to an administrative infraction.[1] Contravention is not an offence, the transaction is not void or unenforceable and no
separate right of action for breach of statutory duty arises.[2] The general
prohibition accordingly applies to all persons while the permission requirement
only applies to authorised parties.

1   FSMA 2000, s 20(1).
2   FSMA 2000, s 20(2).

2.56   'Regulated activity' is defined in s 22(1). An activity is a regulated activity for the purposes of the FSMA 2000 if it is of a specified kind and carried on by way of business relating to an investment of a specified kind or carried on in relation to property of any kind. While investment includes any asset, right or interest, specified means listed by order of the Treasury. This was effected under the Regulated Activities Order, which came into effect on N2.[1] The general range of activities and investments that may be included within the Treasury order are listed in Sch 2 to the Act. Under Sch 2, regulated activities may include dealing and arranging deals in investments, deposit taking, safekeeping and administration of assets, managing investments, investment advice, establishing collective investment schemes and using computer-based systems for providing investment instructions.[2] This generally follows the definition of investment activity set out in Part II of Sch 1 to the Financial Services Act 1986 with the addition of deposit taking.

Investments now include securities, instruments creating or acknowledging indebtedness, government and public securities, instruments giving entitlement to investments, certificates representing securities, units in collective investment schemes, options, futures, contracts for differences, contracts of insurance, participation in Lloyd's syndicates, deposits, loans secured on land and rights in investments.[3] This generally follows Part I of Sch 1 of the Financial Services Act 1986 with deposits and secured loans as well as contracts of insurance and Lloyd's syndicate participations.

The scope and meaning of each of these activities and investments is set out in further detail in the Regulated Activities Order. Schedule 2 is only indicative and is non-exhaustive with the definition of regulated activities for the purposes of the FSMA 2000 being as set out in the Order.

1   See Financial Services and Markets Act 2000 (Regulated Activities) Order 2001 (SI 2001/544) as amended by Financial Services and Markets Act 2000 (Regulated Activities) (Amendment) Order 2001 (SI 2001/3544). See Chapter 5.
2   FSMA 2000, Sch 2, Pt I.
3   FSMA 2000, Sch 2, Pt II.

2.57   The draft Regulated Activities Order was initially released for consultation in October 2000.[1] The draft was accompanied by a draft Exemption Order, Appointed Representatives Regulations, Non-Exempt Activities Order and Business Order.[2] These followed an earlier consultation in February 1999. The Exemption Order, in particular, sets out the specified persons or persons within a specified class exempt from the general prohibition under the FSMA 2000.[3] The Non-Exempt Activities Order lists certain regulated activities that do not fall within the exemption provided under Part XX of the Act (members of the professions). The Appointed Representatives Regulations specifies the types of businesses that appointed representatives of authorised persons may carry out. The Business Order sets out the circumstances in which a person is or is not to be regarded as carrying on a regulated activity by way of business. Article 2 of the Business Order was revised to reflect the business tests for deposit-taking formerly set out in s 6 of the Banking Act 1987. Article 3 amends the business test for investment business to reflect s 22 of the Financial Services Act 1986. Article 4 follows s 191 of the Financial Services Act 1986.

1   See HM Treasury, *Financial Services and Markets Act 2000: Regulated Activities – Second Consultation Document* (October 2000).

2 Second Consultation Document, Part IV. See also Financial Services and Markets Act 2000 (Exemption) Order 2001 (SI 2001/1201) as amended by Financial Services and Markets Act 2000 (Exemption) (Amendment) Order 2001 (SI 2001/3623); Financial Services and Markets Act 2001 (Appointed Representatives) Regulations 2001 (SI 2000/1217) as amended by Financial Services and Markets Act 2000 (Appointed Representatives) (Amendment) Regulations 2001 (SI 2001/2508); Financial Services and Markets Act 2000 (Professions – Non-Exempt Activities) Order 2001 (SI 2001/1227); Financial Services and Markets Act 2000 (Carrying on Regulated Activities by Way of Business Order) Order 2001 (SI 2001/1177).
3 FSMA 2000, s 38(1).

2.58 Part II of the FSMA 2000 also imposes restrictions on financial promotion as well as creates the offence of making false claims as to being an authorised or exempt person.[1]

A person must not, in the course of business, communicate an invitation or inducement to engage in investment activity unless authorised or the content of the communication has been approved by an authorised person.[2] 'Engaging in investment activity' means either entering or offering to enter into an agreement the making or performance of which by either party constitutes a controlled activity or exercising any rights conferred by a controlled investment to acquire, dispose of, underwrite or convert a controlled investment. An activity is controlled if it is of a specified kind or falls within a specified class of activity and relates to an investment of a specified kind or specified class. An investment is controlled if it is of a specified kind or falls within a specified class.

The exemptions from this requirement and circumstances in which a person is to be regarded as acting or not acting in the course of business are set out in the Financial Promotions Order.[2] The restriction on financial promotion only applies to communications originating outside the UK where they are capable of having an effect in the UK.

1 See Chapter 5.
2 FSMA 2000, s 21(1) and (2).
3 See Financial Services and Markets Act 2000 (Financial Promotion) Order 2001 (SI 2001/1335).

2.59 It is an offence under FSMA 2000 for any persons who are neither authorised nor exempt to describe themselves as authorised or exempt in whatever terms or behave or otherwise hold themselves out as indicating (or reasonably likely to be understood as indicating) that they are authorised or exempt.[1]

A person may be liable for up to six months' imprisonment or a level 5 fine. Where the conduct constituting the offence has included the public display of any material, the fine is level 5 multiplied by the number of days during which the display continued.

It is a defence to show that a person took all reasonable precautions and exercised all due diligence to avoid committing any offence.

1 FSMA 2000, s 24(1).

2.60 Authorisation is governed by Part III and permission by Part IV of FSMA 2000. Applications are made for permission to carry on one or more regulated activities.[1] Such applications may be made by an individual, a body corporate, a partnership or an unincorporated association although only a body corporate or a partnership may apply to accept deposits.[2] Permission is only granted if the applicant satisfies the threshold conditions set out in Sch 6.[3]

Once a person has obtained a Part IV permission to carry on one or more regulated activities, they automatically become an authorised person.[4] Authorised persons also include EEA and Treaty firms under Schs 3 and 4 and any person otherwise authorised under the Act.[5]

The separate authorisation regime was generally necessary to allow European authorised firms to conduct regulated activities within the UK. Authorisation is then more concerned with status rather than specific entitlement with the scope of activities that any regulated person may carry out being determined by the terms of their home country licence. It is also for this reason that UK applications are for permission rather than authorisation. The 2000 Act distinguishes between European Economic Area (EEA) and Treaty firms in that Sch 3 (EEA Firms) only applies to those authorised under the European financial directives while Sch 4 (Treaty Firms) includes the exercise of any other rights conferred directly by the European Community Treaty.[6]

1 FSMA 2000, s 40(1).
2 FSMA 2000, Sch 6, Pt I, para 1(2)(a) and (b).
3 FSMA 2000, s 41(1). See Chapter 5.
4 Under FSMA 2000, s 31(1)(a).
5 FSMA 2000, s 31(1)(b), (c) and (d).
6 FSMA 2000, s 417(1).

Rules and guidance

2.61 The detailed requirements applicable with regard to the day-to-day conduct of regulated activities are not set out in FSMA 2000 but rather in the form of rules and guidance issued by the FSA under the Act. The reason for this was to create a more flexible regulatory system that can be quickly revised in response to changes within financial market structure or practice without the need for legislative amendment.

The FSA's general functions under the 2000 Act are defined in terms of its rule-making power,[1] although these also include power to issue codes and guidance and determine general policy and principles.[2]

A number of different types of rules are then provided for under the Act. The FSA may issue general rules applying to authorised persons with respect to regulated or other activities where this is considered necessary or expedient for the purpose of protecting the interests of consumers.[3] The FSA may issue endorsing rules such as with regard to the City Code on Takeovers and Mergers or the Panel on Takeovers and Mergers' rules Governing Substantial Acquisitions.[4] The FSA may also issue other specific Rules such as with regard to insurance business,[5] price stabilising,[6] financial promotion,[7] money laundering,[8] control of information[9] and auditors and actuaries.[10]

1 FSMA 2000, s 2(4)(a).
2 FSMA 2000, s 2(4)(b), (c) and (d). See para 2.62 below.
3 FSMA 2000, s 138(1).
4 FSMA 2000, s 143(1).
5 FSMA 2000, s 141.
6 FSMA 2000, s 144. See Chapter 18, paras 18.108–18.112.
7 FSMA 2000, s 145.
8 FSMA 2000, s 146.
9 FSMA 2000, s 147.
10 FSMA 2000, s 340(1).

2.62 The FSA may provide guidance in support of its rules.[1] The FSA may, in particular, issue such information and advice as it considers appropriate with respect to the operation of the FSMA 2000 or of any of its rules, with respect to any matters relating to its functions, its regulatory objectives or with respect to any other matters where this may be desirable.[2] The guidance may be published and offered for sale at a reasonable charge or a reasonable charge imposed on any specific request made. The guidance may also be issued by third parties with the FSA providing financial or other assistance. Copies of the guidance and any alterations must be given to the Treasury.[3]

1   FSMA 2000, s 2(4)(c).
2   FSMA 2000, s 157(1).
3   FSMA 2000, s 158(1) and (2).

2.63   The FSMA 2000 sets out a special procedure for the issuance of rules and guidance. While the rules have the equivalent effect to secondary instruments, the normal Parliamentary procedures with regard to the production of such measures are dis-applied.

The FSA is generally only required to exercise its powers in writing and specify the provision of the Act under which the rules are made[1] with draft copies having being published in a manner considered to be best calculated to bring them to the attention of the public.[2] The draft must be accompanied by a cost-benefit analysis, an explanation of the purpose of the proposed rules and their compatibility with the FSA's general duties under s 2 and contain notice that representations may be made within a specified time.[3] The FSA is then only required to consider rather than follow the representations made. The FSA is also only required to provide the Treasury with a copy of the rules once they have been made as well as any alteration or revocation.[4]

The effect of these provisions is to confer on the FSA a quasi-lawmaking power although one that operates outside the normal scope of traditional Parliamentary scrutiny and accountability. It must be accepted that it is exceptional for such authority to be conferred on a private body.[5] The accountability regime established under the Act is considered further below.[6]

1   FSMA 2000, s 153(1) and (2).
2   FSMA 2000, s 155(1).
3   FSMA 2000, s 155(2).
4   FSMA 2000, s 152(1) and (2).
5   For further discussion, see M Taylor, 'Accountability and Objectives of the FSA' in M Blair, R Cranston, C Ryan and M Taylor, *Guide to the Bank of England Act 1998* (1998), Ch 2.
6   See paras 2.69–2.79.

Enforcement

2.64   The FSMA 2000 confers on the FSA a range of intervention and enforcement powers. These re-state many of the former powers available under the earlier sector statutes, although a number of these have been consolidated and revised under the new regime. The Act contains more general provisions with regard to information gathering and investigations,[1] disciplinary measures,[2] intervention in connection with incoming firms,[3] injunctions and restitution[4] and general offences[5] as well as a number of other more specific offences such as with regard to contravention of the general prohibition,[6] the making of false claims as to authorisation or exemption,[7] breach of the financial promotions restrictions[8] and provisions on market abuse.[9]

The effect of these provisions is to confer a range of formal powers of intervention on the FSA in connection with regulatory breaches and the prosecution of all other offences under FSMA 2000. This is supported by the range of information and investigation powers provided, with the FSA being able to impose a wide variety of sanctions including private and public censure and financial penalties as well as apply for injunction or restitution orders. In addition to restricting or cancelling permission[10] or the withdrawal of authorisation,[11] the FSA may petition for a winding-up or bankruptcy order[12] and participate in other insolvency proceedings.[13]

While most of these powers are only exercisable against the regulated community, the FSA can proceed against anyone in connection with certain offences such as breach of the core prohibition,[14] market abuse[15] and misleading statements and practices.[16] The FSA has accordingly acquired a significant range of preventative and penal statutory powers under the FSMA 2000.

1   FSMA 2000, Pt XI.
2   FSMA 2000, Pt XIV.
3   FSMA 2000, Pt XIII.
4   FSMA 2000, Pt XXV.
5   FSMA 2000, Pt XXVII.
6   FSMA 2000, s 23(1).
7   FSMA 2000, s 24(1).
8   FSMA 2000, s 25(1).
9   FSMA 2000, ss 118 and 123(1).
10 FSMA 2000, s 44.
11 FSMA 2000, s 33.
12 FSMA 2000, ss 367 and 372.
13 FSMA 2000, Pt XXIV.
14 FSMA 2000, ss 19(1) and 23(1).
15 FSMA 2000, ss 118(1) and 123(1).
16 FSMA 2000, s 397(2) and (3).

2.65   The FSA's proposals with regard to enforcement were originally set out in its Consultation Paper 17 (December 1998) and Consultation Paper 25 (July 1999).[1] The enforcement regime was revised following amendments made to the Bill during the Bill's Parliamentary processes.[2] While a range of formal powers are available, the FSA has stressed that it will not take formal disciplinary action in all cases. Where appropriate, the FSA will respond through 'proactive supervision' and monitoring as well as by maintaining an open and co-operative relationship with firms insofar as possible.[3] Formal action will then be taken where firms fail to respond promptly. Enforcement powers will generally be exercised to secure the statutory objectives set out in the FSMA 2000. The full range of the regulatory tools including enforcement available were also considered by the FSA as part of its new operating framework in January 2000.[4]

1   See FSA, *Financial Services Regulation: Enforcing the New Regime* (December 1998), CP 17; and FSA, *Enforcing the New Perimeter* (July 1999), CP 25. Response papers were issued in July 1999 and December 1999.
2   See FSA, *The Enforcement Manual* (August 2000), CP 65, Ch 1. The full text of the draft Enforcement Manual was first issued as part of CP 65.
3   See CP 65, para 2.2.
4   See FSA, *A new regulator for the new millennium* (January 2000).

2.66   The full range of formal powers available to the FSA and its proposed policies and procedures in connection with the exercise of these powers are set out in the Enforcement manual (ENF) which is included as part of the Regulatory Process Block 3 of the Handbook of Rules and Guidance. This gives effect to specific requirements in the FSMA 2000 to publish its policy and procedures in connection with the exercise of formal powers. Further guidance is also provided.

Following an introduction, the Enforcement manual explains how the FSA will exercise its powers in 18 separate sets of circumstances. These consist of:

(1) information gathering and investigation powers;
(2) decision-making;
(3) variation of Part IV permission on the FSA's own initiative;
(4) intervention against incoming firms;
(5) cancellation of Part IV permission and withdrawal of authorisation;
(6) injunctions;
(7) withdrawal of approval;
(8) prohibition of individuals;
(9) restitution;
(10) insolvency proceedings and orders against debt avoidance;
(11) general discipline of authorised and approved persons;
(12) public statements of misconduct;
(13) discipline of authorised firms and approved persons and financial penalties;
(14) sanctions for market abuse;
(15) prosecution of criminal offences;
(16) collective investment schemes;
(17) disqualification of auditors and actuaries; and
(18) disapplication orders against members of the professions.

The Enforcement manual accordingly provides considerable assistance in clarifying the nature of the specific sanctions or offences concerned and the manner in which the FSA will enforce them. While a powerful range of retaliatory provision is available, the FSA would still appear to be concerned to act in as transparent and accountable a manner as possible.

2.67 One of the particular complaints that arose during the Bill stage was that with its full range of powers, the FSA would effectively act as prosecutor, judge and jury in connection with any enforcement action. Concerns also arose as to whether specific offences such as in connection with market abuse and the disciplinary regime as a whole complied with the European Convention on Human Rights. To the extent that the proceedings were considered to be criminal in nature, under article 6 of the Convention, a number of additional safeguards would have to be provided including a clear presumption of innocence and privilege against self-incrimination in disciplinary proceedings. Article 6 also requires that there is an independent and impartial court and a fair trial with a right to proper legal assistance to the extent necessary.

The nature of the proceedings was, in particular, considered by the Joint Committee under Lord Burns. The government also received advice from Sir Sidney Ketridge QC and James Eadie that the disciplinary regime generally was not criminal in nature although a number of further safeguards were introduced in connection with market abuse proceedings to ensure that appropriate criminal safeguards were available.

As part of its internal revision and, in particular, to avoid complaints of bias or abuse, the FSA also decided to establish a separate Regulatory Decisions Committee (RDC) to decide on enforcement actions. The RDC is not provided under for under the FSMA 2000 and was established at the FSA's initiative. The purpose is to separate the enforcement decision process from the internal supervisory and investigatory functions of the FSA. While the RDC has an independent Chairman, it still operates as a part of the FSA.

2.68 A Financial Services and Markets Tribunal was also set up under the 2000 Act to ensure independence in connection with the conduct of hearings and appeals.[1] The Tribunal is independent of the FSA and is administered by the Lord Chancellor's Department. The Lord Chancellor is given power to make rules concerning the conduct of proceedings before the Tribunal[2] with constitutional and procedural matters being dealt with under the Act.[3]

The Tribunal has both a first instance and appellate jurisdiction. The function of the Tribunal is generally to determine the appropriate action to be taken by the FSA with its decisions being remitted back to the FSA for action.[4] The FSA is required to act in accordance with any determination or direction of the Tribunal.[5] The Act also contains separate provision for appeal on a point of law to the courts.[6]

1 FSMA 2000, Pt IX. See Chapter 20.
2 FSMA 2000, s 132(3).
3 FSMA 2000, Sch 13.
4 FSMA 2000, s 133(4) and (5).
5 FSMA 2000, s 133(10).
6 FSMA 2000, s 137(1).

Accountability and transparency

2.69 In light of the essentially rules-based nature of the regulatory system set up under the FSMA 2000 and the extended range of enforcement powers conferred on the FSA, it is essential that appropriate accountability mechanisms are in place. This is particularly necessary as the FSA is only a private limited company and does not act on behalf of the Crown.[1] A number of mechanisms are included within the 2000 Act in this regard. These are essentially based on Treasury oversight and review rather than direct Parliamentary control. This reflects traditional practice with regard to public corporations although the degree of formal accountability secured in practice may be questioned.[2]

1 FSMA 2000, Sch 1, paras 13 and 14. The FSA is exempt from the requirement under the Companies Act 1985 to use 'limited' as part of its name subject to review by the Secretary of State (Sch 1, paras 14 and 15).
2 For general discussion, see M Taylor, 'Accountability and Objectives of the FSA' in M Blair, R Cranston, C Ryan and M Taylor, *Guide to the Bank of England Act 1998* (1998), Ch 2.

Treasury oversight

2.70 The FSA is generally responsible for the conduct of its activities to HM Treasury. The Treasury appoints the Chairman and other members of the governing body of the FSA.[1] The FSA is required to make a report to the Treasury, at least, annually on the discharge of its functions, the extent to which its regulatory objectives and supervisory principles have been secured and any other matters the Treasury may from time to time direct.[2] A separate report must also be prepared by the non-executive members of the governing board of the FSA on the discharge of their functions. The responsibilities of the non-executive members are generally to review the extent to which the FSA acts in the most efficient and economic manner and whether its internal financial controls secure the proper conduct of its financial affairs as well as the remuneration of the Chairman and executive members of the governing body.[3] Copies of these reports are to be laid before Parliament.[4]

1   FSMA 2000, Sch 1, para 2(3).
2   FSMA 2000, Sch 1, para 10(1).
3   FSMA 2000, Sch 1, para 4(3) and (6).
4   FSMA 2000, Sch 1, para 10(2) and (3).

Review or enquiry

2.71   The Treasury may require that either an independent review or inquiry is conducted with regard to the activities of the FSA in certain cases.

The Treasury may appoint an independent person to conduct a review of the economy, efficiency and effectiveness with which the FSA has used its resources in discharging its functions.[1] This may be limited to such functions as are specified although it may not consider the merits of the FSA's general policy, regulatory principles or official listing related functions.[2] The person conducting the review has a right of access at any reasonable time to all such documents or other information and explanations as may be required.[3]

A copy of the written review containing such recommendations as may be considered appropriate is to be delivered to the Treasury, a copy laid before each House of Parliament and published in such manner as the Treasury may consider appropriate.[4]

1   FSMA 2000, s 12(1).
2   FSMA 2000, s 12(3).
3   FSMA 2000, s 13(1).
4   FSMA 2000, s 12(4) and (5).

2.72   The Treasury may also appoint such person as they consider appropriate to conduct an inquiry.[1] An inquiry may be called for where this is considered in the public interest and serious concerns have arisen with regard to either the operation of the financial or regulatory system or the official list.[2]

Directions may be issued by the Treasury with regard to the scope, period, conduct or reporting of the inquiry. The person conducting the inquiry will determine the procedures to be followed and may obtain any such information or documents as may be considered fit.[3]

A written report with recommendations is again to be submitted to the Treasury on conclusion of the inquiry.[4] The Treasury may publish all or part of the report, a copy of which must be laid before each House of Parliament.[5] Anyone who fails to comply with an inquiry request or otherwise obstruct the inquiry is guilty of contempt.[6]

1   FSMA 2000, ss 14(4) and 15(1).
2   FSMA 2000, s 14(2) and (3).
3   FSMA 2000, s 16(2).
4   FSMA 2000, s 17(1).
5   FSMA 2000, s 17(2)–(5).
6   FSMA 2000, s 18(1).

Public meetings

2.73   In addition to providing the Treasury with a copy of its annual report, the FSA must hold a public meeting within three months of the report having been made.[1] The purpose of the meeting is to allow general discussion of the contents of the report and provide a reasonable opportunity for the FSA to be questioned as to the manner in which it has discharged or failed to discharge its functions during the period to which the report relates.[2] Reasonable notice must be given including details of the time and place at which the meeting is to be held, the proposed agenda and duration of the meeting and attendance arrangements. This must be published in the way appearing to be most suitable for bringing the notice to the attention of the public.[3] Reasonable notice of any alterations must also be given.[4] A report of the proceedings of the meeting must be published within one month.[5]

1　FSMA 2000, Sch 1, para 11(1).
2　FSMA 2000, Sch 1, para 11(2).
3　FSMA 2000, Sch 1, para 11(4) and (5).
4　FSMA 2000, Sch 1, para 11(6).
5　FSMA 2000, Sch 1, para 12.

Good governance

2.74　In addition to complying with its regulatory objectives and supplementary supervisory principles, the FSA is required to have regard to such generally accepted principles of good corporate governance in managing its affairs as it is reasonable to regard as relevant.[1] Although drafted in general terms, this is an important requirement in applying the general standards of good corporate governance to the activities of the FSA.[2]

1　FSMA 2000, s 7.
2　See also FSMA 2000, Sch 1, paras 2(1) (constitution) and 3(1) (non-executive members) in para 2.75 below.

Board and committee structure

2.75　The general requirement of good governance is supported by the more specific constitutional requirements imposed on the FSA under Sch 1 of the FSMA 2000. The constitution of the FSA is, in particular, required to make provision for a Chairman and governing body as well as a majority of non-executive members. The governing body must maintain a separate committee of non-executive members.[1]

The non-executive members are appointed by the FSA, with their chairman being appointed by the Treasury from amongst its members.[2] As noted, the purpose of the non-executive members is to review the efficiency of the manner in which the FSA conducts its functions, its internal control systems and the remuneration of the Chairman and the executive members.[3]

With regard to its internal operations, the FSA must make arrangements for any of its functions to be discharged by a committee, subcommittee, officer or member of staff.[4] Legislative functions may only be conducted through the governing body.[5] The FSA must maintain effective monitoring and enforcement arrangements.[6] The FSA must also generally maintain satisfactory arrangements for recording decisions made in the exercise of its functions and the safe-keeping of records to be preserved.[7]

1　FSMA 2000, Sch 1, paras 2 and 3
2　FSMA 2000, Sch 1, paras 3(2) and (3).
3　FSMA 2000, Sch 1, para 4(3).
4　FSMA 2000, Sch 1, para 5(1).
5　FSMA 2000, Sch 1, para 5(2).
6　FSMA 2000, Sch 1, para 6.
7　FSMA 2000, Sch 1, para 9(a) and (b).

Complaints

2.76 Under the applicable constitutional provisions, the FSA must also set up an internal complaints scheme with an independent investigator being responsible for the conduct of investigations.[1] The complaint scheme must ensure that complaints are investigated quickly insofar as reasonably practicable.[2] The appointment or dismissal of the investigator requires Treasury approval.[3] Complaints may also be referred to the Financial Services Tribunal or dealt with through legal proceedings at the FSA's discretion.[4]

The complaints scheme must provide for reference to the investigator of any complaint with all means being made available to allow the investigation to be conducted.[5] The investigator will report on the investigation to the FSA and the complainant and publish the report to the extent considered necessary.[6] The investigator has power to require the FSA to make a compensatory payment to the complainant or otherwise remedy the matter complained of with the FSA to report on the action taken.[7]

These requirements are developed in the Complaints against the FSA (COAF) section of the Handbook.[8]

1 FSMA 2000, Sch 1, para 7(1).
2 FSMA 2000, Sch 1, para 7(2).
3 FSMA 2000, Sch 1, para 7(3).
4 FSMA 2000, Sch 1, para 8(1). See Chapter 20.
5 FSMA 2000, Sch 1, para 8(2)(a) and (b)(i).
6 FSMA 2000, Sch 1, para 8(2)(b)(ii) and (iii).
7 FSMA 2000, Sch 1, para 8(5) and (6).
8 See para 2.132.

Practitioner and consumer consultation

2.77 Under the FSMA 2000, the FSA is further required to make and maintain effective arrangements for consulting practitioners and consumers on the extent to which its general policies and practices are consistent with its general duties as set out in the Act.[1] This will apply to all of its rule-making functions and their compliance with the regulatory objectives and supervisory principles established.

For this purpose, the FSA must, in particular, set up a Practitioner Panel[2] and Consumer Panel.[3] The membership of both Panels is determined by the FSA, although Treasury consent is required for the appointment or removal of the Chairmen. The Practitioner Panel is made up of either authorised persons or representatives of authorised persons or recog-nised investment exchanges or clearing houses.[4] The FSA must also appoint to the Consumer Panel such consumers or persons representing the interests of consumers as it considers appropriate.[5]

The FSA is required to consider any representations made by either the Practitioner or Consumer Panel in connection with their review of its general policies and practices.[6] It would appear that the FSA is also required more generally to have regard to any other representations made by either Panel.[7] Where the FSA disagrees with any views expressed or proposals made, it must provide the relevant Panel with a written statement of its reasons.[8]

1 FSMA 2000, s 8.
2 FSMA 2000, s 9.
3 FSMA 2000, s 10.
4 FSMA 2000, s 9(5).
5 FSMA 2000, s 10(5).

6   FSMA 2000, s 11(2).
7   FSMA 2000, ss 9(4) and 10(4).
8   FSMA 2000, s 11(3).

Competition scrutiny

2.78   The rules and practices of the FSA are subject to separate review by the Director General of Fair Trading for competition purposes. This applies to any 'regulating provisions' which (under s 159(1)) include the FSA rules, general guidance,[1] the statement of principles of approved persons[2] and any codes (issued under ss 64 (approved persons) or 119 (market abuse)).

The standard to be applied is whether the regulating provisions or practices have a significantly adverse effect on competition. This will apply where they have (or are intended or are likely to have) that effect or the effect that they have (or are intended or are likely to have) is to require or encourage behaviour that has (or is intended or likely to have) a significantly adverse effect on competition.[3] Where they have (or are likely to have) the effect of requiring or encouraging exploitation of the strength of a market position they are to be taken to have an adverse effect on competition.[4]

The Director General is generally required to keep the regulating provisions and the FSA's practices under review.[5] The Director may require documentation or information to be provided.[6]

The Competition Commission must consider any report made by the Director General that a regulating provision or practice has a significantly adverse effect on competition.[7] The Commission must produce its own report unless this would serve no useful purpose following a change of circumstances. The report must state whether there has been a significantly adverse effect on competition and if so, whether that effect is justified or what action, if any, should be taken by the FSA.[8] Where the Commission's conclusion is that the adverse effect on competition is not justified, the Treasury must give a direction to the FSA requiring it to take such action as may be specified.[9] The Treasury may decide that directions are unnecessary as a result of action taken by the FSA in response to the Commission's report or that other exceptional circumstances make it inappropriate or unnecessary to do so.[10]

The Chapter I and II prohibitions set out in the Competition Act 1998 are generally dis-applied with regard to agreements between authorised persons or parties otherwise subject to the FSA's regulatory provisions to the extent that these are 'encouraged' by the FSA's regulating provisions.[11]

1   As defined in FSMA 2000, s 158(5).
2   FSMA 2000, s 64(1).
3   FSMA 2000, s 159(2)(a) and (b).
4   FSMA 2000, s 159(3).
5   FSMA 2000, s 160(1), (2) and (3).
6   FSMA 2000, s 161.
7   FSMA 2000, s 162(1).
8   FSMA 2000, s 162(4) and (5).
9   FSMA 2000, s 163(2).
10 FSMA 2000, s 163(3)(a) and (b).
11 FSMA 2000, s 164(1).

Judicial review

2.79   In addition to these statutory mechanisms, the actions of the FSA will be subject to judicial review to the extent that it is performing a public function under statute. Possible liability may also arise under an action for misfeasance in public office where it can either be established that the FSA has acted with 'targeted malice' or 'untargeted malice' in certain circumstances and loss has arisen.[1] The availability of judicial review will in practice be limited due to the general discretion conferred on the FSA in connection with the discharge of its functions under the FSMA 2000.[2]

A number of formal processes have accordingly been established to ensure the proper accountability of the FSA with regard to both its general legislative or rule-making function and practice in individual supervisory or regulatory cases. This accountability is nominally based on Treasury oversight and control. This is secured through a general system of regular reporting, appointments or dismissals approval and review or investigation. While there is no direct Parliamentary control, the Chancellor is answerable to Parliament or Parliamentary committees while individual members of the FSA staff may be interviewed in Parliamentary proceedings. This Treasury oversight is supplemented through internal governance and complaints requirements as well as external competition scrutiny and judicial review. The highly transparent nature of the regime generally as well as specific requirements with regard to publication and annual meetings will also promote larger public scrutiny and accountability.

1 See *Three Rivers District Council v Bank of England (No 3)* 4 All ER 800n [2000] 2 WLR 15 CA; [2000] 3 All ER 1, 2 WLR 1220, HL; and *(No 3)* [2001] UKHL 16 [2001] 2 All ER 513.
2 See paras 2.16–2.21.

Ombudsman and compensation

2.80   As well as establishing a single integrated Financial Services Tribunal for the UK,[1] the FSMA 2000 also contains provision for the creation of a single Financial Services Ombudsman[2] and Financial Services Compensation Scheme.[3]

1 FSMA 2000, Pt IX. See Chapter 20.
2 FSMA 2000, Pt XVI.
3 FSMA 2000, Pt XV.

Ombudsman scheme

2.81   Part XVI provides for the creation of a single Ombudsman scheme. The objective is to allow disputes to be resolved quickly and with minimum formality by an independent person with the scheme being generally administered by a body corporate independent of the FSA.[1]

The scheme's jurisdiction may either be compulsory or voluntary. The FSA rules determine which activities fall within the compulsory jurisdiction which is set out in the Dispute Resolution: Complaints sourcebook (DISP) section of the Handbook.[2] For a respondent to be subject to the compulsory jurisdiction, the complainant must also have been eligible and wish to have the complaint dealt with under the scheme, the respondent must have been authorised at the time and the act or omission must fall within the compulsory jurisdiction rules.[3] Firms may also join the ombudsman scheme on a voluntary basis with regard to activities for which they are not authorised or which fall outside the compulsory jurisdiction.[4] This is referred to as the 'voluntary jurisdiction'.

The Ombudsman will make a decision under the compulsory jurisdiction concerning the complaint on the basis of what he considers to be fair and reasonable in all of the circumstances of the case.[5] If the Ombudsman considers in favour of the complainant, a money award may be made or a direction issued that the respondent takes such steps as may be considered just and appropriate.[6] The money award may compensate for financial loss or other loss or damage of a specified kind. This may not exceed the monetary limit currently set at £100,000. Costs may also be awarded in accordance with the costs rules set by the scheme operator and approved by the FSA.[7]

The Ombudsman has general power to require information or documents to be provided.[8] The Ombudsman may certify to the court any default or failure to provide information or documents requested in which case the defaulter will be treated as if in contempt of court.[9]

The FSMA 2000 sets out further provision with regard to the scheme operator and the compulsory and voluntary jurisdiction in Sch 17.

1   FSMA 2000, s 225(1) and (2).
2   See paras 2.129–2.130.
3   FSMA 2000, s 226(2).
4   FSMA 2000, s 227(12).
5   FSMA 2000, s 228(2).
6   FSMA 2000, s 229(2)(a) and (b).
7   FSMA 2000, s 230(1) and (2).
8   FSMA 2000, s 231(1)).
9   FSMA 2000, s 232(1) and (2).

Financial Services Compensation Scheme

2.82   Part XV makes provision for the establishment of the Financial Services Compensation Scheme. The FSA is required to set up the scheme manager as a separate body corporate to exercise the functions conferred under the FSMA 2000.[1] The constitution of the scheme manager must provide for a Chairman and a Board. The Chairman and members of the board must be persons appointed and liable to removal from office by the FSA with the terms of their appointment being such as to secure their independence from the FSA and the operation of the compensation scheme. The Treasury must be consulted on the appointment or removal of the Chairman. The scheme manager, nor board members, officers nor staff, are to be regarded as acting on behalf of the Crown or Crown servants.

The FSA is to establish the scheme to provide compensation for persons in cases where relevant authorised persons are unable or are likely to be unable to satisfy claims against them.[2] The compensation scheme must, in particular, provide for the scheme manager to assess and pay compensation in accordance with the scheme to claimants in respect of claims made in connection with regulated activities carried on (whether or not with permission) by relevant persons and to have power to impose levies on authorised persons or any class of authorised person for the purpose of meeting its expenses (including those incurred or expected to be incurred in paying compensation, borrowing or insuring relevant risks). The compensation scheme may make a number of specific provisions such as with regard to entitlements, the establishment of different funds for different types of claim, levies, repayment, limits and interim payments.[3] The scheme may make further provision conferring on the scheme manager rights to recovery in the event of a person's insolvency.[4]

The scheme manager is required to issue an annual report on the discharge of its functions.[5] The scheme manager is given power to require information or documents to be provided where these are necessary to make a fair determination of the claim or related claims.[6] The scheme manager may also inspect information held by a liquidator or similar party or documents held by the Official Receiver.[7] Failure to comply with any request for information or documentation may be treated as contempt.[8] Statutory immunity is conferred on the scheme manager or any person acting as board member, officer or other member of staff.[9]

These provisions are developed further in the Compensation (COMP) section of the Handbook.[10]

1 FSMA 2000, s 212(1).
2 FSMA 2000, s 213(1).
3 FSMA 2000, s 214(1).
4 FSMA 2000, s 215.
5 FSMA 2000, s 218.
6 FSMA 2000, s 219.
7 FSMA 2000, ss 220 and 224.
8 FSMA 2000, s 221.
9 FSMA 2000, s 222(1).
10 See para 2.131.

HANDBOOK OF RULES AND GUIDANCE

2.83 The FSMA 2000 creates the statutory framework for the new regime. Specific regulatory provision is then developed through the rules and guidance issued by the FSA under ss 138 and 157 of the Act. The regime is accordingly rules-based (rather than statutory-based). The advantage of this is that the detailed regulatory provisions imposed on financial institutions can be continuously reviewed and revised as regulatory insight and experience develop and as market practice changes. The regime may then be more flexible in terms of regulatory revision as well as more closely related to market practice and activity. While the former institutional uncertainties created under the Financial Services Act 1986 and other separate sector regimes have been removed, flexibility and market input and relevance have been retained especially with the Practitioner and Consumer Panels. To that extent, the new rules-based format can be considered to retain the advantages of the earlier self-regulatory system but, at the same time, remove the inherent difficulties that arose with regard to inconsistency and lack of accountability.

Handbook design and architecture

2.84 The detailed regulatory provisions applicable to all financial services and markets within the UK are now set out in the FSA's Handbook of Rules and Guidance (see Table 2.1). The FSA has a general rule making power under s 138(1) although it may also issue endorsing rules[1] as well other specific rules such as with regard to auditors and actuaries,[2] control of information,[3] financial promotion,[4] insurance business,[5] price stabilisation[6] and money laundering.[7] The largest part of the Handbook is issued as general rules under s 138(1) with supporting guidance under s 157(1).

1 FSMA 2000, s 143(1).
2 FSMA 2000, s 340(1) to (4).
3 FSMA 2000, s 147(1).
4 FSMA 2000, s 145(1).
5 FSMA 2000, s 141(1).

6   FSMA 2000, s 144(1).
7   FSMA 2000, s 146.

2.85   The original design objectives of the Handbook were announced by the FSA in April 1998.[1] The stated objectives were communication, consistency and implementation each of which included a number of sub-functions or activities. The Handbook was also to be based on five main design principles. The intention was that it should constitute a succinct authoritative statement of high level principles beginning with the fundamental obligations to be complied with by regulated businesses. There should then be a solid structure of further rules to facilitate enforceability and other requirements. There should be a major role for guidance. There should be a presumption against differentiation except on policy grounds. Regulatory standards should also focus on firms' outputs and on the adequacy of internal systems and controls.

With regard to architecture, the Handbook was from an early stage to be based on a number of separate blocks.[2] The FSA recognised that it would have to be divided into a number of modules to reflect the variety of activities covered and diversity of the regulated population to which it was to be applied. This would be structured on the basis of substantive regulatory standards being separated from the main regulatory process manuals. Separate provision would be made for consumers including complaints, compensation and information arrangements. Firms that required distinct treatment would be dealt with through separate sourcebooks.

The original handbook was to be based on six blocks comprising high level standards, business standards, regulatory processes, financial consumers, specialists sourcebooks and special guides. Although some structural adjustments have been made, the basic architecture has remained largely intact.

1   See FSA, *Designing the FSA Handbook of Rules and Guidance* (April 1998).
2   Ibid.

2.86   The FSA was also concerned to comply with four further process disciplines. These were identified before the basic accountability and other procedural requirements were set out in the FSMA 2000. These disciplines generally required that the FSA would consult publicly on all significant changes of substance or form, make reasoned proposals by, in particular, relating draft provisions to regulatory objectives, use feedback statements to explain its response to comments received and issue supporting cost-benefit assessments of the proposals announced. Each of these would be complied with in developing the Handbook sections subsequently.

Handbook text

2.87   The draft sections of each part of the Handbook were published separately with supporting feedback statements. The main modules of the Handbook were made by the FSA Board on 21 June 2001.[1] These consisted of all of the main sections of the Handbook including the final High Level Standards, the Business Standards, Regulatory Processes and most of the Specialist sourcebooks. Almost all of this was designated 'final' text which referred to post-consultative text that had been approved by the Board in advance of the necessary legislative powers coming into effect on N2. Further sections of made text were issued on 19 July and 20 September 2001.[2]

Table 2.1: FSA Handbook of rules and guidance

Prefatory material

Readers' guide	
Glossary of definitions	

Block 1: High level standards

PRIN	The principles for businesses
SYSC	Senior management arrangements, systems and controls
COND	Threshold conditions
APER	Statements of principle and code of practice for approved persons
FIT	The fit and proper test for approved persons
GEN	General provisions

Block 2: Business standards

IPRU (BANK)	Interim prudential sourcebook: banks
IPRU (INV)	Interim prudential sourcebook: investment businesses
IPRU (BSOC)	Interim prudential sourcebook: building societies
IPRU (INS)	Interim prudential sourcebook: insurers
IPRU (FSOC)	Interim prudential sourcebook: friendly societies
COB	Conduct of business sourcebook
MAR	Market conduct sourcebook
TC	Training and competence sourcebook
ML	Money laundering sourcebook

Block 3: Regulatory processes

AUTH	Authorisation manual
SUP	Supervision manual
ENF	Enforcement manual
DEC	Decision making manual

Block 4: Redress

DISP	Dispute resolution: complaints
COMP	Compensation
COAF	Complaints against the FSA

Block 5: Specialist sourcebooks

CIS	Collective investment schemes sourcebooks
CRED	Credit unions
ECD	Electronic commerce directive
ELM	Electronic money
PROF	Professional firms sourcebook
LLD	Lloyd's sourcebook
REC	Recognised investment exchange and recognised clearing house sourcebook
MORT	Mortgages (to follow)
UKLA	United Kingdom Listing Authority

Block 6: Special guides

EMPS	Energy market participants
OMPS	Oil market participants
SERV	Service companies
FREN	Small friendly societies

Source: www.fsa.gov.uk/handbook

Certain changes were made in October and November 2001[3] with some further amendments to the Handbook and the UKLA Guidance Manual on 18 October 2001. The Compensation sourcebook and Chapter 7 of the Authorisation manual and Chapter 18 of the Supervision manual were made on 15 November 2001.

Most of the Handbook came into effect on 1 December 2001 (N2) although some parts had come into force on 3 September 2001 to allow the FSA to undertake certain preparatory work in advance. These included receiving and processing applications for Part IV permission, applications from grandfathered firms to vary Part IV permission and applications for waivers. Certain administrative provisions also came into effect on 21 June 2001 although these did not impose obligations on firms as such.

1 See FSA, *Handbook Notice 1* (June 2001).
2 See FSA, *Handbook Notice 2* (July 2001); and FSA, *Handbook Notice 3* (September 2001).
3 See FSA, *Handbook Notice 4* (18 October 2001); and FSA, *Handbook Notice 5* (15 November 2001). See subsequent notices for further revisions and amendments.

2.88 A number of amendments have since been made subsequently with various further provisions also having been added. These are all referred to in the later *Handbook Notices* and are available on the FSA website (www.fsa.gov. uk).

Handbook structure

2.89 The general structure of the final Handbook is as follows:

Prefatory material

2.90 The prefatory material consists of the Reader's Guide and the Glossary:

READER'S GUIDE

2.91 The intention of the Reader's Guide is to provide a user-friendly introduction to the Handbook. This explains the presentation and structure of the Handbook and how it operates. The Guide had originally been published for consultation in November 2000.[1] The final text was published in April 2001 with some amendments being made in July 2001.[2]

1 FSA, *General Provisions* (November 2000), Consultation Paper 71.
2 See FSA, *General Provisions* (April 2001), Policy Statement.

GLOSSARY OF DEFINITIONS

2.92 The Glossary sets out the definitions for all of the main terms used in the Handbook. This has been built up incrementally. Drafts had been released with relevant consultation on particular parts of the Handbook. The Glossary also contains guidance on the main General provisions to be used in interpreting the Handbook. The final text was issued in May 2001 subject to subsequent amendment in relevant Handbook Notices.[1]

1 This was attached to the Policy Statement on the Regulatory Processes Manual. See FSA, *The Regulatory Processes Manuals and Threshold Conditions* (May 2001), Policy Statement, Annex K.

High Level Standards

2.93 The High Level Standards are made up of six modules which set out the general principles to be complied with by all regulated firms including, in particular, the main provisions in connection with management suitability and conduct.

PRINCIPLES FOR BUSINESSES (PRIN)

2.94 The Principles for Businesses contain a statement of eleven core obligations to be complied with by all regulated firms. These develop the main aspects of the 'fit and proper' standards set out in Threshold Condition 5 (suitability) in Sch 6 of the FSMA 2000. The principles are concerned with integrity (Principle 1), skill, care and diligence (Principle 2), management and control (Principle 3), financial prudence (Principle 4), market conduct (Principle 5), customers' interests (Principle 6), communication with clients (Principle 7), conflicts of interest (Principle 8), trust relationships (Principle 9), client assets (Principle 10) and relations with regulators (Principle 11). These replace the earlier statements of principle issued by the SIB.

2.95 The principles are expected to be complied with by firms at all times. They are intended to provide a universal statement of relevant standards. They are not, however, exhaustive and do not give rise to actions for damages but will be available to support disciplinary actions and other interventions.

2.96 The draft Principles had been published for consultation in September 1999 with the final text being issued in October 1999 subject to some subsequent amendments. The changes were generally concerned with confirming that regulatory action may be taken with firms still to comply with the fit and proper test or financial resources requirements and to add guidance on co-operation with overseas regulators in connection with the extra-territorial application of Principle 11.[1]

1 See FSA, *The FSA Principles for Businesses* (September 1999), Consultation Paper 13; FSA, *The FSA Principles for Businesses* (October 1999), Policy Statement; and FSA, *High Level Standards for firms and individuals* (February 2001), Policy Statement.

SENIOR MANAGEMENT ARRANGEMENTS, SYSTEMS AND CONTROLS (SYSC)

2.97 SYSC sets out the main standards applicable to management arrangements and internal control systems. The objective is to encourage firms' directors and senior managers to take appropriate practical responsibility for their firms' arrangements. Firms are expected to assign responsibility for the effective and responsible discharge of each to specific directors and senior managers. This expands Principle 3 (management and control) of PRIN.

2.98 The main provisions of SYSC require firms to take reasonable care to establish and maintain a clear and appropriate apportionment of senior management responsibility.[1] Firms must, in particular, allocate appropriate responsibility and record the arrangements made.[2] Firms must take reasonable care to establish and maintain such systems and controls as are appropriate to their business.[3] Firms must, in particular, establish appropriate systems to secure compliance with all applicable requirements and standards including financial crime,[4] designate a senior manager to be responsible for compliance[5] and maintain adequate records.[6]

1   SYSC 2.1.
2   SYSC 2.1.3 and 2.1.1.
3   SYSC 3.1.1.
4   SYSC 3.2.6.
5   SYSC 3.2.8.
6   SYSC 3.2.20.

2.99   The draft SYSC was published in December 1999 with the final text being issued in June 2000. This was revised in February 2001.[1]

1   See FSA, *Senior Management Arrangements, Systems and Controls* (December 1999) Consultation Paper 35; FSA, *High Level Standards for firms and individuals* (June 2000); and FSA, *High Level Standards for firms and individuals* (February 2001), Policy Statement.

THRESHOLD CONDITIONS (COND)

2.100   The main threshold conditions which firms have to satisfy are set out in Sch 6 of the Act. The meaning and content of each of these is developed in further detail by the FSA in COND. This explains how each of the statutory requirements are interpreted and applied in practice. They are provided in the form of guidance with no separate or additional obligations being imposed.

2.101   The original draft was published in March 1999 with a revised text in August 2000.[1] The final text was published in May 2001.[2]

1   See FSA, *The Qualifying Conditions for Authorisation* (March 1999), Consultation Paper 20; and FSA, *The Authorisation Manual* (August 2000), Consultation Paper 63, Annex.
2   See FSA, *Regulatory processes manuals and the Threshold conditions* (May 2001), Policy Statement.

STATEMENTS OF PRINCIPLE AND CODE OF PRACTICE FOR APPROVED PERSONS (APER)

2.102   The FSA has power to issue statements of principle with regard to the conduct of approved persons under s 64 of the FSMA 2000. This statement must be accompanied by a code of practice for the purpose of determining whether a person's conduct complies with the statements of principles.[1]

1   FSMA 2000, s 64(2). See Chapter 5.

2.103   The Statements of Principle for Approved Persons are set out in s 2 of APER. This generally requires that approved persons act with integrity in carrying out their control functions (Principle 1), act with due skills, care and diligence (Principle 2), observe proper standards of market conduct (Principle 3) and deal with the FSA and other regulators in an open and co-operative manner making full disclosure of all information reasonably expected (Principle 4).

Approved persons carrying out a significant management function must also take reasonable care to ensure that the business of the firm is organised effectively (Principle 5), exercise due skill, care and diligence in managing the business of the firm (Principle 6) and take reasonable steps to ensure that the business complies all relevant requirements and standards (Principle 7). General and specific guidance is provided under the Code of Practice set out in ss 3 and 4 of APER.

2.104   The original version of APER was published in July 1999 with minor amendments in December 1999.[1] The final text was released in June 2000 with minor amendments and high level material in February 2001.[2] The final text was made by the Board in July 2001 subject to some subsequent adjustment.

1 See FSA, *The Regulation of Approved Persons* (July 1999), Consultation Paper 26; and FSA, *Senior management arrangements, systems and controls* (December 1999), Consultation Paper 35.
2 See FSA, *High level standards for firms and individuals* (June 2000); and FSA, *High Level Standards for firms and individuals* (February 2001), Policy Statement.

FIT AND PROPER TESTS FOR APPROVED PERSONS (FIT)

2.105 FIT sets out the general criteria that the FSA will apply in assessing whether an individual is fit and proper to conduct any controlled function. The FSA will generally have regard to such factors as honesty, integrity and reputation, competence and capability and financial soundness.[1] Different factors will be taken into account in assessing each.[2]

1 FIT G1.3.1.
2 FIT G2.1.3, G2.2.1, G2.3.1 and G2.3.2.

GENERAL PROVISIONS (GEN)

2.106 GEN contains matters applicable across the Handbook as a whole. This includes necessary or useful material relevant to all sections of the Handbook. This incorporates matters not suitable to be set out in any particular manual or sourcebook. This includes provisions applicable to all authorised persons,[1] guidance on interpreting the Handbook[2] and FSA fees as well as transitional provisions.

1 GEN 1.
2 GEN 2.

2.107 The original text was published in November 2000 with the final copy being released in April 2001.[1]

1 See FSA, *General Provisions* (November 2000), Consultation Paper 71; and FSA, *General Provisions* (April 2001).

Business Standards

2.108 The business standards are generally made up of the prudential sourcebooks and revised conduct of business rules as well as further training and competence and money laundering requirements. The prudential source-books set out the main financial and related requirements for banks (IPRU (BANK)), securities business (IPRU (INV)), building societies (IPRU (BSOC)), friendly societies (IPRU (FSOC)) and insurers (IPRU (INS)).

The market rules deal with both the market conduct provisions including new market abuse (MAR) requirements and conduct of business (COB) rules. Firms must also generally comply with the training and competence (TC) requirements that develop suitability and the approved persons regime as well as the money laundering (ML) requirements.

INTERIM PRUDENTIAL SOURCEBOOK: BANKS (IPRU (BANK))

2.109 The standards applicable to the adequacy of financial resources and risk management systems and controls for banks are set out in IPRU (BANK).[1] This will apply to banks on an interim basis until the final Prudential Sourcebook (PSB) is issued for all financial firms.[2] IPRU (BANK) is based on the earlier Bank of England Guide to Supervisory Policy which was reissued by the FSA in 1998.[3] This had been developed by the Bank to assist banks understand and implement all of its earlier supervisory papers. An earlier edition had been produced although this was fundamentally rewritten as part of the Bank's post-Barings response.

1 See Chapter 15.
2 See Chapter 6, paras 6.85–6.88.
3 See also FSA, *Guide to Supervisory Policy* (loose leaf) 2 vols.

2.110   The draft sourcebook was published in June 2000 with the final text being released in January 2001.[1]

1 See FSA, *The Interim Prudential Sourcebook for Banks* (June 2000); and FSA, *The Interim Prudential Sourcebooks for Building Societies and Banks* (January 2001), Policy Statement.

INTERIM PRUDENTIAL SOURCEBOOK: INVESTMENT BUSINESSES (IPRU (INV))

2.111   The investment business sourcebook sets out the equivalent financial and systems requirements for securities and investment firms. This is based on the earlier rulebooks of the SIB and SROs, although it also includes some Lloyd's related material. The draft text was issued in June 2000 with further consultation on section 43 exempt business arrangements in October 2000.[1] Final text was produced in March 2001.[2] The text was made by the Board on 21 June 2001 subject to some subsequent amendment.

1 See FSA, *The Investment Business Interim Prudential Sourcebook* (June 2000), Consultation Paper 54; and FSA, *Section 43 Firms: prudential regime* (October 2000), Consultation Paper 68.
2 See FSA, *The Interim Prudential Regime for Investment Firms* (March 2001), Policy Statement.

INTERIM PRUDENTIAL SOURCEBOOK: BUILDING SOCIETIES (IPRU (BSOC))

2.112   The earlier rules issued by the Building Societies Commission with regard to financial resources and management systems and controls have been re-stated in IPRU (BSOC). The main financial and systems requirements are set out in volume 1 with other constitutional matters being dealt with in volume 2 as well as merger and transfer procedures. The draft was issued for consultation in June 2000 with the final text being released in January 2001.[1] Volume 1 was made on 21 June 2001 and volume 2 on 19 July 2001.

1 See FSA, *The Interim Prudential Sourcebook for Building Societies* (June 2000), Consultation Paper 51; and FSA, *The Interim Prudential Soucebooks for Building Societies and Banks* (January 2001), Policy Statement.

INTERIM PRUDENTIAL SOURCEBOOK: INSURERS (IPRU (INS)) AND FRIENDLY SOCIETIES (IPRU (FSOC))

2.113   The financial and systems and control requirements for insurance companies (other than friendly societies and the Society of Lloyd's) are set out in IPRU (INS). This was again based on the former applicable provisions subject to amendment to give effect to the European Insurance Group's Directive and certain other policy changes. The draft text was issued in January 2000 with separate consultation on the European Directive in May 2000 and March 2001.[1] Various further amendments were announced with the final text being made on 21 June 2001.

The separate sourcebook for friendly societies (IPRU (FSOC)) was made on 19 July as amended on 20 September 2001.[2]

1 See FSA, *Insurance Draft Interim Prudential Sourcebook* (January 2000), Consultation Paper 41; FSA, *Implementing the EC Directive on Insurance Groups* (May 2000), Consultation Paper 50;

and FSA, *Interim Prudential Sourcebook: Friendly Societies and Insurance Companies* (March 2001), Consultation Paper 84.
2 See FSA, *Handbook Notice 3* (20 September 2001 and later notices).

CONDUCT OF BUSINESS SOURCEBOOK (COB)

2.114 The main conduct of business rules to be complied with by firms are set out in COB. This generally reproduces the earlier provisions set out in the SIB Rules and the rulebooks of the SROs. These contain the main requirements governing the relationship between investment firms and their clients. These are accordingly of a more private law nature as distinct from the financial and systems requirements imposed under the prudential sourcebooks. COB includes provision with regard to such matters as client identification, terms of business, promotions, financial advice and segregation.

2.115 The original draft was issued in February 2000 and July 2000 with further provisions in February 2001.[1] Separate provisions on polarisation were published in January 2001 with a feedback statement in March 2001.[2] The FSA has since announced that the former polarisation regime will be substantially revised in due course. The final text for COB was issued in February 2001 (except with regard to with profits guides and polarisation amendments).[3] The main sections of the final text were made on 21 June 2001 with further sections and amendments being made subsequently.[4]

1 See FSA, *The Conduct of Business Sourcebook* (February 2000), Consultation Paper 45; FSA, *The Conduct of Business Sourcebook Supplement* (July 2000), Consultation Paper 57; and FSA, *Conduct of Business Sourcebook* (February 2001).
2 See FSA, *Reforming Polarisation: First Steps* (January 2001), Consultation Paper 80; and FSA, *Polarisation: Feedback to CP 80* (March 2001), Policy Statement.
3 See FSA, *Conduct of Business Sourcebooks* (February 2001), Policy Statement.
4 See FSA, *Handbook Notice 5* (15 November 2001) and later notices.

MARKET CONDUCT SOURCEBOOK (MAR)

2.116 MAR explains how the FSA will apply the market abuse provisions contained in Part VIII of the Act. This includes the Code of Market Conduct issued under s 119(1) (MAR 1), the price stabilisation rules (MAR 2) and the inter-professional conduct requirements (MAR 3). MAR 1 sets out how the statutory market abuse test will be applied in practice. MAR 2 creates a safe harbour for price stabilisation. MAR 3 sets out the rules that will apply to firms dealing with other market counterparties.

2.117 The draft Code of Market Conduct was issued by the FSA in June 1998.[1] The Treasury issued a consultation document on prescribed markets in June 1999[2] with the FSA issuing a revised document in the summer of 2000.[3] MAR 2 was originally published for consultation in January 2000 with the final text being released in December 2000.[4] MAR 3 was published in May 2000 and finalised in February 2001.[5]

1 See FSA, *Market Abuse: Consultation a Draft Code of Market Conduct* (June 1998); and FSA, *Feedback Statement* (March 1999).
2 See HM Treasury, *Market Abuse: Prescribed Markets* (June 1999). See also Financial Services and Markets Act 2000 (Prescribed Markets and Qualifying Investments) Order 2001 (SI 2001/996).
3 See FSA, *Market Abuse: A Draft Code of Market Conduct* (July 2000).
4 See FSA, *The Price Stabilising Rules* (January 2000), Consultation Paper 40; and FSA, *The Price Stabilising Rules: Feedback on CP 40 and supplementary consultation* (December 2000), Consultation Paper 78.

5   See FSA, *The Inter-Professionals Code* (May 2000), Consultation Paper 47; and FSA, *Inter-Professional Conduct: Feedback on CP 47 and supplementary consultation* (February 2001), Consultation Paper 83.

TRAINING AND COMPETENCE SOURCEBOOK (TC)

2.118   The standards expected of all employees in the financial sector are set out in the training and competence sourcebook. TC1 contains the commitments that apply to all employees involved with regulated activities with TC2 setting out specific rules and guidance for employees engaged in the oversight of particular activities. The draft sourcebook was originally published in November 1999 with a supplementary consultation in July 2000.[1] The final text was issued in December 2000.[2]

1   See FSA, *Training and Competence Sourcebook* (November 1999), Consultation Paper 34; and FSA, *Feedback Statement to CP 34: Training and Competence Sourcebook* (July 2000), Consultation Paper 60.
2   See FSA, *Feedback Statement to CP 60: Training and Competence Sourcebook* (December 2000), Policy Statement.

MONEY LAUNDERING SOURCEBOOK (ML)

2.119   ML sets out the rules and guidance that apply to authorised firms to ensure that effective control systems are in place to prevent money laundering. The draft was published in April 2000 with the final text being released in January 2001.[1] The text was made by the Board in July 2001 with only minor amendments being made to ML 8.[2]

1   See FSA, *Money Laundering: The FSA's new role* (April 2000), Consultation Paper 46; and FSA, *Money Laundering: The FSA's new role* (January 2001), Policy Statement.
2   See Chapter 10.

Regulatory processes

2.120   The Regulatory Processes block of the Handbook is made up of the three main manuals on authorisation (AUTH), supervision (SUP) and enforcement (ENF) with a further section on decision-making (DEC) having been added subsequently.

The purpose of the manuals is to set out the rules and guidance concerning the main aspects of the FSA's relationship with the regulated community in the UK. This assumes a general chronological approach dealing with initial market entry, ongoing oversight and possible intervention in the event of regulatory or administrative breach. To some extent, all of these functions are supervisory although this creates a clear and valuable structure for these more operational aspects of the FSA's activities. They are then distinct from the more substantive provisions set out in the Business Standards and High Level Standards and the later Redress and specialist sourcebooks. They are accordingly more operational rather than substantive in content. Decision-taking provisions had originally been included in each of the earlier draft manuals although it was decided to draw these together in a separate supplementary manual within the Regulatory Processes Block.

AUTHORISATION MANUAL (AUTH)

2.121   Guidance with regard to applying for Part IV permission under the Act is set out in AUTH. The relevant procedures are explained with further information being provided with regard to fees,[1] qualifying for authorisation[2] and periodical publications, news services and broadcasts.[3]

1 AUTH 4.
2 AUTH 5.
3 AUTH 7.

2.122 The draft authorisation manual was published for consultation in August 2000 with the final text being issued in May 2001.[1] The main sections were made on 21 June 2001,[2] with the rest being made subsequently.[3]

1 See FSA, *The Authorisation Manual* (August 2000), Consultation Paper 64; and FSA, *The Regulatory Processes Manuals and Threshold Conditions* (May 2001), Policy Statement. See Chapter 5.
2 AUTH 1 to AUTH 3, AUTH 6 and AUTH 8.
2 See FSA, *Handbook Notice 5* (15 November 2001) and later notices.

SUPERVISION MANUAL (SUP)

2.123 The rules and guidance that apply with regard to the ongoing supervision or oversight by the FSA of all regulated firms is set out in SUP. This includes the FSA's general approach to supervision,[1] information,[2] and notification and reporting requirements,[3] auditors,[4] actuaries[5] and reports by skilled persons.[6] The manual also contains further provisions with regard to varying or cancelling Part IV permission,[7] individual requirements and guidance[8] and waivers and rules modifications.[9] Further provision is included with regard to approved persons,[10] controllers and close links,[11] appointed representatives,[12] UK passport and EEA firms[13] as well as business transfers and CFTC exemptions.[14]

1 SUP 1. See Chapter 6, paras 6.23–6.25 and 6.26.
2 SUP 2.
3 SUP 15, SUP 16 and SUP 17.
4 SUP 3.
5 SUP 4.
6 SUP 5.
7 SUP 6.
8 SUP 7 and SUP 9.
9 SUP 8.
10 SUP 10.
11 SUP 11.
12 SUP 12.
13 SUP 13 and SUP 14.
14 SUP 18 and SUP 19.

2.124 The original text was published in August 2000 with separate provision on control functions in June 2000 and February 2001.[1] Most of the manual was issued in final form in May 2001.[2] The main sections of the manual were made by the Board on 21 June 2001 with certain sections being made subsequently.[3]

1 See FSA, The Supervision Manual (August 2000), Consultation Paper 64; FSA, The Regulation of Approved Persons: Controlled Functions (June 2000), Consultation Paper 53; and FSA, The Regulation of Approved Persons: Controlled Functions (February 2001), Policy Statement.
2 See FSA, *The Regulatory Processes Manuals and Special Conditions* (May 2001), Policy Statement.
3 See FSA, *Handbook Notice 5* (15 November 2001) and later notices.

ENFORCEMENT MANUAL (ENF)

2.125 The policies and procedures concerning the exercise of the FSA's enforcement powers under the Act are set in ENF. The FSA is required under the Act to issue policy statements on the exercise of specific powers such as the imposition of financial penalties in disciplinary cases or market abuse. The manual then includes guidance on information gathering and investigation[1] and decision-making procedures including the operation of the Regulatory Decisions Committee.[2] Variations or withdrawals are also considered[3] and withdrawal of prohibitions against approved persons.[4] The manual includes provisions with regard to injunctions or restitution,[5] disciplinary action,[6] public censure,[7] criminal proceedings[8] and insolvency.[9] Separate provision is included with regard to disciplinary action in relation to market abuse, collective investment schemes, auditors and actuaries or professional persons.[10]

1 ENF 2.
2 ENF 3. See Chapter 20.
3 ENF 4, 5 and 6.
4 ENF 8 and 9. See Chapter 5.
5 ENF 7 and 10.
6 ENF 12 and 14.
7 ENF 13.
8 ENF 16.
9 ENF 11.
10 ENF 15, 17, 18 and 19.

2.126 The FSA issued two general consultation and response papers on its enforcement policy.[1] The draft manual was published in August 2000 with the final text in May 2001.[2] The text was made by the Board in July 2001 without significant amendment.

1 See FSA, *Financial Services Regulation: Enforcing the New Regime* (December 1998), Consultation Paper 17; and FSA, *Enforcing the New Perimeter* (July 1999), Consultation Paper 25. See also FSA, *Response to CP 17: Financial Services Regulation; Enforcing the new regime* (July 1999), Response Paper; and FSA, *Response to CP 25: Enforcing the New Perimeter* (December 1999), Response Paper.
2 See FSA, *The Enforcement Manual* (August 2000), Consultation Paper 65; and FSA, *The Regulatory Processes Manuals and Threshold Conditions* (May 2001), Policy Statement.

DECISION MAKING MANUAL (DEC)

2.127 The procedures to be followed in taking decisions involving the issuance of supervisory, warning and decision notices under the Act is set out in DEC. This then contains procedural provisions within the larger operational framework created under the Regulatory Processes block. This includes the earlier provisions set out in each of the separate manuals as well as the new provisions added with regard to the Regulatory Decisions Committee and the relationship between the Committee and the FSA. The draft material on DEC was originally issued as part of the consultations on the other process manuals. The final text was issued in May 2001. The text was made by the Board on 21 June 2001.[1]

1 See FSA, *The Regulatory Processes Manuals and Threshold Conditions* (May 2001), Policy Statement.

Redress

2.128 The redress block consists of dispute resolution and complaints (DISP), compensation (COMP) and complaints against the FSA (COAF).

This generally sets out the rights of consumers and other counterparties securing redress either against regulated firms or the FSA directly.

DISPUTE RESOLUTION AND COMPLAINTS SOURCEBOOK (DISP)

2.129 The Complaints sourcebook sets out the general provisions that apply with regard to securing immediate redress against regulated firms. This includes requirements relating to firms' own complaint procedures,[1] the jurisdiction of the Financial Ombudsman Service,[2] ombudsman procedures[3] and standard terms for membership of the voluntary jurisdiction of the Ombudsman Service.[4] The powers to make the complaints rules are shared between the FSA and the body that administers the scheme (FOS Ltd). The scheme rules have accordingly been developed jointly although the objective is to create a single-integrated package of redress provisions.

1 DISP 1.
2 DISP 2.
3 DISP 3.
4 DISP 4.

2.130 Complaints were originally considered by the FSA in Consultation Papers 4 and 33.[1] The draft text of DISP was issued with Consultation Paper 49.[2] The draft funding rules were published in November 2000.[3] The final text was issued in December 2000.[4] Further consultation was required on the transitional arrangements with the Treasury having published a Transitional Order in June 2001.[5] A further policy statement was announced on funding rules. The main sections DISP were made by the Board on 20 September 2001 although these had to be revoked and re-made on 15 November 2001 following a technical error in the earlier list of powers.[6]

1 See FSA, *Consumer Complaints* (October 1997), Consultation Paper 4; and FSA, *Consumer Complaints and the New Single Ombudsman Scheme* (November 1999), Consultation Paper 33.
2 See FSA, *Complaints Handling Arrangements: Feedback Statement on CP33 and draft rules* (May 2000), Consultation Paper 49.
3 See FSA, *Funding the Financial Ombudsman Service* (November 2000), Consultation Paper 74.
4 See FSA, *Complaints handling arrangements: Response to CP 49 (a joint policy statement)* (December 2000).
5 See FSA, *Complaints-handling arrangements: transitional arrangements and other amendments* (June 2001), Consultation Paper 99.
6 See FSA, *Handbook Notice 5* (December 2001) and later notices.

COMPENSATION (COMP)

2.131 The FSA is required to establish a scheme for compensating persons where the authorised person or the appointed representative is unable or likely to be unable to meet claims against it. Provisions in this regard are set out in Part XV of the FSMA 2000. The rules concerning the assessment and payment of claims by the Financial Services Compensation Scheme Limited (FSCS) are set out in COMP. The rules also limit the amount the scheme manager FSCS can levy in respect of management expenses. The rules are supported by a memorandum of understanding entered into between the FSCS and the FSA. The single compensation scheme replaces all of the earlier separate sector arrangements.

COMP follows six separate consultations since December 1997.[1] The final text was issued in September 2001 although amendments had to be made following the Financial Services and Markets Act 2000 (Compensation

Scheme: Electing Participants) Regulations 2001.[2] COMP was made by the Board on 15 November 2001.[3]

1 See FSA, *Financial Services Compensation Scheme Draft Funding Rules* (March 2001); FSA, *Financial Services Compensation Scheme Draft Transitional Rules* (September 2001), Consultation Paper 108; and FSA, *Financial Services Compensation Scheme Management Expenses Levy Limit* (January 2002), Consultation Paper 109. See para 2.104.
2 SI 2001/1783.
3 See FSA, *Handbook Notice 5* (December 2001) and later notices.

COMPLAINTS AGAINST THE FSA (COAF)

2.132 The FSA is required to maintain arrangements for the consideration of complaints against itself under the Act.[1] This must provide for reference to an investigator who has the necessary means to conduct a full investigation and produce a report on the complaint. Guidance on the rules and procedures adopted is set out in COAF. The FSA final text was made by the Board on 19 July 2001.[2]

1 FSMA 2000, Sch 1, paras 7 and 8. See para 2.76.
2 See FSA, *Handbook Notice 2* (August 2001).

Specialist sourcebooks

2.133 The Handbook contains a number of specialist sourcebooks. These provide a number of additional material in connection with the operation of particular products or markets. These are subject to the general provisions set out elsewhere within the Handbook although separate specific material was considered necessary having regard to the particular nature or operations. Separate provisions have since been added to the original Block 5 sourcebooks on credit unions (CRED), the Electronic Commerce Directive (ECD), electronic money (ELM) with further sections to follow on mortgages (MORT) and the United Kingdom Listing Authority (UKLA).

COLLECTION INVESTMENT SCHEMES SOURCEBOOK (CIS)

2.134 CIS is a restatement of earlier product regulation rules applicable to unit trusts and open-ended investment companies. This provides a consolidation and partial rationalisation of the earlier provisions. The main issue on which the FSA consulted was in connection with the extension of the investing powers of open-ended investment companies (OEICs) to treat them on an equal basis with unit trusts and with the ability of operators to charge expenses to capital.

2.135 The draft sourcebook was published for consultation in August 2000 with the final text being issued in February 2001.[1] The FSA consulted on fees separately.[2] The draft sourcebook was amended with regard to warning and decision notices.[3] The text was made by the Board on 21 June 2001 with CIS 18 (fees) being made 19 July 2001.

1 See FSA, *CI Sourcebook* (August 2000), Consultation Paper 62; and FSA, *The Collective Investment Scheme Sourcebook* (February 2001), Policy Statement.
2 See FSA, *Third Consultation Paper on the FSA's Post-N2 Fee-Raising Arrangements* (May 2001), Consultation Paper 95.
3 See FSA, *Collective Investment Scheme Sourcebook: Consultation on warning and decision notices in relation to applications* (March 2001), Consultation Paper 85.

PROFESSIONAL FIRMS SOURCEBOOK (PROF)

2.136 Guidance on the operation of the new regime applicable to members of the professions in Part XX of the Act is set out in PROF. The FSA is required under s 325(1) to keep itself informed about the manner in which designated professional bodies supervise and regulate the carrying on of exempt regulated activities by members of the professions and the way in which such members conduct their activities. Relevant bodies are designated by the Treasury by Order under s 326(1). Professionals are then exempt from the general prohibition under s 327(1) and s 328(1).

2.137 The original text was published for consultation in October 2000 with the final text being issued in May 2001.[1] The sourcebook was made on 21 June 2001 although some minor amendments had to be made in July 2001.[2]

1 See FSA, *The Exempt Professional Firms Sourcebook* (October 2000), Consultation Paper 69; and FSA, *The Professional Firms Sourcebook* (May 2001), Policy Statement.
2 See FSA, *Handbook Notice 1* (July 2001). See also FSA, *Handbook Notice 3* (October 2001) and later notices.

LLOYD'S SOURCEBOOK (LLD)

2.138 Lloyd's of London is dealt with under Part XIX of the Act.[1] The FSA is, in particular, required to keep itself informed of the manner in which the Council of Lloyd's supervises and regulates the market and the way in which regulated activities are carried on.[2] The Society of Lloyd's is an authorised person under s 315(1). LLD then sets out the provisions concerning the prudential supervision of the Society's insurance business, information to be provided by the Society to the FSA, the capacity transfer market, former underwriting members, policyholders' and members' complaints, compensation and guidance on the conduct of regulatory functions by the Society.

1 See generally Walker, 'Lloyd's of London' in Blair et al, Ch 21.
2 FSMA 2000, s 314(1) and (2).

2.139 Draft text was originally published for consultation in May 2000 with further text being released in August 2000.[1] The final text was issued in March 2001[2] although further amendment was required to implement the Insurance Groups Directive.[3] The final text was made by the Board on 21 June 2001.

1 See FSA, *The Lloyd's Sourcebook* (May 2000), Consultation Paper 48; and FSA, *Prudential Requirements for Lloyd's insurance business* (August 2000), Consultation Paper 66.
2 See FSA, *The Lloyd's Sourcebook: feedback on CP 48 and CP 66* (March 2001), Policy Statement.
3 See FSA, *Interim Prudential Sourcebook: Friendly Societies and Insurance Companies* (March 2001), Consultation Paper 84.

RECOGNISED INVESTMENT EXCHANGE AND RECOGNISED CLEARING HOUSES SOURCEBOOK (REC)

2.140 The FSA is given power with regard to the supervision of recognised investment exchanges and clearing houses under Part XVIII of the Act. The regime has been strengthened although it generally continues the earlier arrangements set up under the Financial Services Act 1986.[1]

1 See generally Walker, 'Recognised Investment Exchanges and Clearing House' in Blair et al, Ch 20.

2.141 The draft sourcebook was originally issued for consultation in January 2000 with the fees rules in June 2001.[1] The final text was issued in April 2001.[2] The text was made by the Board on 21 June 2001 and REC 7 (fees) on 19 July 2001.

1 See FSA, *RIE and RCH Sourcebook* (January 2000), Consultation Paper 39; and FSA, *Third Consultation Paper on the FSA's Post-N2 Fee-Raising Arrangements* (May 2001), Consultation Paper 95.
2 See *FSA, RIE and RCH Sourcebooks: Feedback on CP 39* (April 2001), Policy Statement.

Special guides

2.142 The FSA has included further special guides within the Handbook. These were added at a later stage to provide guidance on additional markets or market participants not originally dealt with under the general provisions of the Handbook. At the time of writing, four special guides had been included:

ENERGY MARKET PARTICIPANTS (EMPS)

2.143 The special guide explains which parts of the Handbook apply to energy market participants and includes a form of waiver to be granted where market participants satisfy the statutory criteria set. The amendments are made with regard to such conduct of business rules as the customer dealing protections and some capital adequacy requirements. Energy market participants had to be considered following the introduction of new electricity trading arrangements in 2001 and with the removal of a special Financial Services Act exemption on N2.[1] The FSA issued a consultation paper in June 2001 which was developed with the assistance of a specialist practitioner group from the energy sector.[2] The FSA will conduct a further review of the structure and terms of the EMPS and OMPS regimes in light of its statutory objectives.[3] EMPS was made by the Board on 20 September 2001.

1 See FSA, *Handbook Notice 3* (October 2001), para 3.61.
2 See FSA, *Energy Market Participants and Oil Market Participants: a consultation on the interim regulatory regime for EMPs* (June 2001), Consultation Paper 96.
3 See FSA, *Handbook Notice 3* (October 2001), para 3.61.

OIL MARKET PARTICIPANTS (OMPS)

2.144 A number of the amendments made with regard to energy market participants have been extended to apply to oil market participants under OMPS. OMPS provides guidance on the specific sections of the Handbook that apply to OMPS. The final text was made on 20 September 2001.

SERVICE COMPANIES (SERV)

2.145 Service companies provide trade support services to financial market professionals and are subject to a relaxed regulatory treatment that takes into account the professional nature of their business. Trade support services include order-routing and post-trade processing. The FSA proposed to roll-over the former regime insofar as possible post post-N2.[1] The special guide is aimed at providing an overview of the new regime set up under the Special Guide for Service Companies Instrument 2001. SERV confirms which parts of the Handbook apply.[2]

1 See FSA, *The Service Company Regime* (June 2000), Consultation Paper 55.
2 See FSA, *Handbook Notice 3* (October 2001), paras 3.67–3.69.

SMALL FRIENDLY SOCIETIES (FREN)

2.146   FREN is intended to act as a navigational tool to allow small friendly societies to determine which parts of the Handbook apply to them. These societies are not subject to the European Life or Non-Life Directives. There was no formal consultation on FREN. The text was made by the Board on 15 November 2001.

TERRITORIAL SCOPE

2.147   The application of the FSMA 2000 is limited by way of specifying in what circumstances regulated activities are to be treated as having been carried on in the UK[1] and carried on by way of business.[2] The international scope of the Act is then determined by defining the carrying on of regulated activities in the United Kingdom.

1   FSMA 2000, s 418(1).
2   FSMA 2000, s 419(1).

2.148   Under the FSMA 2000, a person may be considered to carry on a regulated activity in the UK in four additional four cases where it would not otherwise be regarded as doing so.[1] These are generally concerned with the exercise of passport rights, collective investment schemes and local management activities. The Act applies in the following particular situations:

(a)   a person has a registered office in the UK, is entitled to exercise rights under a single market directive as a UK firm and is carrying in another EEA State a regulated activity to which the directive applies;[2]

(b)   has a registered office in the UK, is the manager of a European collective investment scheme and persons in another EEA State are invited to become participants;[3]

(c)   has a registered office in the UK and the regulated activity is managed on a day-to-day basis through the registered office of another establishment maintained in the UK;[4] or

(d)   the head office is not in the UK but the activity is carried on from an establishment maintained in the UK.[5]

1   FSMA 2000, s 418(1).
2   FSMA 2000, s 418(2).
3   FSMA 2000, s 418(3).
4   FSMA 2000, s 148(4).
5   FSMA 2000, s 418(5).

2.149   In each of these cases, the location of the person with whom the activity is carried on is considered irrelevant.[1] These four cases then confirm the 'outward' application of the Act. This relates to regulated activities conducted overseas by a person based in the UK. These generally give effect to the relevant provisions set out in the European financial directives. The 'inward' scope of the Act is limited to the carrying on of any regulated activity within the territory of the UK (unless an exemption or exclusion applies). The inward territorial scope of the Act may be extended or restricted by order under s 22(1). This is considered in further detail in the Regulated Activities Order. The Treasury may also by order specify the circumstances in which a regulated activity is deemed to be carried on by way of business.[2] This allows for certain financial related activities to be excluded from the scope of the core prohibition set out in s 19. This is again developed in the Regulated Activities Order.

1 FSMA 2000, s 418(6).
2 FSMA 2000, s 419. See paras 2.56–2.57 and Chapters 3 and 4.

2.150 Special rules also apply with regard to financial promotions. Under the FSMA 2000, it is a criminal offence for someone to undertake a financial promotion unless they are either authorised or the content of the communication has been approved by an authorised person.[1] The Treasury is given power to make exemptions under s 21(5) which are now set out in the Financial Promotions Order. These generally apply to generic promotions, investment professionals, certain one-off communications and promotions to certified high net worth individuals, sophisticated investors and high net worth companies. Promotions to overseas recipients are exempt.

The scope of the financial promotion rules is dealt with under the Conduct of Business sourcebook (COB) within the FSA's Handbook of Rules and Guidance.[2] The COB distinguishes between real time and non-real time financial promotions. The application, purpose and territorial scope of the rules is set out at the beginning of the COB. Where an authorised firm approves a financial promotion for an overseas firm or unauthorised person, the customer must be warned that the protections that would otherwise apply will not be available.

Guidance is also provided on promotions over the Internet and use of other electronic media. Specific guidance is included with regard to key features, documents, applications forms, the meaning of directed act, hypertext links and banner advertising.

1 FSMA 2000, s 21(1) and (2).
2 See para 2.58 and Chapter 8.

Chapter 3

Regulated activities – investment business

INTRODUCTION

3.1   As has been explained in Chapters 1 and 2, the fundamental purpose of the FSMA is to create a unified framework for the regulation of banking, investment, insurance and other financial services business in the UK. This is reflected in the provisions on regulated activities, which define the activities for which authorisation is required.

3.2   The Banking, Financial Services and Insurance Companies Acts followed significantly different approaches in setting out the activities which they covered. The Financial Services and Markets Act (FSMA) 2000 adopts a single regime. This is modelled largely on that in the Financial Services Act 1986; in particular, it embodies the same building blocks of investment, investment-related activity, exclusion, and business element. As a result, for those familiar with the Financial Services Act 1986, the new regime for investment business will contain few major surprises. Fitting deposit-taking and insurance activities into this framework involves more extensive changes of structure and terminology. In general, however, fundamental changes of substance have not been made – indeed, some of the apparent complications of the new regime (the provisions implementing the 'business' element being a good example) are caused by the desire to replicate the substance of the former position while adhering to the new structure.

THE 'GENERAL PROHIBITION'

3.3 The cornerstone of the FSMA 2000 regime is s 19, which prohibits a person from carrying on a regulated activity in the UK, or purporting to do so,[1] unless he is either authorised or exempt. This is known as the 'general prohibition' and any infringement of it is a criminal offence.[2] Resulting agreements are also unenforceable[3] and the Financial Services Authority (FSA) can obtain injunctions restraining breaches, ordering steps to be taken to remedy breaches and preventing disposal of assets.[4]

1   The reference to 'purporting to do so' follows the corresponding prohibition in the Financial Services Act 1986, but is new in relation to banks and insurance companies. It is supplemented by the offence of describing oneself as an authorised or exempt person or holding oneself out as being so (s 24). This is novel in relation to insurance companies. Section 67 of the Banking Act 1987 prohibited the use by an unauthorised institution of any name which suggested that the institution was a bank or banker. FSMA 2000 takes a different approach and builds on the criminal offence in s 200(2) of the Financial Services Act 1986 of falsely claiming or implying an authorised or exempt status (eg claiming to be authorised as a bank or a building society). The resulting absence of any specific protection of the use of the word 'bank' has been the source of a certain amount of controversy.
2   See FSMA 2000, s 23.
3   See FSMA 2000, s 26. Agreements made by authorised persons (in the course of their business) may also be unenforceable if the agreement is entered into as a result of a third party's unauthorised regulated activities (s 27). Although ss 26 and 27 do not apply if the regulated activity is accepting deposits, s 29 provides that if someone accepts deposits in breach of the general prohibition and the person who made the deposit is not entitled under the deposit agreement to recover the money without delay, that person can apply to the court for the money to be returned to him. However, agreements are not unenforceable when entered into by an EEA firm which does not qualify for authorisation (Sch 3, para 16).
4   See FSMA 2000, s 380. Remedial orders and orders not to dispose of assets can be made against any person 'knowingly concerned' in the breach.

'REGULATED ACTIVITY'

3.4   To constitute a 'regulated activity', an activity must:

(a)   relate to a specified[1] investment or, where the secondary legislation so provides, be carried on in relation to property of any kind;
(b)   be of a specified kind; and
(c)   be carried on by way of business.[2]

The activity must also be carried on in the UK. Each of these key elements of s 22 of the FSMA 2000 is considered in detail below.

1   Ie, specified by the Treasury by secondary legislation – see FSMA 2000, s 22(5).
2   See FSMA 2000, s 22.

WHAT IS A 'SPECIFIED INVESTMENT'?

3.5   As mentioned above, the activity must relate to a specified investment if it is to amount to a regulated activity. The term 'investment' is widely defined in s 22(4) of the FSMA 2000 to include any asset, right or interest. This is supplemented by Part II of Sch 2 to the FSMA 2000, which contains an indicative list of the investments that can be regulated under the new regime.[1] As Sch 2 is indicative only, the Treasury has the power to determine by secondary legislation the precise investments to be regulated under the new regime. On 26 February 2001 the Treasury made the Financial Services and Markets Act 2000 (Regulated Activities) Order 2001[2] (Regulated Activities Order).

1   The Treasury is not limited by the descriptions of investments or activities in Sch 2; s 22 provides that any class of activity and any category of investment may be brought within the regulatory net.
2   SI 2001/544, as amended by SI 2001/3544, the Financial Services and Markets Act 2000 (Regulated Activities) (Amendment) Order 2002 (SI 2002/682) and the Financial Services and Markets Act 2000 (Regulated Activities) (Amendment) (No 2) Order 2002 (SI 2002/1776).

3.6   Part III of the Regulated Activities Order[1] specifies the investments which are relevant when determining whether a person is carrying on a regulated activity. Broadly, these investments correspond to the activities listed in Part II of the Regulated Activities Order (the specified activities) and include deposits, rights under contracts of insurance and all the investments previously included in the Financial Services Act 1986, Sch 1, Part 1, as well as the investments corresponding to the new regulated activities (eg rights under a stakeholder pension scheme and regulated mortgage contracts). The following investments have been specified for the purposes of s 22 of the FSMA 2000.

1   See SI 2001/544, arts 73 to 89.

Deposits (article 74)

3.7   Article 74 of the Regulated Activities Order[1] provides that a deposit is a specified investment. A 'deposit' is defined in article 5 of the Order as a sum of money (other than a sum excluded by virtue of articles 6 to 9 of the Order) which is paid on terms:

(a)   under which it will be repaid either on demand or at a time or in circumstances agreed by or on behalf of the depositor and the person receiving the deposit; and

(b)   which do not refer to the provision of property (other than currency) or services or the giving of security.

1   SI 2001/544.

3.8   Article 5(3) provides that money is paid on terms which *are* referable to the provision of property or services (and therefore does not amount to a 'deposit') if it is paid:

(a)   by way of advance or part payment under a contract for the sale or hire or other provision of property or services, and is repayable only if the property or services is or are not sold, hired or otherwise provided;

(b)   by way of security for the performance of a contract or by way of security in respect of loss which may result from the non-performance of a contract;[1] or

(c)   by way of security for the delivery up or return of any property, whether in a particular state of repair or otherwise.

1   In *SCF Finance Co Ltd v Masri* [1987] QB 1002, [1987] 1 All ER 175, CA it was held that deposits placed with a commodities and futures broker as security for margin purposes were not deposits because they were referable to the provision of property or services under the provision of the Banking Act 1979 which corresponded to (and was in fact somewhat narrower than) SI 2001/544, art 5(3)(b).

Shares etc (article 76)

3.9   The Regulated Activities Order[1] provides that the shares and stock of a company (wherever incorporated) and any unincorporated body constituted under the law of a country outside the UK will be specified investments.

This includes any class of shares which are defined as deferred shares for the purposes of the Building Societies Act 1986 and any transferable shares in UK industrial and provident societies or credit unions (or in a body incorporated under the law of another European Economic Area (EEA) State for equivalent purposes).[2]

However, other shares or stock in industrial and provident societies, credit unions, building societies and open-ended investment companies are excluded from the definition of shares in the Regulated Activities Order.

1   SI 2001/544.
2   Deferred shares are transferable and negotiable in a similar way to other stocks and shares. They are therefore specifically mentioned in SI 2001/544, art 76 because other types of shares issued by mutuals are not transferable and are expressly excluded.

Instruments creating or acknowledging indebtedness (article 77)

3.10   Article 77 provides that debentures (including debenture stock), loan stock, bonds, certificates of deposit and other instruments[1] creating or acknowledging indebtedness are specified investments. However, the following instruments are excluded from the scope of article 77:

(a)   an instrument acknowledging or creating indebtedness for (or for money borrowed to defray) the consideration payable under a contract for the supply of goods or services (ie loan notes and similar documents);
(b)   a cheque or other bill of exchange, a banker's draft or a letter of credit (but not a bill of exchange accepted by a banker);
(c)   a banknote, a bank statement, a lease or other disposition of property, or a heritable security;
(d)   a contract of insurance; and
(e)   any investment excluded by virtue of article 78(2)(b) of the Regulated Activities Order (eg National Savings deposits and products).

It will be noted that the word 'debenture' is not itself defined. This may give rise to uncertainty in some cases, since the scope of the term at common law, though wide, is by no means clear. In practice, the reference to 'other instruments creating or acknowledging indebtedness' should mean that there are relatively few instances where the point is important, since the creation or acknowledgement of indebtedness is regarded as a key feature of a debenture under the test which is perhaps the widest of those suggested in the case law.[2]

1   'Instrument' is defined to include any record whether or not in the form of a document (see SI 2001/544, art 3(1)).
2   See *Levy v Abercorris Slate and Slab Co* (1887) 37 Ch D 260 at 264. For a fuller discussion, reference should be made to standard textbooks on company law.

Government and public securities (article 78)

3.11   Article 78 specifies the following types of investment: loan stock; bonds; and other instruments creating or acknowledging indebtedness issued by or on behalf of any government or local authority,[1] the assemblies for Scotland, Northern Ireland and Wales, or an entity whose members comprise states including the UK or another EEA state (or whose members comprise other entities, the members of which include the UK or another EEA state). The investments excluded from article 77 (see para 3.10 above) are also excluded from article 78.

1 Local authority is defined in the Regulated Activities Order (SI 2001/544) to include a local authority within the meaning of the Local Government Act 1972, the Local Government (Scotland) Act 1973 and the Local Government Act (Northern Ireland) 1972.

Instruments giving entitlement to investments (article 79)

3.12 Article 79 provides that warrants or other instruments entitling the holder to subscribe for shares etc, instruments creating or acknowledging indebtedness, and government and public securities will be specified investments.

The term 'warrant' is not defined in the Regulated Activities Order,[1] possibly because it is used in the market to refer both to instruments within this paragraph, which confer rights to subscribe for new investments, and instruments (sometimes called 'covered' warrants)[2] which confer rights to purchase investments already issued. A 'subscription warrant' is generally taken to refer to an instrument giving the holder the right to subscribe for shares in the issuer's company at a set price within a set time. For the purposes of article 79, it is immaterial whether the instrument to which the entitlement relates is in existence or identifiable. An investment that falls within the scope of article 79 will not be regarded as an option, future or contract for differences for the purposes of the Order (see article 79(3)).

1 SI 2001/544.
2 Probably because the issuer of such warrants frequently 'covers' his position by ensuring that he holds the underlying investments to which the warrant relates, and which he may therefore be obliged to deliver.

Certificates representing securities (article 80)

3.13 Article 80 applies to certificates or other instruments which confer rights (other than rights which constitute options falling within article 83) in respect of the investments specified in articles 76 to 79 and the transfer of which can be effected without the consent of that person (for example, depository receipts). Certificates or other instruments which confer rights in respect of two or more investments issued by different persons, or in respect of two or more different investments of the kind specified by article 78 (ie government and public securities) that are issued by the same person, are specifically excluded from article 80.

Units in a collective investment scheme (article 81)

3.14 Under article 81, units in a collective investment scheme[1] (for example, units in a unit trust scheme, shares in an open-ended investment company and rights in respect of most limited partnerships) are a specified investment.

Although there are no exclusions in the Regulated Activities Order for this category of specified investment, the Treasury has prescribed (in the Financial Services and Markets Act 2000 (Collective Investment Schemes) Order 2001[2]) particular arrangements which do not amount to a collective investment scheme. The result is that units in certain arrangements (for example, closed-ended bodies corporate, franchise arrangements and timeshare schemes) are excluded from being collective investment schemes.

1 The term 'collective investment scheme' is defined in FSMA 2000, Pt XVII.
2 SI 2001/1062.

Options (article 83)

3.15 Article 83 applies to options to acquire or dispose of:

(a) a security or contractually based investment (CBI);[1]
(b) currency;
(c) gold, palladium, platinum or silver; and
(d) an option to acquire or dispose of an investment falling within (a), (b) or (c).

This will include stock exchange traded options, other put or call options over securities, and options over options.

1 This is a new and helpful term which very broadly corresponds to what practitioners refer to as 'derivatives', plus certain life assurance products and funeral protection plans. A 'contractually based investment' is defined in the SI 2001/544, art 3(1) to mean: rights under a qualifying contract of insurance; an option, future, contract for differences or funeral plan contract; and any rights to or interests in any of these investments.

Futures (article 84)

3.16 Article 84(1) applies to rights under a contract for the sale of a commodity or other property under which delivery is to be made at a future date and at the price which is agreed upon[1] when the contract is made.

1 SI 2001/544, art 84(8) specifies that a price is taken to be agreed upon even if it is to be determined by reference to the price at which a contract is to be entered into on a market or exchange (or could be entered into at a time and place specified in the contract). In the case of a contract which is expressed to be by reference to a standard lot and quality, a price will be taken to be agreed even if provision is made for the price to be varied to take account of any variation in quantity or quality on delivery.

3.17 If applied without qualification, this definition would include a vast range of everyday commercial transactions. Article 84, like its predecessor (Financial Services Act 1986, Sch 1, para 8), addresses this point by distinguishing between contracts made for investment purposes (which are included) and those made for commercial purposes (which are not). Paragraphs (3) to (7) set out provisions amplifying and applying this distinction. In two instances these provisions are conclusive; otherwise, they constitute indications which must be taken into account, but the test of 'commercial' or 'investment' purposes will be applied in the light of all the circumstances.

As a result of this, it will sometimes be quite difficult for parties to decide with confidence whether or not a particular contract is to be regarded as an investment. This feature of the old para 8 definition attracted a certain amount of criticism.[1] Some of the concerns were addressed by the introduction of the 'risk management' exclusion, described at para 3.74 below, but the basic difficulty of applying the test in article 84 remains.

1   Guidance was provided by the SIB in Guidance Release 3/88 and, in relation to an area of particular concern – that of forward foreign exchange contracts – by the government in a statement made in January 1988. This expressed the view that on the foreign exchange (and bullion) market, forward contracts were generally made solely for commercial purposes by both contracting parties and did not therefore fall within the scope of the Financial Services Act 1986 provisions. The apparent breadth of this statement was later qualified by further guidance issued by SIB in 1996 (SIB Guidance Release 1/96: Foreign Exchange and the Financial Services Act 1986). This guidance dealt with the provision by some firms of services, primarily for individuals, that were intended either to enable them to speculate in fluctuations in foreign exchange or to enable persons taking out loans to benefit from interest and/or exchange rate variations. These services generally involved contracts which purported to be for delivery within seven days but were intended by both parties to be rolled over or closed out for cash. The SIB expressed the view that firms providing such speculative forex services were likely to be conducting investment business and therefore would need to be suitably authorised. The substance of this additional guidance has now been incorporated into the definition itself through SI 2001/544, art 84(4) – see para 3.22.

3.18   The two conclusive provisions are set out in paras (3) and (4) of article 84. Article 84(3) states that a contract will be deemed to be made for investment purposes if it is made or traded on a recognised investment exchange (such as LIFFE, the London Stock Exchange etc) or is expressed to be traded on such an exchange. The same applies to contracts made off exchange but on equivalent terms. Article 84(4) provides that a contract which does not fall within the scope of article 84(3) will be considered to be made for commercial purposes if, under the terms of the contract, delivery is to be made within seven days.[1]

1   Unless it can be shown that there was an understanding that delivery would not be made within seven days – see para 3.22.

3.19   In relation to contracts not covered by these conclusive tests, article 84(5) sets out factors which are 'two way' indicators – that is, the presence of them is an indication that a contract is made for commercial purposes and the absence of them is an indication that it is made for investment purposes. These factors are as follows:

(a)   one or more of the parties produces the commodity or other property or uses it in his business;
(b)   the seller delivers or intends to deliver the property or the purchaser takes or intends to take delivery of it.

3.20   The remaining factors specified are indicators in one direction only: their presence is an indication of a commercial or investment purpose, but no express significance is attached to their absence. Thus it is an indication that a contract is made for commercial purposes if the price, lot, delivery date or other terms are determined by the parties for the purposes of the particular contract and not, for example, by reference (or not solely by reference) to regularly published prices, standard lots or delivery dates or standard terms (article 84(6)).

3.21   Article 84(7) specifies that the following factors are indications that a contract is made for investment purposes:

(a)   the contract is expressed to be as traded on an investment exchange;

(b)   performance of the contract is ensured by an investment exchange or a clearing house; and

(c)   there are arrangements for the payment or provision of margin.

3.22   Although, as mentioned above, the definition of futures in article 84 reflects the definition in the Financial Services Act 1986, Sch 1, para 8, it has been updated in a number of respects. The first is the qualification of the test now in article 84(4) so that it does not cover cases where it can be shown that there existed an understanding that delivery would not be made within seven days. The purpose of this change is to prevent parties seeking to evade the effect of the article by purporting to structure arrangements as contracts for short-term delivery when in reality the intention is to make them open-ended by repeated 'rollover'.

3.23   Secondly, the Treasury has concluded that, because a large number of commercial purpose contracts are priced 'by reference to' regularly published prices but with contractually agreed variations to reflect differences in quantity or quality of the property, it would be more appropriate to change the phrase included in note 5 of para 8 as an indication of a commercial purpose contract ('not by reference to regularly published prices') to 'not *solely* by reference to regularly published prices'.[1]

1   SI 2001/544, art 84(6).

3.24   Thirdly, the wording in note 6 of para 8 has been changed. Under this note, it was an indication that a contract is made for investment purposes if it was expressed to be made on a market or exchange. A considerable amount of trading in commodities and equipment for physical activity may now be undertaken through arrangements which amount to an electronic market. The phrase 'on a market or exchange' in the Financial Services Act 1986 is therefore changed to 'on an investment exchange' in article 84(7).

Contracts for differences (article 85)

3.25   Article 85 applies to rights under a contract for differences or any other contract the purpose of which is to secure a profit or avoid a loss by reference to fluctuations in either the value or price of property of any description, or of an index or other factor designated for that purpose in the contract. Spread bets, currency and interest rate swaps and commodity swaps are therefore included within the scope of article 85. However, certain rights are specifically excluded; these are:

(a)   rights under a contract if the parties intend that the profit or loss is to be secured/avoided by taking delivery of any property;

(b)   rights under a contract under which money is received by way of deposit on terms that any interest or other return to be paid on the deposit will be calculated by reference to fluctuations in an index or other factor;

(c)   rights under certain contracts connected with the National Savings Bank or National Savings products; and

(d)   rights under a qualifying contract of insurance.

Rights to, or interests in, investments (article 89)

3.26   Article 89 applies to rights to, and interests in, any of the investments that are specified under articles 74 to 87 of the Regulated Activities Order[1] (ie all of the specified investments other than regulated mortgage contracts). However, certain rights and interests are specifically excluded; for example, interests under the trusts of an occupational pension scheme and rights to, or interests in, funeral plan contracts covered by insurance or trust arrangements.

1   SI 2001/544.

Other/new specified investments

3.27   Article 75 provides that rights under a contract of insurance (as defined in the Regulated Activities Order[1]) are specified investments. Rights under a stakeholder pension scheme, the underwriting capacity of a Lloyd's syndicate and membership or prospective membership of such a syndicate, and rights under a funeral plan contract and a regulated mortgage contract are also specified investments pursuant to articles 82, 86, 87 and 88.

1   SI 2001/544.

WHAT IS A 'REGULATED ACTIVITY'?

3.28   To satisfy the criteria in s 22 of the FSMA 2000, an activity must also be of a 'specified kind' if it is to constitute a regulated activity. Part I of Sch 2 to the FSMA 2000 contains an indicative list of the activities that can be regulated under the new regime.[1] As Sch 2 is indicative only, the Treasury has determined the precise scope of the activities that are regulated under the new regime in Part II of the Regulated Activities Order.[2]

1   The Treasury is not limited by the descriptions of investments or activities in FSMA 2000, Sch 2; s 22 provides that any class of activity and any category of investment may be brought within the regulatory net.
2   SI 2001/544.

3.29   The Regulated Activities Order came into force at N2 (ie 1 December 2001), save for (a) the provisions dealing with funeral plans, which came into force on 1 January 2002, and (b) the provisions on mortgages, which were until recently expected to come into force on 31 August 2002, but following the Treasury's announcement of the intention to broaden the scope of regulation to include mortgage advice and general insurance broking, implementation is currently projected for the second quarter of 2004.[1]

1   See further, para 3.57.

3.30   The activities that are regulated include:

(a)   *accepting deposits* (which broadly reflects the activity in the Banking Act 1987, although there are some significant changes in territorial scope);
(b)   *effecting and carrying out contracts of insurance* (which reflects the relevant activity in the Insurance Companies Act 1982, although, again, territorial scope has changed);

(c) *investment activities*, that is: dealing in investments as principal or as agent; arranging deals in investments; managing investments; safeguarding and administering investments; sending dematerialised instructions; establishing, operating or winding up collective investment schemes; advising on investments; and agreeing to carry on any of these activities (except establishing, operating or winding up collective investment schemes). This list reflects the list of activities in Part II of Sch 1 to the Financial Services Act 1986 but, unlike that Act, does not cover offering to carry on any of these activities; and

(d) *certain new activities*, that is: establishing, operating or winding up a stakeholder pension scheme; activities relating to the Lloyd's market (ie advice on syndicate participation, managing the underwriting capacity of a Lloyd's syndicate, and, insofar as carried on by Lloyd's, arranging deals in contracts of insurance written at Lloyd's); providing funeral plan contracts; and providing regulated mortgage contracts.

The regulated activities relating to (a), (c) and (d) are summarised below.

Accepting deposits (article 5)

3.31 Accepting deposits will amount to a specified kind of activity if: the money which is received is lent to others; or the activity of the person who receives the money is financed (wholly or to a material extent) out of the capital or interest on the sum received.

The term 'deposit' is defined in articles 5(2) and (3) of the Regulated Activities Order.[1]

1 SI 2001/544 – see paras 3.7 and 3.8 above.

3.32 Exclusions from the activity of accepting deposits are dealt with in articles 6 to 9 of the Order. These are considered in detail below.

Investment activities

Dealing in investments as principal and agent (articles 14 and 21)

3.33 Articles 14 and 21 of the Regulated Activities Order[1] specify that buying, selling, subscribing for, or underwriting securities[2] or CBIs (other than funeral plan contracts and rights to, or interests in, such contracts) as principal or agent are specified kinds of activity.

The Order defines the term 'buying' to include acquiring for valuable consideration. It defines the term 'selling' to include disposing of an investment for valuable consideration. ('Disposing' is also widely defined in article 3(1) of the Order to include (in the case of an investment consisting of rights under a contract) surrendering, assigning or converting rights under a contract or assuming the corresponding liabilities under the contract and (in the case of any other investment) issuing or creating the investment or granting the rights or interests of which it consists.)

However, an important exception is made in article 18 of the Regulated Activities Order which provides that the issue by a company of its own shares, debentures or warrants is excluded from the activity of dealing in investments as principal. Accordingly, a company issuing equity or debt securities is not treated as dealing in such investments.[3]

1   SI 2001/544.
2   'Securities' are defined in SI 2001/544, art 3(1) as any investments of the kind specified by arts 76 to 82 of the Order (or any rights to, or interests in, those investments), except where the context requires otherwise.
3   See further para 3.73 below.

3.34   Exclusions from these specified activities are set out in articles 15 to 20 and 22 to 24 of the Regulated Activities Order.[1]

1   SI 2001/544.

Arranging deals in investments (article 25)

3.35   Article 25 provides that it is a specified activity to make arrangements:

(a)   for another person (whether as principal or agent) to buy, sell, subscribe for or underwrite securities, CBIs or investments specified by article 86 (ie Lloyd's syndicate capacity and syndicate membership and any rights to or interests in those investments);[1] or

(b)   with a view to a person who participates in the arrangements buying, selling, subscribing for or underwriting the investments referred to in (a) above (whether as principal or agent).[2]

The first activity is aimed at arrangements that would have the direct effect that a transaction is concluded (that is, arrangements that bring about a transaction). The FSA considers that a person brings about or would bring about a transaction only if his involvement in the chain of events leading to the transaction is sufficiently important that, without such involvement, the transaction would not take place.[3]

The second activity is aimed at cases where it may be said that the transaction is 'brought about' directly by the parties to it but where this happens within a standing arrangement or framework set up by a third party with a view to the conclusion of transactions by others, for example through the use of that third party's facilities. This will catch the activities of persons such as exchanges, clearing houses and service companies (for example, persons who provide communication facilities for the routing of orders or the negotiation of transactions). It will also cover arrangements for the payment of introductory commission, where one party, typically a product provider, agrees to pay another party, typically a broker or financial adviser, commission on contracts concluded with persons introduced by the broker or adviser. The activities which are excluded from the scope of article 25 are dealt with in articles 26 to 36 of the Regulated Activities Order.

1   SI 2001/544, art 25(1).
2   SI 2001/544, art 25(2).
3   See the FSA's Authorisation Manual, Appendix 1, para 1.32.2.

3.36   The FSA has commented specifically on the activities of publishers and broadcasters in the context of article 25(2)[1] and has said that such persons will not normally be regarded as making arrangements under this article. However, if the publisher or broadcaster goes beyond what is necessary for him to provide his publishing or broadcasting service then he may fall within the scope of article 25(2). According to the FSA a publisher or a broadcaster is likely to be making arrangements which fall within the scope of article 25(2) (and therefore be unable to use the exclusion in article 27 of the Regulated Activities Order (enabling parties to communicate)) if, for example, he:

(a) enters into an agreement with an investment services provider (such as a broker or product provider) for the purpose of carrying their financial promotion; and

(b) as part of the arrangements, he does one or more of the following:
   (i) brands the investment service or product in his name or joint name with the broker or product provider;
   (ii) endorses the service or encourages readers or viewers to respond to the promotion;
   (iii) negotiates special rates for his readers or viewers if they take up the offer; or
   (iv) holds out the service as something he has arranged for the benefit of his readers or viewers.[2]

The FSA has also specifically considered the position of companies that provide telephone marketing services to investment firms.[3] Merely answering calls, distributing literature and referring queries to a client will not be regarded as making arrangements within the meaning of article 25(2) of the Regulated Activities Order. If, however, such a company makes proactive calls to its client's customers or raises the possibility of a meeting with, or visit by, the client or suggests that the caller will be sent promotional material then the arrangements are likely to fall within the scope of article 25(2) unless an exclusion applies.

1   See the FSA's Authorisation Manual, Appendix 1, paras 1.32.3 to 1.32.7.
2   See the FSA's Authorisation Manual, Appendix 1, para 1.32.6.
3   See the FSA's Authorisation Manual, Appendix 1, para 1.32.10.

Managing investments (article 37)

3.37   The activity of managing investments (which was specified in the Financial Services Act 1986, Sch 1, para 14) has been changed so that it no longer covers all kinds of investment management, but only discretionary investment management (the discretion must be exercised in relation to the composition of the portfolio under management). Under article 37 of the Regulated Activities Order[1] managing assets belonging to another person in circumstances involving the exercise of discretion is a specified kind of activity if it is not an excluded activity[2] and:

(a) the assets consist of (or include) securities or CBIs; or

(b) the arrangements for their management are such that the assets *may* consist of or include such investments and either:
   (i) the assets have done so at any time since 29 April 1988;[3] or
   (ii) the arrangements have at any time been held out as arrangements under which the assets would do so.

1   SI 2001/544.
2   See SI 2001/544, arts 38 and 39.
3   This was the commencement date of the corresponding provisions of the Financial Services Act 1986.

Safeguarding and administering assets (article 40)

3.38   The activity of safeguarding and administering assets[1] belonging to another is a specified activity under article 40 of the Regulated Activities

Order.[2] Arranging for the safeguarding and administration of assets will also be a specified kind of activity where:

(a) the assets consist of (or include) securities or CBIs; or

(b) the arrangements are such that those assets *may* consist of or include such investments and either:
    (i) the assets have done so at any time since 1 June 1997;[3] or
    (ii) the arrangements have at any time been held out as being arrangements under which such investments would be safeguarded and administered.

'Safeguarding' involves acting as custodian of the property, for example, holding any documents evidencing the investments, such as the share certificate, and 'administration' covers services provided to the owner or manager of the property, such as the settlement of sale transactions relating to an investment, dealing with income arising from the investment and carrying out corporate actions such as voting. Article 40 makes it clear that both safeguarding and administration must be carried on for the activity to fall within the article – that is, services which consist only of safeguarding, or only of administration, are not caught.

1 SI 2001/544, art 43 specifies that the following activities will not amount to administration of assets for the purposes of art 40: providing information about the number of units or the value of any assets safeguarded; converting currency; and receiving documents relating to an investment solely for the purpose of onward transmission to, from, or at the direction of the person to whom the investment belongs.

2 SI 2001/544.

3 This was the commencement date of the corresponding provisions of the Financial Services Act 1986.

3.39 Under article 40(2)(a), arranging custody activities in relation to another person's assets will be a specified activity if the assets include securities or CBIs. Accordingly, although the majority of a fund or portfolio may consist of land or other assets which are not specified investments for the purpose of the Regulated Activities Order, the custody activities of the entire fund will be a regulated activity.

Article 40(3) provides that it is immaterial that title to the assets which are safeguarded and administered is in uncertificated form or that the assets are transferred to another person provided that, in the latter case, the person who safeguards and administers the assets (or who arranges their safeguarding or administration) commits that those assets will be replaced by equivalent assets at some time in the future or on request.

3.40 Article 40 is subject to the exclusions in articles 41, 42 and 44.

Sending dematerialised instructions (article 45)

3.41 Article 45 states that the following activities are specified kinds of activity: sending (on behalf of another person) dematerialised instructions relating to a security or a CBI by means of a relevant system in respect of which an operator is approved under the Uncertificated Securities Regulations 2001;[1] or in the case of a system participant, causing (on behalf of another person) such instructions to be sent. This covers members of the CREST dematerialised securities transfer system who are able to input instructions for the transfer of securities belonging to others, either as agents or as 'sponsors'.

1   The references to the Uncertificated Securities Regulations 1995 were changed to the Uncertificated Securities Regulations 2001 (SI 2001/3755) by the Financial Services and Markets Act 2002 (Regulated Activities) (Amendment) Order 2002 (SI 2002/682).

3.42   Exclusions from article 45 are contained in articles 46 to 50 of the Regulated Activities Order.

Collective investment schemes (article 51)

3.43   Article 51 refers to the following specified kinds of activity: establishing, operating or winding up a collective investment scheme; acting as trustee of an authorised unit trust scheme or as a depository or sole director of an open-ended investment company. The term 'collective investment scheme' is defined in s 235 of the FSMA 2000, and s 237 defines the terms 'trustee', 'authorised unit trust scheme' and depositary'.

3.44   There are no exclusions from these specified activities, for the reasons mentioned at para 3.14 above.

Advising on investments (article 53)

3.45   Article 53 provides that certain types of investment advice will amount to a specified activity. To fall within the scope of article 53 the advice must be given to a person in his capacity as an investor or potential investor (or as an agent for such an investor) and must be advice on the merits of his buying, selling, subscribing for or underwriting a particular investment which is a security or a CBI, or exercising any right conferred by such an investment to acquire, dispose of, underwrite or convert an investment.

It will be noted that article 53 uses the phrase 'a particular investment'.[1] This choice of wording is deliberate and is used to emphasise the intention to regulate advice given in relation to specific investments but not general or generic advice about investments. Therefore, advice on the merits of investing abroad rather than in the UK is unlikely to fall within the scope of article 53, but advice that an investor should buy or sell specific stocks will. Similarly, general advice on the merits of investing in different types of investment, such as advice that investing in unit trusts may be safer than investing in equities because there is a better spread of risk, will not amount to a regulated activity.

A further requirement is that the advice must be advice 'on the merits' of buying, selling etc. General advice in relation to an investment, eg advice on where to obtain it or how to buy it, will not be advice 'on the merits' of purchasing that investment.

1   The FSA has also given guidance on the meaning of 'a particular investment'. It has said that this will, for example, include shares in ABC plc, XYZ plc warrants and LIFFE Japanese Government bonds (see the FSA's Authorisation Manual, Appendix 1, para 1.26.4).

3.46   The FSA has issued guidance on the regulated activity of advising on investments.[1] The guidance specifically considers what will constitute giving advice on the merits of buying or selling an investment.[2] The FSA believes that merely explaining the implications of exercising certain rights does not constitute giving advice on the merits of exercising those rights. It also states that advice in the form of rating issuers of debt securities as to the likelihood of their being able to meet their repayment obligations need not of itself involve advising on the merits of buying, selling or retaining that issuer's stock.[3] Similarly, explaining how to complete an application form or advising on terms which are commonly accepted in the market will not in itself amount to advising on the merits of buying and selling an investment.

The FSA also believes that 'advice' requires an element of opinion on the part of the adviser; simply giving information without making any comment or value judgments on it is not advice. However, the mere provision of information may amount to advice if the circumstances in which it is provided give it the force of a recommendation; for example, a person may provide information on a selected basis in an attempt to influence the decision of the recipient.

1   See the FSA's Authorisation Manual, Appendix 1, paras 1.24 to 1.30.
2   See the FSA's Authorisation Manual, Appendix 1, paras 1.29.1 to 1.29.6.
3   This carefully phrased view (note the phrase 'need not of itself' and the reference to the issuer's stock – presumably meaning its equity rather than the rated bonds themselves) is not especially helpful. Rating agencies themselves generally emphasise that they are not advising on the merits of buying, selling or holding any security, including the bonds that they are rating – a view which seems to be supported by the fact that there is frequently a market in (and therefore both buyers and sellers of) rated bonds regardless of whether they have AAA or 'junk' status. The rating will of course be relevant to price and, for some potential investors, suitability; but these are not matters on which rating agencies generally express a view.

3.47 Exclusions from article 53 are contained in articles 54 and 55 of the Regulated Activities Order.

Agreeing to carry on activities (article 64)

3.48 Article 64 of the Regulated Activities Order specifies that agreeing to carry on any of the activities referred to above (other than accepting a deposit or establishing etc a collective investment scheme) will be a specified kind of activity. However, this activity is subject to the exclusion in article 65 of the Order, which deals with overseas persons.

New/potentially new regulated activities

3.49 The Regulated Activities Order also specifies the following activities, which were previously either not regulated by the FSA or not regulated at all, for the purposes of s 22 of the FSMA 2000.

Stakeholder pension schemes (article 52)

3.50 Establishing, operating or winding up a stakeholder pension scheme (as defined in the Welfare Reform and Pensions Act 1999, s 1) is a specified activity.

Lloyd's-related activities (articles 56 to 58)

3.51 The arranging by Lloyd's of deals in contracts of insurance written at Lloyd's is, for the first time, a regulated activity. This covers the operation by the Society of Lloyd's of the central services which underpin the Lloyd's market. Lloyd's has permission to carry on this activity and connected activities under Part XIX of the FSMA 2000.

3.52   Underwriting agents and others carrying on certain Lloyd's-related activities will also need to be authorised under the FSMA 2000. The Regulated Activities Order provides that the following activities are regulated activities:

(a)   advising on syndicate participations at Lloyd's (this includes the activities of Lloyd's members' agents in advising their clients on joining or remaining on particular underwriting syndicates); and

(b)   managing the underwriting capacity of a Lloyd's syndicate as a managing agent.

3.53   As mentioned above, the Regulated Activities Order also extends the scope of regulated investments to include membership of a Lloyd's syndicate and the underwriting capacity of a Lloyd's syndicate.

Funeral plan contracts (articles 9 and 60)

3.54   There is a new regulated activity of entering (as a provider) into a funeral plan contract. This activity involves a customer making one or more payments to another person (ie the provider) and the provider undertaking to provide, or to secure the provision of, a funeral in the UK *unless* the customer and the provider expect the funeral to take place within one month. However, there is an exclusion where:

(a)   the funeral plan contract is backed by appropriate insurance; or

(b)   sums of money paid by the customer are held in a properly constituted trust and managed by an independent fund manager.

Regulated mortgage contracts (articles 61 to 63)

3.55   There are also to be new regulated activities of entering into a regulated mortgage contract or administering a regulated mortgage contract. A regulated mortgage contract is a contract under which the lender provides credit to a borrower and the obligation of the borrower to repay is secured by a first legal mortgage on land in the UK, at least 40% of which is (or is to) be used as, or in connection with, a dwelling by the borrower or related person.

3.56   A person will be held to be administering a regulated mortgage contract if he notifies the borrower of changes in interest rates or payments due under the contract and/or takes any necessary steps for the purposes of collecting or recovering payments due from the borrower under the contract.

However, a person will not be treated as administering a regulated mortgage contract merely because he has or exercises a right to take action for the purposes of enforcing the contract. There is also an exclusion from the activity of administering a regulated mortgage contract where a person either arranges for an authorised person to administer the contract,[1] or administers the contract himself for no more than one month.[2]

1   SI 2001/544, art 62.
2   SI 2001/544, art 63.

3.57   As mentioned above,[1] these provisions did not come into force on N2 (1 December 2001). It was expected that they would be brought into force on 31 August 2002. However, in December 2001 the Treasury announced that it had decided the mortgage advice and general insurance regulation should be brought within the scope of regulation under the FSMA 2000. This will entail further changes to the Regulated Activities Order and other provisions; the changes are currently scheduled to come into force during the second quarter of 2004. The existing provisions of the Regulated Activities Order relating to mortgages are intended to be brought into force at the same time.[2]

1   Para 3.29.
2   See the Treasury's Consultation Paper, 'Regulating Mortgages', February 2002.

Electronic money

3.58   The Financial Services and Markets Act 2000 (Regulated Activities) (Amendment) Order 2002 ('the Amendment Order')[1] amends the Regulated Activities Order[2] to implement the Electronic Money Directive[3] in the UK. It provides for the issuing of electronic money to be a regulated activity under the FSMA 2000 (and also for electronic money to be a specified investment for the purposes of the Regulated Activities Order).

'Electronic money' is defined in the Amendment Order to mean monetary value (as represented by a claim on the issuer), which is stored on an electronic device, issued on receipt of funds and accepted as a method of payment by persons other than the issuer. Sums received in exchange for electronic money are specifically excluded from the definition of a 'deposit' in article 9 of the Regulated Activities Order.

1   SI 2002/682.
2   SI 2001/544.
3   2000/46/EC.

3.59   Articles 4 and 5 of the Amendment Order deal with the exclusions from the regulated activity of issuing electronic money. They provide that certain persons whose operations are conducted on a limited scale and who are certified to that effect by the FSA will be excluded from the scope of the Regulated Activities Order. Furthermore, agreeing to issue electronic money will not be a regulated activity.

Electronic communications

3.60   The draft Financial Services and Markets Act 2000 (Regulated Activities) (Amendment) (No 2) Order 2001[1] (ECD Order) amends the Regulated Activities Order to give effect to the Electronic Commerce Directive.[2]

The ECD Order creates a general exclusion from the definition of 'regulated activity' for activities which consist of the provision of 'information society services' either by persons in EEA States (other than the UK), or from places of establishment in other Member States.[3] The exclusion does not, however, apply to the effecting or carrying out of a contract of insurance as principal where that activity is carried on by an undertaking which has received official authorisation in accordance with the First Life Insurance Directive or the First Non-Life Insurance Directive[4] and the insurance falls within the scope of any of the Insurance Directives.[5]

'Information society services' are defined in the Electronic Commerce Directive as any service normally provided for remuneration, at a distance (ie without the parties being simultaneously present), by electronic means[6] and through the transmission of data on individual request.

1   SI 2002/1776.
2   2000/31/EC.
3   This general exclusion (which applies to several specific kinds of regulated activity) has been
    included in the Regulated Activities Order as art 72A.
4   79/267/EEC and 73/239/EEC.
5   As defined in FSMA 2000, s 425 and Sch 3.
6   'By electronic means' means that the service is sent initially and received at its destination by
    means of electronic equipment for the processing (including digital compression) and storage
    of data, and entirely transmitted, conveyed and received by wire, by radio, by optical means or
    by other electromagnetic means.

EXCLUDED ACTIVITIES

3.61   Part II of the Regulated Activities Order[1] sets out the exclusions
applicable to each specified kind of activity. Exclusions previously contained in
Parts III and IV of Sch 1 to the Financial Services Act 1986 and those in the
Banking Act 1987 and Insurance Companies Act 1982 have broadly been
retained and, in some cases, clarified. Part II of the Order (ie article 4(4)) also
implements the Investment Services Directive by means of a provision
dis-applying some of the exclusions in relation to investment firms that provide
core investment services to third parties on a professional basis.

1   SI 2001/544.

3.62   In an attempt to make the Order as easy to use as possible, exclusions
which relate to specific activities are placed immediately after the relevant
activity. Certain other exclusions which span a variety of activities are then
grouped together at the end of the Order.

Exclusions from accepting deposits

3.63   No exclusions operate directly in respect of the activity of accepting
deposits; instead, the Regulated Activities Order provides that certain sums of
money do not amount to a 'deposit' (see articles 6 to 9). However, certain
persons are exempt persons in relation to the regulated activity of accepting
deposits.[1]

1   These persons are listed in art 4 of the Financial Services and Markets Act 2000 (Exemption)
    Order 2001 (SI 2001/1201), as amended.

Sums paid by certain persons/received by solicitors (articles 6 and 7)

3.64   Article 6 of the Regulated Activities Order provides that sums paid by
certain persons will not amount to a deposit for the purposes of article 5. These
include sums paid by the Bank of England, the central bank of another EEA
state, the European Central Bank, a local authority,[1] the European Investment
Bank or by one company to another at a time when both are members of the
same group[2] or when the same individual is a majority shareholder controller[3]
of both. Article 7 also excludes certain sums received by a practising solicitor in
the course of his profession.

1   The term 'local authority' is defined in SI 2001/544, s 3(1).
2   See *Minories Finance Ltd v Arthur Young (a firm) (Bank of England, third party)* [1989] 2 All ER
    105.

3   A 'majority shareholder controller' is defined in SI 2001/544, art 6(2) as a person who is a controller of a company by virtue of FSMA 2000, s 422(2)(a), (c), (e) or (g) and if the greatest percentage referred to in those sections is (in his case) 50% or more.

Sums received by persons authorised to deal (article 8)

3.65   Sums will not fall within the definition of a 'deposit' if they are received by a person who is either:

(a)   authorised to carry on activities of the kind specified by articles 14 (dealing in investments as principal), 21 (dealing in investments as agent), 25 (arranging deals in investments), 37 (managing investments), 51 (establishing etc a collective investment scheme) and 52 (establishing a stakeholder pension scheme); or

(b)   exempt in relation to such activities, if the sums are received in connection with the carrying on of any such activity with (or on behalf of) the person by whom (or on whose behalf) the sum is paid.

Sums received in consideration for the issue of debt securities (article 9)

3.66   Prior to the new regulatory regime created under the FSMA 2000 there were some rather limited exemptions from the prohibition on accepting deposits for issues of commercial paper and other debt securities. However, there is now a new and much more extensive exclusion in article 9 of the Regulated Activities Order, which provides a general exemption in respect of all issues of debt securities other than commercial paper. Commercial paper is, for this purpose, a debt security which has a maturity of less than one year from the date of issue.[1] In relation to commercial paper, the exclusion applies if the commercial paper is redeemable or transferable in tranches of not less than £100,000 (or equivalent in another currency) and the subscribers are professional investors.

1   See Financial Services and Markets Act 2000 (Regulated Activities) (Amendment) Order 2002 (SI 2002/682), art 12.

3.67   A person who operates a commercial paper programme in an overseas market, but who manages the programme from the UK, will need to comply with this exclusion to avoid carrying on the regulated activity of accepting deposits because of the new territorial scope of s 418 of the FSMA 2000.[1]

1   See further para 3.132.

Exclusions relating to dealing in investments as principal

3.68   The activity of dealing in investments as principal is cut back by the exclusions in articles 15 to 20 of the Regulated Activities Order.[1]

1   SI 2001/544.

Absence of holding out etc

3.69   Article 15 is designed to exclude the activities of investors who deal in investments for their own account and are not to be regarded as providers of investment services. It provides that if a person ('A') enters as principal into a transaction which relates to a security or is the assignment of a qualifying contract of insurance (or a right to, or interest in, such a contract) this activity will not fall within the scope of article 14 unless:

(a)   A holds himself out as making a market in investments of the relevant kind;[1]

(b)   A holds himself out as engaging in the business of buying such investments with a view to selling them;

(c)   A holds himself out as engaging in the business or underwriting such investments; or

(d)   A regularly solicits members of the public[2] for the purpose of inducing them to enter into transactions to which article 14 applies, and the transaction is entered into as a result of the solicitation.

1   A person's 'making a market' for this purpose means being willing, as principal, to buy, sell or subscribe for investments of the relevant kind at prices determined by him generally and continuously rather than in respect of each particular transaction.

2   'Members of the public' is defined in the Regulated Activities Order (SI 2001/544), art 15(2) as comprising persons other than: authorised persons; members of the same group as A; persons who are or who propose to become participators with A in a joint enterprise (as defined in the Order); and any person who is solicited by A with a view to the acquisition by A of 20% or more of the voting shares (as defined in the Order) in a body corporate.

3.70   However, the article 15 exclusion will not apply where A enters into the transaction as bare trustee for another and is acting on that other person's instructions (although the exclusion in article 66(1) will apply if the conditions set out in that article are met).

Dealing in contractually based investments

3.71   Article 16 excludes from the ambit of article 14 certain principal transactions relating to CBIs which are entered into with professional counterparties or through professional intermediaries. If an unauthorised person enters as principal into a transaction relating to a CBI:

(a)   with or through an authorised person or an exempt person;[1] or

(b)   through an office outside the UK which is maintained by a party to the transaction,[2] and with or through a person whose head office is located outside the UK and whose ordinary business involves him in carrying on certain specified activities;[3]

the transaction is excluded.

1   Unless otherwise specified, references in this chapter to 'exempt persons' are references to persons acting in the course of a business comprising a regulated activity in relation to which they are exempt.

2   'Party' here has its technical meaning – that is, it is not sufficient for the relevant office to be maintained by a person who is merely acting as agent or arranger, for such a person would not be regarded as a party. However, it is generally thought that the exclusion does apply if one party is in the UK but deals with an overseas office of the other party.

3   These are the activities specified by any of the Regulated Activities Order (SI 2001/544), arts 14, 21, 25, 37, 40, 45, 51, 52 and 53 or, so far as relevant to any of those articles, art 64 (or who would carry on such activities apart from any exclusion from any of those articles made by the Order).

Acceptance of instruments creating or acknowledging indebtedness

3.72   Article 17 provides that a person who accepts an instrument[1] that creates or acknowledges indebtedness in respect of any loan, credit, guarantee (or other similar financial accommodation) or assurance which he has made, granted or provided will not be deemed to be dealing in investments as principal. This means that a bank which provides another person with finance will be able to accept an instrument acknowledging the debt (and as security for it) without the risk of dealing as principal as a result.

1 A person will be deemed to 'accept an instrument' if, for example, he becomes a party to the instrument otherwise than as a debtor or a surety (SI 2001/544, art 17(2)).

Issue by a company of its own shares etc.

3.73   The issue by a company (ie any body corporate, other than an open-ended investment company) of its own shares or share warrants, and the issue by any person of his own debentures or debenture warrants, are excluded from the activity of dealing in investments as principal (see article 18). The terms 'shares' and 'debentures' include any investment specified by article 76 or 77 and 'share warrants' and 'debenture warrants' are defined as any instrument giving entitlement to shares in the company concerned or the debentures issued by the person concerned.

Risk management exclusion (articles 19 and 23)

3.74   The Regulated Activities Order introduces a new risk management exclusion in respect of the activity of dealing in investments as agent or as principal. This exclusion is designed partly to address the position of certain persons who previously fell within the permitted persons regime contained in para 23 of Sch 1 to the Financial Services Act 1986 and partly to assist in clarifying uncertainties which are not resolved by the 'commercial purposes' test under article 84 of the Regulated Activities Order.[1] It enables a dealer whose (or whose group's) business consists mainly of activities other than regulated activities, to buy or sell derivatives as principal or agent if:

(a)   neither party to the transaction is an individual; and
(b)   the sole or main purpose for which the dealer enters into the transaction is to limit the extent to which the business of the dealer or a group company will be affected by any identifiable risk arising otherwise than as a result of carrying on a regulated activity.

1 See para 3.16.

3.75   The risk management exclusion will only be available where the relevant business of the dealer or a group company consists mainly of activities other than regulated activities (or activities which would be regulated activities but for an exclusion in the Regulated Activities Order). The effect of these conditions is that the exclusion will not necessarily be available to special purpose treasury companies or commodity or energy trading entities in which the relevant activities of a group are concentrated.

Other exclusions

3.76   A person will not be treated as carrying on the activity of dealing in investments as principal if (in certain circumstances) he enters into a transaction as principal:

(a)   while acting as bare trustee (or, in Scotland, as nominee);[1]
(b)   in connection with the sale of goods or supply of services;[2]

(c) where the transaction takes place between members of a group or joint enterprise;[3]

(d) in connection with the sale of a body corporate;[4]

(e) in connection with an employee share scheme;[5] or

(f) as an overseas person.[6]

1 SI 2001/544, art 66.
2 SI 2001/544, art 68.
3 SI 2001/544, art 69.
4 SI 2001/544, art 70.
5 SI 2001/544, art 71.
6 SI 2001/544, art 72. See further below, para 3.119.

Exclusions from the activity of dealing in investments as agent

Dealing with or through an authorised person (articles 22 and 29)

3.77 The Regulated Activities Order introduces a new exclusion under which a person dealing as agent or arranging a transaction for a client with or through an authorised person will not be considered to be carrying on a regulated activity (and therefore will not need to be authorised) where:

(a) the transaction is (or, in the case of arranging, the transaction is to be) entered into on advice given to the client by an authorised person; or

(b) it is clear that the client has not sought advice from the agent or arranger on the merits of entering into the transaction[1] and the agent or arranger does not receive any benefit from the deal from any person for which he does not account to the client.

1 Or, if the client has sought advice, the agent/arranger has declined to give it and recommended that the client obtain advice from an authorised person.

3.78 This exclusion may be of assistance in relation to the establishment of cheap dealing facilities for small shareholders and other similar arrangements.

Risk management exclusion

3.79 This exclusion has already been considered in the context of dealing in investments as principal (see para 3.74 above).

Other exclusions

3.80 A person will not be treated as carrying on the activity of dealing in investments as agent if (in certain circumstances) he enters into a transaction as agent:

(a) in connection with carrying on a profession or a business which does not otherwise consist of regulated activities;[1]

(b) in connection with the sale of goods or supply of services;[2]

(c) that takes place between members of a group or joint enterprise;[3]

(d) in connection with the sale of a body corporate;[4]

(e) in connection with an employee share scheme;[5] or

(f) as an overseas person.[6]

1 SI 2001/544, art 67.
2 SI 2001/544, art 68.

3 SI 2001/544, art 69.
4 SI 2001/544, art 70.
5 SI 2001/544, art 71.
6 SI 2001/544, art 72. See para 3.119.

Exclusions from the activity of arranging deals in investments

3.81 Exclusions from this activity are set out in articles 26 to 36. Of these, some apply only to article 25(1) or to article 25(2), whereas others apply to both paragraphs.

Arrangements not causing a deal and arrangements to which the arranger is a party

3.82 Making arrangements for another person to buy, sell, subscribe for or underwrite particular investments is a specified kind of activity under article 25(1) of the Regulated Activities Order. However, article 26 excludes arrangements which do not or would not bring about the transaction to which the arrangements relate. A person will bring about an investment transaction only if his involvement in the chain of events leading up to the transaction is sufficiently important that without his involvement the transaction would not take place. Article 28 also excludes any arrangements for a transaction into which the arranger enters (or is to enter) as principal or as agent for some other person. This is to avoid overlap between article 25 and articles 14 and 21.

Enabling parties to communicate and arrangements to which the arranger is a party

3.83 Under article 25(2) of the Regulated Activities Order, making arrangements with a view to a person who participates in the arrangements buying, selling, subscribing for or underwriting investments is a specified activity. However, article 27 provides that a person does not carry on an activity of the kind specified by article 25(2) merely by providing the means by which one party to a transaction (or potential transaction) is able to communicate with other such parties. This means that persons such as Internet service providers or telecommunications networks will not be held to be arranging deals in investments if all that they do is to provide communication facilities. Also excluded from article 25(2) are arrangements which a person makes with a view to transactions into which he enters (or is to enter) as principal or as agent for some other person (article 28).

Provision of finance and introductions

3.84 There are two further exclusions which apply only to article 25(2) arrangements; these are contained in articles 32 and 33. Article 32 excludes arrangements the sole purpose of which is to provide finance to enable a person to buy, sell, subscribe for or underwrite investments. Article 33 excludes arrangements which provide for the introduction of clients to another person ('X') if:

(a) X is, broadly, a professional (ie he is authorised or exempt, or he is not unlawfully carrying on regulated activities in the UK and his ordinary business involves him in engaging in an activity of a certain kind[1]); and

(b)   the introduction is made with a view to the provision of independent advice or the independent exercise of discretion in relation to investments generally or in relation to any class of investments to which the arrangements relate.

The FSA is of the view that article 33 will apply where a person is finding potential customers for an independent financial adviser or independent investment manager (ie that in these circumstances the introducer is allowed to receive a payment for making the introduction without being an authorised person). However, article 33 will not apply where the introductions are made to a person who is not independent or are made for the purposes of execution-only dealing.[2]

1   These are activities of the kind specified in the Regulated Activities Order (SI 2001/544), arts 14, 21, 25, 37, 40, 45, 51, 52 and 53 (or, so far as relevant to any of those articles, art 64), or who would carry on such activities apart from any exclusion from any of those articles made by the Order.
2   See the FSA's Authorisation Manual, Appendix 1, para 1.33.5.

Arranging deals with or through authorised persons

3.85   This exclusion has already been considered in the context of dealing in investments as agent (see further para 3.77 above).

Arrangements made by a moneylender/accepting debentures in connection with loans

3.86   Article 30 excludes from articles 25(1) and (2) certain arrangements made by a moneylender.[1] These are arrangements under which either:

(a)   a relevant authorised person[2] ('A') (or a person acting on his behalf) will introduce to the moneylender persons with whom A has entered, or proposes to enter, into a relevant transaction,[3] or will advise such persons to approach the moneylender, with a view to the moneylender lending money on the security of any contract effected pursuant to a relevant transaction; or

(b)   A gives an assurance to the money lender as to the amount which, on the security of any contract effected pursuant to a relevant transaction, will or may be received by the money lender should the money lender lend money to a person introduced to him under the arrangements.

1   A 'money-lender' is a moneylending company within the meaning of s 338 of the Companies Act 1985, a building society or a person whose ordinary business includes making loans or giving guarantees in connection with loans.
2   A relevant authorised person is a person authorised to effect qualifying contracts of insurance or to sell rights to, or interests in, such contracts.
3   That is, effecting a qualifying contract of insurance or the sale of a right to, or interest in, such a contract.

3.87   Article 31 also excludes arrangements under which a person accepts[1] or is to accept an instrument that creates or acknowledges indebtedness in respect of any loan, credit, guarantee, or assurance which is, or is to be, made, granted or provided by that person or his principal.

1   Accepting an instrument includes a reference to a person becoming a party to an instrument otherwise than as a debtor or a surety.

Arrangements for the issue of shares etc

3.88 Article 34 excludes (from both articles 25(1) and (2)) arrangements made by a company for the purposes of issuing its own shares or share warrants and arrangements made by a person for the purposes of issuing his own debentures or debenture warrants. A company/person will not, by reason of issuing its own shares/his own debentures or share warrants/debenture warrants be treated as selling them.[1]

1 The terms 'company', 'shares', 'debentures', 'share warrants' and 'debenture warrants' are defined in SI 2001/544, art 18(2).

International securities self-regulating organisations

3.89 Arrangements which are made by an international securities self-regulating organisation (ISSRO) for the purposes of carrying out its functions are excluded from articles 25(1) and (2) by virtue of article 35.

3.90 The Treasury may approve a body corporate or unincorporated association as an ISSRO provided that certain conditions are met. Among the conditions which must be satisfied are those which specify that the body corporate or association:

(a) must not have its head office in the UK and must not be eligible for recognition under the FSMA 2000, s 287 or s 288[1] (on the basis that the entity is unable to satisfy the requirements of one or both of paras s 292(3)(a) and (b) of the FSMA 2000);

(b) is able and willing to co-operate with the FSA (and also that arrangements exist for co-operation between the FSA and those responsible for the supervision of the body or association in the country or territory in which its head office is situated); and

(c) facilitates and regulates the activity of its members in the conduct of international securities business[2].

Currently the International Securities Market Association (ISMA) is the only organisation approved as an ISSRO.

1 That is, recognition as a recognised investment exchange or clearing house.
2 A term which is defined in SI 2001/544, art 35(4).

Other exclusions

3.91 A person will not be treated as arranging deals in investments if (in certain circumstances) he makes arrangements:

(a) while acting as a trustee or personal representative;[1]

(b) in connection with carrying on a profession or a business which does not otherwise consist of regulated activities;[2]

(c) in connection with the sale of goods or supply of services;[3]

(d) in connection with certain transactions by a group member or a participator in a joint enterprise;[4]

(e) in connection with the sale of a body corporate;[5]

(f) in connection with an employee share scheme;[6] or

(g) as an overseas person.[7]

1 SI 2001/544, art 66.
2 SI 2001/544, art 67.

3   SI 2001/544, art 68.
4   SI 2001/544, art 69.
5   SI 2001/544, art 70.
6   SI 2001/544, art 71.
7   SI 2001/544, art 72. See para 3.119.

Exclusions from the activity of managing investments

Attorneys

3.92   Article 38 provides that a person will not be carrying on the activity of managing investments if:

(a)   he is appointed to manage the investments (which consist of, or include, securities or CBIs) under a power of attorney; and

(b)   all routine or day-to-day decisions relating to the securities or CBIs are taken on behalf of the attorney by a person with permission to manage investments, a person who is an exempt person in relation to activities of that kind, or an overseas person.[1]

1   An overseas person is defined in the Regulated Activities Order (SI 2001/544) as a person who carries on activities of the kind specified by any of arts 14, 21, 25, 37, 40, 45, 51, 52 and 53 or, so far as relevant to any of those articles, art 64 (or activities of a kind which would be so specified but for the exclusion in art 72) but does not carry on any those activities, or offer to do so, from a permanent place of business maintained by him in the UK.

Other exclusions

3.93   Article 37 is also subject to the exclusions in articles 66 (trustees, nominees etc), 68 (sale of goods and supply of services) and 69 (groups and joint enterprises).[1]

1   See paras 3.106, 3.109 and 3.111.

Exclusions from the activity of safeguarding and administering investments

3.94   The exclusions to this activity, which are contained in articles 41 and 42 of the Regulated Activities Order, relate to certain activities involving qualifying custodians.[1] Article 41 excludes any activities which a person carries on as a result of arrangements:

(a)   under which a qualifying custodian undertakes responsibility for the assets which is no less onerous than he would have if he were safeguarding and administering the assets himself; and

(b)   which are operated by the qualifying custodian in the course of carrying on safeguarding and administering activities in the UK.

1   A 'qualifying custodian' is defined in SI 2001/544, art 41(2) as an authorised person who has permission to carry on an activity of the kind specified by art 40 (ie safeguard and administer assets) or an exempt person.

3.95   This means that an authorised person with permission to carry on the regulated activity of safeguarding and administering assets can outsource all or part of the activities without the person to whom they are outsourced needing to be authorised and without loss of protection to the owner of the assets.

3.96 Article 42 also excludes arrangements pursuant to which introductions are made by a person ('P') to a qualifying custodian with a view to the custodian providing safeguarding and administration services in the UK, provided that the custodian (or other person who is to safeguard and administer the assets) is not connected with P. Article 42(2)(b) states that a person will be treated as being connected with P if he is either a member of the same group as P, or P is remunerated by him.

Other exclusions

3.97 A person will not be treated as safeguarding and administering assets if (in certain circumstances) he safeguards and administers assets:

(a) while acting as a trustee or personal representative;[1]
(b) in connection with carrying on a profession or a business which does not otherwise consist of regulated activities;[2]
(c) in connection with the sale of goods or supply of services;[3]
(d) belonging to a group member or a participator in a joint enterprise;[4] or
(e) in connection with an employee share scheme.[5]

1 SI 2001/544, art 66.
2 SI 2001/544, art 67.
3 SI 2001/544, art 68.
4 SI 2001/544, art 69.
5 SI 2001/544, art 71. See para 3.117.

Exclusions from the activity of sending dematerialised instructions

Instructions sent on behalf of participating issuers and settlement banks and instructions sent in connection with takeover offers and in the course of providing a network

3.98 Articles 46 to 49 exclude from article 45 the act of sending, or causing to be sent, a dematerialised instruction:

(a) where the person on whose behalf the instruction is sent (or caused to be sent) is:
    (i) a participating issuer within the meaning of the Uncertificated Securities Regulations 2001[1] (2001 Regulations);
    (ii) a settlement bank;
    (iii) an offeror[2] making a takeover offer;[3] or
(b) as a necessary part of providing a network, the purpose of which is to carry properly authenticated dematerialised instructions (within the meaning of the 2001 Regulations).

1 SI 2001/3755. References to the Uncertificated Securities Regulations 1995 (SI 1995/3272) were changed to references to the 2001 Regulations by the Financial Services and Markets Act 2000 (Regulated Activities) (Amendment) Order 2002 (SI 2002/682).
2 'Offeror' is defined in art 48(2) to mean, in the case of a takeover offer made by two or more persons jointly, the joint offerors or any of them.
3 'Takeover offer' is defined in art 48(2).

Other exclusions

3.99   Article 45 is also subject to the exclusions in articles 66 (trustees, nominees etc) and 69 (groups and joint enterprises).[1]

1   See paras 3.106 and 3.111.

Exclusions from the activity of advising on investments

Advice given in newspapers etc

3.100   The exclusion in article 54 of the Regulated Activities Order provides that investment advice given in a periodical publication, in a regularly updated news or information service or in a television or radio programme will not be a regulated activity if the principal purpose of the publication or the service[1] is not to give advice or to lead or enable persons to buy or sell certain investments.

1   Taken as a whole, including any advertisements and promotional material.

3.101   This exclusion in the Regulated Activities Order differs from the exclusions in the Financial Services Act 1986 in three principal ways. First, the exclusion in the Regulated Activities Order has been updated to cover all media, not just hard copy publications and television etc (the certification process also applies to all media). Second, advice given in a television programme no longer has the benefit of an absolute exclusion but is subject to a similar principal purpose test as advice given in other media (the test also applies to the entire broadcasting service, not an individual programme). Third, the single principal purpose test in the Financial Services Act 1986 has been changed to a double principal purpose test in the FSMA 2000; that is whether the principal purpose of the publication or service is not to give advice or lead the person to buy or sell investments.

3.102   The FSA may, on the application of the proprietor of a publication or service, certify that the publication or service satisfies the criteria in article 54(1) or (2).

Other exclusions

3.103   A person will not be treated as advising on investments if (in certain circumstances) he gives advice:

(a)   while acting as a trustee or personal representative;[1]
(b)   in connection with carrying on a profession or a business which does not otherwise consist of regulated activities[2] (for example, it may be necessary for a tax adviser to advise a client to sell his assets for tax reasons);
(c)   in connection with the sale of goods or supply of services;[3]
(d)   to a group member or a participator in a joint enterprise;[4]
(e)   in connection with the sale of a body corporate;[5] or
(f)   as an overseas person.[6]

1   SI 2001/544, art 66.
2   SI 2001/544, art 67.
3   SI 2001/544, art 68.
4   SI 2001/544, art 69.

Exclusions from the activity of agreeing to carry on activities

3.104   A person who agrees to carry on certain regulated activities does not require authorisation where he is an overseas person and the agreement is reached as a result of a legitimate approach. This exclusion applies to agreements to arrange deals, manage investments, safeguard and administer investments or send dematerialised instructions.[1]

1   SI 2001/544, art 72(6). Art 72 is considered in detail at para 3.119 below.

Exclusions that apply to several kinds of regulated activity

3.105   Chapter XVII of Part II of the Regulated Activities Order sets out the various exclusions that apply to a range of different circumstances. Each of the general exclusions has some application to several regulated activities relating to securities or CBIs. However, they have no effect in relation to the regulated activities of accepting deposits, effecting or carrying out contracts of insurance, advising on syndicate participation at Lloyd's, managing the underwriting capacity of a Lloyd's syndicate as a managing agent at Lloyd's, entering as provider into a funeral plan contract or any regulated activities relating to regulated mortgage contracts.

Trustees, nominees and personal representatives (article 66)

3.106   Article 66 applies to six specified activities. It provides that:

(a)   Article 14 (dealing in investments as principal) will not apply where a person ('X') enters into a transaction as bare trustee for another person ('Y') and X is acting on Y's instructions and does not hold himself out as providing a service of buying and selling securities or CBIs.

(b)   Article 25 (arranging deals in investments) will not apply to arrangements made by a person acting as trustee or personal representative for or with a view to:
  (i)   that person and a fellow trustee or personal representative (acting in their capacity as such); or
  (ii)   a beneficiary under the trust, will or intestacy,
  entering into a transaction.

(c)   Article 37 (managing investments) does not apply to anything done by a person ('X') acting as a trustee or personal representative, unless X holds himself out as providing investment management services or the assets are held for the purposes of an occupational pension scheme and X is treated as carrying on that activity by way of business.[1]

(d)   Article 40 (safeguarding and administering assets) does not apply to any activity carried on by a trustee or personal representative unless the trustee/personal representative holds himself out as providing safeguarding and administration services.

(e)   Article 45 (sending dematerialised instructions) will not apply if the instruction relates to an investment which that person holds as trustee or personal representative.

(f)   Article 53 (advising on investments) does not apply to advice given by trustees and personal representatives to fellow trustees or personal representatives (for the purposes of the trust or estate) or to a beneficiary under the trust, will or intestacy in connection with his interest in the trust fund or estate.

1   By virtue of Financial Services and Markets Act 2000 (Carrying on Regulated Activities by Way of Business) Order 2001 (SI 2001/1177), art 4.

3.107   However, the exclusions in (b) to (d) and (f) above will not apply if the trustee or personal representative is remunerated for the relevant investment activity in addition to any remuneration that he receives for discharging his duties as a trustee or personal representative. This limitation, together with the 'holding out' test referred to in (a), (c) and (d) above, broadly reflect the distinction between activities which can be regarded as merely an integral part of a trustee's functions and activities which amount to a separate and additional investment service.

Activities carried on in the course of a profession or non-investment business (article 67)

3.108   Article 67 of the Regulated Activities Order excludes from articles 21 (dealing in investments as agent), 25 (arranging deals in investments), 40 (safeguarding and administering assets) and 53 (advising on investments) any activity which:

(a)   is carried on in the course of carrying on any profession or business which does not otherwise consist of the carrying on of regulated activities in the UK; and
(b)   may reasonably be regarded as a necessary part of the other services which are provided in the course of that profession or business.

This exclusion is similar to that previously in para 24 of Sch 1 to the Financial Services Act 1986, but has been expanded by the addition of the words 'may reasonably be regarded as'. Its purpose is to avoid professional firms feeling constrained to seek authorisation on a precautionary basis.

Like some elements of the trustee exclusion,[1] this exclusion does not apply if the activity in question is remunerated separately from the other services.

1   See paras 3.106 and 3.107.

Activities carried on in connection with the sale of goods or supply of services (article 68)

3.109   Article 68 excludes certain activities that are carried on for the purposes of (or in connection with) the sale of goods or supply of services by a supplier[1] to a customer[2] (or a related sale or supply).[3] The exclusion is not available where the customer to whom the goods are sold or serviced are supplied is an individual.

1   'Supplier' is defined as a person whose main business it is to sell goods or supply services and not to carry on any activities of the kind specified by any of SI 2001/544, arts 14, 21, 25, 37, 40, 45, 51, 52 and 53 and, where the supplier is a member of a group, also means any other member of that group.
2   'Customer' means a person, other than an individual, to whom a supplier sells goods or supplies services, or agrees to do so and, where the customer is a member of a group, also means any other member of that group.

3   A 'related sale or supply' means a sale of goods or supply of services to the customer other than
    by the supplier but for (or in connection with) the same purpose as the sale or supply.

3.110   This exclusion applies to articles 14 (dealing in investments as
principal), 21 (dealing in investments as agent), 25 (arranging deals in
investments), 37 (managing investments), 40 (safeguarding and administering
assets) and 53 (advising on investments) provided that certain specified
conditions are met.

Groups and joint enterprises (article 69)

3.111   The article 69 exclusions, which apply to seven regulated activities,
relate to intra-group dealings and to activities and dealings involving participators in a joint enterprise.[1] They apply in relation to dealing in investments as
principal and agent, arranging deals in investments and advising on investments where the parties involved either are bodies corporate within the same
group[2] or are (or propose to become) participators in a joint enterprise and the
transaction relates to that enterprise. Article 69 provides that:

(a)   Article 14 (dealing in investments as principal) does not apply to any
      transaction into which a person enters as principal with another person
      ('X') if X is also acting as principal and they are both members of the
      same group or they are participants or proposed participants in a joint
      enterprise and the transaction relates to that joint enterprise.

(b)   Article 21 (dealing in investments as agent) does not apply to any
      transaction into which a person enters as agent for another person ('X') if
      X is acting as principal and they are both members of the same group, or
      participants or proposed participants in a joint enterprise to which the
      proposed transaction relates, provided that:

      (i)   where the investment to which the transaction relates is a security, the
            agent does not hold himself out (other than to other members of the
            group or participants in the joint enterprise) as engaging in the
            business of buying securities of the kind to which the transaction
            relates with a view to selling them, and does not regularly solicit
            members of the public for the purpose of inducing them to buy, sell,
            subscribe for or underwrite securities;

      (ii) where the investment to which the transaction relates is a CBI,
            certain conditions are met (for example, the agent enters into the
            transaction with or through an authorised person or an exempt
            person).

(c)   Article 25 (arranging deals in investments) does not apply to arrange-
      ments made by a person ('X') if:

      (i)   X is a member of a group and the arrangements are made in
            connection with a transaction which is (or will be) entered into, as
            principal, by another member of the same group; or

      (ii) X is (or proposes to become) a participator in a joint enterprise and
            the arrangements are made in connection with a transaction which is
            or will be entered into, as principal, by another person who is or
            proposes to become a participator in that enterprise, for the purposes
            of or in connection with, that enterprise.

(d)   Article 37 (managing investments) does not apply to any activity carried
      on by a person ('X') if: X is a member of a group and the relevant assets
      belong to another group member; or X proposes to become a participator

in a joint enterprise with the owner of the assets, and the assets are managed for the purposes of, or in connection with, that enterprise.

(e)   Article 40 (safeguarding and administering investments) does not apply to any activity carried on by a person ('X') if: X is a member of a group and the relevant assets are owned by another group member; or X proposes to become a participator in a joint enterprise and the relevant assets are owned by another person who proposes to become a participator and the assets are (or will be) safeguarded and administered for the purposes of, or in connection with, that enterprise.

(f)   Article 45 (sending dematerialised instructions) does not apply to a person who is a member of a group and who sends or causes to be sent instructions on behalf of another group member provided that a member of the group is the registered holder of the investment to which the instruction relates or will be so registered as a result of the instruction.

(g)   Article 69 also provides that article 53 (advising on investments) does not apply to the giving of advice by a person ('X') if: X is a member of a group and gives advice to another group member; or X is, or proposes to become, a participator in a joint enterprise and the advice is given to another person who is, or proposes to become, a participator in that enterprise and relates to that enterprise.

1   A joint enterprise means an enterprise into which two or more persons ('the participators') enter for commercial purposes related to a business or businesses (other than the business of engaging in a regulated activity) carried on by them. Where a participator is a member of a group, each other member of the group is also to be regarded as a participator in the enterprise.
2   'Group' is defined in FSMA 2000, s 421. In addition to a parent undertaking and its subsidiary undertakings, it includes associated entities in which the parent undertaking or any subsidiary undertaking holds a 'participating interest'. 'Participating interest' is defined by reference to the accounting provisions of the Companies Acts (and will therefore generally include an interest of 20% or more).

Activities carried on in connection with the sale of a body corporate (article 70)

3.112   Article 70 excludes from the scope of article 14 (dealing in investments as principal), article 21 (dealing in investments as agent), article 25 (arranging deals in investments) and article 53 (advising on investments) certain activities which are carried on in connection with the sale of a body corporate.

3.113   Article 70(1) provides that a person does not carry on an activity of the kind specified by article 14 by entering into a transaction as principal if the transaction is to acquire or dispose of shares in a body corporate[1] (or a transaction that is entered into for the purposes of such an acquisition or disposal) and either:

(a)   certain conditions set out in article 70(2) of the Regulated Activities Order[2] are met (see further below); or

(b)   the object of the transaction may reasonably be regarded as being the acquisition of the day-to-day control of the affairs of the body corporate.

1   Other than an open-ended investment company.
2   SI 2001/544.

3.114   The conditions in article 70(2) are that:

(a)   the shares consist of or include 50% or more of the voting shares[1] in the body corporate; or

(b)   the shares, together with any already held by the person acquiring them, consist of or include at least that percentage of such shares; and

(c)   in either case, the acquisition or disposal is between parties each of whom is a body corporate, a partnership, a single individual or a group of connected individuals.[2]

1   The term 'voting shares' is defined in the Regulated Activities Order (SI 2001/544), art 3(1) to mean the voting rights which are attributable to the share capital of a company and which are exercisable in all circumstances at any general meeting of the company.
2   A group of connected individuals is defined in SI 2001/544, art 70(3); broadly, it means a group of persons who are (or are trustees for) directors and managers of the relevant body corporate or their close relatives.

3.115   The condition in (c) above is quite restrictive, since it appears to have the effect that only one party on each side of the transaction can fall within the specified categories, so that, for example, there cannot be more than one corporate purchaser and there can be no individual seller who is not a member of a group of connected individuals. Under the corresponding provision in Sch 1 to the Financial Services Act 1986, this significantly limited the availability of the exclusion. Under article 70 as currently drafted, this will generally no longer be a problem, since the alternative test (that the object of the transaction may reasonably be regarded as being the acquisition of the day-to-day control of the affairs of the body corporate) is considerably more flexible. It is not clear whether the Treasury intended to broaden the exclusion to this extent.

3.116   The exclusions from articles 21, 25 and 53 are subject to the same conditions.

Activities carried on in connection with employee share schemes (article 71)

3.117   The exclusions in article 71 apply to activities which further an employee share scheme or are carried on in operation of such a scheme. For example, article 71(1) specifies that article 14 (dealing in investments as principal) does not apply where a person ('C'), a member of the same group as C, or a relevant trustee[1] enters into a transaction as principal where the purpose of the transaction is to enable or facilitate:

(a)   transactions in shares in, or debentures[2] issued by, C between or for the benefit of:
   (i)   the *bona fide* employees or former employees of C or of another member of the same group as C; or
   (ii)   their close relatives (eg wives, husbands, children etc); or

(b)   the holding of the investments in C by, or for the benefit of, such persons.

1   'Relevant trustee' means a person who, in pursuance of the arrangements made for the purpose mentioned in paras (a) and (b), holds, as trustee, shares in or debentures issued by C.
2   'Shares' and 'debentures' are defined in SI 2001/544, art 71(6).

3.118   This exclusion also applies to articles 21 (dealing in investments as agent), 25 (arranging deals in investments) and 40 (safeguarding and administering assets).

ADDITIONAL EXCLUSIONS FOR OVERSEAS PERSONS

3.119   Article 72 contains a number of exclusions for overseas persons who carry on particular activities. An overseas person is defined in the Regulated Activities Order as a person who carries on certain investment-related activities[1] but does not carry them on (or offer to do so) from a permanent place of business in the UK.

1   These are activities of the kind specified in the Regulated Activities Order (SI 2001/544), arts 12, 21, 25, 37, 40, 45, 51 to 53 and, so far as relevant to those articles, art 64 (or activities which would be so specified but for the art 72 exclusion).

3.120   The overseas persons exclusions fall into two main categories. The first, which applies to dealing and arranging deals, is where the regulated activity involves an authorised person, or an exempt person acting within the scope of his exemption, as counterparty or intermediary. The second, which applies rather more widely, is where a particular regulated activity is carried on as a result of a 'legitimate approach'.[1]

1   That is, an approach to an overseas person that has not been solicited by the overseas person, or which has been solicited in a way that does not contravene the financial promotion restriction in FSMA 2000, s 21. An approach which is made by the overseas person in a way that does not contravene s 21 is also a legitimate approach.

3.121   Article 72 provides that an overseas person does not carry on an activity of the kind specified by article 14 (dealing in investments as principal) by entering into a transaction as principal:

(a)   with or through[1] an authorised person or exempt person; or
(b)   with a person in the UK if the transaction is the result of a legitimate approach.

1   A transaction is entered into 'through' a person if that person enters into it as agent or arranges, in a manner constituting the carrying on of an activity of the kind specified in the Regulated Activities Order (SI 2001/544), art 25(1), for it to be entered into by another person as agent or principal – see art 3(2) of the Order. The words 'in a manner constituting the carrying on of an activity of the kind specified in article 25(1)' constitute a change from the corresponding provision of the Financial Services Act 1986 (Sch 1, para 29), but it is doubtful whether the change is one of substance.

3.122   An overseas person will not be deemed to be dealing in investments as agent pursuant to article 21 by entering into a transaction:

(a)   as agent for any person with or through an authorised or exempt person; or
(b)   with another party ('X') as agent for any person ('Y'), other than with or through an authorised person or such an exempt person, unless X or Y is in the UK and the transaction is the result of an approach (other than a legitimate approach) made by or on behalf of, or to, whichever of X or Y is in the UK.

3.123   Article 72 also excludes from article 25(1) certain arrangements made by an overseas person with an authorised or exempt person. Article 25(2) arrangements that are made by an overseas person with a view to transactions which are, as respects transactions in the UK, confined to transactions entered into by authorised persons and exempt persons (as principal or agent) are also excluded.

3.124 The overseas persons exclusion also specifies that article 53 does not apply to advice given by an overseas person as a result of a legitimate approach and that article 64 does not apply to any agreement made by an overseas person to carry on an activity of the kind specified by articles 25(1) or (2), 37, 40 or 45 if the agreement is the result of a legitimate approach.

3.125 The scope of the activities covered by the overseas persons exclusion remains broadly the same as in the Financial Services Act 1986. In particular, the overseas persons exclusion does not cover the activities of accepting deposits and effecting or carrying out contracts of insurance or any of the new activities which are specified in the Regulated Activities Order.

WHAT IS MEANT BY 'BY WAY OF BUSINESS'?

3.126 In accordance with s 22(1) of the FSMA 2000, an activity must be carried on 'by way of business' if it is to amount to a regulated activity. However, the Regulated Activities Order does not deal with the business test; this is varied in respect of certain kinds of business in the Financial Services and Markets Act 2000 (Carrying on Regulated Activities by Way of Business) Order 2001[1] (Business Order).

The Treasury has indicated that, in its view, the 'by way of business' test in s 22 of the FSMA 2000 is broader than the business test in the Financial Services Act 1986, similar to the business test in the Insurance Companies Act 1982 and narrower than the business test in the Banking Act 1987. Accordingly, to ensure the business test remains broadly the same as it did under the previous regimes, the Business Order modifies the 'by way of business' test so that it is consistent with the business test for investment business contained in the Financial Services Act 1986 in respect of the regulated activities which correspond to investment business, and with the business test for deposit-taking business contained in the Banking Act 1987 in respect of the regulated activity of deposit-taking.

1   SI 2001/1177.

3.127 In relation to the activities which correspond with the former category of 'investment business',[1] this is achieved by providing that a person is not to be regarded as carrying on such an activity by way of business unless he carries on the business of engaging in one or more such activities.[2] The precise effect of this test has always been difficult to evaluate, but broadly it has the effect that investment activities must be carried on as an identifiable business (or, putting it another way, an investment activity should not be covered if it is a merely incidental part of a non-investment business).

1   Viz, those specified in the Regulated Activities Order (SI 2001/544), arts 14, 21, 25, 37, 40, 45, 51, 52 and 53, and that specified in art 64 so far as it relates to any of those articles – see art 3(2) of the Business Order (SI 2001/1177).
2   SI 2001/1177, art 3(1).

3.128 In relation to deposit-taking, article 2 of the Business Order provides that a person who accepts deposits is not to be regarded as doing so by way of business if he does not hold himself out as doing so on a day-to-day basis and any deposits that he accepts are accepted only on particular occasions, whether or not involving the issue of securities. In applying the 'particular occasions' limb of this test, regard is to be had to the frequency of the occasions and to any characteristics distinguishing them from each other.[1] This test replicates that formerly in s 6 of the Banking Act 1987. The UK authorities have generally interpreted it rather restrictively, as permitting only a small number of transactions in a year before deposit-taking is regarded as sufficiently habitual to fail the test.

1   It should be noted that this provision was not included in the 'particular occasions' limb of the test as originally enacted in the Banking Act 1979. Consequently the decision in *SCF Finance Co Ltd v Masri* [1987] QB 1002, [1987] 1 All ER 175, CA (referred to also in para 3.7, note 2) should be treated with caution insofar as it relates to what is now art 2 of the Business Order.

3.129   The Business Order also provides that the trustees of an occupational pension scheme are to be regarded as carrying on investment management by way of business unless they delegate all routine[1] or day-to-day decisions to an authorised, exempt or overseas asset manager.

The Treasury has also added a new exclusion which provides that the trustees will not be carrying on investment management by way of business where they invest in a fund, the primary purpose of which is to acquire or hold non-publicly traded investments, provided certain conditions are met (eg the trustees' decision to invest in the fund is made in accordance with advice given by an authorised person). This new exclusion implements a recommendation made by Paul Myners[2] which is intended to promote investment in private equity.

1   Cf Financial Services Act 1986, s 191, where the test was 'all decisions, or all day-to-day decisions'.
2   *Institutional investment in the United Kingdom: a review,* 6 March 2001.

WHAT IS MEANT BY 'IN THE UNITED KINGDOM'?

3.130   The territorial scope of the regulated activities regime is defined by ss 19 and 418 of the FSMA 2000. Section 19 prohibits a person from carrying on a regulated activity in the UK unless he is authorised or exempt.[1]

1   Under the Financial Services and Markets Act 2000 (Exemption) Order 2000 (SI 2001/1201), certain persons are exempt from the general prohibition and therefore the requirement to be authorised to carry on regulated activities.

3.131   Section 418 of the FSMA 2000 contains provisions relating to the territorial scope of the authorisation requirement and establishes its 'outward application'. As a result, persons based in the UK and carrying on regulated activities overseas must be regulated in the UK. A person who would not otherwise be regarded as carrying on a regulated activity in the UK will be so regarded if:

(a)   his registered office[1] is in the UK, he is entitled to exercise passporting rights under a single market directive[2] as a UK firm and he is carrying on a regulated activity to which that single market directive applies in another EEA State; or

(b)   his registered office is in the UK, he is the manager of a collective investment scheme which is the subject of particular Community rights[3] and persons in another EEA State are invited to participate in the scheme; or

(c)   his registered office is in the UK and the day-to-day management of the relevant activity is the responsibility of his UK registered office or another establishment maintained by him in the UK; or

(d)   his head office is not in the UK but the activity is carried on from an establishment maintained by him in the UK.

1   Or head office if he does not have a registered office (FSMA 2000, s 418(2)(a), (3)(a) and (4)(a)).
2   That is, the Consolidated Banking Directive, the First, Second and Third Non-Life and the First, Second and Third Life Insurance Directives ('the Insurance Directives') and the Investment Services Directive (Sch 3, para 1).
3   See the FSMA 2000, s 418(4).

3.132   The effect of s 418 is also to bring certain deposit-taking and insurance activities within the scope of regulation for the first time. Under the Banking Act 1987, where a UK-based person accepted a deposit outside the UK, he was not required to be authorised under the Banking Act. It had also been possible for UK-based persons to avoid the requirement to be authorised under the Insurance Companies Act 1982 by effecting insurance contracts outside the UK. Firms which accept deposits or effect or carry out contracts of insurance outside the UK when the day-to-day management of carrying on the regulated activity is in the UK will now need to be authorised.

3.133   The FSMA 2000 also has 'inward application' to the carrying on of regulated activities in the UK from overseas. Overseas persons who carry on regulated activities in the UK therefore need to be authorised unless an exemption or exclusion applies – the most relevant exclusion generally being that for overseas persons in article 72 of the Regulated Activities Order.[1]

1   SI 2001/544. See para 3.119 above.

WHO IS AN 'AUTHORISED PERSON'?

3.134   The FSMA 2000 sets up a single authorisation process for all types of firm that seek to carry on one or more regulated activities in the UK. An applicant for authorisation must apply to the FSA for a Part IV permission to carry on a regulated activity (or activities). Any person who is granted such a permission by the FSA is authorised.

3.135   The FSMA 2000 does, however, provide for the automatic authorisation of:

(a)   firms 'passporting' into the UK under a single market directive (such firms are referred to in the FSMA 2000 as 'EEA firms'); and

(b)   firms exercising Treaty rights, ie rights under the Treaty of Rome (such firms are referred to in the FSMA 2000 as 'Treaty firms' and are defined in Sch 4 as persons whose head office is situated in an EEA State, other than the UK, and who are recognised under the law of that State as its national),

provided that certain conditions are met and certain notifications are given to the FSA.

3.136   Part II of Sch 3 to the FSMA 2000 deals with the exercise of passport rights by EEA firms[1] and therefore applies to entities whose head and registered offices are in an EEA State (ie the EU Member States plus Norway, Iceland and Liechtenstein). Automatic authorisation may be obtained by an EEA firm by virtue of the exercise of passport rights if certain conditions are met (eg, the correct notifications have been given by the relevant home state regulator to the FSA).

The Financial Services and Markets Act 2000 (EEA Passport Rights) Regulations 2001[2] deal with the exercise of passport rights under Sch 3 to the FSMA 2000 and set out the information which must be provided to the FSA in connection with the establishment of a branch, or the provision of services, by an EEA firm in the UK in exercise of its passport rights.[3]

1   FSMA 2000, Sch 3, Pt III deals with the exercise of passport rights by UK firms and has been amended by the Financial Services (EEA Passport Rights) Regulations 2001 (SI 2001/1376).
2   SI 2001/2511.
3   SI 2001/2511 broadly reflects the procedural requirements set out in the Investment Services Directive, the Consolidated Banking Directive and the Insurance Directives.

3.137   Schedule 4 gives effect to rights under the Treaty of Rome. Financial institutions that are authorised in their home state to carry on an activity have the right to carry on that activity in other EU Member States provided certain conditions are met (eg the relevant home state confirmations have been given,[1] the institution notifies the FSA of its intention to exercise such rights and the relevant law of the home state gives equivalent protection to that of the host state[2]).

This is potentially more comprehensive (although, in practice, it is unlikely to be used very often) than the passporting arrangements because a firm established in the EU might not be able to avail itself of a 'passport' but may still be able to qualify under Sch 4. In effect, Sch 4 provides:

(a)   a means equivalent to passporting, by which firms that are not covered by Sch 3 can still gain automatic UK recognition for their home state authorisation; or

(b)   a means by which firms that are covered within Sch 3 can obtain rights for activities that fall outside it.

1   The home-state regulator is required to confirm to the FSA in writing that the relevant institution has home state authorisation.
2   The Treasury is allowed to certify that the law of a particular Member State affords the requisite equivalent protection in relation to the relevant activities.

Chapter 4

Other regulated activities

INTRODUCTION

4.1 One of the effects of the unified regulatory regime introduced by the Financial Services and Markets Act (FSMA) 2000 is that activities which previously fell within a separate regulatory regime have now been incorporated into the single framework of the general prohibition and the definitions of 'investments' and 'regulated activities'.

4.2 In the case of deposit-taking[1] and insurance business, this has involved a certain amount of reorganisation of material, even where (as is in general the case in relation to insurance) there is no intention to make major changes of substance.

1 As to which see Chapter 6.

4.3 The application of the business test for purposes of the general prohibition has also required a policy decision on whether the slightly different tests previously applicable to deposit-taking, investment business and insurance business should be conformed. The decision was not to do this, but broadly to preserve the previous position.

As a result, the Business Order[1] makes use of the power conferred by s 419 of the FSMA 2000 to vary the test of what amounts to carry on an activity by way of business in relation to deposit-taking activities and investment activities formerly regulated by the Financial Services Act 1986. It does not include any special provision for insurance business, since the simple phrase 'by way of business' used in s 22 substantially repeats the wording previously applicable under ss 2 and 95 of the Insurance Companies Act (ICA) 1982.

1 Financial Services and Markets Act 2000 (Carrying on Regulated Activities by Way of Business) Order 2001 (SI 2001/1177).

INSURANCE COMPANIES: AUTHORISATION REGIME

4.4 Under the pre-FSMA 2000 legislation, insurance companies required authorisation under the ICA 1982 to carry on insurance business in the UK. Once authorised under the ICA 1982, they enjoyed the benefit of various exemptions or automatic authorisations under the Banking Act 1987 and the Financial Services Act 1986.

4.5 Under the FSMA 2000, the basic rule is that all the regulated activities of an insurance company are treated in the same way and the scope of its permitted activities is determined, as with any other authorised institution, by the scope of its Part IV permission.[1]

1 This may create uncertainty in relation to branches of European Economic Area (EEA) insurers who do not have a Part IV permission. For example, the express exemption under the Banking Act 1987 for deposits accepted by insurers has not been reproduced under FSMA 2000. While UK insurers can be given a limited permission to cover this activity branches of EEA insurers cannot. It is unclear that the directives enabling insurers to passport would cover the deposit-taking activity. (For the reverse situation applying to banks see para 4.23, note 2.)

4.6 Reference should therefore be made to Chapters 3 and 6 for a description of the regulated activities other than that of effecting and carrying out contracts of insurance, which is described below.

4.7 One feature of the previous regime for regulation of insurance companies which has required special provision under the FSMA is the general prohibition, in s 16 of the ICA 1982, on an insurance company carrying on activities otherwise than in connection with or for the purposes of its insurance business. This requirement is not re-imposed directly by the FSMA 2000, but s 141 empowers the Financial Services Authority (FSA) to make special rules 'prohibiting an authorised person who has permission to effect or carry out contracts of insurance from carrying on a specified activity', and goes on to provide that the specified activities may include activities which are not regulated activities.[1]

1 Under these rule-making powers, ICA 1982, s 16 has been reproduced in the Interim Prudential Sourcebook for Insurers, which provides that 'an insurer must not carry on any commercial business in the UK or elsewhere other than insurance business and activities directly arising from that business'. This wording has been altered slightly from s 16, and now tracks the original European Directive.

Insurance activities

4.8 Apart from activities relating to Lloyd's, the principal insurance activities under the Regulated Activities Order[1] are:[2]

(a) effecting a contract of insurance as principal; and
(b) carrying out a contract of insurance as principal.

1 Financial Services and Markets Act 2000 (Regulated Activities) Order 2001 (SI 2001/544).

2   Certain long-term insurance products, defined as 'qualifying contracts of insurance' in the Regulated Activities Order, are contractually-based investments. There are various other regulated activities which apply to contractually-based investments, such as dealing, arranging or advising. These activities are covered in Chapter 3. In addition, in December 2001 the Treasury announced that the FSA would become responsible for regulating the sale of general insurance products.

4.9   Under the ICA 1982, 'insurance business' comprised 'effecting and carrying out' contracts of insurance and guarantee falling within certain classes. The courts interpreted 'effecting and carrying out' disjunctively,[1] so that either effecting or carrying out an insurance contract could amount to carrying on insurance business. The Regulated Activities Order makes it clear that there are two distinct regulated activities.

1   See *Bedford Insurance Co Ltd v Instituto de Resseguros do Brasil* [1985] QB 966, [1984] 3 All ER 766 and *Stewart v Oriental Fire and Marine Insurance Co Ltd* [1985] QB 988, [1984] 3 All ER 777.

4.10   The requirement that the activity be carried out as principal means, for example, that an agent of an insurance company who has underwriting authority will not be carrying on the regulated activity of effecting contracts of insurance. It is likely, however, that the agent would be regarded as aiding and abetting the insurance company to commit a breach of the general prohibition in the FSMA 2000 if the insurance company did not itself have the necessary authorisation.[1]

1   See *Re a Company* (No 007923 of 1994) and *Re a Company* (No 007924 of 1994) [1995] 1 WLR 953, CA.

4.11   There is no definition in the FSMA 2000 or the Regulated Activities Order of 'effecting' or 'carrying out'. Previous case law on the ICA 1982 is therefore likely to remain relevant in determining what these activities comprise.

4.12   The 'effecting' of contracts of insurance is the activity of contract formation. It is, however, broader than merely concluding the contract, or taking the underwriting decision. In *Stewart*[1] QB Leggatt J stated (obiter) that:

> ' "effecting" a contract of insurance seems to me to involve more than merely making the contract. There may also be involved (as here) the offering of insurance services and the negotiation of the terms of the contract.'

The point was expanded by Evans LJ in *R v Wilson*:[2]

> 'We would hold simply that "effecting" includes the process of negotiation which begins not later than the issue of what the law regards as an invitation to treat. A person who seeks insurance business on the basis of a document such as the brochure . . . in the present case and who holds himself out as having authority both to make insurance contracts and to receive premiums on behalf of an insurer does "carry on [an] insurance business" . . . We would also hold, if necessary, that the statutory definitions are not exclusive and that "carrying on [an] insurance business" clearly does include soliciting such business.'

1   *Stewart v Oriental Fire and Marine Insurance Co Ltd* [1985] QB 988, [1984] 3 All ER 777.
2   [1997] 1 All ER 119, CA.

4.13   'Carrying out' a contract of insurance is the activity of performing the contract once concluded. The courts have not considered the activities comprised in the phrase 'carrying out' in great detail, but they are likely to include receipt of premiums, claims handling and payment of claims.[1]

1 In *Scher v Policyholders Protection Board (No 2)* [1994] 2 AC 57, HL, the court held that the mere act of paying claims to UK based policyholders was insufficient to amount to carrying out a contract of insurance.

4.14 Under the FSMA 2000, both activities (effecting and carrying out contracts of insurance) will be subject to the business test. As stated above, the Business Order does not modify the business test in s 22 of the FSMA 2000 for insurance. Consequently, a company will only require authorisation if it is effecting or carrying out contracts of insurance 'by way of business'.

4.15 This test mirrors the approach of some of the previous cases under the ICA 1982, in which the courts held that the prohibition against unauthorised persons effecting or carrying out contracts of insurance was a prohibition against making and performing a contract of insurance by way of business.[1]

1 *Bedford Insurance Co Ltd v Instituto de Resseguros do Brasil* [1985] QB 966, [1984] 3 All ER 766.

Contracts of insurance

4.16 The regulated activities must, of course, take place in relation to 'contracts of insurance'. The Regulated Activities Order[1] defines 'contract of insurance' as:

'any contract of insurance which is a contract of long-term insurance or a contract of general insurance . . .'.

1 SI 2001/544.

4.17 A 'contract of long-term insurance' is defined as any contract falling within Part II of Sch 1 to the Regulated Activities Order. A contract of general insurance is a contract falling with Part I of Sch 1 to the Order. Parts I and II reproduce the classes of insurance business which were previously set out in Sch 1 (classes of long-term business) and Sch 2 (classes of general business) to the ICA 1982.

4.18 There is no further indication in the FSMA 2000 or the Regulated Activities Order of which contracts are contracts of insurance. Most of the paragraphs of Schs 1 and 2 are themselves prefaced with the words 'contracts of insurance'. This has the effect that the common law definition of what constitutes a contract of insurance will continue to apply. The dictum of Chadwick J in *Prudential Insurance Co v IRC*[1] is a succinct formulation of the common law position:

'It must be a contract whereby for some consideration, usually but not necessarily for periodical payments called premiums, you secure to yourself some benefit, usually but not necessarily the payment of a sum of money upon the happening of some event . . . that event should be one which involves some amount of uncertainty . . . whether the event will happen or not, or . . . as to the time at which it will happen.'

1 [1904] 2 KB 658.

4.19 A reinsurance contract is a contract of insurance at common law. Consequently effecting or carrying out contracts of reinsurance will be regulated activities in the same way as effecting and carrying out contracts of direct insurance.

4.20 Contracts of insurance are distinguished from wagers by virtue of the insured's interest in the property which is the subject matter of the contract (his 'insurable interest').[1]

1 The requirement for an insurable interest also distinguishes certain credit derivatives from insurance. A person can purchase protection through a credit derivative, for example, which will pay out upon the happening of a credit event in relation to a reference portfolio of loans which the protection buyer does not own and in which he has no other interest.

4.21 As was the position under the ICA 1982, contracts of insurance for the purposes of the Regulated Activities Order include:[1]

'fidelity bonds, performance bonds, bail bonds, customs bonds or similar contracts of guarantee, where these are—

(i)   effected or carried out by a person not carrying on a banking business;
(ii)   not effected merely incidentally to some other business carried on by the person effecting them; and
(iii) effected in return for the payment of one or more premiums.'

At common law there is a distinction between contracts of insurance and contracts of guarantee,[2] so the express inclusion of such contracts is an extension of the definition of insurance for regulatory purposes.

1 Contracts of insurance also include: tontines; capital redemption contracts or pension fund management contracts, where these are effected or carried out by a person who (i) does not carry on a banking business; and (ii) otherwise effects or carries out contracts of insurance; contracts to pay annuities on human life; contracts of a kind referred to in art 1(2)(e) of the first life directive (collective insurance etc); and contracts of a kind referred to in art 1(3) of the first life directive (social insurance).
2 *Seaton v Heath* [1899] 1 QB 782, CA; *Re Sentinel Securities plc* [1996] 1 WLR 316.

Exclusions

4.22 There are a number of exclusions from the activities of effecting and carrying out contracts of insurance:

(a)   *community co-insurers* – this exemption applies to contracts of insurance which are effected or carried out by an insurer which is authorised in an EEA country other than the UK and which is a participant in a co-insurance operation;[1]
(b)   *vehicle breakdown* – this exemption applies to persons which only effect or carry out contracts to provide assistance to vehicles in the event of an accident or breakdown.[2]

1 Co-insurance means an arrangement whereby more than one insurer participates in covering a particular risk.
2 The exclusion contains detailed provisions concerning the manner and extent of the assistance which can be provided in the event of a breakdown or accident.

4.23 In contrast to the position under the ICA 1982, the Regulated Activities Order does not include a specific exclusion for certain classes of general insurance contracts (such as credit insurance) when written by banks as part of their banking business.[1] The single authorisation regime under the FSMA 2000 now means that banks which effect or carry out these classes of general insurance contracts as part of their banking business will need to ensure that their permission is phrased in terms broad enough to cover these activities.[2]

1 The exception to this is surety bonds and other similar contracts of guarantee. These contracts, when effected or carried out by banks, are excluded from the definition of contract of insurance and the corresponding class 15 in the Regulated Activities Order (SI 2001/544), Sch 1, Pt I (Suretyship).
2 This approach arguably leaves EEA banks with branches in the UK in an uncertain position. EEA branches do not have permissions as such, and it is not clear that their EEA rights under the banking directive are broad enough to allow them to passport insurance-related activities.

BUILDING SOCIETIES

4.24 Building societies are mutual institutions formed (as the name implies) for the purpose of financing the building of houses for the benefit of their members. They have grown over many years into an important form of UK financial institution and some individual societies are extremely large.

4.25 The formation, constitution and administration of building societies are governed by provisions of the Building Societies Act 1986, and are beyond the scope of this work.

4.26 Before the FSMA 2000, the Building Societies Act 1986 also provided a separate regime for the authorisation and prudential regulation of building societies by the Building Societies Commission (BSC). Building societies were accordingly exempted from authorisation under the Banking Act 1987 in respect of their deposit-taking activities (though many of them obtained authorisation under the Financial Services Act 1986 in respect of investment activities which they undertook in connection with their core lending, deposit-taking and other money-raising activities).

In accordance with its overall objective of establishing a unified system for the regulation of UK financial institutions, the FSMA 2000 has abolished this separate framework and transferred the regulatory functions formerly discharged by the BSC to the FSA.

4.27 Building societies are therefore subject to the same provisions as other institutions as regards regulated activities and the requirement to obtain authorisation. At present, the detailed rules governing their prudential supervision are set out in a separate part of the FSA's Handbook of Rules and Guidance (the Interim Prudential Sourcebook for Building Societies, or IPRU (BSOC)), which in most respects carries forward the regime previously operated by the BSC. The FSA intends in due course to replace this with a single set of rules (the Integrated Source Book) which will apply to all authorised firms.

FRIENDLY SOCIETIES

4.28 Friendly societies are another kind of mutual institution formed for the purpose of making financial provision for their members against contingencies such as unemployment, sickness, retirement, death and funeral expenses.

4.29   The formation, constitution and administration of friendly societies are governed by provisions of the Friendly Societies Act 1992, and are beyond the scope of this work.

4.30   Before the FSMA 2000, the Friendly Societies Act 1992 also provided a separate regime for the supervision of friendly societies by the Chief Registrar of Friendly Societies, which were accordingly exempted from authorisation under the Insurance Companies Act 1982[1] and the Financial Services Act 1986.[2] As in the case of building societies, the FSMA has abolished this separate framework and transferred the regulatory functions formerly discharged by the Chief Registrar of Friendly Societies to the FSA.

1   S 2(2)(b).
2   S 23.

4.31   Friendly societies are therefore subject to the same provisions as other institutions as regards regulated activities and the requirement to obtain authorisation. At present, the detailed rules governing their prudential supervision are set out in a separate part of the FSA's Handbook of Rules and Guidance (the Interim Prudential Sourcebook for Friendly Societies, or IPRU (FSOC)). This also will in due course be replaced by the Integrated Source Book.

CREDIT UNIONS

4.32   Credit unions are a further form of mutual organisation, formed under the Industrial and Provident Societies Act 1965 and the Credit Unions Act 1979 for the purposes of encouraging savings by and loans to their members.

4.33   Credit unions were formerly supervised by the Chief Registrar of Friendly Societies and were granted exemption from the requirement to be authorised under the Banking Act 1987 in respect of their deposit-taking activities.[1]

1   Banking Act 1987, Sch 2, para 10.

4.34   As in the case of building societies and friendly societies, the FSMA 2000 has brought credit unions within the single regulatory framework. They are therefore subject to the same provisions as other institutions as regards regulated activities and the requirement to obtain authorisation.

4.35   The detailed rules governing the supervision of credit unions are set out in a separate part of the FSA's Handbook of Rules and Guidance, the Credit Unions Sourcebook.

PROFESSIONALS

4.36   The Financial Services Act 1986 provided a special regime for the authorisation of members of a profession which was subject to regulation by a professional body recognised for the purpose by the Securities and Investments Board (SIB) (as it then was). Such professionals could obtain authorisation through the issue of a certificate from the recognised professional body rather than through membership of a self-regulating organisation or by direct authorisation from the SIB.

4.37 This regime has not been carried forward under the FSMA 2000, as it was regarded as inconsistent with the overriding objective of unifying the regulatory regime. In principle, therefore, professionals whose activities involve them engaging in regulated activities need to obtain authorisation.

4.38 The government recognised, however, that while some professional firms would engage in substantial investment activities for which they would require to obtain authorisation, there were many firms whose main professional activities involved investments only incidentally, and that it might sometimes be unclear whether these activities amounted to regulated activities.

4.39 It was recognised that it was desirable to minimise the extent to which firms in this position would feel it necessary to seek authorisation on a precautionary basis.

4.40 The FSMA 2000 and the Regulated Activities Order[1] incorporate two sets of provisions directed to this point.

First, article 67 of the Regulated Activities Order sets out an exclusion for any activity which would otherwise fall within articles 21, 25(1) and (2), 40 or 53 of the Order if that activity is carried on in the course of carrying on any profession or business which does not otherwise consist of regulated activities, may reasonably be regarded as a necessary part of other services provided in the course of that profession or business, and is not remunerated separately from the other services. This exclusion reproduces in somewhat wider terms an exclusion formerly contained in the Financial Services Act 1986.[2]

1 SI 2001/544.
2 Sch 1, para 24, which required that the relevant activity 'is a necessary part' of other advice or services. This was a significantly stricter test that the formulation 'may reasonably be regarded as a necessary part' in the Regulated Activities Order (SI 2001/544), art 67.

4.41 Secondly, Part XX of the FSMA 2000 (provision of financial services by members of the professions) creates an exemption for certain activities of professional firms. Section 327 provides that, subject to specified conditions, a member of a profession, or a person controlled or managed by one or more such members, is exempt from the general prohibition (on the carrying on of regulated activities without authorisation). The principal conditions are that:

(a) the person concerned ('P') does not receive from a person other than his client any pecuniary reward or other advantage, for which he does not account to his client, arising out of his carrying on any of the activities in question;
(b) the manner of the provision of any service in the course of carrying on the activities must be incidental to the provision by him of professional services;
(c) P must not carry on, or hold himself out as carrying on, a regulated activity other than one which the rules of his professional body allow him to carry on, or in respect of which he is exempt;

(d) the activities must not be of a description, or relate to investments of a description, specified in an order made by the Treasury for this purpose;

(e) the activities must be the only regulated activities carried on by P (other than activities for which he is exempt).

4.42 The third of these conditions is similar to the article 67 exclusion, though the word 'incidentally' probably makes it slightly wider than the article 67 test of whether the activities 'may reasonably be regarded as a necessary part' of professional services.

EXCHANGES AND CLEARING HOUSES

Introduction

4.43 The terms 'exchange' and 'clearing house' are not defined in the FSMA 2000. Similarly, the operation of an exchange or clearing house is not a separate regulated activity. Instead, the activities of these institutions fall within the general descriptions of regulated activities, so that an exchange or clearing house which acts as a central counterparty, such as OM Exchange and the London Clearing House, carries on the regulated activity of dealing in investments[1] and exchanges and clearing houses which do not provide central counterparty services, such as the London Stock Exchange and CRESTCo, carries on the regulated activity of arranging deals in investments.[2]

1 SI 2001/544, art 14.
2 SI 2001/544, art 25.

4.44 Despite this, the FSMA 2000 and the FSA Handbook contain a special regime for exchanges and clearing houses which have been granted recognition by the FSA.[1] Recognition confers on the body concerned exemption from the need to be authorised under the FSMA 2000.[2] Such exchanges and clearing houses are known as 'recognised investment exchanges' (RIEs) and 'recognised clearing houses' (RCHs) and this regime is referred to in this chapter as the 'recognised body regime'.

The existence of a discrete regime for RIEs and RCHs reflects the fact that exchanges and clearing houses are an essential part of the infrastructure of the financial markets and give rise to different considerations and risks from other market participants. Although investor protection is an important part of the recognised body regime, equally important are market integrity and systemic risk. So, for example, one of the principal reasons stated by the government for the introduction of the market abuse regime[3] was the protection of the integrity of the UK investment exchanges and RIEs and RCHs benefit from special protection on the insolvency of one of their members.[4]

1 FSMA 2000, Pt XVIII and regulations made under that Part and the FSA's RIE and RCH Sourcebook.
2 FSMA 2000, s 285.
3 See Chapter 9.
4 Companies Act 1989, Pt VII, which gives priority to the default rules of a recognised body in the insolvency of a member.

4.45 The recognised body regime is not mandatory in that any person[1] who operates an exchange or trading system or a clearing house has the choice of seeking either recognition, and therefore exemption (in which case the person will not be subject to all of the FSA Rules but only to the provisions of the recognised body regime), or a Part IV permission and authorisation (in which case the person will be subject to the FSA Rules).

As a general rule, the 'traditional' exchanges and clearing houses are recognised bodies[2] while other trading platforms such as electronic communication networks (ECNs) and alternative trading systems (ATSs) are authorised persons.

1 Any body corporate or unincorporated association may apply for recognition as an RIE or RCH.
2 There are seven RIEs (COREDEAL MTS Limited, the International Petroleum Exchange Limited, LIFFE Administration and Management, the London Metal Exchange, the London Stock Exchange plc, OM Exchange and virt-x Exchange Limited); and two RCHs (CRESTCo Limited and London Clearing House Limited).

The recognised body regime

4.46   The recognised body regime prescribes:

(a)   the requirements that must be met in order to obtain recognition;[1]
(b)   the procedure for application for recognition;[2]
(c)   an exemption from liability in damages for anything done or omitted in the discharge of the body's regulatory functions[3] unless it is shown that the act or omission was in bad faith or the act in question was unlawful under the Human Rights Act 1998;[4]
(d)   rules and arrangements for the supervision of recognised bodies;[5]
(e)   powers of the FSA to issue directions and revoke the recognition of recognised bodies in the event that the body fails to meet the recognition requirements;[6]
(f)   a special competition regime for recognised bodies.[7]

1 These are contained in the Financial Services and Markets Act 2000 (Recognition Requirements for Investment Exchanges and Clearing Houses) Regulations 2001 (SI 2001/995); and guidance on the requirements is contained in the recognised bodies sourcebook.
2 The FSA gives guidance on the procedure in ch 5 of the Recognised Investment Exchanges and Recognised Clearing Houses Sourcebook (referred to in this chapter as the 'recognised bodies sourcebook').
3 'Regulatory functions' are the functions of the recognised body so far as relating to, or to matters arising out of, the obligations to which the recognised body is subject under or by virtue of the FSMA 2000. This will include obligations under the FSA's rules for recognised body, which are made under powers granted by the FSMA 2000.
4 FSMA 2000, s 291.
5 Contained in the recognised bodies sourcebook.
6 FSMA 2000, ss 296 to 298.
7 FSMA 2000, ss 302 to 312.

Recognition requirements

4.47   The Financial Services and Markets Act 2000 (Recognition Requirements for Investment Exchanges and Clearing Houses) Regulations 2001[1] ('the Recognised Body Regulations'), prescribe the requirements that a body must satisfy before the FSA will grant a recognition order.

The requirements[2] are wide-ranging and cover: financial resources; fitness and propriety; systems and controls; safeguards for investors; complaints against the recognised body; default rules and procedures; co-operation with regulatory authorities; and margin (for clearing houses and exchanges that provide clearing services). In addition, RIEs must fulfil requirements relating to the disclosure of information by issuers and RCHs requirements relating to the promotion and maintenance of standards, rules and discipline.

Detailed guidance on the application process is contained in chapter 2 of the recognised bodies sourcebook.

1   SI 2001/995.
2   Set out in Sch 1 to the Recognised Body Regulations (SI 2001/995).

Application procedure

4.48   Recognition is obtained upon application to the FSA. An applicant must demonstrate that it fulfils the recognition requirements and must submit copies of its rules and any guidance issued by it together with such other information as the FSA may reasonably require for the purposes of determining the application.[1] In addition, an exchange must provide details of any clearing arrangements for transactions effected on the exchange[2] and a clearing house must provide details of clearing arrangements with an RIE.[3] An application fee is payable.

1   FSMA 2000, s 287 (RIEs) and s 288 (RCHs).
2   FSMA 2000, s 287(2)(c) and (3).
3   FSMA 2000, s 288(2)(c) and (3).

4.49   The FSA may make a recognition order if it appears to it that the applicant satisfies the recognition requirements,[1] but it may only do so with the approval of the Treasury. The Treasury may only refuse its approval on competition grounds.

1   FSMA 2000, s 290.

Competition

4.50   Broadly,[1] the FSA is required to send a copy of an applicant's rules to the Director General of Fair Trading (DGFT). The DGFT and, in some circumstances, the Competition Commission are required to consider the applicant's rules and to determine whether the rules are anti-competitive, ie they have a significantly adverse effect on competition or, if they do, whether that effect is justified.

1   A detailed description of the competition regime is beyond the scope of this work.

4.51   If the DGFT and, where relevant, the Competition Commission conclude that the applicant's rules are not anti-competitive, the Treasury may only refuse to approve the making of a recognition order if they consider that the exceptional circumstances of the case make it inappropriate for them to give their approval.[1] However, if the Competition Commission concludes that the applicant's regulatory provisions are anti-competitive, the Treasury must refuse to give its approval unless they consider that the exceptional circumstances of the case make it inappropriate for them to refuse their approval.[2]

1   FSMA 2000, s 307(2).
2   FSMA 2000, s 307(4).

Recognised overseas investment exchange and clearing houses

4.52   The FSMA also contains a specific regime for non-UK exchanges and clearing houses which, in effect, is a mutual recognition regime. In practice, this regime applies to non-UK bodies which have an office in the UK, since bodies without an office in the UK can rely on the exclusions for overseas persons.[1]

1   See Chapter 3.

4.53   If an exchange or clearing house has neither its head office nor registered office in the UK it may seek recognition as a 'recognised overseas investment exchange' (ROIE) or a 'recognised overseas clearing house' (ROCH). As with RIEs and RCHs, recognition confers on the relevant body exemption from the requirement for authorisation.

4.54   The recognition requirements for overseas exchanges and clearing houses are set out in the FSMA 2000[1] and are broadly that: investors are afforded protection equivalent to that afforded by the UK recognition requirements; the body has adequate default procedures; the body is able and willing to co-operate with the FSA; and adequate arrangements exist for co-operation between the FSA and the relevant overseas supervisor. In assessing whether these criteria are met, the FSA will have regard to the relevant law and practice of the body's home jurisdiction and to its rules and practices.

1   S 292.

Chapter 5

Authorisation and approved persons

INTRODUCTION

5.1   The financial services sector is one of the most heavily regulated industries in the UK. The benefits of regulation include only fit and proper persons being authorised to conduct business; the imposition of minimum standards upon those persons once authorised; effective enforcement procedures to combat malpractice, and a consumer compensation scheme. Authorisation is consequently accepted both in the UK and across the international financial markets as being an important regulatory 'tool' in relation to an institution. The requirement that an individual should be registered with a regulator before performing specified activities on behalf of an authorised firm is also now established in the UK.

> 'Vetting at entry aims to allow only firms and individuals who satisfy the necessary criteria (including honesty, competence, and financial soundness) to engage in regulated activity. Experience in the UK and elsewhere shows that regulatory objectives are more likely to be achieved by setting and enforcing standards for entry, rather than having to deal with major problems later'.[1]

Authorisation is regarded as the first step in risk-based regulation. The UK regulators thus authorise (or exempt) persons carrying on financial services business such as product providers, market participants and advisers; the organised markets upon which securities are traded and the clearing houses; and certain products[2] marketed to the public. They also require certain

120

individuals working in the industry to secure prior approval. Authorised and approved persons are then subject to detailed ongoing prudential requirements, conduct of business rules, supervision visits, reporting requirements and enforcement procedures.

1   FSA, *A New Regulator for a New Millennium* (January 2000).
2   The regulation of collective investment schemes under the Financial Services and Markets Act (FSMA) 2000, Pt XVII and Sch 5, including unit trusts and open-ended investment companies authorised by the Financial Services Authority (FSA) and recognised overseas schemes under the Undertakings for Collective Investments in Transferable Securities (UCITS) Directive (85/611/EEC, December 1985) and 'UCITS qualifiers', is considered in Chapter 7 below.

5.2   Not all commentators accept that detailed regulation and restrained entry is necessary in the financial services industry.[1] Regulation increases costs and can restrict competition through, for instance, the imposition of highly prescriptive authorisation procedures. Regulation can similarly be used to protect national interests by restricting access to local markets or by making life difficult for foreign firms operating in those markets. Restricting competition can reduce the range of products and services available to the consumer and precipitate higher prices. It is thus important, both for London's standing as a leading international financial centre and domestic financial services consumers, that the new Financial Services and Markets Act (FSMA) 2000 regime strikes an appropriate balance between too much and too little regulation. Against that background, this chapter reviews the Financial Services Authority's (FSA) authorisation and approval procedures to which some 10,000 firms and 180,000 individuals are subject.[2]

1   George J Benston, 'Regulating Financial Markets: A Critique and some Proposals' (Institute of Economic Affairs Hobart Paper 135, 1998). In arguing the case for higher levels of capital and fewer rules, Benston comments (at p 18) that 'Regulation has provided and still provides benefits to governments, legislators and regulated financial institutions. That is the principal reason financial service regulation was enacted and is continued although it is generally detrimental to most consumers'.
2   FSA Annual Report 2000/01.

The FSA

5.3   With the benefit of hindsight, the progression from self-regulation to the statutory regulation of the UK's financial services industry appears inevitable. Ultimately, the demise of self-regulation lay in the perception that it equated with self-interest.[1] Under the FSMA 2000, a firm cannot be regarded as a member of a club; it is regulated by the statutory regulator, though the industry, rather than the taxpayer, funds regulation through authorisation and annual fees. Under the Financial Services Act 1986 and the banking and insurance regimes, many firms had to be authorised by, and were subject to the occasionally conflicting demands and inconsistencies of, different regulators for different types of financial business. The Financial Services Act 1986 regulators themselves were often faced with complex questions as to which regulator was responsible for the regulation of a particular activity or whether an activity fell outside all their jurisdictions. Under FSMA 2000, the FSA has adopted a new 'integrated approach' to authorisation.[2] The firm has one authorisation from the FSA based on an appropriate permission to conduct banking, insurance and/or investment business activities within the scope of the permission.

Thus an authorised person will only be able to carry out those particular regulated activities for which it has been granted permission by the FSA. Once authorised, the firm should find it easier to meet the expectations of a single regulator. Obtaining regulatory approval for an additional permission(s) so that it can conduct another FSMA regulated activity will not require the firm to apply for authorisation from another regulator.

1   'Financial Services Regulation: Making the Two Tier System Work' (SIB, May 1993), p 8, para 2(ii). See also the Treasury and Civil Service Committee's 'Sixth Report' on 'The Regulation of Financial Services in the UK' (HMSO, Oct 1995).
2   FSA Annual Report 2000/01.

The FSA's 'regulatory objectives'

5.4   In meeting its 'regulatory objectives',[1] the FSA is concerned that its authorisation procedures should ensure that only a person who meets the FSMA 2000, Sch 6 'threshold conditions' is granted authorisation.[2] This will afford 'the appropriate degree of protection for consumers'[3] by barring those firms not able to meet the threshold conditions from engaging in regulated activities. It also contributes to 'maintaining confidence in the financial system'[4] and to reducing the extent to which regulated activities may be conducted for purposes connected with financial crime.[5] The FSA is concerned to guard against systemic risk without creating an expectation that the regulator can prevent all failures. It is also concerned to minimise the rate of failure among regulated markets and firms without restricting competition and innovation as required under the FSMA 2000 'principles of good regulation'.[6] Under those principles, the FSA must also have regard to 'the principle that a burden or restriction which is imposed on a person, or on the carrying on of an activity, should be proportionate to the benefits, considered in general terms, which are expected to result from the imposition of that burden or restriction'.[7]

1   FSMA 2000, s 2; and Chapter 2 above.
2   CP 20: 'The Qualifying Conditions for Authorisation'.
3   FSMA 2000, s 5.
4   FSMA 2000, s 3.
5   FSMA 2000, s 6.
6   FSMA 2000, s 2(3).
7   FSMA 2000, s 2(3)(c).

A. AUTHORISATION

REGULATED AND PROHIBITED ACTIVITIES: FSMA 2000, PART II

5.5   The authorisation requirement is a key regulatory consideration for any person seeking to conduct financial business.

The question whether authorisation is required depends on whether the firm will be carrying on regulated activities 'in the United Kingdom'. There is a 'general prohibition' against so doing without being authorised or exempt contained in FSMA 2000, s 19. In most instances, it will be clear whether a person is carrying on an activity in the UK because his offices and staff are based in the UK and he solicits investors in the UK. The regulatory implications become more difficult once business is conducted cross-border. A person based outside the UK may be carrying on activities in the UK through, for instance, the Internet or other telecommunications systems or on occasional visits to the UK even if he does not maintain a place of business in the UK. The authorisation requirement can thus apply if a firm and its client/counterparty are based in the UK, or if it provides services from the UK, or provides services into the UK.[1]

The second question is whether the firm's regulated activities are carried on 'by way of business'.[2] Other questions are whether the firm is an EEA or Treaty firm, its activities excluded, or it is exempt.

Finally, a firm may need to extend any existing permission to cover a proposed new activity.

1   FSMA 2000, s 19(1). Considered in Chapter 3 below.
2   FSMA 2000, s 22(1). Considered in Chapter 3 below.

5.6   Under the FSMA 2000, s 19 'general prohibition', 'no person may carry on a regulated activity in the United Kingdom, or purport to do so, unless he is an authorised person or an exempt person'.

A 'person' includes both a legal person, such as a body corporate, and an individual. It is thus the firm, and not its business lines, that requires authorisation. A person who contravenes the 'general prohibition' is guilty of an offence and liable after conviction on indictment to two years' imprisonment and/or an unlimited fine.[1] It is a defence to show that the person 'took all reasonable precautions and exercised all due diligence' to avoid committing the 'authorisation offence'. The FSA 'polices the perimeter' to ensure compliance with the authorisation requirement and has the power to apply to the court for an injunction to stop unauthorised activity.[2] Where the activity has resulted in profits accruing to the unauthorised business or has caused losses or other adverse effects for consumers, the FSA may apply to the court for a restitution order.[3]

1   FSMA 2000, s 23. A false claim to be authorised or exempt is also a criminal offence under FSMA 2000, s 24. If an offence committed by a 'body corporate' can be shown to have been committed with the consent or connivance of a senior officer or controller, or attributable to any neglect on his part, the officer as well as the body corporate will be guilty of the offence under FSMA 2000, s 400.
2   FSMA 2000, s 380.
3   FSMA 2000, s 382.

Enforceability of agreements

5.7   Apart from the criminal law, there is another powerful incentive to see that any necessary authorisation is obtained. Except in relation to accepting deposits, an agreement made by an unauthorised person in contravention of the 'general prohibition' is unenforceable[1] and the aggrieved party is entitled to recover compensation for any loss sustained.[2] Similarly, an authorised person cannot enforce an agreement made through an unauthorised person.[3] Thus an authorised product-provider could not enforce an agreement with an investor made through an unauthorised financial adviser and the investor would be entitled to compensation for loss sustained. However there is provision for the Court to allow the agreement to be enforced if it is just and equitable, and the person providing the service reasonably believed that he was not contravening the general prohibition.[4]

1 FSMA 2000, s 26. Under FSMA 2000, s 29, a depositor may apply to the court for an order directing the deposit-taker to return the money to him.
2 FSMA 2000, s 28.
3 FSMA 2000, s 27.
4 FSMA 2000, s 28.

'Regulated activities'

5.8 The 'general prohibition' focuses on 'regulated activities'. In deciding whether authorisation is required, it is necessary therefore to determine whether the activities are FSMA regulated. Under s 22 of the FSMA 2000, an activity is a FSMA 'regulated activity' if it is specified in an order made by the Treasury; is 'carried on by way of business' and relates to an 'investment' specified by the Treasury (or, for specified activities, 'in relation to property of any kind'). Whilst a sole trader may need to be authorised, an employee does not carry on business and individuals are generally approved rather than authorised under the FSMA 2000 regime.

5.9 Section 22 is supplemented by Sch 2 of the FSMA 2000, which lists, 'in general terms', the 'regulated activities' that can be specified under s 22: 'Dealing in investments'; 'Arranging deals in investments'; 'Deposit taking'; 'Safekeeping and administration of assets'; 'Managing investments'; 'Investment advice'; 'Establishing collective investment schemes' and 'Using computer-based systems for giving investment instructions'. Schedule 2 to the FSMA 2000 also lists, 'in general terms', the 'investments' that can be specified under s 22: 'Securities'; 'Instruments creating or acknowledging indebtedness'; 'Government and public securities'; 'Instruments giving entitlement to investments'; 'Certificates representing securities'; 'Units in collective investment schemes'; 'Options'; 'Futures'; 'Contracts for differences'; 'Contracts of insurance'; 'Participation in Lloyd's syndicates'; 'Deposits'; 'Loans secured on land' and 'Rights in investments'.

5.10 The activities that are 'regulated activities' are specified in the Financial Services and Markets Act 2000 (Regulated Activities) Order 2001.[1] In general terms, a 'regulated activity' is an activity specified in the order carried on in relation to one or more of the investments specified in the order. The Order, which contains exclusions[2] and has been amended, is considered in Chapter 3.

1 SI 2001/544: the 'Regulated Activities Order'.
2 There are, for instance, exclusions for dealing as principal without 'holding out' (art 15) and overseas persons (art 72).

Exclusions and exemptions

5.11 There are various provisions that exclude the FSMA 2000, s 19 'general prohibition' from specific persons in relation to the carrying on by them of particular regulated activities: see Chapter 3 below. As regards exemptions, there is not a general provision that allows a firm to apply for an exemption. A Treasury 'exemption order' may exempt specified persons from the 'general prohibition'.[1] A person cannot be an exempt person as a result of an exemption order if he has a Part IV permission.[2]

1   FSMA 2000, s 38. Eg, the Bank of England is specified in the Financial Services and Markets
    Act 2000 (Exemption) Order 2001 (SI 2001/1201).
2   FSMA 2000, s 38(2).

Recognised investment exchanges and recognised clearing houses

5.12   Exemption provisions apply to the organised investment markets and
clearing houses. These are subject to FSMA regulation and oversight by the
FSA. Under FSMA 2000, Part XVIII,[1] the FSA can make a recognition order
in relation to an investment exchange[2] and a clearing house[3] if the applicant
meets recognition criteria including: operating appropriate market facilities;
being 'fit and proper' with appropriate rules; having sufficient financial
resources; co-operating with regulators and both promoting and maintaining
high standards of integrity and fair dealing.

Recognised investment exchanges (RIEs) (including the London Stock
Exchange, virt-x, LIFFE, the International Petroleum Exchange and the
London Metal Exchange) and recognised clearing houses (RCHs) (The
London Clearing House and CREST) are thereby exempt from the authorisa-
tion requirement. The member firms of an RIE will themselves be FSMA
authorised persons.

The FSA Handbook[4] provides guidance on the recognition criteria, the
notification requirements[5] and how the FSA will supervise RIEs and RCHs.
The FSA can issue directions[6] to RIEs and RCHs 'to take specified steps' to
comply with the recognition requirements and recognition can be revoked.[7]

The proliferation of electronic communications networks providing trading
facilities through the Internet are now providing significant competition to the
established national markets. Increased competition has fragmented the
markets and raises concerns about liquidity, price formation and transparency.
It has also prompted questions about how appropriate it is for exchanges to
retain a regulatory role in relation to their members particularly given the
advent of a unitary regulator. For his part, the regulator is left pondering how to
regulate markets comprising streams of electrons flying across the ether.

The regulation of RIEs and RCHs is considered in Chapter 4.

1   Under FSMA 2000, s 286(1), the Treasury has made regulations setting out the recognition
    requirements.
2   FSMA 2000, s 287.
3   FSMA 2000, s 288.
4   FSA Handbook: Specialist Sourcebook – Recognised Investment Exchanges and Recognised
    Clearing Houses (REC).
5   FSMA 2000, s 293: the obligations of a recognised body to provide information to the FSA.
6   FSMA 2000, s 296.
7   FSMA 2000, s 297.

Appointed representatives

5.13   FSMA 2000, s 39 provides that an 'appointed representative' (typically
a self-employed tied agent marketing life assurance) is exempt from the general
prohibition in relation to any regulated activity for which his FSMA authorised
principal has accepted responsibility in writing. An authorised person cannot
also be an appointed representative.

Lloyd's

5.14 Under FSMA 2000, Part XIX, the Society of Lloyd's is an authorised person[1] with permission to carry on certain regulated activities relating to the insurance markets. The FSA is required to keep a close eye on how 'the Council supervises and regulates the market at Lloyd's' and to keep under review the desirability of exercising its statutory powers to issue directions to the Society.[2]

1 FSMA 2000, s 315(1).
2 FSMA 2000, s 314.

WHO IS AN AUTHORISED PERSON?

5.15 Under FSMA 2000, s 31, the following are authorised persons:

(a) a person who has a 'Part IV permission' to carry on one or more regulated activities;
(b) an 'EEA firm' qualifying for authorisation under Sch 3;
(c) a 'Treaty firm' qualifying for authorisation under Sch 4;
(d) a person who is 'otherwise authorised' under FSMA 2000.

There are thus two main kinds of FSMA authorised person: (1) a person who is authorised because he has a Part IV permission and (2) a person who qualifies for authorisation.

The requirement for permission

5.16 Under FSMA 2000, s 20, an authorised person must have an appropriate 'permission' in carrying on, or purporting to carry on, a regulated activity in the UK. The FSA can restrict an authorised person's activities through the scope of his permission. So whilst a person has to be authorised (or exempt) to engage in regulated activities in the UK, it is his permission that actually sets out the range of activities that he is permitted to conduct. An authorised person who carries on a regulated activity in the UK 'otherwise than in accordance with permission' will 'be taken to have contravened a requirement imposed on him by the [FSA]' but the contravention will not make him guilty of a criminal offence or make any transaction void or unenforceable.[1]

An authorised person who carries on business outside the scope of his permission is liable to be disciplined by the FSA. Authorisation is thus not enough in itself. In considering an extension to its range of products or services, a firm must ensure that its permission covers the proposed activities. Just as the regulator is concerned that once authorised a firm remains fit and proper to carry on the business within the scope of its permission so it is concerned that the authorised firm will be fit and proper to carry on any new activities. Being a 'fit and proper' corporate finance business does not guarantee your fitness to venture into the world of credit derivatives.[2]

1 FSMA 2000, s 20(2).
2 HM Treasury, 'Overview of Financial Regulatory Reform' (July 1998) at para 4.4.

'Permission to carry on regulated activities': FSMA 2000, Part IV

5.17 A firm that has a Part IV permission to carry on one or more regulated activities is an authorised person.[1] A firm authorised under Sch 3 (an incoming

EEA firm) or Sch 4 (an incoming Treaty firm) FSMA can apply for a 'top-up permission' under Part IV.[2] The FSA Handbook sets out the regulator's approach to authorisation applications[3] with both authorisation and approved persons 'application packs' available on the FSA's website.[4] The application pack is designed 'to take account of the needs of everyone applying for Part IV permission . . . regardless of the nature or scale of their business' and 'reflects the single approach to regulation and the common authorisation criteria against which [the FSA assesses] all applicants'.[5]

1   S31 FSMA.
2   FSA Handbook: High Level Standards – Threshold Conditions (COND). FSMA 2000, ss 34 and 35.
3   FSA Handbook: Regulatory Processes – Authorisation (AUTH). AUTH also provides guidance for 'EEA firms', 'Treaty firms' and 'UCITS qualifiers' who qualify for FSMA authorisation.
4   See: www.fsa.gov.uk/pubs/other/application_pack/.
5   AUTH 3.9.3G.

The application

5.18   An application for a Part IV permission 'must contain a statement of the regulated activity or regulated activities which the applicant proposes to carry on and for which he wishes to have permission'.[1] Securing authorisation is a relatively detailed process. The applicant will be required to provide the FSA with all material information. A superficial approach cannot be adopted, for instance, in completing the authorisation application forms.

'Application Pack – Part A'[2] comprises the 'Application Form (Part IV permission)' and captures information about the applicant including 'Core Details' (such as legal status; group structure; management; professional advisers; history; prudential categories and details of any requested 'requirements' together with all relevant supporting documentation); the 'Regulatory Business Plan' setting out how the applicant will satisfy the threshold conditions; a 'Compliance Form' to assist the FSA in determining whether the applicant has the systems and controls necessary to carry on the relevant regulated activities; information on 'Systems' (such as transaction reporting; settlement; accounting and IT) and 'Financial Resources' forms covering the range of regulated activities. Information required from an applicant under Application Form A thus covers (but is not limited to) general information about the applicant including any proposed or current unregulated activities; a business plan; an appropriately analysed financial budget and projections; details of systems, compliance procedures and documentation and details of management.

'Application Pack – Part B' captures information about persons other than the applicant such as proposed controllers, approved persons, appointed representatives and overseas firms.

There are 'Application Pack Notes' in relation to both Part A and Part B providing general information about which applicants should be aware in completing the forms and identifying the documents in the pack that are relevant for each type of business.

1   FSMA 2000, s 51(1).
2   See: www.fsa.gov.uk/pubs/other/application_pack/

5.19   The application must 'be made in such manner as the [FSA] may direct' and must contain 'such other information as the [FSA] may reasonably require'.[1] Effective communications with the regulator are thus essential. The applicant should, for instance, make early contact with the FSA particularly if proposing to undertake complex, high-risk or innovative business. The regulator recognises that it may be appropriate for the applicant to instruct professional advisers to assist with the application. It may also be appropriate to have a pre-application meeting with the FSA's Corporate Authorisation Department to discuss the application and business plan. All applicants are encouraged to take the opportunity to discuss particular issues with the FSA as they arise with a view to tackling those issues before the submission of the application. The FSA 'is keen to encourage an interactive authorisation process'.[2]

The application forms must be completed in full providing all the requested information and supported by all relevant documentation. The applicant must consider whether there is any material information that should be provided about how its business will be funded, conducted, managed and controlled. The FSA will be concerned about whether any person can exert an influence on the applicant that might pose a risk to the applicant satisfying, or continuing to satisfy, the threshold conditions. The regulator will want to meet management and staff and visit the applicant's premises to review its systems and procedures. The applicant must also remember that certain members of staff will have to be registered as approved persons.

There is also an application fee.

1   FSMA 2000, s 51(3).
2   FSA Handbook: Regulatory Processes – Authorisation (AUTH).

Risk assessment

5.20   The FSA has adopted a risk-based approach to regulation. The FSA's assessment of an application is 'proportional to the risks associated with the regulated activities for which permission is sought'.[1] The amount of detailed information that an applicant must submit as part of its application will be related to the risks posed to the FSA's statutory objectives by the regulated activities and the unregulated activities that the applicant intends to carry on. Risk assessments will be made by reference to probability (likelihood of an event happening) and impact (scale and significance of a problem if it occurred) factors:

—   What is the size and scope of the applicant's proposed business?
—   Is the applicant a large deposit taker?
—   Will the applicant be conducting business in the retail sector?
—   Will it be handling client money?
—   Is the applicant a corporate finance boutique?

The outcome of the risk assessment process fashions the relationship that the FSA will maintain with the applicant if permission is granted. The FSA will communicate its risk assessment to the firm but not to the world at large.

1   CP 20 – 'The Qualifying Conditions for Authorisation'.

Determining an application

5.21   Section 52 of the FSMA 2000 requires the FSA to determine a completed application within six months.[1] The burden of proof is on the applicant to demonstrate to the FSA that it is ready, willing and organised to comply, and continue to comply, with the regulatory obligations that are relevant to the regulated activities that it seeks to carry on.[2] The regulator will carry out any enquiries it considers appropriate in assessing an application against the threshold conditions. There may be discussions with other regulators. There may be meetings with the applicant. The FSA may have regard to any relevant 'connected persons'.[3] Information provided by the applicant will be verified. An accountant's report may be required. The FSA may have regard to the cumulative effects of factors which, taken individually, may be regarded as insufficient to enable the FSA to conclude that a particular threshold condition has not been met.

1   AUTH 8 provides an overview of how applications will be determined by the FSA through internal staff procedures or the Regulatory Decisions Committee.
2   The burden of proof is reversed if the FSA seeks to cancel a permission. The application of the Financial Services Act 1986 authorisation regime can be seen in 'In the Matter of Noble Warren Investments' (5 May 1989): *Butterworths Journal of International Banking and Financial Law* (July 1989 334–336).
3   FSMA 2000, s 49.

Giving permission

5.22   Under s 40 of the FSMA 2000, a Part IV permission to carry on one or more regulated activities can be given by the FSA to an individual, a body corporate, a partnership or an unincorporated association.[1]

Under the passporting principle discussed below, an EEA firm cannot apply for a Part IV permission in relation to any regulated activity that it would be entitled to carry on in exercise of an EEA right under Sch 3 of the FSMA 2000.[2]

The FSA enjoys wide discretion in granting a permission. The regulator is under no obligation to permit a person to conduct all, or indeed any of, the regulated activities to which his application relates. In granting an application (or a variation), the FSA must give the applicant written notice stating the date from which the permission (or variation) has effect.[3] The FSA must specify the permitted regulated activities 'described in such manner as the [FSA] considers appropriate' incorporating 'such limitations (for example as to circumstances in which the activity may, or may not, be carried on) as it considers appropriate'.[4] The FSA can give permission for the carrying on of a regulated activity that is not included amongst those activities to which the application relates. A Part IV permission may also include 'such requirements as the [FSA] considers appropriate'.[5] The FSA may impose a requirement to take, or to refrain from taking, specified action. A requirement may extend to unregulated activities and it may be imposed by reference to the person's relationship with other members of his group. Section 48 of the FSMA 2000 sets out the implications for third parties (such as account holding banks) of an assets requirement being imposed on an authorised person. Section 43 of the FSMA 2000 assets requirement may prohibit or restrict the disposal of, or other dealings in, assets or vest assets in an FSA approved trustee. The FSA maintains a public record containing details about all authorised persons including the services they provide.[6]

1   FSMA 2000, s 32 provides for the authorisation of partnerships and unincorporated associations.
2   FSMA 2000, s 40(3); and see below.
3   FSMA 2000, s 52(4) and (5).
4   FSMA 2000, s 42.
5   FSMA 2000, s 43.
6   FSMA 2000, s 347. The register will also provide details of all current approved persons.

Refusing an application

5.23   If the FSA proposes to refuse an application, it must give the applicant a 'warning notice'.[1] In deciding to refuse an application, the FSA must give the applicant a 'decision notice'. An aggrieved applicant can refer his application to the Tribunal.[2] The FSA Handbook sets out details of the FSA's procedures.[3] In this regard, see Chapter 20.

1   FSMA 2000, s 54. If the cancellation of a Pt IV permission means that there is no regulated activity for which an authorised person has permission, the FSA must give a direction under FSMA 2000, s 33 withdrawing that person's status as an authorised person.
2   FSMA 2000, s 55(1).
3   FSA Handbook: Regulatory Processes – Decision Making Manual (DEC).

Variation and cancellation of a Part IV permission

5.24   The FSA can vary and cancel a permission at the request of the authorised person.[1] Bearing in mind the interests of consumers, a permission may, for instance, be varied to add further regulated activities or to cancel or vary a 'requirement'. The FSA can also act on its own initiative.[2] The FSA can, for instance, vary or cancel a permission if it appears that an authorised person is failing, or is likely to fail, to satisfy the threshold conditions or in order to protect consumers. The FSA can impose or vary requirements in the event that a person acquires control over an authorised person with a Part IV permission.[3]

If the FSA proposes on its own initiative to vary a permission, or varies it with immediate effect, it must give the authorised person written notice.[4] The notice must advise the applicant that he may make representations to the FSA and inform him of his right to refer the matter to the Financial Services and Markets Tribunal.[5]

In cancelling an authorised person's permission, otherwise than at his request, the FSA must give him a warning notice and a decision notice as appropriate[6] and the aggrieved authorised person may refer the matter to the Tribunal.[7] The FSA can exercise its own initiative powers to assist an overseas regulator.[8]

1   FSMA 2000, s 44.
2   FSMA 2000, s 45.
3   FSMA 2000, s 46.
4   FSMA 2000, s 53(4).
5   See Chapter 20 below.
6   FSMA 2000, s 54.
7   FSMA 2000, s 55.
8   FSMA 2000, s 47.

Threshold conditions: FSMA 2000, Sch 6

5.25   In giving or varying a permission, or imposing or varying any 'requirement', the FSA must ensure that the relevant person will satisfy, and continue to satisfy, the threshold conditions set out in Sch 6 of the FSMA 2000 in relation to each regulated activity for which he has or will have permission.[1] This duty does not prevent the FSA 'from taking such steps as it considers are necessary in relation to a particular authorised person' in order to protect consumers.

The FSA Handbook provides guidance on the threshold conditions which represent the minimum conditions that a firm is required to satisfy, and continue to satisfy, in order to be given and to retain a Part IV permission.[2] The guidance is not exhaustive and is written at a high level of generality.

Satisfaction of the threshold conditions is considered on a case-by-case basis in relation to each regulated activity that an applicant is seeking to carry on in the context of the size, nature, scale and complexity of its business.[3]

Sch 6 FSMA sets out the threshold conditions:

1   FSMA 2000, s 41.
2   FSA Handbook: High Level Standards' – Threshold Conditions (COND).
3   COND 1.3.2G.

'LEGAL STATUS'

5.26   A person seeking to accept deposits must be a body corporate or a partnership.

'LOCATION OF OFFICES'

5.27   A UK body corporate's head office and any registered office must be in the UK. This provision implements article 6 of the 'Post BCCI Directive'.[1] The key issue in identifying the head office of a firm is the location of its central management and control.[2]

1   Directive 95/26/EC (29 June 1995) amends the directives on banking, insurance, transferable securities and undertakings for collective investment in transferable securities (UCITS) so as to strengthen supervisory authorities' powers.
2   COND 2.2.3G.

'CLOSE LINKS'

5.28   The FSA must be satisfied that any close links (including the parent company; subsidiary; fellow subsidiary or major shareholder) with another person are not likely to prevent the effective supervision of the authorised person by the FSA. For example, might the structure and geographical spread of the group frustrate the provision of adequate and reliable flows of information to the FSA? Is the group subject to consolidated supervision? Can the financial position of the group be assessed with confidence?[1] FSA has stated that

> 'firms whose group structure or internal administrative organisation are subject to the laws and regulations of a territory outside the UK which may be deemed to impede the FSA's ability to supervise the firm effectively or otherwise to discharge its objectives may not meet the requirements of this [threshold condition]'.[2]

This provision also implements requirements of the 'Post BCCI Directive'.[3] The FSA will have regard to all significant relevant matters whether arising in the UK or elsewhere.[4]

1   COND 2.3.3G.
2   CP 20 – 'The Qualifying Conditions for Authorisation'.
3   Directive 95/26/EC (29 June 1995).
4   COND 2.3.4G.

'ADEQUATE RESOURCES'

5.29   Does the firm, in the FSA's opinion, have adequate human, material and financial resources? The FSA will interpret 'adequate' as meaning sufficient in terms of quantity, quality and availability.[1] How will the firm manage those resources? A bank will be given individual guidance by the FSA on its likely capital requirements. The FSA may take into account the impact of other members of a group to which the firm belongs on the adequacy of its resources.[2] Is there any indication that the firm may have difficulty in complying with any of the FSA's prudential requirements? What is the financial history of the firm? Is the business sufficiently viable for consumer funds not to be placed at risk? What provision is made in respect of liabilities? How is risk identified and managed? Newly formed firms should be alive to their susceptibility to teething problems.[3] The FSA would expect a firm to have 'a well constructed business plan' that has been sufficiently tested and resources 'commensurate with the likely risks it will face'.[4]

1   COND 2.4.2G.
2   COND 2.4.3G.
3   COND 2.4.6G.
4   COND 2.4.6G.

'SUITABILITY'

5.30   The FSA Handbook guidance covers a wide range of considerations. The FSA must be satisfied that the person is 'fit and proper' having regard to all the circumstances including connections with any person; the nature of the relevant regulated activity and 'the need to ensure that his affairs are conducted soundly and prudently'.[1]

Relevant questions include: Is the firm likely to conduct its business with integrity and in compliance with proper standards?[2] Has the firm or any associated person been the subject of any regulatory investigations, enforcement proceedings or criminal convictions? How is the firm regarded by UK and overseas regulators? Is the firm's management competent? Will management exercise due skill, care and diligence?[3] Are adequate internal controls in place?[4] How is the firm proposing to manage risk? What account will be taken of the interests of consumers? Has the firm developed procedures to ensure that it only recruits honest staff? Will staff be familiar with the compliance and anti-money laundering requirements?[5]

Suitability to carry on one regulated activity does not mean that the firm is suitable to carry on all regulated activities.

1   COND 2.5.2G.
2   COND 2.5.4G.
3   COND 2.5.7G.
4   FSA Handbook: High Level Standards – Senior Management Arrangements, Systems and Controls (SYSC).
5   FSA Handbook: Business Standards – Training and Competence (TC).

Authorisation through qualification

EEA passport rights: FSMA 2000, Sch 3

5.31   The European Economic Area (EEA) claims to be, and is rapidly becoming, a single market in financial services. A person authorised, and with its head office, in one EEA state qualifies for authorisation to conduct business in any other EEA state through exercising various passport rights agreed by the relevant countries.[1] A person authorised, and with its head office, in an EEA state other than the UK can thus secure FSMA authorisation either under one of the single market directives, [2] or, if the relevant activity is not covered by a directive, pursuant to rights under the Treaty of Rome.[3]

1   Being the contracting states to the 1992 Oporto agreement on the European Economic Area as it has effect for the time being: FSMA 2000, Sch 3, para 8.
2   FSMA 2000, Sch 3.
3   FSMA 2000, Sch 4.

5.32 It should not be assumed that anyone authorised in the UK can take advantage of the single passport. The provisions apply to EEA firms as defined. A firm with its head office in New York or Tokyo cannot take advantage of the passport even if it is UK authorised. Similarly note the difference between branches and subsidiaries. Subsidiaries are separate legal entities and will require their own authorisation even if the parent company is an EEA firm.

5.33 Sch 3 of the FSMA 2000 ('EEA Passport Rights') sets out the authorisation regime in relation to 'the single market directives' covering banking, insurance and investment services. The Member States are required to adopt laws implementing the directives with the aim of creating harmonised minimum requirements across the single market. Each EEA state should, in theory, have the same provisions governing the relevant types of financial business. The essence of this passport regime is that a firm is home state authorised and subject to host state conduct of business rules in relation to the relevant activities. A firm's home state is where it has its head office. Thus an EEA 'investment firm' authorised by its home state regulator has an 'EEA right' to establish a branch or provide services in any other EEA state 'in accordance with the Treaty' and subject to the conditions of the Investment Services Directive,[1] being the relevant single market directive in this instance. Each EEA state must consequently rely upon the other EEA states to authorise only fit and proper persons.

1   Directive 93/22/EEC.

EXERCISE OF PASSPORT RIGHTS BY EEA FIRMS

5.34 An EEA firm consequently has passport rights to establish a branch in or provide services into the UK.[1] Once an EEA firm seeking to set up a branch in the UK has satisfied 'the establishment conditions' it qualifies for FSMA authorisation (and an appropriate permission). The establishment conditions are that:

(a)   the FSA has received an appropriate consent notice from the firm's home state regulator in relation to the firm establishing a branch in the UK that identifies the activities to which the consent relates; and
(b)   the firm has been notified of the relevant UK host state rules with which it must comply or two months have elapsed since the FSA received the consent notice.

There are similar 'services conditions' provisions for EEA firms wanting to provide services cross-border into the UK.

1   FSMA 2000, Sch 3, Pt II.

EXERCISE OF PASSPORT RIGHTS BY UK FIRMS

5.35 Part III of Sch 3 to the FSMA 2000 covers the exercise of passport rights by UK firms into other EEA states. A UK firm may not exercise an EEA right to establish a branch in another EEA state unless:

(a)   the firm has duly given the FSA 'a notice of intention' to establish a branch identifying the activities it wants to carry on through the branch;
(b)   the FSA has duly given 'a consent notice' to the host state regulator; and
(c)   the host state regulator has notified the firm of the host state rules to which it will be subject in conducting business through the proposed

branch or two months have elapsed from the date on which the FSA gave the consent notice.

Similar provisions govern the provision of cross-border services. A breach of the prohibitions relating to the exercise of passport rights by an unauthorised UK firm is a criminal offence.

Treaty Rights: FSMA 2000, Sch 4

5.36   If the activity that a 'Treaty firm' wants to carry on in the UK (whether through a branch or services) is not covered by any of the single market directives (examples include reinsurance business, certain life insurance business and certain business relating to commodities derivatives), it may nevertheless exercise rights under the 'Treaty Establishing the European Community' to secure FSMA authorisation. Schedule 4 to the FSMA 2000 provides that once a Treaty firm satisfies specified conditions, it qualifies for authorisation and an appropriate permission.

5.37   The conditions are that:

(a)   the firm is home state authorised to carry on the relevant regulated activity. A firm will not be regarded as home state authorised until the home state regulator has notified the FSA in writing;

(b)   the home state's laws afford protection at least equivalent to that afforded under the FSMA 2000 to consumers in relation to the relevant activity; and

(c)   there is no available 'EEA right' under the single market directives to carry on the relevant business.

Failure by the firm to give the FSA at least seven days' written notice of its intention to commence business is an offence. It is similarly an offence to provide false or misleading information in a written notice. The relevant local law, and not FSMA, provides for the exercise of Treaty rights by UK firms.

Controlling shareholdings in authorised persons

5.38   Part XII of the FSMA 2000 sets out the requirement to notify the FSA if a person proposes to acquire or increase his control over an authorised person. Part XII focuses upon a person holding 10% or more of the shares; the exercise of voting rights and whether significant control could be exercised over the management of the authorised person or the parent of an authorised person.

A 'notice of control' must be given by the proposed controller to the FSA in writing and include such information as the FSA may reasonably require.[1] The FSA may approve of the person acquiring control[2] or it may impose conditions.[3] Or it might serve a 'warning notice'[4] followed by a notice of objection.[5] The 'approval requirements' are that the person is fit and proper to control an authorised person and that the interests of consumers will not be threatened. The regulator will be concerned that the authorised person continues to satisfy the threshold conditions.[6] The relevant person can refer the matter to the Tribunal.[7] Similar provisions apply in relation to proposed reductions in control. The 'control' regime allows the regulator to freeze a shareholding[8] and it is policed by a range of criminal offences.[9]

1   FSMA 2000, s 182.
2   FSMA 2000, s 184.
3   FSMA 2000, s 185.
4   FSMA 2000, s 183.
5   FSMA 2000, s 186.
6   FSMA 2000, s 186(3); COND 1.2.4G.
7   FSMA 2000, s 186(5).
8   FSMA 2000, s 189.
9   FSMA 2000, s 191.

'THE PRINCIPLES FOR BUSINESSES'

5.39   After securing authorisation the required standards must then be maintained. As already seen, the FSA has to ensure that an authorised person continues to satisfy the threshold conditions. In both securing and maintaining authorisation, the firm must comply with the 'Principles for Businesses'.[1]

The Principles, which apply in whole or part to every firm, are a general statement of the fundamental obligations of firms under the regulatory system. They express the main dimensions of the fit and proper standard set for firms in the suitability threshold condition. The ability to abide by the Principles is therefore a critical factor in Part IV permission applications. Breaching the Principles may jeopardise a firm's authorisation. In applying the Principles to the acceptance of deposits, the FSA will only proceed in a prudential context (where something has gone very seriously wrong). The Principles are also a yardstick for bringing disciplinary proceedings.

1   FSA Handbook: High Level Standards – Principles for Businesses (PRIN).

5.40   The Principles are as follows:

(1)   *Principle 1 – Integrity:* A firm must conduct its business with integrity.

(2)   *Principle 2 – Skill, care and diligence:* A firm must conduct its business with due skill, care and diligence.

(3)   *Principle 3 – Management and control:* A firm must take reasonable care to organise and control its affairs responsibly and effectively, with adequate risk management systems.

(4)   *Principle 4 – Financial prudence:* A firm must maintain adequate financial resources.

(5)   *Principle 5 – Market conduct:* A firm must observe proper standards of market conduct.

(6)   *Principle 6 – Customers' interests:* A firm must pay due regard to the interests of its customers and treat them fairly.

(7)   *Principle 7 – Communications with clients:* A firm must pay due regard to the information needs of its clients, and communicate information to them in a way which is clear, fair and not misleading.

(8)   *Principle 8 – Conflicts of interest:* A firm must manage conflicts of interest fairly, both between itself and its customers and between a customer and another client.

(9)   *Principle 9 – Customers:* relationships of trust: A firm must take reasonable care to ensure the suitability of its advice and discretionary decisions for any customer who is entitled to rely upon its judgment.

(10)   *Principle 10 – Clients' assets:* A firm must arrange adequate protection for clients' assets when it is responsible for them.

(11) *Principle 11 – Relations with regulators:* A firm must deal with its regulators in an open and co-operative way, and must disclose to the FSA appropriately anything relating to the firm of which the FSA would reasonably expect notice.

B. APPROVED PERSONS

5.41 Most authorised persons are legal entities. Investment banks, deposit-takers and insurance companies never really advise on a merger, a savings account, an investment product or a life policy. Although authorised to do so, these bodies corporate can only act through fallible human beings. So the FSA individually registers the individuals that actually do the things for which their corporate masters are authorised. Individual registration in UK financial services can be traced back to individual membership of the Stock Exchange. The exchange spawned The Securities Association (TSA) under the Financial Services Act 1986 self-regulatory regime.

TSA adopted individual registration as a regulatory tool. The idea gradually won favour with the other Financial Services Act self-regulating organisations (SROs). Individual registration and individual accountability, particularly for senior managers, now lies at the heart of the FSMA regime even though it has not, for the moment, been fully adopted in the worlds of retail banking and general insurance business. It has also not yet caught the imagination of all overseas regulators although in a global marketplace this too appears to be a predictable development. If the authorisation requirement restricts entry to the UK financial services industry to firms which are fit and proper to carry on such business, individual registration is similarly intended to keep standards high.[1] It is clearly in the interests of the regulator in pursuing its regulatory objectives that there should be a high level of individual professionalism. Individual registration assists managers in fostering a compliance culture across the firm. It benefits the individual in a highly competitive employment market. In the aftermath of pensions mis-selling, unsuitable home income plans sold to the elderly and guaranteed annuity rates which were not guaranteed, a focus upon professionalism is an important step towards regaining the confidence of the consumer.

1   Evidence of the Securities and Futures Authority to the Treasury and Civil Service Committee (29 June 1994 – 'Financial Services Regulation') at p 384.

APPROVED PERSONS AND 'CONTROLLED FUNCTIONS'

5.42 The FSMA approved persons regime replaced the previous individual registration requirements of the SROs and the notification requirements under the Banking Act 1987. In the days of the Bank of England's Supervision and Surveillance Division, it was the Governor's raised eyebrow that sent a senior officer off to spend more time with his family. The new regime with its prior approval requirements, focused accountability and enforcement procedures will prove to be somewhat different for the banking industry. For those individuals who were previously registered with an SRO, their approval was 'grandfathered' through without having to apply for approval upon the FSA assuming its statutory powers at the end of November 2001. The 'warehousing' of a registration previously allowed an individual to retain his registration even though he was not engaged in an activity that required registration. The new regime prohibits warehousing not least because the individual has to be signed off each year by his manager as being competent to perform the relevant role. There will thus be some individuals who feel diminished under the new regime.

Approval

5.43   Under s 59 of the FSMA 2000, an authorised person ('a firm') must take reasonable care to ensure that no person (in most instances an individual whether employed under a contract of employment or otherwise) performs a 'controlled function' under an arrangement[1] entered into by the firm in relation to the carrying on by the firm of a regulated activity unless that individual is approved by the FSA. The individual registration requirement thus extends beyond the employees of an authorised firm to individuals who act for the firm in a relevant capacity.

The FSA may only specify a function as a 'controlled function' if it is satisfied that one of three conditions is met:[2]

(a)   The first condition is that 'the function is likely to enable the person responsible for its performance to exercise a significant influence on the conduct of the authorised person's affairs'.[3] This covers the most senior managers but it will be a question of fact in each case. What amounts to exercising significant influence in any particular case will depend upon the circumstances. In deciding whether this condition is met, the FSA may take into account 'the likely consequences of a failure to discharge that function properly'.[4] Does the individual play a part in ensuring that effective governance structures, systems and controls are developed and operated? Is he involved in setting the business strategy, regulatory climate and ethical standards of the firm?

(b)   The second condition is that 'the function will involve the person performing it in dealing with customers'.[5] This covers, for instance, financial advisers, salespeople, fund managers and research analysts.

(c)   The third condition is that 'the function will involve the person performing it in dealing with property of customers'.[6] This covers the trader.

Prior approval from the FSA is required for each controlled function to be performed by a person. A firm that fails to take 'reasonable care' to ensure that its staff are duly registered is flirting with liability for breaching the management and control principle.[7] A contravention of the registration requirements 'is actionable at the suit of a private person who suffers loss as a result of the contravention'.[8]

1   FSMA 2000, s 59(10).
2   FSMA 2000, s 59(4).
3   FSMA 2000, s 59(5).
4   FSMA 2000, s 59(9).
5   FSMA 2000, s 59(6).
6   FSMA 2000, s 59(7).
7   FSA Handbook: High Level Standards – Principles for Businesses (PRIN) – Principle 3.
8   FSMA 2000, s 71.

The controlled functions

5.44   Part V of the FSMA 2000 thus sets out the key features of the approved persons regime. The details of that regime, including the descriptions of functions specified by the FSA under s 59(3) of the FSMA 2000, are contained in the FSA Handbook.[1] The Handbook provides how the regime applies to 'overseas firms'[2] and 'incoming EEA firms'.[3] It also provides directions on how a firm should apply for approval on behalf of a candidate and other related procedures such as changing the details held by the FSA about an approved person and withdrawing from approval.

1   FSA Handbook: Regulatory Processes – Supervision (SUP).
2   SUP 10.1.6R and 10.1.7R. The regime 'does not apply to an overseas firm in relation to regulated activities which are carried on in the United Kingdom other than from an establishment maintained by it . . . in the United Kingdom'. The approved persons regime does not therefore apply to cross-border services into the UK.
3   SUP 10.1.9R; SUP 10.1.13R and SUP 10.1.14R.

5.45   FSA has specified 27 controlled functions.[1] By providing detailed descriptions of, and setting out the provisions applicable to, each of those functions,[2] the Handbook marks the boundaries of the approved persons regime. The fact that a person may be approved for one activity does not have the effect of bringing all his activities within the controlled function.[3] Certain controlled functions expressly include other controlled functions.[4] A person can be approved for more than one controlled function.

A table in the Handbook describes in brief terms the controlled functions (CFs):[5] CF 1 through CF 20 are the 'significant influence functions' comprising the 'governing functions', the 'required functions', the 'systems and control functions' and the 'significant management functions'; CF 21 through CF 27 are the 'customer functions'.

1   SUP 10.4.5R.
2   SUP 10.3 to 10.10.
3   SUP 10.4.1R(3).
4   SUP 10.4.4G.
5   SUP 10.4.5R.

'Governing functions'

5.46   CF 1 to CF 7 are the 'governing functions'[1] and cover those persons responsible for directing the firm's affairs such as each director of a company incorporated under the Companies Acts.

—   *CF 1: Director function*
—   *CF 2: Non-executive director function*
—   *CF 3: Chief executive function*
—   *CF 4: Partner function*
—   *CF 5: Director of an unincorporated association function*
—   *CF 6: Small friendly society function*
—   *CF 7: Sole trader function*

1   Details in relation to each of these functions are set out at SUP 10.6.

'Required functions'

5.47   CF 8 to CF 12 are the 'required functions'[1] and cover those functions to which an individual(s) must, as specified, be appointed by the firm.

—   *CF 8: Apportionment and oversight function.* The senior officer(s) responsible for either or both of the apportionment function and the oversight function as required under the Senior Management Arrangements, Systems and Controls Sourcebook ('SYSC') in the FSA Handbook.[2]

— *CF 9: EEA investment business oversight function.* The senior officer responsible under SYSC for overseeing the establishment and maintenance of systems and controls in relation to 'designated investment business' carried on from the branch of an incoming EEA firm in the UK.

— *CF 10: Compliance oversight function.* Under SYSC, a firm that carries on 'designated investment business' must allocate responsibility to a senior officer for oversight of the firm's compliance and for reporting to the firm's governing body in respect of that responsibility.

— *CF 11: Money laundering reporting function.* The senior officer who acts as the money laundering reporting officer as required under the Money Laundering Sourcebook ('ML').

— *CF 12: Appointed actuary function.* Under the Supervision Manual, a long-term insurer must appoint an actuary.

1 Details in relation to each of these functions are set out at SUP 10.7.
2 SYSC 2.1.3R

'Systems and controls functions'

5.48 CF 13 to CF 15 are the 'systems and controls functions'.[1]

— *CF 13: Finance function.* The senior officer responsible for reporting to the firm's governing body about its financial affairs.

— *CF 14: Risk assessment function.* The senior officer responsible for reporting to the firm's governing body about setting and controlling its risk exposure.

— *CF 15: Internal audit function.* The senior officer responsible for reporting to the firm's governing body or audit committee about the firm's adherence to internal systems and controls, procedures and policies.

1 Details in relation to each of these functions are set out at SUP 10.8.

'Significant management functions'

5.49 CF 16 to CF 20 are the 'significant management functions' which apply when a firm apportions a significant responsibility to a senior manager of a significant business unit.[1] The FSA anticipates that there will only be a few firms needing to seek approval for individuals to perform these functions. In most firms, those persons approved for the 'governing functions', 'required functions' and, where appropriate, the 'systems and controls functions', are likely to exercise all the significant influence at senior management level. In determining whether an individual does need to be registered in this capacity, the firm should consider the size and significance of its business in the UK; the range of its regulated activities; its group structure; its management structure and the size of any international operations.[2] There is an annual reporting requirement to FSA in relation to these functions.[3]

— *CF 16: Significant management (designated investment business) function.* A senior manager with significant responsibility for a significant business unit that carries on designated investment business other than dealing in investments as principal.

— *CF 17: Significant management (other business operations) function.* A senior manager with significant responsibility for a significant business unit that carries on dealing in investments as principal or an activity that is not designated investment business.

— *CF18: Significant management (insurance underwriting) function.* A senior manager with significant responsibility for the effecting by an insurer of contracts of insurance other than contractually based investments.

— *CF 19: Significant management (financial resources) function.* A senior manager with significant responsibility for making material decisions on the commitment of a firm's financial resources, its financial commitments, its asset acquisitions, its liability management and its overall cash and capital planning.

— *CF 20: Significant management (settlements) function.* A senior manager with significant responsibility for processing confirmations, payments, settlements, insurance claims, client money and similar matters.

1 SUP 10.9.1R. Details in relation to each of these functions are set out at SUP 10.9.
2 SUP 10.9.3G.
3 SUP 10.9.8R.

'Customer functions'

5.50   CF 21 to CF 27 are the 'customer functions'.[1] These functions apply to giving advice on, dealing and arranging deals in, and managing investments consistent with the scope of the conduct of business regulation.[2] The functions do not apply to banking business such as deposit-taking and lending or general insurance business.[3] It is likely that the FSA will have to clarify how the functions apply as the industry has struggled with the application of the controlled functions to certain activities. A further concern is that, in some instances, an individual now requires multiple registrations to perform an activity that previously required just one registration.

1 Details in relation to each of these functions are provided at SUP 10.10.
2 SUP 10.10.1R; COB1.4.
3 SUP 10.10.3G.

CF 21: INVESTMENT ADVISER FUNCTION

5.51   This function covers the individual who gives advice directly to a customer on investments. Simply having contact with a customer does not require registration if the individual is not providing designated investment advice to the customer. 'Investment advisers' can give advice to clients in connection with 'corporate finance business' as set out in the Supervision Manual[1] but if advising clients only in connection with corporate finance business an individual should be registered under CF 23. CF 21 covers the trader who also advises the customer on the investments[2] without the trader needing to be separately approved for the CF26 'customer trading function'. Note that if the firm has customers who only ever want trades executed (without any advice) and those transactions may be carried out through a CF 21 investment adviser (rather than through a dedicated department) then that individual also requires the CF26 registration. When considering an application for approval in relation to this controlled function, the FSA may ask for evidence of the individual's competence.[3]

1 SUP 10.10.8G.
2 SUP 10.10.7R and SUP 10.10.17G.
3 SUP 10.10.9G.

5.52   The Securities and Futures Authority's '30-day rule' has been retained for investment advisers[1] in that an individual based overseas, who spends no more than 30 days in the UK in a 12-month period, does not need to be approved provided he is appropriately supervised by an approved person for the relevant function. The FSA would, for instance, expect the individual to be accompanied on a visit to a customer. The benefit of this rule has curiously not been extended to CF 23 corporate financiers and it appears to be inconsistent with the examination requirements under the Training and Competence Sourcebook.[2]

1   SUP 10.10.7(3)R.
2   TC 2.4.4R.

CF 22: INVESTMENT ADVISER (TRAINEE) FUNCTION

5.53   The function of advising on investments where the individual performing the function has passed the relevant exams but has not yet been assessed as competent by the firm in accordance with the requirements of the FSA Handbook's Training and Competence Sourcebook. In practice, this function may most readily apply to new entrants into the financial services industry.

CF 23: CORPORATE FINANCE ADVISER FUNCTION

5.54   The function of giving advice to 'clients' only in connection with 'corporate finance business'. In practice, this function is not limited to 'corporate financiers'. Form A[1] describes this category as the 'corporate adviser function' which may be the intended scope of this function. Reference should be made to the 'Glossary of Definitions' in the Handbook in determining whether or not a particular activity falls under the definition 'corporate finance business'.

1   SUP10 Annex 4D.

CF 24: PENSION TRANSFER SPECIALIST FUNCTION

5.55   The function of giving advice or performing related activities in connection with pension transfers or opt-outs for private customers.

CF 25: ADVISER ON SYNDICATE PARTICIPATION AT LLOYD'S FUNCTION

5.56   The function of giving advice to a person to become, or continue or cease to be, a member of a particular Lloyd's syndicate.

CF 26: CUSTOMER TRADING FUNCTION

5.57   The function of dealing, as principal or agent, and arranging deals in investments with or for, or in connection with, 'private customers' and 'intermediate customers' where the person does not advise on or manage investments. Traders who trade solely with market counterparties do not therefore need to be approved. Where a firm's proprietary trader may deal with private or intermediate customers, the firm should ensure that the trader is approved to perform this function.[1] There is no registration requirement for the individual who, on the instructions of the customer, simply inputs the customer's instructions into an automatic execution system where no discretion is or may be exercised by the individual.[2]

1   SUP 10.10.18G.
2   SUP 10.10.19G.

CF 27: INVESTMENT MANAGEMENT FUNCTION

5.58   This function covers discretionary management of investments and, when ancillary to that function, it covers executing trades and providing investment advice.[1] Thus an individual advising on or trading in other investments over which he does not exercise discretion must also have a CF 21 or CF 26 registration as appropriate.

1   SUP 10.10.20R.

APPLICATIONS FOR APPROVAL

5.59   The upshot of this is that as well as the firm requiring authorisation, individuals doing certain jobs must secure prior approval from the regulator.[1]

Applications for approval must contain such information as the FSA may reasonably require[2] and be made by completing FSA's 'Form A' in the manner directed.[3] The form provides for the candidate to confirm the accuracy of the information given by the firm so far as it relates to him. The form must, though, be submitted by, or on behalf of, the firm and not by the candidate. Approval applications are made on behalf of the relevant individual by his firm.[4] In making the application, the firm is responsible for satisfying the regulator that the candidate is fit and proper to perform the relevant controlled function[5] and it will, of course, be concerned for its own reasons to recruit only fit and proper staff. This is fine for routine applications but the interests of the firm and the individual can diverge when things go wrong. If the FSA refuses an application, the implications tend to be much more serious for the individual candidate than the sponsoring firm. The FSMA 2000 thus allows an aggrieved candidate to refer his case to the Tribunal.[6]

Registration is now intended to accord with the individual's job description rather than reflecting the examination that he has passed. The firm will need to decide which is the appropriate controlled function for the individual. Should an investment banker be registered under the CF 21 'investment adviser function' or the CF 23 'corporate finance adviser function'? Should a trader be registered under CF 21 'investment adviser function' or the CF 26 'customer trading function'? The individual must not start working until he has secured approval. Individuals should be reminded that passing any regulatory examination does not constitute registration. The firm should consider an individual's past employment history; written references;[7] credit history; qualifications and whether he has a criminal record.[8] Throughout recruitment, attainment of competence, registration and the probation period, the firm must also be alive to any employment law issues. It is clearly sensible, for instance, that the firm should protect itself by making employment conditional upon attaining and maintaining competence and securing approval.

1   SUP 10.1 sets out how the approved persons regime applies to 'Overseas firms', 'EEA firms', 'Treaty firms' and 'UCITS qualifiers'. SUP 10 does not apply to cross-border service providers (SUP 10.1.6R).
2   FSMA 2000, s 60(2)(b).
3   SUP 10.11.2G provides details of the forms covering applications (Form A); notice to withdraw an application (Form B); notice of ceasing to perform controlled functions (Form C); notification of changes in information (Form D) and internal transfer (Form E).

4   FSMA 2000, s 60; SUP 10.12.3G.
5   SUP 10.12.9G.
6   FSMA 2000, s 62(4).
7   SUP 10.13.12R; SUP 10.13.13G; and see also *Spring v Guardian Assurance plc* [1995] 2 AC
    296 HL.
8   FSA Consultation Paper 133 'Access to criminal records' (April 2002) reviews the implications
    for the financial services industry of the setting up of the Criminal Records Bureau by the
    Home Office under the Police Act 1997 to improve access to criminal records and recent
    amendments to the exceptions provisions under the Rehabilitation of Offenders Act 1974.

Is the candidate 'fit and proper'?

5.60   The FSA will only grant an approval application if it is satisfied that the
candidate 'is a fit and proper person to perform the function to which the
application relates'.[1] Under s 61(2) of the FSMA 2000, the FSA may have
regard (among other things) to whether the candidate is competent to carry out
a controlled function. The FSA Handbook sets out and describes criteria that
the FSA will consider when assessing the fitness and propriety of a candidate
for a controlled function.[2] The criteria are also relevant in assessing the
continuing fitness and propriety of an approved person. The FSA does not
restrict the matters to which it might have regard.

1   FSMA 2000, s 61.
2   FSA Handbook: High Level Standards – The Fit and Proper Test for Approved Persons (FIT).

5.61   There are three important elements to the 'fit and proper' test:

(a)   *Honesty, integrity and reputation:* In considering a person's honesty and
      integrity, the FSA will particularly take into account previous convictions
      for criminal offences involving dishonesty and regulatory enforcement
      actions. The FSA will have regard to whether the person 'demonstrates a
      readiness and willingness to comply with the requirements and standards
      of the regulatory system'.[1] The FSA will consider whether the person's
      reputation might have an adverse impact upon the firm.[2]

(b)   *Competence and capability:* In assessing a person's capabilities, the FSA
      will consider whether the person is 'competent' for the purposes of its
      training and competence regime.[3] Is this individual competent to
      perform this role? The FSA will consider the candidate's qualifications,
      his training and his level of competence. Being a good investment adviser
      will not, for instance, guarantee approval to perform a significant
      influence function.

(c)   *Financial soundness:* The FSA will consider whether the person has any
      outstanding judgment debts and whether he has been adjudged bank-
      rupt. The fact that a person may be of limited financial means will not, in
      itself, affect his suitability to perform a controlled function.[4]

1   FIT 2.1.3G.
2   FIT 2.1.2G.
3   FSA Handbook: Business Standards – Training and competence (TC).
4   FIT 2.3.2G.

Procedure

5.62   Unlike the authorisation process, the FSA cannot impose conditions or
requirements upon a person granted approval. A person is either approved or

not approved. The FSA has three months in which to decide whether or not to grant the application.[1] In most instances applications are turned round much more quickly. The FSA's Individual Vetting and Approval Department looks to process routine customer function applications within four business days and significant influencers within seven business days from receipt. The relevant firm must be authorised before any of its staff can be approved.[2]

In granting an application, the FSA must give written notice 'to each of the interested parties' including the person in respect of whom the approval application is made[3] but in practice the FSA notifies the firm.

The FSA must provide a warning notice if it proposes to refuse an application and a decision notice if it decides to refuse an application. Each of the interested parties can then refer the matter to the Tribunal.

The FSA can withdraw a person's approved status 'if it considers that the person in respect of whom it was given is not a fit and proper person to perform the function to which the approval relates'.[4] The warning notice, decision notice and right to refer to the Tribunal procedures again apply. At a time of increased individual accountability, withdrawal of approval is clearly an important weapon in the FSA's armoury.

1 FSMA 2000, s 61(3).
2 FSMA 2000, s 60(1) and (6).
3 FSMA 2000, s 62(1).
4 FSMA 2000, s 63.

THE STATEMENTS OF PRINCIPLE AND THE CODE OF PRACTICE FOR APPROVED PERSONS

5.63 Securing approval is the first step. The approved person must then ensure that he does nothing to jeopardise his continued approval. The approved person is subject to a wide range of rules, guidance and evidential provisions. And, like the authorised person, he is subject to high-level regulatory principles.

Under s 64 of the FSMA 2000, the FSA has issued the 'Statements of Principle' with respect to the conduct expected of approved persons and a supporting 'Code of Practice for Approved Persons'.[1] The adoption of high-level principles by the FSA not only continues a feature of the self-regulatory regime but also complements the FSA's own risk-based approach to regulation under which the industry has to meet certain standards but is left to decide for itself how best to achieve those standards. There can be little doubt that broadly drafted exhortations to behave are easier grounds upon which to bring enforcement proceedings than complex rules inviting close legal scrutiny.

The Code is new. Its purpose is to help 'to determine whether or not a person's conduct complies' with the Principles.[2] The Code describes conduct taken from regulatory experience that does not, in the FSA's opinion, comply with the Principles. The Code is not exhaustive. In certain cases, the Code sets out factors that, in the FSA's opinion, 'are to be taken into account' in determining whether or not an approved person's conduct complies with a statement of principle.[3] An individual's obligations as an approved person apply wherever he is located in the world but only in relation to carrying on a regulated activity.[4]

1 FSA Handbook: High Level Standards – Statements of Principle and Code of Practice for Approved Persons (APER).

2   APER 3.1.6G.
3   APER 1.2.3G; APER 3.2.1E.
4   APER 1.2.8G.

5.64   The Code provides that a person will only be regarded as breaching a principle if he is 'personally culpable'. Has the person acted deliberately or negligently so that his 'conduct was below that which would be reasonable in all the circumstances'?[1] Breaching the principles will not automatically cost a person his registration but it may leave his relationship with both regulator and employer frayed.

1   APER 3.1.4G.

5.65   The seven principles governing the conduct of approved persons are set out below. Principles 1 to 4 apply to all approved persons; principles 5 to 7 only apply to those senior managers who perform a 'significant influence function'. Extracts from the Code are provided in relation to each principle.

Principles applying to all approved persons

Statement of Principle 1: An approved person must act with integrity in carrying out his controlled function

5.66   To be fit and proper, a person must be honest, be a person of integrity and enjoy a good reputation. Examples from the Code of Practice of conduct by an approved person that would, in the opinion of the FSA, breach this principle include:

—   Deliberately misleading (or attempting to mislead) by act or omission a client, his firm, the firm's auditors or the FSA. This would include deliberately falsifying documents; misleading a client about the risks of an investment; mismarking the value of investments or trading positions and providing false or inaccurate information to the firm or to the FSA.
—   Deliberately recommending an investment to a customer, or carrying out a discretionary transaction for a customer, when the approved person knows that the investment is unsuitable for that customer.
—   Deliberately preparing inaccurate or inappropriate records or returns. This would include deliberately misleading a customer by sending him a statement that deliberately overvalued his portfolio in order to hide losses.
—   Deliberately misusing the assets or confidential information of a client. This would include deliberately front running client orders; churning client accounts and misappropriating a client's assets.
—   Deliberately structuring transactions so that regulatory breaches will be disguised.
—   Deliberately failing to disclose a conflict of interest to a client.

Statement of Principle 2: An approved person must act with due skill, care and diligence in carrying out his controlled function

5.67   Under this principle, the standards expected of an approved person will be determined by a range of factors including the parties involved, the size and complexity of the business, the claimed expertise and any relevant market rules. Examples from the Code of Practice of conduct by an approved person that would, in the opinion of the FSA, breach this principle include:

— Failing to inform a customer or his firm of material information in circumstances where he was aware, or ought to have been aware, of such information, and of the fact that he should provide it. This would include failing to explain the risks of an investment to a customer; failing to disclose details of charges or surrender penalties to a customer; mismarking trading positions and failing to disclose dealings where disclosure is required by the firm's personal account dealing rules.

— Recommending an investment to, or carrying out a discretionary transaction for, a customer when he does not have reasonable grounds to believe that the investment is suitable for that customer.

— Advising on, recommending or undertaking transactions without a reasonable understanding of the risk exposure to a customer or the firm.

— Failing, without good reason, to disclose a conflict of interest when dealing for a client.

— Failing to provide adequate control over a client's assets. This would include failing to segregate a client's assets and failing to process a client's payments in a timely manner.

— Continuing to perform a controlled function despite failing to meet the standards of knowledge and skill set out in the FSA's Training and Competence Sourcebook.

Statement of Principle 3: An approved person must observe proper standards of market conduct in carrying out his controlled function

5.68 A range of issues will be considered in determining what are 'proper' (rather than 'high') standards of market conduct, for example:

— On which market was the transaction carried out?
— What are that market's rules?
— How does the market operate?

The standards acceptable in the commodities markets may, for instance, differ from those acceptable in the equities markets. The market conduct principle applies to conduct on or off market. It thus governs over-the-counter transactions.

A factor to be taken into account in determining whether or not an approved person's conduct complies with this principle is whether he has complied with the FSA's Code of Market Conduct.[1] FSMA 2000 created the new offence of 'market abuse'[2] and required the FSA to issue the Code of Market Conduct[3] as 'appropriate guidance' on 'whether or not behaviour amounts to market abuse'.[4] The market abuse regime applies beyond approved persons. Any person based anywhere whose behaviour abuses the UK's markets can be pursued by the FSA for market abuse.

The market conduct policed by the Principles is not however limited to the 'market abuse' regime's behaviour in relation to 'qualifying investments' traded on 'prescribed markets'.[5]

Another factor to be taken in to account is whether the employee has complied with the FSA's provisions governing 'Inter-Professional Conduct'[6] or any relevant market codes and exchange rules. The authorised firm has its own obligation to observe proper standards of market conduct under 'The Principles for Businesses'.[7]

1 APER 4.3.3E.
2 FSMA 2000, s 118.
3 FSA Handbook: Business Standards – Market Conduct – Code of Market Conduct (MAR).
4 FSMA 2000, s 119.
5 FSMA 2000, s 118. The market abuse regime is considered in greater detail at Chapter 9 below.
6 FSA Handbook: Business Standards – Market Conduct – Inter-Professional Conduct (MAR). The Code is considered in Chapter 11 below.
7 FSA Handbook: High Level Standards – Principles for Businesses (PRIN).

Statement of Principle 4: An approved person must deal with the FSA and other regulators in an open and co-operative way and must disclose appropriately any information of which the FSA would reasonably expect notice

5.69 This principle applies in relation to both the FSA and other regulators including exchanges and overseas regulators.[1] Most staff will satisfy their regulatory obligations by notifying relevant information to their Compliance Department or senior management with whom the duty to report directly to the regulator rests.[2] Examples from the Code of Practice of conduct by an approved person that would, in the opinion of the FSA, breach this principle include:

— Failing to report promptly in accordance with his firm's internal procedures (or if none exist direct to the FSA) information that it is reasonable to assume would be of material significance to the FSA whether in response to questions or otherwise.
— Where the approved person is responsible within the firm for reporting matters to the FSA, failing promptly to inform the FSA of information that it is reasonable to assume would be of material significance to the FSA whether in response to questions or otherwise.
— Failing without good reason to provide a regulator with requested information within a specified time limit. The FSA will look at the reasonableness of any non-cooperation and would, for instance, consider the jurisdiction of an overseas regulator.

1 APER 4.4.2G.
2 APER 4.4.5G.

'Significant influence function' principles

Principles 5 to 7 only apply to senior managers approved to perform a 'significant influence function'

5.70 In applying these principles, the nature, scale and complexity of the business under management and the role and responsibility of the relevant individual within the firm will be relevant to the assessment as to whether his conduct was reasonable in all the circumstances.[1] As approved persons, these senior managers must comply with all the Statements of Principle for Approved Persons and the supporting Code of Practice. As has been noted, the Code sets out specific examples of behaviour drawn from regulatory experience that the FSA regards as breaching the Principles and specifies factors to be taken into account.

The examples given below in relation to each principle are drawn from the Code. Senior management responsibilities are also covered in Chapter 14.

1 APER 3.1.8G; APER 3.3.1E.

Statement of Principle 5: An approved person performing a significant influence function must take reasonable steps to ensure that the business of the firm for which he is responsible in his controlled function is organised so that it can be controlled effectively

5.71 If the firm proposes to undertake high-risk business then the degree of control and level of monitoring reasonably required will be high. The approved person should bear this in mind in organising the business for which he is responsible.

5.72 Examples from the Code of Practice of conduct by a significant influence function approved person that would, in the opinion of the FSA, breach this principle include:

— Failing to take reasonable steps to apportion responsibilities for all areas of the business under his control.
— Failing to take reasonable steps to apportion responsibilities clearly amongst those to whom responsibilities have been delegated. Have confusing or uncertain reporting lines, authorisation levels and job descriptions and responsibilities been implemented? The organisation of the business and the responsibilities of those within it should be clearly defined.
— The individual(s) responsible under SYSC[1] for the firm's apportionment obligation failing to take reasonable care to maintain a clear and appropriate apportionment of significant responsibilities among the firm's directors and senior managers. This would include failing to review regularly the significant responsibilities that the firm is required to apportion.
— Failing to take reasonable steps to ensure that suitable individuals are responsible for those aspects of the business under his control. This would include failing to review staff competence despite unacceptable performance of their duties; giving undue weight to financial performance in determining the suitability of an individual for a particular role and allowing managerial vacancies that jeopardise compliance with regulatory requirements. An adequate investigation of any concerns should be undertaken.

1 SYSC 2.1.3R.

Statement of Principle 6: An approved person performing a significant influence function must exercise due skill, care and diligence in managing the business of the firm for which he is responsible in his controlled function

5.73 Examples from the Code of Practice of conduct by a significant influence function approved person that would, in the opinion of the FSA, breach this principle include:

— Failing to take reasonable steps adequately to inform himself about the affairs of the business for which he is responsible. This includes permitting transactions without a sufficient understanding of the risks involved; permitting expansion of the business without reasonably assessing the potential risks of that expansion; inadequately monitoring highly profitable or unusual transactions; accepting implausible explanations without testing their veracity and failing to obtain independent, expert opinion where appropriate.

— Delegating authority to an individual without reasonable grounds for believing that the delegate is competent. The larger and more complex the business, the greater the need for clear and effective delegation and reporting lines.

— Failing to take reasonable steps to maintain an appropriate level of understanding of the business that he has delegated to an individual. This would include disregarding an issue once it has been delegated; failing to require adequate reports on delegated issues and accepting implausible or unsatisfactory explanations from delegates without testing their veracity.

— Failing to supervise and monitor adequately an individual to whom authority for dealing with an issue has been delegated. Although the approved person can delegate authority, he cannot delegate responsibility.

Statement of Principle 7: An approved person performing a significant influence function must take reasonable steps to ensure that the business of the firm for which he is responsible in his controlled function complies with the regulatory requirements imposed on that business

5.74 The FSA expects a significant influence function approved person to take reasonable steps both to ensure his firm's compliance with the relevant regulatory requirements and to ensure that all staff are aware of the need for compliance.[1]

1 APER 4.7.11G.

5.75 Examples from the Code of Practice of conduct by a significant influence function approved person that would, in the opinion of the FSA, breach this principle include:

— Failing to take reasonable steps to implement (either personally or through a compliance department) adequate and appropriate systems of control to comply with regulatory requirements. The nature and extent of the required systems of control will depend upon the regulatory requirements and the nature, scale and complexity of the business. The individual(s) responsible under SYSC[1] for overseeing that the firm has appropriate systems and controls is specifically subject to this principle. Both the Compliance Officer and the Money Laundering Reporting Officer are also specifically subject to the principle.

— Failing to take reasonable steps to monitor (either personally or through a compliance department) compliance with the regulatory requirements.

— Failing to take reasonable steps adequately to inform himself about why significant breaches of the regulatory requirements may have arisen. Reasonable steps should be taken to deal with regulatory breaches in a timely and appropriate manner.

— Failing to take reasonable steps to ensure that procedures and systems of control are reviewed and, if appropriate, improved following significant breaches of the regulatory requirements. Unless there are good reasons not to, reasonable recommendations should be implemented in a timely manner. What is reasonable will depend upon on the nature of the regulatory breach and the cost of improvement.

1   SYSC 2.1.3R.

GUILTY OF MISCONDUCT?

5.76   Under s 66 of the FSMA 2000, the FSA can bring disciplinary proceedings against an approved person 'if it appears to the [FSA] that he is guilty of misconduct' and the FSA is 'satisfied that it is appropriate in all the circumstances to take action against him'. The FSA may not bring proceedings after two years from when it first knew of the misconduct.[1]

A person is 'guilty of misconduct' if, while an approved person, he has breached a principle or 'he has been knowingly concerned in a contravention by the relevant authorised person of a requirement imposed on that authorised person' by or under the FSMA.[2] The FSA has stated that it will only pursue an individual 'where he is personally culpable' with 'personal culpability arising where an approved person's conduct was deliberate or where the approved person's standard of conduct was below that which would be reasonable in all the circumstances'.[3]

1   FSMA 2000, s 66(4).
2   FSMA 2000, s 66(2); SUP 10 Annex 1G.
3   APER 3.1.4G and ENF 11.5.3G.

Disciplinary powers

5.77   Whilst the FSA enjoys a wide range of disciplinary powers, it will not automatically initiate enforcement proceedings if a rule is broken. In some instances, the regulator may be content to see the breach remedied or to issue a private warning.

In more serious cases, though, it can fine the approved person 'such amount as it considers appropriate',[1] publish a statement of his misconduct or withdraw his approval.[2] The warning notice, decision notice and the right to appeal to the Tribunal procedures will again apply.

1   FSMA 2000, s 66(3)(a).
2   FSMA 2000, s 63.

Prohibition orders

5.78   The FSA can also prohibit an individual from working in the financial services industry. Section 56 FSMA vests the regulator with the power to make a 'prohibition order' banning an individual short on fitness and propriety from performing specified functions or any function.[1] An appeal lies to the Tribunal. An individual who disregards such an order is guilty of an offence.[2] Authorised persons must take reasonable care to ensure that they do not employ a prohibited person.[3]

1   The FSA issued its first prohibition order during April 2002. Richard Vincent Matkin, an independent financial adviser, was banned from working in the financial services industry after

the FSA discovered deficits of up to £1 million in funds he held on behalf of his clients (FSA Press Release, 18 April 2002).
2   FSMA 2000, s 56(4).
3   FSMA 2000, s 56(6). The list of prohibited persons is published on the FSA's website: www.fsa.gov.uk.

Chapter 6

Deposit-taking and banking supervision

INTRODUCTION

6.1 Once a bank has been authorised to carry on deposit-taking business it is necessary to ensure that it conducts its activities in a prudent and safe manner on a continuing basis thereafter. This is necessary to protect the interests of current and potential depositors and other creditors of the bank as well as to protect the stability of the banking and financial system as a whole against the risk of contagion and systemic collapse which arises from the possibility of loss spreading from one institution to another following the collapse of a particular bank.

The objective of bank supervision is accordingly to allow the authorities to confirm that individual banks are either conducting themselves in accordance with accepted standards of market practice or more specific statutory or administrative provisions designed to limit the financial exposures generated by their particular range of activities.

Supervision is consequently a monitoring or review process which ensures that banks comply with recognised market standards or more specific regulatory provisions.

6.2 Bank supervision is effected through a number of parallel processes which generally operate on an informal basis although they are backed by statutory powers in a number of specific regards.

Supervisory data is initially collected from banks through the completion of regular prudential returns on both an individual or solo and a group or consolidated basis. These supplement the more general information provided in the annual accounts or other company filings of the bank. Meetings will also be conducted with the senior management of a particular bank to discuss its business objectives, structure and organisation and control systems. These may be followed by on-site visits conducted by the authorities on the premises of the bank. Reporting accountants or auditors will also be required to provide reports on matters such as the adequacy of internal control systems or the validity of prudential returns on a regular basis. Apart from these commissioned reports, compliance is strengthened through statutory powers to obtain information and documents, appoint investigators or gain entry to premises in certain circumstances.[1]

All of this has now been subsumed within the integrated statutory system set up under the Financial Services and Markets Act (FSMA) 2000 and new more specific regulatory approach and operating framework constructed by the Financial Services Authority (FSA).[2]

1 See Blair et al (2nd edn), Chapter 4.
2 See paras 6.84–6.100.

6.3 One aspect of supervision that has become of particular importance since the late 1970s is ensuring that banks are not only examined individually but that full account is taken of all group or other connected relationships and exposures that may exist.

Early concerns had arisen with regard to the potential impact of more complex group structures on the supervision of individual banks during the 1970s. The matter was considered by the Basel Committee on Banking Supervision at the international level. A statement was issued in 1979 recommending that all supervision be conducted on a consolidated basis which was incorporated into its 1983 Revised Concordat.[1] Within the European Union, the principle of consolidated supervision was given effect to with the adoption of a first Consolidated Supervision Directive in 1983 which was replaced by a more extensive measure in 1992.[2]

The requirements contained in the 1992 Directive were implemented in the UK under the Bank of England's paper on *Implementation in the United Kingdom of the Directive on the Consolidated Supervision of Credit Institutions* of February 1993.[3] Following the collapse of BCCI in 1991 the European provisions were enhanced under the Prudential Supervision Directive[4] which was implemented in the UK by the Financial Institutions (Prudential Supervision) Regulations of 27 June 1996.[5] The 1996 Regulations, *inter alia*, require authorities to refuse to authorise complex groups with opaque structures which obstruct the conduct of their proper supervision.

More recently, attention has focused on the additional risks created by ever more complex banking and financial group structures. While the supervisory response constructed to date has generally involved extending bank supervision to include securities firms with information-gathering requirements being imposed in connection with insurance or other undertakings, serious concerns arise with regard to the increasing growth of complex financial and mixed-activity conglomerate structures. The growth of conglomerates raises a large number of further supervisory and regulatory issues which have still not been fully resolved.[6]

1 See Basel Committee 'Consolidated Supervision of Banks' International Activities' (March 1979); and Basel Committee 'Principles for the Supervision of Banks' Foreign Establishments' (April 1990). See also Basel Committee, 'Consolidation of Banks' Balance Sheets: Aggregation of Risk-Bearing Assets as a Method of Supervisory Bank Solvency' (October 1978); and G Walker 'Consolidated Supervision' BJIBFL, February/March 1996, 74, 131.

2   See Council Directive 83/350/EEC of 13 June 1983 on the supervision of credit institutions on a consolidated basis; and Council Directive 92/30/EEC on the supervision of credit institutions on a consolidated basis.

3   BSD/1993/1.

4   Council Directive amending Directives 77/780/EEC and 89/646/EEC in the field of credit institutions, Directives 73/239/EEC and 92/49/EEC in the field of non-life insurance, Directives 79/267/EEC and 92/96/EEC in the field of life assurance, Directive 93/22/EEC in the field of investment firms and Directive 85/611/EEC in the field of undertakings for collective investment in transferable securities (UCITS) with a view to reinforcing prudential supervision 95/26/EEC OJ No L168, 18.7.95, p 7. All of the main European Directives have since been reissued as a single Banking Consolidation Directive in May 2000 under the European SLIM (Simpler Legislation for the Internal Market) scheme. See Directive 2000/12/EC relating to the taking up and pursuit of the business of credit institutions

5   SI 1996/1669.

6   See G Walker, *International Banking Regulation –Law, Policy and Practice* (2001), ch 3.

6.4   The supervision of banks has been subject to substantial recent review. This pre-dates the larger structural reforms that are currently taking place and are continuing with the new regulatory approach and operating framework under construction by the FSA.

The original catalyst for developments in this area was the collapse of Barings in 1995. The circumstances surrounding the collapse were examined by the Board of Banking Supervision which produced its Report in July 1995.[1] In response to the recommendations contained in the Report, the Bank instituted a number of immediate changes and commissioned a separate report by Arthur Andersen. At the same time as the Arthur Andersen report was produced in July 1996,[2] the Bank published its proposals to give effect to the recommendations made.[3]

A number of consultative documents were subsequently issued by the Supervision and Surveillance division within the Bank during 1997. These were initially concerned with setting out the Bank's opinion as to its proper *Objectives, Standards and Processes of Banking Supervision* and revision to its practices with regard to *Bank's Internal Controls and the Section 39 Process* which were both issued in February 1997.[4]

These were followed by further consultative papers on the introduction of *A Risk Based Approach to Bank Supervision (the RATE Framework)* for UK incorporated banks in March 1997 and *A Revised Method for Measuring Liquidity Mismatches* in June 1997. A separate *Risk Based Approach to the Supervision of Non-EEA Banks (the SCALE Framework)* was announced in July 1997 with a further paper on the creation of *A Risk Based Approach to Supervising Foreign Exchange and Other Market Risks*.

The RATE and SCALE Proposals were subsequently merged in June 1998 in the FSA's final paper on a *Risk Based Approach to Supervision of Banks*. The Bank of England had also been considering further measures in connection with internal policy guidelines, prudential returns, a revised Statement of Principles and consolidating Guide to Banking Supervisory Policy as well as more general Quality Assurance within the conduct of bank supervision.[5] The basic nature of bank supervision was accordingly already in the process of substantial reform pre-FSMA which work has since been continued within the new framework of financial regulation still under construction in the UK.

1   See Board of Banking Supervision, 'Inquiry into the circumstances of the Collapse of Barings', HC (1994–95) 673 ('the BoBS Report').

2   See Arthur Andersen, *Findings and Recommendations of the Review of Supervision and Surveillance*, July 1996 ('the Arthur Andersen Report').

3   See Bank of England, *The Bank's Review of Supervision*, July 1996 ('the Review of Supervision').

4   See Blair et al (2nd edn), paras 2.23–2.25, 2.27–2.38 and 2.85–2.87.
5   See Blair et al (2nd edn), para 4.84–4.92.

6.5   Formal responsibility for banking supervision was transferred from the Bank of England to the FSA under the Bank of England Act 1998.[1] Deposit-taking was then included as a regulated activity within the FSMA 2000 and banks and all other financial institutions are now subject to the general prohibition in s 19(1) and continuing supervision by the FSA under the Act post-N2.[2]

The effect of this has been to create both a new formal statutory framework for all financial services and markets regulation as well as a new single rulebook with the FSA Handbook of Rules and Guidance.[3] Banks are, in particular, required to comply with the High Level Standards set out in Block 1 of the Handbook as well as the main prudential requirements contained in the interim prudential sourcebook (IPRU (BANK)) in Block 2 (Business Standards).[4] The FSA's oversight functions are then developed in the Supervision manual (SUP) which forms part of Block 3 (Regulatory Processes).[5] These provisions are supported by the information collection, investigation and enforcement powers conferred on the FSA under the Act which are expanded within SUP and in the separate Enforcement manual (ENF).[6] The revised complaints (DISP) and compensation (COMP) arrangements are dealt with under Block 4 (Redress).[7] The prudential sourcebook (IPRU (BANK)), in particular, includes the main financial resources and systems and controls requirements applicable to banks which generally restate the earlier provisions set out in the FSA Guide to Banking Supervisory Policy.

These will apply to banks on an interim basis until a revised set of common prudential requirements has been adopted for all sectors under the final Integrated Prudential Sourcebook (PSB).[8] The PSB was to have come into effect in 2004 although it is expected that this may have to be delayed until the proposed revisions to capital adequacy standards being considered at the international and European levels have been finalised. The PSB will operate on a 'risk-by-risk' basis and include separate provisions governing credit risk, market risk, operational risk, insurance risk and group risk.[9]

The FSA has also been developing a new more general regulatory approach and operating framework within which all financial supervision and regulation is to be conducted.[10] A number of announcements have been made in this regard, although the final arrangements have not been confirmed. In practice, while the larger operating framework will relate to the measurement and assessment of compliance by the FSA with its more general statutory objectives, the interim and final sourcebooks will be concerned with regulatory and prudential compliance at the individual firm level. This more specific regulatory function will then operate as one part of the larger operating framework being constructed.

Despite the fundamental nature of the institutional and substantive regulatory reform undertaken, a significant part of earlier banking prudential compliance and supervisory practice has been continued. It has to be expected that further changes will be effected in due course, in particular, as a result of the creation of the new integrated regulatory approach and larger operating framework. Even with this, it has to be hoped that much of the traditional relationship, discretion and judgment based nature of UK banking supervision may remain in place.

1   S 21(a).

2 See paras 6.7–6.10 and 6.11–6.14.
3 See Chapter 2, paras 2.51–2.82 and 2.83–2.146.
4 See para 6.20. See also Chapter 2, paras 2.109–2.110; and Chapter 15.
5 See Chapter 2, paras 2.27–2.30 and 2.123–2.124.
6 See Chapter 2, paras 2.64–2.68 and 2.125–2.126.
7 See Chapter 2, paras 2.128–2.132.
8 See FSA, *Integrated Prudential Sourcebook* (June 2001), Consultation Paper 97; and FSA, *Integrated Prudential Sourcebook, Annex C: Draft Rules and Guidance* (June 2001), Consultation Paper 97a.
9 See paras 6.85–6.88.
10 See paras 6.84–6.100 and Tables 6.2 and 6.3 below. See also FSA, *A New Regulator for the New Millennium*; FSA, *Building the New Regulator – Progress report 1* (December 2001); and FSA, *Building the New Regulator – Progress report 2* (February 2002).

Scope of the chapter

6.6 The purpose of this chapter is to consider the revised statutory basis for bank supervision and the main mechanisms through which supervision is effected in practice.

The development of the new statutory framework for bank supervision is noted and nature of deposit-taking business under the new arrangements explained. The general approach adopted with regard to bank and related supervisory practice in the UK is reconsidered. The general structure and content of the FSA Handbook is examined and the main provisions of the Supervision manual (SUP) considered in further detail.

The further revisions to be introduced under the Integrated Prudential Sourcebook (PSB) are then referred to, and the nature of the new regulatory approach and operating framework assessed.

STATUTORY BASIS FOR BANK SUPERVISION

6.7 The Bank of England was formerly responsible for the supervision of banks in the UK under the Banking Act 1987. This function was subsequently transferred to FSA under s 21(a) of the Bank of England Act 1998.[1]

Under s 1(1) of the Banking Act 1987, as amended by the Bank of England Act 1998, the FSA had the powers conferred on it by the 1987 Act and the duty generally to supervise the institutions authorised to carry on deposit-taking business in the exercise of those powers.[2]

1 See Chapter 2, paras 2.49–2.50.
2 See Blair et al (2nd ed), paras 4.6–4.10.

6.8 The FSA was also charged under the Banking Act 1987 to keep under review the operation of the Act and developments in the field of banking. The duties of the FSA accordingly included a statutory obligation to review the framework of supervision set up under the 1987 Act in addition to its more specific day-to-day regulatory function. In so doing, FSA was to have regard to changes in the banking industry.

Although most of the statutory and more operational developments in the area of bank supervision have generally been crisis-driven (having been adopted in response to particular bank collapse such as the Fringe Banking Crisis in 1972/73, Johnson Matthey in 1984, BCCI in 1991 and Barings in 1995), the Bank of England had at all times been concerned to keep supervisory practices under continuing review. This was, in particular, reflected in the annual reports produced on its activities and non-statutory supervisory papers issued from time to time. As with most other aspects of bank control, supervision has had to be developed as market practices have changed.

6.9 The statutory basis for banking and all other financial services and market control is now the FSMA 2000 which came into effect on 1 December 2001 (N2). The Banking Act 1987 has since been repealed[1] and the Board of Banking Supervision dissolved.[2] The transfer provisions in the Banking Act 1998 have also been repealed, although the other non-supervisory sections of the Act continue in effect with some amendment.[3]

Deposit-taking is included as a regulated activity for the purposes of the Act, with the effect that it is subject to the core prohibition set out in s 19(1) and the requirement for permission in s 20(1).[4] The conduct of such activity is then governed by the provisions set out in the FSA Handbook of Rules and Guidance issued under ss 138 and 157.[5]

1 See Financial Services and Markets Act 2000 (Consequential Amendments and Repeals) Order 2001 (SI 2001/3649), art 3(1). Art 3(2) also provides for repeal of the Banking Coordination (Second Council Directive) Regulations 1992 (SI 1992/3218).
2 See Financial Services and Markets Act 2000 (Dissolution of the Board of Banking Supervision) (Transitional Provisions) Order 2001 (SI 2001/3582).
3 See Financial Services and Markets Act 2000 (Consequential Amendments and Repeals) Order 2001, arts 161–164.
4 See Chapter 2, paras 2.54–2.60.
5 See Chapter 2, paras 2.61–2.63 and 2.83–2.146.

6.10 Many of the underlying powers, such as with regard to information collection, investigations, reports and enforcement, are continued under the FSMA 2000, although these are expanded and developed in the Handbook.[1] UK banking supervision is now principally conducted in accordance with the provisions set out in the FSA's Supervision manual (SUP) which forms part of Block 3 Regulatory processes.

In terms of underlying practice and approach, however, the FSA has stated that it will seek to maintain the general standards of banking supervision formerly practised by the Bank of England and to continue to implement the changes designed to improve its effectiveness following the collapse of Barings and subsequent reviews. This will now be conducted as only one part of the larger integrated regulatory process constructed although a significant amount of the earlier practice should remain in place.

Banks will be subject to more formal regulatory requirements in the form of FSA rules[2] and to a considerably more formal enforcement regime,[3] although it has to be expected that many of the earlier advantages of flexibility and individual supervisory contact and judgment will be preserved within the new regime.

1 See paras 6.20–6.83.
2 See Chapter 2, paras 2.61–2.63. See, for example, the new capital rules imposed under IPRU (BANK). See Chapter 15, paras 15.27–15.48.
3 See para 6.18. See also Chapter 2, paras 2.64–2.68 and Chapter 19.

DEPOSIT-TAKING BUSINESS

6.11 Deposit-taking and deposits are included as regulated activities and investments in Sch 2 to the FSMA 2000.[1]

Under s 22(1), an activity is a 'regulated activity' for the purposes of the Act if it is of a specified kind carried on by way of business and relates to an investment of a specified kind or relates to a specified activity in connection with property of any kind. 'Specified' means specified by order of the Treasury (s 22(5)).

The activities and investments covered are set out Parts II and III of the Regulated Activities Order.[2] The Order follows but extends the earlier definitions of 'deposit' and 'deposit-taking business' set out in ss 5 and 6 of the Banking Act 1987.[3]

'Accepting deposits' is an activity of a specified kind if money received by way of deposit is lent to others or any other activity of the acceptor is financed wholly, or to a material extent, out of the capital of or interest on money received by way of deposit.[4] 'Deposit' means a sum of money paid on terms under which it is to be repaid, with or without interest or premium, and either on demand or at a time or in circumstances agreed by or on behalf of the person making the payment and the person receiving it and which are not referable to the provision of property (other than currency) or services or the giving of securities.[5]

Money is paid on terms which are referable to the provision of property or services or the giving of security if and only if it is paid by way of advance or part payment under a contract for the sale, hire or other provision of property or services and is repayable only in the event that the property or services is or are not in fact sold, hired or otherwise provided.[6] This also includes money paid by way of security for the performance of a contract or by way of security in respect of loss which may result from the non-performance of a contract or is otherwise paid by way of security for the delivery up or return of any property whether in a particular state of repair or otherwise.[7]

A 'deposit' is defined as a specified investment for the purposes of the Act.[8]

1 FSMA 2000, Sch 2, paras 4 and 22.
2 That is, the Financial Services and Markets Act 2000 (Regulated Activities) Order 2001 (SI 2001/544).
3 See Butterworths, *Encyclopaedia of Banking Law* (5 vols, loose leaf), Division A.
4 See Regulated Activities Order, art 5(1)(a) and (b).
5 Regulated Activities Order, art 5(2)(a) and (b).
6 Regulated Activities Order, art 3(a).
7 Regulated Activities Order, art 5(3)(b) and (c).
8 Regulated Activities Order, art 74. 'Deposit' is defined under art 3(1) by reference to art 5. See above.

6.12   A number of further payments are excluded under the Regulated Activities Order. These include sums paid by exempt and other persons including the Bank of England, the central bank of an EEA state or the European Central Bank, another bank or insurance company, a local authority and the main International Financial Institutions.[1] Businesses consisting wholly, or to a significant extent, of the lending money are also excluded[2] as are payments between group companies or close relatives.[3] The Order also excludes sums received by solicitors and persons authorised to deal in investments as well as sums received in consideration for the issue of debt securities.[4]

1 Regulated Activities Order, art 6(1)(a). See para 6.13 below.
2 Regulated Activities Order, art 6(1)(b).
3 Regulated Activities Order, art 6(1)(c) and (d).
4 Regulated Activities Order, arts 7, 8 and 9.

6.13 Under s 22(1) of the FSMA 2000, an activity is only of a 'specified' kind if it is carried on 'by way of business'. The meaning of the reference is set out in the Financial Services and Markets Act 2000 (Carrying on Regulated Activities by Way of Business) Order 2001[1] ('the Business Order'). A person accepting deposits is not to be regarded as doing so 'by way of business' unless he holds himself out as accepting the deposits on a day-to-day basis and provided that he does not only accept them on particular occasions whether or not involving the issue of any securities.[2]

In determining whether deposits are accepted only on particular occasions, regard is to be had to the frequency of those occasions and to any characteristics distinguishing them from each other.[3] These requirements reflect the earlier provisions set out in s 6(2) of the Banking Act 1987. The Business Order also clarifies the application of the Act with regard to investment business and managing investments.

1   SI 2001/1177.
2   Regulated Activities Order, art 2(1)(a) and (b).
3   Regulated Activities Order, art 2(2).

6.14 The list of exempt persons for the purposes of the FSMA 2000 in respect of accepting deposits is now set out in Parts I and II of the Financial Services and Markets Act 2000 (Exemption) Order 2001[1] ('the Exemption Order').

Part I of the Order exempts certain public institutions with regard to any regulated activity other than insurance business. This includes the Bank of England, the central bank of any EEA State and the main International Financial Institutions. Part II exempts certain further bodies from any requirement to be authorised or exempt in connection with the accepting of deposits. This includes a municipal bank, local authority, charity, industrial and provident society and student loan company.

The Exemption Order replaces the earlier regulations issued under s 4(6) of the Banking Act 1987.

1   SI 2001/1201, as amended.

GENERAL SUPERVISORY PRACTICE

6.15 Financial supervision is effected through a number of parallel processes or supervisory mechanisms. Bank supervision has traditionally been conducted through an examination of regular prudential returns and other filings, meetings with bank management, on-site visits and auditor's reports.

The adoption of a specific policy of detailed bank supervision only dates from the early 1970s. Until then the Bank of England had been more concerned with the general stability and efficient operation of the banking and financial markets as a whole. It was only following the Fringe Banking Crisis in 1972/73 that responsibility for supervision was transferred from the Discount Office of the Bank to a new Banking and Money Market Supervision section with increased staff and management involvement.

The range of institutions supervised by the Bank was also extended and new prudential returns introduced. Until then specific bank information was only obtained through the collection of monetary and other statistics and the general review of market operations conducted by the Discount Office depending upon the nature of the institution concerned.

6.16   Supervision was then initially only developed on a non-statutory basis. The statutory basis for banking supervision began with the coming into effect of the Banking Act 1979. This was enacted, in particular, to implement the requirement for the UK to introduce a formal system of bank authorisation under article 3(1) of the European First Banking Directive.[1] The Bank did have a general power to ask banks for information and even to issue directions subject to Treasury approval under s 4(3) of the Bank of England Act 1946. Specific powers in relation to bank supervision were, however, only provided for under the 1979 Act.

Following the Johnson Matthey Bankers crisis in October 1984, it was also decided that more formal powers were required to obtain information from all institutions and not just recognised banks as under the earlier two-tier system set up under the 1979 Act.[2] New powers were also created to require reports by recognised professionals to be prepared on any particular aspect of a bank's business activities. These were generally referred to as 'Section 39 Reports'. The need for sufficient internal control systems was stressed and the use of on-site examinations introduced.

The statutory changes required were given effect to under the Banking Act 1987.[3] These provisions have since been replaced by the new statutory measures and rules that have come into effect under the FSMA 2000.[4]

1   See Council Directive 77/780/EEC of 12 December 1977 on the co-ordination of laws, regulations and administrative provisions relating to the taking-up and pursuit of the business of credit institutions. See also Banking Consolidation Directive, para 2.3.
2   See 'Report of the Committee set up to Consider the System of Banking Supervision', Cmnd 9550, June 1985; and 'Banking Supervision', Cmnd 9695, December 1995.
3   See generally, G Penn, *Banking Supervision* (1989); M Hall, *Handbook of Banking Regulation and Supervision* (1993); C Hadjiemmanuil, *Banking Regulation and the Bank of England* (1996); and R Cranston, *Principles of Banking Law* (1997).
4   See paras 6.26–6.83.

6.17   Much of the former practice with regard to individual bank supervision has been carried forward into the new regime set up under the FSMA 2000.

The FSA is given a general rule-making power under s 138. It is also given revised powers to obtain information and conduct investigations. This includes a general power to require information,[1] commission reports by skilled persons,[2] appoint investigators[3] as well as conduct investigations in support of overseas regulators.[4] The Act also contains further provisions with regard to disciplinary measures,[5] injunctions and restitution,[6] warning, decision and final notices[7] and offences.[8]

The effect of these measures is to create a new statutory framework within which supervision is conducted. Traditional bank supervisory practice has nevertheless been continued insofar as possible within this new regulatory structure.

At this stage, supervision accordingly generally remains to be conducted on the basis of regular returns, management meetings, on-site visits and the commissioning of special reports. This is now supported by the new enhanced enforcement regime in place and will be conducted within the scope of the larger new operating framework currently under construction.[9]

1   FSMA 2000, s 165.
2   FSMA 2000, s 166.
3   FSMA 2000, ss 167 and 168.
4   FSMA 2000, s 169. See Chapter 2, paras 2.71–2.104.
5   FSMA 2000, Pt XIV.
6   FSMA 2000, Pt XXV.

7   FSMA 2000, Pt XXVI.
8   FSMA 2000, Pt XXVII.
9   See paras 6.83–6.100.

6.18   With regard to enforcement, the FSA is given a range of powers under the FSMA 2000. These include imposing prohibitions or restrictions on permitted activities or withdrawing authorisation. The FSA may object to controllers and intervene in connection with EEA or Treaty firms. It may issue private warning or public censure notices and financial penalties. It also has authority to apply for injunctions and restitution or commence or otherwise participate in insolvency proceedings.[1]

All of these powers are exercised in support of the general system of supervision maintained in the UK. While the objective is to ensure that this operates in an effective manner, the general principles on which this has traditionally been based appear to have been fully retained. Bank supervision essentially continues to be conducted on the basis of management responsibility and contact as well as individual supervisory judgment.

The only significant possible change to note in this regard is with regard to the further strengthening of internal management responsibility created under the new regime. One of the stated objectives of the new regulatory system has been to increase the transparency of the management function and importance of management accountability and liability within regulated firms. This has, in particular, been secured through the creation of a separate approved persons regime under the FSMA 2000[2] and the imposition of a number of express requirements on managers through the General Standards contained in the Handbook. This includes general high level principles on businesses (PRIN) and further systems and control requirements (SYSC).[3] The purpose of these provisions is generally to increase management accountability under the threat of enhanced potential management liability.

While much of the attention surrounding the more general design issues that arose with the new regime focused on the rules rather than statutory based nature of the requirements to be imposed, of possibly equal significance has been the shift from external institutional supervision to internal management based compliance and liability. Rather than revise existing bank supervisory practice, however, this can be regarded as simply enhancing or strengthening the continued importance of the management function within regulated institutions and the importance of the close relationship that must exist between management and the supervisory personnel at the FSA.

1   See Chapter 2, paras 2.64–2.68.
2   See Chapter 5.
3   See Chapter 2, paras 2.94–2.99.

6.19   Banking supervision has accordingly then been conducted on the general basis of the examination of regular prudential filings supplemented by management meetings and on-site inspections.[1] This was given statutory effect under both the Banking Acts 1979 and 1987. While this now operates within a more formal rules based framework and is supported by the enhanced enforcement powers available to the FSA, earlier practice has generally been continued under the FSMA 2000.[2] This will be reviewed by the bank supervisory staff within the FSA and will, in particular, have to be reconsidered further as part of the larger new operating framework being constructed,[3] although it is expected that many of the basic operations involved will remain the same.

1   See Blair et al (2nd edn), paras 4.11–4.23.
2   See paras 6.5, 6.10 and 6.26–6.83
3   See paras 6.84–6.100.

FSA HANDBOOK OF RULES AND GUIDANCE

6.20   The FSA initially conducted bank supervision on the basis of the authority transferred by the Bank of England Act 1998. Since N2, this is now carried out under the FSMA 2000.[1] This has created the new statutory framework for banking and all other regulated activities in the UK based on the core prohibition set out in s 19(1) and requirement for permission in s 20(1).[2] The manner in which the powers conferred under the Act are exercised are developed in the Handbook of Rules and Guidance issued under ss 138 and 157.[3] This includes the High Level Standards, the Business Standards, Regulatory Processes, Redress and the Specialist Sourcebooks. Block 3 Regulatory Processes, in particular, consists of the Authorisation manual (AUTH), the Supervision manual (SUP) and the Enforcement manual (ENF) as well as the Decision Making manual (DEC) which was added at a later stage in the drafting process. The Supervision manual sets out the rules and guidance that apply to the conduct of the continuing supervision of all regulated firms within the UK.[4] This gives effect to the requirements set out in the Act at the same time as carrying forward most of the earlier practices developed by each of the former regulatory authorities.

1   See para 6.5.
2   See Chapter 2, paras 2.54–2.60.
3   See Chapter 2, paras 2.83–2.146. See Table 2.1.
4   See paras 6.26–6.83.

6.21   The original draft text of the Supervision manual was published for consultation in August 2000 with separate provisions on controlled functions being issued in June 2000.[1] Earlier related papers had been published on lead supervision, approved persons, guidance and waivers, the permission regime and the regulation of professional firms.[2] The FSA's statement with regard to setting prudential standards also formed part of the consultation process.[3] The approved persons rules on controlled functions were then published in February 2001[4] with most of the manual being issued as final text in May 2001.[5] The detailed proposals with regard to the supervision of authorised firms was set out in the FSA's August 2000 Consultation Paper 64 as subsequently amended.[6]

1   See FSA, *The Supervision Manual* (August 2000), CP 64; and FSA, *The Regulation of Approved Persons: Controlled Functions* (June 2000), CP 53.
2   See FSA, *The FSA's new approach to the co-ordination of its supervision of groups* (June 1999), Information Guide; FSA, *The Regulation of Approved Persons* (July 1999), CP 26 and (June 2000), Response Statement; FSA, *The FSA's approach to giving guidance and waivers to firms* (September 1999), Policy Statement; FSA, *The Permission Regime* (October 1999), CP 29 and (August 2000), Response Statement; and FSA, *The FSA's regulation of professional firms* (October 1999), CP 30 and (June 2000), Response Statement.
3   See FSA, *The FSA's approach to setting prudential standards* (November 1999), CP 31 and (May 2000), Response Statement.
4   See FSA, *The Regulation of Approved Persons: Controlled Functions* (February 2001), Policy Statement.
5   See FSA, *The Regulatory Processes Manuals and Threshold Conditions* (May 2001), Policy Statement.

The Supervision manual

6.22 The objective of the Supervision manual is to construct an integrated approach with regard to the supervision of regulated firms and give effect to the requirements and processes set out in the FSMA 2000. The FSA intended only to produce an interim manual initially with further sections being added at later stages. These would, in particular, reflect developments in the scope of FSA supervision such as with regard to credit unions and mortgage lending as well as to reflect the evolving new regulatory approach being developed.[1] The basic text is, however, substantially complete.

The Supervision manual consists of both rules and guidance. This is distinct from the Authorisation and Enforcement manuals which mainly consist of only guidance.[2]

The reason for the inclusion of rules within the Supervision manual is to allow the FSA to secure its regulatory objectives under the FSMA 2000 as well as fulfil its specific statutory duty to maintain appropriate monitoring and enforcement procedures. Under Sch 1 (para 6(1)), the FSA is required to maintain arrangements designed to enable it to determine whether persons on whom requirements are imposed by or under the Act are complying with them. The FSA must also maintain arrangements for enforcing any provisions set out in the Act or issued under it (para 6(3)).

1 See FSA, *A new regulator for the new millennium* (January 2000). See paras 6.84–6.100.
2 See Chapter 2, paras 2.121–2.122 and 2.125–2.126.

6.23 The general purpose of the Supervision manual is to set out the main elements concerning the FSA's relationship with firms following authorisation. The manual contains material on approach to monitoring and use of regulatory tools, requirements and procedures for dealing with changes in circumstances and information obligations.

With regard to approach, the manual explains risk-based supervision and how the FSA's approach will vary with regard to both the type of firm and individual assessed. This material is generally descriptive and in the form of guidance. The change of circumstances sections are generally concerned with adjustments to the scope of business, rules, waivers or changes in shareholders and controllers. This includes some rules although it is mainly in the form of guidance.

The information requirements are designed to allow the FSA to discharge its monitoring functions. These include financial information reporting and transaction reporting for certain firms. This is made up of both rules and guidance.[1]

The manual also deals with the role and obligations of auditors of authorised firms and actuaries in relation to insurance companies and friendly societies. It is expected that these provisions will be further revised as the FSA develops its new regulatory approach and operating framework.[2]

1 See CP 64, para 3.5.
2 See paras 6.84–6.100. See also www.fsa.gov.uk.

6.24 The structure or content of the Supervision manual may appear to be somewhat unordered on an initial examination. Although information gathering is dealt with after supervisory approach, reporting and transaction reporting is postponed until the end of the Block. Auditors and actuaries are dealt with before approved persons, controllers and appointed representatives with variations, individual requirements and waivers being dealt with in between.

Despite this, the structure is possibly best understood in terms of a supervisory or operational chronology. It must also be stressed that many of the core aspects of general supervisory practice are dealt with in the early sections and then cross-referred to the later more detailed discussions.

The content of the Supervision manual can then most simply be explained in terms of general approach, designated functions, information and reporting, revisions and concessions and special parties.

The manual initially considers the FSA's general approach to supervision (SUP 1). This refers to the FSA's new risk-based approach to supervision based on impact and probability factors. This is nevertheless still sufficiently general at this stage to allow the maintenance of the existing specific sector approaches including bank RATE. This will be revised further over time with the evolution of the FSA's new approach.

In terms of designated functions, the Supervision manual contains further provisions with regard to auditors (SUP 3) and actuaries (SUP 4) as well as reports by skilled persons (SUP 5).

General information collection and reporting is dealt with through information gathering (SUP 2), notifications (SUP 15), reporting requirements (SUP 16), transaction reporting (SUP 17) as well as the skilled persons reports referred to (SUP 5).

Revisions and concessions are dealt with through applications for Part IV permission variation or cancellation (SUP 6), individual requirements (SUP 7), waiver and modification (SUP 8) and individual guidance (SUP 9).

Special parties are then considered under the sections on approved persons (SUP 10), controllers and close links (SUP 11), appointed representatives (SUP 12), passport rights and incoming EEA firms (SUP 13 and 14) as well business transfers (SUP 18) and Commodity Futures Trading Commission Part 30 exemption (SUP 19).

Each of these subsections is considered further below.[1]

1 See paras 6.26–6.83.

The Authorisation, Supervision and Enforcement manuals

6.25   With regard to the relationship between the separate Authorisation, Supervision and Enforcement manuals, the FSA has explained this in terms of their different target audiences.[1]

The Authorisation manual (AUTH) is directed mainly at applicants for permission, persons seeking automatic authorisation or approval under the Act and those considering whether authorisation is necessary. The Supervision manual (SUP) is written for authorised firms although certain provisions are also relevant to approved persons, auditors and actuaries, and potential controllers. The Enforcement manual (ENF) is then directed at those subject to FSA investigation and enforcement. This will principally include authorised firms and approved persons although the criminal prosecution and powers with regard to market abuse will extend against unauthorised persons.

This then reflects the general chronology of market entry, ongoing conduct of business and continuing compliance. Overlapping material is generally dealt with through cross-referencing between the manuals.

1 See CP 64, para 3.9.

THE SUPERVISION MANUAL (SUP)

6.26 The main sections of the Supervision manual[1] were made by the FSA Board on 21 June 2001.[2] Additional transitional provisions were made on 19 July 2001 with the main residual sections being made on 20 September 2001 subject to certain amendments.[3] Some further amendments were made on 18 October 2001 and 15 November 2001.[4] The original draft text had been published in August 2000 with Consultation Paper 64.[5]

The success of the manual has been in consolidating all of the necessary techniques for the effective supervision of all financial firms including banks within a single set of provisions. This will be revised further as the scope of authority of the FSA is extended such as with regard to credit unions although all of the basic operational mechanisms required are already present.

1 See Table 6.1.
2 This included SUP 1 to 4, SUP 6 to 12, SUP 15 to 17 and SUP 19.
3 This included SUP 5, SUP 13, SUP 14 and SUP 15.8.
4 See generally, FSA, *Handbook Notice 1* (July 2001), *Handbook Notice 2* (August 2001), *Handbook Notice 3* (20 September 2001), *Handbook Notice 4* (18 October 2001) and *Handbook Notice 5* (15 November 2001). See also later Handbook Notices available on www.fsa.gov.uk.
5 See FSA, *The Supervision Manual* (August 2000), CP 64; and *Draft Manual* (CP 64a).

6.27 The transitional provisions for the Supervision manual are set out at the beginning (SUP TP1). The main provisions contained in the manual are as follows:

General approach to supervision (SUP 1)

6.28 SUP sets out the relationship between the FSA and authorised persons. This generally relates to material of a continuing post-authorisation nature. ('Authorised persons' are referred to as firms for the purposes of the Handbook.[1]) SUP is issued in implementation of the FSA's requirement to maintain arrangements to ensure compliance with obligations imposed under the FSMA 2000.[2] The design of these supervisory arrangements is then governed by the FSA's regulatory objectives and principles of good regulation.[3]

1 SUP 1 G1.2.1(3).
2 FSMA 2000, Sch 1, para 6(1); SUP 1 G1.1.2.
3 SUP 1 G1.1.3 and 1.1.4. See Chapter 2, paras 2.16–2.21.

Table 6.1: Supervision manual (SUP)

Contents

Transitional provisions

Risk-based supervision

6.29   The purpose of adopting a risk-based approach to supervision is to focus resources on the control or mitigation of risks to the regulatory objectives and to ensure that this is achieved in the most efficient and economic manner possible.[1] The approach is based on the extent to which activities create risks to the regulatory objectives which depends on their impact and probability.[2] This generally continues the earlier Bank of England work carried in constructing the RATE framework but extended to apply to the more general statutory objectives set for the FSA under the Act.[3]

1   SUP 1 G1.3.1. See Blair et al (2nd edn), paras 4.35–4.39.
2   See paras 6.89–6.100.
3   See Blair et al (2nd edn), paras 4.40–4.71.

6.30   The FSA applies a standard risk assessment process to all of its activities. This involves assessing the risk created by a firm against a number of impact and probability factors on an initial and ongoing basis.[1] The impact is assessed by reference to a range of factors derived from the regulatory objectives including, in particular, the degree to which the risk would damage the relevant objectives.[2] Probability is considered in terms of discrete risk groups assessed having regard to the firm's strategy, business risk, financial soundness, nature of customers and products or services, internal systems and controls and compliance culture as well as organisation. Impact and probability assessments are combined to determine necessary priority for the FSA and the nature of the relationship that the FSA will establish with the particular firm.[3]

The choice of supervisory approach and activities is also determined by the degree of confidence in the information available, quality of the home regulatory regime for overseas firms and any anticipated material change in the impact and probability factors.[4] The standard risk assessment process is applied to all firms although the detail required will vary between them.[5] Firms considered to have a high possible impact will require more detailed assessments. Consistency is ensured through a peer review process. This is carried out through a preliminary assessment of potential impact; a probability assessment (depending on impact rating and complexity); peer review by a validation panel (of risk grading and resource allocation); letter to firm detailing assessment and remedial action required and continuing review as necessary.[6]

1   SUP 1 G1.3.2.
2   SUP 1.3.39.
3   SUP 1.3.4 and 1.3. 5. See also FSA, *A new regulator for the new millennium* (January 2000), paras 25–36; and FSA, *Building the new regulator* (December 2000) Progress Report 1, chs 2 and 3.
4   SUP 1 G1.3.6.
5   SUP 1 G1.3.7.
6   SUP 1 G1.3.8.

6.31   The nature of the FSA's relationship with firms is then dependent on the risk categorisation assigned and the particular circumstances such as whether the firm is applying for permission or is currently being investigated by the FSA.[1] The FSA will have to determine satisfaction with threshold conditions on application. Baseline monitoring has to be conducted to ensure that firms comply with regulatory requirements on a continuing basis.[2] Sectoral reviews and thematic work may have to be carried out to validate information and collect up-to-date data. Specific programmes may then be applied to particular firms. Further corrective or response work may also be undertaken after particular risks have escalated or crystallised.

1   See paras 6.97–6.98 below.
2   SUP 1 G1.3.11.

Supervisory tools

6.32   The FSA has identified a range of supervisory tools available to secure its regulatory objectives. These are generally classified as being diagnostic (to identify, assess and measure risks); monitoring (to follow the development of identified risks); preventative (to limit or reduce identified risk and prevent them increasing or crystallising); and remedial (to respond to risk that have crystallised).[1] These are generally then identification (diagnostic and monitoring), preventative and corrective in nature.

Tools may, of course, serve more than one purpose and may be used either for general information dissemination or educational purposes or as part of a direct relationship with a particular firm. Compliance may be secured, for example, through desk-based reviews, liaison with other agencies or regulators, meetings with management and other representatives of a firm, on-site inspections, review and analysis of period returns and notifications, *pass* business reviews, transaction monitoring, use of auditors and skilled persons. Specific risks may also be dealt with through preventative or remedial recommendation, individual guidance or requirements or varying permission in some other way.[2]

The effect of these provisions is to incorporate some of the main elements of bank RATE into the new operating framework although the specific underlying regulatory obligations imposed and statutory basis for the supporting enforcement powers have, of course, changed.[3]

1 SUP 1 G1.4.2.
2 SUP 1 G2.4.3–1.4.6.
3 See Blair et al (2nd edn), paras 4.52–4.67, 4.68–4.69 and 4.70.

Lead supervision

6.33 Lead supervision applies where firms are members of a larger group with more than one supervisory contact at the FSA. Lead supervision is designed to secure a co-ordinated approach to the supervision of groups. This should achieve more efficient and effective supervision of both individual firms and the group as a whole.[1] This operates through the appointment of a lead supervisor for the group based on the predominant business of the group. The functions of the lead supervisor are to produce an overall assessment of the group, co-ordinate the supervision programme and act as a central contact point. Lead supervision had been developed at the international level in response to the difficulties that had arisen in establishing effective mechanisms for the monitoring of activities of cross-border groups. A college system had been adopted in response to BCCI. The possible adoption of lead regulation was considered at the 1996 G7 Summit in Lyons in light of the deficiency that arose with college supervision. The objective was to appoint a single national authority to co-ordinate the activities of all others involved and to ensure that proper information was being properly collected and distributed. The idea had originally been proposed by the British Government. Although it was supported by a number of countries, others had expressed certain reservations. Certain US agencies were, in particular, concerned that they could not be party to any formal allocation (surrender) of function beyond improved information exchange. Lead supervision was nevertheless maintained at the national level within the UK as a co-ordination device between all of the separate authorities involved with the supervision of a large complex group. This has since been continued as an internal (rather than external) arrangement within the FSA following its formal assumption of authority across all financial sectors.

1 SUP 1 G1.5.2. On the nature of lead supervision generally, see GA Walker, 'Conglomerate Law and International Financial Market Supervision', *Boston University Annual Review of Banking Law* (1998, Vol 17: 287); and 'Lead Regulation and International Financial Market Supervision', ch 4 of Walker, *International Banking Regulation Law, Policy and Practice* (2001).

Information (SUP 2)

6.34 SUP sets out the FSA's rules and guidance on the collection of information from firms for supervisory purposes. This explains how firms should co-operate with the FSA to enable it to discharge its responsibilities to monitor compliance. The FSA has noted that each of the main financial sectors were formerly supervised in different ways. Banking supervision, in particular, has generally been conducted through meetings, visits and commissioned reports from reporting accountants.[1] The approach proposed did not envisage any material changes to the current practice[2] and the core elements of traditional UK banking supervision have accordingly been continued in effect.

1 See Blair et al (2nd edn), paras 4.11–4.23.
2 See Consultation Paper 64, paras 4.4 and 4.6.

6.35 SUP 2 is issued under the FSA's requirement to ensure compliance[1] and its obligation to co-operate with other regulators.[2] Part XI of the Act (Information Gathering and Investigations) also gives the FSA statutory powers to require information,[3] commission reports from skilled persons,[4] appoint investigators[5] and apply for warrants to enter premises.[6] Principle 11 of the Principles for Business (PRIN) also requires firms to deal with regulators in an open and co-operative way and disclose to the FSA appropriately anything relating to the firm to which the FSA would reasonably expect notice. Principle 11 is, in particular, developed through SUP 2.2 and 2.3.

1 FSMA 2000, Sch 1, para 6(1).
2 FSMA 2000, s 354.
3 FSMA 2000, s 165; and ENF 2.
4 FSMA 2000, s 166; and SUP 5.
5 FSMA 2000, ss 167, 168 and 169; and ENF 2.
6 FSMA 2000, s 176; and ENF 2.

6.36 The FSA may obtain information in co-operation with firms either through visits, meetings at the FSA's officers or elsewhere or request information or documents by telephone, during meetings or in writing including by electronic communication.[1] Meetings or access to business premises will only be requested during reasonable business hours and subject to reasonable notice. The FSA expects firms to make themselves readily available for meetings and provide FSA representatives or appointees reasonable access to any records, files, tapes or computer systems or facilities which may be reasonably requested.[2] The FSA also expects firms to produce any specified material as reasonably requested, print information in the firm's possession or control, permit the copying of documents or other material and answer truthfully, fully and promptly all reasonable questions or enquiries.[3]

1 SUP 2, G2.3.1.
2 SUP 2, G2.3.3(1) and (2).
3 SUP 2, G2.3.3(3), (4), (5) and (6).

6.37 A firm must permit representatives of the FSA or its agents to access, with or without notice, during reasonable business hours to any of its business premises in relation to the discharge of its functions under the Act. A firm must also take reasonable steps to ensure that its agents, suppliers under material outsourcing arrangements and appointed representatives permit such access to the business premises.[1] Reasonable notice will generally be provided. A firm must also take reasonable steps to ensure that each of its suppliers under material outsourcing arrangements deals in an open and co-operative way with the FSA in the discharge of its functions.[2] The FSA will generally only seek information from the firm although it reserves the right to approach the supplier under a material outsourcing arrangement if considered appropriate.[3]

1 SUP 2, R2.3.5(1) and (2).

2   SUP 2, R2.3.7.
3   SUP 2, G2.3.10.

6.38   The FSA may ask a firm to provide information on behalf of another regulator including the Takeover Panel or an overseas authority to assist it discharge its functions. The FSA may disclose information already in its possession subject to the banking confidentiality and legal privilege. As noted, the FSA has a statutory right to obtain information under s 169 of the FSMA 2000 and to appoint investigators for overseas regulators if required (ENF 2).

6.39   Breach of Principle 11 or SUP 2 makes a firm liable to regulatory sanctions including discipline under Part XIV (Disciplinary Measures) and subject the firm to information gathering and investigation. A breach is not a criminal offence nor contempt.[1] The information gathering provisions are subject to bank confidentiality[2] subject to the exceptions listed and protected items.[3] On receipt of confidential information, the FSA is subject to the obligation of no further disclosure under the Act[4] unless a permitted exception or consent applies.[5] Information obtained by the FSA in a permitted manner may be admissible in evidence in any proceedings.[6] Compliance should be facilitated by all employees, agents and appointed representatives as well as any other members of the relevant group and their employees or agents.

1   FSMA 2000, s 177.
2   FSMA 2000, s 175(5).
3   FSMA 2000, s 413.
4   FSMA 2000, s 348(1).
5   See FSMA 2000, s 349(1)(a) (public function) and (b) permitted by the Financial Services and Markets Act 2000 (Disclosure of Confidential Information) Regulations 2001 (SI 2001/2188). These generally replicate in the banking area the former provisions set out Pt 4 (Restriction on Disclosure of Information) of the Banking Act 1987.
6   SUP 2, G2.2.1–2.2.5.

6.40   Under SUP 2, the FSA may carry out 'mystery shopping' with other programmes or focused visits to obtain information concerning suspected practices and in so doing use recording devices, telephonic or other communications.[1] 'Mystery shopping' involves approaching firms, their agents or appointed representatives as potential retail customers. This is used to protect consumers by ensuring that they are sold appropriate products and services.[2]

1   SUP 2, G2.4.3.
2   SUP 2, G2.4.2.

Auditors (SUP 3)

6.41   SUP 3 develops the role of auditors in supporting the FSA's supervision of firms. It contains appointment rules (SUP 3.3.), minimum qualifications (SUP 3.4) and the rights and duties of auditors (SUP 3.5–3.10). This chapter contains both rules and guidance.

6.42   The statutory basis for the FSA's powers is Part XXII (ss 340–346) of the FSMA 2000. The FSA may require a firm to appoint an auditor if is not already under an obligation to do so under the Act.[1] The FSA may issue rules requiring an authorised person to produce periodic financial reports and have them reported on by an auditor.[2] The rules may impose such duties on auditors as may be specified.[3] The rules may also specify the manner and time of the appointment, require notification, allow the FSA to make the appointment and make provision for remuneration and the terms of office, removal and resignation.[4] The FSA may disqualify auditors where they have failed to comply with any duty imposed under the Act.[5] It is an offence to provide false or misleading information to an auditor.[6]

1   FSMA 2000, s 340(1).
2   FSMA 2000, s 340(2).
3   FSMA 2000, s 340(3).
4   FSMA 2000, s 340(4).
5   FSMA 2000, s 345(1).
6   FSMA 2000, s 346.

6.43   Auditors are provided with a statutory right of access to books, accounts and vouchers and require any information and explanation as may be required.[1] The auditor is also given statutory immunity to inform the FSA of any matters or opinion given in good faith and reasonably believed to be relevant to any of the FSA's functions.[2] This right is extended to apply to close links.[3] The circumstances in which auditors must communicate matters to the FSA are set out in Treasury Regulations.[4] Auditors must also notify the FSA where they have been removed from office, resigned before the expiry of term or are not reappointed.[5]

1   FSMA 2000, s 341(1).
2   FSMA 2000, s 342(3)(a) and (b).
3   FSMA 2000, s 343.
4   FSMA 2000, s 342(5).
5   FSMA 2000, s 344.

6.44   The FSA has confirmed that it intends to continue to use auditors in a manner substantially unchanged from previous sector practices with regard to reporting responsibilities[1] although some harmonisation has been effected especially with regard to appointment and notification requirements and amendments to reflect the new common statutory base.

1   Consultation Paper 64, para 4.13.

6.45   The application of SUP 3 varies depending on the category of firm. Banks are subject to SUP 3.1 (Application), SUP 3.2 (Purpose), SUP 3.3 (Appointment of auditors), SUP 3.4 (Auditors' qualifications), SUP 3.5 (Auditors' independence), SUP 3.6 (Firms' co-operation with their auditors) and SUP 3.7 (Notification of matters raised by auditor). Bank auditors are then subject to SUP 3.1 (Application), SUP 3.2 (Purpose) and SUP 3.8 (Rights and duties of auditors).

SUP 3.8, in particular, requires that auditors co-operate with the FSA in the discharge of its functions under the Act,[1] give any skilled person appointed by the firm all assistance reasonably required,[2] be independent of the firm in performing its duties,[3] take reasonable steps to satisfy itself that it is free from any conflict of interest in respect of the firm from which bias may reasonable be inferred,[4] notify the FSA without delay of removal, resignation before term or non-reappointment[5] and (in the event of termination of appointment) notify the FSA without delay of any matter which ought to be draw to its attention (or that there is no such matter).[6]

1   SUP 3, R3.8.2.
2   SUP 3, R3.8.4.
3   SUP 3, R3.8.5.
4   SUP 3, R3.8.6.
5   SUP 3, R3.8.11.
6   SUP 3, R3.8.12.

Actuaries (SUP 4)

6.46   The statutory provisions set out in Part XXII generally apply equally to actuaries. The rules and guidance relating to the role of an appointed or appropriate actuary are developed in SUP 4. These generally only apply to insurers or friendly societies that carry on long-term insurance business.

Skilled persons reports (SUP 5)

6.47   The earlier Section 39 Reports under the Banking Act 1987[1] have been replaced by new skilled persons reports issued under Part XI of the FSMA 2000. The FSA may by notice in writing require a report to be provided on any matter reasonably required in connection with the exercise of its functions under the Act.[2] Such reports may be requested from any authorised person, member of the firm's group, a partnership of which it is a member or any such person provided that it was carrying on business at the relevant time.[3] The report may be in such form as may be specified in the notice[4] and will be conducted by a person nominated or approved by the FSA having the necessary skills to make the report.[5] Such reports were formerly carried out by lawyers, accountants or persons with similar expert skills. The purpose of these provisions is to replace the former separate sets of rules providing for the appointment of reporting accountants under varies statutes including, in particular, reports under s 39 of the Banking Act 1987. No major changes are proposed to the use of reporting accountants.[6] The FSA has only indicated that the former practice of preparing full scope reports every year on the adequacy of systems and controls under s 82 of the Building Societies Act 1986 would be drawn into line with equivalent bank practice.[7] Practice in this area would then be further reviewed in light of the FSA's development of its new regulatory approach.

1   See Blair et al (2nd edn), paras 4.19–4.23.
2   FSMA 2000, s 166(1).
3   FSMA 2000, s 166(2).
4   FSMA 2000, s 166(3).
5   FSMA 2000, s 166(4)(a) and (b).
6   Consultation Paper 64, para 4.39.
7   See FSA, *The Interim Prudential Sourcebook for Building Societies* (June 2000), Consultation Paper 51; and FSA, *The Interim Prudential Sourcebook for Banks* (June 2000), Consultation Paper 52.

6.48   The FSA's rules and guidance in connection with reports by skilled persons are developed in SUP 5. The chapter applies to every firm.[1] The provisions apply to the persons set out in s 166 of the FSMA 2000 (firms, group members and partnerships).[2] Reports may either be commissioned for diagnostic or reporting, preventative or remedial purposes.[3] This will generally be prompted by a specific requirement for information, analysis of informa-

tion, assessment of a situation or provision of expert advice or recommendation. Reports will generally be requested for verification purposes or as part of
a risk mitigation programme or in response to a specific event or development.
The appointment and reporting process is set out in SUP 5.4. This is
summarised in SUP 5 Annex 2. The duties of firms to co-operate with a skilled
person are set out in SUP 5.5. SUP 5.6 then contains further provision with
regard to confidential information and legal privilege.

1 SUP 5, R5.1.1.
2 SUP 5, G5.2.1.
3 SUP 5, G5.3.1.

Part IV permission variation or cancellation (SUP 6)

6.49 SUP 6 contains guidance on Part IV of the Act and the FSA's powers
with regard to variation and cancellation of permission. Further guidance is
provided with regard to ending authorisation and on the form and content of
applications. Revocation and restriction of banking authorisation was previously dealt with under ss 11 and 12 of the Banking Act 1987.[1] The general
objective of SUP 6 is to consider each application for variation or cancellation
on an individual basis with the relevant information with regard to the specific
firm being required in each case. Firms will hold single Part IV permission
although the permission will specify the activities the firm is entitled to carry
on, the investment covered and any relevant requirements.[2] Applications for
Part IV permission are set out in the Authorisation manual.

1 See Blair et al (2nd edn), paras 3.36–3.50.
2 SUP 6 G6.2.1.

6.50 A firm that wishes to amend its Part IV permission may apply for a
variation under s 44(1) of the FSMA 2000. This may apply to the activities or
investments covered or relevant limitations or requirements.[1] A firm wishing to
vary its Part IV permission must apply in writing. Applications are to be dealt
with by the firm's supervision team. Firms wishing to cease to carry on any Part
IV permission activity can apply for cancellation under s 44(2).[2] Cancellation
relates to the whole of Part IV permission and cannot only relate to specific
elements. If the Part IV permission is cancelled, the status of the firm as an
authorised person will also be removed. If a firm wishes to have its status
terminated, it would normally apply for a cancellation of the Part IV
permission.[3] The FSA may refuse an application for cancellation where the
interests of consumers or potential consumers may be adversely affected or it
would otherwise be desirable in their interests for the application to be
refused.[4]

1 SUP 6 G6.2.3 and SUP G6.3.1.
2 SUP 6 G6.4.1.
3 See Consultation Paper 64, paras 4.48 and 4.49.
4 FSMA 2000, s 44(4); SUP 6 G6.4.2.

6.51 SUP 6 specifies its application (SUP 6.1) and introduces the relevant
statutory provisions (SUP 6.2). Guidance is provided with regard to applications for a variation (SUP 6.3) and cancellation (SUP 6.4) as well as ending
authorisation (SUP 6.5). The procedure for applying for a variation or

cancellation is summarised in SUP 6 Annexes 1, 2 and 3. Additional guidance on firms winding down their business is set out in SUP 6 Annex 4.

Individual requirements (SUP 7)

6.52 The FSA may place requirements on a firm's permission under FSMA 2000, s 45. Guidance on the exercise of this power is provided under SUP 7.[1] Waivers or modification of specific rules is considered under SUP 8 and individual guidance under SUP 9. Specific requirements may be imposed where a firm is not fully complying with a specific requirement such as with regard to systems and controls or where a firm is exposed to specific risks that are not fully dealt with under the FSA's rules and guidance.[2] The FSA will continue as a matter of general practice to set variable minimum capital ratios for banks and building societies under this power. This will be subject to further review with the development of the Integrated Prudential Sourcebook (PSB).[3] The FSA may also use its powers under s 45 for enforcement purposes.[4] The FSA will generally act by issuing a supervisory notice under DEC 3.[5] Criteria for varying a firm's permission are set out in SUP 7.3.

1 See SUP 7 G7.2.1 and 7.2.2.
2 Consultation Paper 64, para 4.58.
3 Consultation Paper 64, para 4.59.
4 See SUP 7 G7.2.3 and ENF 3.
5 The procedure is summarised in DEC 3 ANN 2 G.

Waiver and modification of rules (SUP 8)

6.53 Guidance on how firms may apply for a waiver is provided under SUP 8. Waivers are used by the FSA to provide a flexible and differentiated risk based approach to regulation.[1] The application of rules may be modified or waived under s 148 of the Act.[2] The rules that may be waived are listed in s 148(1) of the Act and SUP 8.2.7 G. This includes the auditors and actuaries rules (s 340), financial promotion rules (s 145) and general rules (s 138).

1 Consultation Paper 64, para 4.61. See also FSA, *The FSA's approach to giving guidance and waivers to firms* (September 1999), Policy Statement.
2 Rules may also be waived with regard to collective investment schemes under s 250 of the Act and regulation 7 of the OEIC Regulations.

6.54 Applications for waiver must in writing.[1] Waiver decisions will generally be considered within 20 business days of receipt.[2] Reasons for refusing to issue a waiver will be given.[3] Modifications or conditions may also be used in place of waivers.[4] Waivers may be given with consent following a decision by the FSA to make a waiver available to a particular group or firm.[5] The manual contains further provisions with regard to reliance (SUP 8.4), notification of a change of circumstances (SUP 8.5), publication (SUP 8.6), variations (SUP 8.7), revocation (SUP 8.8) and decision-making (SUP 8.9). The procedure for applying for a waiver is summarised in SUP 8 Annex 1.

1 SUP 8 D8.3.3.
2 SUP 8 G8.3.5.
3 SUP 8 G8.3.7.

4   SUP 8 G8.3.6.
5   SUP 8 G8.3.10.

Individual guidance (SUP 9)

6.55   The FSA may issue individual guidance to a specific firm. This is distinct from general guidance or guidance applicable to a class of regulated persons The statutory basis is s 157(1) of the FSMA 2000. Where general guidance or the guidance relates to a class of regulated persons, the FSA must comply with the consultation requirements set out in s 155 of the Act.[1] The FSA may publish its guidance, offer copies for sale at a reasonable price and make a reasonable charge if the request is from an individual.

1   FSMA 2000, s 157(3).
2   FSMA 2000, s 157(4).

6.56   A person may apply to the FSA for individual guidance as to how rules and general guidance in the Handbook or specific regulatory requirements apply to their particular circumstances.[1] Requests may made in writing or orally.[2] The FSA will generally not consider a request on a 'no name' basis.[3] The guidance may relate, in particular, to the amount or type of financial resources to be maintained by a firm with regard, for example, to individual capital ratios for banks or building societies.[4]

1   SUP 9 G9.1.3.
2   SUP 9 G9.2.1.
3   SUP 9 G9.2.4.
4   SUP 9 G9.3.2(5).

6.57   Where a firm has acted in accordance with the individual guidance given, the person will be considered to have complied with all aspects of the rule or other requirement to which the guidance relates.[1] This is stated only to relate to individual guidance. The Handbook adds, however, that the extent to which a person may rely on individual guidance will depend on a number of factors including the degree of formality of the original enquiry and guidance given and whether all relevant information was submitted.[2] If circumstances change, a person may ask for further guidance.[3]

1   SUP 9 G9.4.1.
2   SUP 9 G9.4.2.
3   SUP 9 G9.4.3.

Approved persons (SUP 10)

6.58   Firms wishing to employ a person to carry out any controlled function must apply for prior approval under Part V of the FSMA 2000. An application must also be made where another control function is to be carried on or the person moves to another firm to carry on the same function or functions. The importance of the approved persons regime is that it effectively creates a parallel authorisation and permission system for individuals in addition to regulated firms. This allows the FSA to obtain specific information to allow it to assess the adequacy and suitability of individuals to carry on specific key functions relating to the interests of potential investors and depositors. This strengthens the earlier registration system established under the Financial Services Act 1986. Assessing individual management suitability is not a new practice in the banking area although the creation of a formalised notification and registration regime is.

6.59 Controlled functions are divided into governing functions, required functions, systems and controls functions, significant management functions and customer functions.[1] Applications for variation or transfer are dealt with by the Individual Vetting and Registration Department of the FSA.

1 See SUP 10 R10.4.5. The FSA, *The Regulation of Approved Persons* (July 1999), Consultation Paper 26; and FSA, *The Regulation of Approved Persons: Controlled Functions* (June 2000), Consultation Paper 54. See also Chapter 3.

6.60 The Supervision manual contains specific rules and guidance with regard to application (SUP 10.1), purpose (SUP 10.2), statutory base (SUP 10.3), specified functions (SUP 10.4) and each of the main functions (SUP 10.5–10.10), procedures and forms (SUP 10.11), applications (SUP 10.12), changes to an approved person's details (SUP 10.13) and frequently asked questions (SUP 10.14 and SUP Annex 1G). The application procedures are summarised in SUP 10 Annex 3G). SUP 10.11 also refers to the relevant forms.[1]

1 Form A: Application to perform controlled functions under the approved persons regime (SUP 10 Annex 4D); Form B: Notice to withdraw an application to perform controlled functions under the approved persons regime (SUP 10 Annex 5R); Form C: Notice of ceasing to perform controlled functions (SUP 10 Annex 5R); Form D: Notification of changes in personal information or application details (SUP 10 Annex 7R); and Form E: Internal transfer of an approved person (SUP 10 Annex 8G).

Controllers and close links (SUP 11)

6.61 Any person proposing to acquire control or increase their level of control over an authorised person must notify the FSA under s 178(1) of the FSMA 2000. This replaces the earlier provisions set out in ss 21–26 of the Banking Act 1987.[1] This again extends the scope of the general suitability assessment applied by the FSA to controllers of regulated firms. The factors relevant in determining whether a person acquires control are listed in s 179(2). A person holds or can exercise or control the exercise of 10% or more of the shares in a company or its parent or exercises significant influence over the management of the company or its parent. The 'acquirer' means the acquirer, any of its associates or the acquirer and any of its associates. Increasing control is dealt with under s 180. This relates to increases between 10% and 20%, 20% and 33%, 33% and 50% and over 50% in either the company or its parent.[2] Control again relates to either holding, exercising or controlling the voting of the relevant shares. Notice must be given to the FSA in writing and contain such information or be accompanied by such documentation as may be reasonably required.[3] The FSA must either approve the acquisition or change in control or serve a warning notice within three months.[4] Approvals must be notified without delay[5] and may be subject to such conditions as may be considered appropriate.[6] Acquirers must generally be fit and proper persons to exercise control and the interests of consumers must not be threatened.[7] The FSA may issue a warning notice and a decision notice if it is not satisfied that the approval requirements referred to have been met.[8] Decision notices may be referred to the Financial Services Tribunal.[9]

1 See Blair et al (2nd edn), paras 3.25–3.29 and 3.40.
2 FSMA 2000, s 180(2).
3 FSMA 2000, s.182(1).
4 FSMA 2000, s 183(1) and (3).
5 FSMA 2000, s 184(1).
6 FSMA 2000, s 185(1).
7 FSMA 2000, s 186(2)(a) and (b).
8 FSMA 2000, ss 187(1) and 188(1).
9 FSMA 2000, s 187(4).

6.62   The FSA may issue a restriction notice where shares have been improperly acquired.[1] This may include a prohibition on transfer, voting, further acquisition or payment. Notice of reductions in control must also be given to the FSA.[2]

1 FSMA 2000, s 189(2).
2 FSMA 2000, s 190(1).

6.63   Guidance with regard to the exercise of the FSA's powers with regard to controllers and close links are set out in SUP 11 (SUP 11.2). The relevant requirements are summarised (SUP 11.3 and 11.4). The form of notification is specified (SUP 11.5) with the subsequent notification requirements (SUP 11.6), approval procedures for acquisition or increase in control (SUP 11.7), changes in circumstances of existing controllers (SUP 11.8) and changes in close links (SUP 11.9). The notification procedures are summarised in SUP 11 Ann 3G.

Appointed representatives (SUP 12)

6.64   The FSA may exempt appointed representatives from the scope of the general prohibition under s 39(1) of the FSMA 2000. Guidance on the operation of s 39 and the rules on appointment, operation and termination of appointed representatives are set out in SUP 12. This replaces the earlier provisions set out in the SIB and SRO rulebooks.[1] SUP was drafted to attempt to preserve the existing rules insofar as possible while removing any minor areas of inconsistency or uncertainty pending further consultation.[2]

1 See Consultation Paper 64, para 4.102.
2 Consultation Paper 64, para 4.106.

6.65   The Supervision manual contains specific provision with regard to a firm responsibility (SUP 12.3), appointment requirements (SUP 12.4), required terms of contracts (SUP 12.5), continuing obligations (SUP 12.6), notification requirements (SUP 12.7), termination of appointment (SUP 12.8) and record keeping (SUP 12.9). Guidance on the assessment on the financial position of an appointed representative and their fitness and proprietary are set out in the annexes (SUP 12 Annex 1 and SUP 12 Annex 2).

6.66   The FSA has announced that the operation of the appointed representative regime will be revised following earlier recommendations by the Director General of Fair Trading with regard to its distortion on competition.

Exercise of passport rights by UK firms (SUP 13)

6.67 Guidance on the exercise of the Sch 3 rights by UK firms to establish a branch or provide cross-border services into another EEA State is provided in SUP 13. This applies both to the establishment of a first branch or first provision of services as well as amending existing details.[1] The chapter applies to UK firms that are authorised persons under the FSMA 2000 as well as wholly owned subsidiaries of credit institutions capable of exercising the right of establishment and services under the Banking Consolidation Directive.[2] SUP 13 replaces the earlier guidance provided in the Statement of Principles formally issued by the Bank of England.[3]

1 SUP 13 G13.1.5 and SUP G13.1.6.
2 SUP 13 G13.2.1.
3 See Blair *et al* (2nd edn), paras 3.9 and 3.31.

6.68 Guidance is provided with regard to the establishment of a branch in another EEA State (SUP 13.3), the provision of cross-border services (SUP 13.4), notices of intention (SUP 13.5), changes to branches (SUP 13.6), changes to cross-border services (SUP 13.7), changes of details (SUP 13.8), application (SUP 13.9), applicable provision (SUP 13.10), record keeping (SUP 13.11) and further information (SUP 13.12). Details of relevant information is set out in the annexes. This includes branch information (SUP 13 Annex 1), branches of insurance undertakings (SUP 13 Annex 2) and cross-border services (SUP Annex 3).

Incoming EEA firms (SUP 14)

6.69 The FSMA provides for automatic authorisation of UK firms and EEA firms under either the financial market directives or the Treaty directly as well as collective investment schemes recognised under the UCITS Directive.[1] The procedures for obtaining automatic authorisation are set out in the Authorisation manual.[2] SUP 13 and SUP 14 generally only deal with notification issues for UK firms and amending information or cancelling qualification for EEA firms. The former legislation implementing the European financial directives was repealed at N2 and replaced by new secondary legislation. The relevant chapters of the Authorisation and Supervision manuals have been prepared to attempt to collate and clarify the guidance relevant across all financial sectors. The chapter design generally follows Schs 3 and 4 of the Act although further guidance is provided in response to industry requests.[3]

1 See Council Directive 85/611 on the co-ordination of laws, regulations and administrative provisions relating to undertakings for collective investment in transferable securities.
2 See Chapter 3.
3 See Consultation Paper 64, paras 4.115, 4.116 and 4.117.

6.70 SUP 14 applies to incoming EEA firms that have already established a branch or are already providing cross-border services into the United Kingdom under one of the European financial directives. The chapter provides guidance for incoming EEA firms that wish to change the details of the branch or services provided or cancel their qualification for authorisation under the Act.[1] Specific guidance is provided with regard to changes to branch details (SUP 14.2) and cross-border services (SUP 14.3), notices

(SUP 14.4), variation of top-up permission (SUP 14.5), cancelling authorisation qualification (SUP 14.6) and top-up permission (SUP 14.7) and further guidance (SUP 14.8).

1 SUP 14 G14.1.1 and SUP 14 G14.1.4.

FSA notifications (SUP 15)

6.71 The Supervision manual contains three chapters concerned with information reporting. General notifications are specified in SUP 15 with general reporting requirements in SUP 16 and transaction reporting for specific firms in SUP 17. The general notification requirements set out in SUP 15 are concerned with identifying particular circumstances or events in which appropriate notifications should be made to the FSA not specifically dealt with under either SUP 16 or SUP 17.

Principle 11 of the Principles for Businesses (PRIN) requires firms to deal with their regulators in an open and co-operative manner and to inform the FSA promptly of anything relating to the firm of which the FSA would reasonably expect prompt notice.[1] The FSA considers that Principle 11 applies to unregulated as well as regulated activities including those relating to other members of a group.[2] The FSA expects to be notified of such matters as any proposed restructuring, reorganisation or business expansion, any significant failure of a firm's systems or controls or any action that would result in a material change in its capital adequacy or solvency position.[3] The FSA, of course, also has general power to gather information and investigation under Part XI of the Act. The FSA may, in particular, require information or documentation to be provided by notice in writing under s 165(1). Part XI is not used as the statutory base of SUP 15 although it is referred to in ENF.

1 See generally, FSA, *The FSA's Principles for Businesses* (September 1998), Consultation Paper 13; and Response Statement (October 1999).
2 SUP 15 G15.3.7.
3 SUP 15 G15.3.8.

6.72 SUP 15 creates a number of new rules with regard to FSA notification. These include any matters having a serious regulatory impact,[1] breaches of rules or any other requirement under the Act,[2] any civil, criminal or disciplinary proceedings against the firm,[3] fraud, errors and other irregularities[4] and of any insolvency, bankruptcy or winding-up.[5] These are important provisions that create a range of new disclosure obligations for firms.

1 SUP 15 R15.3.1.
2 SUP 15 R15.3.11.
3 SUP 15 R15.3.15.
4 SUP 15 R15.3.17.
5 SUP 15 R15.3.21.

6.73 Firms must provide the FSA with reasonable advance notice of certain core information requirements. These include change of name,[1] change in address,[2] change in legal status[3] and changes with regard to supervisory authority.[4]

1 SUP 15 R15.5.1.
2 SUP 15 R15.5.4.

3 SUP 15 R15.5.5.
4 SUP 15 R15.5.7.

6.74 Overseas firms are subject to a 30-day notification requirement. This includes notification of any change of position of the worldwide chief executive, any person with a purely strategic responsibility for UK operations and any two or more persons that effectively direct a bank's business.[1] Such persons would fall outside the scope of the FSA's other reporting requirements. The persons listed are not subject to the Statements of Principles or the Code of Practice for Approved Persons (unless they are also an approved person). Notification is to be made on Form F (SUP 15 Annex 2R).

1 SUP 15 R15.4.1.

6.75 Firms are separately required to take all reasonable steps to ensure that information provided under the Handbook is factually accurate and complete.[1] If a firm becomes aware that it may have provided false, misleading or incomplete or inaccurate information or any information has changed in a material respect, it must notify the FSA immediately.[2] Such notification must include the correct information, failing which it must be submitted as soon as possible thereafter.[3] This prohibition on the provision of inaccurate, false or misleading information is in addition to the general offence created under s 397 of the FSMA 2000 (misleading statements and practices).

1 SUP 15 R15.6.1.
2 SUP 15 R15.6.4.
3 SUP 15 R15.6.5.

6.76 SUP contains further guidance with regard to the form and method of notifications (SUP 15.7). Notification must also be made in respect of particular products and services (SUP 15.8). The application of the rules is adjusted with regard to incoming Treaty firms that do not have a top-up permission (SUP 15 Annex 1).

Reporting requirements (SUP 16)

6.77 Guidance on the requirements that apply with regard to regular reporting to the FSA is set out in SUP 16. As well as containing general provisions on reporting (SUP 16.3), this contains specific guidance concerning annual controllers reports (SUP 16.4) and annual close links reports (SUP 16.5), compliance reports (SUP 16.6) and financial reports (SUP 16.7). Guidance is also provided with regard to insurance companies' persistency reports (SUP 16.8). These amplify Principle 11 and allow the FSA to ensure compliance with the other provisions set out in PRIN.[1] The general objective is to continue existing reporting requirements at this stage except where certain provisions may be harmonised to reduce the reporting burden on financial groups.[2] This may be subject to further review.

1 SUP 16 G16.2.1(2).
2 Consultation Paper 64, para 4.130.

6.78 SUP 16 creates a number of new rules with regard to reporting requirements. Unless a rule states otherwise, a report must be submitted in writing.[1] The report must provide the institutions' FSA firm reference number and where it is submitted in paper form use the required cover sheet (SUP 16 Annex 13R).[2] Written reports must be given or addressed to the firm's usual supervisory contact and delivered by post, hand (with a time-stamped receipt), electronic mail, handed to the usual supervisory contact or fax.[3] Reports must generally be submitted by their due dates or quarter ends calculated having regard to the firms' accounting reference date.[4] Failure to submit a report in accordance with these rules may lead to the imposition of a financial penalty or other disciplinary sanction.[5] Firms must notify the FSA of any changes to its accounting reference date.[6]

1   SUP 16 R16.3.6.
2   SUP 16 R16.3.7.
3   SUP 16 R16.3.9 and SUP 16 R16.3.10.
4   SUP 16 R16.3.13.
5   SUP 16 G16.3.14.
6   SUP 16 R16.3.17.

6.79   Separate rules are imposed with regard to the individual reports listed in SUP 16. Firms must submit an annual controllers report.[1] This must include a list of all controllers as at the firms' accounting reference date and all relevant information as to the identity and holding. Firms must also submit an annual close links report.[2] Where firms are not aware that they have any controllers or close links, this must be specified in the relevant report. Firms must also submit annual or quarterly compliance reports. Banks must, in particular, submit an annual list of all overseas regulators for each legal entity in the firm's group and an organogram showing the authorised entities in the firm's group. These must be submitted six months after the firm's accounting reference date.[3] A UK bank must also submit relevant financial reports either annually, quarterly or half yearly in accordance with the relevant due date.[4]

Forms BSD3, LR, SLR1, B7 and M1 are to be submitted to the Financial Statistics Division Domestic Banking Group (HO-4) of the Bank of England. All other reports are to be sent to the bank's usual supervisory contact at the FSA.[5]

Bank of England submissions may either be made on paper or in an electronic format.[6] Electronic submissions may be made by AT&T Global Network, by email (to mfsd_beers@bose.co.uk) or on disk. Separate provisions apply with regard to EEA banks[7] and to building societies, service companies, securities and future firms, investment management firms, personal investment firms, authorised professional firms and Society of Lloyd's.[8] Certain additional requirements are imposed under the Annexes.[9]

1   SUP 16 R16.4.5.
2   SUP 16 R16.5.4.
3   SUP 16 R16.6.4 and SUP 16 R16.6.5.
4   SUP 16 R16.7.7. See Blair *et al* (2nd edn), paras 4.14–4.15.
5   SUP 16 R16.7.13.
6   SUP 16 R16.7.15.
7   SUP 16 R16.7.9 and SUP 16 R16.7.11.
8   SUP 16 R16.7.16 and SUP 16 R16.7.19, R16.7.20, R16.7.22, R16.7.23–R16.7.33, R16.7.35–R16.7.41, R16.7.43–R16.7.51, R16.7.54 and R16.7.55–R16.7.59.
9   SUP 16 Annex 1 (Section 5: Personal investment firms requirements applying to the completion of reports); SUP 16 Annex 2 (Section 6: Securities and futures firms form and content of reports); and SUP 16 Annex 3 (Reports from trustees of AUTs and depositories of ICVCs).

Transaction Reporting (SUP 17)

6.80   Certain firms are required to submit reports on their transactions concerning securities and related derivatives. These were formerly imposed under the rules of SFA, PIA and IMRO. These generally corresponded with the provisions imposed under article 20 of the Investment Services Directive. Under the interim arrangements set out in SUP 17, the former transaction reporting rules imposed under the FSA, PIA and IMRO have generally been continued pending further review.

6.81   SUP 17 contains rules and guidance in connection with the operation of these provisions. This includes a general obligation to make a transaction report subject to certain exemptions (SUP 17.4). Reportable transactions are specified (SUP 17.5) with the required transaction reports (SUP 17.6) and method of reporting (SUP 17.7). Relevant exchanges, mandatory fields for reporting systems, the manual transaction reporting form, market identified codes and relevant regulated markets are set out in the Annexes.

Transfers of business (SUP 18)

6.82   The Supervision manual contains guidance on the procedures applicable to the transfer of insurance business and friendly society transfers and amalgamations (SUP 18.2, SUP 18.3 and SUP 18.4). Guidance on building society transfers and mergers is provided in the interim prudential sourcebook for building societies (IPRU (BSOC)).

CFTC Part 30 Exemption (SUP 19)

6.83   Non-US firms are prohibited from trading on behalf of US customers on non-US futures and options exchanges unless registered with the US authorities or otherwise exempt from registration. Applications for exemption are dealt with under the Part 30 Exemption Order granted by the Commodity Futures Trading Commission (CFTC) in May 1989. The Part 30 Order requires applications to be sponsored by the FSA. The scope of the exemption is limited to firms trading in non-US futures and options on behalf of US customers on non-US futures and options exchanges other than a contract market designated as such under s 5 of the US Commodity Exchange Act. Registration is not required if a firm is trading for US customers through a futures commission merchant on an omnibus basis.[1] Where a firm has been granted a Part 30 exemption order, it must comply with certain requirements and standards including segregation and risk warnings under the COB. The FSA is generally responsible for supervising compliance.[2]

1   SUP 19 G19.3.1, G19.3.2 and G193.3.
2   SUP 19 G19.4.1–G19.4.4.

Figure 6.1: The operating framework

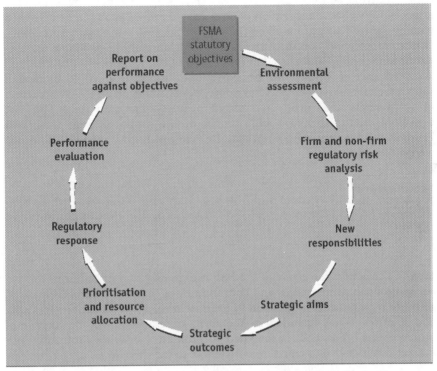

Source: FSA, *Building the New Regulator – Progress Report 2* (February 2002), Fig 1, p 6.

INTEGRATED SOURCEBOOK AND NEW REGULATORY APPROACH

6.84 The FSA originally confirmed that the earlier supervision by risk framework based on bank RATE would continue in operation until the new integrated framework had been constructed.[1] The new supervision by risk methodology (referred to as risk by risk) will form part of the proposed Integrated Prudential Sourcebook (PSB) which the FSA is currently working on. This is also being considered as part of the larger new regulatory approach and supporting operating framework that the FSA is developing. The earlier sector based risk assessment processes (including RATE and FIBSPAM) are to be integrated into the new approach which will form part of the 'firm and non firm regulatory risk analysis' stage within the new operating framework.[2]

1 See FSA, *A New Regulator for the New Millennium* (January 2000). See also FSA, *Building the New Regulator – Progress Report 1* (December 2002); and FSA, *Building the New Regulator – Progress Report 2* (February 2002). See paras 6.29–6.31.
2 See para 6.89; and Figures 6.1 and 6.2. On RATE, see Blair et al (2nd edn), paras 4.35–4.84.

Integrated Prudential Sourcebook

6.85 Most of the financial and solvency (prudential) requirements imposed under the earlier sector regimes have been continued within the FSA

Handbook as interim prudential sourcebooks. This includes, for example, the bank prudential sourcebook, IPRU (BANK).[1] This sets out many of the core financial as well as management control related requirements to be complied with by banks. This was based on the earlier FSA Guide to Supervisory Policy (which was originally produced by Bank of England) although certain sections have been removed and placed in other parts of the Handbook. The FSA had accepted that it would not be possible to produce a single integrated sourcebook for all sectors by N2 although work had begun on the construction of a new single set of prudential related measures at an early stage. The FSA consulted on the structure and content of the proposed draft Integrated Prudential Sourcebook (PSB) in June 2001 to which draft rules and guidance were attached.[2]

1 See Chapter 15.
2 See FSA, *Integrated Prudential Sourcebook* (June 2001), Consultation Paper 97; and FSA, *Integrated Prudential Sourcebook, Annex C: Draft Rules and Guidance* (June 2001), Consultation Paper 97a.

6.86   The general objective of the PSB is to require authorised firms to have adequate financial resources and appropriate systems and controls. Financial resource requirements have generally been set as rules with material on systems and controls being included in the form of guidance on the high level requirements.[1] The PSB is intended to promote consumer protection and market confidence in a manner consistent with the '*New Regulator for the New Millennium*' and '*Building the New Regulator*' proposals. Rather than continue the earlier sector approach contained in the interim sourcebooks, the PSB has adopted a new 'risk by risk' approach. This sets requirements for each of the main risks that could cause a firm major loss or insolvency including credit risk, market risk, operational risk, insurance risk, liquidity risk and group risk.

Consultation Paper 97 stated that the PSB would only develop the general risk by risk framework with the specific requirements to be imposed on individual firms being set out in the Supervision manual. The monitoring of compliance would also be dealt with through the Supervision manual rather than in the PSB. How this will operate in practice is still not entirely clear. The PSB is also stated to be based on EU directives and other relevant international standards.

It was originally proposed that the PSB would be implemented by 2004 although with the delayed consultation on the Basel New Accord,[2] it has been accepted that full implementation will have to be postponed to, at least, 2006. The FSA has nevertheless consulted on the possible adoption of selected 'criteria' for early implementation by the beginning of 2004 with the balance being implemented in stages thereafter.[3] The proposed provisional criteria include systems and controls, insurance firms, investment firms outside the scope of the European Investment Services Directive (ISD), operational risk, market risk and certain other general matters.[4]

1 See Chapter 2, paras 2.93–2.107.
2 See Chapter 15.

Figure 6.2: Risk assessment framework

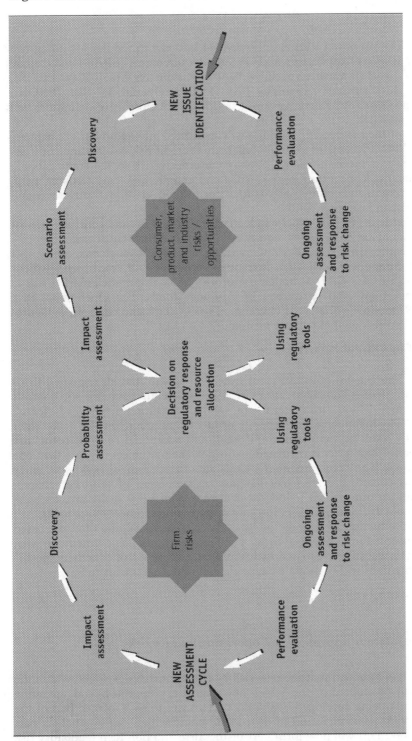

Source: FSA, *Building the New Regulator – Progress Report 2* (February 2002), Fig 2, p 9.

3 See FSA, *Integrated Prudential Sourcebook – timetable for implementation* (November 2001), Consultation Paper 115.
4 Consultation Paper 115 (supra), para 1.4 and Section 4.

6.87   The proposed PSB is to be divided into eight modules including two general sections (Application and General Requirements (PRAG) and Capital (PRCA)) and six further specific sets of provisions on Credit Risk (PRCR), Market Risk (PRMR), Liquidity Risk (PRLR), Operational Risk (PROR), Insurance Risk (PRIR) and Group Risk (PRGR). A glossary of definitions will also be attached.

Each of the risk specific modules will be divided into a number of chapters. Credit Risk (PRCR), for example, will include credit risk systems and controls, credit risk in the non-trading book, counterparty risk in the trading book, provisioning, concentration risk, collateral (credit and counterparty risk), netting (credit and counterparty risk), securitisation, credit derivatives risk and credit risk in insurance funds.

Market Risk (PRMR) will include market risk systems and controls, interest rate risk capital component, equity risk capital component, commodity risk capital component, securities underwriting, foreign exchange risk, option risk capital component, collective investment schemes and traded endowment policies, use of a CAD 1 model, use of a value at risk model, market risk in insurance funds and derivatives in insurance funds. The Operational Risk (PROR) module will include operational risk systems and controls, outsourcing and professional indemnity insurance.[1]

1 See FSA, Consultation Paper 97a.

6.88   The general objective is, as noted, to ensure that all regulated firms maintain adequate financial resources as well as adequate systems and controls at all times. These clearly represent significant common objectives for all sectors. The maintenance of separate prudential requirements for each sector may also result in confusion, duplication and additional costs of regulatory compliance with specific regulated institutions being subject to more than one sourcebook. The development of a single integrated framework is accordingly to be welcomed. It is of particular interest that many of the basic chapter headings set out in PSB follow those already contained in the interim bank sourcebook IPRU (BANK)[1] (and similar parts of the other sourcebooks).

The production of a single integrated set of financial and controls based requirements for all financial firms will be a significant achievement. To what extent this will still have to maintain a number of core sector or activity specific differentiations within module chapters and modules remains to be seen.

1 See Chapter 15.

New regulatory approach and operating framework

6.89   It is intended that the new risk by risk approach developed within the PSB will be built into the larger new regulatory approach and operating framework being developed by the FSA.[1] This was to have formed part of the earlier 'risk assessment and prioritisation' phase within the original six-part framework. This will now form part of the 'firm and non firm regulatory risk analysis' within the new ten-part operating framework.[2]

1   See Tables 6.2 and 6.3.
2   See FSA, *A new regulator for the new millennium*, Fig 1, p 14; and FSA, *Building the New Regulator – ProgressRreport 1*, Fig 1, p 4. For the revised framework, see FSA, *Building the New Regulator – Progress Report 2*, Fig 1, p 6.

6.90   The new approach and framework will, in particular, involve scoring relevant risk against a number of defined 'probability' and 'impact' factors. The probability factors relate to the likelihood of an event happening and the impact factors to the scale and significance of the result or possible loss caused. The combination of probability and impact factors then provides a measure of the total risk created to the FSA objectives. This will be used by the FSA to prioritise risk, set (inform) decisions on regulatory responses and determine resource allocation. While the same overall operating framework was discussed in the FSA's *Progress Report 1*,[1] a more substantial and complex operating framework had been constructed by *Progress Report 2*.[2]

Within this extended framework, risk assessment is incorporated at the 'firm and non-firm regulatory risk analysis' stage 2. This will follow the more general 'environmental assessment' which is to be based on the FSA's new periodic publication, *Financial Risk Outlook*. Firm and consumer as well as industry-wide (CIW) risks are aggregated to form a comprehensive 'risk map'. This is to used to set 'strategic aims' and 'strategic outcomes' in terms of which resources can be allocated and an appropriate regulatory response developed. This will be followed by a 'performance evaluation' and a final 'report on performance against statutory objectives'.[3]

1   See FSA, *Building the New Regulator – Progress Report 1* (December 2000), p 4. See Table 6.2.
2   See FSA, *Building the New Regulator – Progress Report 2* (February 2002), p 6. See Table 6.3.
3   See FSA, *Building the New Regulator – Progress Report 2*, section 2. See paras 6.92–6.98.

New operating framework

6.91   The objective of the new operating framework is to translate the statutory objectives and principles of good regulation into a transparent, integrated and risk-based system. A revised risk map had been prepared by the time that *Progress Report 2* had been issued in February 2002. The FSA's statutory objectives are considered in terms of the impact and probability of a number of risks or events arising. A set of strategic aims are developed to achieve the statutory objectives. These flow from an assessment of the wider environment within which the FSA operates, the output of the risk assessment frameworks and any new assigned responsibilities. The strategic outcomes identified are then used to determine prioritisation and resource allocation in terms of regulatory response at both the firm level and consumer, product, market or industry-wide level.

Revised risk map

6.92   By *Progress Report 2*, the FSA had constructed a ten-part operating framework based on:

(1)   the identification of statutory objectives;
(2)   environmental assessment;
(3)   firm and non-firm regulatory risk analysis;
(4)   new responsibilities;
(5)   strategic aims;
(6)   strategic outcomes;

(7)   prioritisation and resource allocation;
(8)   regulatory response;
(9)   performance evaluation; and
(10) report on performance against objectives.[1]

1   See Table 6.2.

Environmental assessment and regulatory risk analysis

6.93   The risk map only forms part of the overall operating framework. In considering the risks and opportunities that may arise with regard to the statutory objectives, the FSA will initially conduct a larger environmental assessment. This is based on the *Financial Risk Outlook* and will take into account such key external issues as government and European Union policy as well as economic, financial, legal, social and demographic development.[1] Risks and opportunities are then assessed using a firm and consumer and industry-wide (CIW) risk assessment framework. This consists of two separate risk assessment frameworks developed with regard to firm risks and for consumer, product, market and industry risks and opportunities.[2] These are based on impact assessment, discovery, probability assessment, decision on regulatory response and resource allocation, use of regulatory tools, ongoing assessment and response to risk change as well as final performance evaluation. These are aggregated to form the comprehensive risk map although it will be used in a flexible or dynamic manner to allow for further changes in the external environment.

1   See para 6.90.
2   See FSA, *Building the New Regulator – Progress Report 2* (February 2002), Fig 2, p 9. See Table 6.3.

Strategic aims and outcomes

6.94   The objective of the risk map is to set strategic aims and outcomes and then allocate resources based on regulatory priorities. The strategic aims represent the areas of focus in setting out regulatory plans. Each aim will have a strategic outcome. The outcomes are to explain what is to the delivered, allow prioritisation and allocation and demonstrate compliance with the statutory objectives. The strategic aims and outcomes will be set for a three-year period subject to annual revisions based on the yearly environmental analysis. The environmental assessment, strategic aims and outcomes will be published in the first quarter of every year with the annual *Plan and Budget*.

Prioritisation and resource allocation

6.95   Prioritisation and resource allocation will be conducted annually as part of the budget process subject to changes in relevant risks. The objective is to act in as efficient a manner as possible. The use of resources will, in particular, be monitored by the non-executive board committee which will report to the Treasury annually.

Regulatory response and performance evaluation

6.96   Regulatory responses are to be dependent on the significance of the underlying risk or opportunity having regard to the statutory objectives and prioritisation in terms of the FSA's strategic aims and outcomes. Regulatory tools will be set having regard to the principles of good regulation. This may either involve developing firm specific programmes or more general action programmes to deal with consumer and industry-wide issues.

Performance evaluation is designed to determine whether the statutory objectives have been secured and the principles of good regulation complied with. This will be conducted having regard to the strategic aims and outcomes as well as the individual action programme set.

Performance evaluation will be based on a number of information factors which will published. These will include high-level proxy indicators, focusing on strategic aims and outcomes, activity-based measures and performance results and process measures (including speed and efficiency of regulatory processes). Firm-specific evaluation will be used to assess the effectiveness of the programme set and to assist as part of the following risk assessment cycle.

With regard to more general risk monitoring, the risk map will be updated to provide senior management and the FSA board with information on risk concentrations, risk trends and emerging risks. A 'watch list' system will also be used as an internal management tool. Senior management will monitor firms that historically have tended to create problems as well as those requiring immediate remedial action. These results will not be published.

Impact bands and baseline monitoring

6.97   The FSA considers that the revised operating framework will enable it to focus on achieving its statutory objectives, act in a risk-based manner, achieve a consistent assessment of risks as well be proactive, integrated and transparent.[1]

With regard to the risk based policy, firms will be placed into four internal relationship categories of A, B, C and D.[2] This will be based on impact data and a provisional desktop probability assessment for firms in the High, Medium High and Medium Low impact bands. Base supervisory activity will be conducted through the receipt and monitoring of returns and notifications. This is referred to as 'baseline monitoring'.[3]

It is expected that over 80% of the total of 11,000 regulated firms will be low impact with supervision generally being conducted through baseline monitoring and visits. The visits may be conducted in response to identified risks, sample visits to monitor compliance standards or as part of a sector-wide review.[4]

1   See FSA, *Building the New Regulatory – Progress Report 2*, Ch 3, para 30.
2   Ibid, para 37.
3   Para 6.31.
4   The impact indicators and thresholds are available on www.fsa.gov.uk/pubs/other/27.pdf.

Common risk assessment and RTO groups

6.98   A common risk assessment process is then to be adopted with regard to non-low impact firms. Forty risk elements will be grouped into either business risks (strategy; market, credit, insurance underwriting and operational risks; financial soundness; and nature of customers and products or services) or control risks (treatment of customers; organisation; internal systems and controls; board, management and staff; and business and compliance cultures).[1]

Identified risks will then be assessed against the statutory risks effected. The FSA has already identified fifteen generic risks which have since been split into seven 'Risk to The Objective' groups (RTO groups). These consist of financial failure (market confidence and consumer protection), misconduct or mismanagement (consumer protection and market confidence), consumer understanding (consumer protection and public awareness), fraud or dishonesty (financial crime and market confidence), market abuse (financial crime, consumer protection and market confidence), money laundering (financial crime and market confidence) and market quality (market confidence and consumer protection).[2]

Risk elements will be scored against the RTO groups listed to create a 'multi-dimensional' risk picture. A separate common approach is also being developed with regard to consumer and industry-wide (CIW) risks.

1   Para 41.
2   Para 42.

Regulatory comment

6.99   A significant amount of work has accordingly been taken forward on the development of the new operating framework. The FSA has, in particular, developed the new planning framework to set out the strategic aims and outcomes over a three-year period and provide a yearly view of regulatory priorities. The full firm risk assessment framework announced has been tested on an internal desktop basis with sample institutions. Work has also been completed on what the FSA refers to as the jurisdictional implications of the new regime in terms of the risk assessment process and how the FSA will work with other regulators internationally. All of this is developed in *Progress Report 2*.

6.100   It remains to be seen how this new regulatory approach and operating framework will be finalised. A number of substantial changes have already been effected. With each subsequent discussion document, the framework appears to have become increasingly complex and arguably more removed from day-to-day supervisory and regulatory practice.

The desire to create a new single process is understandable following the integration of all supervisory and regulatory function within the FSA post-N2. The final arrangements adopted, however, must still be capable of proper and useful application. It is essential that the FSA settles on a final methodology that is both sufficiently sophisticated to be effective in practice but also necessarily simple enough to be properly understood and applied.

Hopefully much of the value and simplicity of the earlier risk assessment models used such as bank RATE can be retained within both the new PSB and the larger new regulatory approach and operating framework still under construction.

Chapter 7

Investment management

INTRODUCTION

7.1   Managing investments is a regulated activity within the Financial Services and Markets Act (FSMA) 2000, as it was under the Financial Services Act 1986. The FSMA 2000, following the language of the Financial Services Authority (FSA), regulates the managing, or offering or agreeing to manage, of assets belonging to another person where:

(a)   the assets consist of or include investments, or

(b)   the arrangements for their management are such that the assets may consist of or include investments at the discretion of the person managing or offering or agreeing to manage them.[1]

This applies to most portfolio management activities undertaken for clients whether private, corporate or institutional, and whether provided by a bank or a separately incorporated subsidiary of a bank or by a free-standing investment management firm. Many entities engaged in investment management offer a range of products and services offering a variety of investment objectives and levels of risk and aimed at differing sectors of the market.

1   FSMA 2000, s 22(2) and Sch 2, Pt 1, s 6.

7.2   This chapter identifies key regulatory aspects of the main products and services. The amount of detailed regulation, particularly that attaching to some retail products, is extremely extensive, and it would exceed the scope of this book to set out the regulations in all their details.

PORTFOLIO MANAGEMENT

7.3   The level of detailed regulation affecting portfolio management depends on the categorisation of the client to whom the services are being provided or offered. The prime objective of the FSA and most other national regulators is to protect private investors in the retail market, with lower levels of protection for non-private clients. However, in practice most institutional investors, such as pension funds, insist upon high levels of protection through the contractual obligations assumed by their portfolio managers under the investment management agreements. This reflects their own obligations to the underlying beneficiaries of or investors in their funds. Most large institutional investors have detailed standard forms of investment management agreements, of which only minor variations are usually negotiated. Topics covered by such agreements typically include the powers and duties of the manager, soft or directed commissions, reports and records, execution of purchases and sales, custody arrangements, confidentiality, termination, investment guidelines and restrictions, and of course the manager's fees. An investment manager whose clients are largely or entirely institutional may therefore feel almost as constrained and as closely supervised as one in the retail sector. The investment management agreement may construct what is tantamount to a private self-regulatory regime, monitored by the client or by consultants or auditors appointed by the client.

7.4   The main features of the FSA's rules relating to investment management for private clients are centred upon the requirement to 'know your customer', set out in COB 5.2 of the FSA's Handbook. These rules flow from the FSA's Principle 9, which obliges a firm to take reasonable care to ensure the suitability of its advice and discretionary decisions. It is impossible to achieve this without sufficient information about the client's circumstances and investment objectives; hence the FSA's guidance that:

> 'a firm acting as a discretionary investment manager for a private customer should ensure that before acting in the exercise of its discretion it has sufficient information about its private customer to enable it to act in a way which is suitable for that private customer'.[1]

In mandatory terms this finds expression in COB 5.2.5 R, which states:

> 'Before a firm gives a personal recommendation concerning a designated investment to a private customer, or acts as an investment manager for a private customer, it must take reasonable steps to ensure that it is in possession of sufficient personal and financial information about that customer relevant to the services that the firm has agreed to provide.'

1   COB 5.2.4 G.

7.5   The key to compliance with this requirement clearly lies in the firm's procedures for taking on new customers and in ensuring that information held on existing customers is kept up-to-date through a system of regular review. However, not all customers are as co-operative as they might be, as is recognised by the FSA's guidance note at COB 5.2.7 G, which states:

> 'If a private customer declines to provide relevant personal and financial information a firm should not proceed to provide the services . . . without promptly advising that customer that the lack of such information may affect adversely the quality of the services which it can provide. The firm should consider sending written confirmation of that advice.'

Many firms in that situation will wish to consider whether to act for the customer at all.

7.6 The use of information collected under COB 5.2.5 R is prescribed by COB 5.3.5 R, which requires a firm to take reasonable steps to ensure that it does not effect a discretionary transaction for a private customer unless the transaction is suitable for him having regard to the facts disclosed by him and other relevant facts about him of which the firm is, or reasonably should be, aware.

A similar requirement applies to pooled funds for private customers, where the firm 'must take reasonable steps to ensure that a discretionary transaction is suitable for the fund, having regard to the stated investment objectives of the fund'.[1] In practice, however, the objectives and investment guidelines and restrictions of most pooled funds, whether retail or institutional, are so closely defined in the prospectus or other offering documents that the requirement of suitability adds little to the manager's obligations.

The greatest impact of the general requirement of suitability is on investment management for individual private clients. As COB 5.3.5 (2) R makes clear, suitability is to be judged not just at the moment of the initial investment decision but on a continuous basis. The customer's objectives or circumstances may change, or the characteristics of an investment may alter so that although once suitable it ceases to be so. Investment managers must, therefore, have procedures to ensure that suitability is kept under frequent review.[2]

1   COB 5.3.5(3) R.
2   For further material on suitability, see Chapter 11.

7.7 Just as the investment manager has to understand the private customer's objectives, so it is essential that the private customer understands the firm and the service which he is contracting to receive. In particular, the manager must take reasonable steps to ensure that the private customer understands the nature of the risks involved.[1]

If the portfolio is permitted to include warrants or derivatives, the manager must give a risk warning in the prescribed form [2] and require the customer to acknowledge receipt of the notice and confirm acceptance of its contents, in writing.[3] A risk warning is also required[4] if the manager is permitted to invest in non-readily realisable investments: the manager must tell the customer that there is a restricted market and that in consequence dealing in the investment or obtaining a reliable valuation may be difficult, and must disclose any position held by the firm or any of its associates in the investment or a related investment. Should the manager be authorised to invest in penny shares there must be risk warning about fluctuations in value.[5] In the case of securities which may be subject to stabilisation a risk warning notice must be sent unless the firm 'has taken reasonable steps to establish that the customer requires an oral explanation only'.[6] However, few firms will wish to rely on an oral explanation, which gives little practical protection to a manager.

Finally, a manager should not engage in stock lending activity with or for a private customer unless it has notified him that this may affect his tax position and that he should consult a tax adviser before proceeding, and also of the consequences of the stock lending activity including what impact it may have on the rights of the holder of the investments concerned.[7] In practice, if any of these warnings or notices is required, most investment managers will include it in the account opening documents, whether as part of the investment management agreement or as an associated document.

1   COB 5.4.3 R.
2   The form is prescribed in COB 5 Annex 1.
3   COB 5.4.6 R.
4   COB 5.4.7 R.
5   COB 5.4.8 R.
6   COB 5.4.9 R.
7   COB 5.4.10 R.

Churning and switching and allocations

7.8   An investment manager is of course subject to duties of client care, such as best and timely execution, customer order priority, and conflicts of interests and material interests, the rules as to which are set out in COB 7 and which are discussed in Chapter 11 below. Two topics merit specific mention in the context of investment management, namely (a) churning and switching and (b) allocations.

Both of these issues have their roots in the FSA's Principle 6, which requires a firm to pay due regard to the interests of its customers and treat them fairly, and indeed Principle 1 on the conduct of business with integrity. Both may also be seen in the context of the manager's fee structure. A manager whose charges are based on the volume of transactions rather than on fixed rates or performance ratios is much more exposed to allegations of generating excessive activity on an account (churning) or of unnecessary switching within a packaged product or between packaged products.[1] In relation to allocations of shares between accounts, a manager must avoid any temptation to favour accounts carrying higher fee rates. Unfair preferences of any kind contravene COB 7.7.9 R, but a regulator may scrutinise particularly carefully allocations as between accounts with different methods or scales of charging. A firm, for example, which manages hedge funds alongside institutional or private client accounts might be tempted to give preference to the hedge funds whose fees will usually be higher than other accounts or be performance based as opposed to fixed fees. The reasons for any departure from pro rata allocation must therefore be carefully documented, so that the manager can demonstrate fairness; for example, in terms of differences in accounts' investment restrictions or of divergent investment objectives or suitability.

1   COB 7.2.3 R.

COLLECTIVE INVESTMENT SCHEMES GENERALLY

7.9   An investment manager may be engaged to manage investments for a pooled vehicle to which investors have individually contributed. The manager's client is the pooled vehicle and not the underlying investors. Such vehicles are generally described as collective investment schemes, which are defined in s 235 of the FSMA 2000 in broad terms:

> 'any arrangements with respect to property of any description, including money, the purpose or effect of which is to enable persons taking part in the arrangements (whether by becoming owners of the property or any part of it or otherwise) to participate in or receive profits or income arising from the acquisition, holding,

management or disposal of the property or sums paid out of such profits or income'.

7.10 The section goes on to explain that the participants are not to have day-to-day control over the management of the property, although they may have the right (in practice rare) to be consulted or to give directions. Section 235(3) states that the arrangements must also have either or both of the following characteristics:

'(a) the contributions of the participants and the profits or income out of which payments are to be made to them are pooled;

(b) the property is managed as a whole by or on behalf of the operator of the scheme'.

In practice, both (a) and (b) are usually present. Section 235(4) provides that if the arrangements provide for such pooling in relation to separate parts of the property, 'the arrangements are not to be regarded as constituting a single collective investment scheme unless the participants are entitled to exchange rights in one part for rights in another'. The Treasury is empowered[1] to provide that certain arrangements do not amount to a collective investment scheme. It has excluded a number of activities of which perhaps the most significant are occupational pension schemes, employee share schemes, insurance contracts and deposit-taking business.

1 FSMA 2000, s 235(5).

7.11 Collective investment schemes are perhaps most commonly associated with the retail market, through products such as authorised unit trusts. However, they are frequently designed for and used by institutional investors, for example those wishing to place with a manager assets too small to justify a separate account. A manager who provides a separate account service for clients investing, say, a minimum of £100 million may set up a collective investment scheme to accommodate smaller initial investments, thereby drawing in funds without acquiring a cost-ineffective layer of small separate accounts. A collective investment scheme may be a much more realistic institutional product than high minimum separate accounts if a manger is seeking to develop business in a country or region where it lacks an established client base.

AUTHORISED UNIT TRUSTS

7.12 In the UK perhaps the best-known form of collective investment scheme is the authorised unit trust, under which the property is held in trust for the participants and which is authorised under the FSMA 2000. The crucial benefit of authorisation to a promoter and manager is that it enables promotion of the scheme to the general public.

Section 235(1) of the FSMA 2000 states that an authorised person must not communicate an invitation or inducement to participate in a collective investment scheme, but that prohibition does not apply (*inter alia*) to an authorised unit trust scheme. From the perspective of the investor, authorisation of the scheme brings a level of structural control which should provide a measure of protection from abusive practice.

Authorisation

7.13   The FSA is the body by which authorisation is granted, in the form of an authorisation order made under s 243 of the FSMA 2000. Application for an authorisation order must be made by both the manager and the trustee, or the proposed manager and the proposed trustee, who must be different persons. The application must be made in such manner as the FSA may direct and contain such information as it may reasonably require for determining the application.

7.14   There are a number of requirements which must be satisfied if the FSA is to grant an authorisation order. They are:

— The manager and the trustee must be independent of each other.
— The manager and the trustee must each be a body corporate incorporated in the UK or another European Economic Area (EEA) state, and have a place of business in the UK.
— The affairs of each of the manager and the trustee must be administered in the country in which it is incorporated.
— If the manager is incorporated in another EEA state, the scheme must satisfy the requirements for recognised overseas schemes.
— The manager and the trustee must each be an authorised person and must each have regulatory permission to act as a trustee.
— The name of the scheme must not be undesirable or misleading.
— The purposes of the scheme must be reasonably capable of being successfully carried into effect.
— The participants must be entitled to have their units redeemed in accordance with the scheme at a price (a) related to the net value of the property to which the units relate and (b) determined in accordance with the scheme; as to which it is sufficient if the manager is required to ensure that a participant is able to sell his units on an investment exchange at a price not significantly different from (a) and (b).
— The scheme complies with the requirements of the trust scheme rules.
— The FSA has been provided with a copy of the trust deed and with a certificate signed by a solicitor to the effect that it complies with s 243 and the trust scheme rules.
— The FSMA 2000 confers on the FSA power to make rules relating to the constitution, management and operation of or authorised unit trust schemes ('trust scheme rules') and the publication of particulars of such schemes ('scheme particulars rules').

The FSA's supervisory powers

7.15   Once a unit trust is authorised, the FSA has a range of important supervisory powers.

7.16   First, a scheme cannot be altered and the manager or trustee cannot be changed without the FSA's approval (or the elapse of one month from notice of the proposed change having been given to the FSA without the FSA having served a warning notice on the manager or trustee). The FSA cannot approve a proposal to replace the manager or trustee unless it is satisfied that the scheme would continue to comply with s 243 above.

7.17 Second, the FSA may revoke authorisation if it appears to the FSA that one or more specified circumstances apply. They are:

— One or more of the requirements for the making of the authorisation order are no longer satisfied.

— The manager or trustee has contravened a requirement imposed on him by or under the FSMA 2000.

— The manager or trustee in purported compliance with any such requirement has knowingly or recklessly given the FSA information which is false or misleading in a material particular.

— No regulated activity is being carried on in relation to the scheme and the period of that inactivity began at least twelve months earlier.

— It is desirable to revoke the authorisation order in order to protect the interests of participants or potential participants in the scheme.

This power of revocation is widely drawn. In particular, it should be noted that the FSA can proceed on the basis of any breach of the FSMA 2000 by the manager or trustee the breach need not be connected with the operation of the scheme. A revocation order may be made at the request of the trustee or manager; but the FSA is entitled to (and it is submitted should) refuse to make the order if it considers that the public interest requires an investigation before a decision is taken as to revocation or that revocation would not be in the interests of participants or would be incompatible with a European Community obligation.

7.18 The third key supervisory function of the FSA arises in similar circumstances to that of revocation. It is a power to make a direction to require the manager to cease the issue or redemption, or both, of units under the scheme, or to require the manager and trustee to wind up the scheme.

7.19 Fourthly, again in similar circumstances to a revocation or direction, the FSA may apply to the High Court or the Court of Session in Scotland for an order removing the manager or trustee or both and replacing them with a suitable nominee or nominees of the FSA. If it appears to the FSA that there is no person it can nominate, it may apply to the court for an order appointing an authorised person to wind up the scheme.

7.20 A further valuable safeguard is contained in s 253 of the FSMA 2000, which renders void any provision in the trust deed insofar as it would have the effect of exempting the manager or trustee from liability for any failure to exercise due care and diligence in the discharge of his functions in respect of the scheme.

INVESTMENT COMPANIES WITH VARIABLE CAPITAL (ICVC)

7.21 Another common form of authorised collective investment scheme is the investment company with variable capital (ICVC), the name adopted in the FSA's Collective Investment Schemes Sourcebook for what previously was known as (and is still often called) an OEIC (open-ended investment company). In contrast to a unit trust, the assets of the scheme are held by a company in which the investor holds shares. The company is established through an instrument of incorporation which covers both constitutional matters such as requirements for board meetings and the issue of share certificates and the characteristics of the fund such as investment restrictions and classes of shares. At least one director must be an authorised corporate director, and there must also be a depository responsible for the safekeeping of the scheme's property.

THE COLLECTIVE INVESTMENT SCHEMES SOURCEBOOK

7.22   Detailed rules relating to authorised unit trusts and ICVCs are contained in the FSA's Collective Investment Schemes Sourcebook. This extensive document contains material on their constitution and management, including the key topics of: (i) responsibility for and content of prospectuses, (ii) valuation and pricing arrangements, (iii) investment and borrowing powers and information to be provided to investors and (iv) the authorisation process.

7.23   Thus, the Sourcebook contains provisions which stipulate material to be included in the trust deed of an authorised unit trust and the instrument of incorporation of an ICVC. The permitted categories of an authorised fund are also set out (securities schemes, money market schemes, futures and options schemes, geared futures and options schemes, property schemes, warrant schemes, feeder funds, fund of funds schemes, and umbrella schemes).

The provisions on investment and borrowing powers (CIS 5) are central to the protection of consumers, in prescribing minimum standards for investments that may be held in an authorised fund. There are, for instance, restrictions on the proportions of transferable securities and derivatives that can be held which are not listed on eligible markets, and a number of provisions designed to procure the spreading of risk.

In addition to general rules on investment and borrowing, there are detailed specific provisions relating to the permitted categories of fund. CIS 7 apportions responsibilities between directors and the depository of an ICVC and between the trustees and manager of an authorised unit trust. There are provisions on changes when investors buy or sell units, and on the calculation and distribution of income. The content and publication of half-yearly and annual account are covered, as are requirements for shareholders meetings and other constitutional matters. There are rules on the suspension and resumption of dealings in units and on the winding up and termination of funds.

UNREGULATED SCHEMES

7.24   Many collective investment schemes fall outside the scope of authorisation by the FSA, because they are not designed to comply with the requirements and restrictions which authorisation and regulation involves. Most hedge funds, for example, operate with very wide (in some cases almost unlimited) powers of investment and borrowing which far exceed those of an authorised unit trust or ICVC, or indeed of a UCITS qualifying fund. Indeed, it would defeat the object of most hedge funds were they to be so constrained.

Private equity and venture capital funds are other examples. Such funds are not illegal; on the contrary, many are of high standing in their respective fields.

7.25 The principal consequence of the unregulated status is inability to promote the fund to the general public in the UK. Since most hedge funds and other unregulated schemes are conceived for very different markets than the retail one, this restriction, while entirely appropriate, is not generally seen as a commercial burden. Promotion in the UK is permitted to investment professionals (which include authorised persons, exempt persons, governments, and local and public authorities), in limited circumstances to 'high net worth' and 'sophisticated' investors and to certain companies and associations.

Conduct of Business Rules obligations

7.26 It should be noted that a UK manager of an unregulated scheme continues to have obligations under the Conduct of Business Rules notwithstanding the scheme's unregulated status.

Thus, he must take reasonable steps to ensure that transactions which he undertakes for the scheme and the overall portfolio under his management are suitable for the scheme,[1] having regard to the scheme's stated investment objectives. He can disregard the 'best execution' rule only if expressly permitted by the scheme documents and if no participant in the scheme is or on joining was a private customer.[2] He cannot accept a private customer as a participant in the scheme without having taken reasonable steps to offer and, if requested, provide to the potential participant scheme documents which adequately describe how the operation of the scheme is governed.[3] Periodic statements of the value and composition of the portfolio must be sent to participants,[4] and there are record-keeping requirements.[5]

1 COB 10.4.3 R.
2 COB 10.5.3 R.
3 COB 10.6.2 R.
4 COB 10.7.2 R.
5 COB 10.7.6 R, and see Chapter 13.

UNDERTAKINGS FOR COLLECTIVE INVESTMENT IN TRANSFERABLE SECURITIES (UCITS)

7.27 The European Directive on Undertakings for Collective Investment in Transferable Securities (UCITS)[1] was designed to facilitate the retail promotion of qualifying collective investment schemes across the European Community. A scheme which satisfies the UCITS qualifying criteria may be marketed to private investors in any Member State, subject to the marketing regulations of that state. Local marketing laws are, however, not uniform, and require careful analysis supported by local legal advice before a European marketing strategy can be implemented.

1 Directive 85/611/EEC.

The Management and Product Directives

7.28   Furthermore, the investment restrictions which a UCITS qualifying fund must meet are currently conservative, limiting the investment powers of UCITS schemes to transferable securities, principally shares and bonds. These impediments have been addressed by two important amending Directives of the European Parliament and the Council, which were formally adopted on 21 January 2002. These are known respectively as the 'Management Directive'[1] and the 'Product Directive'.[2] Both of these Directives are expected to be finally implemented by Member States by 13 August 2003, although transitional arrangements in relation to the Product Directive are likely to enable existing schemes to operate under existing rules for an extended period after that date.

1   Directive 2001/107/EEC.
2   Directive 2001/108/EEC.

7.29   The Management Directive adopts the approach of the Investment Services Directive by introducing a 'passport' to enable collective investment scheme management companies to operate throughout the European Economic Area. It also provides for a simplified prospectus to be used as a marketing document in all EEA countries. These changes should significantly reduce the current irksome variations in local marketing requirements, although from a commercial standpoint the extent to which even with their assistance operators are able to overcome retail customers' understandable preference for local products remains to be seen. This Directive also introduces new prudential rules and new rules on delegation.

7.30   The Product Directive when implemented will amplify the investment powers of UCITS schemes to embrace money market instruments, derivatives, deposits and other collective investment schemes; the latter extension enabling funds of funds to qualify.

In April 2002 the FSA published a consultation paper (CP 135), in which the FSA set out its proposals for implementing the Product Directive. The FSA there describes its general approach to implementation of this Directive as being 'to provide maximum flexibility in terms of a scheme's investments that the directive allows' and 'to ensure we are not super-equivalent to the directive's requirements'.[1] This indication that the FSA will not impose additional requirements on UK authorised funds is welcome.

1   FSA Consultation Paper 135, para. 2.5

7.31   The outcome of the consultation process and the extent of consequential amendments to the Collective Investment Schemes sourcebook remain to be seen, but the FSA's consultation paper is a strong indication that these two directives will effect a significant improvement in the commercial attractiveness of UCITS funds to investment management firms.

Other prospective developments

7.32   The FSA's consultation paper 135 contains two other proposals designed to lead to the development of new collective investment scheme products: (i) first, to permit authorised funds to be set up as Limited Issue

Funds ('LIFs'); and (ii) second, to permit the use of the words 'guaranteed' or 'capital protected' in the name of an authorised collective investment scheme where a third party is providing protection against falls in the value of the fund.

7.33   The FSA's current rules on authorised collective investment schemes reflect the concept of such schemes as open-ended, issuing and redeeming units at the request of investors without restriction. This obliges funds to expand or contract the number of units in issue on a daily basis. The idea of a LIF is that the issue of units or shares is limited, either to a single issue or to a series of issues and, if desired, by a monetary amount. This makes it easier to develop a product with a degree of protection against falls in value, which the increased investment powers to be conferred pursuant to the Product Directive should facilitate. In the FSA's view, a LIF may also be an appropriate vehicle through which to give investors improved access to less liquid investments or markets.

7.34   The second proposal, to permit the use of 'guaranteed' or 'capital protected' in the name of an authorised fund, flows from the first, in that it may enable the element of downside protection to be reflected in the name of the fund.

Chapter 8

Marketing and financial promotion

INTRODUCTION

8.1 A key objective of the Financial Services Authority (FSA) is to ensure that those who purchase investments or obtain banking or investment services do so on the basis of fair and accurate information and without pressure from over-zealous or unscrupulous salespeople. No reputable bank or financial services firm would wish to attract business by improper means. All such entities, however, operate in exceptionally and increasingly competitive markets, in which marketing and selling skills play a crucial part. The regulator's task is to provide an appropriate level of protection for investors without unreasonably restricting the ability of banks and others to promote their products and services. This reflects the requirements of the Financial Services and Markets Act (FSMA) 2000 that in making rules the FSA must have regard to the desirability of facilitating innovation and the need to minimise the effect on competition[1] and in parallel to the regulatory objective of the protection of consumers.[2]

This chapter deals with the main steps in the process of finding and securing customers, from the first stage of advertising to the consummation of the relationship by the making of a customer agreement.

1 FSMA 2000, s 2(3)(d) and (f).
2 FSMA 2000, s 2(1)(a) and (4)(a).

WHAT IS FINANCIAL PROMOTION?

8.2 'Financial promotion' is a new concept in the FSMA 2000 that covers the marketing of financial services. It replaces the concepts of 'advertisement' and 'unsolicited call' that appeared in the previous statutes. The Act itself speaks of the communication of 'an invitation or inducement to engage in investment activity', and the term 'financial promotion' is confined to headings and side-notes (for example, in the heading and side-note to s 21). For convenience (and in accordance with other writings on this subject) this chapter will use the latter term to describe the former activity.

It seems at first sight strange that the Act should, in s 21, seek to change concepts with which firms and their advisers were well familiar. But throughout the consultation process on the new regime the Treasury emphasised that their aim was to move to a more 'media neutral' concept. Recent technological developments in communications (in particular, the growth of the Internet) had meant that the existing legislation was becoming increasingly strained to accommodate electronic media within 'advertisements' and 'unsolicited calls'. It was a key Government aim that the financial services system in the UK should be best placed to reflect, and continue to reflect, the opportunities afforded by electronic commerce.[1]

1 See HM Treasury, *Financial Promotion – A Consultation Document* (March 1999) ('First Consultation Document'), Part One, paras 1.2–1.3; *Financial Promotion – Second Consultation Document: A New Approach for the Information Age* (October 1999) ('Second Consultation Document'), Part One, paras 1.2, 3.3; *Financial Promotion – Third Consultation Document* (October 2000) ('Third Consultation Document'), para 1.7.

8.3 The restriction on making a financial promotion (referred to in this chapter as 'the financial promotion restriction'), and the main circumstances in which the financial promotion restriction is lifted, are set out in s 21(1) and (2) of the FSMA 2000:

'(1) A person ("A") must not, in the course of business, communicate an invitation or inducement to engage in investment activity.

(2) But subsection (1) does not apply if–

(a) A is an authorised person; or
(b) the content of the communication is approved for the purposes of this section by an authorised person.'

Section 21(5) gives the Treasury the power to create by order further exclusions, by specifying circumstances in which the financial promotion restriction will not apply. The Treasury made the first order under this section on 2 April 2001, the Financial Services and Markets Act 2000 (Financial Promotion) Order 2001[1] (the 'FPO'). The FPO has since been amended by a number of further orders, in part reflecting the wide scope of the financial promotion restriction and the need for exclusions to ensure that the regime is workable.[2] A consolidated version of the FPO is available on the Treasury's website.[3]

1 SI 2001/1335.
2 At the time of writing the amending orders are:
    (1) Financial Services and Markets Act 2000 (Financial Promotion) (Amendment) Order 2001 (SI 2001/2633);
    (2) Financial Services and Markets Act 2000 (Miscellaneous Provisions) Order 2001 (SI 2001/3650);
    (3) Financial Services and Markets Act 2000 (Financial Promotion) (Amendment No 2) Order 2001 (SI 2001/3800);

(4)   Financial Services and Markets Act 2000 (Financial Promotion and Miscellaneous Amendments) Order 2002 (SI 2002/1310); and

(5)   Financial Services and Markets Act 2000 (Financial Promotion) (Amendment) (Electronic Commerce Directive) Order 2002 (SI 2002/2157).

3   See www.hm-treasury.gov.uk under Documents; Financial services; Regulating financial services; Financial Services and Markets Act; Secondary legislation ordered by date of laying; Consolidated Orders.

8.4   Breach of s 21 of the FSMA 2000 is a criminal offence under s 25. This reflects the previous position regarding advertisements issued in breach of statutory requirements, but is tougher (at least compared to the Financial Services Act 1986) on a person who makes what would previously have been classified as an 'unsolicited call' in breach of regulatory requirements.[1]

A person in breach of s 21 is subject to a maximum sentence of two years' imprisonment and an unlimited fine. The offence is one of strict liability, although it is a defence under s 25(2) to show that the person making the communication believed on reasonable grounds that the communication was prepared or approved by an authorised person, or that he took all reasonable precautions and exercised all due diligence to avoid committing the offence.

Any agreements made as a result of a communication that is in breach of the financial promotion restriction are generally unenforceable against the person who has entered as a customer into the agreement. In addition, the customer is entitled to recover any money or other property that he has paid or transferred under the agreement, as well as compensation for any loss that he has suffered as a result.[2] Likewise, if as a consequence of an unlawful communication a person exercises any rights conferred by an investment, any obligation to which he is subject as a result is unenforceable against him and he has a similar entitlement to recover money, property and compensation.[3] Only if the court decides that in the circumstances it is just and equitable will the agreement or obligation be enforced or the money or property be allowed to be retained.[4]

As 'communicate' includes causing a communication to be made,[5] it follows that an unauthorised person who causes a communication to be made is in breach of the financial promotion restriction unless the contents of the communication are approved by an authorised person. A literal reading of s 21 with article 6 of the FPO thus indicates that if the unauthorised person causes the communication to be made, he will be in breach of the financial promotion restriction even if the communication is actually made by an authorised person, unless the authorised person also approves the content of the promotion. Given that the authorised person will be subject to the FSA's rules in relation to the making of the communication, it would seem illogical to require the authorised person to approve the content also, which provides no extra protection for the general public. Furthermore, if the authorised person is being regulated in this situation, it is pointless to seek to control the action of the unregulated person as well, since the promotion can be controlled by regulating the authorised person alone. This dual regulation can scarcely have been the intention of the legislation; it therefore seems unlikely that any action would be taken against the unauthorised person in this example, although the possibility cannot be ruled out.

1   Under the Financial Services Act 1986, a person who entered into an agreement with an investor following an unsolicited call in breach of s 56(1) did not commit a criminal offence, though in general he could not enforce the agreement against the investor. By contrast, breach of the unsolicited calls provision in respect of deposits was a criminal offence under s 34(3) of the Banking Act 1987.

2   FSMA 2000, s 30(2).

3   FSMA 2000, s 30(3).
4   FSMA 2000, s 30(4).
5   FSMA 2000, s 21(13); see para 8.7 below.

The key concepts

8.5   Section 21(5) of the FSMA 2000 introduces four concepts that are key to whether the financial promotion restriction applies or not:

(1)   'in the course of business';
(2)   'communicate';
(3)   'invitation or inducement'; and
(4)   'engage in investment activity'.

These will be examined in turn.

1. A person must be acting in the course of business

8.6   The Treasury has the power to specify by order, under s 21(4) of the FSMA 2000, circumstances in which a person is to be regarded as acting, or as not acting, in the course of business. At the time of writing, this power has not been exercised. The Treasury has indicated that it has no present intention to do so, and that in the absence of such an order the phrase 'in the course of business' is intended to have its ordinary meaning.[1] It will thus be for the courts to decide, in the light of the circumstances concerned, whether or not a person is acting in the course of business.

The FSA considers that 'in the course of business' requires a commercial interest on the part of the communicator, though not necessarily a direct interest. So correspondence from one close relative to another, conversations between friends, and emails posted on a bulletin board or sent to an Internet chat room will not be covered, provided that there is no commercial motivation behind the communication. Even communications made in the pre-formation stage of a small private company by the intended founders to family, friends and acquaintances with a view to obtaining start-up capital will not, in the FSA's view, be made in the course of business, unless the raising of capital for small private companies is done so frequently that the founders would be regarded as carrying on the business of forming companies, or they already carry on the business which the company will carry on.[2]

The requirement to act in the course of business is not limited to the carrying on of a regulated activity. Firms making communications to their employees, for example, may be affected by s 21(1), even if their business is not a financial services business: for example, when making promotions in relation to employee share schemes or stakeholder pension schemes.

1   Second Consultation Document, Part One, paras 4.5–4.6.
2   FSA Handbook, AUTH App 1 (Financial promotion and related activities), paras 1.5.2–1.5.3.

2. A person must communicate

8.7   Under s 21(13) of the FSMA 2000, 'communicate' includes causing a communication to be made. So the range of potential communicators includes the author of the communication, the person who communicates (if a different person) and any third party who passes on the communication. Thus publishers and broadcasters who transmit a communication on the author's behalf will 'communicate' the communication, whilst the author will cause the communication to be made.

The Oxford English Dictionary definition of 'communicate' as 'transmit' suggests that the scope of the word is very wide and would cover any process whereby information is passed from one person to another. However, it seems doubtful whether A could, for the purposes of s 21(8), make a communication to B without intending to do so. Thus if B overhears a conversation between A and C, it would appear that neither A nor C is communicating to B. This result is consistent with the 'directed at' test in article 12(4)(e) of the FPO (where the fact that a communication is included in a newspaper or magazine principally accessed in or intended for a market outside the UK is to be taken into account in determining whether the communication is directed at the UK, even if the communication was in fact received by someone in the UK). It also accords with the Treasury's view of the meaning of 'invitation or inducement', discussed below.

3. The communication must consist of an invitation or inducement

8.8   Neither 'invitation' nor 'inducement' is defined in s 21 of the FSMA 2000. The Treasury has indicated that the intention:

> 'is to catch only promotions containing a degree of incitement and not communications comprising purely factual information where the facts are presented in such a way that they do not amount to an "invitation or inducement" '.[1]

This reflects the views given by a Government Minister during the Parliamentary debates on what is now s 21 of the FSMA 2000,[2] where the view taken was that 'inducement', as it appears in the Act, already incorporates an element of design or purpose on the part of the person making the communication. On this interpretation, the facts of the case determine whether a communication is caught or not.

The difficulty with the Treasury's view is that the dictionary definition of 'inducement' suggests that a communication amounts to an inducement if the result is that a person takes a particular course of action as a consequence, regardless of the intention of the person making the communication. *The Oxford English Dictionary* defines 'inducement' as including 'something attractive by which a person is led on or persuaded to action'. This definition is reflected in the case law, where 'to induce' in the context of the Race Relations Act 1976 was held to mean 'to persuade or to prevail upon or to bring about'.[3]

There seems less scope for doubt over the word 'invitation'. An invitation in this context would appear to be a direct invitation to someone to do something that results in investment activity. So invitations include prospectuses with application forms or promotions from brokers urging the recipient to 'register with us and begin dealing'. But an invitation does not include an enquiry from a professional adviser as to whether his client would be willing to sign an agreement, or a request to sign an agreement when the client has already agreed to its terms.[4]

---

1   Third Consultation Document, para 2.2.
2   613 HL Official Report (5th Series) (18 May 2000) cols 387–388 (Lord McIntosh of Haringey); and compare 611 HL Official Report (5th Series) (20 March 2000) cols 105 and 612 HL Official Report (5th Series) (18 April 2000) col 567.
3   *Commission for Racial Equality v Imperial Society of Teachers of Dancing* [1983] ICR 473 at 476.
4   FSA Handbook, AUTH App 1 (Financial promotion and related activities), paras 1.4.5–1.4.6.

8.9   The FSA believes that the purpose of s 21 is to regulate communications which have a promotional element, rather than those which seek merely to inform or educate about the mechanics or risks of investment; and that the courts would be likely to take account of the statements made in Parliament if there were any doubt over the true meaning of 'invitation or inducement', following the doctrine in *Pepper (Inspector of Taxes) v Hart*.[1] However, since that doctrine applies only where the meaning of the text is ambiguous, a court could conclude that the meaning of 'invitation or inducement' was abundantly clear and that it had no need to look outside the statute for aids to interpretation. It therefore remains to be seen whether the dictionary definition, or the view of a Minister in Parliament, will prevail if the meaning of the expression falls to be determined by a court.

1   [1993] AC 593, HL; see FSA Handbook, AUTH App 1 (Financial promotion and related activities), para 1.4.3G.

8.10   The FSA considers that it is appropriate to apply an objective test to decide whether a communication is an invitation or an inducement. The test is whether a reasonable observer, taking due account of all the circumstances, would:

(a)   consider that the communicator intended the communication to persuade or induce the recipient to engage in investment activity, or that that was its purpose; and

(b)   regard the communication as seeking to persuade or incite the recipient to engage in investment activity.[1]

1   FSA Handbook, AUTH App 1 (Financial promotion and related activities), para 1.4.4G.

8.11   The FSA's guidance[1] contains analysis of several circumstances in which communications may (or may not) constitute invitations or inducements. Among the areas considered are:

(a)   *Directory listings:* Mere lists of names and contact details (for instance a list of 'fund managers' or 'stockbrokers') will not be inducements, but sources of information only. Where the directory incites recipients to contact a firm or firms contained in the directory in order to make an investment, that part of the directory (but only that part) will constitute an inducement to engage in investment activity.

(b)   *Tombstone advertisements:* These announcements of past achievements are likely to be intended to create awareness of what a particular firm can offer. If they contain contact details, that in itself may turn the advertisements into inducements; but not inducements to engage in investment activity, rather inducements to contact the firm concerned. If the advertisement contains other promotional material, it may be capable of being an inducement to engage in investment activity; if the inducement is directed at investment professionals, the exemption in article 19 of the FPO may be available.[2]

(c)   *Publication or broadcast of prices of investments (historic or live):* Historic prices on their own will not be invitations or inducements, and will not become invitations or inducements to engage in investment activity simply by the addition of contact details. But any additional wording seeking to persuade persons to contact firms so that they can buy or sell investments may make them so.

(d) *Company statements and announcements, and analyst briefings:* Statements of fact about a company's performance will not, in themselves, be inducements to engage in investment activity (even if they may lead persons to buy or sell shares in the company). But statements which speculate about the company's future may have the intention to encourage persons to act. In this case, whether they are inducements will depend on their contents.

(e) *Decision trees (flow charts):* If used as an educational tool doing no more than enabling persons to identify generic investment options, a decision tree will not constitute an inducement. But if it is intended to procure business for a firm, it will be likely to constitute an inducement.

(f) *Image advertising:* Advertisements which are purely profile raising, such as logos on umbrellas, sponsorship of teams or sporting events, or names on diaries or pens will not be inducements. Even if the advertising material contains contact details and were to be considered an inducement, this would be an inducement only to contact the firm, not to engage in investment activity (compare (b) above).

(g) *Introductions:* These may be inducements if the introducer is seeking to persuade the person he is introducing to do business with the person to whom the introduction is made, and will be inducements to engage in investment activity if that is the purpose behind the introduction. So a person who seeks to persuade people to let him introduce them to a firm so that they can take advantage of the firm's cheap dealing rates will be making an inducement to engage in investment activity.

(h) *Invitations to attend meetings or to receive telephone calls or visits:* These are clearly invitations or inducements; their purpose and content will determine whether they are invitations or inducements to engage in investment activity.

(i) *Instructions or guidance on how to invest:* The purpose of such material is explanatory only and as such it is unlikely to constitute an invitation or inducement to engage in investment activity.

1 FSA Handbook, AUTH App 1 (Financial promotion and related activities), paras 1.4.9–1.4.34.
2 For this exemption, see para 8.54 below.

8.12 Whatever the meaning of 'invitation or inducement' for the purposes of s 21, it is clear that the expression covers a far wider area than the 'advertisements' and 'unsolicited calls' of the previous regimes. In particular, and in marked contrast with the regimes that s 21 replaces, it includes circumstances where the invitation or inducement is made orally (for instance, via a personal visit) and is solicited by the recipient of the communication. The thinking behind this is that solicited oral communications are potentially no less harmful than those that are unsolicited, so it would be anomalous to exclude them.[1]

1 First Consultation Document, Part One, para 3.2.

4. The invitation or inducement must be to engage in investment activity

8.13 'Engage in investment activity' is defined in s 21(8) as:

'(a) entering or offering to enter into an agreement the making or performance of which by either party constitutes a controlled activity; or

(b) exercising any rights conferred by a controlled investment to acquire, dispose of, underwrite or convert a controlled investment.'

Section 21(9) and (10) gives the Treasury the power to specify what constitutes a 'controlled activity' or a 'controlled investment', and the Treasury has done so in Sch 1 to the FPO.

8.14 In general, controlled activities and controlled investments are the same as regulated activities and specified investments under the Financial Services (Regulated Activities) Order[1] (the 'RAO'), but this is not always the case. In most cases, the exemptions that apply in the RAO do not apply to the corresponding controlled activity, so the scope of the controlled activity will be wider. And some controlled investments have a wider scope than their counterparts in the RAO. For instance, the controlled activity of providing qualifying credit, which applies to all secured loans, is far wider than the regulated activity of entering into a regulated mortgage contract as lender or administering regulated mortgage contracts, which applies only to loans secured by a first legal mortgage and which meet other conditions.[2] Conversely, electronic money (e-money), though a specified investment,[3] is not a controlled investment, which means that invitations or inducements relating to e-money fall outside the financial promotion restriction.

It would seem to follow that invitations or inducements not to do any of the things listed in s 21(8)(a) or (b) are not caught by the financial promotion restriction. So advertisements urging persons not to invest in a particular company would not be within the scope of s 21, unless they were in addition to constitute inducements to existing shareholders of the company to sell their shares.

1   SI 2001/544, as amended.
2   Compare Sch 1, para 10 of the FPO with art 61 of the RAO.
3   RAO, art 74A.

FINANCIAL PROMOTION BY AUTHORISED PERSONS

8.15 The financial promotion restriction does not apply to promotions made by an authorised person. The authorised person does not commit a criminal offence and any contract that results will be enforceable. However, the authorised person will be subject to the FSA's rules in respect of the communication.[1]

The fact that an authorised person has made a communication to a third party that falls within s 21(1) does not, in itself, relieve the third party from the financial promotion restriction if he is unauthorised and wishes to communicate the promotion to a wider group of recipients. In order for this to occur, the authorised person will need to approve the content of the communication under s 21(2)(b). Should the third party materially alter the communication after it has been approved, the original approval will no longer apply and the third party will be committing an offence under s 25, unless he can show that an exemption in the FPO applies.[2] Where there has been a material alteration, the defence provided by s 25(2)(a) (belief on reasonable grounds that the content had been approved by an authorised person) is unlikely to be available.

1   See paras 8.33–8.45 below.
2   Third Consultation Document, para 2.18.

TERRITORIAL SCOPE

8.16   As far as communications from within the UK are concerned (sometimes referred to as 'outward promotions'), the financial promotion restriction applies without limitation. Some respondents to the Treasury's consultations on financial promotion had argued that s 21 should not apply to communications made to persons in an overseas jurisdiction, if those communications were lawfully made in that jurisdiction; but the Treasury has maintained the position that although this might extend the scope of regulation when compared to the previous regime, the result is justified on the grounds that this 'will help to maintain the highest confidence in the UK as a safe place to do business'. Unsurprisingly, the UK Government attaches the utmost importance to safeguarding the UK's reputation as a financial centre.[1]

1   First Consultation Document, Part Two, para 1.4; cf Second Consultation Document, Part Two, paras 2.7–2.9; Third Consultation Document, para 2.6.

8.17   Where the communication originates outside the UK, s 21(3) provides that the financial promotion restriction applies only if the communication is capable of having an effect in the UK. 'Capable of having an effect' means that the scope of the financial promotion restriction is potentially extremely wide, since communications which do not actually have an effect would appear to be caught provided that they are capable of doing so. The opportunity for communicators to rely on the exemption created by s 21(3) is thus limited. However, article 12 of the FPO provides an exemption for communications made to overseas recipients.[1] This has the effect that, in general, s 21 will not apply to communications which are not directed at persons in the UK.

1   See further para 8.54(1) below.

8.18   Communications made by persons in another European Economic Area (EEA) state made to or directed at persons in the UK will be subject to relevant Directives. The Electronic Commerce Directive (ECD)[1] prevents, with limited exceptions, Member States from imposing restrictions on incoming financial promotions in relation to 'information society services', and this has been implemented in the UK via an order made under s 21 of the FSMA 2000.[2] In general, information society services are services provided for remuneration, at a distance, by means of electronic equipment for the processing and storage of data, and at the individual request of the person who receives the services.[3] Information society services are subject to 'country of origin' regulation, which means that a communication subject to the ECD that originates in France will not be subject to UK regulation. Conversely, communications in respect of information society services for which the UK is the 'country of origin' will be subject to UK regulation, even if they are not directed at persons in the UK.[4]

The Television Without Frontiers Directive[5] would also appear relevant in this context. This Directive prevents the UK restricting the re-transmission in the UK of television broadcasts from other Member States. The FSA has indicated that, despite the lack of references to this Directive in the FPO, it will take the Directive into account in interpreting the FPO and enforcing the financial promotion restriction.[6] This reflects the fact that the Treasury cannot have intended the FPO to be interpreted contrary to the requirements of European law.

1 Directive 2000/31/EC.
2 Financial Services and Markets Act 2000 (Financial Promotion) (Amendment) (Electronic Commerce Directive) Order 2002 (SI 2002/2157).
3 ECD, art 2(a).
4 FPO, art 12(7).
5 Directive 89/552/EEC.
6 FSA Handbook, AUTH App 1 (Financial promotion and related activities), para 1.8.3G.

8.19 Section 21(7) of the FSMA 2000 gives the Treasury the power to repeal s 21(3). This power should be read together with the power in s 21(6) which allows the financial promotion restriction to be disapplied in respect of communications of a specified description originating in specified countries or groups of countries outside the UK. The Treasury has indicated that in light of developments in the European Union towards a 'home state' regime for financial services (as illustrated in the 'country of origin' approach to transactions falling within the scope of the ECD) it wished to retain in s 21 the flexibility to make the financial promotion regime in the UK a pure 'home state' regime when the time is right (that is, when other Member States agree to operate on a 'home state' basis). Whilst in theory the UK could do so unilaterally, this is not in practice acceptable, since it could leave UK consumers vulnerable to unregulated financial promotions communicated from outside the UK. And in any event, since it is unlikely (whatever the ultimate position within the European Union) that all countries will adopt a 'country of origin' approach, it will remain appropriate for s 21 to apply to some communications, at least, made into the UK from abroad.[1]

1 See Third Consultation Document, paras 2.10–2.13.

DIFFERENT TYPES OF FINANCIAL PROMOTION

8.20 The FPO distinguishes between two types of communication: real time and non-real time.[1] Real time communications are in turn subdivided into solicited and unsolicited communications.[2] As the availability of an exemption under the FPO can depend on whether a communication is a particular type of communication, these distinctions are important.

The FPO uses the word 'communication' rather than 'financial promotion', but the two concepts are identical.

1 FPO, art 7.
2 FPO, art 8.

Real time and non-real time communications

8.21 A 'real time communication' is 'any communication made in the course of a personal visit, telephone conversation or other interactive dialogue'.[1] All other types of communication are non-real time.[2] 'Non-real time communications' include 'communications made by letter or email or contained in a publication'.[3] Article 7(3) appears designed to clarify the position over whether communications made by the Internet could constitute real time communications under the FPO; and though not expressly covered in article 7(3), it would seem that other types of electronic communication (such as via WAP phones and to Internet chat rooms) would also constitute 'non-real time communications'. Broadcasts (whether sound or via television) come within the definition of 'publication' and will therefore also be non-real time communications, even when they are live recordings.

1 FPO, art 7(1).
2 FPO, art 7(2).
3 FPO, art 7(3).

8.22 Article 7(5) sets out a number of factors which are to be treated as indications that a communication is non-real time. These are:

(1) the communication is made to more that one person in identical terms (save for details of the person's identity);
(2) the system of communication normally creates a record of the communication which is available to the recipient to refer to at a later time; and
(3) the communication is made or directed by way of a system which in the normal course does not enable or require the recipient to respond immediately to it.

Although it seems clear that not all of these indicators have to be satisfied for a communication to be classified as non-real time, it is not clear whether a communication that satisfied none of these indicators could still be a non-real time communication. Given, however, that they are indicators only rather than factors that determine the issue, it would appear that in theory at least this should be possible.

8.23 The phrase 'personal visit, telephone conversation or other interactive dialogue', as the FSA notes,[1] clearly implies that interaction is crucial to a real time communication (although, as noted in para 8.21, an interactive dialogue by exchange of emails cannot be a real time communication). Consequently, communications by telephone where direct contact is established with the party at the other end of the line would be a real time communication; the same communication left on an answering machine would not be. And communications made by machines which do not allow the opportunity for dialogue to take place will likewise not be real time communications, even if they are made in real time with the recipient (for instance, when the recipient answers the telephone and listens to a recorded message). Conversely, telephone communications made by real people using scripts will be real time communications, since an interactive dialogue is bound to result. Even if the script contains prompts on what to say to typical responses from the recipient, it cannot predict the response of the recipient in advance, as the recipient will not have read the script nor be subject to it. This categorisation is important, as the FSA's rules prevent authorised persons from approving the content of unsolicited real time communications communicated by persons who are not authorised,[2] which means that authorised persons cannot approve scripts for use by unauthorised persons intending to cold-call prospective clients.

1 FSA Handbook, AUTH App 1 (Financial promotion and related activities), para 1.10.4G.
2 FSA Handbook, COB 3.12.2R.

8.24 An interesting issue arises regarding the type of communication being made when a person in the course of a presentation invites or receives a question from the audience (for example, a company director at a company's annual general meeting). Depending on the nature of the response, the type of communication will vary. For instance, if the response is not personal to the questioner and does not call for any interaction, the communication will be non-real time, even if given in real time. If, on the other hand, the person questioned enters into a dialogue with the questioner (for instance, asking for his thoughts on a particular issue in order to provide an answer relevant to the questioner's circumstances), this will be interactive and thus be a real time communication with the questioner. In this context, the phrase 'non-real time' is confusing, since the circumstance in which the communication is made is clearly 'real time', as generally understood, so far as the audience is concerned. Perhaps a distinction in the FPO between 'interactive' and 'non-interactive' communications would have been less likely to mislead the reader.

8.25 The circumstances described in para 8.24 raise the question whether the communication made to the questioner, but also received by the rest of the audience, could be both real time (with the questioner, involved in an interactive dialogue) and non-real time (with the rest of the audience, who are not involved in any interaction with the person questioned). Although in the abstract this would appear possible, a close reading of s 21(13) of the FSMA 2000 with article 6 of the FPO indicates that a communication is either real time or non-real time, but not both. Section 21(13) indicates that communications are 'made', and article 6(e) provides that a recipient of a communication is the person to whom a communication is made (or, in the case of non-real time communications directed at persons generally, anyone who reads or hears the communication). A communication is made to another person if it is addressed to a particular person (article 6(b)), and directed at persons if it is addressed to persons generally (article 6(c)). In this case, the response to the questioner would have been made only to the questioner, as it would have been addressed to him. It could therefore not have been 'made' to or 'directed at' any other party; the other members of the audience are therefore irrelevant to the question of whether the communication is real time or non-real time. They are, as it were, eavesdroppers on a conversation between the questioner and the respondent, where the respondent's reply is not addressed to them.

It is, however, possible for a real time communication to be issued subsequently in non-real time form. For instance, a real time communication made in a meeting may be recorded and made available to others on a later occasion. The broadcast version will be a non-real time communication, which will need to be approved by an authorised person if it is not exempt.

Real time communications: solicited and unsolicited

8.26 Under article 8 of the FPO, a real time communication is solicited when made in the course of a personal visit, telephone call or other interactive dialogue which was initiated by or made in response to an express request from the recipient of the communication. It is unsolicited in any other case.

Article 8(3) provides that the following do not amount to an express request:

(1) a failure by a person to indicate that he does not wish to receive any or any further visits or calls or to engage in any or any further dialogue; and

(2) an agreement by a person to standard terms that state that such visits, calls or dialogue will take place, unless he has signified clearly that in addition to agreeing to the terms, he is willing for them to take place.

These provisions are clearly designed to prevent arguments that real time communications are 'solicited' because the recipient has failed to tick a box, or has 'agreed' to pages of small print which contain, among the many terms and conditions, authority for calls to be made upon him. In practice, however, 'signified clearly' may amount to little more than a person providing a separate signature beside the relevant term.

Article 8(3) also prevents a communication being classified as 'solicited' when the call, visit or dialogue is initiated ostensibly with one purpose in mind, but then moves to a different area. For example, a customer may have agreed to visits being made to discuss investments in units in collective investment schemes. If, however, the caller in the course of the communication turned to discuss the possibility of the customer investing in futures, that part of the communication would be unsolicited.

8.27   Article 8(4) allows a real time communication to qualify as a solicited communication if it is made to a person who has not requested it, provided that that person is a close relative of, or expected to engage in any investment activity jointly with, a person who has solicited the communication. This will enable, for example, solicited real time communications to be made to both a husband and wife if only one party has asked for the communication to be made.

The FSA has indicated that a financial promotion which is solicited by a person, but is received not only by him but also by a third party support or adviser outside the scope of article 8(4), will not be a solicited communication to the former and an unsolicited communication to the latter.[1] This is because the communication is not addressed to the third party, and therefore cannot be a financial promotion to him.

1   FSA Handbook, AUTH App 1 (Financial promotion and related activities), para 1.10.13G; see para 8.25 above.

THE INTERNET AND FINANCIAL PROMOTION

8.28   The Internet provides swift and easy global access to a vast array of information, including information concerning investments. Neither the FSMA 2000 nor the FPO make any special provision for financial promotions made via the Internet.

Websites and hypertext links

8.29   It therefore follows that whether the contents of a particular website constitute a financial promotion must be judged in the same way as any other communication. Thus the person who causes the website to be created will be a communicator in respect of its content, and will need to establish whether he falls within the scope of the financial promotion restriction or not. A manager of a website for another person will not be communicating any financial promotion contained on the website, unless he has control over or responsibility for its contents.

8.30   Hypertext links, which allow a person who clicks on the link to move to one site on the Internet from another, were initially considered by the Treasury to require a specific exemption in the FPO.[1] However, the Treasury's final conclusion was that such an exemption was unnecessary:

> 'In our view, a hypertext link will be caught only if the link itself, *not* the website to which it leads, constitutes an invitation or inducement to engage in investment activity. The name of a site or a logo and any surrounding narrative may constitute an invitation or inducement, but only to click on the hypertext link and reach a website. That does not amount to causing the communication of an invitation or inducement to engage in investment activity contained in that website. This is in line with our intention that responsibility for a promotion should lie with its originator. Only if the link by itself invites or induces someone to engage in investment activity would it be caught by the financial promotion restriction – in the same way as an invitation or inducement by any other means.'[2]

The Treasury view would appear to depend on a narrow view of 'inducement', which is consistent with their approach elsewhere, if seemingly at odds with the dictionary definition and decided case law.[3] There must therefore remain some doubt over whether this view is in fact correct, although the FSA also does not regard a hypertext link in isolation as a financial promotion.[4] However, if the website hosting the hypertext link contained text that sought to encourage persons to activate the link with a view to engaging in investment activity, that *would* be regarded as a financial promotion.[5]

1   For the history, see Third Consultation Document, para 2.27.
2   Third Consultation Document, para 2.29 (emphasis in the original text).
3   See further para 8.8 above.
4   FSA Handbook, AUTH App 1 (Financial promotion and related activities), para 1.22.3G(1); compare 1.22.3G(4).
5   FSA Handbook, AUTH App 1 (Financial promotion and related activities), para 1.22.3G(2).

FSA guidance

8.31   The growing importance of the Internet as a medium for firms to market their products and services has prompted the FSA to include within its financial promotion rules specific guidance on the communication of financial promotions via the Internet and other electronic media.[1]

Firms are reminded that material displayed on a website and sound and television broadcasts are non-real time financial promotions, that they need to keep in mind the requirements of legislation such as the Data Protection Act 1998 and the Computer Misuse Act 1990, and that when designing websites and other electronic media, they should be aware of the difficulties that can arise in the reproduction of certain colours and the printing of certain types of text.[2] This last point is linked to the possibility that required information will not be easily intelligible to the recipient, which would mean that the basic requirement of the FSA's rules – that the promotion should be clear, fair and not misleading – would be unlikely to be satisfied.[3]

1   COB 3.14.
2   COB 3.14.3–4.
3   COB 3.8.4R; see para 8.40 below.

8.32   COB 3.14.5G contains specific guidance on a number of areas relevant to financial promotion via the Internet:

(1)   If the promotion is a direct offer financial promotion for a packaged product, the general position is that the promotion must contain the

contents required by the FSA's key features rule.[1] Where the promotion is
an Internet promotion, firms should make it clear that this information is
available and easily obtainable before an application is made. The text of
all the information required by the FSA's rules can be accessed via a
hypertext link, though the link should not be hidden away in the text
where the reader could miss it. Where feasible, the reader should be
allowed to print off this material, and the firm should endeavour to
provide a hard copy if so requested.

(2)   Firms need not deny access to an application form until the reader has
read the key features and other contractual terms, but the application
form or the preceding text must draw attention to the importance of
reading it.

(3)   Firms are reminded that the availability of certain exemptions from the
FSA's rules depends on whether a promotion is made to or directed at
certain persons only, and what 'made to' or 'directed at' might mean in
this context.[2]

(4)   If firms want to take advantage of exceptions in the FSA rules which
allow the promotion of unregulated collective investment schemes, they
must design the website to reduce, as far as possible, participation in the
scheme by those who are not permitted to participate.

(5)   Firms may include a reference or hyperlink to the FSA website, which
contains a range of material specifically relevant to customers. However,
the inclusion of such a reference or link will not replace any requirements
of the FSA's financial promotion rules.

1   COB 3.9.10R.
2   See further para 8.25.

FSA'S FINANCIAL PROMOTION RULES

8.33   Under s 145 of the FSMA 2000, the FSA may make rules governing the
communication by authorised persons, or their approval of a communication
by others, of invitations or inducements to engage in investment activity or to
participate in a collective investment scheme. In particular, the FSA's rules
may make provision about the form and content of communications. The
FSA's financial promotion rules are contained in chapter 3 of the Conduct of
Business Sourcebook ('COB').

Section 145(3)(a) prevents the FSA from imposing rules on authorised
persons in respect of communications to which an exemption applies under the
FPO. This reflects the Treasury's desire that authorised persons should not be
at a disadvantage in this area when compared to unauthorised persons. In
theory, at least, the FSA could bypass this restriction and use its general
rule-making power under s 138 to regulate promotions that are exempt under
the FPO, if that seemed 'necessary or expedient for the purpose of protecting
the interests of consumers'; but in practice it has not done so, recognising the
fact that the Act clearly envisages financial promotion rules being made under
the power in s 145, not that in s 138.

8.34   In addition to the exemptions contained in the FPO, COB 3.2.4–3.2.5
provides that the FSA's rules will not apply to a number of other categories of
financial promotions. As with the exemptions in the FPO, different exemptions
can be combined in respect of the same financial promotion:

(1) Communications made to persons whom the firm has taken reasonable steps to establish are market counterparties or intermediate customers, or which may reasonably be regarded as directed at them. Promotions to expert private customers classified as intermediate customers are also exempt, provided that the promotion relates to the investments or type of business for which the customer has been so classified. Firms which do not deal with private customers will therefore not need to concern themselves about the financial promotion rules, unless they are approving financial promotions (where certain rules will apply: see COB 3.2.4R(2)).

(2) Communications from outside the UK which would be exempt under articles 30–33 of the FPO if the office from which the communication was made were a separate unauthorised person.

(3) 'One-off' non-real time or solicited real time communications. These are already exempt in part under article 28 of the FPO; the effect of the exemption in the FSA's rules is to extend the FPO exemption to communications relating to deposits and all contracts of insurance. A financial promotion is to be regarded as 'one-off' if it satisfies all of conditions (a) to (c) below. If one or two of the conditions are satisfied, this fact will be taken into account in determining whether a financial promotion is 'one-off'. But a financial promotion can still be regarded as 'one-off' even if none of the conditions is satisfied. The conditions are:

    (a) the financial promotion is communicated only to one recipient or only to one group of recipients in the expectation that they would engage in any investment activity jointly;

    (b) the identity of the product or service to which the financial promotion relates has been determined having regard to the particular circumstances of the recipient;

    (c) the financial promotion is not part of an organised marketing campaign.

So correspondence written especially for a particular recipient will be excluded from the financial promotion rules, though other FSA COB rules may be relevant, such as those dealing with 'know your customer' and suitability.[1]

(4) 'Image' promotions (promotions containing only such items as firm or appointed representative name, address, logo, or brief factual description of the firm's activities and products) or price lists (such as are found in the business sections of national newspapers). In the latter case, the firm's name and contact details may be added.

(5) Personal quotations or illustration forms (which will be subject to the protections provided elsewhere in the FSA's COB rules, such as those in COB 5.3 dealing with suitability).

(6) Promotions in connection with takeovers subject to the Takeover Code or to other EEA requirements.

(7) Promotions in the form of a decision-tree for a stakeholder pension scheme, provided that the text, content and format comply with the requirements of COB 6.5.8R.

1 COB 3.2.7G(3)(a); compare COB 5.2 and 5.3.

8.35 The FSA's rules in COB 3 apply generally to firms in respect of all financial promotions. However, this principle is subject to a number of qualifications in specific circumstances.

First, the rules do not apply to an authorised professional firm if the financial promotion is incidental to the promotion or provision by the firm of professional services or of non-mainstream regulated activity, and is not communicated on behalf of another person who could not lawfully make the communication if he were acting in the course of business.[1] However, even if the communication is exempt from the rules in COB 3, the authorised professional firm will be subject to COB 2.1.3R. This requires the firm to take reasonable steps to communicate information to customers in a way that is clear, fair and not misleading, if the communication is made in the course of or in connection with the firm's designated investment business.

Secondly, only certain rules apply to financial promotions concerning deposits, general insurance contracts, pure protection contracts (long-term insurance contracts without an investment element, such as permanent health insurance) and reinsurance contracts, the most important of which is that the promotion be clear, fair and not misleading.[2] Financial promotions concerning these types of investments are, in particular, exempt from the provisions relating to direct offer financial promotions in COB 3.9, unless the promotion relates to a cash deposit ISA.[3]

Thirdly, the rules have a territorial limitation on the promotions to which they apply, mirroring article 12 of the FPO. In general, they apply only in relation to:

(a)   the communication of a financial promotion to a person inside the UK; or

(b)   the communication of an unsolicited real time financial promotion to a person outside the UK, unless the communication is made from a place outside the UK and made for the purposes of a business which is not carried on in the UK; and

(c)   the approval of a non-real time financial promotion for communication to a person inside the UK.

However, certain of the rules apply in any event where a firm approves a financial promotion (even if that promotion is a promotion exempt under the FPO).[4] This has the result that a firm cannot approve a real time financial promotion, wherever that promotion is intended to be made, and that it must take reasonable steps to ensure that the promotion it approves is clear, fair and not misleading. It also means that communications to participate in unregulated collective investment schemes, wherever made, will be subject to the rules in COB 3.11.

1   COB 3.1.5R.
2   COB 3.2.3R.
3   COB 3.2.3R; compare COB 3.9.4G.
4   COB 3.3.1R, 3.3.3R(2) and 3.3.4G.

8.36   The fact that the FSA's rules do not apply to a particular promotion will not inevitably mean that the promotion is free from all restrictions. Apart from regulations or guidelines outside the FSA's remit (such as Advertising Standards Authority or broadcasting codes, and regulations of overseas regulators), the FSA's Principle 7 (Communications with clients), which requires a firm to pay attention to the information needs of its clients and communicate information to them in a way which is clear, fair and not misleading, and COB 2.1.3R (Clear, fair and not misleading communication) may also be relevant.

The detailed provisions

8.37   The FSA's rules adopt the language found in the FPO. Thus the use of the concepts of real time/non-real time, solicited/unsolicited, and 'made', 'directed at' and 'recipient' is common to both. The main terminological difference is that the FSA rules speak of a 'financial promotion', whereas the FPO and the FSMA 2000 use the word 'communication'; but this is not a distinction of substance, as the two expressions describe the same concept. In keeping with the Treasury's emphasis on the need for the financial promotion regime established by the FSMA 2000 to reflect developments in electronic commerce, the FSA's rules contain a separate guidance section on the use of the Internet and other electronic media to communicate financial promotions.[1]

1   COB 3.14; see paras 8.28–8.32.

8.38   Before communicating or approving a non-real time communication, a firm must confirm that the communication meets the requirements of the FSA's rules. It must also ensure that the person who confirms that this is so is someone with appropriate expertise. What 'appropriate expertise' means will vary depending on the nature of the promotion. Where a firm employs a number of individuals to confirm compliance, who may themselves have various levels of expertise, whether they have authority to confirm the compliance of a particular promotion may also depend on the nature of the promotion. The task of confirmation may be subcontracted to a third party, but the firm remains responsible for any promotion that it communicates or approves.[1]

If a firm becomes aware that a financial promotion that it has confirmed as compliant with the rules in COB 3 is no longer compliant, it must ensure that the promotion is withdrawn as soon as reasonably practicable. This it should do by ceasing to communicate it or (where applicable) withdrawing its approval, and notifying any person that the firm knows to be relying on the firm's confirmation or approval.[2] The last seems potentially a very onerous requirement. However, the FSA has noted that this will have little application to promotions that are by their very nature ephemeral (such as mobile phone text messages). Furthermore, promotions such as an analyst's report, which clearly speak as at a particular date, will not be rendered non-compliant merely by the passage of time.[3]

The FSA has indicated that, where a firm becomes aware that private customers may have been misled by a financial promotion, the firm should consider whether those private customers who have responded to it should be contacted with a view to explaining the position and to offering appropriate form of redress to those who have suffered financial loss.[4] Whilst this reaction might be appropriate for communications which the firm itself communicates (and therefore over which it has control), it is submitted that this would not, in general, be appropriate for communications which the firm had approved. An exception to that might be where the firm ought to have spotted that the content of the promotion was misleading at the time it gave its approval. Where a promotion which a firm had approved was not misleading at the time of approval, but became misleading over time, and where the identity of the private customers who had responded to the promotion will be known to the third party and not the approving firm, it would seem reasonable for the third party to resolve any difficulties arising from respondents to the promotion being misled, and not the approving firm.

A firm is expected to monitor the financial promotions that a firm communicates or approves, and the FSA has suggested that each promotion is given a 'shelf life', at the end of which the promotion should be rechecked against the rules in COB 3.[5] However, a firm that merely communicates a financial promotion produced by another will not need to check the promotion against the FSA's rules, provided that it takes reasonable care to establish that:

(a)   another authorised person has done so;

(b)   the promotion is directed only at those types of person for whom the original promotion was intended;

(c)   the promotion remains clear, fair and not misleading following the confirmation of compliance with the FSA's rules by the other authorised person; and

(d)   the other authorised person has not withdrawn its approval of the promotion.[6]

1   COB 3.6.1–2.
2   COB 3.6.3R.
3   COB 3.6.4G(1).
4   COB 3.6.4G(3).
5   COB 3.6.4G(2).
6   COB 3.6.5R.

8.39   Firms also need to retain 'adequate' records of all non-real time communications they have confirmed as complying with the FSA's rules (ie both those communications issued by themselves and those whose contents they have approved). The time for which the records should be kept varies depending on the nature of the investment which is the subject of the communication, but it will be for three years in any event.[1] By 'adequate' the FSA means that the record should include, among other things, the name of the person who confirmed that the promotion complied with the rules, the date of confirmation, and the evidence supporting any material factual statements in the promotion.[2] Records may be kept in any form that the firm chooses, provided that they are readily accessible by the FSA when required for inspection. The FSA would regard a record as being 'readily accessible' if it were available for inspection within 48 hours of the request being made.[3] A published version of the promotion should be retained where practicable.[4]

1   COB 3.7.1R.
2   COB 3.7.2G.
3   COB 3.7.4–5.
4   COB 3.7.3G.

8.40   The basic obligation for non-real time financial promotions is that the firm must be able to show, in respect of any such financial promotion that it communicates or approves, that it has taken reasonable steps to ensure that the promotion is clear, fair and not misleading.[1] Where the promotion includes a comparison or contrast, the promotion must satisfy various requirements designed to ensure that like is compared with like and that no 'passing off' of other person's investments or services as one's own can occur. These include a requirement that a non-real time financial promotion including a comparison or contrast must objectively compare one or more material, relevant, verifiable and representative features of those investments or services, which may include the price; and must not denigrate the trademarks, trade names, services or activities of a competitor.[2]

In the context of deposit-taking, the FSA has indicated that firms may find it helpful, when seeking to comply with the basic obligation mentioned above, to take account of the Code of Conduct for the Advertising of Interest Bearing Accounts.[3] The contents of the Code are described in more detail below.[4]

1   COB 3.8.4R(1).
2   COB 3.8.4R(2)(b) and (d).
3   COB 3.8.6G.
4   See paras 8.46–8.51.

8.41   The remaining rules that apply to non-real time financial promotions in COB 3.8 are little more than expansions of the clear, fair and not misleading concept, fleshed out and applied to specified circumstances. So specific non-real time financial promotions – promotions which identify and promote a particular investment or service – must:

(a)   include a fair and adequate description of the nature of the investment or service, the commitment required, and the risks involved;[1]
(b)   where the promotion relates to designated investments other than non-packaged products, disclose any position or holding the firm or its associate might have in the investment or a related investment, or any material interest in the investment;[2]
(c)   where past performance of specified investments or of a firm is given, include text, specifically designed as suitable for the type of financial promotion concerned and its target audience, which draws attention to the fact that past performance will not necessarily be repeated, as well as information that relates to a relevant and sufficient period of past performance so as to provide a fair and balanced indication of the performance.[3] If past performance information is given in relation to a packaged product, the information must cover the previous five years, or the entire life of the product if that is less than five years.[4] Past performance information must not be presented in a way that suggests that this is a projection of future performance.[5]

1   COB 3.8.8R(1).
2   COB 3.8.10R(1)–(2).
3   COB 3.8.11R.
4   COB 3.8.13R.
5   COB 3.8.15R.

8.42   The same principle lies behind the FSA's treatment of real time financial promotions. Here there is no risk that the recipient might be influenced by what is included in or omitted from written promotional material. But there is a clear risk that, left to its own devices, a firm might bring unfair pressure to bear on the recipient, particularly in the context of a personal visit. COB 3.8.22R therefore requires the firm to take reasonable steps to ensure that, where a person makes a real time financial promotion on the firm's behalf, a number of requirements are satisfied, such as:

(1)   the promotion is made in a way that is clear, fair and not misleading;
(2)   the promoter does not make untrue claims;
(3)   the promoter makes clear the purpose of the promotion at the outset and identifies himself and the firm that he represents;
(4)   the promoter respects the right of the individual to terminate matters at any time and to refuse any request for another appointment; and

(5)   the promotion is not made at an unsocial hour, unless the recipient has previously agreed to contact at that time.

These requirements apply to all individuals who initiate the communication, and all forms of real time financial promotion. They thus affect equally door-to-door salesmen and staff in telephone call centres.

COB 3.10.3R prohibits firms from making unsolicited real time financial promotions (other than promotions which are exempt under COB 3.2.4– 3.2.5) unless there is an established customer relationship with the recipient under which the recipient envisages receiving such promotions, or the promotion relates to a generally marketable packaged product which is not a higher volatility fund or a life policy linked or potentially linked to a higher volatility fund; or the financial promotion relates to a controlled activity to be carried on by an authorised person or exempt person, and the only controlled investments involved or which reasonably could be involved are readily realisable securities (other than warrants) and generally marketable non-geared packaged products.

8.43   COB 3.9 deals with 'direct offer financial promotions'. A direct offer financial promotion is a non-real time financial promotion that:

(a)   contains either an offer by the firm (or another person) to enter into a controlled agreement with anyone who responds to the promotion, or an invitation to anyone who responds to make an offer to the firm (or another person) to enter into such an agreement; and

(b)   specifies the manner of response or includes the means for the recipient to respond to the promotion (for example, by providing a tear-off slip which the recipient completes).

Firms cannot communicate or approve direct offer financial promotions that relate to broker funds, and can do so where the promotion relates to unregulated collective investment schemes, derivatives or warrants only if the firm has adequate evidence to suggest that the investment may be suitable for the person to whom the promotion is communicated.[1] The FSA's rules therefore prevent indiscriminate mailing to private customers of promotions relating to these latter types of investment.

The rules in this section set out various contents requirements, some of which apply to all direct offer financial promotions, others to specific types only. All direct offer financial promotions need, for instance, to contain sufficient information to enable a person to make an informed assessment of the investment or service to which the promotion relates; to set out details of charges and expenses which the recipient might bear and of commission which might be payable by the firm to a third party; and to include a summary of the taxation of any investment to which it relates and the taxation consequences for investors generally.[2] In addition, there are specific contents requirements for promotions relating to such investments as packaged products (where key features are required), investments that can fluctuate in value (where this fact must be made clear in language suitable for the target market – examples of wording that the FSA regards as potentially suitable are provided), and investments that attract cancellation rights.[3]

As noted above, COB 3.9 does not in general apply to financial promotions relating to deposits,[4] although direct offer financial promotions relating to cash deposit ISAs are required to contain the information set out in COB 6.5.42R, unless the direct offer financial promotion includes the information that is suggested in the January 2001 edition of the 'Guidance for subscribers' to the Banking Code. COB 6.5.42R requires the giving of such information as:

(a) a comparison with the CAT standards[5] (for cash deposit ISAs which are said to satisfy the CAT standards), or a statement clearly indicating that the CAT standards are not satisfied;

(b) the minimum amount needed to open the account;

(c) the maximum yearly deposit;

(d) the interest rate earned, and how it may vary;

(e) how to make withdrawals, and any limits on withdrawals;

(f) cancellation, complaints, and compensation arrangements;

(g) a warning that mini- and maxi-ISAs may not be opened in the same tax year.

1 COB 3.9.5R.
2 COB 3.9.6R(1), 3.9.7R(5)–(6), and 3.9.19R.
3 COB 3.9.10R, 3.9.15–3.9.17, and 3.9.21R.
4 See para 8.35.
5 CAT (Changes, Access and Terms) standards for ISAs prescribed by the Treasury on 22 December 1998.

8.44 Section 21(2) of the Act envisages the possibility that an unauthorised person can make a real time financial promotion that is not in breach of the basic prohibition, by having the content of the promotion approved by an authorised person. However, the effect of COB 3.12.2R, which prevents a firm from approving such a promotion, is to ensure that unauthorised persons can make real time financial promotions only where an exemption exists under the FPO. The reasoning behind this restriction is not stated in the rules, but it is likely to relate to the difficulty of ensuring that the content that was approved by the firm was not altered or embellished when the promotion was actually made.

Firms are also prohibited from communicating or approving specific non-real time financial promotions relating to an investment or service of an overseas person, unless they have no reason to doubt that the overseas person will deal with private customers in the UK in an honest and reliable way, and the promotion discloses that the protections under the FSMA 2000 do not apply and contains a statement of the compensation position.[1]

1 COB 3.12.6R.

8.45 Finally, COB 3.13 contains provisions that apply where a firm communicates or approves promotions relating to life policies for overseas long-term insurers. The firm must not communicate or approve such promotions unless the insurer falls within one of the categories listed in article 10 of the FPO (which, broadly speaking, requires the insurer to be an authorised person or regulated in an EEA or approved third country state). The promotion must also satisfy various contents requirements designed to make it clear to the recipient, where this is the case, that the overseas long-term insurer is not subject to regulation under the FSMA 2000 (such as a warning that holders of policies issued by the insurer will not be protected by the compensation arrangements under the FSMA 2000 in the event of the insurer's insolvency).

MARKETING OF INTEREST BEARING ACCOUNTS

8.46 As we have seen, the principal requirements in relation to financial promotions for deposits are that the promotions be clear, fair and not misleading.[1] There are no detailed provisions explaining what these concepts might mean in particular circumstances. However, as stated in para 8.40 above, the FSA has indicated that, in assessing whether these requirements are satisfied, firms may find it helpful to take account of the Code of Conduct for the Advertising of Interest Bearing Accounts (the 'Code'), published jointly by the British Bankers' Association and Building Societies Association.

The Code has been in place since 1985. It was revised in 1990 to take account of the abolition of composite rate tax arrangements for interest bearing accounts, and further revised and updated in January 1999. The Consumers' Association and the Advertising Standards Authority were consulted on the latest revision. The Code applies to the advertising of all interest bearing accounts maintained within the UK.[2] A copy of the Code can be obtained from the website of the British Bankers' Association.[3]

'Advertisement' is, appropriately, widely defined in the Code so as to include press and broadcast advertisements, direct marketing, window displays, posters, brochures, leaflets, advertisements delivered by electronic means (for example, via the Internet) and automated teller machines.[4] The Code, by reference, also embraces the British Codes of Advertising and Sales Promotion, the Radio Authority Advertising Code, the Independent Television Commission Code on Advertising Standards and Practice and any relevant legislation. It requires compliance with its spirit as well as its letter.[5]

1   See para 8.35 above.
2   COB 3.8.6G.
3   See www.bba.org.uk.
4   Code, para 1.
5   Code, para 2.

8.47   The main provisions of the Code can be summarised shortly. Advertisers of interest bearing accounts must take care to inform potential customers of the nature of any commitment they may enter into as a result of responding to an advertisement, particularly if the advertisement is 'off the page'.[1] There is a requirement that the registered or business name (and in the case of press advertisements, direct marketing, brochures and leaflets, the address) of the deposit-taking institution must be stated clearly.[2] Any agent/principal relationship must be unambiguously explained.[3] Explanatory phrases and statements must be clearly audible or legible, as appropriate.[4]

1   Code, para 3. This provision is supplemented by the 14-day cooling-off period in the Banking Code for firms that adhere to that Code.
2   Code, para 4.
3   Code, para 5.
4   Code, para 6.

8.48   The key provisions, however, relate to the description of rates of interest and the terms and conditions attaching to deposits. In relation to the rates of interest, the Code's objective is to ensure that they are appropriately described. The Code[1] requires the use of the following terms where interest rates are advertised:

(a)   'W% gross';
(b)   'X% net';
(c)   'Y% tax free';
(d)   'Z% Annual Equivalent Rate ("AER")'.

Where:

(a) W is the contractual rate of interest payable before the deduction of income tax at the rate specified by law (the 'specified rate'); an explanatory phrase conveying this meaning must be used in conjunction with this expression.

(b) X is the rate which would be payable after allowing for the deduction of income tax at the specified rate; an explanatory phrase conveying this meaning must be used in conjunction with this expression. Where both gross and net rates are given, only the net rate need be defined, provided the gross rate can be inferred.

(c) Y is the contractual rate of interest payable where interest is exempt from income tax. An explanatory phrase conveying this meaning must be used in conjunction with this expression.

(d) Z is a notional rate which illustrates the contractual interest rate (excluding any bonus payable) as if paid and compounded on an annual basis. An explanatory phrase conveying this meaning must be used in conjunction with this expression. Any assumptions made in calculating the rate should be stated. Guidance on calculating the AER is given in an Appendix to the Code.

The AER must be quoted, in respect of the gross rate only, in every advertisement where an interest rate is quoted. This will enable consumers to compare rates across providers regardless of how interest is calculated and paid. Advertisements which do not quote a specific interest rate (such as those that say that the interest rate will be X% below base rate) are not required to quote an AER. The Code reinforces the primacy of the AER by stipulating that 'no rate or return shall be given greater prominence than the AER' and that the AER 'must be given at least equal prominence as the contractual rate'.[2]

1 Code, para 7.
2 Code, para 8.

8.49 Advertisements quoting a rate of interest must contain the following specific information:

(a) the frequency of payment of interest;
(b) either a statement that the rate quoted is fixed for any term specified, or that the rate is subject to variation; and
(c) the minimum amount that must be deposited to achieve the advertised rate of interest.[1]

Advertisements quoting a return which includes the original investment must explain this fact in the main part of the advertisement. Thus returns of, say, '110%' or '150% over five years' need to be clearly explained, not buried in the small print.[2]

Advertisements quoting a rate of interest or yield which are intended for media or direct mail with long copy dates must contain a suitable qualification, such as 'rates correct at date of going to press', and must state that date.[3]

A general notice to customers of changes in rates (or a simple list of the range of accounts and their rates) need only comply with paragraphs 7 and 8 of the Code.[4] In the case of such notices or lists, the words 'gross', 'net', 'tax free' and 'AER', as appropriate, need not appear after each rate. However, it must be clear from the whole of the notice or list which term applies to which rate, for example, by the use of column headings or footnotes.[5]

1   Code, para 8.
2   Code, para 9.
3   Code, para 10.
4   Set out in para 8.48 above.
5   Code, para 11.

8.50   In relation to terms and conditions, the Code seeks to achieve clear indications of the type of deposit being advertised.[1] The following conditions must be satisfied:

(a)   Advertisements must contain a clear statement of the conditions (if any) for withdrawal or transfer, including the period of any notice required, the amount of any charges payable, and any limitation on the amount which may be withdrawn or transferred in a single transaction.

(b)   For accounts which do not allow withdrawals before the end of the term, even after notice, without forfeiting interest, the text of the advertisement must include a statement indicating that, if a withdrawal is made, the stated interest rate or return will not be achieved.

(c)   Where interest is forfeited on any withdrawal without notice, words such as 'instant access' or 'immediate withdrawal' must not be displayed without clearly stating the qualification in the main body of the advertisement.

(d)   'Instant access' and similar wording should be used only where it is possible to make cash withdrawals without charge.

1   Code, paras 12 ff.

8.51   Advertisements which invite deposits by immediate response, such as by coupon, must include the full terms and conditions (or state that they are available on request), and clearly state in the part of the advertisement to be retained by the consumer a full postal address at which the advertiser can be contacted during normal business hours and the description and details of the advertised product, including the information required by the Code.[1]

1   Code, para 16.

EXEMPTIONS

8.52   An extensive series of exemptions in relation to financial promotions is set out in the FPO, on which the FSA has provided helpful guidance to be found in Appendix 1 of the Authorisation section of the Handbook. There is also a useful overview of the exemptions in tabular form in Annex 1 to chapter 3 of the Conduct of Business section, although it does not purport to be exhaustive or to replace the Order itself.

8.53   As the FSA's Guidance explains,[1] the exemptions established by the Order are in three categories, namely those applicable to:

(a)   all controlled activities (Part IV of the Order);

(b)   controlled activities concerning deposits and contracts of insurance other than life policies (Part V); and

(c)   certain specific controlled activities (Part VI).

The FPO permits[2] exemptions to be combined for the purposes of a particular communication: Part IV exemptions may be combined with each other or with

Part V or VI ones; Part V exemptions may be combined with each other, as may Part VI ones; but Part V exemptions cannot be combined with Part VI exemptions. This may sound complicated, but the intent of the combination provisions is to maximise the effect of the exemptions.

1   AUTH Appendix 1.11.36.
2   FPO, art 11.

Part IV exemptions

8.54   The Part IV exemptions, applicable to all controlled activities, are as set out below.

(1) Communications to overseas recipients

8.55   The restrictions on financial promotions do not apply to a communication made to a person who receives it outside the UK or which is directed only at persons outside the UK.[1] However, the scope and commercial value of the exemption are to some extent reduced by its being disapplied in respect of unsolicited real time communications made from within the UK or for the purposes of business carried on in the UK.

1   FPO, art 12(1).

8.56   The FPO sets out[1] a number of conditions which are likely to assist in establishing the applicability of the exemption in a particular case, although it is careful to say that a communication may still be regarded as directed only at persons outside the UK even if none of the conditions applies. The conditions are:

(a)   the communication is accompanied by an indication that it is directed only at persons outside the UK;

(b)   the communication is accompanied by an indication that it must not be acted upon by persons in the UK;

(c)   the communication is not referred to in, or directly accessible from, any other communication which is made to a person or directed at persons in the UK by or on behalf of the same person;

(d)   there are in place proper systems and procedures to prevent recipients in the UK (other than those to whom the communication might otherwise lawfully have been made) engaging in the investment activity to which the communication relates with the person directing the communication, a close relative of his or a member of the same group;

(e)   the communication is included in:
(i) a website, newspaper, journal, magazine or periodical publication which is principally accessed in or intended for a market outside the UK;
(ii) a radio or television broadcast or teletext service transmitted principally for reception outside the UK.

If conditions (a), (b), (c) and (d) are met a communication from inside the UK is to be regarded as directed only at persons outside the UK. If conditions (c) and (d) are met, a communication from outside the United Kingdom is to be regarded as directed only at persons outside the UK. In any other case, where any of the conditions is met, it is a factor to be taken into account in deciding whether the exemption is brought into effect. In practice firms seeking to rely on this exemption will wish to deploy as many of the conditions as practicable; for example, the language of conditions (a) and (b) is easy to include as a matter of routine.

A useful extension of the exemption is that a communication will be treated as directed only to persons outside the UK even if it is also directed at investment professionals as defined in the FPO[2] or to high net worth persons in circumstances described in the FPO.[3]

1   FPO, art 12(4).
2   FPO, art 12(5)(a), and art 19.
3   FPO, art 12(5)(b), and art 49.

(2) Communications from customers and potential customers

8.57   This covers communications *from* actual or potential customers seeking information about or acquiring a controlled investment, or seeking information about or in order to be supplied with a controlled service (that is, a service the supply of which constitutes a controlled activity).[1]

1   FPO, art 13.

(3) Follow-up non-real time communications and solicited real time communications

8.58   This exempts[1] a communication (other than an unsolicited real time one) which follows up a communication protected by an exemption. It must be made by and to the parties to the prior communication, must relate to the same controlled activity and controlled investment as before, and be made within 12 months of the recipient receiving the first communication.

1   FPO, art 14.

(4) Introductions

8.59   This[1] covers real time financial promotions made with a view to or for the purposes of introducing the recipient to:

(a)   an authorised person who carries on the controlled activity to which the communication relates; or
(b)   an exempt person where the communication relates to a controlled activity which is also a regulated activity in relation to which he is an exempt person.

1   FPO, art 15.

8.60   There are important safeguards designed to prevent abuse of the exemption. The exemption is available only if:

(a)   the maker of the communication is not a close relative of, nor a member of the same group as, the person to whom the introduction is, or is to be, made;
(b)   the maker of the communication does not receive from any person other than the recipient any pecuniary reward or other advantage arising out of his making the introduction; and
(c)   it is clear in all the circumstances that the recipient, in his capacity as an investor, is not seeking and has not sought advice from the maker of the

communication as to the merits of the recipient engaging in investment activity (or, if the client has sought such advice, the maker of the communication has declined to give it, but has recommended that the recipient seek such advice from an authorised person).

(5) Exempt persons

8.61 Unsurprisingly this exempts non-real time or solicited real time communications made or directed by exempt persons, if they are for the purposes of the exempt person's business in relation to which he is exempt.[1] Similarly, there is an exemption for unsolicited real time communications by appointed representatives[2] if the communication is made by the appointed representative in carrying on business for which his principal has accepted responsibility and in relation to which the appointed representative is exempt; the communication must also be one which, if it were made by the principal, would comply with any rules made by the FSA.

1 FPO, art 16.
2 As defined in FSMA 2000, s 39(2).

(6) Generic promotions

8.62 Article 17 of the FPO exempts communications which neither directly nor indirectly identify (a) the person who provides the controlled investment to which the communication relates or (b) any person as someone who carries on a controlled activity in relation to that investment.

(7) Mere conduits

8.63 Communications by 'mere conduits' are exempted by article 18 of the FPO. For this purpose a person is a mere conduit if he makes the communication in the course of his business, the main purpose of which is transmitting or receiving material provided by others, if the content of the communication is wholly devised by someone else, and if the nature of his service is such that he does not select, modify or otherwise exercise control over its content.

(8) Investment professionals

8.64 An important exemption[1] is that for communications (a) made only to recipients whom the communicator believes on reasonable grounds to be investment professionals or (b) reasonably regarded as directed only at such recipients.

1 FPO, art 19.

8.65 An 'investment professional' for this purpose is:

(a) an authorised person;
(b) an exempt person where the communication relates to a controlled activity which is a regulated activity in relation to which the person is exempt;
(c) any person whose ordinary activities involve him in carrying on the controlled activity to which the communication relates for the purpose of a business carried on by him, or who it is reasonable to expect will carry on such activity for the purposes of a business carried on by him;

(d)   a government, local authority (whether in the UK or elsewhere) or an international organisation;

(e)   a director, officer or employee of any of (a) to (d) if the communication is made to him in that capacity and if his responsibilities in that capacity involve him in the carrying on by his company or firm of controlled activities.

8.66   The FPO provides three conditions. If all of them are met, sole direction at investment professionals is conclusively presumed; if one or more of them is met, that is to be taken into account in deciding whether the communication is directed only at investment professionals; and if none of them is met, all is not lost, for the FPO states that the communication may still be regarded as so directed, although in practice it is difficult to see how that may reliably be achieved. The three conditions[1] are:

(a)   the communication is accompanied by an indication that it is directed at persons having professional experience in matters relating to investments and that any investment or investment activity to which it relates is available only to such persons or will be engaged in only with such persons;

(b)   the communication is accompanied by an indication that persons who do not have professional experience in matters relating to investments should not rely on it; and

(c)   there are in place proper systems and procedures to prevent recipients other than investment professionals engaging in the investment activity to which the communication relates with the person directing the communication, a close relative of his or a member of the same group.

1   FPO, art 19(4).

(9) Communications by journalists

8.67   Article 20 of the FPO provides for an exemption for non-real time communications by journalists, subject to a number of conditions and safeguards.

(10) Promotions broadcast by company directors and others

8.68   This exemption[1] covers communications by a director or employee inviting or inducing the recipient to acquire a controlled investment issued by his company, if he does so as part of a service which is broadcast or transmitted in the form of television or radio programmes or is displayed on a website (or similar system for the electronic display of information) comprising regularly updated news and information. The communication must comprise spoken words or words which are displayed in writing only because they form part of an interactive dialogue in the course of which the director or employee is expected to respond immediately to questions; the communication must not be part of an organised marketing campaign; and it must be accompanied by an indication that the communicator is a director or employee of the company.

1   FPO, art 20A.

Part V exemptions

8.69   The Part V exemptions, as stated above in para 8.53, relate to deposits and contracts of insurance other than life policies. In both cases, real time communications, whether solicited or unsolicited, are exempt from the financial promotion restriction. Non-real time communications are exempt if they are accompanied by certain statements. In the case of deposits these are 'an indication' of:

(a)   the full name of the deposit-taker;
(b)   the country or territory of the deposit-taker's incorporation;
(c)   if different, the country or territory of the deposit-taker's principal place of business;
(d)   whether the deposit-taker is regulated in respect of his deposit-taking business;
(e)   if the deposit-taker is so regulated, of the name of the regulator in the principal place of business, or, if there is more than one such regulator, of the prudential regulator;
(f)   whether the transaction to which the communication relates would fall within any dispute resolution or deposit guarantee scheme and, if so, identifying the scheme;
(g)   what is called 'the necessary capital information', which in relation to any incorporated deposit-taker is the amount of its paid-up capital and reserves or a statement that the amount of its paid-up capital and reserves exceeds a particular amount; if the deposit-taker is not a body corporate the required information is the amount of the total assets less liabilities or a statement that the total assets exceeds a particular amount and that total liabilities do not exceed a particular amount.

8.70   In the case of insurance contracts the requirements are essentially the same, without the requirement for the necessary capital information. There is a further exemption for non-real time communications relating to insurance contracts or to contracts covering 'large risks' as defined in article 25(2) and (3) of the FPO.

Part VI exemptions

8.71   Part VI of the FPO contains a variety of miscellaneous exemptions, some of which are in substance covered earlier in this chapter. The principal items in Part VI are:

(1)   One-off non-real time communications and solicited real time communications.
(2)   Communications required or authorised by an enactment other than the FSMA 2000.
(3)   Solicited real time communications made by an overseas communicator from outside the UK.
(4)   Non-real time communications by an overseas communicator from outside the UK to a previously overseas customer of his.
(5)   Unsolicited real time communications by an overseas communicator from outside the UK to a previously overseas customer of his.

(6) Unsolicited real time communications by an overseas communicator from outside the UK to knowledgeable customers.

(7) Non-real time or solicited real time communications communicated by and relating only to controlled investments issued by a government, a local authority (in the UK or elsewhere), an international organisation, the Bank of England, the European Central Bank, or the central bank of any country or territory.

(8) Non-real time or solicited real time communications communicated by and relating only to an investment issued by an industrial and provident society.

(9) Non-real time or solicited real time communications by nationals of an EEA state other than the UK in the course of a controlled activity lawfully carried on in that state and conforming with any rules made by the FSA which are relevant to such communications.

(10) Non-real time or solicited real time communications communicated by a market, which relate only to the market's facilities and do not identify a particular investment or person through whom transactions may be effected.

(11) Communications made to persons whose business it is to place or arrange the placing of promotional material, if made for the purpose of the material being so placed.

(12) Communications by one participant in a joint enterprise to another in connection with or for the purposes of the enterprise.

(13) Non-real time or solicited real time communications by an operator of certain recognised collective investment schemes to participants in the scheme, relating only to such recognised schemes as are operated by the operator or to units in such schemes.

(14) Non-real time or solicited real time communications relating to bearer instruments made by a company (other than an open-ended investment company) to persons reasonably regarded as entitled to such instruments issued by the company, its parent or a subsidiary, and required or permitted to be made by the rules of a market.

(15) Non-real time or solicited real time communications to existing holders of bearer instruments, relating to those instruments or to a class of instruments which includes either the bearer instruments or instruments in respect of which those bearer instruments confer rights.

(16) Non-real time or solicited real time communications by a company (other than an open-ended investment company) to members or creditors of the company or of an undertaking in the same group.

(17) Non-real time or solicited real time communications by an open-ended investment company to its members or creditors in relation only to an investment issued or to be issued by the company.

(18) Communications by one company to another in the same group.

(19) Communications made only to persons reasonably believed to be in the business of disseminating information concerning controlled activities through a publication, or a director, officer or employee of such a business.

(20) Subject to certain conditions, non-real time or solicited real time communications to 'high net worth individuals', who hold a current certificate of high net worth signed by their accountant or employer and who have signed a statement in prescribed terms.[1]

(21) Subject to certain conditions, communications to companies with a called-up share capital or net assets of not less than £500,000 (if the

company has, or is a subsidiary of a company which has, more than 20 members), or otherwise £5 million, to an unincorporated association or partnership with net assets of not less than £5 million, to a trustee of a high value trust, or to a director, officer or employee of any such company, association, partnership or trust acting in such capacity.

(22) Subject again to specified conditions, communications to 'sophisticated investors' who are currently certified as such by an authorised person and who have signed a statement in prescribed terms.[2]

(23) Non-real time solicited real time communications to associations of high net worth or sophisticated investors.

(24) Non-real time solicited real time communications to members of a 'common interest group' of a company in relation to investments issued by the company, if certain conditions are met; a common interest group for this purpose is an identified group of persons reasonably regarded as having an existing and common interest with each other and the company in the company's affairs and in what is done with the proceeds of any communication to which the communication relates.

(25) Communications between a settlor or grantor of a trust, a trustee, a personal representative and a fellow trustee or personal representative if made for the purposes of the estate.

(26) Communications between a settlor or grantor of a trust, trustee or personal representative, and a beneficiary under the trust, will or intestacy, or between beneficiaries if the communication relates to the management or distribution of the trust fund or estate.

(27) Communications by members of professions, where the controlled activity to which the communication relates is an excluded activity which would be undertaken for the purposes of and incidental to the provision of professional services to or at the request of the recipient of the communication.

(28) Non-real time communications by members of professions in specified terms.[3]

(29) Communications following a report by the Parliamentary Commissioner for Administration, for the purpose of enabling an injustice to be remedied.

(30) Receipt of a publication in which the recipient has placed an advertisement.

(31) Non-real time or solicited real time communications in relation to an interest in a management company managing the common parts of or servicing premises.

(32) Subject to conditions, a company's annual accounts and directors' report.

(33) Communications relating to employee share schemes.

(34) Non-real time or solicited real time communications relating to the sale of goods or the supply of services.

(35) Subject to conditions, communications relating to the sale of a body corporate (other than an open-ended investment company).

(36) Communications relating to takeovers of an unlisted company, which has been an unlisted company throughout the period of ten years immediately preceding the date of the offer.

(37) Non-real time or solicited real time communications required or permitted by market rules.

(38) Non-real time or solicited real time communications in connection with admission to certain EEA markets.

(39) Non-real time or solicited real time communications by a company (other than an open-ended investment company) in relation to securities of the company traded or dealt in on a relevant market, if not constituting or accompanying an invitation or advice to underwrite a controlled investment or engage in investment activity; any reference to the price at which the investments have been bought or sold in the past or to their yield must be accompanied by an indication that past performance cannot be relied on as a guide to future performance.

(40) Non-real time or solicited real time communications in relation to listing applications.

(41) Non-real time communications in relating to listing particulars, supplementary listing particulars, prospectuses, supplementary prospectuses, and any other document required or permitted to be published by listing rules made under Part VI of the FSMA 2000.

(42) Non-real time communications included in a prospectus or supplementary prospectus issued in accordance with the Public Offers of Securities Regulations 1995.[4]

(43) Non-real time communications relating to a prospectus or supplementary prospectus which may be an invitation or inducement only because it gives the name and address of the person by whom the securities are to be offered or other details for contacting that person, states the nature and nominal value of the securities and the number offered and the price of the offer, states that a prospectus or supplementary prospectus is or will be available (or when it is expected to be) or gives instructions for obtaining a copy of the prospectus or supplementary prospectus.

1   FPO, art 48(2)(b).
2   FPO, art 50(1)(b).
3   FPO, art 55A.
4   SI 1995/1537.

AGREEMENTS WITH CUSTOMERS

8.72   It is often wrongly assumed by practitioners that the need for a customer agreement is primarily driven by regulation. In principle, this is not so. The need for a customer agreement is driven by the law of contract. Traditionally, legal advisers to the industry have had to grapple with a hair-raising tendency amongst practitioners to offer their services as soon as a customer demands and then worry about the 'paperwork' later. As with so many areas of the business, this approach is commonly justifiable where the customers are sophisticated users of the services on offer. Such users are aware of general custom and practice amongst those who offer the services. They may be taken to have accepted certain terms by their conduct, even if, in doing so, they cause any lawyers involved to have nightmares.

8.73   The same approach cannot be taken, however, with customers who are new to the market and are not necessarily versed in its customs and practices. The FSA's primary intention in this area of regulation is to ensure that those customers are sufficiently protected. To that end, in relation to private and intermediate customers, there are rules stating when a written agreement is required and what it should contain. These rules have their root in the FSA's Principle 7, which requires a firm to have due regard to the information needs of its customers. A customer's central information need is to know the basis on which the firm will provide services to him. A customer agreement and terms of business fulfil that function.

8.74 The FSA's rules on terms of business and customer agreements are to be found in COB 4.2 of the Handbook. Terms of business must be provided to a private customer before conducting designated investment business with him (except in the case of an ISA or a stakeholder pension scheme, where the terms must be provided within five business days of the offer).[1] The timing is less stringent for an intermediate customer, where the firm has a reasonable period after beginning to conduct business with or for the customer to send the terms.[2] Such terms of business are sent 'one way', that is from the firm to the customer without any need for a response by the customer. Some types of business with private customers, however, require two-way agreements, to which the customer has consented.[3] They are:

— discretionary management of investments;
— transactions in a contingent liability investment, when it is designated investment business;
— stock lending;
— underwriting (except life policies), when it is designated investment business.

However, a two-way agreement can be dispensed with if the private customer is habitually resident outside the UK and the firm has taken reasonable steps to establish that he does not wish to enter into one.[4] Terms of business (including customer agreements) can be in more than one document, so long as it is clear that collectively they constitute the terms of business and the use of more than one document does not materially detract from the information which the firm is required to give or the ease with which it can be understood.[5]

1 COB 4.2.5R(2).
2 COB 4.2.5R(3).
3 COB 4.2.7R(1).
4 COB 4.2.7R(2).
5 COB 4.2.12R.

8.75 There are some exceptional cases in which terms of business and customer agreements are not required.[1] Perhaps the most notable are execution-only transactions. Others include:

— transactions as a result of direct offer financial promotions;
— a life insurer's effecting of a life policy issued or to be issued as a principal;
— various actions by the operator of a collective investment scheme, namely scheme management activity, other services to the trustee or depository, and the sale or purchase of units as a principal;
— acting as a trustee of a unit trust or a depository of an ICVC (investment company with variable capital);
— acting as an operator of an investment trust savings scheme, in bringing about a transaction in the shares of the trust or in conducting designated investment business as part of its activities as operator;
— supplying a published recommendation;
— designated investment business carried on by an occupational pension scheme firm in relation to an occupational pension scheme of which it is the trustee.

Nor are terms of business or a customer agreement required in relation to advice preliminary to or actions subsequent to the termination of the relationship between firm and customer: that is to say providing advice or information solely for the purpose of preparing or providing terms of business or of entering into a customer agreement, or fulfilling outstanding obligations under terms of business which have been terminated.

1 COB 4.2.9R.

8.76 The FSA requires terms of business (including customer agreements) to 'set out in adequate detail the basis on which designated investment business is to be conducted'.[1] To facilitate compliance with this requirement, the FSA has provided a table of contents to be included to the extent that they are relevant to the particular case. Compliance with the table will tend to establish compliance with the requirements to provide adequate detail, as will non-compliance have the contrary effect. This is merely an evidential provision as a firm may be able to demonstrate compliance with the rule by other means. But in practice the evidential effect will be strong.

Since this table[2] is central to the FSA's regulation of terms of business, it is worth setting out the list in full, as follows:

(1) *Commencement of the terms of business:* When and how the terms of business are to come into force.
(2) *Regulator:* The fact that the firm is regulated or authorised by the FSA.
(3) *Investment objectives:* The customer's investment objectives.
(4) *Restrictions:*
   (a) Any restrictions on:
      (i) the types of designated investment in which the customer wishes to invest; and
      (ii) the markets on which the customer wishes transactions to be executed; or
   (b) that there are no such restrictions.
(5) *Services:* The services the firm will provide.
(6) *Payments for services:* Details of any payment for services payable by the customer to the firm, including where appropriate:
   (a) the basis of calculation;
   (b) how it is to be paid and collected;
   (c) how frequently it is to be paid;
   whether or not any other payment is receivable by the firm (or to its knowledge by any of its associates) in connection with any transaction executed by the firm, with or for the customer, in addition to or in lieu of any fees.
(7) *Disclosure of polarisation status:* Where the firm is to transact business in packaged products with private customers, a statement, in accordance with COB 5.1.17R (Disclosure of polarisation status generally) whether advice on investments about packaged products will be:
   (a) independent; or
   (b) restricted to the packaged products of one product provider or marketing group; or
   (c) restricted to the packaged products of one product provider or marketing group but inclusive of adopted packaged products; or
   (d) given for the purposes of managing a portfolio with discretion.
(8) Investment manager: If the firm is to act as an investment manager:

(a) the arrangements for giving instructions to the firm and acknowledging those instructions;

(b) the initial composition of the managed portfolio;

(c) the initial value of the managed portfolio; and

(d) the period of account for which statements of the portfolio are to be provided in accordance with COB 8.2.4R (Requirements for a periodic statement) (where periodic statements are required).

(9) *Accounting:* The arrangements for accounting to the customer for any transaction executed on his behalf.

(10) *Right to withdraw:* In the case of a non-packaged product ISA or PEP, an explanation of any right to withdraw (see COB 6.7 (Cancellation and withdrawal)) or, if it is the case, a statement that such rights will not apply.

(11) *Unsolicited real time financial promotions:* In the case of a private customer, the circumstances, if any, in which the firm or its representatives or employees may communicate an unsolicited real time financial promotion to the private customer.

(12) *Acting as a principal:* That the firm may act as principal in a transaction with the customer, if this is the case.

(13) *Conflict of interest and material interest:* When a material interest or conflict of interest may or does arise, the manner in which the firm will ensure fair treatment of the customer as required by COB 7.1.3R (Fair treatment).

(14) *Broker fund adviser:* If the firm acts as a broker fund adviser for a private customer, a statement explaining the nature of the firm's dual role as adviser to the customer and adviser to the life office or operator in question.

(15) *Use of soft commission agreements:* If the firm is to be authorised under the terms of business to undertake transactions with or through the agency of another person with whom the firm has a soft commission agreement, the prior disclosure required by COB 2.2.16R (Prior disclosure).

(16) *Customer's understanding of risk:* When a firm chooses to fulfil any of its obligations under COB 5.4.3R (Requirement for risk warnings) in the terms of business in relation to any of the following:

(a) warrants or derivatives;

(b) non-readily realisable investments;

(c) penny shares;

(d) securities which may be subject to stabilisation;

(e) stock lending activity;

the relevant risk warning.

(17) *Unregulated collective investment scheme:* That the services to be provided by the firm will or may include advice on investments relating to, or executing transactions in units in unregulated collective investment schemes, if this is the case.

(18) *Underwriting:* That the firm may enter into transactions for the customer, either generally or subject to specified limitations, when the customer will incur obligations as an underwriter or sub-underwriter, if this is the case.

(19) *Stock lending:* In the case of a private customer, that the firm may undertake stock lending activity with or for the private customer (if this is the case), specifying the assets to be lent, the type and value of relevant collateral from the borrower and the method and amount of payment due to the private customer in respect of the lending.

(20) *Right to realise a private customer's assets:* The information required by COB 7.8.3R (Contractual rights to realise a private customer's assets), if applicable.

(21) *Complaints procedure:* How to complain to the firm, and a statement, if relevant, that the customer may subsequently complain directly to the Financial Ombudsman Service.

(22) *Compensation:* If applicable, an explanation of the compensation arrangements available to customers under the Financial Services Compensation Scheme if the firm is unable to meet any of its liabilities, or the availability of an explanation describing those arrangements.

(23) *Termination method:* How the terms of business may be terminated, including a statement:

    (a) that termination will be without prejudice to the completion of the transactions already initiated, if this is the case;

    (b) that the customer may terminate the terms of business by written notice to the firm and when this may take effect;

    (c) that if the firm has the right to terminate the terms of business, it may do so by notice given to the customer, and specifying the minimum notice period, if any; and

    (d) of any agreed time after which, or any agreed event upon which, the terms of business will terminate.

(24) *Termination consequences:* The way in which transactions in progress are to be dealt with upon termination.

(25) *Contracting out of best execution:* When the obligation to provide best execution can be and is to be waived, a statement:

    (a) that the firm does not owe a duty of best execution; or

    (b) the circumstances in which it does not owe such a duty.

(26) *Authorised professional firms:* If the firm is an authorised professional firm and may conduct a non-mainstream regulated activity with or for the customer (whether with or without any other regulated activity for the same customer), an explanation, with respect to that activity, of:

    (a) how to complain to the firm, where the customer may subsequently complain and the mechanisms that operate in respect of such a subsequent complaint; and

    (b) what, if any, compensation arrangements are available to the customer if the firm is unable to meet any of its liabilities, or the availability of an explanation describing those arrangements.

In respect of discretionary management, terms of business (including a client agreement) provided to a customer should, in addition, cover:

(1) *Extent of discretion:*

    (a) The extent of the discretion to be exercised by the firm, including any restrictions on:

        (i) the value of any one investment; and

        (ii) the proportion of the portfolio which any one investment or any particular kind of investment may constitute; or

    (b) that there are no such restrictions

(2) *Periodic statements:*

    (a) The frequency of any periodic statements, except when a periodic statement is not required by COB 8.2.7R (Promptness, suitable intervals and adequate information); and

    (b) whether those statements will include some measure of performance, and if so, what the basis of that measurement will be.

(3)   *Valuation:* The basis on which assets comprised in the portfolio are to be valued.

(4)   *Borrowings:* That the firm may commit the customer to supplement the funds in the portfolio, including borrowing on his behalf, if this is the case, and, if it may:

 (a)   the circumstances in which the firm may do so;

 (b)   whether there are any limits on the extent to which the firm may do so and, if so, what those limits are; and

 (c)   any circumstances in which such limits may be exceeded.

(5)   *Underwriting commitments:* If it is the case, that the firm may commit the customer to any obligation to underwrite or sub-underwrite any issue or offer for sale of securities; and:

 (a)   whether there are any restrictions on the categories of securities which may be underwritten and, if so, what these restrictions are; and

 (b)   whether there are any financial limits on the extent of the underwriting and, if so, what these limits are.

1   COB 4.2.10R.
2   COB 4.2.15E, 4.2.15 16E.

Chapter 9

Market misconduct

INTRODUCTION

9.1 Measures to prevent or punish abuses of UK investment markets are not new. The common law offence of 'conspiracy to defraud' was invoked for the purpose nearly 200 years ago.[1] More recently the legislature has intervened with statutory provisions creating offences of (i) insider dealing,[2] (ii) false or misleading statements,[3] and (iii) false or misleading practices.[4] In addition, securities exchanges[5] and regulators[6] have also introduced rules on the subject.

1   See *R v de Berenger* (1814) 3 M & S 67 – a case which concerned a conspiracy to manipulate the market in UK government securities by the circulation of false rumours about the death of Napoleon and the imminent conclusion of a peace treaty ending the Napoleonic wars. See also *Scott v Brown Doering & Co* [1892] 2 QB 724, another interesting example of the use of conspiracy to defraud in relation to facts which would now fall within the Financial Services and Markets Act (FSMA) 2000 market abuse regime.
2   First introduced by the Companies Act 1981, the relevant provisions of which were re-enacted in the Company Securities (Insider Dealing) Act 1985; this was replaced, as part of the implementation of the EC Insider Dealing Directive, by the current provisions of Criminal Justice Act 1993, Pt V.
3   See the Prevention of Fraud (Investments) Act 1939, s 12, re-enacted in an expanded form in Prevention of Fraud (Investments) Act 1958, s 13 and further expanded in Financial Services Act 1986, s 47(1), now FSMA 2000, s 397(1).
4   See Financial Services Act 1986, s 47(2), now FSMA 2000, s 397(3).
5   The London Stock Exchange, for example, has for many years had a rule prohibiting practices which create a false market in securities listed on the Exchange. The relevant rules are currently rules 3300 and 3301.
6   The statements of principle promulgated by the Securities and Investments Board under Financial Services Act 1986, s 47A included (as Principle 3) the requirement 'to observe high standards of market conduct'. Principle 3 of the FSA's Statements of Principle for Businesses requires firms to observe 'proper standards of market conduct'.

9.2 The Financial Services and Markets Act (FSMA) 2000 retains all these measures. In addition, it introduces an entirely new regime for the imposition

(*) Chpt 9. Market Misconduct
- Inside Dealing 241
- Market Abuse 251

(*) Chapt 10. Prevention of
money laundering.

(*) Chapt 16 Financ. Derivatives
- derivatives 481

of civil 'penalties' on those who engage in behaviour which constitutes 'market abuse'. The market abuse regime is described in paras 9.50ff below.

9.3   The importance attached to protecting the integrity of UK markets is also reflected in the regulatory objectives which, for the first time, the FSMA 2000 lays down for the Financial Services Authority (FSA). These objectives define the central policy focus of the new regulatory regime introduced on 1 December 2001; they include ensuring that confidence in the UK financial markets is maintained and reducing the extent to which the financial markets can be used for the purposes of financial crime.

A. CRIMINAL OFFENCES

INSIDER DEALING

9.4   Section 52 of the Criminal Justice Act (CJA) 1993 creates three offences[1] of insider dealing. An individual who has information as an insider commits an offence if:

(a) he deals in price-affected securities in circumstances where the dealing occurs on a regulated market or he is acting as, or relies on, a professional intermediary;

(b) he encourages another person to deal in securities that are price-affected (whether or not the other person knows this) knowing or having reasonable cause to believe that the dealing would occur in the circumstances mentioned above; or

(c) he discloses the information, otherwise than in the proper performance of the functions of his office, employment or profession, to another person.

1   The penalties are: (a) on summary conviction, imprisonment for up to six months, a fine of up to the statutory maximum, or both; (b) on conviction on indictment, an unlimited fine, imprisonment for up to seven years, or both: CJA 1993, s 61(1).

9.5   These offences can be committed only by an individual. This does not mean, however, that securities dealings by a corporation cannot contravene the prohibition. This is because the word 'deal' is defined as including procuring another person to deal. An individual officer of a corporation may therefore commit an offence by entering into a dealing on behalf of the corporation.

Definitions

9.6   A number of defined terms are crucial to an understanding of the offences under the CJA 1993:

Possession of information 'as an insider'

9.7   First, a person has information 'as an insider' if the relevant information is, and he knows that it is, inside information and he has it, and knows that he has it, from an inside source.[1]

1   CJA 1993, s 57(1).

9.8   The implication of the definition of 'insider' is that the 'insider' must know that the information satisfies all the elements of the definition of 'inside information'.[1] For example, if he honestly believes that the information, if released, would not have a significant effect on the price of the securities in which he wishes to deal, it is difficult to see how he can commit an offence if he deals.[2]

1   See paras 9.11–9.12 below for the elements of that definition.
2   Though if the alleged belief is sufficiently perverse it may, of course, be difficult to convince a jury that it was genuinely held.

Possession 'from an inside source'

9.9   A person has information from an 'inside source' if he has it:

(a)   through being a director, employee or shareholder of an issuer of securities or through having access to it by virtue of his employment, office or profession; or
(b)   if the direct or indirect source of his information is a person within (a) above.[1]

1   CJA 1993, s 57(2).

9.10   In relation to the definition of 'inside source', it should be noted that the use of this phrase is, perhaps, somewhat misleading. As noted above, it is not necessary that the source of the information be a person inside the company to which the information relates; it is sufficient that the relevant individual has it by virtue of his own employment, office or profession. Thus information received at work by an employee of, say, an investment bank or other securities dealer will almost always be held 'as an insider'. This position, which differs from that which prevailed before the CJA 1993, stems from the policy approach of the EC Insider Dealing Directive, which focuses on inequality of information between dealing parties rather than on breach of confidentiality or the misappropriation of company information.

'Inside information'

9.11   The next key defined term is 'inside information'. This is information which:

(a)   relates to particular securities or to a particular issuer or issuers, and not to securities or issuers generally;
(b)   is specific or precise;
(c)   has not been made public; and
(d)   if it were made public, would be likely to have a significant effect on the price of any securities.

9.12   It will be noted that the securities whose price is affected (which are termed 'price-affected securities'[1]) need not be the same securities, or securities of the same issuer, as the securities or issuer to which the inside information relates. Thus a person who acquires inside information about company A which is also price sensitive in relation to company B, another company in the same business sector, may commit an offence by dealing in securities of company B.

1   See below, paras 9.13–9.14.

'Price-affected securities'

9.13   Securities are 'price-affected securities' in relation to inside information if the information would, if made public, be likely to have a significant effect on the price of those securities. As noted above, this definition is not restricted to the securities of issuers to which the inside information actually relates.

9.14   The 1993 Act does not specify what amounts to a 'significant' effect, and the UK authorities have consistently declined to offer guidance on the question, taking the not unreasonable view that what is significant will depend on the circumstances of the particular case and the characteristics of the particular securities – for example on whether a particular price movement is within the normal range of volatility for the securities in question, which may vary considerably between different markets and between individual securities. It is probably prudent to assume that price movements which, in percentage terms, are comparatively small can nevertheless be 'significant' if they are unusual for the relevant security and likely to generate large profits for those dealing at the relevant time.

'Made public'

9.15   Section 58 of the CJA 1993 contains guidance on the circumstances in which information will be treated as made public. The guidance, which is not exhaustive,[1] is of two kinds.

1   CJA 1993, s 58(1): information may therefore be shown to have been made public, in accordance with the ordinary meaning of those words, in cases not covered by s 58.

9.16   First, there are cases where the information is conclusively treated as made public. These are:

(a)   where the information is published in accordance with the rules or a regulated market for the purpose of informing investors and their professional advisers (for example, it is announced through the London Stock Exchange's Regulatory News Service);

(b)   where it is contained in records which by virtue of any enactment are open to inspection by the public (for example, on a company's file at the Companies Registry);

(c)   where it can readily be acquired by those likely to deal in any securities to which it relates, or of an issuer to which it relates;

(d)   where it is derived from information which has been made public.

9.17   The second list set out in s 58 is of circumstances which might otherwise be thought to count against the suggestion that information has been made public. Thus it is provided that information can be treated as made public even though:

(a)   it can be acquired only by persons exercising diligence or expertise;

(b)   it is communicated to a section of the public and not to the public at large;

(c)   it can be acquired only by observation;

(d)   it is communicated only on payment of a fee; or

(e)   it is published only outside the UK.

'Dealing' and related terms

9.18   The term 'deal' is expanded to cover any acquisition or disposal, whether as principal or agent. In addition, a dealing directly or indirectly procured by a person is treated as a dealing by that person.

Furthermore, 'acquire' includes agreeing to acquire and entering into a contract which creates the security (for example, entering into an option), and 'dispose' includes agreeing to dispose and bringing to an end the contract by which the security was created (for example, releasing an option).

Scope: securities and markets

9.19   The provisions of the CJA 1993 apply to securities which:

(a)   fall into any of the categories described in Sch 2 to the CJA 1993 (broadly, shares, debt securities, warrants, depositary receipts, options, futures and contracts for differences); and

(b)   satisfy conditions set out in the Insider Dealing (Securities and Regulated Markets) Order 1994[1] as amended.[2]

The main condition is that the securities are officially listed in a state within the EEA or admitted to dealing on a regulated market. A regulated market is any market which is established under the rules of an investment exchange specified in the schedule to the 1994 order as amended.[3]

1   SI 1994/187.
2   Amended by the Insider Dealing (Securities and Regulated Markets) (Amendment) Order 1996 (SI 1996/1561) and the Insider Dealing (Securities and Regulated Markets) (Amendment) Order 2000 (SI 2000/1923).
3   This lists broadly all the operators of EEA regulated markets, plus NASDAQ.

9.20   To fall within the CJA prohibitions, a dealing must either:

(a)   occur on a regulated market; or

(b)   be made by a person who is relying on a professional intermediary or is himself a professional intermediary.

The first of these is relatively straightforward, but the second needs some explanation, since it covers a broad range of off-market dealings and is wider than one would expect from the natural meaning of the words used. A 'professional intermediary' is a person who either himself carries on a business consisting of specified activities and holds himself out to the public as willing to engage in such a business, or is employed by such a person to carry on any of the specified activities.[1] The specified activities are acquiring or disposing of securities and acting as an intermediary between persons taking part in any dealing in securities. A person dealing in securities 'relies' on a professional intermediary if a person who is acting as a professional intermediary carries on one of the specified activities in relation to that dealing. Thus a deal with a professional securities firm as counterparty will always be caught, even if the firm is not acting as 'intermediary' in the ordinary sense (for example where it is dealing as principal for its own book and no third party is involved) and even if there is no advisory or other relationship which would ordinarily be described as involving 'reliance'.

1   By CJA 1993, s 59(3), a person is not to be treated as carrying on such a business if he carries on a specified activity which is merely incidental to some other activity, or merely because he occasionally conducts a specified activity.

Territorial scope

9.21 The territorial application of the insider dealing offences is dealt with in s 62 of CJA 1993. In accordance with the normal pattern of modern UK regulatory offences, the insider dealing legislation applies if the prohibited behaviour either takes place in the UK or has effects there. An individual can therefore commit the dealing offence if either:

(a) he is within the UK at the time when he is alleged to have done any act constituting or forming part of the dealing; or

(b) the regulated market on which the dealing is alleged to have occurred is one which is treated as regulated in the UK;[1] or

(c) where a professional intermediary is involved, the professional intermediary is in the UK at the time when the intermediary is alleged to have done anything by means of which the offence is alleged to have been committed.[2]

In the case of the disclosure and encouragement offences, either the individual encouraging or disclosing or the recipient of the disclosure or encouragement must be within the UK at the time of the alleged offence.

1 The markets which satisfy this condition are listed in Insider Dealing (Securities and Regulated Markets) Order 1994 (SI 1994/187) (as amended by SI 1996/1561 and SI 2000/1923), art 10. They comprise the markets operated by UK recognised investment exchanges.

2 This last phrase presumably covers the situation where the professional intermediary is the counterparty to the dealing, though it is perhaps odd as a matter of language to describe the professional intermediary as doing something 'by means of which the offence is committed'.

Defences to insider dealing

9.22 The CJA 1993 sets out six defences.[1] The first three are contained in s 53 and are based on the principle in the Insider Dealing Directive[2] that the behaviour prohibited is 'taking advantage' of inside information. The other three defences are set out in Sch 1.

1 In addition, CJA 1993, s 63(1) excepts from s 52 anything done by an individual acting on behalf of a public sector body in pursuit of monetary policies or policies with respect to exchange rates or the management of public debt or foreign exchange reserves.

2 See art 2(1) and the twelfth recital.

No profit

9.23 For all three offences (that is, dealing, encouraging and disclosure) it is a defence to show that the person concerned did not expect what he did to result in a dealing profit attributable to the price sensitive nature of the information.[1] This would apply, for example, if the dealing was 'against' the information, as where the information suggested that the current market price was lower than the real value, but the person nevertheless sold at the current market price.

1 CJA 1993, s 53(1)(a), (2)(a) and (3)(b). In the case of a charge of disclosure, it is also a defence for the person to show that he did not expect the disclosure to result in a dealing at all: CJA 1993, s 53(3)(a).

Adequate disclosure ('equality of information')

9.24 For the dealing and encouragement offences, it is a defence for the person accused to show that he believed on reasonable grounds that the information had been (or, in the case of the encouragement offence, would be) disclosed widely enough to ensure that none of those taking part in the dealing would be prejudiced by not having the information.[1] The most obvious example of this defence is where the person with the information discloses it to another person and then enters into a dealing with that other person. For this reason, the defence is often referred to as the 'equality of information' defence.

1   CJA 1993, s 53(1)(b) and (2)(b).

'Would have done it anyway'

9.25   For the dealing and encouragement offences, it is a defence for the person accused to show that he would have done what he did even if he had not had the information.[1] This is a defence which, with the benefit of hindsight, may be approached by the authorities, and perhaps by a court, with some scepticism.

1   CJA 1993, s 53(1)(c) and (2)(c).

Market making

9.26   Under the first of the special defences set out in Sch 1 to the CJA 1993, it is a defence for a person accused of dealing or encouraging to show that he acted in good faith in the course of his employment in the business of a market maker (or his own business as a market maker).[1] A 'market maker' for this purpose is a person who holds himself out at all normal times in accordance with the rules of a regulated market or approved organisation as willing to acquire or dispose of securities, and is recognised as doing so under those rules.

1   CJA 1993, Sch 1, para 1. The reference to an individual carrying on his own business as a market maker is at first sight puzzling, but could cover the case of a partner in a firm which was a market maker.

Market information

9.27   There are two defences available in cases where the relevant information constitutes 'market information'. 'Market information' is defined in para 4 of Sch 1; broadly, it is information about past or possible future dealings, including information about the securities covered, the parties involved and the price or prices. The fact that a dealing has not taken place or will not do so is also 'market information' for this purpose.

9.28   The first market information defence is a general defence dependent only on the person's showing that 'it was reasonable for an individual in his position to have acted as he did despite having that information as an insider at the time'. This is potentially broad. It is also, however, somewhat uncertain, since it will often be difficult to predict what will be regarded as 'reasonable' – a test on the application of which no further guidance is given. One of the interesting side-effects of the introduction of the market abuse regime is that the FSA's Code of Market Conduct is likely to be invoked as evidence of what can be regarded as reasonable for purposes of the general market information defence as well as for those of market abuse itself. The provisions of the Code about 'trading information'[1] are therefore of particular interest.

1   See below, para 9.99.

9.29 The second market information defence applies where an individual shows:

(a) that he acted:
    (i) in connection with an acquisition or disposal which was under consideration or the subject of negotiation, or in the course of a series of such acquisitions or disposals; and
    (ii) with a view to facilitating the accomplishment of the acquisition, disposal or series; and
(b) that the information which he had as an insider was market information arising directly out of his involvement in the acquisition, disposal or series.

9.30 This defence is most frequently used to permit the acquisition of a significant stake in a target company in preparation for the intended launch of a takeover offer, and is therefore often referred to as the 'bid facilitation' defence.

9.31 The phrase 'with a view to facilitating the accomplishment' needs to be construed carefully. Probably it implies a direct and causative connection between the actions for which the defence is invoked and the intended acquisition, so that actions which merely bring economic benefits which help finance, or offset the costs of, the acquisition are unlikely to be covered by the defence. This certainly seems to be the view of the FSA. In its Guidance Release 4/96, the SIB (as it was then called) advised as follows:[1]

> 'The SIB takes the view, on the advice of leading counsel, that in the context of a takeover bid [the 'facilitation' defence] is not available for indirect stakes which provide a purely economic exposure to movements in the price of the underlying securities which are the subject of the proposed acquisition, or other securities in relation to which unpublished information concerning the proposed takeover bid is price-sensitive. In these circumstances, the dealing which it is claimed 'facilitates' the acquisition provides only a cash benefit which may be used by the bidder to offset the costs of a proposed bid.'

Such an indirect, economic exposure contrasts with the direct acquisition of a stake in the target company, which will not only reduce the costs of the bid (by enabling the bidder to accumulate a partial stake at a lower price than will be possible once the bid is announced) but also directly contribute to its success by enabling the bidder to progress towards the minimum required percentage of share ownership or acceptances.

1 Guidance Release 4/96 (December 1996), para 15.

Stabilisation

9.32 The final defence applies where a person acts in conformity with price stabilisation rules made under s 144 of the FSMA 2000.

MISLEADING STATEMENTS AND PRACTICES

9.33 Section 397 of the FSMA 2000 creates two offences, relating respectively to (i) misleading statements or dishonest concealment and (ii) misleading practices.

Misleading statements

9.34   Section 397(1) and (2) provides that a person who:

— makes a statement, promise or forecast which he knows to be misleading, false or deceptive in a material particular; or
— recklessly makes (dishonestly or otherwise) a statement, promise or forecast which is misleading, false or deceptive in a material particular; or
— dishonestly conceals any material facts;

is guilty of an offence[1] if he does so for the purpose of inducing (or is reckless as to whether it may induce) another person (whether or not the person to whom the statement, promise or forecast is made or from whom the facts are concealed) to enter or offer to enter into, or to refrain from entering or offering to enter into, a relevant agreement or to exercise, or refrain from exercising, any rights conferred by a relevant investment.[2]

1   The penalties are: (a) on summary conviction, imprisonment for up to six months, a fine of up to the statutory maximum, or both; (b) on conviction on indictment, an unlimited fine, imprisonment for up to seven years, or both: FSMA 2000, s 397(8).
2   These relevant agreements and investments are set out in Financial Services and Markets Act 2000 (Misleading Statements and Practices) Order 2001 (SI 2001/3645).

9.35   It will be seen that this is a complicated offence embodying three main elements: an action (an *actus reus,* in the technical terminology of the criminal law) and two mental elements (elements of *mens rea*).

The act

9.36   The act can take one of two forms:

(a)   the making of a statement which is misleading, false or deceptive, or
(b)   the concealment of material facts.

9.37   The phrase 'misleading, false or deceptive' is wide – even without the addition of 'misleading or deceptive', the word 'false' is taken to include a statement which is literally true but which is misleading when account is taken of what is not stated.[1]

1   See for example *R v Lord Kylsant* [1932] 1 KB 442 (prospectus containing table of past dividends paid held false because it omitted to refer to the fact that payments were made out of reserves rather than current profits); and *Gluckstein v Barnes* [1900] AC 240 at p 250: 'everybody knows that sometimes half a truth is no better than a downright falsehood'.

9.38   As to concealment of material facts, it is unclear whether the word 'concealment' imports some positive step to obscure the position or prevent discovery, or will include mere non-disclosure. It is generally thought, however, that it will include mere non-disclosure at least in cases where there is some legal or regulatory duty of disclosure (for example, the duty of disclosure of substantial holdings in a UK public company under Part VI of the Companies Act 1985).

'Material' facts are, in the context of the section, clearly facts relevant to the decision whether or not to enter into the contemplated agreement or exercise of rights.

Mental elements

9.39 Of the mental elements, the first relates to the act itself and the second to its consequences.

9.40 Where the act is the making of a misleading, false or deceptive statement, promise or forecast, the mental element is knowledge or reckless-ness, the latter having its normal meaning of failing to give any thought to, or proceeding in spite of, an obvious risk.[1] In the context, this is likely to cover the making of statements without directing any attention to the issue of their accuracy, for example by taking steps to verify the facts stated or to confirm that an appropriate verification process has been carried out. Where the act is concealment of material facts, the mental element is dishonesty. This too has its ordinary criminal law meaning.[2]

1 See *R v Lawrence* [1982] AC 510, HL; and *Metropolitan Police Comr v Caldwell* [1982] AC 341, HL.
2 See *R v Ghosh* [1982] QB 1053, CA, where it was held, in the context of the Theft Act 1968, that the test of whether a person has acted dishonestly is (a) whether his actions were dishonest according to the ordinary standards of reasonable and honest people and (b) if so, whether he himself realised that his actions were, according to those standards, dishonest.

9.41 The second mental element relates to a decision by another person whether to enter into a relevant agreement or exercise specified rights. Here either intention (to induce such a decision) or recklessness (as to whether such a decision will in fact be induced) will suffice.

Misleading practices

9.42 Section 397(3) of the FSMA 2000 concerns the creation of false or misleading impressions relating to securities. The elements of this offence[1] are as follows:

— an act or course of conduct which creates a false or misleading impression as to the market in or price or value of relevant investments; and
— the purpose of creating that impression; and
— the purpose of thereby inducing another person to acquire, dispose of subscribe for or underwrite those investments or to refrain from doing so or to exercise or refrain from exercising rights attaching to those investments.

1 The penalties are the same as those for an offence under FSMA 2000, s 397(1): see para 9.34, note 1.

9.43 As with s 397(1) of FSMA 2000, therefore, the offence involves an act and two mental elements.

The act

9.44 The act is the creation of a false or misleading impression as to the price or value of, or market in, relevant investments. The word 'impression' is not defined and is not easy to interpret. In particular, it is unclear whether it requires a person to speculate about the inferences which particular market participants are likely to, or may, draw from a particular course of action, or whether the offence requires conduct which, objectively considered from the standpoint of a typical market participant, can be regarded as creating a false appearance of fact. Probably the latter is the correct view, though the distinction is easier to state than to apply in practice.

Mental elements

9.45　In relation to the first mental element, the reference to the purpose of creating 'that impression' has the result that it is irrelevant whether the person creating the impression intended or appreciated that it would be false or misleading. This is clear both from the words used and from the FSMA 2000, s 397(5)(a) defence described below.

9.46　The second mental element is self-explanatory; it should be noted that, in contrast to the position under s 397(1), recklessness as to the result is not sufficient.

Defences

9.47　By s 397(5)(a) of the FSMA 2000, it is defence for a person accused of contravening s 397(3) to show that he reasonably believed that his act or conduct would not create an impression that was false or misleading as to the matters mentioned in s 397(3). This may be quite a difficult test to satisfy in view of the requirement that the belief be reasonable and the overall difficulty of the concept of 'impression'. It also requires the person relying on the defence to have identified clearly the intended impression and directed his mind to the issue of its accuracy – a person who has not thought about the issue, or has not done so with sufficient clarity, will not be able to rely on the defence.

9.48　Two further defences, relevant to both offences, are provided in respect of price stabilising rules[1] and control of information rules.[2]

It is a defence for a person charged with knowingly[3] making a misleading, false or deceptive statement, promise or forecast to show that he made it in conformity with price stabilising or control of information rules. Likewise it is a defence for a person charged under s 397(3) to show that he acted for the purpose of stabilising investments and in accordance with price stabilising rules, or that he acted in conformity with control of information rules. The main function of the defence for control of information rules is to protect corporate bodies from liability based on the attribution or aggregation of information which is in fact held in different parts of the firm behind 'Chinese walls'. Without such protection, there would be concerns that the firm could breach the section as a result of, for example, statements made by an individual on one side of the Chinese wall, which, taking into account information known to the firm but not known to that individual, are false or misleading.

1　Ie rules made by the FSA under FSMA 2000, s 144, dealing with the permitted stabilisation of investments around the time of an offer. The defences are set out in FSMA 2000, s 397(4) and (5)(b).
2　Ie rules made by the FSA under FSMA 2000, s 147, dealing with the disclosure and use of information held by an authorised person. These are the rules which will deal with 'Chinese walls' and other procedures for the control of dissemination of information within a firm. The defences are set out in FSMA 2000, s 397(4) and (5)(c).
3　Curiously, the defence does not apply to the reckless making of a statement which is misleading, false or deceptive. This seems particularly odd in the case of control of information

rules, since an individual operating behind a 'Chinese wall' will generally not know that a statement he makes is false or misleading as a result of other information held on the other side of the Chinese wall. Possibly the thinking is that the firm as a corporate body (which is the person which the defence is mainly aimed at protecting) will 'know' of the falsity of the statement.

Territorial scope

9.49 Like the insider dealing legislation, FSMA 2000, s 397 applies if the prohibited behaviour either takes place in the UK or has effects there. Thus an offence may be committed if:

(a) the person making a statement, promise or forecast, concealing material facts or engaging in a course of conduct is in the UK at the relevant time;

(b) the recipient of a statement, promise or forecast is in the UK, or a false or misleading impression is created there; or

(c) in the case of an offence under s 397(1), the contemplated agreement is or would be entered into, or the contemplated exercise of rights takes place or would take place, in the UK.

B. CIVIL OFFENCES

MARKET ABUSE

Introduction

9.50 The market abuse provisions in Part VIII of the FSMA 2000 are the most radical and controversial of all the innovations made by that Act. They are the product of a long-standing and widely expressed dissatisfaction with the perceived ineffectiveness of the criminal law on insider dealing[1] and misleading statements and practices,[2] to which a number of factors have contributed:

— the criminal offences are expressed in detailed and precise language and include a substantial and in some cases complex[3] mental element;

— the criminal offences have to be established to the criminal standard of proof – that is beyond reasonable doubt;

— the criminal offences have to be tried under the rules of criminal procedure, before the criminal courts and usually by a jury;

— responsibility for investigating and prosecuting breaches of the criminal offences has been divided among a number of public and regulatory authorities.

1 See paras 9.4–9.32 above.
2 The most important offences are those in Financial Services Act 1986, s 47 (now FSMA 2000, s 397, described at paras 9.33–9.49 above). Also important is the common law offence of conspiracy to defraud (see para 9.1 above), which continues to apply in addition to the statutory offences.
3 For example, both offences under FSMA 2000, s 397 require proof of either intention or recklessness both as to the principal prohibited act and as to the intended, expected or actual consequences – see paras 9.39–9.41 and 9.45–9.46, above.

9.51 The market abuse regime incorporates changes directed to all these difficulties:

— the civil 'offence'[1] of market abuse is couched in very general language and is amplified in an FSA Code of Market Conduct (CoMC) which is itself constructed and worded very differently from the language of the criminal law, sometimes in rather general and subjective terms;

— the market abuse regime is 'effects based'; proof of intention or recklessness is not generally required;[2]

— because the market abuse regime is classed as 'civil' rather than criminal,[3] the standard of proof is the civil standard of proof on the balance of probabilities;[4]

— in spite of its classification as a civil regime, the market abuse regime applies to everyone, regardless of whether they require or have obtained any form of regulatory authorisation;[5]

— decisions on market abuse are made in the first instance by the FSA's Regulatory Decisions Committee and, if the defendant chooses to take them further, by the Financial Services and Markets Tribunal. Both bodies contrast strongly with a jury in terms both of size and of experience and sophistication, and will operate under more flexible procedural rules than under the criminal law;

— the FSA is now responsible for all aspects of both the investigation and the prosecution of regulatory rules, market abuse and the criminal law.

1 The word 'offence' is not used in FSMA 2000, Pt VIII and is strictly perhaps inaccurate outside the context of the criminal law. It is, however, both convenient and frequently used in discussion of the market abuse provisions.

2 Though in a number of cases the Code of Market Conduct (CoMC) incorporates varying levels of mental element, ranging from intention through culpable blindness to negligence, presumably on the basis that the regular user will often not be prepared to condemn unintentional behaviour as failing to meet an acceptable standard purely on the basis of its results. See below, in particular paras 9.132 ff.

3 It should be noted, however, that the regime is likely to be classed as criminal for purposes of the European Convention on Human Rights (ECHR). This point was one of those hotly debated during the passage of the Bill. While the government never entirely accepted it, it did concede that the possibility of the regime being classed as criminal for ECHR purposes was sufficiently real to make the special safeguards required under the Convention in the context of criminal proceedings – notably the inadmissibility of evidence obtained under compulsion – appropriate.

4 This point is, however, perhaps less significant than some commentators imply, since even under the civil standard cogent proof is required for serious allegations. See *Re H (minors)* [1996] AC 563, HL, where the principle was expressed by Lord Nicholls as follows: 'the more serious the allegation, the less likely it is that it occurred and hence, the stronger should be the evidence before the court concludes that the allegation is established on the balance of probabilities'.

5 This is, indeed, one of the reasons why it is thought likely to be regarded as criminal for ECHR purposes – see note 3 above. The fact that the regulatory powers under the Financial Services Act 1986 could not be used, in the case of the Sumitomo copper affair, against unregulated parties was a factor that contributed to the authorities' frustration with the old regime.

9.52   The cumulative effect of these changes is to place in the hands of the authorities enormously strengthened powers to investigate cases of suspected misbehaviour and to impose sanctions where misbehaviour is regarded as established. While this will be widely welcomed, it is also true that the novelty of the new regime, as regards both its structure, its conceptual framework and the language in which its requirements are couched, has given rise to a significant amount of apprehension among market participants. There are areas where it is difficult for them to judge with confidence whether practices which have hitherto been accepted aspects of market practice will now expose them to accusations of market abuse. The FSA has taken pains to address such concerns by extensive formal and informal consultation and by an expressed preference for correcting practices which are widespread, but which it regards as unacceptable, by announcement rather than by making examples. It is to be hoped that this approach, together with a developing familiarity with the new regime, will over time allay the most acute worries that have been expressed in the market.

What is market abuse?

9.53　Section 118 of FSMA 2000 defines 'market abuse' as behaviour[1] by any person:

(a)　which occurs in relation to qualifying investments traded on a specified market;

(b)　which satisfies any of the following three conditions:

   (i)　it is based on information which is not generally available to those using the market in question but which, if available to a regular user of that market, would or would be likely to be regarded by him as relevant when deciding the terms on which transactions in investments of the kind in question should be effected (the 'misuse of information limb');

   (ii)　it is likely to give a regular user of the market in question a false or misleading impression as to the supply of, or demand for,[2] or as to the price or value of, investments of the kind in question (the 'false or misleading impression limb');

   (iii)　a regular user of the market in question would, or would be likely to, regard it as behaviour which would, or would be likely to, distort the market in investments of the kind in question (the 'distortion limb'); and

(c)　which is likely to be regarded by a regular user of the market in question as a failure on the part of the person or persons concerned to observe the standard of behaviour reasonably expected of a person in his or their position in relation to the market (the 'regular user test').

1　'Behaviour' includes inaction as well as action: FSMA 2000, s 118(10).
2　It is unclear to what extent, if at all, the reference here to 'supply and demand' is intended to be different from the reference to 'market' in FSMA 2000, s 397(3) – see para 9.42 above.

9.54　It will be seen that this definition is couched in very broad and general terms. While it covers broadly the same ground as the criminal legislation on insider dealing and false or misleading practices,[1] it lacks the substantial mental element embodied in those offences, concentrating on the nature and effects of a person's behaviour rather than on what he intends or foresees – though, as discussed below, this may be qualified to some extent by the application of the 'regular user' test, since in some cases the regular user may not regard behaviour as falling below an acceptable standard unless some mental element is present (for example, the behaviour is deliberate or reckless).

1　Though it should be noted that the distortion limb extends into ground not covered by either set of criminal provisions.

9.55　The FSMA 2000 recognises that substantially greater detail and clarity is required if the regime is to be acceptably predictable in its operation. It also recognises that a range of defences will need to be provided. Both objectives are promoted in a novel way, through the use of a code to be issued by the FSA.

9.56   The FSA is required[1] to issue a code containing 'such provisions as the [FSA] considers will give appropriate guidance to those determining whether or not behaviour amounts to market abuse'. This code, which forms part of the FSA's Handbook of Rules and Guidance, is known as the Code of Market Conduct (CoMC).

1   FSMA 2000, s 119.

9.57   The CoMC contains descriptions of behaviour which, in the opinion of the FSA, amount to market abuse, descriptions of behaviour which, in the FSA's opinion, do not amount to market abuse, and factors which, in the FSA's opinion, are to be taken into account in determining whether or not behaviour amounts to market abuse.

Material in the second of these categories has a special status: behaviour described in the CoMC as not amounting to market abuse is taken not to do so – in other words, such a description creates a conclusive 'safe harbour'.[1] Otherwise, the CoMC has evidential force: it may be relied on so far as it indicates whether or not behaviour amounts to market abuse, but the indication is not conclusive.[2] The text of the CoMC set out in the MAR part of the FSA's Handbook also contains explanatory guidance. Technically this does not form part of the CoMC and does not have the evidential force provided by FSMA 2000, s 122. Instead, it constitutes guidance issued under the FSA's general powers given by s 157 of the FSMA 2000.[3] It is doubtful whether this distinction will be of great significance in practice.[4]

1   See FSMA 2000, s 122(1). Such provisions are identified in the CoMC by the marginal letter 'C' (for conclusive).
2   See FSMA 2000, s 122(2). Provisions of this kind are identified by the marginal letter 'E' (for evidential).
3   See the FSA's explanation in MAR 1.1.12. Such provisions are identified by the letter 'G'.
4   The FSA has also issued a Guidance Note (No 1 (2001), effective from 1 December 2001) on 'frequently asked questions on the code of market conduct'; this is referred to in this chapter as the 'FAQ Guidance Note'. In addition, the Markets and Exchanges Division also issues a regular newsletter called 'Market Watch', aimed at updating market participants on market conduct issues as they arise. The newsletter does not have any formal status as guidance, but is nevertheless a useful indicator of the FSA's thinking.

The 'regular user' test

9.58   The 'regular user' test constitutes a key control on the application of the market abuse regime – indeed, it was introduced during the passage of the Bill as a result of concerns that the test as originally formulated could create an offence of strict liability or otherwise operate unfairly or perversely. As an element of the definition of 'market abuse' itself, the test also controls and in principle prevails over the CoMC.[1] It is therefore worth examining in some detail, as the CoMC itself does in section 1.2.

1   Except in relation to the CoMC's 'safe harbour' descriptions of behaviour which does not amount to market abuse. Behaviour described in one of these would not be market abuse even if, in theory, the regular user would otherwise conclude that it fell below an acceptable standard. This is very unlikely to be an issue in practice.

9.59   The 'regular user' is defined in the FSMA as 'in relation to a particular market, . . . a reasonable person who regularly deals on that market in investments of the kind in question'.[1] The CoMC glosses this by stating that:

'in determining whether behaviour amounts to market abuse, it is necessary to consider objectively whether a hypothetical reasonable person, familiar with the market in question, would regard the behaviour as acceptable in the light of all the relevant circumstances'.[2]

1   FSMA 2000, s 118(10).
2   MAR 1.2.2E.

9.60   The emphasis on the objective nature of the test and the status of the regular user as a hypothetical person (rather than an actual user, or an amalgam of actual users, of the market) are key features of the FSA's approach to the test, which, though not universally supported by commentators, appear to be justified by the wording of the FSMA.[1] One important consequence is that standards actually accepted, even generally accepted, by actual users cannot always be regarded as acceptable; in the FSA's words,[2] 'the regular user is likely to consider it relevant, although not determinative, that the behaviour conforms with standards that are generally accepted by users of the market'.

1   FSMA 2000, s 118(10) refers to the regular user as 'a reasonable person etc'. It is hard to see how this can be taken to refer to any particular actual user. If actual users had been intended, one might have expected a reference to 'persons' in the plural.
2   MAR 1.2.4E. Arguably this formulation is somewhat elliptical, the more important point being that the Tribunal and the courts, as the ultimate arbiters of the regular user test, are likely to regard the views of actual users as relevant, but not determinative, in arriving at the views of the (hypothetical) regular user.

9.61   It follows that the FSA may use its powers under the market abuse regime to penalise conduct which is generally thought by market users, but not by the FSA, to be acceptable. This possibility has given rise to some unease among practitioners and commentators. The FSA seeks to address this (but without ruling out the possibility of using its enforcement powers) by the following guidance:[1]

'The FSA does not anticipate that divergences between standards that are generally accepted by users of the market and the standards expected by the regular user will be frequent. In future, the FSA may identify a practice which is accepted in the market, but which, in the FSA's opinion, is likely to fall short of the standards expected by the regular user. In such cases the FSA will consider whether to signal its views on the practice in the form of guidance (making use of its power to do so under section 157 of the Act), or through some other statement, or by revising the Code, or to take enforcement action. The FSA recognises that the former approach will often be more appropriate, and where this is the case the FSA will work with relevant market participants and regulatory bodies (including the RIEs) to address the causes of concern. However, for those occasions where the appropriate response will be to take enforcement action, the FSA's enforcement policies in relation to market abuse as set out in ENF 14 will be relevant.'

1   MAR 1.2.11G.

9.62   A further consequence of the nature of the 'regular user' test is that the FSA's function in promulgating the CoMC, and any future changes to the CoMC, differs from its general rule-making function in being ultimately declaratory. In making rules, the FSA decides as a matter of policy what the requirements ought to be, and, subject to normal principles governing the scope of powers and the manner of exercising them, the Tribunal and the courts will recognise that this policy decision is a matter for the FSA. In relation to the CoMC, however, the CoMC sets out what the FSA considers to be the standards expected by the regular user. No doubt these will generally be the same as the standards which the FSA considers, as a matter of policy, should be applied, but in this case it is open to the Tribunal and the courts to disagree and to hold that the CoMC fails properly to reflect the views of the regular user. This distinction is not expressly referred to in the CoMC, but it is apparent that it is recognised by the FSA; in particular, the draftsman is in a number of places careful to make clear that what is described is the likely or perceived views of the regular user.[1]

1 See for example MAR 1.4.9E: 'Whether, in a particular case, a particular piece of information would, or would be likely to, be regarded as relevant information by the regular user will depend on the circumstances of the case. In making such a determination, the regular user is likely to consider the extent to which . . .'

9.63 The regular user will be different depending on the market in question; for example, the regular user of the London Stock Exchange may well be different from the regular user of the London Metal Exchange. This is important when considering a regular user's reaction to any given behaviour.

9.64 As mentioned above,[1] the absence of an express mental element in the definition of market abuse was one of the most discussed aspects of the new regime. In discussing the regular user test, the CoMC addresses this issue in the following terms:

'The statutory definition of market abuse does not require the person engaging in the behaviour to have intended to abuse the market. Accordingly it is not essential for such an intention or purpose to be present in order for the behaviour to fall below the objective standards expected. However, in some circumstances the determination of whether the behaviour falls short of those standards will depend on the purpose of the person in question . . . In those circumstances, the regular user is likely to consider the purpose of the person in question in addition to the other relevant consideration listed at MAR 1.2.3E . . .
A mistake is unlikely to fall below the objective standards expected where the person in question has taken reasonable care to prevent and detect the occurrence of such mistakes.'[2]

1 Para 4.5.
2 MAR 1.2.5E and 1.2.6E.

9.65 The FSA has also used the discussion of the regular user test to address two other controversial subjects, namely the extent to which compliance with rules of other regulators, or with the standards applicable in an overseas market, determines whether market abuse has occurred.

9.66 In relation to other rules of the FSA itself, and rules of other regulators such as recognised investment exchanges and the Panel on Takeovers and Mergers, the FSA has come under some pressure to create a safe harbour which would avoid the need for firms to take account of multiple requirements. It has declined to include any general provision to that effect: in the wording of the CoMC:

'compliance with such rules may not be sufficient for the behaviour not to amount to market abuse, since those rules may not specifically be directed at the types of behaviour prohibited by the Act or because compliance with those rules is only one consideration among others'.[1]

However, the CoMC does state that it will often be appropriate to take into account the extent to which behaviour is in compliance with such rules, and that greater weight is likely to be given to compliance with a rule that expressly requires or permits certain behaviour. It also states that the FSA is satisfied that RIE rules, the Takeover Code and the Substantial Acquisition Rules do not permit or require behaviour that amounts to market abuse.[2] In limited cases, compliance with requirements of the Takeover Code or the Substantial Acquisition Rules creates a 'safe harbour'.[3]

1 MAR 1.2.8G.
2 MAR 1.2.12G, 1.7.6E.
3 See below, paras 9.123–9.124. 'Safe harbours' for the Takeover Code are governed by a special procedure set out in FSMA 2000, s 120; the FSA requires the approval of the Treasury before it may include them.

9.67 In relation to standards in overseas markets, the CoMC cautiously states that 'where a person's behaviour occurs on an overseas market, but has an impact on a prescribed market, the regular user is likely to consider that it will be relevant to have regard to the local rules, practices and conventions prevailing in the relevant market, and whether or not the person is in the United Kingdom. However, compliance with such rules will not of itself be determinative.'[1]

1 MAR 1.2.9G. The possibility of the FSA's imposing sanctions on an overseas firm for behaviour occurring primarily in its own market is not therefore ruled out.

Scope of the market abuse regime: subject matter

9.68 The market abuse regime applies to behaviour in relation to qualifying investments which are traded on prescribed markets. The scope of 'prescribed markets' and 'qualifying investments' is determined by Treasury Order.[1] The Financial Services and Markets Act 2000 (Prescribed Markets and Qualifying Investments) Order 2001[2] prescribes all markets established under the rules of a UK recognised investment exchange (ie those exchanges recognised under s 289(1) of the FSMA 2000).

1 FSMA 2000, s 118(3).
2 SI 2001/ 996.

9.69 The Order also prescribes, for the purposes of the market abuse regime, all investments of a kind specified for the purposes of s 22 of the FSMA 2000 (ie those specified in the Financial Services and Markets Act 2000 (Regulated Activities) Order 2001).[1]

1 SI 2001/544.

9.70 The application of the CoMC to investments which have been admitted to trading, but have not yet traded, on a prescribed market, and of investments which have traded in the past and can still be, but in practice are not, traded is considered in MAR 1.11.3E. The FSA takes the view that both categories are to be regarded as 'traded on' the prescribed market, though in the latter case it is pointed out that, if there is no significant ongoing market in the investments, it is unlikely that behaviour relating to the investments will be regarded as amounting to market abuse.[1]

1   MAR 1.11.5G. This topic is discussed further in the FAQ Guidance Note, Q1.

9.71   On the face of it, the definition of the scope of the regime by reference to investments traded on a prescribed market might appear to have the result that off-market behaviour generally falls outside its scope. Any such impression would, however, be misleading, the effective scope of the regime being significantly expanded both by express provisions in FSMA 2000, s 118(6) and more generally by the effects-based nature of the concept of market abuse.

9.72   Section 118(6) of the FSMA 2000 provides that behaviour is regarded as occurring in relation to qualifying investments if it:

(a)   occurs in relation to anything which is the subject matter, or whose price or value is expressed by reference to the price or value, of those qualifying investments; or

(b)   occurs in relation to investments (whether qualifying or not) whose subject matter is those qualifying investments.

9.73   Investments and other property falling within these paragraphs are referred to in the CoMC as 'relevant products'. Examples of relevant products are:

—   the individual shares (whether or not themselves traded on a prescribed market) which are the subject matter of an index option traded on such a market, for example the individual components of the FTSE Eurotop index option traded on LIFFE;

—   conversely, an over-the-counter (OTC) option whose subject matter is a basket of shares listed on a prescribed market such as the LSE;

—   a spread bet in relation to a basket of such shares;

—   a physical commodity which is the subject of a futures contract traded on a prescribed market (eg gas or oil, both of which are the subject of IPE-traded futures contracts);

—   an OTC total return swap the payments on which are expressed by reference to the value of a share traded on a prescribed market.

9.74   Furthermore, the provisions of s 118(6) of the FSMA 2000 are not exhaustive. Behaviour may still relate to a qualifying investment even if it falls outside s 118(6). The CoMC expresses the view[1] that there needs to be a clear relationship between the behaviour and the qualifying investment in question. It goes on to point out, however, that where behaviour is engaged in *for the purpose* of abuse in relation to a qualifying investment, it may be regarded as having occurred in relation to the qualifying investment even though it is not in a qualifying investment or related product – in other words, the purpose may itself supply the necessary clear relationship.

1   MAR 1.11.7.

Territorial scope of the market abuse regime

9.75   Like the corresponding criminal offences, the market abuse regime applies if the prohibited behaviour either takes place in the UK or has effects there. Thus behaviour is to be disregarded unless it occurs in the UK or in relation to qualifying investments traded on a market which is either situated in or accessible electronically in the UK.[1]

1   FSMA 2000, s 118(5). The extension to markets which are accessible electronically makes the potential scope of the regime extremely wide, although, as mentioned above, only UK recognised investment exchanges (RIEs) are currently prescribed.

'Behaviour'

9.76   The FSMA 2000 does not give a great deal of guidance on the meaning of 'behaviour', except to provide that behaviour includes inaction as well as action.[1] The CoMC[2] expands on this reference by observing that, for example, inaction may amount to market abuse in circumstances where a person is under a legal or regulatory obligation to make a particular disclosure and fails to do so – a view which reflects that generally taken in relation to s 397 of the FSMA 2000.[3] It also sets out[4] a number of examples of behaviour. These include dealing in qualified investments, dealing in commodities or investments which are the subject matter or whose price is determined by reference to a qualifying investment, arranging deals in qualifying investments, causing or procuring or advising others to deal in qualifying investments and managing qualifying investments which belong to someone else.

1   FSMA 2000, s 118(1).
2   MAR 1.3.2.
3   See paras 9.33ff above.
4   MAR 1.3.1.

Market abuse: (1) Misuse of information

9.77   The first of the three heads of market abuse is misuse of information, expressed in s 118(2)(a) of the FSMA as follows:

> 'behaviour . . . based on information which is not generally available to those using the market but which, if available to a regular user of the market, would or would be likely to be regarded by him as relevant when deciding the terms on which transactions in investments of the kind in question should be effected'.

9.78   This description is extremely wide. It is, in fact, significantly narrowed by the CoMC, which states that behaviour will amount to misuse of information where a person deals or arranges deals[1] in a qualifying investment or relevant product where all four of the following circumstances are present:

—   the dealing or arranging is based on information which is in the possession of the person concerned and has a material influence on his decision to engage in the dealing or arranging. The information must be one of the reasons for the dealing or arranging, but need not be the only reason;
—   the information must not be generally available;
—   the information must be likely to be regarded by a regular user as relevant when deciding the terms of transactions in the investments in question; and
—   the information must relate to matters which a regular user would reasonably expect to be disclosed to users of the market on an equal basis.

1   Curiously, the CoMC does not include as a description of behaviour amounting to market abuse anything corresponding to the disclosure offence under the CJA 1993. In practice, disclosure in circumstances falling within the CJA offence is likely to be regarded as also amounting to requiring or encouraging market abuse – see below, paras 9.149–9.154.

9.79 It will be noted that the last of these four circumstances is not to be found in FSMA 2000, s 118 itself; it is presumably based on the view – which seems sound – that the regular user would not regard behaviour based on information which is not generally available as a 'misuse' of the information unless there is a reasonable expectation of general disclosure.

9.80 The CoMC subsequently identifies more closely the circumstances in which such a reasonable expectation of disclosure is regarded as arising. These are where the information:

(a) has to be disclosed in accordance with any legal or regulatory requirement (such information being called 'disclosable information'); or

(b) is routinely the subject of a public announcement, though not subject to any formal disclosure requirement ('announceable information').[1]

1 MAR 1.4.12E.

9.81 It will be seen that the 'misuse of information' limb of market abuse covers broadly the same kind of conduct as the criminal offences of insider dealing. However, there are important differences of substance, and the terminology used, though on many points addressed to essentially the same issues, is different.

9.82 One difference of substance which is characteristic of the market abuse regime is the lack of a mental element corresponding to that required under the CJA. Whereas it is an essential element of the offence of insider dealing that the person dealing know that the information he has is inside information, and that he has it as an insider, there is no corresponding requirement that a person alleged to have misused information under the market abuse regime know that the information in question is not generally available; it is enough for the information merely to be in his possession.

9.83 Further differences apply to the main concepts used in defining the prohibited behaviour under the two regimes: 'relevant' information compared with 'price-sensitive' information, and information 'not generally available' compared with information not 'made public'. Likewise, the main defences under the CoMC (dealing required for other reasons, dealing not based on information, trading information, facilitation of takeover bids) correspond to, but are not the same as, some of the CJA 1993 defences ('would have done it anyway', market information, bid facilitation). The following paragraphs examine these differences and also consider the areas where the misuse of information provisions differ more significantly from the scheme of the insider dealing legislation.

RELEVANT INFORMATION

9.84 Information is 'relevant information' if it is likely to be regarded by a regular user as relevant when deciding the terms on which transactions in the investment in question are to be entered into. It is not necessary to show that the disclosure of the information would significantly have affected the price. There may therefore be 'relevant information' which would not be regarded as price sensitive under the CJA 1993.

9.85 The CoMC states that, in determining whether information is relevant information, a regular user is likely to consider the extent to which:

— the information is specific or precise;[1]
— the information is material;
— the information is current;
— the information is reliable, including how near the person providing the information is, or appears to be, to the original source of the information and the reliability of that source;[2]
— there is other information generally available to inform other users of the market;
— the information differs from information which is generally available and can therefore be said to be new or fresh information.

1 This corresponds to one of the elements of the definition of 'inside information' (see paras 9.11–9.12), but is here merely a factor expected to be taken into account by the regular user. The difference may be partly attributable to the FSA's view of the limitations of its role under the CoMC (see para 9.62), but may also reflect a difference of substance, indicating that the FSA considers that penalties should in some cases be imposed for the misuse of unspecific or imprecise information.
2 This element has a somewhat distant connection with the CJA 1993 requirement of knowledge that information is held as an insider. The thinking is presumably that it will often not be appropriate to regard behaviour based only on a market rumour of doubtful provenance as misuse of information.

9.86 Where the information relates to future developments, the CoMC states that the regular user will also consider whether the information provides, with reasonable certainty, grounds to conclude that the possible future developments will in fact occur and the significance that the occurrence of those events would assume for other market users. This excludes information which is too imprecise or speculative to form the basis of any useful conclusion, though it may sometimes be difficult to identify the point at which information first falls into this category.

9.87 Specific examples of relevant information given in the CoMC[1] are information concerning the business affairs and prospects of a company, information or events affecting the deliverable supply of a commodity (where the relevant investment is a derivative relating to that commodity), information about official statistics and fiscal and monetary policy announcements.

1 MAR 1.4.11.

9.88 As mentioned above, relevant information comprises both information which has to be disclosed in accordance with a legal or regulatory requirement (disclosable information) and information which is routinely the subject of a public announcement without being subject to any formal disclosure requirement (announceable information).

Examples of announceable information include information which is to be the subject of official announcement by governments, changes to published credit ratings and changes to the constituents of an index, but not surveys or research based on publicly available information, eg CBI surveys or MORI polls.

Disclosable information includes information which is required to be disseminated under the Takeover Code or SARs on, or in relation to qualifying investments traded on, a prescribed market, information relating to officially listed securities which is required to be disclosed under the Listing Rules, and information which must be disclosed to a prescribed market under the rules of an RIE.

Disclosable and announceable information are expressed to include matters which are likely to be the subject of future announcements, provided that there is reasonable certainty that the disclosure will be made.

INFORMATION 'NOT GENERALLY AVAILABLE'

9.89   Section 118(7) of the FSMA provides that information which can be obtained by research or analysis conducted by, or on behalf of, users of a market is to be regarded as being generally available to them. This provision is the only clarification in the FSMA 2000 itself of what is meant by 'generally available'. It is interesting to compare it with s 58(2)(c) of the CJA 1993 (which provides that information is made public if it can be readily acquired by those likely to deal in any securities, or securities of any issuer, to which it relates) and s 58(3)(a) (which provides that information may be treated as made public even though it can be acquired only by persons exercising diligence or expertise). The two statutes appear to reach approximately the same result, but it is characteristic of the way in which the market abuse regime has been constructed that they do so with different words.

9.90   Further indications of the application of the test of 'generally available', which helpfully use language closer to that of the CJA 1993, are given in the CoMC. MAR 1.4.5E expresses the view that information is to be regarded as generally available where one or more of the following is satisfied:

— the information has been disclosed to a prescribed market through an accepted channel for dissemination of information, for example an announcement made through the London Stock Exchange's Regulatory News Service;
— the information is contained in records which are open to inspection by the public;[1]
— the information has otherwise been made public (for example through being included in a written publication or made available on the Internet) or is derived from information made public;[2]
— the information can be obtained by observation.

1   This reproduces, in slightly wider terms, CJA 1993, s 58(2)(b) (see para 9.16(b)).
2   The last phrase reproduces CJA 1993, s 58(2)(d) (see para 9.16(d)).

9.91   These factors are further amplified in MAR 1.4.6E and 1.4.7E as follows:

'People are free to use information that they have obtained through research, analysis or other legitimate means. Legitimate means include the observation of a public event. Observation of a public event includes any information which is discussed in a public area or can be observed by the public without infringing rights of privacy, property or confidentiality. Such information will be considered generally available. The fact that in practice other users of the market cannot obtain the information because of limitations on their resources, expertise or competence does not mean that the information cannot legitimately be obtained. Examples of information which might be obtainable through legitimate research include:

(1) information which is available only overseas and has not been published, or otherwise been made available to the public, in the United Kingdom;[1] and

(2) information which is only available on payment of a fee.'[2]

1 Compare CJA 1993, s 58(3)(e) (see para 9.17(e)).
2 Compare CJA 1993, s 58(3)(d) (see para 9.17(d)).

9.92   The CoMC gives as an example of legitimate dealing based on observation of a public event that of a railway passenger who sees a factory burning and telephones his broker on a mobile telephone in order to sell shares of the company which owns the factory.[1]

1 MAR 1.4.8G.

DEFENCES

9.93   The CoMC sets out a number of safe harbours in relation to the misuse of information limb. As already mentioned, these broadly correspond to some of the defences to insider dealing provided by the CJA 1993, but there are significant differences, and not all the CJA defences are reproduced.

9.94   Dealing or arranging deals does not amount to market abuse where:

(a)   the dealing or arranging was required to comply with a pre-existing legal (including contractual) or regulatory obligation in circumstances where the obligation existed before the relevant information was in the person's possession;[1] or

(b)   the person's possession of the information did not influence the decision to deal or arrange.[2]

1 MAR 1.4.20C.
2 MAR 1.4.21C.

9.95   It will be presumed that possession of the information did not influence the decision to deal or arrange if the person had taken a firm decision before the information came into his possession and the terms of the transaction did not alter after receipt of the information.

9.96   The same presumption applies where the person dealing is an organisation and one or more individuals within the organisation are in possession of relevant information, if none of the individuals in possession of the information:

(1)   had any involvement in the decision to deal;

(2)   behaved in such a way as to influence that decision, directly or indirectly; or

(3)   had any contact with those involved in the decision to deal whereby the information could have been transmitted.[1]

1 MAR 1.4.23E.

9.97   These presumptions do not appear to be conclusive, since they are identified as 'E', rather than 'C', provisions. The second of them is paralleled by a further provision which is a conclusive safe harbour. This applies where either the information in question was held behind an effective Chinese wall and the individual or individuals who dealt or arranged deals were on the other side of the wall, or arrangements equivalent to effective Chinese walls[1] had been established and maintained in respect of the information, and the individuals who dealt or arranged deals did not, therefore, have access to the relevant information.

1 The scope of 'arrangements equivalent to Chinese walls' is not entirely clear. Probably its primary focus is on arrangements within entities which are not regulated financial services institutions and, where they have arrangements serving the same purpose as Chinese walls as understood in regulated institutions, may not structure them or describe them in quite the same way. The phrase may possibly be wide enough to include *ad hoc* arrangements (sometimes called 'Chinese boxes') for the segregation of information, provided that they satisfy the test of 'effectiveness'. However, that test has in practice been very strictly interpreted by the courts in relation to *ad hoc* arrangements; and since the defence requires it to be demonstrated that the individuals did not in fact have access, it is unclear how useful this limb will be in practice.

9.98 The CoMC includes two 'safe harbours' which parallel, though not precisely, the market information defences under the CJA 1993.[1]

1 See para 9.27–9.31.

9.99 The first[1] relates to 'trading information', and provides that a person's dealing or arranging deals will not amount to a misuse of information solely because it is based on information as to that person's intention, or any other person's intention, to deal or arrange deals in relation to a qualifying investment, or information concerning deals that have taken place. This safe harbour does not include dealing or arranging which is based on information as to a possible takeover bid[2] or on information relating to new offers, issues, placements or other primary market activity.

The comparison between this defence and the general market information defence under the CJA is of great interest. Prior to the introduction of the market abuse regime, it would generally have been regarded as doubtful whether the category of dealings based on market information was as wide as that covered by the 'trading information' category described. In particular, it is doubtful whether trading while in possession of price sensitive information relating to the dealing intentions of other persons (as opposed to one's own) would always pass the 'reasonableness' test. Since, however, the CoMC will itself clearly be influential as a benchmark of acceptable standards, it is possible that the 'trading information' defence will indirectly affect the scope of the general market information defence under the CJA.

The exclusion from the 'safe harbour' of dealing based on information about 'primary market activity' is the subject of a great deal of continuing consultation and controversy, both as to its precise scope (that is, as to what is generally understood by 'primary market activity') and as to the merits. There appears to be a range of views in the market about whether the extent to which and circumstances in which some practices, notably the practice of 'pre-hedging' exposures expected to arise from impending transactions, are acceptable.

1 MAR 1.4.26C.
2 Information on takeover bids is covered by the second 'safe harbour' – see below.

9.100 The second of these 'safe harbours'[1] deals with the facilitation of takeover bids and other market operations. It therefore parallels the 'bid facilitation' defence under the CJA 1993, but, as with other provisions which have already been described, does not do so precisely. It applies where:

(a) the dealing or arranging was in connection with the acquisition or disposal of an equity stake in a company and was engaged in for the sole purpose of making that acquisition or disposal and by or for the benefit of the potential bidder; and

(b)   the information in question consists of one or more of the following matters:

— that investments of a particular kind have been or are to be acquired or disposed of, or their acquisition or disposal is under consideration or the subject of negotiation;

— that investments of a particular kind have not been or are not to be acquired or disposed of;

— the number of investments in question;

— the price or range of prices involved;

— the identity of the persons involved or likely to be involved; and

— in the case of a takeover bid, any information legitimately obtained by the bidder in relation to the target company.

The last item goes beyond the category of 'market information' as defined for purposes of the CJA.[2] It makes it clear that the bidder's making of its offer will not amount to misuse of information because the bidder has non-public information, provided that this has been legitimately obtained.[3] The inclusion of the item may also have some relevance to stake-building, because of the difference between the concepts of 'inside information' and 'relevant information'. The Takeover Code permits a prospective bidder to receive information from a target company in certain circumstances, and subject to safeguards.[4] However, the receipt of any information which is unpublished price sensitive information will generally preclude a prospective bidder from stake-building, since the 'bid facilitation' defence applies only where the only such information possessed by the person dealing is market information.[5] The additional item in the CoMC list prevents this constraint being extended to situations where information provided is not price sensitive, but is nevertheless 'relevant'.

The types of activity covered by the safe harbour include seeking irrevocable undertakings, making arrangements for the issue of securities to be used as consideration for an offer or to fund an offer (including making arrangements for underwriting or placing and any associated hedging arrangements) and making arrangements to offer a cash alternative as consideration.

1   MAR 1.4.28 to 1.4.30.
2   See para 9.27.
3   So that, for example, information obtained in breach of confidence would not be covered.
4   See rule 20 of the Takeover Code. The main safeguard is that any information which has been provided to one bidder or potential bidder must also be given, on request, to another bidder or *bona fide* potential bidder, even if the second bidder is less welcome.
5   See above, para 9.29.

9.101   Finally, there is a more general safe harbour for agreeing to underwrite an issue of securities. This has been included in the CoMC to deal with situations where, as will often happen, underwriters are given more information than just the fact of the issue (for example, where they are underwriting a rights issue to fund an acquisition).

9.102   It should be noted that there is no equivalent in the CoMC of the 'no profit' and 'equality of information' defences to insider dealing.[1]

1   See above, paras 9.23 and 9.24.

Market abuse: (2) False or misleading impressions

9.103   The second limb of market abuse occurs where:

> 'the behaviour is likely to give a regular user of the market a false or misleading impression as to the supply of, or demand for, or as to the price or value of, investments of the kind in question'.

9.104   MAR 1.5.4E expands on two elements of this definition. It states, first, that in order for behaviour to fall within this limb of the regime the impression must be materially false or misleading; and secondly, that, in order for the stated effect to be regarded as 'likely', there must be a real and not fanciful likelihood that the behaviour will have the stated effect, although the effect need not be more likely than not.[1]

1   This approach has considerable support in case law (see for example *R v Wills* [1990] Crim LR 714, CA ('likely to cause . . . suffering or injury' meant only excluding what could fairly be described as highly unlikely) and *Re SCL Building Services Ltd* (1989) 5BCC 746 ('likely' meant 'having a real prospect'), though there is also support for a more stringent approach (see for example *Taplin v C Shippon Ltd* [1978] ICR 1068, EAT (more than 51% probable) and *Bailey v Rolls Royce (1971)* [1984] ICR 688, CA (more probable than not). The New Oxford Dictionary gives 'such as might well happen or be true; probable' – arguably supporting either approach.

9.105   The FSA's view of the policy underpinning this limb and the third limb of market abuse is described in MAR 1.5.3E, which repays a careful reading. It includes the following:

> 'Prescribed markets provide a mechanism by which the price or value of investments may be determined according to the market forces of supply and demand. When market users trade on prescribed markets they expect the price or value of investments and volumes of trading to reflect the proper operation of market forces rather than the outcome of improper conduct by other market users.'

9.106   The CoMC then sets out[1] a number of general factors that are to be taken into account in determining whether or not behaviour is likely to give a regular user a false or misleading impression:

(a)   the experience and knowledge of market users;
(b)   the structure of the market, including its reporting, notification and transparency requirements;
(c)   the legal and regulatory requirements of the market concerned and accepted market practices;
(d)   the identity of the person concerned; and
(e)   the extent and nature of the visibility or disclosure of the person's activity.

1   MAR 1.5.5.

9.107   The remainder of this section of the CoMC consists of examples of behaviour which the FSA considers to fall within the false or misleading impressions limb. Two of these relate to false or misleading impressions created by conduct, while the other two deal with dissemination of information by statements.

ARTIFICIAL TRANSACTIONS

9.108   The more important example of conduct creating a false or misleading impression is that of artificial transactions. The CoMC expresses the view[1] that behaviour will amount to market abuse as an artificial transaction where a person enters into a transaction the principal effect of which will be, or will be likely to be, to inflate, maintain or depress the apparent supply or demand or price or value of a qualifying investment or relevant product so that a false or misleading impression is likely to be given to a regular user *and* the person knows or could reasonably be expected to know that this will be, or will be likely to be, the principal effect of the transaction.

1   MAR 1.5.8E.

9.109   This is, however, subject to a qualification which recognises that a formulation which looks simply to the actual or probable result of the trading would unduly restrict trading activity by catching trades which are entered into for purposes other than their expected market impact and which are of a kind which would generally be regarded as legitimate. The qualification states that a transaction will not be regarded as an artificial transaction amounting to market abuse if the regular user:

— would regard its principal rationale as a legitimate commercial rationale; and
— would regard the way in which it is to be executed as proper.

9.110   This qualification, while welcome, is likely to be difficult to apply in some cases, since both 'legitimate commercial rationale' and execution 'in a proper way' are concepts which admit of considerable differences of view. In relation to 'legitimate commercial rationale', the CoMC states[1] that:

— a transaction which has as its sole purpose, or as an actuating purpose,[2] that of inducing others to trade, or of positioning or moving the price, will not normally be considered to have a legitimate commercial rationale;
— the fact that the purpose of a transaction is to make a profit or avoid a loss does not mean that it will automatically be considered to have a legitimate commercial rationale.

1   MAR 1.5.9E.
2   The phrase 'actuating purpose' is defined as 'a purpose which motivates or incites a person to act' – see the FSA's Glossary of Definitions.

9.111   As to execution in a proper way, the CoMC states[1] that a transaction will be executed in a proper way where it is executed in a way which takes into account the need for the market as a whole to operate fairly and efficiently. This phrase is itself difficult to interpret, but it seems prudent to suppose that, where it is possible to minimise the market impact of a particular trading strategy, it will be advisable to do so. It also suggests that there may be circumstances in which a trading stategy cannot be executed without engaging in market abuse, however legitimate its commercial rationale, where it is of such a size or nature as to overwhelm the market and prevent its operating effectively at all.

1   MAR 1.5.10E. The same phrase is used in MAR 1.6.10E in relation to the distortion limb – see para 9.133 below.

9.112   The CoMC sets out[1] a number of factors to be taken into account when determining whether a transaction amounts to market abuse as an artificial transaction.[2] These are:

—   whether the transaction causes or contributes to an increase or decrease in the supply of, or the demand for, or the price or value of a qualifying investment or relevant product and the person concerned has an interest in the level of supply, demand, price or value;

—   whether the transaction involves the placing of buy or sell orders at prices higher or lower than the market price or which increase the volume of trading;

—   whether the transaction coincides with a time at or around which supply, demand, price or value is relevant (whether for the market as a whole or for the particular person) to the calculation of reference prices, settlement prices or valuations (examples of such times being close of trading and the end of a quarter);

—   whether those involved are connected parties;

—   whether the transaction causes the price to increase or decrease following which the price returns to its previous level (ie causes a temporary 'spike' or dip on the market price); and

—   whether a person places a bid (or offer) which is higher (or lower) than the previous bid or offer but removes it from the market before execution.

1   MAR 1.5.11E.
2   It continues 'although the presence of one or more of these factors does not automatically mean the behaviour amounts to market abuse'. This phrase seems unfortunate, as it could be read as suggesting that the presence of one of the factors is at least an indication of market abuse.

9.113   Most of these factors are self-explanatory. The most difficult is the third, which focuses on an area which has received a great deal of attention, namely that of heavy trading at times of particular significance. Such times include the close of trading on a particular day (which may be significant, for example, as a trigger or benchmark for payments under an exchange-traded or OTC derivative) or the close of a quarter (when the composition of indices may be rebalanced, with possible knock-on effects on supply and demand for investments coming into, or falling out of, the index). It can be particularly difficult at such times to distinguish (at least by reference only to parties' actions, as distinct from their motives) trading which should be viewed as legitimate from trading which could be thought manipulative or abusive.

9.114   The CoMC also states[1] that the extent to which the transaction generally opens a new position or closes an existing position so as to create or remove an exposure to market risk will also be relevant; if it does, this will tend to suggest the existence of a legitimate commercial rationale.

1   MAR 1.5.12E.

9.115   Specific examples given of behaviour which may give rise to a false or misleading impression and may not be for a legitimate commercial rationale are:

—   arrangements for the sale or purchase of an investment where there is no change in beneficial interests or market risk (other than repos or stock loans);

—   a transaction or series of transactions designed to conceal ownership of an investment in order to circumvent disclosure requirements; and

—   fictitious transactions.[1]

1   MAR 1.5.14E.

9.116   Conversely, the following are given as examples of behaviour which will not give rise to a false or misleading impression, even though it has the characteristics described at paragraph 9.108 above, provided that the tests of 'legitimate commercial rationale' and 'execution in a proper way' are satisfied:

—   transactions which effect the taking or unwinding of a position so as to take legitimate advantage of differences in income or capital taxation or differences in the price of investments or commodities as traded in different locations[1] (ie tax and inter-market arbitrage);
—   borrowing or lending of investments or commodities to meet underlying commercial demand.

This provision[2] is expressed to be a conclusive 'safe harbour', though it is perhaps less clear-cut than this might suggest when one takes into account the use of the phrase 'legitimate advantage' and the incorporation of the difficult 'legitimate commercial rationale' and 'execution in a proper way' tests.

1   Presumably the same applies to trading to take legitimate advantage of price differences between different markets (for example between cash and futures markets) in the same location.
2   MAR 1.5.24C.

COURSE OF CONDUCT

9.117   MAR 1.5.21E sets out a head of conduct creating a false or misleading impression which in most respects parallels that of artificial transactions, but is more broadly and generally expressed. It states that behaviour will constitute market abuse where a person engages in a course of conduct, the principal effect of which will be, or is likely to be, to give a false or misleading impression to the regular user as to the supply or demand or price or value of a qualifying investment or relevant product *and* the person knows or could reasonably be expected to know that this will be, or will be likely to be, the principal effect of the conduct on the market.

This formulation is similar to that for artificial transactions,[1] and it too is subject to the tests of legitimate commercial rationale and execution in a proper way. Its very wide scope makes it open-ended and difficult to interpret. The only examples given[2] are movements of physical commodity stocks and of empty cargo ships, either of which might create a false or misleading impression as to the supply of, demand for or price or value of a commodity deliverable into a commodity futures contract.

1   MAR 1.5.8, described at paragraph 9.108 above.
2   MAR 1.5.22E.

DISSEMINATION OF INFORMATION

9.118   The CoMC contains two provisions dealing with the dissemination of false or misleading information. The first applies to anyone who disseminates information, the second only to those responsible for the dissemination of information through an 'accepted channel of communication'.

9.119   A person is stated to engage in market abuse under the first of these heads where he disseminates information which is, or if true would be, 'relevant information' in circumstances where he knows or could reasonably be expected to know that the information is false or misleading and disseminates it in order to create a false or misleading impression. An example of such behaviour is posting false or misleading information on an Internet bulletin board about the takeover of a company.[1] It will be seen that this formulation produces a result similar to that under s 397(3) of the FSMA 20000.[2]

1 MAR1.5.17E.
2 See paras 9.42–9.46 above. The phrase 'or could reasonably be expected to know' (that the information is false or misleading) differs from the wording of s 397(3), but arguably produces a result close to that of the defence in s 397(5)(a), which requires a person accused to demonstrate a *reasonable* belief that his act or conduct would not create a false or misleading impression. Interestingly, s 397(1) is actually wider than the CoMC formulation, since recklessness both as to the falsity of the information and as to the result is sufficient – see paras 9.40 and 9.41.

9.120 By contrast, a person responsible for the submission of information to an accepted channel for the dissemination of information is stated[1] to engage in market abuse if the information is (or if true would be) relevant information, it is likely to give a regular user a false or misleading impression as to supply, demand, price or value and the person who submits it has not taken reasonable care to ensure that it is not false or misleading. This provision therefore imposes a negligence standard on persons responsible for the submission of, among other things, trade reports and company announcements.

1 MAR 1.5.18E.

9.121 The rationale for this provision is explained as follows:

'The FSA recognises the importance of information disseminated through accepted channels for the dissemination of information. Users of such information should be able to rely on the accuracy and integrity of information carried through these channels. It is, therefore, appropriate that those who disseminate information through them, for example, the company itself, its financial advisers or its public relations advisers, take reasonable care to ensure that the information is not inaccurate or misleading.'[1]

1 MAR 1.5.20E.

9.122 This explanation exposes an element of ambiguity in the word 'responsible'. One would expect it to be used in the strict sense, as referring to the person on whom the requirement to disseminate the information in question falls – in the case of a listed company, the company itself. It seems, however, that the FSA regards the negligence standard as also applying to advisers who in fact assist the company in providing the information.

SAFE HARBOURS

9.123 The CoMC sets out two safe harbours applicable to the dissemination of information. The first[1] states that making a report or disclosure will not of itself give rise to a false or misleading impression[2] if the report or disclosure was made in accordance with the way specified by any applicable legal or regulatory requirement and was expressly required or permitted by FSA rules, the rules of a prescribed market, the Takeover Code or Substantial Acquisition Rules or the rules of any competent statutory, governmental or regulatory authority.

1 MAR 1.5.25C.

2 Strictly, this should perhaps read 'will not constitute market abuse' – one of the concerns is that compliance with some disclosure requirements will indeed give rise to a false or misleading impression because of the terms of the requirement. For example, under s 198 of the Companies Act 1985 a firm is required to disclose a long position as an interest in a public company's voting share capital even if it has a matching short position. Arguably this gives a misleading impression as to the true level of its interest.

9.124   This is amplified in guidance[1] as follows:

'Examples of disclosure that is expressly required or permitted include rule 9.10(j) of the listing rules, which permits a company to delay certain announcements at its discretion, and section 198 of the Companies Act 1985 which requires disclosure of certain interests in shares. See also MAR 1.7.7C concerning rules of the Takeover Code which relate, among other things, to the timing of announcements and MAR 1.7.3E(3)–1.7.3E(4) concerning the listing rules.'

This is helpful as indicating that the FSA regards the rules in question as negativing market abuse in cases where it is the deferred timing of an announcement, rather than its content as such, which creates the possibility of a false or misleading impression being created.

1 MAR 1.5.25G.

9.125   The second safe harbour, which relates to Chinese walls, is set out in three paragraphs. The first[1] notes that an organisation may be aware of information that is not known to all the individuals within the organisation. It then states that if an individual within the organisation disseminates information which he would know, or could reasonably be expected to know, is false or misleading if he were aware of information held by other individuals within the organisation, he will be taken not to know, or to be reasonably expected to know, that it is false or misleading if the other information is held behind an effective Chinese wall or is restricted using other similarly effective arrangements[2] and there was nothing which was known or ought reasonably to have been known to the individual who disseminated the information which should have led him to conclude it was false or misleading. This paragraph therefore provides a defence to the individual concerned.

1 MAR 1.5.27C.
2 See para 9.97, note 1 above.

9.126   The second paragraph[1] reads as follows:

'For the purposes of MAR 1.5.27C, the fact that the person did not know, or could not reasonably have been expected to know, that the information was false or misleading can be demonstrated by showing that the requirements identified in MAR 1.4.23E[2] have been satisfied. Where it can be demonstrated that the individual disseminating the information did not know, or could not be reasonably expected to know, that the information was false or misleading, behaviour will not fall within the description of market abuse set out in MAR 1.5.15E.'

This paragraph therefore provides protection to the firm.

1 MAR 1.5.28C.
2 The text refers to MAR 1.4.22E, but it seems clear that this is an error.

9.127   The third paragraph[1] states that 'the circumstances described in MAR 1.4.23E(1) to MAR 1.4.23E(3)[2] are capable of giving rise to a presumption that the other information in question is held behind an effective Chinese wall or is restricted using other similarly effective arrangements'. The references to MAR 1.4.23E in this and the preceding paragraph are not easy to interpret, since MAR 1.4.23E relates to influence on decisions to deal rather than to the dissemination of information as such. Presumably the references should in this context be treated as references to the decision to disseminate the relevant information.

1 MAR 1.5.29E.
2 See para 9.96 above.

Market abuse: (3) Market distortion

9.128 The final head of market abuse is behaviour which:

'a regular user of the market would, or would be likely to, regard . . . as behaviour which would, or would be likely to, distort the market in investments of the kind in question'.

9.129 Unlike the other two limbs, this has no close parallel under the pre-existing criminal law, though there is a substantial degree of overlap between this limb and the false and misleading impressions limb.[1]

1 A point which is made in the CoMC at MAR 1.5.6G.

9.130 The CoMC makes some of the same introductory points in relation to distortion as in relation to false and misleading impressions. Thus it stresses the key element of interference with the proper operation of market forces and glosses the word 'likely' with the view that there must be a 'real and not fanciful' likelihood that the behaviour will have a distorting effect, but that the effect need not be more likely than not.

9.131 The CoMC gives two examples of distortion: (i) price positioning and (ii) abusive squeezes.

PRICE POSITIONING

9.132 The CoMC states that behaviour will constitute market abuse where a person enters into a transaction with the purpose[1] of positioning the price of a qualifying investment or relevant product at a distorted level.

1 This is, therefore, another example of the effect of the regular user test in reintroducing a mental element. As in the case of false and misleading impressions, 'purpose', in the view of the FSA, need not be the sole purpose but must be an 'actuating purpose' – MAR 1.6.9E.

9.133 It follows, in the FSA's view, that 'behaviour which incorporates a purpose of positioning the price at a distorted level cannot have a legitimate commercial purpose'. The CoMC states that it does not restrict market users trading significant volumes where there is a legitimate purpose for the transaction, helpfully citing the case of index tracking, which can involve significant trading at the close (especially at the time of a rebalancing of the index). This is, however, subject to the test of execution 'in a proper way, that is, a way which takes into account the need for the market as a whole to operate fairly and efficiently'.[1]

1 MAR 1.6.10E – compare the same sentiment in para 9.111.

9.134   The overall effect of these provisions is difficult to judge precisely, given the breadth and lack of precision of the key concept of 'distortion'. It seems that any trading effected with a purpose of affecting the price is viewed with suspicion, though MAR 1.6.10 also uses the somewhat higher test of 'trading significant volumes with the purpose of *controlling* the price . . . and positioning it at a *distorted* level' (emphasis added). It also seems, as under the false and misleading impressions limb, that where trading is likely to have an effect on the price it is prudent to assume that the 'execution in a proper way' requirement dictates that the effect be minimised.

9.135   Some reassurance can be gained from the statement that:

'it is unlikely that the behaviour of market users when trading at times and in sizes most beneficial to them (whether for the purpose of long term investment objectives, risk management or short term speculation) and seeking the maximum profit from their dealings will itself amount to distortion. Such behaviour, generally speaking, improves the liquidity and efficiency of markets.'[1]

It is, however, difficult to judge how far this statement can be taken in relation to speculative trading in volatile markets, where at least the expected effect of trades on the price will inevitably enter into a trader's calculations.

1   MAR 1.6.5E.

9.136   Factors relevant when determining whether price positioning has occurred include:

— whether the transaction coincides with a time at which the price or value is relevant to the calculation of reference prices or valuations;
— the extent to which the person had an interest in the price or value of the investment;
— the volume or size of the transaction in relation to the depth and liquidity of the market at the time;
— the extent to which the price, rate or option volatility movements are outside normal ranges;
— the extent to which the transaction causes the price to increase or decrease following which the price returns to its previous level; and
— whether a person has successively and consistently increased or decreased his bid or offer or the price he has paid.

9.137   Examples of price positioning include:

— simultaneously buying and selling investments in order to position the price of an investment in order to affect the settlement value of an option;
— placing a large sell order in a stock in order to force the stock out of an index, thereby realising a large gain on a short position in the stock;
— a fund manager placing a large buy order in illiquid shares in order to drive up the price of the shares so as to improve the fund manager's performance.

ABUSIVE SQUEEZES

9.138   An abusive squeeze is stated to occur where a person with significant influence over the supply of, or demand for, or delivery mechanisms for an investment or relevant product and a position in the investment under which it is deliverable engages in behaviour with the purpose of positioning at a distorted level the delivery price for that investment or product.[1]

1   MAR 1.6.13E. As in the case of other provisions of the CoMC, 'purpose' need not be the sole purpose, but must be an 'actuating purpose'.

9.139   Not every squeeze is regarded as abusive; indeed the CoMC states that 'squeezes occur relatively frequently when the proper interaction of supply and demand leads to market tightness'. It also makes clear that having a significant influence over supply, demand or delivery mechanisms is not itself abusive.

9.140   What is less clear is when a squeeze crosses the boundary of what is 'abusive'. Factors to be taken into account include:

—   the extent to which a person is willing to relax his control or influence in order to help maintain an orderly market and the price at which he is willing to do so;
—   the extent to which the person's activity causes or risks causing settlement failure by other users on a multilateral basis;
—   the extent to which prices for delivery under the market's delivery mechanisms diverge from those under other delivery mechanisms; and
—   the extent to which the spot market compared to the forward market is unusually expensive or inexpensive or the extent to which borrowing rates are unusually expensive or inexpensive.

9.141   The CoMC expresses the view[1] that the extent to which other market users have failed to protect their own interests or fulfil their obligations will influence the effects of an abusive squeeze and a regular user is likely to expect other market users to fulfil their obligations and not put themselves in a position of having to rely on holders of long positions when they may not be inclined to lend and may be under no obligation to do so. This suggests that the concept of an 'abusive squeeze' is not regarded as imposing an obligation to lend in all circumstances, and possibly that a refusal to lend, or a willingness to do so only on onerous terms, may be regarded as legitimate at least in cases where the borrowing demand itself results from short selling which could be regarded as abusive.

1   MAR 1.6.17G.

SAFE HARBOURS

9.142   The only safe harbour specifically for market distortion relates to the LME document 'Market Aberrations: the Way Forward' published in October 1998.[1]

1   MAR 1.6.19C.

General defences and safe harbours in respect of market abuse

9.143   The FSMA 2000[1] provides that where an FSA rule includes a provision to the effect that behaviour conforming with that rule does not amount to market abuse, then behaviour which conforms with that rule will not constitute market abuse. The rules which include such a provision are listed in MAR 1.7.3E; they are:

(a)   the price stabilising rules;
(b)   the rules relating to Chinese walls;

(c)   listing rules relating to the timing, dissemination or availability, content and standard of care applicable to a disclosure, announcement, communication or release of information; and

(d)   rule 15.1(b) of the Listing Rules, which relates to share buy-backs.

These safe harbours apply to all three limbs of the definition of market abuse (discussed above).

1   See s 118(8).

9.144   Under s 120 of the FSMA 2000, the FSA also has the power to include in the CoMC a provision to the effect that behaviour which in its opinion conforms with the Takeover Code does not amount to market abuse whether generally, in specified circumstances or in relation to specified persons. This section differs from the other safe harbour provisions in requiring the approval of the Treasury for the inclusion of such a provision.

9.145   In relation to the false and misleading impression and distortion limbs of market abuse (but not the misuse of information limb), the CoMC includes two specific safe harbours for provisions of the Takeover Code and the SARs. Conformity with:

(a)   the provisions relating to the timing, dissemination or availability, content and standard of care applicable to a disclosure, announcement, communication or release of information;

(b)   the provisions of rule 4.2 of the Takeover Code (restrictions on dealings by offeror and concert parties);

provides a safe harbour insofar as the behaviour is expressly required or permitted by the relevant rules and does not breach the Takeover Code's general principles.[1]

1   MAR 1.7.7C, 1.7.8C and 1.7.10E.

9.146   MAR 1.7.9G gives an illustration of how the safe harbours are intended to operate. It states that if a rule of the Takeover Code is about timing of an announcement, the safe harbour confers protection in so far as timing is relevant. This means that disclosure of a dealing after the event will be sufficient where this is what the Takeover Code requires or permits. But the method of dissemination, the content and the standard of care will not be protected unless they are in compliance with the relevant provisions of the Takeover Code or SARs.

9.147   The CoMC also states[1] that the FSA is satisfied that none of the other provisions of the Takeover Code (ie the provisions not referred to in the safe harbours) permits or requires behaviour which amounts to market abuse.

1   MAR 1.7.6E.

9.148   However, the CoMC also points out[1] that, in cases where no safe harbour applies, the regular user may not necessarily consider that complying with applicable requirements of the Takeover Code or the SARs will be sufficient to demonstrate that behaviour does not amount to market abuse, although it may be relevant in assessing whether a person's behaviour has fallen below reasonably expected standards. It gives as an example a case where a person builds a stake in conformity with the SARs, but his decision to do so was based on relevant information and none of the safe harbours in the misuse of information section of the CoMC applies.

1 MAR 1.7.13E.

'Requiring and encouraging'

9.149 Section 123 of the FSMA 2000 empowers the FSA to impose penalties not only on a person who engages or has engaged in market abuse, but also on a person who, by taking or refraining from taking any action, has required or encouraged another person or persons to engage in behaviour which, if engaged in by the person requiring or encouraging, would amount to market abuse.

9.150 This provision is amplified in section 1.8 of the CoMC. It is of great importance, the more so because of the broad interpretation placed on it by the FSA.

9.151 Straightforward examples given of requiring or encouraging are:

— a director instructing an employee to deal in investments at a time when the director has relevant and disclosable information;
— a person advising or recommending another person to engage in behaviour which would be market abuse if engaged in by the adviser;[1]
— a person who has relevant and disclosable information about a company advising another person to acquire shares in the company.[2]

1 MAR 1.8.3G.
2 MAR 1.8.9. This example of course corresponds to the encouraging offence under the CJA 1993.

9.152 It is also made clear that the FSA will generally regard selective dissemination of information about a listed company in circumstances not permitted by the relevant provisions of the listing rules as amounting to requiring and encouraging. This shows that the FSA interprets 'encouraging' as extending to communications which do not contain any explicit element of encouragement but clearly have that flavour in the context in which they are made.

9.153 The guidance also suggests, however, that the FSA interprets the concept of encouragement through inaction widely, and will approach it, like the definition of market abuse itself, by reference to its effects and without the inclusion of any mental element. MAR 1.8.8G provides that:

'Where the originator of the transaction appears to have engaged in market abuse and, in the course of doing so, has acted through an intermediary, the intermediary's behaviour will not amount to either requiring or encouraging or market abuse unless the intermediary knew or ought reasonably to have known that the originator was engaging in market abuse.'

This suggests that negligent failure to detect market abuse on behalf of a client can amount to 'requiring or encouraging' the abuse. This is, at best, a strange use of language; it is open to question whether the ordinary meaning of either word can be stretched to cover this situation.

9.154   Other guidance on circumstances which will not amount to requiring or encouraging, while helpful in itself, also indicates a broad and effects-based approach to the concept. Thus MAR 1.8.6G cites various examples of disclosures which the FSA will not regard as requiring or encouraging the recipient to deal. These include disclosures to employees, advisers, negotiating counterparties and public and regulatory bodies – exclusions which, while in themselves helpful, would not naturally be assumed to be needed unless a very broad view of the scope of requiring and encouraging were taken.

'Reasonable belief' and 'due diligence' defences

9.155   Section 123 of the FSMA 2000 confers protection against some of the consequences of market abuse, and of requiring or encouraging market abuse, where there are reasonable grounds for the FSA to be satisfied, after taking into account any representations made by the person concerned, that a person reasonably believed that he was not doing either of those things or took all reasonable precautions and exercised all due diligence to avoid doing them.

9.156   This section does not technically constitute a defence, since it does not prevent the behaviour from amounting to market abuse (or requiring or encouraging). It does, however, preclude the imposition of a penalty, the issue of a public statement or the making of a restitution order. The FSA's powers of investigation and the possibility of an injunction to restrain the behaviour are not affected.

9.157   The FSA's Enforcement Manual[1] gives some guidance on the factors which the FSA will take into account in determining whether a person had reasonable grounds for believing that their behaviour did not amount to market abuse. These include:

—   the extent to which the person took reasonable precautions to avoid market abuse;
—   the treatment of the relevant behaviour in the CoMC and any relevant FSA guidance;
—   the rules of any relevant market or any other relevant regulatory requirements or codes of conduct or best practice;
—   the level of knowledge, skill and experience to be expected of the person concerned; and
—   whether the person can demonstrate a legitimate purpose for the behaviour.

1   See ENF 16.5.1G.

9.158   In relation to the test of reasonable precautions and due diligence, the FSA states that it will take into account:

—   the extent to which the person followed established internal consultation and escalation procedures;
—   the extent to which he sought and followed legal and other expert professional advice;
—   the extent to which he sought and followed advice from the relevant market authorities or, where relevant, the Takeover Panel;
—   any relevant FSA guidance; and

— the rules of any relevant market or any other relevant regulatory requirements for codes of conduct or best practice.

Sanctions for market abuse

9.159 The FSMA provides a range of sanctions in cases of market abuse or expected market abuse.

The basic sanction is the imposition by the FSA of a 'penalty' (in effect, a fine, but one imposed outside the framework of the criminal law). The FSMA 2000 does not impose any limit on the amount of such a penalty.

Alternatively, the FSA may make a public statement to the effect that a person has engaged in market abuse.[1]

1 See FSMA 2000, s 123.

9.160 Sections 384 and 383 of the FSMA 2000 empower the FSA on its own initiative, and the court on the application of the FSA, to make restitution orders, aimed at compensating those who have been affected by market abuse, provided that they are satisfied that the person in question has engaged in market abuse, or required or encouraged another person to engage in market abuse, and that as a result profits have accrued to that person or one or more persons have suffered loss or been adversely affected. The FSA or the court may order the person concerned to pay such sum as appears to be just, having regard to the profits that have accrued to the person concerned and, where one or more persons have suffered loss or other adverse effect, the extent of that loss or adverse effect. This is a potentially costly remedy for the person against whom it is ordered, since that person may be required to recompense those who have suffered loss as a result of the relevant behaviour without any offset for any benefit received by other market participants.

9.161 Section 381 of the FSMA 2000 gives the court the discretionary power to grant an injunction on the application of the FSA to prevent market abuse or deal with the consequences of abusive behaviour or to prevent the disposal of assets.

9.162 Where the same facts constitute an offence under Part V of the CJA 1993 or s 397 of the FSMA 2000 and market abuse, the FSA will need to decide whether to take action in respect of the criminal offence or in respect of market abuse. As regards criminal offences, the FSA considers whether there is sufficient evidence to provide a realistic prospect of conviction and whether, having regard to the seriousness of the offence and all other circumstances, a criminal prosecution is in the public interest. There are a number of additional factors which the FSA will take into account, namely:

— whether the misconduct is serious and prosecution is likely to result in a significant sentence;
— whether there are victims who have suffered loss and the extent and nature of their losses and whether the person concerned made a profit or avoided a loss;
— the effect on the market and/or market confidence;
— whether the misconduct may be continued or repeated and a financial penalty is unlikely to deter further misconduct;

— previous cautions, convictions or other action for market misconduct;
— whether the misconduct involves dishonesty or an abuse of position of authority or trust;
— where the misconduct is carried out by a group, whether a particular individual has played a leading role; and
— the circumstances of the individual.

9.163 However, the FSA has confirmed that it will not pursue a criminal prosecution and impose a civil sanction for market abuse in respect of the same behaviour.

The FSA has also given guidance on the approach it will adopt to the exercise of its powers to impose civil sanctions

Power to fine and censure publicly

9.164 The FSA's enforcement manual gives guidance on how the FSA will exercise its power to impose fines or publicly censure for market abuse. It will consider all relevant circumstances, but has specifically indicated that the following will be relevant to a decision whether or not to take action:

— the nature and seriousness of the behaviour (including, where it was deliberate or reckless, its duration and frequency, its market impact, the amount of any benefit gained or loss avoided and risk of loss to others);
— the conduct of the person concerned (including how quickly and completely it was brought to the attention of the FSA or another regulator, the degree of co-operation shown by the person to the regulators, any remedial steps taken to address the behaviour and how promptly those have been taken and whether the person has complied with the requirements of another regulator);
— the degree of sophistication of the users of the market in question, its size and liquidity and its susceptibility to market abuse;
— action taken by other regulatory authorities;
— action taken by the FSA in similar cases;
— the impact a financial penalty or public statement might have on the market or on the interests of consumers;
— the likelihood of repetition; and
— the disciplinary record and general compliance history of the person concerned.

9.165 Once the FSA has decided to take action, it will need to decide which form of sanction is appropriate. In general terms the FSA's policy is to consider issuing a public statement that market abuse has occurred where it believes that a statement will more appropriately address the behaviour in question. It will consider all relevant circumstances, but has specifically set out the factors which it will consider in deciding whether to impose a penalty or publicly censure a person for engaging in market abuse. For example, if the person concerned has gained a financial advantage from their abusive behaviour this will tend to indicate a penalty, but if the person has admitted their behaviour and taken steps to compensate anyone who has suffered loss as a result, the FSA will be inclined to censure that person. In addition, the FSA has conceded that the more serious the behaviour, the more likely that it will impose a penalty.

9.166   If the FSA concludes that a penalty is appropriate, it will take into account all relevant circumstances in determining the level of that penalty. It has indicated, in particular, that it will take account of:

—   the adverse effect of the behaviour on the markets and the seriousness of that effect (including the risk of loss, the duration and frequency of the behaviour and its impact on the orderliness of markets);
—   the extent to which the behaviour was deliberate or reckless;
—   whether the person on whom the penalty is to be imposed is an individual;
—   the amount of any profit made or loss avoided;
—   conduct following the behaviour (including whether the person alerted regulators, his degree of co-operation with them, whether he took remedial steps and whether he complied with the requirements of other regulators);
—   the person's disciplinary record and compliance history;
—   previous action undertaken by the FSA in respect of similar behaviour; and
—   action taken by other regulatory authorities.

9.167   These provisions reflect s 124 of the FSMA 2000, which requires the FSA to issue a statement of its policy with regard to, amongst other things, the amount of its penalties for market abuse. The FSA must also have regard to this policy when deciding upon the level of penalty it plans to impose in each particular case.

Restitution orders

9.168   When deciding whether to seek a restitution order from the court, or to make an order on its own initiative, the FSA will consider all relevant circumstances, but has specifically indicated that the following will be relevant:

—   whether the profits are quantifiable;
—   whether the losses are identifiable;
—   the number of persons affected and whether they have contributed to their own loss or failed to take reasonable steps to protect their interests;
—   the costs likely to be incurred by the FSA;
—   whether practicable redress is available elsewhere (for example through the ombudsman scheme) or through another regulator;
—   whether persons can bring their own proceedings; and
—   whether the person is solvent.

Injunctions

9.169   In deciding whether to seek an injunction the FSA will consider all relevant circumstances, but has specifically indicated that the following will be relevant:

—   the nature and seriousness of the misconduct or expected misconduct (including its impact on the financial system and the extent and nature of any losses or likely losses);
—   whether the conduct has stopped or is likely to stop;

—   whether there are any remedial steps which could be taken;
—   whether there is a danger of assets being dissipated;
—   the relationship between the FSA's likely costs and the likely benefits;
—   the person's compliance record and disciplinary history;
—   whether other FSA powers adequately address the matter;
—   whether another regulator can adequately address the matter; and
—   whether there is information to suggest financial crime.

Other remedies against authorised and approved persons

9.170   Principle 5 of the FSA's Principles for Businesses (which are made by the FSA under s 118 of the FSMA 2000 and apply to all authorised persons) requires an authorised person to observe proper standards of market conduct. Breach of this principle may result in disciplinary and other sanctions, including a penalty, censure, alteration of the relevant person's permissions or, in an extremely serious case, the removal of authorisation. The FSA has indicated that where the principal mischief arising from the behaviour is market abuse, it will take action under the market abuse regime rather than under the Principles for Businesses. However, it has also indicated that it may take action under both where it is unclear or arguable where the principal mischief lies.

9.171   An individual who is an approved person under the regime established by Part V of the FSMA 2000[1] is subject to Principle 3 of the Statements of Principle for Approved Persons, which requires an approved person to observe proper standards of market conduct in carrying out his controlled function. Breach of this statement of principle exposes the person concerned to sanctions which include penalty, censure and the withdrawal of approval.

1   See Chapter 5.

Interaction between the FSA and other regulators

9.172   In circumstances where behaviour occurs on a prescribed market, the FSA will refer the matter to the relevant RIE and give due weight to its views. However, the FSA does have power to require RIEs not to investigate or terminate or suspend an existing investigation. As a result of this overlap, the FSA and the RIEs have agreed operating arrangements for the enforcement of market abuse cases.

9.173   Where behaviour occurs in the context of a takeover bid to which the Takeover Code or SARs are relevant, the FSA will refer to the Panel and will give due weight to its views. It expects people to exhaust procedures available for complaint under the Takeover Code and the SARs and expects to take action before exhaustion of these procedures or during the course of a takeover bid only in exceptional circumstances (broadly where the Panel asks it to intervene, consistency requires it, the matter covers securities outside the Panel's jurisdiction or there are financial stability issues). It considers that the Takeover Panel's informal powers will often be sufficient to address concerns, although, of course, the Panel does not have power to impose a financial penalty. As with the RIEs, the FSA has agreed operating arrangements with the Takeover Panel in relation to enforcing market abuse cases.

Chapter 10

The prevention of money laundering and terrorist finance

INTRODUCTION

10.1 Most people would not quarrel with the view that customers have a right to expect that their financial affairs will be kept private. Under English law, the nature of the contract between a bank and its customer imports a legal duty not to disclose information about the customer's account to third parties. This is known as the duty of confidentiality. As regards retail customers, the duty is expressly set out in the Banking Code. The duty has always been subject to qualification, including situations where disclosure is under compulsion at law, or under a duty to the public.[1]

1 *Tournier v National Provincial and Union Bank of England* [1924] 1 KB 461, CA.

10.2 In recent years, attention has been focused less on customer rights to privacy, and more on the prevention of misuse of the financial system by criminal elements. Banking confidentiality, or as it is often called bank secrecy, has become associated with money laundering and dubious off-shore bank accounts. The result increasingly is that banks are not merely entitled under certain circumstances to report suspicious activity on their customer's account to the authorities, but are obliged to do so under pain of criminal penalty.

Concern was initially focused on the proceeds of drugs dealing. The anti-money laundering provisions of the UN Convention against Illicit Traffic in Narcotic Drugs and Psychotropic Substances concluded in Vienna in 1988 are a landmark in this respect.

Then came the Financial Action Task Force on Money Laundering (FATF), established by the G-7 Summit held in Paris in 1989. It has actively sought to promote the fight by taking on centres deemed lax on money laundering, and imposing sanctions on miscreants.

Another trend is that measures originally restricted to the proceeds of drug dealing have been increasingly extended to cover the proceeds of crime generally.

A further extension is as regards the use of the financial system to salt away the proceeds of corruption by political leaders.

Finally, the attacks on the United States on September 11 brought all these issues into focus. The attacks clearly required considerable funding. In the aftermath, the inhibition of terrorist finance has become an important international objective.

10.3   The result of all this is that financial institutions have been required to take a much closer interest in their customer's affairs than was previously the case. Whilst the principle is clear and laudatory,[1] the practical difficulties are not always appreciated. For one thing, money laundering rarely presents itself in a neatly recognisable form. There are rarely identifiable proceeds of a specific crime, let alone a crime committed by someone whose guilt has been established in a court of law. Banks and financial institutions are not set up as private detectives. At the same time, it is important that action should take place within a proper legal framework.

A balance has to be struck between the very necessary fight against the abuse of the financial system, and issues of privacy, the right to property and due process. Some of those working in the field believe that the anti-money laundering regime requires pruning and refocusing. But the confusing array of statutes, secondary legislation, industry guidance notes and international standards is probably here to stay for the time being.

1   A point which has been made by the courts: see *Governor and Company of the Bank of Scotland v A Ltd* [2001] Lloyd's Rep Bank 73.

10.4   This chapter examines the rules that apply to banks carrying on business in the UK. In this regard, there is a strong interest in a level playing field internationally. Little can be achieved by the implementation of high standards in one jurisdiction if lower standards are applied elsewhere. That leads to an immediate problem. The enactment of suitable laws is only one stage in the process: The laws then have to be implemented by proper practices within banks; supervisory authorities have then to be properly vigilant to see that the rules are kept; and the courts of all countries concerned have to provide effective procedures to enforce the rules if necessary.

10.5   An appreciation of the above points underlies the work of the FATF. As a result of this work, there has been a general tightening of standards, particularly in countries which it 'blacklists'. The FATF has issued forty recommendations as regards money laundering. These are aimed as much at national policy-makers and supervisors as at financial institutions. An important private initiative complementing the work of the FATF at the operational level is found in the so-called 'Wolfsberg AML Principles'. These were formulated by a group of international banks.[1]

1   Named after Wolfsberg, in Switzerland, where the working group met. Global anti-money laundering guidelines for private banking were published in October 2000. A statement as regards the Suppression of the Financing of Terrorism was published in January 2002.

10.6   The body of recommendations and principles produced by these international initiatives are an example of 'soft law'. They have no legal effect in themselves. On the other hand, they have appeared indirectly in the standards applied in the UK. For example, according to the Guidance issued by the Joint Money Laundering Steering Group (JMLSG), firms offering private banking facilities should consider adopting the Wolfsberg principles.[1] Another example is the requirement in the FSA's money laundering sourcebook that firms are required to 'make proper use' of findings of inadequacy made by the FATF.[2] So although a UK banking business is entitled to look to local law to define its obligations, the international element cannot be ignored.

1   Guidance Notes, para 2.24.
2   ML 5.1.2.

10.7   Over time, a number of key tools have been developed, namely:

(a)   *The 'know your customer' (KYC) requirement.* This involves establishing the identity of a prospective customer and the expected origin of the funds to be used in the proposed relationship. Where relevant, beneficial owner- ship must be established.

(b)   *The recognition and reporting of suspicious transactions.* Financial institu- tions are not expected to act as prosecutors. Their key role is to report suspicious transactions to the authorities, who then must decide what action to take. Suspicious transaction reports (STRs) in the UK are made to the National Criminal Intelligence Service (NCIS). In the US, reporting requirements go further than to file a report of suspicious activity (SAR). There is an automatic requirement to file a Currency Transaction Report (CTR) in respect of cash transactions exceeding a specified threshold.[1] This approach has not been adopted in Europe.

(c)   *Staff training.* Anti-money laundering measures are only as effective as the staff who have the responsibility to administer them.

(d)   *Record keeping.* Investigators refer to the 'audit trail' that should in theory enable even complex transactions to be pieced together. In the UK, records are retained for a five-year period.

1   In the US, the threshold is currently US$10,000.

10.8   Clearly, these tools cannot be applied mechanically. They have to be applied intelligently in a way commensurate with the size of the particular financial business, and the degree of risk posed by the transaction concerned. Some transactions will obviously be very low risk and conversely others will be high risk.

The Wolfsberg principles contain a checklist of situations which may require particular attention:

(a)   *Numbered or alternate name accounts.* These, it is said, should only be accepted if the bank has established the identity of the client and the beneficial owner.

(b)   *High-risk countries.* A bank should apply heightened scrutiny to clients and beneficial owners resident in and funds sourced from countries identified by credible sources as having inadequate anti-money launder- ing standards or representing high-risk for crime and corruption.

(c)   *Offshore jurisdictions.* Risks associated with entities organised in offshore jurisdictions are covered by due diligence procedures laid out in the guidelines.

(d)   *High-risk activities.* Clients and beneficial owners whose source of wealth emanates from activities known to be susceptible to money laundering will be subject to heightened scrutiny.

(e)   *Public officials.* Individuals who have or have had positions of public trust such as government officials, senior executives of government corporations, politicians, important political party officials, etc and their families and close associates also require heightened scrutiny.

ANTI-MONEY LAUNDERING: LAW AND LIABILITY

Sources of anti-money laundering law in the UK

10.9   There are five primary sources of law: (i) statutes, (ii) the EU Directive, (iii) the Money Laundering Regulations 1993,[1] (iv) the FSA's money laundering sourcebook and (v) the JMLSG's Guidance Notes. These are discussed in turn below.

1   SI 1993/1933.

Statutory offences

10.10   Criminal offences under UK primary legislation fall into three main categories: First, there is the offence of dealing with criminal property, which is itself subdivided into a number of constituents. Second, there is the offence of failing to disclose suspected money laundering to the authorities. Third, there is the offence of tipping off a suspect that disclosure has been made.

   Until 2002, offences relating to drugs were contained within the Drug Trafficking Act 1994. Offences relating to the laundering of the proceeds of other crimes were mostly found in the Criminal Justice Act 1988 (as amended). These provisions are now consolidated in Part 7 of the Proceeds of Crime Act 2002 (which is before Parliament at the time of writing). A controversial aspect of the Act is that as regards banks and other financial institutions, the offence of failing to disclose money laundering to the police arises in the situation where there are reasonable grounds for knowledge or suspicion of money laundering. This is an extension of the traditional 'knows or suspects' test. Special provisions as regards terrorism are contained in the Terrorism Act 2000.

The EU Directive

10.11   The current instrument is the Council Directive of 10 June 1991 on Prevention of the Use of the Financial System for the Purpose of Money Laundering.[1] This provides basic Europe-wide rules applicable to credit and financial institutions. It is presently limited to criminal activity contrary to the 1988 Vienna Convention (ie drugs dealing). The ML Directive has been amended by Directive 2001/97/EC. Amongst other things, this will extend the scope of the ML Directive to cover the proceeds of all serious crime. It also extends the scope of the directive beyond banks and financial institutions. Implementation is required by 15 June 2003. In the UK, the ML Directive as implemented already covers crimes other than drug dealing. The scope of the duties has already been extended to certain categories of money service business, including bureaux de change, by the Money Laundering Regulations 2001.[2]

The Money Laundering Regulations 1993[1]

10.12   These regulations implement the 1991 EU Directive, though as indicated they are not restricted to drugs dealing. In the ML Regulations, 'money laundering' is defined as doing any act which constitutes an offence under the above statutes. The ML Regulations require banks and investment businesses to maintain systems and training to prevent money laundering, and to maintain identification, record-keeping and internal reporting procedures. The Money Laundering Regulations 2001[2] extend the regime to bureaux de change, cheque cashers and money transmission agents.

1   SI 1993/1933.
2   SI 2001/3641.

Regulatory requirements: the FSA's money laundering sourcebook

10.13   These requirements are new in the UK, and follow from the fact that one of the FSA's general duties is the reduction of financial crime. Since FSMA came into force therefore, the prevention of money laundering has become one of the responsibilities of the financial regulators. The money laundering sourcebook sets out a mix of regulatory rules and guidance in this regard. But there is a considerable degree of overlap with the Guidance Notes; see below.

Guidance Notes for the UK Financial Sector

10.14   These are issued by the Joint Money Laundering Steering Group and consist of a number of associations with members in the financial sphere. Whilst their application is not mandatory, in determining whether the ML Regulations have been complied with, a court may take account of this guidance.[1]

1   SI 2001/3641, reg 5(3).

Legal liability

10.15   It follows that a bank may incur legal liability of three kinds in respect of money laundering:

(a)   *Criminal liability:* Naturally, the potential criminal liability of banks and their officers is of overriding concern, though in fact prosecutions are likely to be extremely rare.

(b)   *Regulatory liability:* Failure to maintain proper systems and controls is likely to be taken increasingly seriously by the regulators.

(c)   *Civil liability:* Civil claims by the victims of fraud against banks handling the money are quite common, and potentially costly. Insofar as the money laundering sourcebook consists of rules (rather than guidance), the civil liability of banks has been potentially widened under the new regulatory regime. A private person suffering loss as a result of the contravention of such a rule may have an action for damages under s 150 of the Financial Services and Markets Act (FSMA) 2000.

For all these reasons, banks are increasingly likely to demand clarity in the rules, and safe harbours so as to avoid incurring liability for what can be difficult operational judgments.

PRACTICAL COMPLIANCE

10.16 What is required by way of policies and procedures will depend on the nature of the institution's business. The discussion below is intended to highlight some of the practical considerations, rather than provide a template. Common sense and proportionality are required in applying the rules. Financial institutions will probably need to adopt a risk-based approach to compliance.[1] In practice this may require the firm to focus, for instance, on business conducted through 'non co-operative countries and territories',[2] and on its higher-risk products. The firm's business lines will obviously want to minimise disruption to clients.

Balancing the needs of the business against money laundering prevention may require the classification of countries and products by level of risk, and the use of procedural requirements tailored to each class.

1   Also advocated in the JMLSG Guidance Notes (December 2001).
2   JMLSG Guidance Notes (December 2001), Appendix D.

10.17 An individual of appropriate seniority within the firm must be appointed as the Money Laundering Reporting Officer (MLRO). See below. He or she must have the authority to act, adequate resources, an appropriate degree of autonomy and access to the Board and the Audit Committee. In practice, the Compliance Officer or another member of the Compliance Department currently tends to act as the MLRO. A competent deputy should be appointed to provide cover in the MLRO's absence.

10.18 Whilst the MLRO has the key role in ensuring that the firm complies with the anti-money laundering regime, responsibility for compliance rests with the firm, its management and staff. The firm's organisational structure should clearly identify the MLRO, and short reporting lines should be maintained. The MLRO must monitor and document adherence to procedures by staff across the firm, and maintain appropriate records so that the annual reporting obligation to management can be fulfilled, as well as the demands of any external investigation. In larger financial institutions, a separate department may be responsible for new client take-on procedures including the verification of identity. Some firms are now requesting documentation from the firms upon whom they have relied in meeting the identification requirements. Computer programs may be used to try to identify suspicious transactions, a consequence of the fact that when transaction volumes are high, there may be little contact between the product provider and its customer.

THE MONEY LAUNDERING REGULATIONS

10.19 The Money Laundering Regulations 1993[1] can be considered as the core rules. They apply to banking and investment businesses carried on in the UK. The effect of reg 5 is to require anyone carrying on such a business to maintain certain defined systems and training to prevent money laundering. Failure to do so is an offence. By reg 6, senior managers who connive at the committing of an offence may themselves incur criminal liability. It is also to be noted that the requirements relate to maintaining *procedures*. Criminal liability in respect of specific instances of money laundering will be incurred, if at all, under the primary legislation. In addition to the requirement to maintain procedures, there is a requirement to make employees aware of such procedures, and provide training.

1   SI 1993/1933.

10.20   The imposition of criminal penalties may have practical consequences. As pointed out above, reg 5(3) specifically provides that a court may take account of guidance issued by a trade association. The relevant guidance is that issued by the JMLSG. However given the fact of criminal liability, it is questionable whether such guidance could ever operate to *extend* liability. For example, the Guidance states that 'information collected at the outset might include the expected origin of funds to be used within the relationship'. That may be good practice, but the obligation under the Money Laundering Regulations is to identify the prospective customer. Clearly however, a key issue is whether the procedures adopted by an institution are adequate bearing in mind the type of institution it is, and the type of business it transacts. The court may also take into account supervisory guidance, but the FSA Handbook makes it clear that the money laundering sourcebook is not relevant regulatory or supervisory guidance for these purposes.[1]

1   ML 1.2.4.

Required procedures

10.21   For a detailed description of the complexities of the required procedures (particularly in relation to identification) see Division 4 of *Butterworths Money Laundering Law*, edited by D Allen. In summary, the procedures are as follows.

Identification procedures

10.22   Procedures must be in place to identify an applicant for business as soon as reasonably practicable after contact is first made.[1] One-off transactions of less than EUR15,000 are excluded. If payment is to be made from a personal account held in the customer's name (or jointly with one or more other persons) at an authorised financial or credit institution (eg an EU or UK bank or a UK building society) no further evidence of identity is necessary.[2] This is the 'payment by post' exception, which applies where it is reasonable in all the circumstances for a payment made by the applicant for business to be sent by post or by any electronic means which is effective to transfer funds. Where the applicant for business is or appears to be acting otherwise than as principal, identification procedures must require reasonable measures to be taken for the purpose of establishing the identity of any person on whose behalf the applicant for business is acting.[3] The obligation to identify does not apply if the applicant for business is also a UK or EU credit or financial institution.[4] In other circumstances, unless the client is another regulated firm acting on behalf of another person from within the UK, EU or a country listed by the FATF as having equivalent legislation and financial sector standards, identification evidence should usually be obtained for the named account holder, any known beneficial owner, all signatories, and any intermediate parties.

See generally JMLSG Guidance Section 4.

1 SI 1993/1933, reg 7.
2 SI 1993/1933, reg 8.
3 SI 1993/1933, reg 9.
4 SI 1993/1933, reg 10.

Record-keeping procedures

10.23 Regulation 12 requires the maintenance of record-keeping procedures. Evidence of identity and a record of transactions must be kept. The prescribed period is five years from the date on which the relevant business was completed. There are special provisions in the case of insolvency.

Internal reporting procedures

10.24 Regulation 14 provides that internal reporting procedures must be maintained identifying a money laundering reporting officer. Procedures must provide for reports to be considered in the light of all other relevant information, and with that in mind the MLRO must have reasonable access to other information which may be of assistance. The procedures must secure that in the case of knowledge or suspicion of money laundering, an appropriate disclosure is made to the police.

FSA MONEY LAUNDERING SOURCEBOOK

10.25 The FSMA 2000 regulatory objectives charge the FSA with reducing the extent to which regulated firms are used in connection with financial crime.[1] In considering that objective, the FSA 'must have regard to the desirability of regulated persons taking adequate measures to prevent money laundering, facilitate its detection and monitor its incidence'. This objective 'will command a clear regulatory response for non-compliance'.[2] The risk to market confidence, the importance of public awareness and consumer protection are also cited in the FSA's Money Laundering Sourcebook[3] as justifying the priority attached by the regulator to combating money laundering.

The FSA conducts what is called a 'Money Laundering Theme'.[4] One of the aims of the theme is to inform firms of 'the consequences of failing to meet the minimum requirements'. The theme identifies international and domestic banking as sectors particularly vulnerable to the money launderer. Under the FSMA 2000, the FSA is armed with a range of powers in this area for the first time. Section 402 allows the FSA to 'institute proceedings for an offence under . . . prescribed regulations relating to money laundering' regardless of whether the person is FSA regulated. Section 146 allows the FSA to 'make rules in relation to the prevention and detection of money laundering in connection with the carrying on of regulated activities by authorised persons'. A 'threshold condition' for FSMA authorisation is that the relevant person has 'in place the appropriate money laundering prevention systems and training'.[5]

In an indication of the regulator's attitude, in 2001 Paine Webber was disciplined by the Securities and Futures Authority[6] for failings in the organisation of its internal affairs as regards a wide range of money laundering requirements. It is significant that no instances of money laundering were identified (a fact that was taken into account in the size of the fine).

1 FSMA 2000, s 2.
2 FSA, 'Money Laundering Theme: tackling our responsibilities' (July 2001), 1.13.
3 FSA Handbook of Rules and Guidance: Business Standards – Money Laundering Sourcebook (ML).
4 FSA 'Money Laundering Theme: tackling our responsibilities' (July 2001), 1.13.
5 FSA Handbook of Rules and Guidance: High Level Standards – Threshold Conditions (COND 2.5).
6 SFA Board Notice 597: Paine Webber International (UK) Limited (28 August 2001).

10.26   The Sourcebook requirements should be read with other parts of the Handbook. For example, the 'Principles for Businesses' (particularly Principle 3 on 'Management and Control'), 'Statements of Principle and Code of Practice for Approved Persons', 'Senior Management Arrangements, Systems and Controls' (which states as a rule that an authorised firm must take 'reasonable care to establish and maintain appropriate systems and controls for compliance with its regulatory obligations and to counter the risk that it might be used to further financial crime'[1]), and the Training and Competence Sourcebook.

Compliance is not limited to the MLRO. The firm, senior management, and each approved person are also responsible.

1 FSA Handbook of Rules and Guidance: High Level Standards – Senior Management Arrangements, Systems and Controls (SYSC 3.2.6R).

10.27   The Sourcebook is about regulatory requirements not prohibitions imposed by the criminal law. It is parallel to, but separate from, the Money Laundering Regulations. It 'is therefore not relevant regulatory or supervisory guidance for the purposes of regulation 5(3) of the Money Laundering Regulations'.[1]

On the other hand, a court would presumably not disregard a firm's compliance with the Sourcebook in determining whether the firm had complied with the systems and training requirements of the Regulations. Similarly, compliance with the Sourcebook arguably constitutes taking 'all reasonable steps' and the exercise of 'all due diligence' to avoid breaching the Money Laundering Regulations.[2]

In any case, the Sourcebook repeats large portions of the Money Laundering Regulations. Nor is the relationship of the Sourcebook and the Joint Money Laundering Steering Group's Guidance Notes completely clear. The Guidance Notes provide guidance on the Sourcebook, much of which is itself guidance.

1 Money Laundering Regulations 1993 (SI 1993/1933), reg 5(4).
2 Money Laundering Regulations 1993 (SI 1993/1933), reg 5(4).

Scope

10.28   The scope of the Sourcebook is very wide. It applies to all firms except those only conducting certain insurance activities and 'UCITS qualifiers'. In accordance with the application of the Money Laundering Directive[1] on a host state basis, it covers incoming firms such as branches of institutions established elsewhere in the EEA except those only providing cross-border services into the UK. The Sourcebook thus only applies to activities carried on from an establishment maintained by the firm in the UK.

1   No 91/308/EEC.

Purpose

10.29   The purpose of the Sourcebook 'is to require [firms] to have effective anti-money laundering systems and controls, in order to reduce the opportunities for money laundering'.[1] The Sourcebook also requires firms 'to ensure that approved persons exercise appropriate responsibilities in relation to these anti-money laundering systems and controls'. Whilst the Sourcebook obligations thus apply to the firm, an approved person will be vulnerable not least for breaches of the Statements of Principle.

1   ML 1.2.1G.

The MLRO

10.30   A firm 'must set up and operate arrangements', including the appointment of an MLRO (Money Laundering Reporting Officer) to ensure that it complies with the Sourcebook.[1] In keeping with the high priority afforded to combating money laundering, the MLRO is a 'significant influence function' requiring prior approval under the approved persons regime.

The MLRO 'is responsible for the oversight of the [firm's] anti-money laundering activities and is the key person in the [firm's] implementation of anti-money laundering strategies and policies'.[2] The MLRO's responsibilities cover receiving internal reports; reviewing 'know your business information'; making external reports; obtaining and using national and international findings; establishing and maintaining adequate arrangements for awareness and training (whether by himself or someone else) and making annual reports to senior management. In acting as the focal point within the firm for the oversight of all activity relating to anti-money laundering, the MLRO must be senior, properly resourced, free to act on his own authority and have his ear close to the ground. He should be based in the UK and should establish effective working relationships with the law enforcement authorities. Whilst some duties can be delegated, the FSA 'will expect the MLRO to take ultimate managerial responsibility'.[3]

1   ML 2.1.1R.
2   ML 2.1.2G.
3   ML 7.1.3G.

10.31   At least once a year the firm should commission a report from its MLRO that assesses compliance with the Sourcebook; indicates, in particular, the way in which new national and international findings have been used during the year. The following type of issues might be covered:

—   How many reports have been made to the National Criminal Intelligence Service (NCIS)?

— What changes have been made in respect of new legislation, rules or industry guidance?
— Have there been any serious compliance deficiencies?
— How risky is any new business?
— Have any issues arisen from the staff training?
— Does the MLRO have sufficient resources?
— Are any particular parts of the firm failing, for instance, to make reports?
— Are adequate records being retained?

Senior management should consider and 'take any necessary action to remedy deficiencies identified by the report'.[1]

1 ML 7.3.3G.

10.32 Many MLROs will currently be drawn from the ranks of a firm's in-house lawyers and compliance staff. In time, larger firms may have separate money laundering departments. Unfortunately, the stage has been reached at which familiarity with the regulatory jargon is as important as an intelligent approach aimed at combating the problem. The industry appears, for instance, to have accepted the theoretical analysis of money laundering in terms of 'placement, layering and integration'. In reality, there are many variations on these concepts. It may be questioned whether money launderers think in these terms, and whether these concepts really help staff to identify suspicious transactions. Similarly, although 'knowing your client' is not a difficult proposition in itself, applying the complexities of the identification regime can be difficult. The fight against money laundering will have best prospects of success if the focus is practical rather than theoretical.

Identification

10.33 Chapter 3 of the Sourcebook requires a firm to 'know its clients'. It must obtain sufficient evidence of the identity of any client to be able to show that the client is who he claims to be.

In assessing compliance with this duty, the FSA will consider whether the firm has complied with the JMLSG Guidance Notes. The client must be identified 'as soon as reasonably practicable'. Unless the NCIS has been notified, the firm must stop acting if the client does not provide evidence of identity as required. There are 'special provisions . . . for cases where the person with whom the [firm] has contact is acting for another', which broadly require the firm to enquire into the identity of both persons, unless an exemption allows the firm to focus solely on the person it is actually in contact with.

Internal reporting

10.34 Chapter 4 of the Sourcebook covers 'internal reporting'. The firm:

'must take reasonable steps to ensure that any member of staff who handles, or is managerially responsible for handling, transactions which may involve money laundering makes a report promptly to the MLRO if he knows or suspects that a client, or the person on whose behalf the client is acting, is engaged in money laundering'.

This includes establishing and maintaining arrangements for disciplining any member of staff who fails, without reasonable excuse, to make a report of the kind envisaged. The focus on the money laundering responsibilities of the management is new and in keeping with the FSA's approach to management accountability generally. A firm's internal systems can allow staff to consult with their line manager before sending a report to the MLRO. Whilst the manager may be able to dispel suspicion, the firm should ensure that its systems 'are not used to prevent reports reaching the MLRO whenever staff have stated that they have knowledge or suspicion that a transaction may involve money laundering'.[1] The firm must take reasonable steps to make information about a client and his transactions ('know your business information') 'readily available' to the MLRO. The MLRO will require this information in deciding whether or not to make a report to NCIS. Internal reports to the MLRO must be considered in the light of all relevant information and, where appropriate, an external report must be promptly made to NCIS. The MLRO must enjoy autonomy in making a suspicious transaction report.

1 ML 4.1.3G.

Non–co-operative jurisdictions

10.35 Significantly, firms must take account of findings by governments and the Financial Action Task Force about the inadequacies of individual countries or jurisdictions in relation to restraining money laundering. The awareness and training provisions require this information to be disseminated to staff. The FSA website sets out the current findings.[1]

1 See www.fsa.gov.uk.

Awareness

10.36 The Money Laundering Regulations 1993 require firms to maintain 'such other procedures of internal control and communication as may be appropriate for the purposes of forestalling and preventing money laundering', to provide awareness training to staff on its procedures to prevent money laundering, and to provide staff 'from time to time with training in the recognition and handling of transactions carried out by . . . any person who is . . . engaged in money laundering'.[1] Contravention of this requirement is an offence.

1 Money Laundering Regulations 1993 (SI 1993/1933), reg 5.

10.37 It would not be enough for example to show staff a video once a year. Staff must be both aware of and given regular training about 'what is expected of them in relation to prevention of money laundering, and what the consequences are for the [firm] and for them if they fall short of that expectation'.[1] Staff need to have a clear understanding of their own potential liability. On the other hand, there is little point in telling staff again and again of the penalties imposed by the criminal law. A better approach is to focus upon the commercial benefits to the bank of knowing its customer and keeping proper records, and encourage proper compliance.

1 ML 6.

10.38   A firm 'must take reasonable steps' to ensure that staff who handle, or are managerially responsible for the handling of, transactions which may involve money laundering are aware of their responsibilities under the firm's procedures, 'the identity and responsibilities of the MLRO', and the law and the implications of breaching that law.[1] Appropriate information (in whatever form) must be, and remain, available to staff. Guidance provides that 'staff are likely to need information about the ways in which their clients' involvement in money laundering may affect bank and other accounts and other assets, in particular if a [firm] decides it is unable to process transactions because of the risk of committing a money laundering offence. They are also likely to need information about the ways in which the [firm] may itself be at risk if (without the consent of NCIS) it processes transactions which involve the proceeds of crime'.[2]

1   ML 6.2.1R.
2   ML 6.2.4G.

10.39   In fostering staff awareness, a firm will focus on a broad range of issues, for example:

—   What are the money laundering risks to the business?
—   How vulnerable is the firm?
—   Where is the firm vulnerable?
—   Do staff follow the procedures?
—   How effectively are national and international findings on material deficiencies used within the firm?
—   What happens if staff do suspect money laundering?
—   How does the firm handle the client, counterparty, transaction and police once an internal or external report has been made?
—   What is said to the client if the firm decides not to process a transaction?
—   How does it end a relationship that has become too high a risk?

10.40   A practical issue is maintaining staff enthusiasm year-in year-out, which can be difficult. The compliance manual is an obvious place to set out the procedures.

Information can also be made available in a user-friendly format through a company intranet. Larger firms may like to follow this checklist:

—   Does it have a money laundering site?
—   Does it issue a staff handbook and awareness raising updates?
—   Does its procedures manuals (such as new client take-on procedures) cover money laundering?

There are other means of maintaining awareness, such as emailing messages to staff, posters around the office, etc. On the other hand, the position will vary from firm to firm. A small branch cannot be expected to have the same processes as a large multinational. It is a question of what is adequate in the circumstances.

Training

10.41   As well as staff awareness, there is an overlapping obligation as regards training. A firm 'must take reasonable care to provide appropriate anti-money laundering training for its staff who handle, or are managerially responsible for the handling of, transactions which may involve money laundering'.[1]

The training should cover the law and the responsibilities of staff under the firm's arrangements. The training should take place 'with sufficient frequency to ensure that within any period of 24 months it is given to substantially all [relevant] staff'.[2] In adopting high-level standards throughout the Handbook, the FSA has largely avoided pedantry but guidance[3] provides that the training requirements 'do not preclude a rolling programme of training, under which training on different subjects takes place on different dates'. This guidance envisages not just training on money laundering but separate sessions on various different elements of the money laundering regime.

1 ML 6.3.1R.
2 ML 6.3.2(c)E.
3 ML 6.3.3G.

10.42 In designing a staff training programme, the firm's obligations under the FSA's Training and Competence Sourcebook may be kept in mind.[1] Staff have to be, and have to be seen by the regulator to be, competent. What skills are expected of the staff concerned in relation to their area of the business?

One approach to providing effective money laundering training is to allow money laundering issues to feature generally in the compliance training programme, including staff induction. Retaining staff interest in a subject upon which training has to be provided so regularly is not surprisingly a major problem. The earliest training videos were not considered effective, particularly on repeated showing to staff. A sensible approach needs to be taken to delivery of training, for example by mixing the medium of delivery and varying it from year to year, keeping the message fresh, and trying to make training relevant. The banks themselves may have a better idea of what is required than external training providers. Given the focus on managerial responsibilities, bespoke training programmes will have to be conducted for different categories of staff. Some staff, such as the MLRO and the private bankers, will need more regular training than others.

1 FSA Handbook of Rules and Guidance: Business Standards – Training and Competence Sourcebook (TC).

10.43 It is noticeable that under the Proceeds of Crime Act 2002, an individual has a defence to not reporting a knowledge or suspicion of money laundering if he can show that the firm did not provide him with adequate training. In establishing such a defence, an individual will inevitably render the firm liable for failing to provide adequate training. It follows that a firm needs to be able to demonstrate that it has provided adequate training.

One way of doing that is by keeping good training records[1] relating to the training, the topics covered, methods of delivery, timing, supporting documentation etc. It may be helpful to know which staff failed to attend the training, and whether there is a policy of suspension as regards staff failing to complete the training. Staff should be required to record an acknowledgement of the date and nature of the training received, and encouraged to ask for further training if they do not think that they have had adequate training. An employee could confirm in his annual appraisal that he has had adequate training. Again it is emphasised that the position will vary from firm to firm. It is a question of what is adequate in the circumstances.

1 ML 7.3.3G.

Records

10.44   A firm must make and retain adequate records for specified periods in relation to evidence of identity, transactions carried for the client, internal and external reports, and the information considered by the MLRO in the event that a report is not made to NCIS.[1]

1   ML 7.3.

FINANCE OF TERRORISM: THE UK LEGAL REGIME

10.45   As regards banks in the UK, measures against terrorism are dealt with by the Sanctions Unit of the Bank of England. Various Notices are issued from time to time listing terrorist suspects, and requiring the assets of the persons named to be frozen. Some are specific to particular groupings, such as those applicable to the Taliban and Osama bin Laden. These are imposed pursuant to UN Security Council Resolutions, applied in the UK by statutory instruments made pursuant to s 1 of the United Nations Act 1946. In summary, the making of funds available to or for the benefit of the persons named is an offence. An institution which knows or suspects that a customer is a person named commits an offence if it does not disclose to the Treasury the information as soon as is reasonably practicable.

10.46   After the September 11 tragedy, a further freeze resolution was adopted by the UN Security Council on 28 September 2001.[1] This applies to terrorist funds generally. It calls on states to freeze terrorist funds and other assets, and to prohibit their nationals or persons and entities within their territories from making funds available to terrorists. This is given effect to by the Terrorism (United Nations Measures) Order 2001[2] also made under s 1 of the United Nations Act 1946. In summary, the making of funds available to or for the benefit of persons involved in terrorism is an offence under article 3. The Treasury has power to direct the freezing of funds under article 4. Article 7 makes failure to disclose knowledge or suspicion an offence.

1   Resolution 1373.
2   SI 2001/3365.

10.47   In practice, banks also have regard to lists of terrorist suspects issued by overseas authorities, such as the US Office of Foreign Assets Control (OFAC). The US freezes assets by Executive Order pursuant to powers contained in the International Emergency Economic Powers Act, 50 USC 1701–1706. In the European context, there is also Council Regulation EC/467/2001 of 6 March 2001 (as amended) which freezes accounts of persons/entities designated by the Security Council Sanctions Committee listed in the Annex. Overlapping lists are an unfortunate feature of the regime.

10.48   There are statutory provisions applicable in the context of terrorism: see ss 17 and 18 of the Terrorism Act 2000 relating to funding and money laundering. 'Terrorist property' includes money which is likely to be used for the purposes of terrorism.[1] By s 21(2), there is a defence under these provisions if disclosure is made to the police. Even if these provisions do not apply directly, disclosure duties may arise. There are specific duties to disclose information to the police contained in s 19. These need to be read along with the duties to make disclosure to the Treasury within the terms of article 7 of the Terrorism (United Nations Measures) Order 2001.[2]

1 Terrorism Act 2000, s 14(1).
2 SI 2001/3365.

CIVIL LIABILITY

10.49 A bank owes a duty of care to its customer both in contract and in tort. The duty extends to making payments out of the account. However, the courts have not recognised any duty of care owed to non-customers. The constructive trust doctrine has been developed in this respect. In brief, when a bank knows that money received by it, or actions taken by it, are in breach of trust, it may incur liability as 'constructive trustee' equivalent to an obligation to compensate for loss. Where a bank has beneficially received funds which it knows have been paid in breach of trust, it may incur liability for 'knowing receipt' type constructive trust. The funds must have been received beneficially (for example, in repayment of indebtedness). Constructive notice is probably sufficient to found liability. In other words, dishonesty is not a necessary ingredient of liability. Where however a bank has not received funds beneficially, its potential liability is considerably narrower. It may incur liability as an accessory for 'knowing assistance' type constructive trust. In such circumstances, dishonesty must be proved against the bank: see *Royal Brunei Airlines Sdn Bhd v Tan*[1] and *Twinsectra Ltd v Yardley*.[2]

1 [1995] 2 AC 378, PC.
2 [2002] UKHL 12, [2002] 2 AC 164.

10.50 A problem encountered in practice is the extent to which the making of a suspicious transaction report may be relevant to constructive trust liability. There appears to be no necessary connection. For reasons that are unclear, the standard NCIS Disclosure Report includes a box entitled 'Constructive Trust'. In practice, a bank will not proceed with a transaction until a response has been received from NCIS. Two situations have come before the courts.

10.51 First, in *C v S*,[1] in the course of proceedings in which it was not directly involved, a disclosure order was made against a bank. Unknown to the plaintiff, the bank had already made money laundering reports relating to one of the defendants to NCIS. It was concerned that by disclosing the information, it might be guilty of 'tipping off'. The court set out the procedure to be followed in such circumstances, It said in effect that the burden was on the NCIS to show how disclosure would prejudice an investigation so as to amount to 'tipping off'.

1 [1999] Lloyd's Rep Bank 26, CA.

10.52 The second case is *Governor and Company of the Bank of Scotland v A Ltd*.[1] There, the relationship between constructive trust liability and 'tipping off' was considered. It was held that it was not appropriate for a bank itself to seek an order freezing an account on the grounds that it might be liable as constructive trustee. However the court did indicate that though a decision as regards the account was normally a commercial decision to be taken by the bank itself, in some circumstances it would be prepared to grant an interim declaration. In the case in question, the information as regards suspected fraud had come from the Serious Fraud Office. It was held that the appropriate defendant to any application for directions was the SFO, rather than the customer. The court also made it clear that where guidance is sought from the court and acted upon, that will be sufficient to avoid subsequent accessory liability.

1   [2001] Lloyd's Rep Bank 73, CA.

Chapter 11

Customer care

INTRODUCTION

11.1 The protection of customers sits at the heart of the system of financial regulation. Indeed one of the four statutory obligations imposed on the Financial Services Authority (FSA) by the Financial Services and Markets Act (FSMA) 2000 is 'securing an appropriate degree of protection for consumers'.[1] In considering what is appropriate the FSA are required to relate the appropriateness of the information provided to consumers to the risks they are undertaking and the experience they possess. It would however present an unbalanced picture to see customer protection as purely a consequence of legislation and regulation. All financial businesses operate in a fiercely competitive market and a failure by a business to provide a competitive degree of customer care could cause a potentially serious loss of business. The purpose of this chapter is to focus on the legal and regulatory issues. This involves considering regulation that is directly related, such as those parts of the FSA Conduct of Business rules that protect private customers. In addition there are also those laws which are indirectly related in that they minimise the risks of a conflict of interest arising, such as the laws and regulations relating to market abuse and insider dealing.

1   FSMA 2000, s 5.

11.2   This chapter seeks to look at the parts of the rules and relevant law that are relevant in the context of customer care. It then proceeds to examine the same in the circumstances prior to contact between a firm and the prospective customer, the process of making contact and finally those that apply once a customer relationship has been established.

CUSTOMER CLASSIFICATION

11.3   Customer classification is the key to understanding how the system works. The Conduct of Business rules divide clients into three main categories:[1] market counterparties, intermediate customers and private customers. Firms are required to take reasonable steps to ascertain which category a client is prior to carrying on designated investment business with, or for them. This is to make certain that the appropriate FSA conduct of business rules are applied and that the degree of regulatory protection offered to a client is appropriate. Dealings with market counterparties are not dealt with under the Conduct of Business rules, but a separate set of rules – the Inter-Professionals Code. This Code (which also governs brokers and market makers) contains a light regulatory touch as the parties involved are believed to be capable of protecting their own interests. The same approach informed regulation by the Bank of England under the so-called 'Grey Paper' regime (covering business that was exempt from the 1986 Act). The FSA however reserves the right to take disciplinary steps if the Code is breached. The remaining two categories of client are the ones on which this chapter will focus. It should be stated at the outset that the bulk of the rules are aimed at private customers and that intermediates thus carry a much heavier risk.

1   COB 4.1.

11.4   In essence market counterparties are central banks, other national monetary authorities and FSA authorised firms. Many will be large corporates and overseas financial services firms. Firms may also opt to move up to this level from intermediate status, though such firms must still be able to meet any regulatory obligations they have towards their own customers. In the case of expert private investors, special FSA dispensation is needed to upgrade market counterparty status. Intermediates will be local and public authorities together with trustees of smaller pension funds. It may also include the corporate treasury departments of companies in other sectors and skilled private investors who have opted up. Private customers will be any other category of person, the commonest of which will be ordinary private investors. (See para 11.12 for a definition.) Firms which opt up must be regarded by the firm agreeing to treat them as such as being capable of operating at such a level. In addition they must provide them with a written list of the protections they will lose under the Conduct of Business rules as a result and give them sufficient time to consider the implications of this prior to acting[1] and obtain written consent. It is also possible for customers to agree to opt down. This involves no extra steps to be taken as the customer concerned will gain extra protection as a result.

1   COB 4.1.9(b)(ii).

11.5 In ascertaining whether a firm can operate at intermediate rather than private level the firm must consider the customer's knowledge and understanding of the investments and markets that will be involved and any associated risks. A key factor here will be the length of time the customer has been engaged in the markets concerned and the extent during this time that he has relied on the firm's advice. The customer's financial standing will also be relevant.

11.6 The protections at issue where firms opt up to intermediate status and of which they must be notified are:

— protections in relation to direct offer financial promotions (COB 3.9);
— those relating to the customer's understanding of risk (COB 5.4);
— disclosure of charges, remuneration and commission (COB 5.7);
— disclosure in relation to packaged products and ISAs (COB 6.1);
— protections relating to making loans to private customers (COB 7.9);
— margin requirements in relation to contingent liability investments (COB 7.10); and
— sales to customers of securities that are not traded on recognised or designated investment exchanges or regulated markets where the firm holds itself out as a market maker (COB 7.11).

11.7 In addition, explanations must be provided explaining the consequences to the client in respect of the limits or modifications that will be made to the rules applying to them once they are an intermediate. These are:

— financial promotions (COB 3);
— polarisation and status disclosure (COB 5.1);
— confirmation and transactions (COB 8.1); and
— periodic statements (COB 8.2).

Together with these issues, the consequences of certain rule modifications should also be pointed out; specifically:

— best execution (COB 7.5);
— custody (COB 9.1);
— client money (COB 9.3); and

the requirement that communications must be clear, fair and not misleading will be modified according to the customer's newly recognised level of expertise.

Finally the customer should be warned that they will lose their right of access to the Ombudsmen scheme.

11.8 Where large corporations who are currently intermediates wish to become market counterparties certain prerequisites apply. The client must be a body corporate whose share capital (or that of its group) exceeds £10 million, or one who meets two of the following criteria. Where the balance sheet total exceeds the equivalent of €12.5 million, where the net turnover exceeds €25 million or there have been an average number of employees of 250 over the previous year.

THE FSA CONDUCT OF BUSINESS RULES

11.9 Appointed representatives are not directly regulated,[1] though the firm on whose behalf the appointed representative operates will be responsible for their agent's acts. This excludes from regulation anyone who satisfies the description of an approved person[2] in s 39(1) as qualified by the Financial Services and Markets Act 2000 (Appointed Representatives) (Amendment) Regulations 2001.[3] As a consequence the principal will be responsible for their appointed representatives' acts. There is a limit to the extent of this in s 39(6) which states that 'nothing . . . is to cause the knowledge or intentions of an appointed representative to be attributed to his principal for the purpose of determining whether the principal has committed an offence, unless in all the circumstances it is reasonable for them to be attributed to him.' The FSA rules set out additional requirements for firms which use appointed representatives.[4]

1 See s 19(1) and s 39.
2 See FSMA 2000, s 39(4).
3 SI 2001/2508.
4 SUP 12.

11.10 A guidance note[1] states that in any communication with customers which takes place electronically must satisfy certain criteria. These are that the customer must have shown that they wish to use this method of communication and that it has been made clear to the customer that a contractual relationship can be created in this manner. The firm must have in place appropriate arrangements to facilitate sending and receiving such messages and in the process authenticate and satisfy itself as to the integrity of the communication concerned. Such arrangements must be proportionate to the risk involved.

1 COB 1.8.

11.11 The first step in communications with customers is that of communicating information. Under rule 2.1.3 firms must communicate in a way which is 'clear, fair and not misleading'. A critical factor here will be the customer's understanding of the investment business concerned. Communications will include: client agreements, periodic statements, financial reports, telephone calls and any correspondence other than financial promotions which are covered by separate rules.

POLARISATION

11.12 Polarisation has been a key part of the financial services regime since the coming into force of the Financial Services Act 1986, although it has been amended in its specifics by a recent statutory instrument.[1] In essence it requires those who sell packaged products either to be independent of all the product providers and to act independently of any; or alternatively to act as a representative of one company, or at least its marketing group. 'Packaged products' are defined[2] as life policies, units in regulated collective investment schemes, interests in investment trust savings schemes, (whether or not any of these are held within a Personal Equity Plan or Individual Savings Account) and stakeholder pension schemes. Polarisation only applies however where the client is a private customer. They are defined as:[3]

'a client who is not a market counterparty or an intermediate customer, including:

(a) an individual who is not a firm;
(b) an overseas individual who is not an overseas financial services institution;
(c) a regulated collective investment scheme;

(d) a client when he is classified as a private customer. . .

but excluding a client, who would otherwise be a private customer, when he is classified as an intermediate customer.'

It does not impact where the client is an intermediate or market counterparty. The status of the advising firm must be communicated to the prospective client so that they do not have any misconceptions about the basis on which they are receiving advice.

1 Financial Services (Conduct of Business) (Modification of Polarisation) Rules 2001.
2 FSA Glossary of Definitions.
3 FSA Glossary of Definitions.

11.13 FSA COB rule 5.1 sets the FSA's requirements in this area. An independent intermediary has two key obligations. The first is to act in the best interests of its private customers when it provides advice on packaged products.[1] Thus an independent intermediary cannot enter into commercial agreements with third parties that might adversely affect their capacity to provide independent advice to the customers. They must also take reasonable steps to make sure their appointed representatives do the same. The status that any firm enjoys must be communicated to their private customers[2] on a timely basis if a firm is advising on packaged products. The status they declare may be that they are independent, restricted to the packaged products of one provider or marketing group, restricted to the packaged products of the firm's marketing group and adopted products, or that the advice will be given for the purposes of discretionary fund management. If a firm is a provider firm advising on packaged products it must take reasonable steps to communicate to private customers that the firm can give advice on adopted packaged products, if this is the case.

1 COB 5.1.16.
2 COB 5.1.17.

11.14 It is also necessary for provider firms and their introducers to take reasonable steps when making contact with private customers to communicate[1] key facts. These are: the firm's name, the fact that the person is an introducer or representative of the provider firm or its marketing group. They must also make clear that the firm can only provide advice on its own products or those of its marketing group or ones which are adopted. Where the first communication with a client is by electronic means, the firm must make sure that its polarisation status is clearly set out. There is an overlap here with the financial promotion rules (see below) in that provider firms must disclose their polarisation status in any specific non-real time financial promotion relating to a packaged product.[2]

1 COB 5.1.19.
2 COB 5.1.19R.

11.15 As discussed above the FSA Conduct of Business Rules contain significant provisions about the advice given to private customers in relation to packaged products. These represent the core of the polarisation principle. These provisions have a profound effect upon a marketing group which offers only a limited range of products, for example a banking group which contains one or more unit trust managers but no life company. Such a marketing group may advise only upon its own products and may therefore offer no advice on life policies at all. So far as the major retail banking groups are concerned, the effect has had two major consequences. The first is to oblige these groups to organise themselves, as far as possible, so that they have a full range of products to market, even if that means forming alliances with life companies and unit trust managers that might not otherwise have featured in the groups' plans. The second is to lead them to consider including within the corporate group (but outside the marketing group) an IFA who can look after those customers who would prefer to receive advice from an independent adviser or who may need advice in relation to any gaps that may remain in a group's product range.

11.16 However, the rule does not require a tied firm to draw to the customer's attention any packaged product outside that firm's marketing group range of products which might better suit the customer. Nor does it require the tied firm to tell him that there may be such a product and that an independent intermediary might be able to identify it. This is a weakness. A marketing group will have its range of packaged products. Some may be highly regarded and others less so, perhaps due to higher price or poorer performance compared with like products offered by competitors. They do, however, complete the range of products which satisfy the likely needs of potential customers and are capable of meeting the suitability requirement. A company in that marketing group will satisfy the regulatory requirements if it recommends a product to a private customer which is suitable. If considered suitable a member of a marketing group is obliged to recommend the product which satisfies the 'front rank' rule when compared with the rest of that marketing group's range of products and irrespective of what products might be available outside the group.

11.17 The FSA has considered the polarisation rule at some length. In its most recent communication on the subject[1] they concluded: 'there are significant market failings in the life assurance and collective investment scheme market and that these failures cannot be dealt with simply by the way in which the industry is permitted to distribute its products'. Six key conclusions followed:

— the commission system secures IFA distribution power for the product providers in a way which is detrimental to consumers;
— that despite polarisation the current system has not delivered good value for many middle-market consumers;
— the remuneration system for both independents and tied agents give an incentive to sell, which may not always be in the client's best interests;
— too few consumers were making provision for retirement or their future in a wider sense;
— the combination of the cost of advice and the product makes it impossible for customers to form a clear view of what the advice is really costing; and
— the current system does not encourage consumers to shop around.

1 FSA Consultation Paper No 121 'Reforming Polarisation: Making the market work for consumers'.

11.18 The key conclusion is that in due course polarisation should be abolished and a system of improved disclosure made. The consequence is likely to be that the market would break into four categories:

(i) *provider firms offering their own products.* They would do this directly, through tied agents and independent financial advisers;
(ii) *provider firms which also adopt products from other such firms.* They would distribute in the same ways as those that do not so adopt;

(iii)   *distributor firms* which distribute and provide advice on a range of products of various providers; and

(iv)   *independent advisers.*

Those firms that offer independent advice would not then be able to charge on a commission basis, but would have to charge on a defined basis. They would also have to disclose to clients any stake a product provider has in the firm or connected firms. A further suggestion has also been put forward to the effect that there should be a two-tier system of advisers. The lower tier would be made up of people who were less well qualified and only be able to advise on lower-risk products. As a result the approach to this aspect of client care may see significant change. The end result should be that the general public finds a system that is fairer and more transparent, but one in which they will have to start paying normal professional fees as they would for other professional services.

INDUCEMENTS

11.19   Firms must not offer or accept inducements if this is likely to conflict to a material extent with the duties which the firm owes to its customers. Nor can a firm direct that investment business be carried on by another person where this may not be in the best interests of customers affected. In the case of arrangements entered into with intermediaries in relation to packaged products where commission disclosure to the client is required,[1] the following are banned:

—   Volume overrides that are paid on any basis other than a simple multiplication of the transactions concerned.

—   Arrangements to pay commission that is increased in excess of the amount disclosed to the customer. The one exception here is where it occurs as a result of an increase in the premiums paid by the customer concerned.

—   Agreements to indemnify commission payments where this would confer a financial benefit on the recipient if the commission were to become repayable. This would be most likely to occur where the policy that gave rise to the commission lapsed within the first 12 months.

—   Arrangements to pay commission other than to the firm responsible for the sale, unless: they have passed the right to receive commission on to the current recipient; another firm has given advice on the investments concerned to the same customer after the sale; or the firm is a provider who responded to a direct offer financial promotion relating to a packaged product which the firm had communicated to a customer of an independent intermediary who is the recipient.

1   For this see COB 6.2.

11.20   It is acceptable to provide reasonable hospitality and prizes and indirect benefits of a reasonable value. Indirect benefits that are permissible are fairly extensive in range and cover:

—   Generic product literature that can be distributed by the recipient (who must be an independent intermediary) to prospective customers. However, the intermediary's name must feature less prominently than that of the provider and the intermediary must be responsible for the cost of distributing the literature. The arrangement must not promote a broker funds service by the intermediary.

— Provider firms can also provide freepost envelopes for application forms and other relevant documentation. If this is done, the provider firm must make them available to all the independent intermediaries they carry on business with.

— Product literature, of which key features documents are probably the most common, can be issued by provider firms provided they are not designed to promote the independent adviser's service, it does not name an independent intermediary or if it does appear, it is less prominent than that of the provider.

— Where an independent intermediary publishes a magazine a provider firm can supply news items, draft articles and financial promotions but they must be provided at no more than market rate excluding distribution costs.

— Independent intermediaries can organise seminars and pay towards their costs where provider firms attend provided it is for genuine business purposes, the contribution is reasonable and proportionate and (if it is organised by a third party) is open to independent intermediaries generally.

— Freephone links can be provided by provider firms, but they must be available to independent intermediaries generally.

— Provider firms can provide independent intermediaries with quotations, projections, advice on completing their documentation, access to data processing or third party dealing or quotation facilities related to the provider's business and software giving information about the provider firm's packaged products or which is relevant to its business.

— Provider firms can provide broker funds advisers and their customers with periodic statements relating to the broker fund concerned if the broker fund adviser cannot provide it.

— Provider firms can supply independent intermediaries with information concerning mortgage finance.

— Provider firms can act as independent intermediaries providing generic technical information and this does not have to be related to the provider firm's business, provided it is available generally to independent intermediaries or is specialist information and clearly states that it was produced by the provider firm.

— Training facilities can be provided by independent intermediaries but again they must be made generally available to all intermediaries.

— Reasonable travel and accommodation expenses can be provided where the independent intermediary receiving them participates in market research, attends an annual national event, participates in the provider firm's training facilities or visits the provider firm's UK office. This meeting must be related to the provider firm's administrative services or be for a meeting with that firm and a prospective customer.

SOFT COMMISSION

11.21   A soft commission agreement is defined in the FSA Glossary as an agreement in any form under which a firm receives goods or services in return for designated business put through or in the way of another person. There are requirements imposed when a soft commission agreement is in place. Essentially these state that such agreements are only acceptable where there is already a written agreement in place, the broker has agreed to provide best execution to the firm, the terms of business of the services concerned do not involve a comparative price disadvantage for their customer and adequate prior disclosure of the state of affairs is made. Goods provided under a soft commission agreement do not amount to inducements provided they are directly relevant to and are used to help the firm's customers. Such customers must be using investment management services, taking advice on investments, custody services or portfolio valuation. Client agreements where the firm will be operating under a soft commission agreement must be notified to the client along with an explanation of the firm's policies. There are additional rules governing periodic disclosure where another member of a firm's group operates under a soft commission disclosure.

11.22   An important topic to be addressed with a customer at or before the start of his relationship with the firm is the firm's use, if any of soft commission arrangements. In order to promote increased order flow, brokers may be prepared to pay for goods or services that an investment manager or adviser uses to perform or enhance its investment function. The broker benefits from having access to additional business, even if it is at a lower margin. Figure 11.1 illustrates what happens.

Figure 11.1

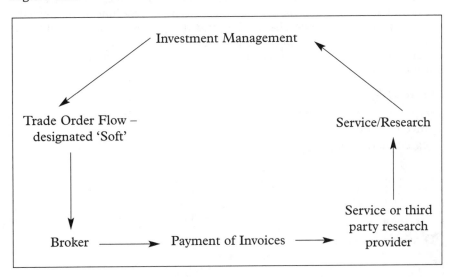

11.23   Soft commission arrangements may be contrasted with directed commission and commission recapture arrangements, which are increasingly common, particularly in the United States with pension fund clients. The idea of directed commission is similar to soft; however the fund itself directly benefits instead of reserving the indirect benefit of research and other services under a soft commission arrangement. Brokers establish an arrangement with third parties, typically consultants advising the client on overall investment strategy and selection of investment managers, whereby they agree to return a proportion of commission 'directed' by the investment manager to this third party who in turn passes on those commissions to the underlying fund concerned. The third party would typically keep a proportion of the commission as a fee. This is shown in Figure 11.2.

Figure 11.2

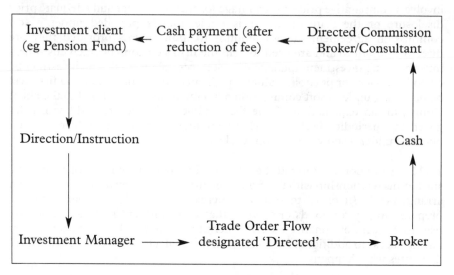

11.24   A commission recapture arrangement channels benefits directly to the underlying fund. However, in this case there is a direct relationship between the broker and the underlying client. The third party consultant is cut out. The broker agrees to return a proportion of the commission back to the client; either in cash or through the payment of invoices for the fund. Figure 11.3 illustrates this.

Figure 11.3

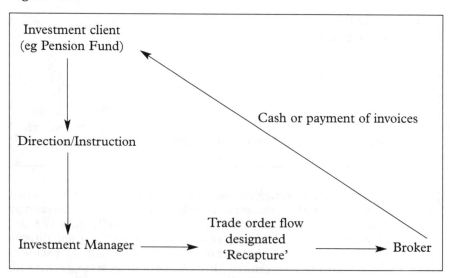

11.25   Directed commission and commission recapture arrangements are not covered by the FSA's soft commission rules.[1] A firm engaging in them must have regard to the prohibition on inducements.[2] The soft commission rules provide a safe harbour for soft commission arrangements in relation to that prohibition. A compliant soft commission arrangement will not be an improper inducement. As directed commission and commission recapture do not have the benefit of that safe harbour, particular care must be taken to ensure that they are not likely to cause a conflict with a firm's duty to its customers. Such conflicts are certainly not inevitable, and legitimate directed commission and commission recapture arrangements are often seen; but a cautious approach is appropriate.

1   COB 2.2.8R.
2   COB 2.2.3R.

11.26   Much has been written elsewhere about the commercial need for soft commissions and, conversely, about the perceived danger that they may lead firms to put their own interests above those of their customers. For example, the report of the Myners Committee[1] recommended that:

> 'it is good practice for institutional investment mandates to incorporate a management fee inclusive of any external research, information or transaction services acquired or used by the fund manager rather than those costs being passed to the clients'.

In the Committee's view this inclusive approach would better serve the interests of clients. The Report states:

> 'Clients' interests would be better served if they required fund managers to absorb the cost of any commissions paid, treating these commissions as a cost of the business of fund management, as they surely are. Fund managers would of course seek to offset this additional cost through higher fees; this would be a matter for them to agree with their clients. Under this system, the incentives would be different. Institutional clients would see more clearly what they were actually paying to have their funds invested. Incentives for them to manage costs would apply equally to all costs, as opposed to acting on some more than on others, as at present. Fund managers would choose which services to buy and which to provide themselves.'[2]

1   Published 6 March 2001, Recommendations.
2   Myners Committee Report, Summary, para 61.

11.27   Arguments of this kind have led to a conduct of business rule which states:[1]

> 'A firm must not deal in investments for a customer, either directly or indirectly, through any broker under a soft commission agreement unless:
>
> (1)   the agreement is a written agreement for the supply of goods or services described in COB 2.2.12 which do not take the form of, or include, cash or any other direct financial benefit;
>
> (2)   the broker has agreed to provide best execution to the firm;
>
> (3)   the firm has taken reasonable steps to ensure that the terms of business and methods by which services will be supplied by the broker do not involve any potential for comparative price disadvantage to the customer;
>
> (4)   for transactions in which the broker acts as principal, the firm has taken reasonable steps to ensure that commission paid under the agreement will be sufficient to cover the value of the goods or services to be received and the costs of execution; and
>
> (5)   the firm makes adequate prior and periodic disclosure to the customer in accordance with COB 2.2.16 and COB 2.2.18R.'

1   COB 2.2.8R.

11.28 The first of these five conditions is elaborated later in the rules[1] which define the permissible benefits to be provided under a soft commission agreement. The FSA requires the goods or services to be directly relevant to and in fact to be used to assist in the provision to the firm's customers of:

(1) investment management services; or
(2) advice on dealing in or on the value of any designated investment; or
(3) custody services relating to designated investments belonging to or managed for customers; or
(4) services relating to the valuation or performance measurement of portfolio.

1 COB 2.2.12R.

11.29 By way of guidance, the FSA goes on to provide a more specific list of examples of goods and services which may be provided under a soft commission agreement and also a list of examples of goods and services which may not be provided. It should be emphasised that these lists are not definitive or exhaustive and may be amended at any time.

11.30 The current illustrative lists are as follows:

(a) *Likely to be permitted:*[1]
— research, analysis and advisory services, including those on economic factors and trends;
— market price services;
— electronic trade confirmation systems;
— third party electronic dealing or quotation systems;
— computer hardware associated with specialised computer software or research services;
— dedicated telephone lines;
— seminar fees (if the subject matter is relevant to the provision of the services set out in COB 2.2.12R); and
— publications (if the subject matter is relevant to the provision of the services set out in COB 2.2.12R).
(b) *Unlikely to be permitted:*[2]
— travel, accommodation or entertainment costs, whether or not related to the conduct of designated investment business;
— any seminar fees not falling within COB 2.2.13G(7);
— any subscription for publications not falling within COB 2.2.13G(8);
— office administrative computer software, for example, word processing or accounting programs;
— computer hardware not associated with specialist computer software;
— membership fees to professional associations;
— purchase or rental of standard office equipment or ancillary facilities;
— employees salaries; and
— direct money payments.

1 COB 2.2.13G.
2 COB 2.2.14G.

11.31 When a firm is able to and does reclaim or offset all or part of the VAT payable on benefits received, the firm should ensure that its soft commission account with the broker is charged only with the net amount at the firm's effective rate. Disclosure of the value of benefits received, in accordance with COB 2.2.18 R, should be expressed net of VAT reclaimed, when appropriate.[1]

1   COB 2.2.15G.

11.32   The second proviso outlined in COB 2.2.8R(2) is that the broker concerned has agreed to provide best execution to the firm. It is not entirely clear what 'best execution' means in this context. The rule appears to contemplate that the broker will assess what constitutes best execution in any particular case. If the broker is entitled to assess best execution other than in terms of price alone, the substitution of the broker's assessment for that of the firm in question is not particularly helpful. Moreover, that interpretation would appear to be inconsistent with the requirements of subparagraph (3) of the Rule. Subparagraph (3) requires a firm to have taken reasonable steps to ensure that the terms of business and methods by which the relevant broker's services will be supplied 'do not involve any potential for comparative price disadvantage to the customer'. The meaning of the phrase 'comparative price disadvantage' is unclear and yet it appears to mean something other than 'best execution'. It is tempting to wonder if the intention is for the regulator to have available a sufficiently general clause that can be used whenever a practice emerges in relation to the pricing of transactions which it finds distasteful but which does not obviously fall foul of the requirement to provide best execution. Perhaps the two subparagraphs can be reconciled on the basis that (2) requires the firm to obtain the broker's agreement to provide best execution and (3) requires the firm to be satisfied that best execution is being provided. But until the regulator has established its practice in relation to this provision, firms will face an awkward period of uncertainty. It would also be an odd result if firms which offer soft commission services, and firms which take advantage of those services, were placed under a more stringent requirement with respect to price than firms who offer and receive no such services. It is also notable that, in this context, price is the only and overriding criterion.

11.33   Subparagraph (4) of the Rule prevents a broker who is remunerated solely by his 'spread', ie the difference between his bid and offer price for a security, from offering soft commission services (so-called 'soft for net' agreements). The FSA makes it clear that a broker may be remunerated by a combination of spread and commission as long as commission forms a sufficient part of his remuneration. Other practical issues concern the effect of COB 2.2.8(4) above, and are the subject of guidance from the FSA. One arises where the soft commission broker is part of an integrated house. In such a case, the FSA indicates[1] that a firm may be able to satisfy the rule 'if it is able to monitor the individual transaction prices obtained by the broker and has taken reasonable steps to ensure that the broker has complied with its best execution obligation'. 'Alternatively', continues the guidance note, 'a firm should select a soft commission broker who is able to demonstrate independence of action in the market place.' As the FSA has observed, this independence is unlikely to be demonstrated if the broker deals exclusively, or we would add predominantly, with a single market maker. The guidance from the FSA also addresses the situation in which a broker is only partly remunerated by commission. Here the firm 'should take reasonable steps to ensure that the commission element that should be disclosed constitutes the greater part of that broker's remuneration'.[2] For its part, continues the guidance note, 'a broker firm should also set its multiple at a level which it can demonstrate would generate sufficient commission income from softing transactions to cover the costs of the goods and services provided, and the costs of dealing and settling the associated transactions, together with the specialised softing administration. When considering whether the commission is sufficient to cover the costs of the services provided, the broker firm may have regard to the aggregate number of bargains transacted rather than each individual transaction.'

1   COB 2.2.9G.
2   COB 2.2.10G.

11.34   An important development relating to this issue occurred in the US on 27 December 2001, when the Securities and Exchange Commission issued interpretative guidance[1] on s 28(e) of the Securities Exchange Act of 1934. Much in the same way as with the FSA's rules, s 28(e) provides a safe harbour for investment managers' use of soft commissions to obtain payment for research and other brokerage services. It excludes a breach of fiduciary duty if certain conditions are met. Prior to 27 December 2001, the value of the safe harbour was to some extent reduced by the Commission's view that it was available only in relation to commissions paid to a broker acting as agent and not as a principal. This excluded transactions with market makers. At the request of the NASDAQ Stock Market the Commission has relaxed this restrictive approach. A principal's transaction will now be included if two conditions are met: (1) the broker's confirmation note discloses the transaction price and any markup, markdown or other commission equivalent or fee paid by the investment manager to the broker, and (2) as in the case of NASDAQ, 'the transaction is reported under conditions that provide independent and objective verification of the transaction price subject to self-regulatory organisation oversight'. The guidance is not confined to NASDAQ and will apply to transactions on any exchange where the above conditions are met.

1   Securities Exchange Act Release No 45194 (27 December 2001): www.sec.gov/rules/interp/34-45194.htm.

11.35   In COB 2.2.16R and 2.2.18R and related guidance notes the FSA elaborates on the requirement contained in subparagraph (5) of Rule 2.2.8R to provide adequate prior and periodic disclosure. Prior disclosure to customers of the existence of soft commission agreements and of the firm's (or its group's) policy on soft commission agreements is normally effected through client agreements. The FSA states that it is acceptable to make a general disclosure that soft commission agreements are or may be in place.[1] In addition to prior disclosure, a firm must provide reports to relevant customers on its soft commission arrangements at least once a year. Such annual disclosures are not required for customers habitually resident overseas who have requested the firm not to provide them or where the firm has information from which it is reasonable to conclude that the customer does not wish to receive this disclosure.[2] These annual disclosures are otherwise mandatory. They are required to cover:

—   the percentage paid under soft commission agreements of the total commission paid by or at the direction of the firm and any other member of the firm's group which is a party to those arrangements;

—   the value (on a cost-price basis) of goods and services, received by the firm under soft commission agreements, expressed as a percentage of the total commission paid by or at the direction of the firm or other members of the firm's group;

— a summary of the goods and services received by the firm;
— a list of the brokers who are parties to the soft commission agreements; and
— the total commission paid from the portfolio of that customer.

1   COB 2.2.17G.
2   COB 2.2.19R.

11.36   At the same time, or in a separate document, the firm should explain its policy on soft commission (or state that its policy has not changed), explain any changes in its policy and confirm (if it is so) that the goods and services which it receives are expected to assist only in the conduct of investment business with or for other customers.

FINANCIAL PROMOTIONS

11.37   A further set of rules that are relevant in the context of circulating information are the new financial promotion rules. These govern what has traditionally been the regulation of advertising and cold calling. However, with the emergence of electronic communication and the Internet as a significant part of the business environment, it was felt necessary to alter fundamentally the legal approach to business communications with both prospective and existing customers. Section 21 of the FSMA 2000 states that:

'(1)   A person ("A") must not in the course of business communicate an invitation or inducement to engage in investment activity.
(2)   But subsection (1) does not apply if—

(a)   A is an authorised person; or
(b)   the content of the communication is approved for the purposes of this section by an authorised person.'

In this context 'communicate' seems to mean the same thing as 'promote'. Breach of the section is a criminal offence.[1] It is a strict liability offence but it is a defence for the accused to show that they believed on reasonable grounds that the communication was prepared or approved by an authorised person, or that they had taken all reasonable precautions and exercised due diligence. As far as civil consequences are concerned, the normal common law approach applies, namely that agreements entered into as a consequence of behaviour that is in breach of the section are enforceable against them but may not be enforced by them, at the discretion of the judge. This area is covered in depth in Chapter 8. For the purposes of customer care however it should be borne in mind that it is an area of law and regulation that has impact.

1   S 25.

11.38   In addition the FSMA 2000 states at s 397 that it is a criminal offence to make a statement, promise or forecast which is known to be misleading, false or deceptive.[1] It is also an offence to conceal dishonestly any material fact, whether in connection with such a statement or otherwise.[2] Finally, the offence extends to such statements, promises or forecasts where they are made recklessly, whether they are dishonest or not.[3] This last point is important as enforcement of the section would be much more difficult if a dishonest state of mind had to be proved. In all three instances the offence is committed if the statement or concealment is made for the purposes of inducing another to enter into, or refrain from entering into a contract relating to a relevant investment.[4] There is a further offence which occurs when someone engages in a course of conduct which creates a false or misleading impression as to the price of a relevant investment with a view to inducing someone to buy or sell an investment, or refrain from doing either.[5] Some defences are added by the Act to the effect that it is a defence where:

— the person charged can show that they acted in conformity with price stabilising rules or control of information rules;[6]

— in the case of reckless statements being alleged, that the person charged reasonably believed that their act or conduct would not create an impression that was false or misleading, or that they acted for the purpose of stabilising investments in conformity with price stabilisation rules or control of information rules.

1   S 397(1)(a).
2   S 397(1)(b).
3   S 397(1)(c).
4   S 397(2).
5   S 397(3).
6   S 397(4).

PUBLISHING RESEARCH

11.39   Many larger investment banks and financial advisory firms carry out market research. In part this is for their own use, but it is often also distributed to key customers and sometimes target customers to impress them as to the firm's abilities. The circulation of such research has the potential to affect the market price of some investments and for this reason both the Conduct of Business Rules and the FSMA 2000 deal with the issue.

11.40   Dealing ahead of the publication of material that could affect the price of investments could put a firm in a position where having purchased investments it then published and benefited from such an increase in price. As a consequence COB 7.3 states that wherever a firm or one of its associates intends to publish a written recommendation relating to investments it must not undertake a transaction on its own account in either that investment or a related one. It must also take all reasonable steps to ensure that its associates do not carry out any such transaction. This requirement not to trade terminates once the clients for whom the publication was principally intended have had a reasonable opportunity to act on it. There are exceptions however. For example, if the publication could not reasonably be expected significantly to change the price of an investment, or where the firm is a market maker in the investment concerned and it undertakes the transaction in good faith and in the normal course of market making. (A market maker is someone who holds themselves out as able and willing to buy and sell certain types of investments on an ongoing basis. It does not extend to those operating collective investment schemes.)[1] The firm can also act when it does so to fulfil an unsolicited client order. The firm may also proceed where it has taken reasonable steps to ensure that it needs to deal to fulfil a client's order that is likely to arise from the publication. However, in such cases the firm must be sure that the publication will not cause the price of the investment to move against the client's interest by a material amount. Finally, the firm can proceed where they have disclosed in the publication that they or an associate can or has traded in a relevant investment.

1   FSA Glossary of Definitions.

11.41   'Publish' is not defined in COB 7.3 or the FSA Glossary of Terms. However, *The Oxford English Dictionary* defines it as 'Make generally known, noise abroad; announce formally, promulgate. . .' It is clearly therefore going to include releasing information on the internet and sending emails and email attachments as well as more traditional forms of publication. Neither is 'recommendation' or 'research' defined. No undue complication arises as a result of this. Both terms are being used in an understood context and for firms circulating information it is safest to interpret them in a wide sense. The fact that the extensive definition of 'published recommendation' in the old IMRO rules was not retained is a sign that the FSA felt that to do so was unnecessary.

11.42   FSA Principles 6 and 8 (both discussed below) will be relevant here. Of the two, no. 8 is the most relevant. As highlighted in the guidance note to COB 7.3 it '. . . aims to ensure that either a firm pays due regard to the interests of its customers by postponing an own account transaction where the firm or its associate publishes a written recommendation or, when this is not practicable or desirable generally in the interests of the firm's customer, that any dealing does not unfairly disadvantage the customer'.

11.43   A further step taken by the FSMA is the creation of the new crime of market abuse. This is covered in detail in Chapter 8. As a result only a few relevant points are made here. The crime extends to unauthorised as well as authorised people. However, unauthorised people will only be concerned with the criminal ramifications whereas those who are authorised will also be concerned about potential regulatory steps. It is in many ways an unsatisfactory crime in that it is very widely and vaguely defined. As a consequence, the FSA, which has the legal power to police the offence, has issued a Code of Practice.[1] This has a statutory basis[2] and was intended to assist by clarifying the meaning of the crime and the FSA have made clear that they will use it, *inter alia*, to describe behaviour that they believe will, or will not be caught by the definition. The Code adds that the standards expected from a regular user of the market will depend on that user's experience, skill and level of knowledge. It also adds that if behaviour was reasonable at the time but ceases to seem so with the benefit of hindsight, it may still be safe from being adjudged to be market abuse. The Code acknowledges that the motivation for the behaviour will also be a crucial factor.

1   Now republished as MAR 1 in the Market Conduct Handbook.
2   FSMA 2000, s 122.

11.44   The crime itself falls into three separate primary offences:

(i)   misusing information that is not generally available to the market, but which if it were would be regarded by them as relevant when determining the terms of a contract;

(ii)   giving a false or misleading impression as to the supply, demand, or price of the investments concerned; and

(iii)   engaging in behaviour which a regular user of the market would regard as being likely to distort the market.

Note that there is no requirement that the person concerned intended any of these as the consequences of their act.[1] There is also a secondary offence of requiring or encouraging someone else to commit market abuse.[2] This is presumably aimed at firms employing those who commit market abuse, together with their directors and senior managers.

1   Code of Market Conduct 1.2.5E.
2   S 123(1).

11.45   Information is taken to be generally available where it can be obtained by research or analysis conducted by or on behalf of users of the market. Typical examples would be where the information has been disclosed through an approved channel of communication on a prescribed market; when it is obtainable from records that are open to inspection by the public; where the information has been made public or can be derived from information that has; where it can be obtained by observation; where it has been published overseas; where it has been made available to a section of the public; or where it is available on the publication of a fee. Factors that would be relevant would include how specific the information was, how material, how current, how reliable, how new it is and its relationship with other information already on the market.

SUITABILITY

11.46   Prior to acting on behalf of, or advising a client, a firm must obtain full details of all relevant information pertaining to that client's financial position. This will need to cover the current and probable future position regarding income, capital, investments, protection cover and inheritance. Such information should also be obtained relating to any spouse or partner. Without such information any advice given would probably prove inappropriate and could give rise to civil proceedings were loss to result. In addition the FSA rules prescribe such client research as a first step prior to acting. The general FSA requirements are set out at COB 5.3.5:

'(1)   A firm must take reasonable steps to ensure that it does not in the course of designated investment business—

(a)   make any personal recommendation to a private customer to buy or sell a designated investment; or

(b)   effect a discretionary transaction for a private customer (except as in (3));

unless the recommendation or transaction is suitable for the private customer having regard to the facts disclosed by him and other relevant facts about the private customer of which the firm is, or, reasonably should be aware.

(2)   A firm which acts as an investment manager for a private customer must take reasonable steps to ensure that the private customer's portfolio or account remains suitable, having regard to the facts disclosed by the private customer and other relevant facts about the private customer of which the firm is or reasonably should be aware.

(3)   Where, with the agreement of the private customer, a firm has pooled his fund with those of others with a view to taking common discretionary

management decisions, the firm must take reasonable steps to ensure that a discretionary transaction is suitable for the fund, having regard to the stated investment objectives of the fund.'

11.47 The most onerous issue here appears to be the imposition on fund managers at (2) and (3). The requirement to take 'reasonable steps' with regard to suitability of investments may be a problem. In many instances it will not be practical for a fund manager to know whether a precise investment is appropriate for a customer even though the overall fund may be generically appropriate, particularly where the fund manager is not directly advising the customer. It remains to be seen how precisely the FSA will interpret this rule.

11.48 Where packaged products are concerned the rule is slightly different. Here the obligation on a provider firm making a personal recommendation to a private customer to buy a packaged product is that they must be satisfied that it is the most suitable. In ascertaining this the key issue is the products that are available from the marketing group and the packaged products that the firm is able to sell. Independent advisers will need to ascertain the best product from everything available on the market. The availability of a special price or special terms are not regarded as the crucial issue.[1] In the case of independent advisers there will be a much greater burden than in the case of tied agents who are only able to sell the products of the party to whom they are tied. Independents can only recommend a packaged product if they do not have reasonable grounds for believing that there is an alternative product available which would be more appropriate. In the case of managers of occupational pension schemes and stakeholder pension schemes, reasonable steps must be taken to make sure the transactions of the portfolio are suitable, bearing in mind the investment objectives of that portfolio.

1 COB 5.3.7.

11.49 Where the customer buys, sells, surrenders, cancels or suspends payments to a life policy or a stakeholder pension scheme a suitability letter must be sent. It is also required where the customer decides to make income withdrawals, and where he acquires or sells a holding in such a scheme, or enters into a pension transfer or opt-out from an occupational pension scheme. The purpose of this is to highlight the risk of potential long-term loss arising as a consequence of the steps being taken. The letter itself does not have an exactly prescribed form but there are clear requirements as to the minimum information that must be included. This must identify the person in the firm authorised to deal on the product concerned and:

— explain why the firm believes the transaction to be suitable for that customer;
— include a summary of the main consequences and any possible disadvantages;
— where relevant, state why the firm believes that a personal pension scheme is more appropriate than a stakeholder scheme;
— in the case of free standing additional voluntary contributions to a pension being taken out the letter must explain why the arrangement is at least as suitable as additional voluntary contributions, a stakeholder scheme or additional payments to an occupational pension scheme.

It is not necessary to send a suitability letter in certain specific instances. There are also differences in the content in certain specific areas, notably broker funds[1] and personal pension schemes.[2]

1   COB 5.3.20.
2   COB 5.3.28.

BEST EXECUTION

11.50   In essence this consists of making sure that the client obtains the contract on the best reasonably available terms. There are however exceptions. The rule does not apply where a customer order relates to a life policy, or the purchase or sale of units in a regulated collective investment scheme from, or to the operator of that scheme. Nor does it apply where the firm has agreed with an intermediate customer that it does not owe them such a duty, unless the customer is the trustee of an occupational pension scheme or an OPS collective investment scheme, or the trustee of a trust for which the firm acts as a permitted third party. Finally, the rule does not apply where the firm relies on another person to execute a customer's order.

11.51   Best execution specifically involves taking reasonable care to find out the price which is the best available for the customer in the market concerned, bearing in mind the type of contract and its size. It also involves executing the order at such a price unless it is in the client's best interests not to do so.[1] In this context 'reasonable care' has a specific meaning.[2] It requires that the firm should:

—   disregard charges and commission disclosed to the client;
—   where different exchanges or trading platforms offer comparable prices the order should be carried out at the best available price, provided that this is in the customer's best interests. Such comparative prices will not always be available.

The execution price is that which should be charged to the customer.

In the case of programme trading a general duty of care is also a component of best execution. Where the customer order relates to securities priced in euros and the firm will be executing the contract in sterling, the best price must be obtained in sterling.

1   COB 7.5.5.
2   COB 7.5.5 E.

11.52   Best execution does not apply to the purchase of life policies or the purchase or sale of units in a regulated collective investment scheme to or from its operator.[1] It is also possible for a firm to agree with an intermediate customer that it does not owe a duty of best execution to them. However, this option does not exist where the customer is the trustee of an occupational pension scheme or an OPS collective investment scheme, or where the customer is the trustee of a trust and the firm is acting as a permitted third party. It is possible for a firm to pass the duty of best execution along to a party to whom they have passed a customer order for execution, provided this is reasonable in the circumstances.

1   COB 7.5.3.

11.53   Matters are somewhat simplified in the case of trades on SETS (the Stock Exchange Electronic Trading Service). If the customer's order relates to shares that are traded on SETS it is sufficient that the firm executes the order through SETS. If the firm does not trade through SETS in such a situation then the firm must:

— Trade at a price which matches the best bid or offer price on SETS where the order is for normal settlement.

— Where a customer order is larger than the limit orders available on SETS but there is sufficient market depth to trade, the price obtained must at least match the weighted average on SETS for the security concerned.

— If the procedure described immediately above is not an option due to the customer order being larger than the totality of orders displayed on SETS, the firm must use due skill and care to ascertain the best available price. In so doing the firm must have regard to the price at which transactions of that general size have been executed recently and prevailing market conditions.

— Where there are no bid or offer prices available, the firm must refer to the best prices previously quoted and to the latest published trades and then form a view as to the current value.

— If the customer order is subject to a special condition the price should still at least match that available on SETS.

Executing an order at a price that is less advantageous to the client may be acceptable provided that the firm reasonably believes that it will be able to obtain corresponding advantages for the customer over time.

11.54   In the case of non-standard settlement any charges and commission may either be stated on the contract or confirmation note or be in a separate written statement sent to the client before the contract is executed. If it cannot be done that quickly then it should at least be disclosed orally, straight away and then a written confirmation be sent on as soon as possible after the contract has been executed.

TIMELY EXECUTION

11.55   When a firm agrees to exercise an order for a customer on a discretionary basis it must do so as soon as is reasonably practicable unless postponing appears to be in the client's best interests.[1] The issue of timing is particularly sensitive where the firm receives a client order outside normal trading hours for a particular market and the firm intends trading on that market. It will also arise where there are grounds for anticipating an improvement in the liquidity in the investment concerned that is likely to improve the price or terms of trading. Finally, situations could arise where executing the order as a series of smaller contracts could improve the terms on which the client can trade. Aggregated trades are acceptable provided this will not operate to the disadvantage of a client, even where this means one or more clients having their trades delayed. Postponement therefore is permissible if it is in the best interests of the client. The rule does not apply to customer orders that are to be executed on the fulfilment of a condition.[2]

1   COB 7.6.4 and 7.6.5.
2   COB 7.6.3G.

11.56 FSA Principle 2 requiring a firm to act with due skill, care and diligence and Principle 6 relating to customers' interests are specifically noted in the guidance made to the rules.[1] It requires that the firm must act with due skill, care and diligence and to act in the customer's best interests in choosing the most appropriate time to execute customers' orders.

1   COB 7.6.2.

CHURNING AND SWITCHING

11.57 Churning is a term that describes the activity that occurs where a fund manager or investment adviser arranges to buy and sell contracts on behalf of a client on a scale that does not reflect the investment needs of the client concerned. Rather the trades are carried out to generate commission for the manager or adviser. It extends to situations where discretionary fund managers trade within their portfolio on the same immoral basis. Switching extends the same concept to retail packaged products, eg, life policies, units in a regulated collective investment scheme, interests in an investment trust savings scheme and stakeholder pension schemes. It used to be the case in the pre-FSA regulations that these two activities were dealt with separately. However, their nearly identical nature has resulted in COB 7.2 dealing with both in a joint rule.

11.58 The FSA rule is fairly straightforward. It states[1] that a firm must not engage in a number of activities unless it has taken reasonable steps to ascertain what is in their clients' best interests. One factor to be considered in this respect are the previous transactions carried out on that client's behalf. The activities concerned are:

— dealing or arranging deals when exercising discretion for a client;
— making recommendations to a private customer to deal or arranging a deal on the basis of such a recommendation;
— making or arranging a switch in a packaged product, or between packaged products in the carrying out of a discretionary activity for a private customer; or
— making personal recommendations to private customers to switch within a packaged product or between packaged products or to make or arrange a switch that has the same effect.

1   COB 7.2.3.

11.59 A key issue arising in this context is the difficulty of proving that churning has occurred. There is always difficulty in proving that a 'crime' has occurred where the argument focuses on the motivation of an act rather than on whether that act has taken place. Thus in marginal cases it may be impossible to prove that churning has occurred. The manager or adviser will no doubt present evidence from the customer file that the activity was carried out on a plausible basis that should have benefited the client, which regrettably did not work out. In some instances though the scale of the trading and the circumstances and nature of the investment background may render it apparent that churning has taken place. In such instances, not only is there a serious breach of the Conduct of Business rules but it is also potentially a criminal offence. Fraud and obtaining a pecuniary advantage by deception are the two most obvious candidates. It is beyond the remit of this chapter to enter into a lengthy analysis of criminal law. Suffice to say that a manager or adviser finding themselves falling foul of the anti-churning provisions of the rules could find themselves in serious trouble.

11.60 The FSA Principles are also an issue here. Principle No 1 states that 'a firm must conduct its business with integrity'. Further No 6 states that 'a firm must pay due regard to the interests of its customers and treat them fairly'. Finally, No 8 adds 'a firm must manage conflicts of interest fairly, both between itself and its customers and between one customer and another'. The Statements of Principle for approved persons continue at No 1 'An approved person must act with integrity in carrying out his approved function.' At No 7 it adds 'An approved person performing a significant influence function must take reasonable steps to ensure that the business of the firm for which he is responsible in his controlled function complies with the regulatory require-ments imposed on that business.' Thus in addition to any breaches of COB 7.2 the FSA have a strong armoury of potential lines of attack on both the firm and the individual concerned as well as its senior managers and directors. This could help to force a firm to settle any disciplinary proceedings that are brought as those being regulated may well be concerned at the range of broadly drafted principles that could be applied to them, even if they could protect themselves on technical grounds from steps taken under the Conduct of Business rules.

INSIDER DEALING

11.61 One further area of law that deals with abuse of position is that of insider dealing. This area provides some customer protection in that those dealing in securities, as defined by the Criminal Justice Act 1993, can do so in the knowledge that the price they are paying or receiving is not distorted by transactions in the marketplace being undertaken by those who have inside knowledge. That at least is the theory. The reality is that there has been an average of less than one conviction a year for the crime since 1980. Nonetheless, any consideration of customer care needs to refer to this area. This is dealt with in detail in Chapter 9.

MATERIAL INTERESTS AND DISCLOSURE

11.62 Any firm that provides financial services in a sophisticated market is likely to have to deal with its own material interests and potential conflicts of interest on an everyday basis. For example, an investment management firm may own or be owned by a broker through which it deals on behalf of clients. A broker, in recommending a particular line of stock to a client, may be aware that it has another client who wishes to sell such a line. In such circumstances, a firm must pay close attention to the FSA rules. In addition, however, this is an area where the firm will also be subject to duties that are imposed by the general law, because of its agency relationship with the client. In this field, there is a strong temptation for firms to focus too closely on their FSA requirements and, in doing so, to lose sight of the more general restrictions.

11.63 The handling of material interests and conflicts of interest is an exception to the general position and because of the structural changes that have taken place within the industry in recent years, a range of new problems has arisen. As explained above, financial services groups have developed. They can offer a wide range of services to their clients. There is no doubt that many clients have come to appreciate the 'one-stop' or full-service approach to the provision of services. Yet a firm whose client has come to it for one particular service will generally be materially interested if that client decides to use another service offered by a firm within its corporate group. As the client begins to use a third, fourth or fifth service, a complex web of material interests may build up. At times, the immediate interests of a client may potentially conflict with those of the firm or of another client, eg where an advisory or investment management firm deals through a related broker or with a related market maker.

11.64 A detailed discussion of the law of agency is outside the scope of this book. In general terms, however, the basic position of common law is that an agent must not profit by his agency except through any fee that he may charge to his principal.He must also account to his principal for any other income received which is attributable to the agency. In addition, an agent may not act where he has a material interest in a transaction or an interest which potentially conflicts with that of his principal. In all these cases, there is an exception to the strict, general rule where the agent specifically discloses in advance the additional income that may be received and/or the material interests or potential conflicts of interest and where the principal gives his informed consent to the agent retaining the income concerned and/or to his acting despite the material interest or potential conflict.

11.65 In short, the general rule is that any profit, material interest or potential conflicts of interest of an agent must be the subject of specific prior disclosure to the principal and must have received the principal's informed consent. The courts have recognised, however, that there are circumstances where the general rule may operate too harshly. There are circumstances where it is recognised that a specific disclosure on each occasion when a profit or interest may arise may be impractical and where as a result a general disclosure and consent in advance will suffice. In these cases the nature of the income that may arise and the kinds of interests and conflicts that may be involved must be described to the principal in sufficient detail to enable any consent given by the principal to be an informed consent. There are also circumstances where the courts have recognised that the general rule may be modified by particular custom and practice in an industry or commercial sector. The extent, if any, to which the court will recognise any such modification will depend upon the circumstances. It is against this background of common law that the FSA rules on conflicts of interest and material interests must be viewed.

11.66 If a firm has a material interest in a transaction to be entered into with, or for a customer; or a relationship that gives, or may give rise to a conflict of interest in relation to such a transaction; or an interest in a transaction that is, or may be in conflict with the interest of any of the firm's customers; or customers with conflicting interests in relation to a transaction; the firm must not knowingly advise or deal in the exercise of discretion in relation to that transaction unless it takes reasonable steps to ensure fair treatment for the customers.[1] The note to the rule adds that:

'For the purposes of CoB 7.1.3 a firm may manage a conflict of interest by taking on or more of the following reasonable steps:

(1)   disclosure of an interest to a customer;
(2)   relying on a policy of independence;
(3)   establishing internal arrangements (Chinese walls);
(4)   declining to act for a customer.'

1   COB 7.1.3.

11.67   The main conceptual difference between the approach of the common law and the approach of the rule is that, at common law, certain arbitrary prohibitions and sanctions are imposed in order to deter an agent from abusing his position. The rule is more concerned to be reasonable in striking a balance between the interests of a firm and those of its customers. For example, the use of the word 'knowingly' leaves open the question how far the knowledge of individual employees may be attributable to the firm and of how far the regulators will regard the knowledge of the employee who is responsible for the advice or transaction in question to be the determining factor. In other words, it leaves open the question of the effectiveness of an independence policy. Further, there is clearly a difference between the rule's concern to ensure 'fair treatment' for customers and the strict common law duty of an agent to account to his principal for profits.

Chapter 12

Client money

SOURCE AND GENERAL PRINCIPLES

12.1 The Financial Services and Markets Act (FSMA) 2000 sets the framework for the Financial Services Authority's (FSA) detailed client money rules. The FSMA 2000 makes provision for the FSA to make rules in relation to the handling of money by authorised persons.[1] Broadly, the legislation provides for the FSA to make provision for money to be held on trust. In addition, the legislation covers the treatment of accounts as a single account (see distribution rules) and for rules relating to interest, both payable to clients and retained by the firm. Importantly, the legislation states that:[2]

> 'an institution with which an account is kept in pursuance of rules relating to the handling of clients' money does not incur any liability as constructive trustee if money is wrongfully paid from the account, unless the institution permits the payment –
>
> (a) with knowledge that it is wrongful; or
> (b) having deliberately failed to make enquiries in circumstances in which a reasonable and honest person would have done so'.[3]

1 FSMA 2000, s 139.
2 See FSMA 2000, s 139(2).
3 In the application of the FSMA 2000, s 139(1) to Scotland, 'the reference to money being held on trust is to be read as a reference to its being held as agent for the person who is entitled to call for it to be paid over to him or to be paid on his direction or to have it otherwise credited to him', as set out in the FSMA 2000, s 139(3).

12.2 The FSA is required to act in a way which is compatible with its regulatory objectives. These objectives include the protection of consumers.[1] The FSA has defined its principles which are a general statement of the fundamental obligations of firms under the regulatory system.[2] These principles derive from the FSA's rule-making powers as set out in the FSMA 2000. The principle that deals with clients' assets is Principle 10. This states that:

> 'A firm must arrange adequate protection for clients' assets when it is responsible for them'.

Breaching a principle makes a firm liable to disciplinary sanctions.[3] Some of the detailed rules and guidance in the FSA Handbook deal with the bearing of

324

the principles upon particular circumstances but the principles are also designed as a general statement of regulatory requirements (for example, in new or unforeseen circumstances).

1   FSMA 2000, s 5.
2   FSA Handbook, PRIN 2.1.1R.
3   FSA Handbook, PRIN 1.1.7G.

THE FSA HANDBOOK AND THE CONDUCT OF BUSINESS RULES

12.3   The FSA has sought to document all its rules and guidance in a single document known as the FSA Handbook. This Handbook is divided into sections dealing with high level standards, business standards (ie detailed rules), regulatory processes (eg the authorisation process), redress (eg compensation arrangements) and specialist sourcebooks (eg a sourcebook for collective investment schemes).

The principles are located in the high level standards section of the FSA Handbook.

The detailed rules and guidance relating to the protection of assets for which a firm is responsible are located within the business standards section of the FSA Handbook. These rules are known as the 'client asset' rules and are located within the 'Conduct of Business Sourcebook' (COB) within the business standards section of the FSA Handbook. The client asset rules are divided into five sections. The first four sections deal with custody, mandates, client money and collateral respectively. The final section deals with client money distribution, that is, the rules applicable when events such as the failure of the firm occur.

In this chapter the term 'firm' is used to mean an authorised person.[1] This is the convention adopted within the FSA Handbook. Within this chapter no distinction has been made between rules, guidance and evidential provisions, although the references in the footnotes show whether the requirement takes the form of a Rule (R), of Guidance (G), or Evidential provision (E).[2]

1   FSA Handbook, Glossary.
2   The status of the different types of provisions depends on the terms of the FSMA 2000 and the particular power exercised to create that provision. An introductory description to the terms is provided in the Reader's Guide section of the FSA Handbook.

Scope of the client asset rules

12.4   Whilst a few of the conduct of business rules are applicable to firms carrying on all types of regulated activities (including deposit-taking and insurance related activities) the majority of the rules in this section of the FSA Handbook are limited in their scope to firms which are carrying on designated investment business.[1] In relation to deposits, pure protection contracts and general insurance contracts, COB has only limited application.[2] Individual sections of COB set out the extent of their application to different types of regulated activities. The application rules differ for the client money and custody rules within COB. The client money rules apply to 'a firm that receives or holds money from, or on behalf of, a client in the course of, or in connection with its designated investment business', except where otherwise provided by the rules.[3] The disapplications are set out below.

1   The definition of 'designated investment business' is provided in the Glossary section of the
    FSA Handbook. The activities described in this definition derive from activities specified in the
    Financial Services and Markets Act 2000 (Regulated Activities) Order 2001, SI 2001/544.
    Note that not all the activities specified in the Order are included within the 'designated
    investment business' definition.
2   COB 1.3.2G(2).
3   COB 9.3.1R.

12.5   There are a number of disapplications to the client money rules. The
most important for a bank is that, broadly, the client money rules do not apply
to 'money held by a firm which is an approved bank where this money is held by
the bank in an "account with itself"'.

It is important to understand the limits of this disapplication. It is easy for
those working within banks to fall into the 'trap' of believing that 'banks do not
hold client money'. This is not the case and a number of banks hold substantial
sums of money which fall within the FSA's client money rules.

Money of clients held by banks (COB 9.3.2(3), 9.3.5–9.3.6)

12.6   It should be noted that where a firm is an approved bank and the money
is held on behalf of a client 'in an account with itself',[1] then the client money
rules do not apply. However, if the firm then transfers money from that account
to another approved bank or another authorised person, then that money will
have to be treated as client money. Where a bank wishes to rely on this 'banking'
exemption it must be able to account to all of its clients for amounts held on
their behalf at all times. Normally a bank would comply with this requirement
by recording the amount due to a client in a current account on the firm's
balance sheet. Such accounts can be 'pooled' accounts but where this is the
case the bank must clearly identify the pooled account as an account for clients
and must be able to identify individual clients' entitlements within the pool at
any time.[2] Specific examples illustrate the extent to which this 'exemption'
applies in different circumstances.

1   COB 9.3.2R.
2   COB 9.3.5G.

12.7   Where a bank places money of its investment business clients in
accounts with another bank, this may be client money, depending on the way in
which and the purpose for which, it has been deposited. Consider the following
scenarios.

(1)   Bank A passes money to Bank B in the form of an overnight deposit in the
      normal course of banking business (eg as part of its treasury manage-
      ment activities) – the money passed to Bank B is not within the scope of
      the client money rules.
(2)   Bank A opens an account with Bank B for the purpose of depositing
      money on behalf of its investment business clients (eg because Bank B
      offers a preferential rate of interest for deposits over £X,000) – the money
      in this account is within the scope of the client money rules.
(3)   Bank A passes money of its investment business clients to a futures broker
      or exchange in the course of undertaking futures business on behalf of
      these clients – once passed to the broker or exchange, this money is within
      the scope of the client money rules.

Money passed on in the normal course of banking business is not deemed to be client money – here, it is important to distinguish between the liability (ie the liability of the bank to its account holders) and the underlying asset (which the bank may use in the normal course of banking business).

12.8   Where a firm (which is a bank) relies on this 'banking exemption' it must notify the client in writing that money held for that client will be held by the firm as banker and not as trustee, and as a result the money will not be held in accordance with the client money rules.[1]

1   COB 9.3.2R(3).

12.9   The application of the client money rules to European branches of UK firms and to UK branches of European firms is governed by the Investment Services Directive (ISD).[1] Where firms are 'passporting'[2] their activities under the Investment Services Directive then the home state is responsible for prudential supervision of investment firms. This 'prudential supervision' includes a requirement for proper client money arrangements. Consequently, where a UK-regulated entity opens a branch in an European Economic Area (EEA) state (eg Germany) then the FSA's client money rules are the rules applicable to the activities of the branch. Similarly, if a German investment firm were to open a branch in the UK then this branch would be subject to German rather than UK requirements in relation to client money arrangements.

1   Council Directive 93/22/EEC.
2   FSMA 2000, Sch 3.

Further issues concerning the scope of the client money rules

12.10   A new Inter-Professional Conduct (IPC) regime[1] will apply to dealings which a firm has with a market counterparty where the activity relates to an inter-professional investment. This area of the rules may be particularly relevant to a bank's treasury activities. The list of inter-professional investments is broadly:

- shares;
- debentures;
- government and public securities;
- certificates representing certain securities;
- futures;
- warrants;
- options;
- contracts for differences;
- rights to, or interests in, investments falling within the other categories listed above.

Transactions relating to deposits, general and long-term insurance contracts and units in collective investment schemes will fall outside the inter-professional conduct regime.

1   FSA Handbook, Market Conduct (MAR 3).

12.11   The IPC regime covers the activities of dealing and arranging deals in IPC investments with advice covered only to the extent that it is given for the purposes of dealing or arranging services that the firm is already providing, or which it wishes to provide.[1]

1   MAR 3.1.2R.

12.12   Whilst most of the provisions in the conduct of business sourcebook (COB) will not apply to inter-professional business, the requirements in COB 9 (client assets) will apply where a firm provides safekeeping and administration of assets. In particular, the COB requirements in relation to holding money for clients will apply in connection with inter-professional business.

Money that is not client money

12.13   Even where a bank cannot rely on the disapplication for banks (explained at para 12.5 above) there may be other reasons why the money is not client money.

12.14   The definition of client money provided in the FSA Handbook reads:

'subject to the client money rules, money of any currency which, in the course of carrying on designated investment business, a firm holds in respect of any investment agreement entered into, or to be entered into, with or for a client, or which a firm treats as client money in accordance with the client money rules'.[1]

The following notes set out the variety of ways in which a firm, including a bank, might hold money which, whilst it belongs to clients, falls outside the scope of the FSA's client money rules.

1   FSA Handbook, Glossary.

Type of business – business that is not designated investment business (COB 9.3.1)

12.15   The client money rules apply to a firm that receives or holds money from or on behalf of, a client in the course of, or in connection with, its 'designated investment business', except where otherwise provided in the rules.[1] Client money can only arise in relation to designated investment business activities, so activities which fall outside this definition such as lending or deposit-taking cannot give rise to client money to which the COB client money rules will apply.

1   COB 9.3.1R.

12.16   Although firms undertaking regulated activities must be authorised under the FSMA 2000, they are not precluded from undertaking activities which are not regulated activities. In addition, a regulated firm may carry out regulated activities that fall outside the definition of designated investment business. Any firm involved in activities other than designated investment business is not considered to hold client money in respect of those activities.

Money due and payable to the firm (COB 9.3.19–9.3.24)

12.17   Money which is properly due and payable to the firm for its own account is not client money.[1] An evidential provision provides guidance on the term 'due and payable' in the context of fees and commissions.[2] Broadly, fees and commissions can be treated as due to the firm from five business days after a statement showing the fees have been sent to the customer, provided these fees were accurately calculated on a basis previously disclosed to the client and the FSA-regulated firm has no reason to believe that the client questions the amount of the fees or commissions shown on that statement.[3]

1   COB 9.3.19R.
2   COB 9.3.20E and COB 9.3.21G–9.3.22G.
3   COB 9.3.20E.

Money from an affiliated company (COB 9.3.17–9.3.18)

12.18   Affiliated companies are considered to be so closely related to the firm that their money should be treated as the firm's money and should be held separately from any client money. However, where money from an affiliated company belongs to an underlying client the segregation of this money would be in accordance with the principle of investor protection. Hence, the rules specify that the money from affiliated companies should not be given client money protection unless:

(1)   the firm has been notified by the affiliated company that the money belongs to a client of the affiliated company; or
(2)   the affiliated company is a client dealt with at arm's length; or
(3)   the affiliated company is a manager of an occupational pension scheme or is an overseas company and the money has been given to the firm in order to carry on designated investment business for or on behalf of the clients of the affiliated company and the firm has been notified by the affiliated company that the money is to be treated as client money.[1]

Whilst the general principle is that group company money should not be treated as client money, in fact the result of these exemptions, in particular those for money belonging to underlying clients of the affiliated company and for situations where the affiliated company is treated on an 'arm's length' basis, is that, in fact, most group company money is held in protected accounts.

1   COB 9.3.18R.

DVP transactions (COB 9.3.15–9.3.16)

12.19   Even where a transaction constitutes investment business and, *prima facie*, client money could arise, it is necessary to consider the settlement process involved in the transaction. Delivery versus payment (DVP) transactions are those transactions where it is intended that the transfer of securities and cash will take place on the same day. Clearly, if a client delivers securities to the firm or pays for the purchase of securities without receiving an asset (in the form of cash or securities) from the firm in exchange, then the client is at risk.

12.20   The client money rules provide a concession where there is a short-term delay in the delivery to, or payment of, a client in relation to a DVP transaction since these delays are not considered to represent a significant risk to the client. Where the client delivers securities or cash to the firm on day one, the firm must provide client money protection to the client's funds only if delivery or payment by the firm has not occurred by the end of day four. Hence the firm effectively has a 'three (business) day window' in which to resolve the mismatch of delivery and payment before it is required to protect the client's money.[1]

1   COB 9.3.15R.

12.21   A similar principle applies for money received by a firm in relation to the issue of units in a regulated collective investment scheme. This money will only need to be treated as client money if the price of the units has not been determined by the close of business on the next business day after receipt. If the money was received by an appointed representative of the firm, some time is allowed by the rules for transmission to the firm. In addition, if money is held in the course of redeeming units it need not be treated as client money if the redemption proceeds are paid within the timeframes specified in the Collective Investment Scheme sourcebook within the FSA Handbook.[1]

1   COB 9.3.16R and 9.3.49R.

Client opt-outs

12.22   The rules recognise the fact that not all clients require the same level of protection and they therefore aim to provide the greatest protection to inexperienced clients. Applying this principle, the client money rules include provisions allowing firms to disapply the rules to certain types of client, provided strict conditions have been satisfied.

Private customers – no opt-out

12.23   Private customers (eg individuals) require the greatest protection and therefore the firm cannot opt out these clients of client money protection. An exception to this general rule occurs in the case of individuals and small business investors who are classified as 'expert' customers for the purposes of the Conduct of Business Rules and are treated as intermediate customers. The client money rules do not need to be applied to money held for these customers where their written consent has been obtained. The written consent will only be effective if it is in the required form.[1]

1   See para 12.24.

Other clients – two-way opt-out (COB 9.3.8–9.3.9)

12.24   The client money rules do not need to be applied to money held for intermediate customers and market counterparties if their written agreement has been obtained. This written agreement will only be effective if it contains the matters specified in COB 9.3.9, that is, if it states that:

(1)   the client's money will not be subject to the protection of the client money rules; and

(2)   the client's money will not be segregated from the firm's own money; and

(3)   the client's money will be used by the firm in the course of its own business; and

(4)   the client will rank as a general creditor of the firm.[1]

1   COB 9.3.9R.

Non-European business – one-way opt-out (COB 9.3.10–9.3.11)

12.25   Where a firm is carrying on designated investment business which is not a core investment service, a non-core investment service,[1] or a listed activity,[2] and where the counterparty (ie the client) is not an authorised person or a private customer, a one-way opt-out from client money protection may be used. The written form of the opt-out must be the same as that used for the two-way notice described above.[3] The FSA is not permitted by European legislation to treat 'ISD type' business of a non-ISD investment firm with branches in the UK any more favourably than business of an ISD firm so two-way opt-outs should be used in relation to such 'ISD type' business.[4]

1   Core investment services and non-core investment services are defined in the Investment Services Directive and in the Financial Services and Markets Act 2000 (Regulated Activities) Order 2001 (SI 2001/544), Sch 2.
2   A 'listed activity' is an activity listed in Annex 1 to the Banking Consolidation Directive, Council Directive 2000/12/EC.
3   COB 9.3.11R.
4   COB 9.3.10G.

Money transferred – no opt-out (COB 9.3.13–9.3.14)

12.26   Where a firm transfers client money to another person, the firm must not allow itself to be 'opted out' of client money protection on either a one-way or two-way basis.[1]

1   COB 9.3.13R.

Type of bank account – mandated accounts

12.27   Money held in a bank account in the name of an individual client is not client money since it is not 'held by the firm'. There is a normal banker/customer relationship between the customer and the bank with which the money is placed, although for practical reasons the firm will usually have a mandate to transfer money to or from the account. Even though such money is not client money for the purposes of the rules, it should be noted that the FSA has specific requirements relating to the operation of mandated accounts: these are set out in COB 9.2.

No banking exemption – standard rules

12.28   Where the banking exemption does not apply the standard client money rules apply and the usual considerations in respect of the treatment of the money should be addressed; whether the clients have been opted out of client money protection, whether the accounts opened with other banks are in the name of the client only, or in the form 'Bank A, Client account'. Trust status is required as normal. The client money rules are extremely detailed and a full review of all these detailed requirements is beyond the scope of this book. The following notes therefore provide an overview of some of the provisions which are likely to be of relevance to banks and banking groups.

Segregation

Purpose of segregation and rules applicable (COB 9.3.36–9.3.41)

12.29   The purpose of the client money rules is to keep clients' money separate from the firm's money. In the event of a default, such as the firm's failure, it is important that the money belonging to clients is held in such a way as to distinguish it from the money available for general creditors. Further, the funds belonging to clients must actually be 'ring-fenced' in a way that provides protection from their being distributed to the general creditors.

12.30   The rules explicitly state that the firm must hold client money separate from the firm's money except as specified in the rules.[1] To achieve this a firm must not hold money other than client money in a client money bank account except as follows:

(1)   it is a minimum sum required to keep the account open;
(2)   it is temporarily held in that account in accordance with the rules on mixed remittances;[2]
(3)   it represents interest paid into the account in excess of the amount due to clients.[3]

1   COB 9.3.37R.
2   See para 12.53.
3   COB 9.3.39R.

12.31   A firm is permitted to deposit its own money into a client bank account where it deems it prudent to do this for the protection of clients.[1] These amounts are commonly referred to as 'buffers' and the regulator will expect a firm to be able to explain the reasons for such buffers. The guidance to the rules makes it clear that the use of a 'buffer' does not reduce in any way the firm's responsibility to properly perform the daily calculations of client money requiring segregation.[2]

1   COB 9.3.40R.
2   COB 9.3.41G.

12.32   The rules seek to protect client money by ensuring that it can be easily identified as money belonging to clients. The definition of a 'client bank account' demonstrates this. The definition is:

'(a)   an account at a bank which:

    (i)   holds the money of one or more clients;
    (ii)   is in the name of the firm;
    (iii)   includes in its title an appropriate description to distinguish the money in the account from the firm's money; and
    (iv)   is a current or a deposit account; or

(b)   a money market deposit of client money which is identified as being client money'.[1]

Merely identifying the money as client money does not represent adequate protection and consequently the rules provide for a trust to be established, as set out below.[2]

1   FSA Handbook, Glossary.
2   See para 12.33.

Statutory trust (COB 9.3.30–9.3.31)

12.33 The FSMA 2000, s 139 provides that the FSA's rules may make provisions that result in money being held by a firm on trust (in England and Wales) or as agent (in Scotland). The FSA rules provide that:

'A firm (other than [a trustee firm]) receives and holds client money as trustee (or agent in Scotland) on the following terms:

(1) for the purposes of and on the terms of the client money rules and the client money distribution rules;

(2) subject to (3), for the clients for whom that money is held, according to their respective interests in it;

(3) on failure of the firm, for the payment of the costs properly attributable to their respective interests in it;

(4) after all valid claims and costs under (2) and (3) have been met, for the firm itself.'[1]

1   COB 9.3.31R.

Holding client money

General and designated client bank accounts (COB 9.3.32)

12.34 Although different types of client money exist (money held pending investment, money held in the course of settlement etc) all client money can be held in a single type of account known as a general client bank account.[1] Firms may use names such as 'client settlement money' or 'client free money' in naming their client money bank accounts notwithstanding the fact that these accounts all take the form of general client bank accounts. An alternative type of account, a designated client bank account, is available but is rarely seen in practice. The purpose of these designated accounts is to establish different pools of client money in the event of the failure of a bank at which the firm holds client money.

1   COB 9.3.32G.

Currency in which funds are held (COB 9.3.38)

12.35 A firm can hold segregated client money in a different currency from that of receipt. Daily translations must be performed to ensure that the amount held is equivalent to the value in the currency of receipt (or where different, equivalent to the currency in which the liability to the client is due).[1]

1   COB 9.3.38R.

Client bank accounts (COB 9.3.67–9.3.68 and 9.3.74–9.3.79)

12.36 The rules in relation to bank accounts aim to ensure that clients' money is properly protected. With this objective the rules specify that client money can only be held in accounts with approved banks except in specified exceptional circumstances, as described below.[1] A detailed definition of an 'approved bank' is provided in the Glossary section of the FSA Handbook. A regulated firm wishing to open a client bank account with an approved bank must carry out a detailed risk assessment of the bank to be used.[2] This assessment must be performed even where the bank is within the same group as the firm.[3] Reviews should then be performed on a continuing basis with a review performed at least once in every financial year. Guidance is provided on the factors to be considered in the assessment.[4] A concession is provided in relation to a bank authorised by an EEA regulator whereby the continuing assessment is not required provided the bank remains authorised.[5]

1   COB 9.3.68R. See also para 12.37.
2   COB 9.3.76R.
3   COB 9.3.80R.
4   COB 9.3.78G.
5   COB 9.3.79G.

12.37   A firm may hold money with a bank which is not an approved bank only where the applicable law or market practice of that overseas jurisdiction prevents the holding of client money in a client money bank account with an approved bank. This 'concession' is available only in relation to the settlement of transactions or the distribution of income. Hence money held pending investment could not be held with a non-approved bank. The use of such a non-approved bank is permitted only for as long as required to effect the relevant transactions and notifications to the client (or consent for a private customer) is required. This type of account must be established as a designated bank account, thereby creating a separate pool of funds for distribution in the event of the failure of the firm.[1]

1   COB 9.3.74R.

12.38   Where a firm uses a group bank to hold client money it must disclose in writing to its client at the outset of the relationship, or not less than 20 days before it begins to hold client money of that client with the group bank, the identity of the bank and that it is a group bank.[1] If a client notifies the firm in writing that he does not wish his money to be held at the group bank the firm must either move the money to a client bank account with another bank or return the money to the client.[2]

1   COB 9.3.80R.
2   COB 9.3.81R.

Euroclear

12.39   Confusion often arises over the treatment of client money held with Euroclear which is commonly used by authorised persons as custodian for their holdings of client investments. Since settlement of securities transactions is effected through Euroclear, cash accounts as well as securities accounts are operated. Money, including client money, held within the Euroclear system is held by Morgan Guaranty Trust Company of New York which is an approved bank for the purpose of the client money rules.

Notifications

Notifications to banks (COB 9.3.82–9.3.85)

12.40   The protected status of a client bank account is established by obtaining from the bank at which the account is held a written acknowledgement of the following matters:

(1) that the money in the account is held by the firm as trustee;

(2) the bank cannot combine the money with any other account or offset the money against any of the firm's own accounts;

(3) the title of the account sufficiently distinguished that account from any account containing money of the firm; and

(4) the account title is in the form requested by the firm.[1]

1   COB 9.3.82R.

12.41   If a UK bank has not acknowledged the trust status of an account within 20 business days, the account cannot be used for client money and any money held in the account must be removed.[1] If a non-UK bank has not acknowledged the trust status of the account within 20 business days the firm must notify the client of this fact.[2]

1   COB 9.3.83R.
2   COB 9.3.84R.

Notifications to exchanges, clearing houses, intermediate brokers or OTC counterparties (COB 9.3.86–9.3.89)

12.42   A firm that carries out any contingent liability investment for clients through an exchange, clearing house, intermediate broker or OTC counterparty must confirm the protected status of the account. The confirmation must:

(1) notify the third party that the firm is under an obligation to keep client money separate from the firm's own money and is under an obligation to 'hold' client money in a client bank account;

(2) instruct the person with whom the account is to be opened that any money paid to it in respect of a contingent liability investment is to be credited to the firm's client transaction account;

(3) require the person with whom the account is opened to acknowledge in writing that they cannot combine the client transaction account with any other account nor is there any right of set-off available against other amounts owed to them.[1]

As with the notifications to banks regarding client money accounts, time limits apply to the receipt of a response to a confirmation request.[2]

1   COB 9.3.86R.
2   COB 9.3.87R.

12.43   It is important to note that the 'trust status' notification in respect of securities accounts which hold safe custody investments does not also cover the client money trust status confirmation required for accounts at custodians which hold client money (ie custodians which are banks).

Notification to clients (COB 9.3.90–9.3.97)

12.44   Where a bank account outside the UK is used to hold client money, clients must be notified (in advance) of the fact that their money may be deposited outside the UK and must be warned that the legal and regulatory regime applicable to such overseas banks will be different from that of the UK and that in the event of default on the part of the overseas bank their money may be treated differently from the position which would apply if the bank were a bank in the UK.[1]

1   COB 9.3.90R.

12.45   This disclosure must also warn clients of the additional risks which may result from the use of an overseas account where a bank has *not* accepted that it has no right of set-off or counterclaim against money held in a client bank account.[1]

1   COB 9.3.90R(3).

12.46   A similar notification is required in relation to the use of an intermediate broker, settlement agent or over-the-counter (OTC) counter-party outside the UK.[1]

1   COB 9.3.95R.

12.47   In both cases (banks and others) if a client notifies a firm that it does not wish money to be held by a bank or other third party in a particular jurisdiction then the money must be held in a protected account in another jurisdiction (to which the client does not object) or the money must be returned to the client.[1]

1   COB 9.3.93R and 9.3.97R.

Notification to the FSA (COB 9.3.98)

12.48   The client money rules seek to protect investors in situations where there is a failure of the firm. The rules are not intended (nor could they be) to protect investors in the event of a default of a third party such as a bank with which the firm deposits its client money. The rules do require firms to perform reviews of the institution with which funds are deposited, but this checking cannot provide guarantees against subsequent failures of these institutions.

12.49   On the failure of a third party with which client money is held the firm must notify the FSA of the failure and then, as soon as reasonably practical after this time, the firm must inform the FSA whether it intends to 'make good' any shortfall which has or may arise.[1]

1   COB 9.3.98R.

Payments into client money bank accounts

General rules (COB 9.3.42–9.3.44)

12.50   A firm can organise the segregation of client money under one of two approaches. These approaches are known as the 'normal' and the 'alternative' approaches.[1]

1   COB 9.3.42R.

12.51   The normal approach requires firms to pay client money directly into their client money accounts on receipt. The rules require a firm using this approach to pay money which it receives into a client bank account as soon as possible and in any event no later than the business day following receipt.[1]

The alternative approach is seen in practice only very occasionally but can be particularly useful to firms holding client money in many jurisdictions/currencies. The alternative approach is dealt with later in this chapter.

1   COB 9.3.44R.

Automated transfers (COB 9.3.45)

12.52   If client money is received in the form of an automated transfer then the firm must take steps to ensure that where possible the money is received directly into a client bank account. In the event that the money is received directly by automated transfer into the firm's account, the money which is client money must be paid into a client bank account no later than the next business day after receipt.[1]

1   COB 9.3.45R.

Mixed remittances (COB 9.3.47–9.3.48)

12.53   Where a firm receives mixed remittances (for example dividend cheques representing the firm's and clients' money) these must be paid into a client money account initially and then the firm's money must be withdrawn within one business day of the date the remittance is expected to be cleared.[1] Where the money is due and payable to the firm in respect of fees and commissions, the firm should follow the specific rules for these amounts.[2]

1   COB 9.3.47R.
2   COB 9.3.20E.

Appointed representatives, field representatives and other agents (COB 9.3.49–9.3.52)

12.54   Where a firm has appointed representatives, field representatives and other agents, it must have procedures in place which ensure that any money received by these parties on behalf of the firm is paid into a client bank account no later than the next business day after receipt, or forwarded to the firm (or a specified business address of the firm in the case of a field representative) to ensure that it arrives by the close of the third business day after receipt.[1]

1   COB 9.3.49R.

12.55   Appointed representatives, field representatives and other agents must keep client money separately identifiable from other money until the client money is paid into a client bank account or sent to the firm.[1]

1   COB 9.3.51R.

12.56   For the purpose of the rules on receipt of funds by agents, a firm that operates a number of small branches but handles or accounts for all client money centrally (for example, regional stockbroking operations), may treat its small branches as appointed representatives.[1]

1   COB 9.3.52G.

Client entitlements

Notification of entitlements (COB 9.3.53)

12.57 A firm must take reasonable steps to ensure it receives information on the receipt of client money in the form of client entitlements (eg dividends) promptly.[1]

1 COB 9.3.53R.

Overseas entitlements (COB 9.3.54–9.3.55)

12.58 Firms often receive entitlements (dividends, coupons, and other distributions with similar characteristics) relating to clients' assets into their own overseas bank accounts in order to avoid opening client bank accounts in numerous overseas locations. These dividends must be transferred to client money accounts or paid to clients. The client money rules recognise the fact that it may be difficult to arrange the transfer on a same or next day basis and they provide a window of five business days following receipt of notification from the overseas bank for the transfer to be effected.[1]

1 COB 9.3.55R.

Allocation of entitlements (COB 9.3.56–9.3.57)

12.59 A firm should allocate client entitlements due to the individual clients within a period of ten business days.[1]

1 COB 9.3.56R and 9.3.57E.

Payments out of client money bank accounts

Timing of payments to clients (COB 9.3.58–9.3.59)

12.60 Where a firm is liable to pay money to a client then it must make this payment as soon as possible, and no later than one business day after the money is 'due and payable', either by paying the money into a client bank account or by paying it to the client or to the order of the client.[1]

1 COB 9.3.58R.

Interest (COB 9.3.60–9.3.62)

12.61 Any interest due to a client is client money. The FSA regard interest on client bank accounts to be a matter of contract between the firm and its clients. All clients, except private customers, are deemed able to negotiate their own arrangements regarding interest. In relation to private customers, the firm must specify in writing its policy on the payment of interest and whether interest is or is not payable and, if so, on what terms and at what frequency. A firm does not need to disclose actual rates prevailing at any particular time to the customer, rather it must explain its policy for the payment of interest.[1] The example given by the FSA Handbook is LIBOR plus or minus 'X' per cent. If a firm does not provide a private customer with the required information then the firm must pay all interest earned on client money of a customer to that customer.[2] The inference here is that a firm may, provided they have made the proper disclosure, pay a rate of interest to private customers which is less than that actually earned by the firm on the client money bank accounts.

1   COB 9.3.62G.
2   COB 9.3.60R.

Payments of money to a third party (COB 9.3.63–9.3.66)

12.62   The rules in relation to payment of money to a third party are designed to address situations where the firm passes money to a third party without discharging its fiduciary duty to the client. The specific circumstances in which a firm may allow money to be held or controlled by an exchange, clearing house or intermediate broker are:

(1)   where the firm transfers the money for the purpose of a transaction for a client through or with that person;
(2)   where the firm transfers the money to meet a client's obligation to provide collateral for a transaction (eg initial margin for a derivative transaction);
(3)   in the case of a private customer, where the customer has been notified that the client money may be transferred to the other person.[1]

1   COB 9.3.64R.

12.63   The guidance to this section of the rules states that firms should not hold excess client money in its client transaction accounts with intermediate brokers, settlement agents, and OTC counterparties.[1]

1   COB 9.3.66G.

Money which ceases to be client money (COB 9.3.133–9.3.136)

12.64   Money ceases to be client money if it is paid:

(1)   to the client;
(2)   to a third party on the instruction of the client;
(3)   into a bank account of the client;
(4)   to the firm itself, when it is due and payable to the firm;
(5)   to the firm itself, when it is an excess in the client bank account.[1]

1   COB 9.3.133R.

12.65   When a firm draws a cheque, or equivalent payable order, to discharge its fiduciary duty, it must continue to treat the sum concerned as client money until the cheque or order is presented and paid by the bank.[1] Similarly, where a firm makes payment to, or on the instruction of a client, from an account other than the client bank account, no equivalent sum may be removed from the client bank account until the payment has cleared.[2]

1   COB 9.3.135R.
2   COB 9.3.136R.

Allocated but not unclaimed money (COB 9.3.138–9.3.140)

12.66   A firm may cease treating money as client money if it can demonstrate that it has taken reasonable steps to trace the client concerned and to return the balance.[1] An evidential provision sets out the steps which the FSA would consider to be reasonable steps. These steps include undertaking to make good any valid claim against any released balances.[2] Where a firm makes such an undertaking it should make arrangements authorised by the firm's relevant controllers that are legally enforceable by any person with a valid claim to the previously unclaimed money.[3]

1   COB 9.3.138R.
2   COB 9.3.139E.
3   COB 9.3.140G.

Reconciliations

Method and frequency (COB 9.3.123–9.3.131)

12.67   Reconciliations must be performed at least once every 25 business days by comparing independent third-party statements (such as bank statements) to the firm's own records for the following:

(1)   client money bank accounts;
(2)   client transaction accounts with exchanges, clearing houses and intermediate brokers; and
(3)   approved collateral holdings where these are held in accordance with the client money rules.[1]

1   COB 9.3.123R and 9.3.126R.

12.68   A firm must identify the reason for any discrepancy resulting from a reconciliation. Corrections must be made as soon as possible except where differences result solely from timing differences.[1] Firms should perform reconciliations more frequently if the risks to which the business is exposed (eg the volume of business) warrant this.[2] The firm must make this judgment in the context of its overall risk management systems.

1   COB 9.3.128R.
2   COB 9.3.124G.

12.69   Where, however, the FSA-regulated firm is unable to resolve a difference arising from a reconciliation and it appears that one of the sets of records indicates that there is a need to 'top up' the relevant client bank accounts or approved collateral, the FSA-regulated firm must assume that this set of records is correct and pay its own money into the client bank account until such time as the matter is conclusively resolved.[1]

1   COB 9.3.129R.

12.70   All these reconciliations must be performed within ten business days of the date to which they relate.[1]

1   COB 9.3.125R.

12.71   Where a firm is unable to comply with the rules on the timing of reconciliations, dealing with discrepancies and unresolved differences, it must notify the FSA as soon as possible.[1]

1   COB 9.3.131R.

Alternative approach

Benefits and requirements of this approach (COB 9.3.42–9.3.43, 9.3.46 and 9.3.103)

12.72   As noted above, a firm which is holding client money in many jurisdictions may find that significant savings in operational costs can be achieved by adopting the 'alternative approach'. Under this approach, client money is received into and paid out of the firm's own bank accounts.[1] In order to achieve the necessary protection of client money, a single transfer is made to or from a client money bank account each day.

1   COB 9.3.43G.

12.73   If a firm wishes to use the alternative approach it must provide the FSA with a report from its auditor that the firm has in place systems and controls adequate to enable it to operate the alternative approach effectively.[1]

1   COB 9.3.42R.

12.74   In addition, a firm wishing to use this approach must appoint a manager with responsibility for client money rules.[1] A firm can choose to operate the alternative method for some types of business (eg overseas equities) whilst adopting the normal approach for other types of business (eg derivatives).[2] A firm would need to be able to demonstrate that its systems were adequate to permit these two approaches to apply in parallel.

1   COB 9.3.42R.
2   COB 9.3.46R(5).

Commodity Futures Trading Commission Part 30 exemption order

Special requirements (COB 9.3.141–9.3.144)

12.75   Those firms who are subject to a Commodity Futures Trading Commission (CFTC) Part 30 exemption order in relation to trading on behalf of US customers on non-US futures and options exchanges are generally required by the CFTC to offer all US customers segregation in accordance with the client money rules.[1] These firms trade on behalf of US customers on non-US futures and options exchanges and have obtained an exemption under Part 30 of the General Regulations of the US Commodities Exchange Act. Where firms trading as clearing members on the London Metals Exchange (LME) have LME bond arrangements in place they must exclude the US clients' equity balances from the calculation of the sum of all the positive client equity balances (as described in 'stage 2' of the daily calculation of client money).[2]

1   COB 9.3.141R.
2   COB 9.3.142R.

12.76   Firms that have a bond arrangement in place must not reduce the amount of, or cancel, a letter of credit issued under an LME bond arrangement where this will cause them to be in breach of their Part 30 exemption order.[1] In addition, firms must notify the FSA immediately if they arrange the issue of an individual letter of credit under an LME bond arrangement.[2]

1   COB 9.3.143R.
2   COB 9.3.144R.

Client money and Europe

Inward passports (European institutions branching into the UK)

12.77   Article 10 of the Investment Services Directive (ISD)[1] provides that each home Member State is responsible for drawing up prudential rules which investment firms must observe at all times. These prudential rules, mandated by the Directive, require each Member State to require each investment firm to have, *inter alia*, adequate arrangements for funds belonging to investors with a view to safeguarding the investor's rights and, except in the case of credit institutions, preventing the investment firm from using investors' funds for its own account. The basic principle then is that the prudential regulation of clients' money is the responsibility of the home state regulator (eg FSA rules do not apply to a German bank's UK branch investment business activities – these are subject to German requirements).

1   Council Directive 93/22/EEC.

12.78   It is important to note that these provisions only apply to investment firms subject to the ISD and to client money held in respect of investment services within the passport.

12.79   Non-ISD firms 'branching' into the UK continue to be subject to the FSA's client money rules and in respect of services outside the passport (eg commodities derivatives) the FSA's client money rules will continue to apply.

Outward passports

12.80   On the principle stated in the ISD, art 10,[1] all UK incorporated banks or investment firms are subject to and should apply the relevant UK client money rules to their activities in branches outside the UK unless the activities are non-ISD activities for which the firm is not authorised in the UK and the services are therefore outside the passport.

1   Council Directive 93/22/EEC.

Chapter 13

Record-keeping and notifications

INTRODUCTION

13.1   An essential part of the regulatory process is the gathering by the Financial Services Authority (FSA) of accurate and up-to-date information on regulated firms' business activities. This turns on the rules which have been put in place in relation to the keeping of records by firms and to reporting of material events to the FSA.

It is easy to fall into the trap of regarding these rules as a routine and even bureaucratic aspect of regulatory compliance. On the contrary, they are a central component of the regulatory structure and a key element of the relationship between the FSA and a regulated firm. A firm with weak records cannot adequately demonstrate compliance with the rules or possession of effective controls and will not enjoy the regulator's confidence. Even if the necessary documents exist in some form, slow retrieval of ill-organised records can also damage regulatory relationships: an inspection team from a regulator will be unimpressed if a firm produces requested documents only after an unseemly delay. Late or incomplete reporting will also undermine the firm's relationship with the regulator. As illustrated in paras 13.3 and 13.4 below, deficiencies in record-keeping and notifications to regulators can lead to or exacerbate disciplinary action. Compliance with the requirements relating to record-keeping and reporting is therefore essential. The burden of doing so has, however, been slightly eased by the creation of the single regulator, which has, happily, brought about harmonisation of the requirements and has eliminated the sometimes irritating variations in the rules of the former regulators, notably IMRO (Investment Management Regulatory Organisation) and the SFA.

13.2   The FSA's requirements on record-keeping and reporting are tied at high level into the FSA's Principles and the Approved Persons regime. Although record-keeping is not expressly mentioned in the FSA's eleven Principles, basic record-keeping may give rise to a breach of Principles 2 (the duty to conduct the business with due skill, care and diligence) and 3 (the duty

343

to take reasonable care to organise and control the firm's affairs responsibly and effectively, with adequate risk management systems).

In relation to reporting, Principle 11 states: 'A firm must deal with its regulators in an open and co-operative way, and must disclose to the FSA appropriately anything relating to the firm of which the FSA would reasonably expect notice.' This Principle is carried forward into the Principles for Approved Persons (where it is Principle 4). The latter Principles again do not specifically mention records, but an approved person performing a significant influence function who presided over an inadequate system of records would be unlikely to be exercising due skill, care and diligence in managing the business of the firm (Approved Persons Principle 6).

Deliberately falsifying documents or deliberately preparing misleading or inappropriate records, or destroying documents in order to remove an audit trail or to compromise an investigation, are of course very grave regulatory offences.

13.3   To emphasise the importance of record-keeping it is worth noting that deficiencies in record-keeping have led to a number of regulatory penalties in recent years, a trend which is likely to continue. In most cases, the failures in record-keeping have been combined with other shortcomings, with a compendious penalty not allocated separately to specific items. Nevertheless, in each case the terms of the disciplinary announcement have made clear that the failure to keep proper records was a significant element in the regulatory penalty. Examples are:

(1)   On 26 October 2000, IMRO announced[1] that it had fined Yorkshire Bank plc £100,000 for breaches of regulatory rules between December 1996 and June 1999 in relation to its PEP unit. The breaches consisted of failures to complete customer asset reconciliations and to keep proper records and failures in internal organisation and control. The record-keeping deficiencies cited by IMRO were failures to:
— retain records of dealing instructions received from customers;
— make and/or retain a record on all occasions of decisions to deal for discretionary managed portfolios in the PEP unit and to record the time of any such decisions;
— make and/or retain records on all occasions of instructions to third parties to deal on the unit's behalf;
— make and/or retain copies of contract notes on all occasions, evidencing transactions;
— make and/or retain records on all occasions of intended and factual allocations between customers of aggregated transactions;
— identify on all occasions what stockholdings were held on behalf of PEP clients;
— keep records on all occasions of customer asset transactions; and
— record on all occasions the amount of dividend to which each customer was entitled on receipt of dividends.

(2)   A month later, on 23 November 2000, IMRO announced[2] another £100,000 fine, on that occasion imposed on Lloyds TSB Bank plc. This disciplinary action concerned failures in the completion of customer asset reconciliations in the bank's Securities Services Division. Those failures included deficiencies in record-keeping, notably failures to maintain accurate records of holdings in the custody system and records of the handling of bearer and negotiable items.

(3) In April 2002, the FSA fined a much smaller entity, Sharelands Financial Services Limited, £140,000 for record-keeping and associated compliance breaches.[3] The company was found by the FSA to have failed to keep sufficient records of client information or instructions received from clients, with the consequence that it was unable to provide evidence of the suitability of its investment recommendations to clients.

1   IMRO Press Release 007/2000, 26 October 2000.
2   IMRO Press Release 009/2000, 23 November 2000.
3   FSA Press Release FSA/PH/036/2002, 11 April 2002.

13.4   A failure to notify the regulator of material information can also lead to disciplinary action. An example is the fine of £300,000 imposed by IMRO on BISYS Fund Services Limited in March 2001.[1] A variety of compliance-related misdemeanours included failure to ensure that all information provided to IMRO was accurate and promptly to inform IMRO of all relevant matters. The precise matters found by IMRO in those respects were:

(a) having assured IMRO some months earlier that its compliance officer would be returned from operational work to compliance work, BISYS failed to ensure that IMRO was made aware that he had once again become so involved in operational matters that he had insufficient time to carry out effective compliance monitoring; and

(b) having assured IMRO that external consultants had been engaged to assist with the production of a compliance monitoring programme, BISYS failed to provide IMRO with information sufficient to make IMRO aware that a decision had been taken to delay the work.

That type of situation apart, late submission of routine reports and notifications may lead to more modest fines.

1   IMRO Press Release 001/2001, 29 March 2001.

13.5   In practical terms, most banks and financial services firms will not approach the FSA's record-keeping requirements in isolation and will incorporate them into a comprehensive policy on the retention and destruction of documents.

Such a policy should embrace a number of issues, for example the preservation of documents likely to be relevant to potential litigation, and the obligation under the Data Protection Act 1998 not to keep personal data for longer than necessary for the purpose for which the data was originally obtained. An international organisation will also need to address the differing requirements of jurisdictions outside the UK. Any policy on the retention and destruction of documents must cover electronic as well as paper communications, notably email and pages on websites. Electronic storage systems materially lighten the logistical burden of storing large volumes of paper. Systems for the storage and retrieval of documents will in turn link into a firm's arrangements for operational recovery from natural or man-made disasters. Unsurprisingly, in the light of terrorist activity in the US on 11 September 2001, disaster recovery is a high priority for regulators in the UK, the US and elsewhere.

RECORDS

13.6   The FSA requires[1] a firm to take reasonable care to make and retain adequate records (including accounting records). The FSA lists in its

Handbook the various events and matters which must be recorded and retained by member firms. These can be placed under the following headings (each of which are discussed below):

—   market conduct;
—   supervision;
—   senior management arrangements, systems and controls;
—   training and competence;
—   conduct of business (where the most numerous requirements are located);
—   money laundering;
—   complaints; and
—   accounting.

These records may be kept in any form (including computer disk, tape or some other form) and in any language, but must be capable of prompt reproduction in English on paper. However, if a firm's records relate to business carried on from an establishment in a country or territory outside the UK, an official language of that country or territory may be used instead of English.

The records must, in the main, be retained for a minimum period of three years, although other periods apply in some cases.

A customer is entitled to inspect any record relating exclusively to him but not those which are not exclusive to him, although such records may be inspected by the FSA.

1   SYSC 3.2.20 R (Records).

Market conduct

13.7   The FSA notes[1] two specific requirements, namely (i) full details of price stabilisation action and (ii) details of steps taken in consideration of non-market price transactions. In each case the record must be kept for a retention period of three years from, respectively, initiation of the stabilising action and considering the transaction.

1   MAR Sch 1.

Supervision

13.8   A variety of items appear under this heading. Under SUP 4.3.17R(3) any data required by an appointed actuary must be recorded for an unspecified period. SUP 12.19.1 and 2 R require records to be kept in relation to appointed representatives, covering the appointed representative's name, a copy of the contract with the appointed representative and any amendments, and the date and reason for terminating or amending the contract; all this to be kept for three years from the termination or amendment of the contract.

Under SUP 13.11 a UK firm exercising an EEA right must record the services or activities it carries on from a branch in, or provides cross-border into, another EEA state under that EEA right, with details relating to those services or activities. This record must be kept for three years from the earlier of the date on which (a) it is superseded by a more up-to-date record or (b) the firm ceases to have a branch in or carry cross-border services into any EEA state under an EEA right. The exercise of passport rights by a UK firm must be recorded for a similar three-year period (SUP 13.11.1R).

Finally, under SUP 16.8.23R there must be kept (for an unspecified period) records to enable a firm to monitor regularly the persistency of life policies effected through its representatives and to make the required reports to the FSA.

Senior management arrangements, systems and controls

13.9 The FSA requires[1] there to be a record of the apportionment of significant responsibilities among a firm's directors and senior managers and of the allocation to one or more individuals of the functions of dealing with the apportionment of responsibilities and overseeing the establishment and maintenance of systems and controls. This record must be made on making the arrangements and when they are updated and be kept for six years from the date on which the record is superseded by a more up-to-date record.

1 SYSC Sch 1.

Training and competence

13.10 The FSA has published[1] a schedule of record-keeping requirements relating to training and competence. Despite a disclaimer that it is not a complete statement of the requirements, it is a good summary. This is shown in Table 13.1.

1 TC Sch 1.

Conduct of business

13.11 Liberally scattered throughout the Conduct of Business section of the FSA's Handbook are numerous record-keeping requirements. They cover a wide range of topics, examples of which are advertising and other promotional materials, client classifications, terms of business, soft commissions, aggregation and allocation of orders, execution of orders, confirmations of transactions, client money, safe custody arrangements, and personal account dealing. Retention periods are mainly either three or six years, with indefinite periods in some instances.

In COB Schedule 1 the FSA has provided a table of record-keeping requirements relating to conduct of business, the stated purpose of which is to give 'a quick overall view'. As in the case of the training and competence schedule (see Table 13.1), the FSA states that it is not a complete statement of those requirements and should not be relied on as if it were. Despite that disclaimer, the table does provide a convenient summary of record-keeping obligations. This information is shown in Table 13.2.

Table 13.1: FSA's training and competence record-keeping requirements

Handbook reference	Subject of record	Contents of record	When record must be made	Retention period
TC 2.4.9 G	Attaining competence	Data on competence	On a continuing basis	Employment plus 3 years. For pension transfer specialist ('PTS') indefinite
TC 2.5.1 R	Approved examinations	Examination time limits	When employee begins in the activity	Employment plus 3 years or for PTS indefinite
TC 2.5.2 G	Approved examinations	Examination passes and dates and other relevant data such as periods of absence	Duration of time limits for that activity	Employment plus 3 years or for PTS indefinite
TC 2.5.6 G	Approved examinations – regulatory module only	Criteria for application of TC 2.5.5 R to the employee	At the time of the application of the rule	Employment plus 3 years or for PTS indefinite
TC 2.6.4 G	Maintaining competence	Criteria for and application of assessment	On a continuing basis after competence	Employment plus 3 years or for PTS indefinite
TC 2.7.6 G	Supervising and monitoring	Criteria in deciding level of supervision and how it is carried out	When the employee begins in the activity and on an ongoing basis	Employment plus 3 years or for PTS indefinite
TC 2.8.1 R (1)	Compliance with sourcebook	Data on competence, relevant to compliance with the sourcebook	When the employee begins in the activity and on a continuing basis	Employment plus 3 years or for PTS indefinite

Table 13.2: FSA Handbook record-keeping requirements

Handbook reference	Subject of record	Contents of record	When record must be made	Retention period
COB 2.2.20R(1)	Periodic reports	Details of soft commission agreements	Date of periodic statement	3 years (from termination of relevant soft commission agreement)
COB 2.2.20R(2)	Disclosable commission	Each payment	Date of payment	6 years
COB 2.2.20R(3)	Indirect benefits given to an independent intermediary	Each benefit	Date from which benefit was conferred	6 years
COB 3.7.1R	Non-real time financial promotion – each: Pension transfer Pension opt-out FSAVC	Name of Individual who confirmed compliance or approved the financial promotion. See COB 3.7.2(1) to (4) for other contents	Date of confirmation or approval	Indefinitely
COB 3.7.1R	Non-real time financial promotion – each: Life policy Pension contract Stakeholder pension scheme	Name of individual who confirmed compliance or approved the financial promotion. See COB 3.7.2(1) to (4) for other contents	Date of confirmation or approval	6 years

Table 13.2: FSA Handbook record-keeping requirements – *contd*

Handbook reference	Subject of record	Contents of record	When record must be made	Retention period
COB 3.7.1R	Non-real time financial promotion – any other case	Name of individual who confirmed compliance or approved the financial promotion. See COB 3.7.2(1) to (4) for other contents	Date of confirmation or approval	3 years
COB 4.1.16R	Classification of each client – if relevant to: Pension transfers Pension opt-outs FSAVCs	Sufficient information to support classification	When the client relationship begins or upon reclassification, to include annual review where necessary	Indefinitely
COB 4.1.16R	Classification of each client – if relevant to: Life policies Pension contracts	Sufficient information to support classification	When the client relationship begins or upon reclassification, to include annual review where necessary	6 years (from end of client relationship)
COB 4.1.16R	Classification of each client – any other case	Sufficient information to support classification	When the client relationship begins or upon reclassification, to include annual review where necessary	3 years (from end of client relationship)

Table 13.2: FSA Handbook record-keeping requirements – *contd*

Handbook reference	Subject of record	Contents of record	When record must be made	Retention period
COB 4.2.14R	Terms of business for: Pension transfer Pension opt-out FSAVC	Each term of business provided and any amendments	As soon as in force	Indefinitely
COB 4.2.14R	Terms of business for: Life policy Pension contract Stakeholder pension scheme	Each term of business provided and any amendments	As soon as in force	6 years (from the date on which the customer ceases to be a customer)
COB 4.2.14R	Terms of business: Any other case	Each term of business provided and any amendments	As soon as in force	3 years (from the date on which the customer ceases to be a customer)
COB 5.1.4R(3)	Adoption of a packaged product	Decision to adopt	On making the decision to adopt	Throughout the period the adoption remains in effect and for 6 years thereafter
COB 5.2.9R	Private customer's details for a pension transfer, pension opt-out, FSAVC	Personal and financial circumstances	On giving advice	Indefinitely
COB 5.2.9R	Private customer's details for a life policy, pension contract	Personal and financial circumstances	On giving advice	6 years

351

Table 13.2: FSA Handbook record-keeping requirements – *contd*

Handbook reference	Subject of record	Contents of record	When record must be made	Retention period
COB 5.2.9R	Private customer's details for any other case	Personal and financial circumstances	On giving advice	3 years
COB 5.2.10R	Private customer: Opt out or transfer from an OPS on an execution only basis	Execution only transaction, no investment advice given	Upon execution	
COB 5.3.25R	Private customer instructs a pension opt-out or transfer contrary to advice of firm	Firm's advice to customer and customer instructions to firm to proceed	Upon execution	Indefinitely
COB 5.3.26R(2)	Statistics of pension opt-out or transfer transactions involving private customers	Details of the notification required by COB 5.3.26R(1)	On making the notification	Indefinitely
COB 5.3.27R	Statistics of pension opt-out, pension transfer or FSAVC transactions involving private customers	Separate records per customer	On arranging the transaction	Indefinitely
COB 6.6.19R	Projections relating to a life policy, pension contract or stakeholder pension scheme	A projection provided to a customer	As soon as proposal proceeds	6 years

Table 13.2: FSA Handbook record-keeping requirements – *contd*

Handbook reference	Subject of record	Contents of record	When record must be made	Retention period
COB 6.6.19R	Projections relating to a pension transfer or pension opt-out	A projection provided to a customer	As soon as proposal proceeds	Indefinitely
COB 6.6.19R	Projections relating to any other case	A projection provided to a customer	As soon as proposal proceeds	3 years
COB 6.7.47R	Cancellation or withdrawal: Pension Transfer, opt-out or FSAVC	To include a copy of any receipt of notice issued to the customer and the customer's original notice instructions	Upon notice of cancellation or withdrawal being served to firm, its appointed representative or agent	Indefinitely
COB 6.7.47R	Cancellation or withdrawal: Life policy, pension contract or stakeholder pension scheme	To include a copy of any receipt of notice issued to the customer and the customer's original notice instructions	Upon notice of cancellation or withdrawal being served to firm, its appointed representative or agent	6 years (from the date when the firm became aware that notice of cancellation had been served)
COB 6.7.47R	Cancellation or withdrawal: Any other case	To include a copy of any receipt of notice issued to the customer and the customer's original notice instructions	Upon notice of cancellation or withdrawal being served to firm, its appointed representative or agent	3 years (from the date when the firm became aware that notice of cancellation had been served)

Table 13.2: FSA Handbook record-keeping requirements – *contd*

Handbook reference	Subject of record	Contents of record	When record must be made	Retention period
COB 6.8.18R(1)	Firm effecting or carrying out pure protection contracts	Adequate details of information provided	After information provided	6 years
COB 6.8.18R(2)	Firm effecting or carrying out general insurance contracts	Adequate details of information provided	After information provided	3 years
COB 7.7.6E(4)	Allocation of aggregated transactions in a series of transactions all executed within one business day	The time each transaction is made	On executing an aggregated transaction	
COB 7.7.14R(1)	An aggregated transaction that includes a customer order	Identity of each customer; whether transaction is in whole or in part for discretionary managed investment portfolio and any relevant proportions	On executing an aggregated transaction	3 years
COB 7.7.14R(2)	Firm aggregated a number of client orders that include a customer order	Intended basis of allocation	As soon as is practicable	3 years
COB 7.7.14R(3)	Aggregation of one or more customer orders and own account order	Intended basis of allocation	Before the transaction is executed	3 years

Table 13.2: FSA Handbook record-keeping requirements – *contd*

Handbook reference	Subject of record	Contents of record	When record must be made	Retention period
COB 7.7.16R	Allocation of an aggregated transaction that includes the execution of a customer order	Date + time of allocation; relevant designated investment; identity of each customer and market counterparty and the amount allocated to each customer and market counterparty; agreement to extend allocation period for intermediate customers under COB 7.7.6E(2)(b)	Date on which the order is allocated	3 years
COB 7.7.17R	Re-allocation	Basis and reason for any re-allocation	At the time of the re-allocation	3 years
COB 7.9.7R	Lending to private customers	Assessment of a private customer's financial standing and the date when the information was last updated/checked	Upon assessment	3 years (from the date on which the credit arrangement ceased)

Table 13.2: FSA Handbook record-keeping requirements – *contd*

Handbook reference	Subject of record	Contents of record	When record must be made	Retention period
COB 7.12 3R and COB 7.12.6E(1)	Customer orders	Customer's name (or other designation)/account number; date and time of receipt or decision by the firm to deal; who received the order or made the decision to deal; the designated investment; the number of/total value of the designated investment including any price limit; whether sale or purchase; any other instructions received	When the order arises	3 years (after the date of completion of the transaction)

Table 13.2: FSA Handbook record-keeping requirements – *contd*

Handbook reference	Subject of record	Contents of record	When record must be made	Retention period
COB 7.12.3R and COB 7.12.6E(2)	Execution of a transaction by a firm	Name/other designation of client (if any); name of counterparty (if known); date and time of execution; who executed the transaction; the designated investment; number of/total value of the designated investment; price and other significant terms; whether sale or purchase; whether the firm was acting as principal	When the firm executed a transaction	3 years (after the date of completion of the transaction)
COB 7.12.3R and COB 7.126E(3)	The firm instructs another person to deal	Name of the person instructed; terms of instruction and date and time of instruction	When the firm instructs another person to deal	3 years (after the date of completion of the transaction)
COB 7.13.11R(1)(a)	Personal account dealing	The restrictions upon PA dealing and the basis upon which any permission to deal is made	Whenever the restrictions are placed and from the date of consent	3 years (from the date that the restrictions or basis were communicated to the employee)
COB 7.13.11R(1)(b)	Personal account dealing	Each permission to deal given by the firm	From the date of consent	3 years (from the date that the permission was given)

Table 13.2: FSA Handbook record-keeping requirements – *contd*

Handbook reference	Subject of record	Contents of record	When record must be made	Retention period
COB 7.13.11R(1)(c)	Personal account dealing	Each notification of the transaction made by the employee to the firm	From the date of notification	3 years (from the date that the notification was made)
COB 7.13.11R(1)(d)	Personal account dealing	The basis upon which the firm has determined that an employee will not be involved in, or have access to information about, the firm's designated investment business	On determining the basis	3 years (from the date on which the individual ceases to be an employee)
COB 8.1.14R	Confirmation of transaction	Information provided	On dispatch of confirmation	3 years
COB 8.2.9R	Periodic statements	Copy of any periodic statement	On date on which it is provided	3 years
COB 9.1.9R	A personal investment firm that temporarily holds a client's designated investments	Client details and any action taken by firm		3 years (from the making of the record)
COB 9.1.53R(3)	Safe custody: arrangements for clients ordinarily resident outside the United Kingdom	The steps taken and result under COB 9.1.53R(2)	On determination that client does not wish to execute agreement	

Table 13.2: FSA Handbook record-keeping requirements – *contd*

Handbook reference	Subject of record	Contents of record	When record must be made	Retention period
COB 9.1.98R	Client custody assets held or received by or on behalf of a client or which the firm has arranged for another to hold or receive	Full details	On receipt	3 years
COB 9.1.99R	Safe custody investments used for stock lending activities	The identify of safe custody investments available to be lent, and those which have been lent	On receipt	3 years
COB 9.2.5R	Adequate records and internal controls in respect of the firm's use of mandates (see COB 9.2.5R(1) to (4))	Up-to-date list of firm's authorities, all transactions entered into, important client documents held by firm	Maintain current full details	
COB 9.3.145R	Client money	Sufficient records to show and explain firm's transactions and commitments	Maintain current full details	3 years (after records made)
COB 9.5.24R(3)	Client money shortfall	Each client's entitlement to client money shortfall at the failed bank	Maintain up-to-date records	Until client repaid

Table 13.2: FSA Handbook record-keeping requirements – *contd*

Handbook reference	Subject of record	Contents of record	When record must be made	Retention period
COB 9.5.25R(3)	Client money shortfall	Each client's entitlement to client money shortfall at the failed bank	Maintain up-to-date records	Until client repaid
COB 9.5.31R(3)	Client money shortfall	Each client's entitlement to client money shortfall at the failed intermediate broker, settlement agent or to a counterparty	Maintain up-to-date records	Until client repaid
COB 10.3.3E(3)	Allocation of aggregated transactions in a series of transactions all executed within one business day	The time each transaction is made	On executing an aggregated transaction	
COB 10.3.5R(1)	Aggregated transaction on behalf of a number of schemes	Identity of schemes concerned, whether transaction was effected proportionally or if a stated proportion was effected for some schemes under its management	On executing an aggregated transaction	
COB 10.3.5R(2)	Aggregated customer orders on behalf of a number of schemes	The intended basis of allocation	As soon as is practicable	

Table 13.2: FSA Handbook record-keeping requirements – *contd*

Handbook reference	Subject of record	Contents of record	When record must be made	Retention period
COB 10.3.5R(3)	Aggregated orders of schemes under its management and own account orders	The intended basis of allocation	Before the transaction is executed	
COB 10.7.6R	Periodic statements in relation to unregulated collective investment scheme	Operator to retain copy of any periodic statement it has provided to participants in the scheme	On providing the period statement	3 years
COB 11.7.1R	PTP appointment	Details of the written delegation to a PTP, PTP's undertaking under COB 11.6.1R(3) and of any variation in the documentation	On the PTP's appointment	3 years (from date of end of the PTP's appointment)
COB 11.8.7R	Trustee firm following (or rejecting) proper advice in relation to exercise of power of investment	Evidence of compliance with COB 11.8.5R	Date on which proper advice is received	3 years

Money laundering[1]

13.12 The FSA's money laundering rules contain specific record-keeping requirements, which reinforce the requirements relating to customers set out above. In view of the importance attached by the FSA and other regulators around the world, in part in response to terrorist atrocities in the United States on 11 September 2001, meticulous adherence to these rules should be of the highest priority for all regulated firms. The FSA's requirements focus upon evidence of identity of clients, transactions, recovery of debt from insolvent clients, handling of suspicious activity, training of staff, and the activities of the money laundering reporting officer.

1 For money laundering generally, see Chapter 10.

13.13 In relation to evidence of identity, the firm must make the following records and retain them for five years from the end of its relationship with the client:[1]

(a) a copy of the evidence of identity obtained under ML3; or
(b) a record of where a copy of the evidence of identity can be obtained; or
(c) when it is not reasonably practicable to comply with either of the above, a record of how the details of the evidence of identity can be obtained; and
(d) when it has concluded that it should treat a client as financially excluded, a record of the reasons for doing so.

1 ML 7.3.2R.

13.14 The firm must keep a record containing the details of every transaction carried out by the firm with or for the client in the course of regulated activity, for five years from the date when the transaction was completed.[1] Records of action taken by way of internal or external reporting of suspicious activity must be kept for five years from the obtaining of the information or the creation of the record.[2] A trap for the unwary money laundering reporting officer is the requirement[3] that, where he has considered information on other matters concerning knowledge or suspicion that someone has engaged in money laundering but he has not made a report to the National Criminal Intelligence Service (NCIS), a record of that information or matter must be kept for five years from the obtaining of the information or matter. Since most firms rightly require their staff to report to the money laundering reporting officer even the slightest suspicion, he will inevitably receive a number of spurious reports where in fact no realistic ground for suspicion exists. In the current climate, the safest approach to this rule is to record everything, however tenuous.

1 ML 7.3.2R(I)(b). Note that a transaction for this purpose does not include advice given to a client unless such advice is followed by a transaction with monetary value (ML 7.3.2(3)R).
2 ML 7.3.2R(1)(d).
3 ML 7.3.2R(I)(e).

13.15 Many national regulators now publish, with frequent updates, increasingly long lists of the names of suspected terrorists or terrorist organisations. Some, for example the Ontario Securities Commission, require monthly or other periodic reports as to whether a firm has had any contact with any of the names on the list. A regulated firm would be well advised to keep a record of its periodic checks to ensure that it is not conducting business with anyone on the list.

Complaints

13.16 In order to support the FSA's arrangements in relation to recording complaints by clients, a regulated firm must make and retain records of complaints which are subject to DISP 1.4–1.6 for a minimum of three years from the date of its receipt of the complaint.[1] The purpose of this requirement is not only to facilitate monitoring by the FSA but also to ensure effective co-operation with the Financial Ombudsman Service.

By way of guidance the FSA has stated[2] that the records should include the name of the complainant, the substance of the complaint, and any correspondence between the firm and the complaint, including details of any redress offered by the firm. To those particulars we suggest most firms will wish to add the customer's address, the identity of the business unit within the firm and any specific individuals against whom the complaint was directed, the resolution of the complaint, and the dates of the making and final disposal of the complaint. Those are all items of information which a regulator will scrutinise on an inspection. The FSA also requires an annual report of complaints against a firm, as described in para 13.52 below.

1   FSA DISP 1.5.1.
2   FSA DISP 1.5.2

Accounting

13.17   The FSA's Interim Prudential sourcebooks contain a series of requirements on accounting records, augmenting the general requirements of the Principles described in para 13.2 above. In relation to banks, these are to be found in the Interim Prudential sourcebook for Banks; other types of investment business are covered by the Investment Business Interim Prudential sourcebook.

Banks

13.18   The FSA's overall approach to banks' accounting records is not to be over-prescriptive on matters of detail; it looks to a bank to put in place records which are 'commensurate with its needs and particular circumstances',[1] having regard, *inter alia*, 'to the manner in which the business is structured, organised and managed, and to the nature and complexity of its transactions and commitments'. Consequently, the FSA has not published a definitive and comprehensive schedule of requirements. This approach allows a welcome element of flexibility.

13.19   Nevertheless, the FSA has included in the Banks' sourcebook a list of features which should feature in accounting and other related records.[2] This states that the records should:

(a)   capture and record on a timely basis and in an orderly fashion, every transaction and commitment which the bank enters into, with sufficient information to explain:

      (i) its nature and purpose;

      (ii) any asset or liability, actual or contingent, which respectively arises or may arise from it; and

      (iii) any income or expenditure, current or deferred, which arises from it;

(b) provide details, as appropriate, for each transaction and commitment, showing:

      (i)   the parties, including, in the case of a loan, advance or other credit exposure, whether (and if so to whom) it is sub-participated;

      (ii) the amount and currency;

      (iii) the contract, rollover, value and settlement or repayment dates;

      (iv) the contracted interest rates of an interest rate transaction or commitment;

      (v) the contracted exchange rate of a foreign exchange transaction or commitment;

      (vi) the contracted commission or fee payable or receivable, together with any other related payment or receipt;

      (vii) the nature and current estimated value of any security for a loan or other exposure; the physical location and documentary evidence of such security; and

      (viii) in the case of any borrowing, whether it is subordinated, and if secured, the nature and book value of any asset upon which it is secured;

(c) be maintained in such a manner that financial and business information can be extracted promptly to enable management to:

      (i)   identify, measure, monitor and control the quality of the bank's assets and safeguard them, including those held as custodian;

      (ii) identify, measure, monitor and control its exposures by related counterparties across all products;

      (iii) identify, measure, monitor and control its exposures to liquidity risk, and foreign exchange and other market risks across all products;

      (iv) monitor the performance of all aspects of its business on an up-to-date basis; and

      (v) make timely and informed decisions;

(d) contain details of exposure limits authorised by management which are appropriate to the type, nature and volume of business undertaken; these limits should, where relevant, include counterparty, industry sector, country, settlement, liquidity, interest rate mismatch and securities position limits as well as limits on the level of intra-day and overnight trading positions in foreign exchange, futures, options, future (or forward) rate agreements (FRAs) and swaps;

(e) provide information which can be summarised in such a way as to enable actual exposures to be readily, accurately and regularly measured against these limits;

(f) contain details of the factors considered, the analysis undertaken and the authorisation or rejection by management of a loan, advance or other credit exposure; and

(g) provide, on a memorandum basis, details of every transaction entered into in the name of or on behalf of another party on an agency or fiduciary (trustee) basis where it is agreed that the bank itself is not legally or contractually bound by the transaction.

---

1 IPRU (BANK) AR 3.2.1.
2 IPRU (BANK) AR 3.2.2.

13.20   Apart from specific items as above, a bank's record-keeping arrangements should be viewed not in isolation but as part of its overall control environment. The Interim Prudential sourcebook stresses the need for the provision of information to directors and management to enable them to 'monitor, assess and control the performance of the business, the state of its affairs and the risk to which it is exposed', on both an individual company and where appropriate a consolidated basis.[1] The sources of such management information are the bank's accounting and other related records. Their ability to generate complete, accurate and timely information is crucial to the management process.

In the FSA's view,[2] such information should:

— show the state of affairs of the bank;
— show the operational results of the business both on a cumulative basis and by discrete period, and give a comparison with budgets and previous periods;
— provide an analysis of assets and liabilities showing how they have been valued;
— provide an analysis of off-balance sheet positions showing how they have been valued;
— provide an analysis of income and expenditure showing how it relates to different categories of asset and liability and off-balance sheet positions; and
— show the bank's exposure to each type of risk, compared to the relevant limits set by management.

1   IPRU (BANK) AR 3.2.3.
2   IPRU (BANK) AR 3.2.3.

13.21   An important additional point arises where a bank has outsourced part of its operations to another part of its group or to an external supplier of services. The FSA requires[1] the bank to ensure that its records and controls adequately cover the outsourced business. 'Banks should put in place procedures for monitoring and controlling the outsourced operations, and/or ensuring that the information requirements of the authorised bank's management with respect to the outsourced operations are satisfied.'[2]

1   IPRU (BANK) AR 3.2.8.
2   IPRU (BANK) AR 3.3.8.

Non-bank investment businesses

13.22   No less important requirements relating to accounting records for non-bank investment businesses are to be found in the Interim Prudential Sourcebook for Investment Businesses. This investment management firms' records must:[1]

(a)   be up-to-date and must disclose, with reasonable accuracy, at any time the firm's financial position at that time;
(b)   enable the firm to demonstrate its continuing compliance with its financial resources requirements; and
(c)   provide the information:
(i)   which the firm needs to provide such financial statements and periodical reports as may be required by the FSA; and

(ii) which the firm's auditor (where the FSA requires one to be appointed) needs to form an opinion on any statements of the firm on which the auditor is required to report.

1   IPRU (INV) 5.3.1(1) R.

13.23   Accounting records (in English) must also show and explain any own account transactions by the firm, distinguishing between trading book and non-trading book transactions.[1] In relation to customers, the accounting records must:[2]

(a)   record all purchases and sales of customers' assets effected by the firm;

(b)   record all receipts and payments of money belonging to customers which arise from transactions effected by the firm;

(c)   in relation to client money, have regard to the requirements of the Client Money rules;[3]

(d)   disclose the assets and liabilities of a firm's customers individually and collectively, to the extent they are managed by the firm; and

(e)   record all customers' assets (including customer investments) in the possession of the firm or of another person who is holding such assets for, or to the order of, the firm, showing the location of the assets, their beneficial owner and the extent to which they are subject to any change of which the firm has been notified.

1   IPRU (INV) 5.3.1(3) R.
2   See COB 9.3.
3   IPRU (INV) 5.3.1(4) R.

13.24   All of the above accounting records must be kept for a minimum of six years, during the first two of which they must be kept either at a place where the firm carries on business or in such a manner that they can be produced there within 24 hours of their being requested.[1]

1   IPRU (INV) 5.3.1(6) R.

Securities and futures investment firms

13.25   Securities and futures firms which are investment firms are subject to a comparable range of requirements. In particular such firms must[1] keep records in such a manner that they are sufficient to show and explain the firm's transactions and commitments (whether effected on its own behalf or on behalf of others) and in particular so that they:

(a)   disclose with reasonable accuracy the financial position of the firm at any point in time within the previous six years when the firm was authorised by the FSA or a predecessor regulator;

(b)   demonstrate whether or not the firm is or was at that time complying with its financial resources requirement; and

(c)   enable the firm to prepare within a reasonable time any financial reporting statement as at the close of business of any date within the previous six years when the firm was authorised by the FSA or a predecessor regulator, and such that the statement complies with the requirements of the rules of the FSA.

1   IPRU (INV) 10–10(2) and (3) R.

13.26   A firm must ensure that its records contain as a minimum:

(1)   *Financial:*
    (a)   entries from day to day of all sums of money received and expended by the firm whether on its behalf or on behalf of others, and the matters in respect of which the receipt and expenditure takes place;
    (b)   a record of all income and expenditure of the firm explaining its nature;
    (c)   a record of all assets and liabilities of the firm including any commitments or contingent liabilities;
    (d)   entries from day to day of all purchases and sales of investments by the firm distinguishing those which are made by the firm on its own account and those which are made by or on behalf of others;
    (e)   any working papers necessary to show the preparation of any reporting statement or any other periodic return to the FSA.
(2)   *Risk management:*
    (a)   details of exposure limits for trading positions and counterparty credit limits which are appropriate to the type, nature and volume of business undertaken, in such a way that they are capable of being summarised to enable actual exposures to be measured readily and regularly against these limits;
    (b)   management information records maintained in a manner such that they disclose, or are capable of disclosing, in a prompt and appropriate fashion, the financial and business information which will enable the firm's management to:
      (i)   identify, quantify, control and manage the firm's risk exposures;
      (ii)   make timely and informed decisions;
      (iii)   monitor the performance of all aspects of the firm's business on an up-to-date basis;
      (iv)   monitor the quality of the firm's assets; and
      (v)   safeguard the assets of the firm, including assets for which the firm is accountable belonging to other persons.

13.27   As with banks, the above list is not intended to be exhaustive. The FSA's requirements of an individual firm will depend on its structure, organisation and size, and on the nature, volume and complexity of its transactions and commitments. Records may be kept in any form provided that they can be reproduced promptly in hard printed form in English.[1] An important point, easy to overlook, is that if records relating to a counterparty are kept in different locations, each location must indicate that there are other records relating to the counterpart and how they can be accessed.[2] A firm may accept and rely on records supplied by a third party if they can be and are reconciled with records held by the firm.[3] The records must be kept for six years from the date on which they are first made or prepared.[4] All records relating to the current year must be arranged, filed and indexed so as to permit prompt access to any particular record.[5] During the most recent year, the records must be kept either at a place where the firm carries on business or in such a manner that they can be produced at such a place within 24 hours of their being requested, and thereafter within 48 hours.[6]

1   IPRU (INV) 10–12(1) R.
2   IPRU (INV) 10–12(2) R.
3   IPRU (INV) 10–12(3) R.
4   IPRU (INV) 10–12(5)(c) R.

NOTIFICATIONS AND REPORTING

Principle 11

13.28   As stated in para 13.2 above, the overriding principle (FSA Principle 11) is that a firm must deal with its regulators in an open and co-operative way, and must disclose to the FSA appropriately anything relating to the firm of which the FSA would reasonably expect notice. It is important to keep in mind that Principle 11 covers unregulated as well as regulated activities, and also the activities of other members of the regulated entity's group of companies. Accordingly, it is capable of operating beyond the confines of banking and investment business.

13.29   Helpfully the FSA has given guidance[1] as to the type of event within Principle 11, in the form of a list. Obviously, the list is not exhaustive, and there will be a wide range of other circumstances which should trigger a notification. Nevertheless, the FSA's guidance is valuable, not least because it sets a standard of materiality for notifications under the Principle. The list of notifiable items is as follows:

(1)   any proposed restructuring, reorganisation or business expansion which could have a significant impact on the firm's risk profile or resources, including, but not limited to:
   (a)   setting up a new undertaking within a firm's group, or a new branch (whether in the United Kingdom or overseas); or
   (b)   commencing the provision of cross-border services into a new territory; or
   (c)   commencing the provision of a new type of product or service (whether in the United Kingdom or overseas); or
   (d)   ceasing to undertake a regulated activity or ancillary activity, or significantly reducing the scope of such activities; or
   (e)   entering into, or significantly changing a material outsourcing arrangement (a bank should also see IPRU (BANK) OS 4.2 and a building society should also see IPRU (BSOC) 12 OS 4.2 for further details); or
   (f)   a substantial change or a series of changes in the governing body of an overseas firm (other than an incoming firm); or
   (g)   any change to the firm's prudential category or subcategory, as used in the Interim Prudential sourcebooks and SUP and on which guidance is given in SUP App 1;
(2)   any significant failure in the firm's systems or controls, including those reported to the firm by the firm's auditor;
(3)   any action which a firm proposes to take which would result in a material change in its capital adequacy or solvency, including, but not limited to:
   (a)   any action which would result in a material change in the firm's financial resources or financial resources requirement; or
   (b)   a material change resulting from the payment of a special or unusual dividend or the repayment of share capital or a subordinated loan; or

(c) for firms which are subject to the rules on consolidated financial supervision, any proposal under which another group company may be considering such an action; or

(d) significant trading or non-trading losses (whether recognised or unrecognised).

1　SUP 15.3.8 G.

13.30　Despite the guidance provided by this list, a principle expressed in such general terms inevitably from time to time gives rise to questions of judgment as to whether a particular matter should be notified. On the one hand, no one wants to be criticised for having withheld material information; on the other, it is clearly undesirable for both the firm and the FSA to inundate the regulator with numerous trivial reports. A firm's best protection in these circumstances is the cultivation of an appropriate relationship with its regulator, which should enable it better to recognise the matters of which the regulator is likely to expect notice. In some cases it may be helpful to contact the regulator informally to seek an indication as to whether a formal notification is required.

Other notification requirements

13.31　Apart from the guidance on Principle 11, the FSA has established rules which require notification in specific circumstances. These are:

Matters having a serious regulatory impact

13.32　A firm must notify[1] the FSA immediately it becomes aware, or has information which reasonably suggests, that any of the following has or may have occurred or may occur in the foreseeable future:

— the firm failing to satisfy one or more of the threshold conditions;

— any matter which could have a significant adverse impact on the firm's reputation;

— any matter which could affect the firm's ability to continue to provide adequate services to its customers and which could result in serious detriment to a customer of the firm;

— any matter in respect of the firm which could result in serious financial consequences to the financial system or to other firms.

1　SUP 15.3.1R.

13.33

By way of guidance, the FSA recognises[1] that the 'circumstances which may give rise to any of the above events are wide-ranging and the probability of any matter resulting in such an outcome, and the severity of the outcome, may be difficult to determine'. 'However', continues the FSA's guidance,[2] 'the FSA expects firms to consider properly all potential consequences of events', and 'In determining whether an event that may occur in the foreseeable future should be notified to the FSA, a firm should consider both the probability of the event happening and the severity of the outcome should it happen.'

1   SUP 13.3.26.
2   SUP 15.3.2 and 3.3G.

Breaches of rules and other requirements of the Financial Services and Markets Act (FSMA) 2000

13.34   A firm must notify[1] a significant breach of a rule or Principle, a breach of any requirement of the Act or an order made under the FSMA 2000, or the bringing of a prosecution for or a conviction of an offence under the Act, by the firm or any of its directors, employees, approved persons or appointed representatives. Again, the notification must be immediate on the firm becoming aware or having information which reasonably suggests that any of the above matters has or may have occurred or may occur in the foreseeable future.

1   SUP 15.3.11 R.

13.35   By way of guidance as to which breaches are significant, the FSA states[1] that 'significance should be determined having regard to potential financial losses to customers or the firm, frequency of the breach, implications for the firm's systems and controls and if there were delays in identifying or rectifying the breach'.

1   SUP 15.3.12 G.

Civil, criminal or disciplinary proceedings against a firm

13.36   Immediate notification[1] is required of:

—   civil proceedings against the firm which are significant in relation to the firm's financial resources or its reputation;
—   an action against the firm for damages for breach of statutory duty under the FSMA 2000 or of rules made under the Act;
—   disciplinary measures or sanctions imposed on the firm by any statutory or regulatory authority, professional organisation or trade body, or the firm becoming aware of an investigation by one such body;
—   prosecution or conviction of the firm for an offence involving fraud or dishonesty, or the imposition of penalties for tax evasion;
—   removal of an Occupational Pension Scheme firm as trustee by a court order.

1   SUP 15.3.15 R.

Fraud, errors and other irregularities

13.37   The FSA requires[1] immediate notification of significant instances of fraud, where the firm:

—   becomes aware that an employee may have committed a fraud against a customer, or that any person may have committed a fraud against the firm;
—   considers that any person is acting with intent to commit a fraud against it;
—   identifies irregularities in its accounting or other records (whether or not there is evidence of fraud);

— suspects that one of its employees may be guilty of serious misconduct concerning his honesty or integrity and which is connected with the firm's regulated or ancillary activities.

1 SUP 15.3.17 R.

13.38 By way of guidance as to which instances are significant, the FSA states[1] that a firm should have regard to:

'(1) the size of any monetary loss or potential monetary loss to itself or its customers (either in terms or a single incident or group of similar or related incidents);

(2) the risk of reputational loss to the firm; and

(3) whether the incident or a pattern of incidents reflects weaknesses in a firm's internal controls.'

1 SUP 15.3.18 G.

(5) Insolvency, bankruptcy and winding up

13.39 A firm must notify[1] the FSA immediately of any of the following events:

(a) the calling of a meeting to consider a resolution for winding up the firm;

(b) an application to dissolve the firm or to strike it off the Register of Companies;

(c) the presentation of a petition for the winding up of the firm;

(d) the making of, or any proposals for, the making of, a composition or arrangement with any one of more of its creditors;

(e) an application for the appointment of an administrator or trustee in bankruptcy to the firm;

(f) the appointment of a receiver to the firm (whether an administrative receiver or a receiver appointed over particular property);

(g) an application for an interim order against the firm under s 252 of the Insolvency Act 1986 (or, in Northern Ireland, s 227 of the Insolvency (Northern Ireland) Order 1989);

(h) if the firm is a sole trader:
(i) an application for a sequestration order on the firm; or
(ii) the presentation of a petition for bankruptcy; or

(i) anything equivalent to (a) to (h) above occurring in respect of the firm in a jurisdiction outside the UK.

1 SUP 15.3.21 R.

(6) Core information requirements

13.40 The FSA requires[1] reasonable advance notice of a change in a firm's name or business name, or in the address of a firm's principal place of business in the UK (or, in the case of an overseas firm, of its registered or head office), or of a proposed change in its legal status which limits the liability of any of its members or partners. A firm must also notify the FSA immediately if it becomes subject to or ceases to be subject to the supervision of any overseas regulator (including a Home State regulator).[2]

1 SUP 15.5.1, 4 and 5 R.
2 SUP 15.5.7 R.

(7) Notified persons

13.41   In SUP 15.5.4.1 R there are requirements for overseas firms to notify the FSA within 30 business days of a person taking up or ceasing to hold the positions of worldwide chief executive, the holder of strategic responsibility for UK operations, in the case of a bank the two or more persons who effectively direct its business, and in the case of an insurer the authorised UK representative.

(8) Inaccurate, false or misleading information

13.42   A regulated firm must do all it reasonably can to ensure that information it provides to the FSA is accurate and up to date. It must therefore notify the FSA immediately if it becomes aware or has information which reasonably suggests that information which it has given to the FSA is inaccurate or has materially changed.[1]

1   SUP 15.6.4 R.

(9) Particular products and services

13.43   There are specific reporting requirements[1] relating to some individual products. These relate to the management of occupational pension scheme assets, the administration of individual pension accounts, and insurers' indemnity commission clawbacks.[2]

A manager of the assets of an occupational pension scheme must notify the FSA as soon as reasonably practicable if it receives a request or instruction from a trustee which it knows or on substantial grounds suspects or has cause reasonably to suspect is at material variance with the trustee's duties.[3] If a firm begins or ceases to administer individual pension accounts, it must notify the FSA as soon as reasonably practicable that it has done so.[4] An insurer must notify the FSA in respect of any firm (the 'intermediary') as soon as reasonably practicable if:[5]

(a)   any amount of commission due from the intermediary to the insurer in accordance with an indemnity commission clawback arrangement remains outstanding for four months after the date when the insurer gave notice to the intermediary that the relevant premium had not been paid; or

(b)   any amount of commission due from the intermediary to the insurer as a result of either the cancellation of an investment agreement or overpayment of commission remains outstanding for four months after the date on which the insurer gave notice to the intermediary that cancellation or overpayment had occurred.

However, such a notification need not be given unless the total amounts outstanding in respect of the intermediary exceed £1,000.

1   SUP 15.8.
2   An indemnity commission clawback arrangement is an arrangement under which an insurer pays commission to an intermediary before the date on which the premium is due under the relevant investment agreement, and the insurer requires repayment of the commission if the investment agreement is terminated by reason of a failure to pay a premium.
3   SUP 15.8.1 R.
4   SUP 15.8.2 R.
5   SUP 15.8.3 R

Reporting requirements

13.44 In addition to the notification requirements described above, the FSA requires a number of specific reports, the underlying purpose of which is to enable the FSA to assemble a profile of each regulated firm. These reporting requirements are mainly to be found in SUP 16 of the Handbook, where they are arranged in five sections (each of which is discussed below), namely:

(a) annual controllers reports;
(b) annual close links reports;
(c) compliance reports;
(d) financial reports; and
(e) persistency reports.

Failure to submit a report may incur a fine or other disciplinary penalty.

(1) Annual controllers reports

13.45 With certain specified exceptions, a regulated firm must[1] provide an annual report on its controllers, the report to be submitted within four months of the firm's accounting date. If the firm is not aware that it has any controllers, or is not aware of any changes in the identity of its controllers or in the percentage of shares or voting power in the firm held by a controller since it submitted its previous report, then the report need only confirm that. Otherwise, the report must list the controllers as at the accounting reference date, with percentages of voting power and of shares held in the firm or its parent, the country of incorporation and address and registered number of corporate controllers, and the date and place of birth of individual controllers. Information may be provided in the form of an organisation chart, and for a group of companies the information required in relation to the members of the group can be incorporated in a single report.

1 SUP 6.4.5 R.

13.46 Reports are *not* required at all from: ICVCs, incoming EEA firms, incoming treaty firms, non-directive friendly societies, partnerships, sole traders, service companies and UCITS qualifiers.

A friendly society or building society need submit a report only if its is aware that it has a controller.

(2) Annual close links report

13.47 Similar reporting requirements[1] relate to a regulated firm's close links[2] with another person. The close links report can be combined with the controllers report in a single document.

1 SUP 16.5.4 R.
2 'Close links' are defined in the FSA Handbook's Glossary of Definitions.

(3) Compliance reports

13.48   The requirement to produce compliance reports[1] applies only to:

(a)   *Banks:* The obligation on banks is merely to list all overseas regulators for each legal entity in the firm's group and to provide an organogram showing the authorised entities in the group.[2] This must be done annually within six months after the firm's accounting reference date.

(b)   *Trustees of authorised unit trusts:* A trustee of an authorised unit trust must provide quarterly reports (within one month after the quarter end) on failures by the manager in relation to the creation or cancellation of units or the pricing of units.[3]

(c)   *Depositories of ICVCs:* Similarly, a depository of an ICVC must make quarterly reports on failures by the authorised corporate director in relation to the issue or cancellation of shares or the pricing of shares.[4]

(d)   *Occupational pension scheme (OPS) firms:* OPS firms must provide annual reports (within seven months after the end of the scheme year) in the form of annual accounts of each occupational pension scheme and audited annual accounts of each OPS collective investment scheme in respect of which the firm is acting.[5] An OPS firm must also notify the FSA of any change in the date of commencement of the scheme year of an OPS or OPS collective investment scheme in respect of which the firm is acting, not less than 15 business days before the date on which such change is to become effective.[6]

1   SUP 16.6.
2   SUP 16.6.4 and 5 R.
3   SUP 16.6.6, 7 and 8 R.
4   SUP 16.6.6, 7 and 8 R.
5   SUP 16.6.6, 7 and 8 R.
6   SUP 16.6.8 R.

(4) Financial reports

13.49   Financial reports are essential material from which the FSA can evaluate the financial soundness and performance of regulated firms. It is of course important that all reports of any kind are submitted on time; but in the case of financial reports timely submission is essential. The specific requirements vary from one type of firm to another. Those relating to banks, securities and futures firms and investment management firms are summarised in Tables 13.3.1 to 13.3.5, which are taken from section SUP 16.7 of the FSA's Handbook.

(5) Persistency reports

13.50   This is a requirement[1] on insurers to submit an annual report, by 30 April each year, on life policies promoted or issued during the year.

1   SUP 16.8.

Table 13.3.1: Financial reports: Banks

Content of report	Form (Note 1)	Frequency	Due date
Annual report and audited accounts	N/A	Annually	3 months after the firm's accounting reference date
Adequate information on capital adequacy (Unconsolidated, solo consolidated)	BSD3	Quarterly	10 business days after quarter end (Note 6) (12 business days if submitted electronically)
Adequate information on capital adequacy (Consolidated)	BSD3 (Note 2)	Half yearly	20 business days after period end (22 business days if submitted electronically)
Analysis of large exposures (Unconsolidated, solo consolidated)	LE2	Quarterly	10 business days after quarter end (Note 6)
Analysis of large exposures (Consolidated)	LE2 (Note 2)	Quarterly	20 business days after period end
Adequate information on holdings of credit and financial institutions and non-financial companies capital instruments (Unconsolidated, solo consolidated)	M1 (Note 3)	Quarterly	10 business days after quarter end (Note 6) (12 business days if submitted electronically)
Adequate information on holdings of credit and financial institutions and non-financial companies capital instruments (Consolidated)	M1 (Note 2 & Note 3)	Half yearly	20 business days after period end (22 business days if submitted electronically)
Adequate information on sterling stock liquidity	SLR1 (Note 4)	Monthly (Note 5)	6 business days after second Wednesday of the month

Table 13.3.1: Financial reports: Banks – *contd*

Content of report	*Form (Note 1)*	*Frequency*	*Due date*
Adequate information on mismatch liquidity	LR (Note 4)	Quarterly	10 business days after quarter end (Note 6) (12 business days if submitted electronically)
List of companies included in the bank's consolidated large exposure reporting	N/A	Annually	6 months after the firm's accounting reference date
Annual confirmation that all companies included in solo consolidation meet the criteria for such consolidation as set out in IPRU (BANK) CS 9.2	N/A	Annually	6 months after the firm's accounting reference date

Note 1: When giving the report required, a bank must use the form indicated, if any. The content of the form has the status of guidance on the type of information that should be provided to meet the reporting obligation. A copy of the form is located in SUP 16 Ann 1R.

Note 2: The requirement to submit consolidated reports applies only to a bank which calculates its capital requirements on a consolidated basis. See IPRU (BANK) GN 3.3.13R(2) and IPRU (BANK) CS 4. All consolidated reports required on a half-yearly basis must be prepared as at the end of June and December of each year.

Note 3: This report is only required from a bank which reports either on a solo or consolidated basis and: (i) has been granted a trading book concession as explained in IPRU (BANK) CA 3; or (ii) has qualifying holding in non-financial companies as explained in IPRU (BANK) CA 10.4.

Note 4: A bank is not required to submit both the SLR1 and LR. A bank which monitors its liquidity according to the maturity mismatch approach as set out in IPRU (BANK) LM must submit the LR. A bank which monitors its liquidity according to the sterling stock liquidity approach as set out in IPRU (BANK) LS must submit the SLR1.

Note 5: This report must be prepared as at the second Wednesday of each month. See IPRU (BANK) LS 5.2(2) regarding submission of an SLR1 on breach of various limits.

Note 6: Reports required on a quarterly basis must be prepared as at the end of March, June, September and December of each year, except that a bank, which submits the BT report to the Bank of England monthly, must prepare the Form LR (Adequate information on mismatch liquidity) as at the end of February, May, August and November each year.

Table 13.3.2: Financial reports: Securities and futures firms

Report	Frequency	Due date
Audited annual financial statements	Annually	3 months after the firm's accounting reference date
Annual reporting statement	Annually	3 months after the firm's accounting reference date
Annual reconciliation (Note 1)	Annually	3 months after the firm's accounting reference date
Audited accounts of any subsidiary, unless the rules in this chapter require that subsidiary to submit accounts to the FSA	Annually	3 months after the firm's accounting reference date
Consolidated reporting statement (Note 2)	Half yearly	1 month after period end
Large exposures quarterly reporting statement (Form LEM 1 or LEM 2) – solo (Notes 3 and 4)	Quarterly	15 business days after quarter end
Large exposures quarterly reporting statement (Form LEM 1 or LEM 2) – consolidated (Notes 2 and 4)	Quarterly	1 month after quarter end
Monthly reporting statement	Monthly	15 business days after month end

Note 1: Every year a firm must submit: (a) a reconciliation and explanation of any differences between amounts shown in the balance sheet in the audited annual financial statements and the annual reporting statement; and (b) a reconciliation and explanation of any differences between the annual reporting statement and the monthly reporting statement prepared as at the same date.

Note 2: Only for category A and B firms which are subject to the consolidation rules set out in IPRU (INV) 10-200R – 10-203R, and are not exempt from the consolidation rules under IPRU (INV) 10-200R(2) or IPRU (INV) 10-204R.

Note 3: Only for category A and B firms.

Note 4: A firm which was required to submit Form LEM1 in the relevant period immediately prior to the commencement must continue to do so. A firm which was required to submit Form LEM2 in the relevant period immediately prior to the commencement must continue to do so. A category A or B firm authorised after the commencement must submit Form LEM1.

Table 13.3.3: Financial reports: Securities and futures firms which are category C or D firms or arrangers or venture capital firms

Report	Frequency	Due date
Audited annual financial statements	Annually	3 months after the firm's accounting reference date
Annual reporting statement	Annually	3 months after the firm's accounting reference date
Annual reconciliation (Note 1)	Annually	3 months after the firm's accounting reference date
Audited accounts of any subsidiary unless the rules in this chapter require that subsidiary to submit accounts to the FSA	Annually	3 months after the firm's accounting reference date
Consolidated reporting statement (Note 2)	Half yearly	1 month from period end
Large exposures quarterly reporting statement (Form LEM 1 or LEM 2) –solo (Notes 3 and 4)	Quarterly	15 business days after quarter end
Large exposures quarterly reporting (Form LEM 1 or LEM 2) – consolidated (Notes 2 and 4)	Quarterly	1 month after quarter end
Quarterly reporting statement	Quarterly	15 business days after quarter end

Note 1: Every year a firm must submit: (a) a reconciliation and explanation of any differences between amounts shown in the balance sheet in the audited annual financial statements and the annual reporting statement; and (b) a reconciliation and explanation of any differences between the annual reporting statement and the monthly reporting statement prepared as at the same date.

Note 2: Only for category C firms (as defined in the glossaries located in IPRU (INV) 10), which are subject to the consolidation rules set out in IPRU (INV) 10-200R – 10-203R, and are not exempt from the consolidation rules under IPRU (INV) 10-200R(2) or IPRU (INV) 10-204R.

Note 3: Only for category C firms (as defined in the glossaries located in IPRU (INV) 10).

Note 4: A firm which was required to submit Form LEM1 in the relevant period immediately prior to commencement must continue to do so. A firm which was required to submit Form LEM2 in the relevant period immediately prior to commencement must continue to do so. A category C firm authorised after commencement must submit the Form LEM1.

Table 13.3.4: Financial reports: Securities and futures firm which are advisers or locals, or traded options market makers (as referred to in IPRU (INV) 3-60R (4))

Report	Frequency	Due date
Solvency statement (sole traders only)	Annually	2 months after the firm's accounting reference date
Audited annual financial statements (Partnerships and bodies corporate only)	Annually	3 months after the firm's accounting reference date
Audited accounts of any subsidiary unless the rules in this chapter require that subsidiary to submit accounts to the FSA	Annually	3 months after the firm's accounting reference date

A securities and futures firm which is an ISD investment firm, and which is a sole trader, or a partnership formed under the laws of England and Wales, must submit a solvency statement for the sole trader or each partner to the FSA every year.

Table 13.3.5: Financial reports: Investment management firms which are not one of the types of firm specified in SUP 16.7.37R

Report	Frequency	Due date
Annual Financial Return (Note 1)	Annually	4 months after the firm's accounting reference date
Annual accounts (Note 1)	Annually	4 months after the firm's accounting reference date
Annual solvency statement (only for individuals in partnership) (Note 2)	Annually	At the same time as the Annual Financial Return
Quarterly Financial Return (only for firms subject to a Liquid Capital Requirement as set out in IPRU (INV) 5.2.3(1)(a) or (b))	Quarterly	1 month after quarter end
Monthly Financial Return (only for ISD firms (Note 3) subject to the Own Funds Requirement of Euro 730,000 as set out in IPRU (INV) 5.2.3(1)(b)) (Note 4)	Monthly	1 month after month end

Note 1: The Annual Financial Return and the annual accounts of a firm must together give a true and fair view of the state of affairs of the firm (or in the case of a sole trader, of his regulated activities) and of the firm's profit and loss.

Note 2: The annual solvency statement is a statement from each partner in the following form: 'I certify that I have sufficient assets to cover my personal liabilities.'

Note 3: The definition of ISD firm for this purpose is provided in the glossary located in IPRU (INV) 5.

Note 4: A firm need not prepare a Monthly Financial Return as at the same date as a Quarterly Financial Return. A firm must therefore prepare eight Monthly and four Quarterly Financial Returns each year. One Quarterly Financial Return must be prepared to the same date as the Annual Financial Return (but submitted earlier). Monthly and Quarterly Financial Returns are not cumulative, and must relate only to the period concerned. A firm may need to prepare more frequent accounts, including financial resources statements, for its own internal use to ensure that it complies at all times with the rules in IPRU (INV).

Other reporting requirements

13.51   In addition to the above categories, the following reporting obligations are noteworthy:

COMPLAINTS

13.52   Twice a year a regulated firm must report to the FSA on complaints which it has received during the periods respectively of 1 April to 30 September and 1 October to 31 March, the reports to be submitted within one month of the end of the relevant reporting period.[1] The reports must cover the total number of complains received, broken down into categories and product types, the total number of complaints closed by the firm (a) within four weeks or less of receipt, (b) within four to eight weeks of receipt and (c) more than eight weeks after receipt, and the total number of complaints outstanding at the end of the reporting period.

A firm which does not do business with eligible complaints and has no reasonable likelihood of doing so may obtain exemption from these reporting requirements if it notifies the FSA of those facts.[2]

1   DISP. 1.5.4R.
2   DISP 1.1.7R.

EMERGENCIES

13.53   If there occurs an emergency which makes it impracticable for a firm to comply with an FSA rule, as soon as practicable the firm must notify the FSA of the emergency and of the steps it is taking and proposes to take to deal with its consequences.[1]

1   GEN 1.3.2R.

TRANSACTION REPORTING

13.54   The FSA has rules relating to reporting transactions (including own account transactions) in securities. The stated purposes of these requirements are 'to implement article 20 of the Investment Services Directive which has the true aims of protecting investors and ensuring the smooth operation and transparency of the markets in transferable securities'.[1] 'Transaction reports', continues the FSA, 'also form a useful part of the FSA's arrangements for monitoring . . . and can assist the FSA in assessing the type and conduct of business carried on by the firm'.

From the perspective of monitoring, transaction reports provide the FSA with an effective audit trail to ensure that, for example, a firm has complied with its best execution obligations and other aspects of propriety in its dealings. A report is not required if the firm complies with a requirement to report the transaction to its Home State regulator or if the transaction is transacted on one of the exchanges specified by the FSA[2] and the firm reports the transaction to that exchange.[3] An investment management or a personal investment firm need not make a report if the reportable transaction is transacted on a regulated market and the firm reports the transaction to that market or satisfies itself that it will be so reported, or if the firm is a seller or is acting on behalf of the seller and the counterparty is another regulated firm, or if the firm has reasonable grounds to believe that another firm is obliged to make a transaction report to the FSA and that other firm is not entitled to rely on this exemption.[4] A firm may appoint another person to make transaction reports on its behalf if the firm has informed the FSA of the appointment in writing and the reports made on its behalf comply with the rules, distinguishing each individual transaction and using the firm's identifying code.[5]

1   SUP 17.2.1 G.
2   Listed in SUP 17 Annex 1R.
3   SUP 17.4.2 R.
4   SUP 17.4.3 R.
5   SUP 17.4.7 R.

13.55   The FSA specifies[1] which transactions must be reported and the permitted reporting systems to be used, which include Cresto Limited, the FSA's Direct Reporting System, the SEQUAL 2000 system of Thomson Financial Services and the Trax system of the International Securities Market Association. If a reporting system fails (whether an external system, the firm's own system or the system of a person reporting on its behalf) the firm must:[2]

(a)   make the transaction report through another reporting system, if it considers it reasonably practicable to do so; or

(b)   make the report by the end of the business day after the day on which the failure is remedied if the firm does not consider it reasonably practicable to comply with (a).

The firm must notify FSA in writing which of (a) or (b) it will adopt, and of any failure of its own system or that of a person reporting on its behalf which prevents a report being made in time.[3]

1   SUP 17.5, 17.7.
2   SUP 17.7.10 R.
3   SUP 17.7.11 and 12 R.

Chapter 14

Ensuring compliance: managing regulatory and reputational risk

RESPONSIBILITY: THE BANK, SENIOR MANAGEMENT AND THE COMPLIANCE FUNCTION

The Board and senior management

14.1   Responsibility for a bank's compliance with all regulatory requirements has always rested with the Board and the holder of the chief executive function. It is the bank (or its subsidiary) which is authorised to conduct its regulated activities. It is, therefore, the duty of the bank's Board and its most senior management to ensure that the bank meets the obligations which its authorisation brings. Generally, they are ultimately responsible for the regulatory good standing and reputation of the bank. That responsibility covers all operations of the bank, in every country in which it does business. The bank's reputation with its regulators, counterparties and customers is fundamental to its well-being. Ensuring that the bank's businesses are conducted lawfully and with integrity is as much a part of the Board's and management's responsibilities as ensuring that they are conducted profitably. Indeed, except in the shortest of terms, profitability cannot be achieved without a strong reputation for probity. The Board and management must, therefore, be constantly alert to the risk of damage to that reputation. It is their duty to ensure that appropriate arrangements are in place for the management of that risk.

14.2   Well-established though the principle of the Board's and senior management's responsibility has been, in the aftermath of the fall of the house of Barings in 1993, it became apparent that the regulatory regime established by the Financial Services Act 1986 and the Banking Act 1987 needed strengthening if senior management were always to be held fully to account.[1] The machinations of a rogue trader in a distant country in another time zone thus precipitated a major change in the UK's regulation of its financial markets. A key feature of the Financial Services and Markets Act (FSMA) 2000 statutory regime is the strengthening of responsibility and accountability of senior management. The Financial Services Authority (FSA) regards:

> 'members of senior management of firms [as having] a crucial role to play in ensuring that effective governance structures and systems and controls are operated. [Senior management] is responsible for setting the business strategy, regulatory climate and ethical standards within a firm'.[2]

As the FSA enjoys a daunting set of enforcement powers with which to enforce this principle, the senior individual performing the 'Apportionment and Oversight Function' in each firm will not be the only person apportioning responsibility under the new regime.

1 'The Chairman of Barings plc, Peter Baring, described the failure of controls with regard to Barings Futures (Singapore) as "absolute". We agree. It was this lack of effective controls which provided the opportunity for Leeson to undertake his unauthorised trading activities and reduced the likelihood of their detection. We consider that those with direct executive responsibility for establishing effective controls must bear much of the blame': from *Report of the Board of Banking Supervision Inquiry into the circumstances of the collapse of Barings* (18 July 1995).
2 FSA Consultation Paper 26: 'The Regulation of Approved Persons' (July 1999).

The Regulator and senior management: *modus vivendi*

14.3   The FSA's senior management regime applies to large and small firms alike, whether they conduct business as an independent financial adviser, a provincial building society, a high street deposit-taker, an investment manager, a general insurer or a global investment bank. The challenges of managing a financial institution should not be underestimated. The senior manager may preside over a multinational business providing a diverse range of complex products in a hugely competitive and innovative global market. The fear for such a manager and regulator alike is that a financial institution in apparent robust health in one country can be laid low by the failings of an individual in a distant outpost. Even firms of more modest size and less elaborate structure are likely to face a wide range of regulatory and reputational issues; and their ability to withstand the shock of a regulatory crisis may be much less than that of a larger and more robust concern.

A challenge for the regulator is to maintain a regime that meets its regulatory objectives whilst remaining sympathetic to the demands placed upon the senior management of firms. Another challenge is that regulatory powers are constrained within the borders of the relevant jurisdiction whilst business (and fraud) knows no boundaries. Similarly, the FSA regulates by legal entity whilst a firm may be managed through global business lines. What are the UK authorised firm's responsibilities to the FSA in conducting business, for instance, through overseas offices?

14.4   Successful management is not simply about making money. It is often stated that good compliance is good business. It is the senior managers who, more than anyone else, can foster a corporate culture under which compliance with ethical principles and regulatory requirements becomes an accepted part of the day-to-day conduct of business by the firm. As senior management will always be best placed to identify failings within a firm, the FSA regards management as the first line of defence against, and potentially accountable for, such failings. The new regime also offers management the incentive of a lighter supervisory relationship for managing the risks inherent in their business effectively.

14.5 The FSA links the responsibilities of authorised firms and individuals registered as approved persons by focusing upon the responsibilities of senior management. The FSA's senior management regime sets high-level standards for firms and managers rather than prescriptive rules. Those standards are not limited to compliance matters but cover the range of management responsibilities. The regulator professes to want neither to be intrusive nor to frustrate a firm's legitimate commercial ambitions. Whilst interested in the viability of a firm's business, the FSA will not tell management how to manage. The FSA has promised that there will be no disproportionate interference in the internal management of firms and that it is not seeking to be too prescriptive about the particular arrangements in a firm. An authorised firm is required to apportion responsibilities clearly across senior management and to establish and maintain appropriate systems and controls. The nature of those systems and controls will depend upon the business conducted by the firm. An individual registered as an approved person through performing a 'significant influence function' must meet certain standards in managing the business of the firm for which he is responsible in his controlled function.

> 'The FSA believes that by providing high level rules and guidance the requirements form a framework within which firms will have a culture of compliance instilled in the highest level of management. The compliance culture can be expected to filter downwards throughout the firm'.[1]

1 FSA Consultation Paper 35: 'Senior Management Arrangement, Systems and Controls' (December 1999).

The FSA's regulatory objectives

14.6

> 'The FSA's regulatory approach to the senior management of authorised firms reflects its key goals to set standards which reflect the pivotal role of senior management in determining whether their firms live up to regulatory expectations and to leave the senior management of each firm with the freedom they need to devise business structures and processes in accordance with their own commercial objectives.'[1]

The FSMA 2000 sets out the FSA's regulatory objectives. As discussed in Chapter 2, those objectives are (i) maintaining market confidence; (ii) promoting public awareness; (iii) protecting consumers; and (iv) reducing financial crime. As the debate over whether the FSA should have a competition objective revealed, the objectives are not just window-dressing. The FSA's accountability will turn upon whether it is achieving those objectives.

To that end, the FSA must take account of the FSMA's 'principles of good regulation'. Under s 2(3)(b) of the FSMA 2000, the FSA must have regard to '. . . the responsibilities of those who manage the affairs of authorised persons'. Senior management is responsible for the authorised firm's activities and for ensuring that its business is conducted in accordance with the regulatory requirements. The FSA has stated that this principle 'is designed to guard against unnecessary intrusion by the regulator into firms' business and requires [FSA] to hold senior management responsible for risk management and controls within firms'.[2]

1　FSA Handbook Development Special Edition (June 2000).
2　FSA: 'A New Regulator for a New Millennium' (January 2000).

14.7　How will the FSA translate the FSMA's regulatory objectives and principles of good regulation into regulatory activities? Of the regulatory objectives, the main considerations for the FSA in relation to senior management responsibilities are (i) confidence in the financial system; (ii) the fair treatment of firms' customers; (iii) the protection of the consumer; and (iv) preventing the use of the financial system in connection with financial crime.[1]

In carrying out 'the business of regulation from day to day, and year to year', the FSA will preside over a regulatory regime that 'is founded on a risk-based approach to the regulation of all financial business' and 'recognises the proper responsibilities . . . of firms' own management'.[2] How well does a firm assess, understand and respond to the risks it faces? By the very nature of their business, some firms, however well managed, will always be more heavily supervised than others. An international bank will be seen as a greater risk in the context of the FSA's regulatory objectives than a corporate finance boutique. Although the FSA does not publish its risk assessments, the firm will be told the basis for the assessment and the direction in which the assessment appears to be moving. The firm will be told what type of supervisory relationship it will enjoy with the FSA.

> 'Well-managed firms whose own assessment of risk is sophisticated and effective will require less supervisory attention than a firm conducting similar business whose controls are not of the same quality.'[2]

The incentive for firms to manage their own risks effectively is a promised reduction in the burden of regulation as the regulator steps back. The compliant, and thus less risky, firm may enjoy a lighter form of supervision such as remote desk-based monitoring of management information, fewer on-site regulatory inspection visits or even a reduction in capital requirements. For those firms regarded by the FSA as posing a threat to its regulatory objectives, regulation will be more intensive and intrusive, as some have already discovered.

1　FSA Handbook of Rules and Guidance: 'Senior Management Arrangements, Systems and Controls' – SYSC 1.2.2G.
2　FSA, *A New Regulator for a New Millennium* (January 2000).

The responsibilities of the authorised firm

14.8　The FSA regards authorisation as the first step in risk-based regulation. Under the 'Threshold Conditions' which a firm is required to satisfy (and continue to satisfy) in order to be given and to retain a permission,[1] authorisation will be granted by reference to a broad range of factors including:

— 　the quality of its management;
— 　the identity of major shareholders;
— 　how it proposes to conduct its business;
— 　the viability of that business;

— the procedures that management has put in place to control the business;
— whether it has adequate resources;
— the competence of its staff; and
— how effectively it will manage risk.

Such questions that will be considered are:

— Does the governing body have the skills and experience to understand the firm's activities and to cope when the going gets tough?
— Is the governing body organised so that it can address and control the activities of the firm including those activities carried on by managers to whom particular responsibilities have been delegated?
— Will its staff comply with the regulatory requirements? Will the firm comply with 'The Principles for Businesses'?

1 FSMA 2000, Sch 6 – 'Threshold Conditions'; FSA Handbook of Rules and Guidance: 'Threshold Conditions'. Also FSA Consultation Paper 20: 'The Qualifying Conditions for Authorisation'.

'The Principles for Businesses'

14.9 'The Principles for Businesses'[1] have been issued under the FSA's rule-making powers and reflect the regulatory objectives. The Principles are a general statement of the fundamental obligations of authorised firms under the regulatory system and their purpose is to formulate succinct high-level precepts stating the fundamental obligations of regulated businesses which will provide a basic yardstick by which firms should order their behaviour and provide a basis for supervisory and enforcement activity by the FSA itself. In keeping with the FSA's risk-based approach to regulation, the Principles define the standards that must be achieved by firms rather than prescribing detailed processes.

Liability for breaching the Principles will only arise where the FSA can show that the firm was at fault.

1 FSA Handbook of Rules and Guidance: 'Principles for Businesses'.

14.10 Under the 'Management and Control Principle' (Principle 3), 'a firm must take reasonable care to organise and control its affairs responsibly and effectively, with adequate risk management systems'.[1] By focusing on 'reasonable care', the regulator has adopted an objective test. The bank will not be liable if it can show that it acted in accordance with the standards of the reasonable bank. 'Adequate risk management systems' does not mean just financial risk but covers any form of risk to which the firm might be subject. The requirement 'to organise and control its affairs responsibly and effectively' is the link to the responsibilities of individual senior managers. 'The Management and Control Principle' has spawned a range of FSA rules and guidance including the new regime governing staff competence[2] as well as the 'Senior Management Arrangements, Systems and Controls' (SYSC) regime.[3]

1 FSA Handbook of Rules and Guidance: 'Principles for Businesses'.
2 FSA Handbook of Rules and Guidance: 'Training and Competence'.
3 FSA Handbook of Rules and Guidance: 'Senior Management Arrangements, Systems and Controls' – SYSC. See also FSA Consultation Paper 35: 'Senior Management Arrangement, Systems and Controls' (December 1999); FSA Consultation Paper 53: 'Feedback Statement to

CP35' (June 2000); FSA Policy Statement: 'Issues arising out of CP26 and CP35' (June 2000) and FSA Policy Statement: 'Grandfathering of Firms, Individuals and Products' (December 2000).

Senior Management Arrangements, Systems and Controls (SYSC)

14.11   The SYSC regime bites upon the authorised firm. SYSC supports the Principles for Businesses by amplifying the Management and Control Principle. Except as set out in its 'application' provision,[1] SYSC applies to the 'regulated activities' and certain other activities of every firm. The 'Systems and Controls' provisions ('SYSC 3') also apply to the carrying on of 'unregulated activities' in a 'prudential context' and take into account any activity of other members of a group of which the bank is a member.[2] This requires a bank to assess the appropriateness of its systems and controls in the light of the potential impact of a group member's activities.

The regime essentially 'applies with respect to activities carried on from an establishment maintained by the firm in the United Kingdom'.[3] In relation though to a 'UK domestic firm', for instance, SYSC applies in a prudential context 'with respect to activities wherever they are carried on'. In considering whether to take regulatory action in relation to activities carried on outside the UK, the FSA will take into account the standards expected in the market in which the firm is operating. For European Economic Area (EEA) firms, the regime will operate in a modified form in relation to their UK branches. As prudential regulation is reserved to the home state regulator, the apportionment requirement will not apply to EEA firms' branches in the UK and the systems and controls requirements will only apply in relation to UK conduct of business. Individuals exerting significant influence over the conduct of designated investment business must be approved. The UK branch of a firm based outside the EEA is covered by the senior management regime for most purposes. The branch must comply with the apportionment and systems and controls requirements. Senior managers of the UK branch performing controlled functions involving designated investment business must be approved.

The purposes[4] of SYSC are:

(a)   to encourage senior management 'to take appropriate practical responsibility for their firms' arrangements on matters likely to be of interest to the FSA because they impinge on the FSA's functions under the Act';

(b)   to amplify Principle 3 ('Management and control');

(c)   'to encourage firms to vest responsibility for effective and responsible organisation in specific directors and senior managers'.

1   SYSC 1.1.
2   SYSC 1.1.5R (SYSC 3 applies only so far as responsibility for the matter in question is not reserved to a firm's 'Home State' regulator).
3   SYSC 1.1.7R.
4   SYSC 1.2.1G.

The Apportionment and Oversight Function

14.12   The bank 'must appropriately allocate' to one or more individuals the functions of dealing with the apportionment of responsibilities and overseeing the establishment and maintenance of appropriate systems and controls: 'There is no magic number which is "appropriate" – it is any number which enables the firm to deliver compliance with Principle 3 and its other major regulatory obligations'.[1] If the bank has a chief executive or equivalent, that individual must be, alone or with others, one of those by whom the above functions are carried out. If the responsibility is shared then the division of responsibilities between the individuals should be clear and documented. All relevant individuals must be FSA-registered as they will be performing the 'Apportionment and Oversight Function' (CF 8), which is a 'Required Function' under the Approved Persons regime.[2] (They will have to comply with the 'Statements of Principle for Approved Persons' and the Code of Practice.) For an incoming EEA firm, the role is called the 'EEA investment business oversight function'. The bank must make, and take reasonable care to maintain, records of its apportionment and allocation arrangements. In the aftermath of Barings, there was concern about how firms employing matrix management systems could be regulated. The FSA's regime is designed to be consistent with the operation of matrix management structures in international corporate groups. Thus a firm can vest the Apportionment and Oversight Function either in individuals employed in that firm and/or in individuals elsewhere in the group whose responsibilities (whether defined by product or geography) extend to that firm. Either way the individuals concerned will need to be approved persons.

1   FSA Handbook Development Special Edition (June 2000).
2   FSA Handbook of Rules and Guidance: 'Regulatory Processes' – 'Supervision' – SUP 10.

Apportionment of significant responsibilities

14.13   Under SYSC, a bank 'must take reasonable care to maintain a clear and appropriate apportionment of significant responsibilities among its directors and senior management' so that their individual responsibilities are clear and the business 'can be adequately monitored and controlled' by senior management.[1] The board and any subcommittees should have detailed terms of reference. Each senior manager's sphere of personal responsibility should be clearly delineated and documented by the firm and understood within it. Senior managers should have appropriate job descriptions. Organisation charts should show each individual's personal sphere of responsibility. Appropriate records must be maintained. The regulatory obligations of the individual senior manager are bounded by the responsibilities apportioned to him in the firm and it is 'the firm's apportionment of responsibilities to its senior people' that drives their regulatory accountability as individuals'.[2]

1   SYSC 2.1.1R.
2   FSA Handbook Development Special Edition (June 2000).

Systems and controls

14.14   The authorised firm must take reasonable care to establish and maintain such systems and controls as are appropriate to its business. The FSA's expectations for a small independent financial adviser will differ from those for a listed bank. Guidance in the FSA Handbook[1] lists the factors to be considered by the bank in deciding the 'nature and extent' of the required systems and controls:

(a)   the nature, scale and complexity of its business;
(b)   the diversity of its operations, including geographical diversity;
(c)   the volume and size of its transactions; and
(d)   the degree of risk associated with each area of its operation.

Although there are some rules, the Handbook relies predominantly upon guidance in setting out the main issues that a bank is expected to consider in establishing and maintaining systems and controls appropriate to its business. This accords with the FSA's policy of setting high-level standards (rather than prescriptive rules) and then leaving the authorised firm and its management with a wide discretion in deciding how best to meet those standards. The FSA will expect the bank to have a detailed and comprehensive framework of systems and controls in place covering all of the SYSC rules and guidance. Maintaining appropriate systems and controls will require the bank to undertake regular reviews:

—   Has the range of business conducted by the bank changed?
—   Have you moved into the retail sector?
—   Are more complex products now being marketed?
—   Has there been a merger?
—   Have offices been opened in new overseas jurisdictions?

1   SYSC 3.1.2G.

14.15   The SYSC 'rules' govern the firm's compliance with regulatory requirements and 'countering the risk that the firm might be used to further financial crime';[1] the firm's appointment of a senior officer to perform the 'Compliance Oversight Function'[2] and the making and retention of adequate records.[3] A bank will be expected to have a separate compliance function to establish systems and controls to monitor its compliance with its regulatory obligations and to be responsible for establishing documented policies and procedures such as a compliance manual. The focus upon record-keeping permeates the FSA Handbook.[4] Organisation charts and job descriptions will rapidly become out-of-date and checking their accuracy and date controls is a soft target for any regulator. In the event of enforcement proceedings, such records will be amongst the first documents requested by the FSA as it seeks to establish what you knew and when you knew it.

1   SYSC 3.2.6R.
2   SYSC 3.2.8R.
3   SYSC 3.2.20R.
4   See generally Chapter 13.

Guidance

14.16   Guidance[1] is provided to the firm on its systems and procedures in relation to:

—   'organisation';
—   'risk assessment';
—   'management information';
—   'employees and agents';
—   'audit committee';

— 'internal audit';
— 'business strategy';
— 'remuneration policies'; and
— 'business continuity'.

1 SYSC 3.

14.17 The SYSC guidance[1] on organisation provides that the bank's 'reporting lines should be clear and appropriate having regard to the nature, scale and complexity of its business'. The reporting lines, together with clear management responsibilities, should be appropriately communicated within the firm. Organisation charts should be available to staff and kept up-to-date. A job description should record the individual's reporting lines, set authorisation levels and facilitate compliance with the attainment and maintenance of competence requirements. In delegating a function, the firm should put appropriate safeguards in place and 'should assess whether the [individual] is suitable to carry out the delegated function or task, taking into account the degree of responsibility involved'. Problems should be dealt with at an appropriately senior level. Regulatory obligations must be met in relation to outsourced activities as a firm cannot contract out of its regulatory obligations. The bank is also encouraged, in words echoing the fall of Barings, to segregate the duties of individuals and departments to reduce the opportunities for fraud.

1 SYSC 3.2.2G *et seq.*

14.18 Guidance[1] provides that, depending upon the nature, scale and complexity of the bank's business, 'it may be appropriate' for senior management to be advised by a separate risk assessment function 'who are sufficiently independent to perform their duties objectively' in monitoring the bank's key risks including market risk, credit risk, operational risk and legal risk:

— How relevant, reliable and timely is the management information furnished to the governing body to facilitate compliance with the bank's regulatory obligations? (The bank should be able to satisfy itself of the suitability of its staff.)
— What level of responsibility will the individual be assuming within the bank?
— How effective are the bank's recruitment procedures?
— Does the bank ensure that relevant individuals are appropriately registered?
— Does the bank comply with the FSA's training and competence requirements?

A key feature of the new regulatory regime is the focus on individual competence. The introduction of a higher degree of professionalism into both the wholesale and the retail financial services sectors would contribute significantly towards the FSA achieving its 'regulatory objectives'.

1 SYSC 3.2.10G.

14.19 Other guidance[1] focuses upon audit committee procedures; the internal audit function; business strategy (does the bank have a formal and documented procedure for planning its strategy and business?); remuneration policies (what level of risk-taking is being promoted?); and business continuity (what would happen if the bank did hit an iceberg?).

1   SYSC 3.

Whistleblowing

14.20   The Public Interest Disclosure Act (PIDA) 1998 is the subject of guidance issued by the FSA to regulated firms.[1] The object of the PIDA 1998 is to protect from victimisation by their employer employees and other workers (such as agency workers or trainees on work experience) who make disclosures in the public interest. Effective arrangements to comply with the PIDA are the responsibility of a firm's senior management, and 'the FSA would regard as a serious matter any evidence that a firm had acted to the detriment of a worker because he had made a protected disclosure about matters which are relevant to the functions of the FSA'.[2] 'Such evidence', states the FSA, 'could call into question the fitness and propriety of the firm or relevant members of its staff and could therefore, if relevant, affect the firm's continuing satisfaction of threshold condition 5 (Suitability) or, for an approved person, his status as such'.[2] The FSA has, therefore, directly linked the PIDA 1998 with the fundamental regulatory principles of fitness and propriety.

1   SYSC 4. See also FSA Consultation Paper 101 'Whistleblowing, the FSA and the financial services industry', and the FSA's Policy Statement of April 2002 containing feedback on CP 101.
2   SYSC 4.2.3G.

14.21   The PIDA protects disclosures, made in good faith, of information which in the reasonable belief of the worker making the disclosure tends to show that any of the following failures has been committed:

— a criminal offence;
— a failure to comply with any legal obligation;
— a miscarriage of justice;
— the putting of the health and safety of any individual in danger;
— damage to the environment; or
— deliberate concealment of any of the above.

14.22

The FSA's guidance encourages firms to adopt appropriate procedures to encourage members of their staff with concerns to blow the whistle internally about matters relevant to the functions of the FSA.[1] The FSA recognises that the extent of such procedures may depend on the size of the firm and that smaller firms may not need written procedures.[2] However, a bank or financial services firm of any size would, in our view, be at risk of adverse comment if it did not have a written procedure.

In its guidance the FSA has indicated[3] what internal processes might appropriately include, as follows:

(1)   *Larger firms:*
— a clear statement that the firm takes failures seriously;
— an indication of what is regarded as a failure;

— respect for the confidentiality of workers who raise concerns, if they wish this;

— an assurance that, where a protected disclosure has been made, the firm will take all reasonable steps to ensure that no person under its control engages in victimisation;

— the opportunity to raise concerns outside the line management structure, such as with the Compliance Director, Internal Auditor or Company Secretary;

— penalties for making false and malicious allegations;

— an indication of the proper way in which concerns may be raised outside the firm if necessary;

— providing access to an external body such as an independent charity for advice;

— making whistleblowing procedures accessible to staff of key contractors; and

— written procedures.

(2) *Smaller firms:*

— telling workers that the firm takes failures seriously and explaining how wrongdoing affects the organisation;

— telling workers what conduct is regarded as a failure;

— telling workers who raise concerns that their confidentiality will be respected, if they wish this;

— making it clear that workers will be supported and protected from reprisals;

— nominating a senior officer as an alternative route to line management and telling workers how they can contact that individual in confidence;

— making it clear that false and malicious allegations will be penalised by the firm;

— telling workers how they can properly blow the whistle outside the firm if necessary;

— providing access to an external body for advice such as an independent charity; and

— encouraging managers to be open to concerns.

1   SYSC 4.2.2G(1).
2   SYSC 4.2.2G(2).
3   SYSC 4.2.2G(3).

14.23   The FSA states[1] that firms should also consider telling workers that they can blow the whistle direct to the FSA. However, the FSA strongly encourages workers to blow the whistle internally in the first instance, and to contact the FSA only if the whistleblower is concerned by the response or lack of response from the firm.

1   SYSC 4.2.2G(3).

The responsibility of the individual senior manager

14.24   To this point, we have reviewed the responsibilities of the authorised bank. But it is only through its staff that the bank will ever give investment advice, sell a life policy, trade in the derivatives markets or manage a business line. It is employees who actually carry out the bank's transactions. It is the individual(s) performing the 'Apportionment and Oversight Function' who will apportion significant responsibilities amongst senior management and oversee the maintenance of appropriate systems and controls. The FSA thus requires creatures of flesh and blood to be registered to carry out the business for which the bank is authorised.

Regulatory responsibilities

14.25   What are the regulatory responsibilities of the senior manager? As discussed in Chapter 5, an individual performing a function which 'is likely to be able to exert significant influence over the conduct of the firm's affairs in so far as they relate to a regulated activity' must be registered as an approved person.[1] An individual 'dealing directly with the firm's customers' or their property must also be registered. There are 20 'significant influence' controlled functions[2] covering:

(a)   *'governing functions':* directors, non-executive directors and the chief executive;

(b)   *'required functions':* the 'Apportionment and Oversight Function', the 'Compliance Oversight Function' and the 'Money Laundering Reporting Officer';

(c)   *'systems and controls functions':* heads of finance, risk control and internal audit; and

(d)   *'significant management functions':* heads of product lines such as research, sales and trading; of operational functions such as settlement, custody, information technology and financial control; and heads of business operations such as retail banking, corporate lending, credit cards, proprietary trading.

The 'Apportionment and Oversight Function' is thus an essential function and many of the individuals to whom responsibilities are apportioned will fall into the other categories.

1   FSMA 2000, s 59(5).
2   SUP 10.4.

14.26   As an approved person, the senior manager must comply with the Statements of Principle for Approved Persons and the supporting Code of Practice.[1] The Code sets out specific examples of behaviour drawn from regulatory experience that will breach the Principles and specifies factors to be taken into account.

Whilst all approved persons must comply with the first four principles, individuals registered to perform a 'significant influence' function must also comply with the senior manager principles set out below:

(a)   Under Principle 5, 'an approved person performing a significant influence function must take reasonable steps to ensure that the business of the firm for which he is responsible in his controlled function is organised so that it can be controlled effectively'.

(b)   Under Principle 6, 'an approved person performing a significant influence function must exercise due skill, care and diligence in managing the business of the firm for which he is responsible in his controlled function'.

(c)   Under Principle 7, 'an approved person performing a significant influence function must take reasonable steps to ensure that the business of the firm for which he is responsible in his controlled function complies with the regulatory requirements imposed on that business'.

1   FSA Handbook of Rules and Guidance: 'Statements of Principle and Code of Practice for Approved Persons'. See Chapter 5 above for a discussion of the obligations under the Statements of Principle and the Code of Practice.

How can the senior manager comply?

14.27   The responsibilities of the senior manager under the FSA's new regulatory regime must not be viewed in isolation. The FSA Handbook's many rules, guidance and evidential provisions are interwoven. As we have seen, the registered senior manager works for an authorised firm subject to its own Principles and other regulatory obligations including training and competence requirements. Moreover, the FSA's regulatory obligations themselves do not, of course, operate in a vacuum. UK-incorporated companies listed on the London Stock Exchange, for instance, are subject to the Combined Code developed by the Committee on Corporate Governance, whose internal control provisions are amplified in the Guidance for Directors issued by the Institute of Chartered Accountants in England and Wales. Credit will be given by the FSA for following the Code and the related guidance.

How do the regulatory obligations relate to corporate governance principles and the collective responsibility of the board? The FSA maintains that its regulatory arrangements for senior management are consistent with the collective responsibility of boards of directors, in the sense of a collegiate approach on the part of the board to strategy and decision-making. However, the FSA's requirements can be addressed only to the authorised person or to individual approved persons; the FSA has no power to make rules binding on a board as a body. The idea of guilt by association has no place in FSA's regulatory arrangements: an individual member of a board cannot have any disciplinary liability in the absence of a culpable act or omission of his own. When the board does get things wrong, it will be the authorised firm that will be accountable. The director himself has statutory duties under the Companies Acts and many other pieces of legislation. The company and its employees can be called to account by Parliamentary Select Committees and both can incur liability under the civil and criminal law.

14.28   In the event of a regulatory failing, the FSA will not automatically seek to hold an individual liable. It is the liability of the authorised firm that will be considered in the first instance. If it does consider the potential liability of a senior manager, the FSA will take account of the size and complexity of the business for which the individual was responsible; his role and responsibility, the knowledge that he had or should have had, and whether he has taken reasonable care. Although this is not a strict liability regime, senior individuals will be judged by an appropriately high standard.[1] As we have seen, the firm's apportionment of responsibilities to its senior people drives their regulatory accountability as individuals. The personal regulatory obligations of non-executive directors will reflect their non-executive status.[2] Provided that non-executive directors take due care in their roles, they will not be held liable for failings of either the firm or its executive directors. No doubt many senior managers will nonetheless be checking their insurance cover.

1   SFA Board Notice 592 Disciplinary Action (July 2001): Sir Michael Richardson.
2   CP 35 – 'executive summary'.

14.29   Just as the FSA assesses the risks to its regulatory objectives, so senior management must assess the risks faced by the bank. What could sink the bank? Where are the icebergs? How effectively are its risks being managed? The FSA has stressed that the new regime complements best business practice. Complying with high-level standards is, though, much more demanding than ticking off detailed rule requirements. Mechanical compliance is not now an option, as senior management must exercise judgment to ensure compliance. It is imperative that management is proactively involved in fashioning a compliance culture rather than simply reacting to compliance failings as they happen. It is crucial that the firm both establishes and maintains appropriate systems and procedures that are accepted as part of how the bank conducts its business from day to day. It is important to maintain effective ongoing supervision and monitoring programmes.

Compliance responsibilities should therefore be written into the senior manager's job description. Manuals and training must clarify the range of his responsibilities. The senior manager must appreciate his responsibilities and understand that complying with regulatory obligations cannot simply be left to the compliance officer.

The compliance function

14.30   The Board and the chief executive may, of course, delegate compliance functions to other executives of the bank. In this respect compliance is no different from any other aspect of the management of a bank's business. The invariable practice of British banks and other sizeable financial services institutions is to appoint a senior person to manage regulatory affairs. Indeed, the FSA requires a firm which carries on designated investment business to allocate to a director or senior manager the function of having responsibility for oversight of the firm's compliance and of reporting to the governing body in respect of that responsibility.[1]

Any temptation, however, to suppose that a bank has fulfilled its regulatory obligations by making such an appointment, and that the appointee alone is responsible if anything goes wrong, must be resisted. The appointee is not a guarantor of the firm's compliance. The Board and senior management have continuous overall responsibility. The purpose of the compliance function is to assist them to discharge it, as part of the process of regulatory and reputational risk management. They are responsible for the adequacy of the resources of the compliance function.

1   SYSC 3.2.8R

Reporting lines and access to top management

14.31   The head of the compliance department should not merely have access to senior management. As is required by SYSC 3.2.8R, he should be a director or member of senior management. This is reinforced by his status as an 'Approved Person'. Seniority is essential both to mark the bank's commitment to compliance with its regulatory obligations and to give him and his department the authority within the bank to enable them to discharge their often difficult duties effectively. It is also an important factor in ensuring that the compliance department is promptly and fully informed of developments in the business. The form and substance of the senior compliance officer's position in his firm are plainly of significant interest to FSA in its assessment of the firm's fitness and properness to conduct investment business. Without genuinely holding a position in senior management, it is hard to see how he could provide the regulators with the assurance of his firm's compliance which they require.

14.32   Within his own firm the senior compliance officer must have, and be clearly seen to have, the full support of the Board and chief executive. However constructive his approach, he will sometimes be obliged to take unpopular action. He may have to insist on the introduction and observance of burdensome procedures. He may have to halt or significantly modify profitable projects or transactions; or insist on changes to an advertising programme. He may have to take the customer's side in a disputed complaint. Without established authority, he cannot hope to succeed. The support of the Board and the chief executive is all the more important in view of the demands which are placed on the compliance officer's judgment. That judgment must be seen to have the full weight of the institution behind it.

14.33   The compliance officer's authority must extend to every nook and cranny of the bank. Staff involved with compliance must have access, in carrying out their duties, to all business units and to all records, paperwork and meetings, however confidential. This right of unrestricted access is of the essence of the compliance officer's role as an active and interventionist adviser and monitor of the bank's compliance. It is the compliance officer who should determine whether his sight of a document or presence at a meeting is or may be relevant to the performance of his duties. He should not be excluded on the basis that someone else, however senior, judges the matter at issue to be unaffected by considerations of compliance.

14.34   In a comparatively compact organisation, for example a typical investment bank, the senior compliance officer should report directly to the chief executive. In a very large institution, for example a clearing bank, this may not be practicable. Even there, however, the reporting line between the chief executive and the senior compliance officer should be short. Typically, the compliance officer might report to the executive director responsible for administration, or perhaps to the company secretary or General Counsel. It is hard to envisage any circumstances, in which it would be appropriate for the compliance officer to report to an individual directly engaged in day-to-day banking operations or investment services. Were he to do so, his independence would be compromised. He must, so far as practicable, be independent of those directly involved in regulated activity.

14.35   Whatever the reporting line, it is essential that the senior compliance officer has free and direct access to the chief executive and to the Board. From time to time there will be issues so important and pressing that a routine reporting line must be bypassed. This right of direct access may need to be exercised only sparingly, but its existence should be clearly established. Only in an extreme case would the compliance officer need to go directly to the Board; but if he were to consider that his chief executive was acting, or proposing to act, unlawfully or improperly, and could not otherwise be restrained, it would be his duty to do so. In such circumstances members of the bank's Audit Committee, normally non-executive directors, would be an appropriate first point of contact.

14.36   Apart from reporting lines and rights of access, it is essential that the firm's top management and the Board are fully informed of the compliance department's plans, of the principal issues affecting compliance and of any significant breach of regulatory requirements.

The best practice is that, in addition to any *ad hoc* reports required by particular events, the senior compliance officer should make regular reports on compliance affairs to the senior management group (however it is constituted) and to the Board. Every three or six months are suitable periods. Where there is an Audit Committee of the Board, that is normally the most appropriate means through which to keep the Board informed. The Audit Committees of most banks contain non-executive directors experienced in regulatory matters and in corporate governance. The Audit Committee's terms of reference should expressly empower it to review compliance arrangements. The senior compliance officer should present his report in person and be questioned on it by the members of the Committee. The periodic reports should cover the main events of the period under review, including, for example, regulatory inspections, material breaches, significant initiatives taken by the compliance department (for example, in relation to training or monitoring) and key regulatory changes and issues. The Audit Committee should be given an opportunity to examine the compliance department's plans, objectives and resources for each coming year.

In addition to the regular periodic reports, the senior compliance officer should present to the Audit Committee *ad hoc* reports on specific topics or events of major importance. The Audit Committee should approve the senior compliance officer's reporting and communication lines and his terms of reference, and periodically review their operation. For his part, the compliance officer should find the independence, wisdom and experience of the members of the Audit Committee a valuable source of advice and support. It is desirable that from time to time he should meet members of the Audit Committee informally, outside the structure of Audit Committee meetings, in order to exchange thoughts and information.

ORGANISATION OF A BANK'S COMPLIANCE FUNCTION

The function's origins

14.37   Until the mid-1980s compliance officers were almost unknown in British banks and financial services institutions. For many years they had been a familiar presence in the US; indeed, the term 'compliance officer' is of American origin. But until the advent of the Financial Services Act 1986 very few British bankers acknowledged any role for a compliance officer in their organisations. Now, however, compliance officers are firmly rooted in British banking and financial services. Their contribution to the proper management of banking and financial services businesses is fully accepted. Crucially, as paras 14.1–14.10 above describe, they are seen by the FSA as central in the system of regulation established by the FSMA 2000. A vigorous and authoritative compliance function is a critical factor in establishing that a bank is fit and proper to conduct regulated business.

14.38   It was the Financial Services Act 1986 which brought about the creation of most British banks' compliance departments. The heads of those departments had the task of establishing a new function from scratch, in organisations whose understanding and expectations of their role varied widely. Some precedent could be drawn from established American compliance departments; indeed, some of the new wave of British compliance officers spent time undergoing training in the US. For the most part, however, compliance officers and their employers were engaged in what was to them a wholly novel exercise.

The emergence of both formal and informal discussion groups for compliance officers facilitated exchanges of views and experience between banks, but even today there is no uniformity in the way in which banks' compliance departments are organised. Differences of approach are inevitable. They reflect various factors, notably the different internal structures of the individual banks, the range, mix and geographical spread of their businesses, and the type of work on which the department concentrates. There is no single 'right way' to organise a compliance function. Each bank has its own requirements. What follow are general guidelines, which should be adapted to particular circumstances.

Structure

14.39   In most banks the main features of the organisation of the compliance function are:

(1)   a central department, led by the senior compliance officer; and
(2)   individual compliance departments or officers in particular business units or subsidiaries, whether in the UK or overseas.

In the smaller firms this structure may be too elaborate; a single department may be able to discharge all aspects of the compliance function. But, in the great majority of banks and other major financial institutions, a single, monolithic department is unlikely to be close enough to day-to-day events in the various units. It will tend to lack knowledge of the fine details and nuances of the businesses and, however good its lines of communication, cannot intervene or respond as quickly as a compliance officer in the business unit. It is likely to become overburdened and bureaucratic. On the other hand, individual compliance officers scattered around business units and subsidiaries are not in a position to decide the bank's policies and standards on compliance issues, although, of course, their views are a valuable contribution. That should be done at the centre. For example, the central department should give guidelines to the local compliance officers on the degree of flexibility which they should adopt under the three-tier rule structure.

14.40   One of the more difficult aspects of structuring a compliance function is ensuring satisfactory coverage of small branches, particularly those in remote locations. For example, a bank's presence in a country may consist of just one or two branches of modest size. If an international bank has a single branch in, say, Bangladesh, Venezuela or Nigeria, with perhaps only a dozen or so employees, there is unlikely to be sufficient regulatory risk or volume of work to justify the appointment of a full-time compliance officer. Yet hardly ever is the regulatory risk so minute that it can be ignored.

There are several ways in which this dilemma can be addressed. One is to allocate compliance responsibilities to a local executive whose existing role is broadly compatible, for example a legal adviser or the senior person engaged in operational support services. This sometimes works well, but the danger is that the individual designated as the compliance officer does not, perhaps is unable to, give adequate time to these new duties, and the appointment in practice is a token one. There is a particular risk that he will at best merely react to compliance issues as they arise and will not think creatively or take initiatives to prevent problems arising. If a part-time appointment is to be successful, clear commitments must be secured from local management to ensure that sufficient priority is given to compliance work. Another approach is to appoint a full-time compliance officer to cover two or more adjacent countries. This regional approach can be very effective, if care is taken not to create too large a geographical area of responsibility; otherwise the compliance officer's efforts may be too thinly spread. Outsourcing compliance work to, for example, a local law firm is also sometimes tried. While valuable advice is of course often obtained from such a source, the loss of immediate contact with the branch's employees is a severe handicap. In practice, outsourcing of this sort rarely does more than mitigate the lack of a compliance officer and does not provide an adequate substitute for one.

14.41   The main tasks of the central department are to develop and communicate compliance policy and standards for the bank as a whole, to monitor the arrangements for ensuring compliance in individual business units and subsidiaries, to support individual compliance departments and officers and their managements with advice and information, and to advise and act in projects and transactions substantial enough to be of significance to the group as a whole. The central department should ensure that individual compliance officers operate to common standards and with a cohesive methodology, subject to any specific local variations that it accepts are appropriate. This will often involve training as well as supervision. These are major responsibilities; but, if there is an adequate network of local compliance officers in the business units and subsidiaries, the number of staff required to discharge them need not be large. Indeed, the bigger the central department becomes, the less likely it is to stick to its core tasks and more likely to duplicate unnecessarily the work of local compliance officers. Precise numbers of personnel are for individual banks to determine. A single figure complement at the centre is, however, feasible even in many large and complex banking and financial services groups.

14.42   Local compliance officers should concentrate on the day-to-day problems and issues which arise in their units, following the policies and standards established by the central department. Whether the local compliance officers should report directly to the senior group compliance officer, as their manager, or to the chief executives of their own business units or should have a dual reporting line is a matter for individual banks to decide, in the light of their overall management structures. In most cases there is a reporting line to the group compliance officer. There is, however, merit in there being also a reporting line to the business unit heads; this emphasises their prime responsibility for their units' own compliance. In any event there must be a strong line of communication between local compliance officers and the central department, fully used on both sides.

The central department should also ensure that the local compliance officers' terms of reference and powers are sufficiently clear and strong to enable them to operate effectively and in accordance with the group's standards for compliance officers. No local compliance officer should be employed or dismissed without the approval of the group compliance officer. There should be close consultation between the group compliance officer and the local chief executive or business head on local compliance officers' annual appraisals, remuneration and other employment-related issues.

14.43 The quality of communication between the central compliance department and the local compliance officers is in any case crucial, whatever reporting lines are adopted. It is a useful discipline to hold regular (at least monthly) meetings between the central compliance department and the head of each local compliance unit; and in addition there should be frequent written and oral communications on specific matters. A periodic, perhaps annual, conference of all the group's compliance officers gives a valuable opportunity to share ideas and experiences and to ensure uniformity of approach to common issues. To avoid misunderstanding of roles, the respective responsibilities and tasks of the central compliance department and local compliance units should be agreed in writing with the Board and the heads of the business units or subsidiaries concerned. The central department should regularly review the effectiveness of these arrangements and of the local compliance units' performances. Such a review programme should include visits to each location, however remote. It is essential to observe a local compliance officer in action, and to talk directly to local managers and staff of all levels of seniority in order to assess their awareness of compliance-related issues.

Skills and experience

14.44 In assembling a central compliance team, the aim should be to produce a mixture of talents and experience suitable for the needs of the businesses concerned. A blend of legal and practical experience is usually desirable. Senior and other compliance officers in banks and financial institutions located in the UK come from a variety of backgrounds. Some are lawyers, some are former practitioners, and others have a background in auditing or regulation. All of these strands of expertise and experience are valuable. Since much of the subject matter of compliance is to be found in, or is derived from, statute, a lawyer is an essential member of the team. Without one, the team would be ill-equipped to deal with the FSMA 2000, the rules and regulations made under it and other applicable legislation. There is not always time to consult outside lawyers. Equally, understanding of the practicalities of the businesses is crucial. This is best provided by one or more individuals with relevant experience as practitioners. It is also helpful to have a member of the team who has worked for, a regulator, either as an employee or a secondee. Indeed, there is a distinct trend for younger compliance officers to gain two or three years' experience with a regulator and then to move to a compliance department in a bank or financial services firm.

14.45 In an individual business unit or subsidiary, a similar mix of skills and experience is obviously desirable, although in some smaller operations not always attainable. If there is a strong legal element in the central team, it may not always be necessary to replicate it at business unit level where compliance officers with a business or regulatory background will often be more effective. In any event, the central department should ensure that local compliance officers have sufficient skills and resources, and that they (and members of the central department themselves) follow an appropriate programme of continuing education so that they stay abreast of regulatory changes and other current issues.

14.46 Whatever a compliance officer's formal qualifications, he must be able to deploy a wide range of personal qualities and skills. Obviously the technical ability to understand the rules and their application to his bank's business is essential; but it is not enough. Strong communication skills are vital. The compliance officer must be able to communicate the regulatory requirements clearly and attractively to an audience whose attention may not always be rapt. A practical commercial sense is also important. The task is to turn the text of rules and regulations into practical effect in the almost infinitely variable circumstances of daily life in the business of banking and financial services. Above all, the compliance officer must display natural authority and integrity. He must be accepted within his bank and by the regulators as an independent and authoritative figure, whose advice and decisions are respected for not only their technical soundness but also their objectivity and freedom from extraneous influences. This authority is all the more important in view of the demands which the FSA's Principles and the concept of market abuse are making on the compliance officer's judgment.

PRINCIPAL ACTIVITIES OF THE COMPLIANCE DEPARTMENT

General: regulatory and reputational risk management

14.47 A compliance department should provide an active, interventionist advisory and monitoring service. We use the word 'service', since the department's objective should be to support the bank's businesses by enabling them to be conducted lawfully and with integrity. The service comprises a number of activities, the balance between which will vary according to the needs and circumstances of the bank. The main activities are listed below, although the list is not necessarily exhaustive.

The sum of these activities is a process of risk management: management of the bank's regulatory and reputational risk. Bankers are familiar with the concept of credit risk management, embodied in the policies and arrangements which the bank has in place to ensure that its credit risks are properly controlled. The concept of regulatory and reputational risk management is essentially similar: the development of policies and arrangements designed to control the risk of damage to the bank's regulatory status and to its reputation for lawful conduct and integrity. A bank's good standing with its regulators and its reputation are amongst its most precious assets. Damage to them can undermine a bank at least as much as a defective credit policy. No compliance officer can guarantee that his bank will never commit a regulatory breach or suffer a setback to its reputation. But his activities should materially reduce the risk of such an occurrence, and ensure that any mishap is appropriately handled. Critical to the successful performance of all these activities is a clear understanding by members of the compliance department of the complexities and dynamics of the bank's businesses. Unless the compliance officer really understands the business, he cannot be fully effective; he is likely to find himself firefighting after compliance errors have been made, instead of being in tune with the practitioners and so able to anticipate and forestall any such errors.

Education

14.48 Senior management are responsible for ensuring that staff are fully aware of compliance requirements.[1] A compliance officer's first task, therefore, is to ensure that the relevant legal and regulatory requirements and in-house policies are clearly communicated to the managers and members of staff who may be affected by them. This is obviously not achieved by simply giving them copies of the FSA's Handbook and leaving them to struggle forward on their own. The compliance officer must identify those aspects of the rules which are or may be relevant to each business and see that they are explained to management and staff in language as straightforward and attractive as possible.

Most compliance officers use a variety of methods to achieve this. The formal compliance manual is one, but its main value tends to be as a point of reference rather than as a means of first instance education. A good compliance manual will expound the principles and core policies, and set out the procedures which the bank requires to be followed. It is essential to keep it up-to-date. This is more easily done if the manual is maintained and distributed electronically rather than in a paper version.

It is, however, not enough just to issue a manual. Most members of staff will also need direct, personal instruction. Most banks now conduct full training courses in compliance matters for their staff. Talks and workshops are invaluable; and more sophisticated training techniques, including the use of video programmes and interactive computer based training packages are now frequently seen. Electronic mail and internal Internet (or intranet) sites are increasingly used. Regulators' own workshops and seminars are usually well received; so far they have concentrated on particular topics and have not aimed to be comprehensive. External training courses can also be valuable, although they may in some cases suffer from a lack of direct connection with the bank's particular business unless the bank works with the training company to produce material specifically tailored to the bank's needs.

1   Principle 7 for Approved Persons.

14.49 Effective compliance education should embrace not only matters of detail, but also the principles and rationale of the regulatory requirements, and the critical importance of the bank's reputation. Most managers and other members of staff respond well to the proposition that compliance is not merely a negative process of avoiding regulatory penalties but a positive contribution to the commercial success of the business. A strong reputation for legality and integrity is a strong commercial advantage; just as a weak one is a severe impediment. In recent years there have been enough well-publicised examples of reputational damage in financial services for this to be a convincing message.

14.50 Compliance officers need not themselves design and deliver training courses; although many do, and those who are good communicators are well placed to do so. At the very least, however, they should satisfy themselves that the content and frequency of training given to staff is appropriate. Good training can significantly enhance the standing of the compliance function and fortify the firm's compliance culture. In most banks it is helpful to devise a core syllabus based on the FSA's high level principles and generally applicable topics such as money laundering and insider dealing, which, perhaps with minor additions, may be used for most staff at most levels, and to which additional elements can be added for specialised business units or particular levels of staff. For example, senior managers and approved persons will need specific training in senior management responsibilities and the approved persons regime. Compliance staff require their own training programme. Some coverage of the principles of overseas regulation may be necessary in international companies.

A key part of any training programme is the induction process for new recruits when joining the bank. Working with the personnel department, the compliance department must ensure that incoming staff at all levels acquire a clear understanding of the regulatory requirements applicable to them. This is not just a matter of the rules. It is at least as important that new joiners receive an unmistakable statement of the bank's commitment to compliance matters. They will form their impression of the bank's regulatory culture in the first few weeks or even days. One way of giving or at least reinforcing the message is an early meeting with the most senior compliance officer available. If numbers permit, the senior compliance officer may be able to meet all new joiners, at least those in his main location, individually or in small groups to convey the central principles.

14.51 Communicating compliance requirements and policy to staff is, of course, a continuous process. Under the pressures of day-to-day business, business units' awareness of these topics can swiftly deteriorate, unless efforts are made to keep it at a high level. Updating of written material, such as compliance manuals, and refresher sessions are essential tasks. Some formal testing of groups of staff is a valuable check. Multiple-choice computer-based questionnaires are a useful way of doing this. Opportunities to maintain and raise the profile of the compliance department should be sought out. For example, it is useful to secure inclusion of compliance-related items in internal publications, such as the house magazine, and at management conferences.

14.52 Compliance training, as described above, is but one facet of the FSA's requirements relating to training and competence. In all professions, it is recognised that continual training is important in attaining and maintaining competence. It is clearly in the commercial interests of any financial services business that its staff should be competent. Employees should also appreciate the benefits of continuing education in a competitive employment market. Political concerns saw the introduction of a training requirement into the Money Laundering Regulations 1993.[1] In the aftermath of Barings and pension mis-selling, regulators across the financial markets are now focusing upon the competence of staff and senior management.[2]

1   Money Laundering Regulations 1993 (SI 1993/1933).
2   SFA Board Notice 597 Disciplinary Action (August 2001): Paine Webber. Paine Webber was fined for failing 'to organise and control its internal affairs in a responsible manner in that it failed to adequately train and supervise staff' in relation to the money laundering regime.

Ensuring trained and competent staff

14.53 The FSA Handbook 'Training and Competence Sourcebook' rules and guidance 'are less prescriptive on firms and yet maintain proper levels of protection for consumers and markets'.[1] They give rise to a number of questions:

— What are the implications of this new regime for a bank?
— What standards must the firm aspire to?
— Which employees are subject to the rules?
— Which rules apply to business conducted with non-private customers?
— Does the employee have to pass an 'approved examination'?
— When can an employee be regarded as having attained competence?
— What are the firm's responsibilities for maintaining staff competence?
— How can the firm demonstrate compliance?
— How will the FSA exercise its supervisory powers?
— What are the respective and interrelated responsibilities of senior management, Personnel and the Compliance Department?

It is a key role of the compliance officer to ensure that the firm meets the FSA's extensive requirements on training and competence.

1 FSA Policy Statement 60: 'Feedback Statement to Consultation Paper 34 – Training and Competence Sourcebook'.

'The Commitments'

14.54 'The Commitments' are set out in Chapter 1 of the Sourcebook.[1] The Commitments are 'guidance' with respect to the operation of the 'Management and Control Principle' as well as the authorisation and approval criteria. Under the 'Management and Control Principle', the 'Senior Management Arrangements, Systems and Controls' provisions and the 'Principles for Approved Persons', the FSA is imposing responsibilities upon those performing a 'significant influence function' within a firm. Both the firm and such senior managers are responsible for ensuring that staff are, and remain, competent.

1 FSA Handbook of Rules and Guidance: Business Standards – 'Training and Competence' (TC).

14.55 The Commitments[1] set out 'some general, high level, commitments which every firm should make and fulfil'. 'The guidance . . . is addressed to firms wherever their activities may be carried on'[2] covering 'any person associated with a regulated activity carried on by the firm'.[3] It remains to be seen[4] whether the FSA is really intending, for example, to police Indian traders dealing with Indian investors in India, though clearly a bank must consider carefully what training programmes it should provide in its overseas offices. The Commitments provide 'a statement of the underlying purpose' of the 'Rules and Guidance' set out in Chapter 2 of the Sourcebook. Under the Commitments, the firm should 'achieve, maintain and enhance' the competence of its employees including senior management; ensure employees remain competent for the work they do; ensure appropriate supervision; regularly review the competence of employees and should ensure that the level of employee competence is appropriate to the nature of the business. Training on compliance and regulatory requirements is therefore only part of the story.

1 TC 1.
2 TC 1.1.2G.
3 TC 1.1.3G.
4 CP 137 sets out proposed amendments to the scope of TC.

14.56   Guidance the Commitments may be, but to meet their standards a firm will have to maintain a demonstrably effective staff training programme. This will require a competence assessment at the point of recruitment; appropriate job descriptions; a careful ongoing consideration of staff competencies; effective probation and appraisal procedures; the administration and delivery of appropriate training; appropriate supervision, monitoring and controls; the active commitment and participation of line management and the maintenance of appropriate records. Regulated firms will need continually to address a series of issues:

— Is there an established training programme for new staff?
— Is good quality training being provided?
— Does the training help staff to reach a higher standard of performance?
— Is it enough to send staff on external courses?
— Do the trainers understand the business?
— Have explicit standards of performance and job competencies been set for each category of staff?
— Do systems and procedures indicate promptly whether an employee is failing to maintain his competence?

In adhering to the Commitments, the firm will have to take account of 'the level of competence that is appropriate to the nature of the business'[1] and the work carried out by its employees. All this requires a high commitment to training and competence.

1   TC 1.2.1G.

Rules and Guidance

14.57   The Chapter 2 'Rules and Guidance'[1] apply to a 'UK domestic firm in respect of its employees who engage in or oversee [the specified] activities . . . wherever they are carried on'.[2] Again the FSA presumably envisages monitoring competence in respect of business that has little or no connection with the UK. Chapter 2:

> 'applies to an overseas firm in respect of its employees who engage in or oversee [the specified] activities . . . from an establishment maintained by the firm in the United Kingdom'.[3]

The rules and guidance only apply in respect of employees engaged in specified activities such as advising and dealing in securities or derivatives; managing investments; giving investment advice (without dealing) and 'overseeing on a day-to-day basis' the provision of custody services.[4] Do not assume that the competence required of an 'Approved Person' is mirrored in the requirements imposed under the training and competence rules.

The frustrating distinctions between the two regimes appear to be without justification. You can be subject to one regime and but not the other. 'Significant influence function' senior managers must be competent to be approved but they are not subject to the training and competence TC 2 rules. Overseers in the back office are important enough to be subject to the training and competence TC 2 rules but are not so important that they are subject to the competence requirements of the approved persons regime. No doubt regulatory inspection visits will focus on the competence of the back office overseer because he is most likely to fall through your net through not being registered. Surely it would have been simpler and no less effective for the two regimes to have ensured that all approved persons are and remain competent? These distinctions will complicate, for instance, the completion of annual appraisals and the administration of training programmes despite the Commitments being more broadly applicable than the rules. The FSA is proposing to issue a leaflet to employees explaining the new regime. It will be interesting to see what senior management, the traders and the 'overseers of administrative functions' make of the distinctions.

1   TC 2.
2   TC 2.1.2R. For two years from N2, 'the section 43 listed money market institution' will be subject only to the requirements of 'The Commitments' and not the rules. Despite the rearguard action being mounted by the trade associations of the wholesale markets, 'Section 43 employees' can look forward to a future of exams and competency requirements.
3   TC 2.1.2R.
4   TC 2.1.4R.

14.58   The rules[1] focus upon those activities where there is a direct interface between the firm's employee and the consumer. The rules on 'Recruitment and Training' and 'Supervising and Monitoring' only apply in relation to business carried on with or for 'private customers'. The investment bank dealing with non-private customers must comply with the 'Attaining Competence'; 'Approved Examinations'; 'Maintaining Competence'; 'Record Keeping' and 'Transitional' rules.

1   TC 2.

Attaining Competence

14.59   The 'Attaining Competence' rule[1] requires the employee to have been assessed as competent or to be appropriately supervised. Do probation procedures ensure that new staff are properly supervised? Is the supervisor competent? In making the competence assessment, the manager must regard the individual as having the appropriate level of expertise and the individual must also have passed the appropriate 'Approved Examination' within the specified time limit. An exam exemption of sorts is available to the seasoned campaigner.[2]

1   TC 2.4.
2   TC 2.5.5R.

14.60   Guidance[1] on the competence assessments of an employee provides that 'technical knowledge and its application'; 'skills and their application' and 'changes in the market and to products, legislation and regulation' should be taken into account. Guidance also provides that the firm should use 'methods of assessment that are appropriate to the activity and to the employee's role'. Under the rules, the firm 'must make and retain appropriate records to demonstrate compliance'.[2] Records should demonstrate who is responsible for determining whether an employee is competent; whether the employee is aware of his key job responsibilities; what criteria have been applied in assessing competence; and how and when the competency decision was arrived at. Records evidencing the passing of (or exemption from) the examination within the stipulated time limit and the successful completion of a probationary period will have to be maintained.

Assessing an individual as competent will require the careful consideration by management of the individual's knowledge and skills against his job description and his competency framework rather than simply the ticking of a number of boxes. Is this individual competent for this role? It may not be much use recruiting a pensions industry expert as a securities trader.

1 TC 2.4.6G.
2 TC 2.8.

Maintaining Competence

14.61 The 'Maintaining Competence' rule[1] requires that the firm 'must have appropriate arrangements in place to ensure that an employee who has been assessed as competent to engage in . . . an activity maintains competence'. Guidance[2] provides that the firm should maintain systems to monitor an employee's competence and specifies factors to be taken into account in maintaining employee competence. Management again has a key role to play. A competency assessment within the annual appraisal will allow management to review the employee's knowledge and skills against his role and his competency framework. The firm will have to address a number of questions, for example:

— Is an appropriate competency framework with explicit benchmarks being used for this employee?
— How does the employee continue to be competent?
— Has the employee's role changed during the course of the year?
— Have new responsibilities been assumed in a different business line?
— Have new regulations governing the conduct of business been introduced?
— What training does this employee require?

Thankfully there is no requirement that an employee should do a set number of hours' training each year, although the FSA is keeping this under review. For the moment, it is accepted that 'the firm is best able to determine what is required'. One line tucked away in FSA Policy Statement 60 floats the idea of retesting, about which we shall no doubt hear more in the years to come.[3]

1 TC 2.6.
2 TC 2.6.
3 Morgan Stanley Dean Witter was fined US$750,000 by the NYSE in 2000 over employee education failures. Morgan Stanley improperly allowed employees to continue working after they had missed an ethics refresher course. The course has to be taken two years after becoming registered and then every three years (Complinet, 2 October 2000).

Record-keeping

14.62 Under the record-keeping rules,[1] the firm 'must make appropriate records to demonstrate compliance' and keep the relevant records both for the duration of the individual's employment and 'for a minimum period of three years' after the employee leaves the firm. The making and retaining of adequate records is a rule requirement under the 'Senior Management Arrangements, Systems and Controls' provisions[2] and records will be evidence during an FSA supervision visit that the regulatory requirements have been met.

1 TC 2.8.
2 SYSC 3.2.20R.

Supervising training and competence

14.63 One of the banking and financial services industry's main concerns is whether the FSA will adopt a consistent approach in supervising the new regime, particularly given its significant enforcement powers. Will an unstated and evolving benchmark be imposed upon firms? The regulator will be training its own supervisory staff to ensure consistency. The FSA will provide industry support through helplines, workshops and it has produced 'a generic toolkit template'[1] for trade bodies and institutes to develop to meet the needs of the various market sectors.

1 Available through the FSA website under 'industry training': www.fsa.gov.uk.

14.64 Training and competence requirements are an important element of senior management responsibilities under the UK's new regulatory regime. The regulator has set out the required staff competence 'outputs' but left the means of achieving those outputs to the firm. In keeping with its risk-based, and thus less prescriptive, approach, the FSA accepts that firms will 'make their own arrangements' in achieving its standards. The regulator will not though allow any flexibility in the standards that firms must achieve. 'The approach demands careful thought and mature judgement, by individuals, firms and regulators – there is no refuge for those expecting to get by through mechanical compliance.'[1] The FSA has set out its goal of industry competence; now the firm must ensure that the ball regularly hits the back of the net.

1 FSA Consultation Paper 34: 'Training and Competence'.

Advice

14.65 A prime activity is advising management and staff on regulatory matters. This will cover advice on individual transactions and projects, and broader issues of policy and principle. Advisory work is not just a matter of responding to requests for advice, important though it is that that be done accurately and promptly. The compliance department should actively seek out problems and issues, and proffer unsolicited advice. Much of the value of an expert in-house advisory function is its ability to anticipate difficulties and trends in relation to the idiosyncrasies of the bank's business. So far as possible, without compromise of the bank's commitment to adherence to the rules, advice should be constructive. The object should be to find appropriate solutions to difficulties and not, unless it is unavoidable, simply to produce bald prohibitions. However, the compliance officer must insist that the applicable laws and regulations and the bank's standards are fully observed, in spirit as well as in the letter. A 'solution' which contravenes that principle is not a solution at all. Blandishments from bankers along the lines that a breach should be tolerated because 'everyone else is doing it' or because of 'market practice' must be firmly rejected. 'Market practice' is too often a euphemism for sharp practice.

Procedures

14.66 The compliance department is responsible for ensuring that there are in place well-defined procedures to enable staff to comply with relevant regulatory requirements. The more that such procedures can be integrated with the bank's existing systems the easier they are for staff to follow and, therefore, the more effective they prove to be. The procedures must extend to the maintenance of adequate written records to enable a regulator or internal or external auditor to see that the rules have been observed; in other words, the creation of an audit trail. External auditors, in discharging their own obligations, will seek to draw comfort from the work of internal compliance and audit departments, but they cannot do so unless there is a clear audit trail for them to follow. In this connection it is easy for a busy compliance department to overlook the need to keep reasonable records of its advisory work. During a typical day members of the compliance team will give numerous pieces of advice on a range of issues. It is unrealistic to expect every such item to be recorded – otherwise compliance officers will spend too much time on record-keeping and not enough on substantive compliance work. But if nothing is recorded, the result will be dissatisfied regulators and auditors and over time a loss of knowledge and consistency within the department. A balance needs to be struck, with trivial or truly ephemeral issues excluded and points of difficulty or which are likely to recur included.

In-house rules

14.67   All banks should have internal policies and rules on matters relating to the personal conduct of their staff; for example, in relation to personal transactions in securities and to the receipt of gifts, entertainment and hospitality. These are normally necessary to comply with regulatory require-ments, and in any event are an essential part of the prudent conduct of a financial business. The compliance department should ensure the appropriate-ness of, and will often design and implement, these arrangements. So too with other issues relating to the conduct of business, such as the containment of confidential information and the identification and management of conflicts of interest.

Monitoring

14.68   The compliance officer is not merely a creator of and adviser upon policies and procedures. He must also monitor compliance with them. To some extent, monitoring work may be delegated to the internal audit function; but far from totally.[1] It is rare for internal auditors to visit a branch or business unit with the frequency which is appropriate for the FSA's rules, the subject matter of which is still seen as requiring a specialised system of review. Compliance departments must, therefore, undertake a planned and regular programme of monitoring.

The monitoring programme is best conducted on a continuous rolling basis, rather than as individual set piece reviews. The programme should be underpinned by a risk analysis of the rules to which the bank is subject, that is to say an assessment of the likelihood of a breach occurring and of the probable consequences of such a breach. The higher the risk rating attached to a rule, the more frequent and more extensive will be the monitoring checks attached to it. The risk-based programme will then have a range of checks to be conducted over varying periods, typically some daily and others weekly, monthly, quarterly and even annual.

1   See also para 14.81 below.

14.69   The FSA rightly attaches importance to monitoring programmes. It is important that they be carefully planned and clearly documented. Records of a monitoring programme should cover:

—   the rules covered by the programme;

— the extent to which those conducting the checks can rely on work done by others, for example internal audit, external auditors or local compliance officers in the business unit concerned;
— the tests carried out, including the size of any samples and the sampling techniques used;
— the strengths and weaknesses and other issues identified;
— the remedial action required to be taken;
— management's response.

Working papers should be retained. Visitors from the FSA and external auditors will wish to review them to ensure that they support the conclusions expressed. The compliance department will, of course, conduct follow-up checks to ensure that appropriate remedial actions have indeed been taken. The compliance department should also use the programme as a check upon itself. Errors or weaknesses detected may indicate that the regulatory requirements have not been communicated to staff clearly enough, or that refresher training is required, or that compliance procedures need to be strengthened. It is much better to have an internal programme which throws up such points than to have them identified for the first time by a visiting regulator.

Reporting to regulators

14.70   FSA requires a number of reports and also notification or clearance of specific events. Other than with reports on financial resources, it is usually convenient for the compliance department to make these reports and communications itself, having established internal systems to ensure that it promptly receives the necessary information. Alternatively, arrangements may be made for at least some notifications, for example changes of directors and senior executives, to be given by others, for example the company secretary or the personnel department; in that event the compliance department should satisfy itself that adequate procedures are in place and monitor their observance.

Customers' complaints

14.71   The FSA requires there to be in place procedures for the prompt handling of customers' complaints.[1] The compliance officer is particularly well qualified to adjudicate upon complaints, and it will often be appropriate for the bank's complaints procedure to ensure that complaints not speedily resolved by the business unit are referred to him. The compliance officer's ability to bring an independent mind to the complaint is a valuable asset. At the very least, if the complaints procedure does not establish him as the arbiter, he should ensure that the procedure in place is adequate and monitor its operation.

1   See also Chapters 11 and 19.

Other activities

14.72   The activities described above are those generally regarded as forming the core of the compliance function. There are, however, additional activities which may be undertaken.

14.73   One is the approval of advertising. FSA requires the appointment of an individual within the bank to approve financial services advertisements before issue.[1] The compliance officer, with his knowledge of the advertising rules and his independent approach, is often the best person to do this. Breaches of the advertising rules are highly visible, and competitors are not always slow to point them out to the regulators. The compliance officer's involvement should markedly reduce the risk of embarrassment.

1 See also Chapter 8.

14.74 Another crucial role frequently undertaken by the compliance officer is that of the Money Laundering Reporting Officer, a position required by FSA.[1] The FSA explains that the job of the money laundering officer is to act as the focal point within the firm for the oversight of all activity relating to anti-money laundering. This includes reporting to and liaison with the National Criminal Intelligence Service (NCIS), for example reporting suspicious transactions and resolving whether or not to proceed with particular transactions. Key aspects of the function of the money laundering reporting officer include formulating and monitoring the day-to-day operation of anti-money laundering policies and procedures, ensuring that staff are appropriately trained in relation to them and at least annually providing internal reports to senior management on the firm's compliance with anti-money laundering requirements.[2] In a large organisation it may be necessary for the money laundering reporting officer to delegate some duties to qualified staff while of course retaining responsibility and accountability.

1 FSA Money Laundering Rule 7.1.5. For money laundering generally, see Chapter 10.
2 SYC 3.2.6R.

14.75 Other activities which may be undertaken may include, for example, ensuring compliance with the City Code on Takeovers and Mergers, handling complaints by customers to the Financial Ombudsman Service and monitoring compliance with the Code of Banking Practice. In some cases the compliance officer may be the Data Protection Officer for the purposes of the Data Protection Act 1998.

14.76 It is essential that the allocation of activities and tasks to the compliance department is carefully assessed and controlled. If the firm uses its compliance department as a receptacle into which to deposit a variety of tasks which have no obvious home elsewhere, but which have little or nothing to do with core compliance work, it will end up with a function dangerously lacking in focus and incapable of performing its key obligations to an appropriate standard.

RELATIONSHIP BETWEEN COMPLIANCE AND OTHER CONTROL AND SUPPORT FUNCTIONS

14.77 The compliance department should be seen not in isolation but as one of a number of support and control functions which contribute to the bank's prudent management and regulatory performance. Other areas of the bank which are part of the overall picture normally include operational risk management, credit control, trade control and settlements, information technology, personnel, and, not least, internal audit.

The interaction of, and division of responsibilities between, these functions should be assessed and defined, to ensure that particular topics or areas of work are not being overlooked or left unattended through misplaced assumptions that some other department is addressing them. The compliance department should establish close working relationships with all support and control departments in the bank.

Compliance and internal audit

14.78 All banks have an internal audit or inspection department. In most cases this was established long before the advent of the compliance department, and remains structurally separate from it. This dichotomy reflects fundamental differences in the functions of the internal audit and compliance teams. The differences in the roles of internal auditors and compliance officers are now generally understood and accepted. This was not always so. The first compliance officers had to overcome an assumption in some business units in their firms that they were a new, and perhaps obnoxious, breed of inspector; and it is fair to say that the arrival of separate compliance departments was not received with unqualified enthusiasm by some internal auditors. These adverse perceptions over time have largely evaporated.

14.79 The main activities of a compliance department are more fully described in paras 14.47–14.71 above. The essential difference between a compliance officer on the one hand and an internal auditor on the other, however, is that the compliance officer is primarily an adviser and active participant in transactions and projects, whereas the internal auditor is mainly engaged in retrospective review of adherence to the bank's procedures and controls. The compliance officers should provide an active and interventionist advisory and monitoring service, designed to ensure that developments in the business and specific transactions meet the required standards of legality and integrity. This produces a high degree of direct involvement with business managers and staff on a day-to-day basis. The bank's internal auditors, on the other hand, conduct a programme of periodic reviews normally detached from any particular project or transaction, although, of course, they will be involved in the event of a major breach of procedure or control.

14.80 Furthermore, the subject matter of the compliance officer's work is usually more specialised than that of an internal auditor. Although he should not confine himself to matters arising from the FSMA 2000, the compliance officer's prime concern is with the legality and integrity of the firm's conduct of business, that is to say with the manner in which the firm promotes and transacts business with customers and counterparties and in which it handles confidential information and conflicts of interest. Internal auditors are responsible for reviewing the adequacy of and level of adherence to the entire range of the bank's controls and procedures. This covers many matters which normally fall outside a compliance officer's remit, for example limits on authorities for lending or other transactions, internal security procedures, and standards of accommodation in offices and branches. The compliance officer is, by comparison, a specialist.

14.81 These distinct functions are, if properly conducted, complementary. Together they should provide comprehensive assurance to the bank's regulators, shareholders and customers that the bank's affairs are lawfully and prudently managed. To achieve this, however, it is essential that the compliance and internal audit departments communicate and co-operate. If they see each other as rivals, their effectiveness will be greatly impaired. What should bring them together is a shared commitment to the development and spread of best practice in the bank. Good communications between the compliance and internal audit departments are critically important. In the course of their work, each department will come across material or information of interest to the other; this may be from external or internal sources. It is usually helpful for the senior inspector and compliance officer to meet regularly; but, in addition to fixed meetings of that sort, there should be frequent contact at all levels. The importance of communication can be reinforced at Board level, if the senior inspector's and compliance officer's periodic reports (to the full Board or the Audit Committee as the case may be) are taken at the same meeting. This enables the Board or Audit Committee to see a full picture of the effectiveness of the bank's controls and regulatory arrangements. It is desirable to record the respective roles of the compliance and internal audit departments in a document agreed with the bank's top management and approved by the Audit Committee.

14.82   The point at which the functions of the compliance and internal audit departments come closest to overlapping is the monitoring of compliance with the FSA's rules. Although most compliance officers rightly emphasise the advisory and training aspects of their work, monitoring business units' observance of the rules is an important element – not least in the eyes of the FSA.[1] Here the compliance officer may look like an internal auditor; indeed, he may look like a busy one, since he will normally need to check a unit's compliance more frequently than an internal auditor will visit in the course of a typical bank's inspection plan and, as described in para 14.68, may be conducting a rolling monitoring programme. In some banks it may be possible for the compliance officer to delegate a portion of his monitoring work to the internal auditors. Usually it is not feasible to do this completely. The internal audit departments in particular rarely have the resources to be able to visit affected branches and units with sufficient frequency. Nevertheless, compliance monitoring will be strengthened if regulatory rules are covered in internal audit programmes. Whenever there is an audit of a branch or business unit, it should encompass compliance matters as much as any other aspect of management. If the internal auditors are to make an effective contribution to compliance monitoring, they must be trained in at least the basic elements of the FSMA 2000 and the FSA Handbook. Some aspects of the rules can readily be assimilated into audit programmes: for example, the use of customer agreements and risk warnings, timely execution of orders, priority of customers' orders, records of transactions, and the issue of contract notes. It is good practice for auditors to discuss a forthcoming audit with the compliance officers and to maintain contact as the audit progresses. Both compliance and audit reports should be freely exchanged, even if an audit report has not raised any exceptions in relation to compliance matters or vice versa.

1   See also para 14.67 above.

14.83   In view of the internal audit department's overall responsibility for the bank's procedures and controls, there is no reason why it should not audit the compliance function both centrally and in the business units. Indeed, it would be remiss if it were to fail to do so. That is not to imply that audit is the senior function. It is not; but its responsibility extends over the entire operations of the bank, of which the compliance function is a part. The effectiveness of such an audit depends, of course, on the extent to which the auditors understand the compliance function. Provided an adequate level of understanding exists, an audit would usefully cover the terms of reference and resources of the compliance officers and the effectiveness with which they discharge their key tasks, described in paras 14.47–14.71 above.

Compliance and the personnel departments

14.84   In recent years there has been increasing interaction between compliance and personnel departments. This trend is likely to continue in consequence of the greater regulatory focus on individuals as Approved Persons and on staff training. The FSMA 2000 regime will require compliance and personnel to work closer together than ever before. Two important areas under the new regulatory regime are: (i) the focus on staff competence and (ii) the registration of approved persons.

Whilst previous regulators had competency rules that were enforced with varying degrees of enthusiasm, the FSA has made it clear that training and competence is now a priority. Compliance with the individual registration requirements remains as important as ever. These two regulatory strands are closely (though imperfectly) tied together. From the moment the bank is minded to employ an individual, the regulatory obligations will bite. In conducting interviews, management and Personnel must focus upon competency issues (Is this individual competent to perform this role? Will the individual need to pass an exam? Does the individual need training?). Offer letters must be clear about the individual's regulatory obligations. The manager must appropriately supervise the employee pending his competency sign off (For what, if any, controlled function must the individual be registered? Is the individual aware that passing an exam does not constitute registration? Is the individual 'fit and proper' to be registered? Has Personnel taken appropriate references?). Once registered, the bank will have its own probation period to police. Having attained competence, the employee must then maintain that competence to safeguard his registration.

Details of the training and competence regime are set out at paras 14.54 to 14.64 above; the individual registration requirements are covered in Chapter 5.

Relationships with regulators and external auditors

Regulators

14.85   One of the most important tasks of a bank's compliance department is to ensure the health of the bank's relationship with its regulators: in relation to the FSMA 2000, with FSA. In the UK, the opportunities to develop a strong relationship should be greater than in a more overtly authoritarian regulatory environment, such as that of securities and investments business in the US. That is not to say that a bank should seek, or FSA would grant, a favoured or privileged position. But the bank should aim to establish a constructive relationship, based on clear communication and mutual understanding of the bank's and the regulator's objectives. This, of course, requires a positive response by the regulators. They must reciprocate. They cannot expect co-operation from banks and other providers of financial services unless they are themselves constructive and open.

On the whole, British regulators have so far achieved a reasonable balance in their relationships with those they regulate. It would, however, be unfortunate if the FSA's enforcement powers and the sharper tone of inspection visits in recent years were to betoken a contrary trend.[1] The confrontational approach which exists in some other countries – that of the Securities and Exchange Commission in the US might be regarded as an example – would be counter-productive.

1 For further material on disciplinary policy and fines, see Chapter 20 below.

14.86 The regulators' expectations of their members are summarised in FSA's Principles, which declare:

'A firm should deal with its regulator in an open and co-operative manner and keep the regulator promptly informed of anything concerning the firm which might reasonably be expected of it.'[1]

This is an unexceptionable statement, but it leaves at large precisely what are the matters of which the regulator would reasonably expect to be informed. The safe course for a regulated firm is to err on the side of giving too much information rather than too little, relying on the regulator to indicate if it is being burdened with unnecessary communications. However, if there is a sound relationship between a member and its regulator, that should lead to a mutual understanding of what is material information and what is not. The information given to the regulator should not be restricted to matters arising from the regulatory legislation or the FSA's rules. Other matters may be relevant to the regulator's continuous assessment of the member's general fitness and properness to conduct banking and investment business.

1 Principle 10.

14.87 The FSA's Handbook requires prior clearance or subsequent notification of various specified events, and the submission of various reports. Communication with the FSA should not, however, be confined to these mandatory items. There should be more frequent contact, through meetings, correspondence and telephone conversations. It is important, from both parties' points of view, that the FSA should be fully aware of developments or changes in its member's business. This can be achieved only by open communication. All compliance departments from time to time will wish to approach the FSA for clearance or guidance on a difficult point of construction or practice. This is itself an important element of the process of communication, and the more the regulator already knows of the member's business and circumstances, the easier it is to give a constructive response to the query. Without a good knowledge of the member's business the regulator may have difficulty in assessing the appropriate degree of flexibility under the rules and in particular the effect of FSA's Principles in specific situations.

14.88 Opportunities to develop the relationship with the regulators may occur in a variety of ways. For example, it may be possible to second staff to a regulator for short periods or to take in a member of a regulator's own staff for a short-term secondment for training and experience. A member of the compliance department may be able to sit on one of the FSAs' committees for rule-making or other policy matters. Attending or contributing to seminars or other training courses conducted or approved by the FSA is inherently valuable, and may also help in building the relationship with the regulator. The FSA also welcomes constructive responses to consultative papers and draft rules issued by them. Banks that are members of the British Bankers Association or the London Investment Banking Association can contribute to their Association's collective discussions with the regulators, but this neither precludes nor should inhibit individual submissions.

14.89   The bank's approach to regulatory visits and inspections is an important factor in the development of the regulatory relationship.[1] The frequency of such visits largely depends upon the regulator's perception of the supervisory complexity and risk attendant upon the firm's operations. Normally a visit or inspection takes place on notice. The length of notice varies from a few days to three or four weeks. Unannounced visits are, of course, within the FSA's powers, but usually occur only if there is a major concern as to the firm's compliance. Whatever the immediate cause of a visit or inspection, the bank's approach should be open and constructive. So far as possible, the bank should view the occasion as an opportunity for guidance on the enhancement of its controls and compliance systems, rather than taking a defensive posture designed to keep the regulators at bay. The FSA has comprehensive powers to compel the production of documents, but normally the bank should make voluntary disclosure. In any event, if the bank has been communicating effectively with the FSA in the preceding months, the inspection should produce few surprises on either side. It does, however, remain to be seen whether banks can continue to sustain this co-operative approach in the face of the regulators' growing emphasis on disciplinary process.

1   For regulatory inspections generally, see Chapter 19.

14.90   The FSA's overall purpose is to satisfy itself of the continued fit and proper status of its members, and reviews may be wide-ranging. Greater emphasis, however, is now being given to concentration on particular topics most likely to produce regulatory concerns. The object is to achieve a sharper focus on problem areas and on the characteristics of the member and its businesses. This should not result in more frequent visits (unless the FSA believes these are necessary), and for some firms visits will become relatively less frequent. However visits will generally focus in greater detail on certain specific issues and follow less of a standard pattern.

The FSA also intends from time to time to concentrate on the same specific issues with a particular segment of its membership, in the form of themed visits. The tone of inspection visits is widely perceived to have become more inquisitorial and detailed over the last few years. The range of topics covered has also widened, progressing beyond Conduct of Business matters into broader issues relating to controls and systems. There is also increasing focus on the role and performance of the compliance department. In this respect it is crucial that the regulators continue to recognise that compliance officers are not guarantors of their firm's compliance. It is all too easy, with the wisdom of hindsight, for a regulator to place unwarranted responsibility on a compliance officer in the event of a breach of rule.

COPING WITH ENFORCEMENT PROCEEDINGS

14.91 It is increasingly likely that at some stage in his career the compliance officer will become embroiled in enforcement proceedings[1] whether as a result of the bank's actions; those of its officers and employees; those of a counterparty or a client, or as a witness. Enforcement proceedings can be protracted and expensive. Badly managed enforcement proceedings can be as damaging to the bank's reputation as any findings in relation to the subject matter of the investigation. Senior management will naturally treat enforcement proceedings as a priority. As a member of senior management, the compliance officer must have the vision to identify the potential ramifications of an investigation.

1 For enforcement proceedings generally, see Chapter 20.

14.92 Despite the advent of a unitary financial services regulator, the compliance officer must still be familiar with the powers of numerous agencies each with its own rules and enforcement powers. Enforcement under the FSMA 2000 must not be viewed in isolation, as those who conduct regulated activities are invariably also subject to the jurisdiction of other regulatory authorities, government departments and law enforcement agencies. A person snared by one strand of the regulatory framework can be fairly certain that the other regulators will be alerted to his activities and that documents and information will pass from one agency to another. A single transaction can consequently give rise to a series of enforcement proceedings. The Stock Exchange may look into the transaction. A person authorised under the FSMA 2000 might find the FSA conducting an investigation. Alternatively the Department of Trade and Industry (DTI) might appoint inspectors to investigate the transaction under its statutory powers. Any report might be referred to the Serious Fraud Office. The National Criminal Intelligence Service may become involved. A police inquiry may be conducted followed by a prosecution in the criminal courts. A House of Commons Select Committee might conduct its own review. Fuelled by information obtained through an investigation, claims might be brought by administrators, liquidators, employees and others leading to litigation in the civil courts. If there is an international element in the matter under investigation, foreign regulators and law enforcement agencies may become involved.

Each investigation would be pursued under different legislation. Each would be pursued by a different agency exercising different powers. Each would be time-consuming and costly. Each would be likely to engender adverse publicity. All could result in significant enforcement measures being taken.

14.93 What can the compliance officer do?

In the first instance, he must know his regulators and ensure that he is familiar with the range of external agencies. As much as possible, the compliance officer should develop meaningful working relationships with those agencies. In an age of risk-based regulation, how he is perceived by the regulator will be important. He should establish procedures to enable the firm to deal effectively with enforcement proceedings.

Together with other members of senior management, he will have to face a range of urgent issues:

— Should an internal inquiry be conducted and, if so, by whom?
— Can the independence of that inquiry be challenged?

— Should any report be disclosed to the regulator?
— Should legal professional privilege be claimed?
— Should disciplinary action be taken against any members of staff?
— Are they being made scapegoats or will they become hostile witnesses?
— What are the powers of any investigator?
— Can the bank be required to provide documents or to give evidence?
— Should the police be notified?

14.94 Great care must be taken with the collation and copying of documents. At all times the compliance officer must ensure that close contact is maintained with the regulator through clear lines of communication. He should make careful notes of any discussions with the regulator.

The bank should form a senior management committee to deal with the investigation, and manage the implications for the bank's day-to-day conduct of business:

— Can the bank rebut adverse press speculation?
— Is the bank's position tenable?
— Should individual members of staff have separate legal representation?

The bank must establish the factual background:

— What happened?
— Who was involved?
— Was the bank at fault?
— To what extent can the compliance officer speak to employees and others about an investigation?
— Can the evidence of witnesses be rehearsed?
— Should the bank stand by its employee?

These are just a few of the issues that the compliance officer will have to consider.

14.95 A financial institution's involvement in enforcement proceedings will be a 'loss limitation' exercise. There is no possibility of being awarded damages or having a costs order made in its favour. If the bank itself is being investigated, it will be almost permanently on the back foot in defending its conduct, monitoring any potential legal liability and trying to safeguard its authorisation to conduct business. In addressing the issues outlined above, the compliance officer can play a major role in helping the bank to come through the crisis. As compliance officer, his colleagues will be relying upon his expertise in this field. As a senior manager, colleagues will be looking to him for leadership. For any employee, enforcement proceedings will be an unusual and worrying experience. For those closely concerned with the matters under investigation, it will be a frightening experience with their careers and possibly their solvency and even liberty, at stake. Any investigating agency is adept at using its authority and the uncertainty of those under investigation to pressure them into answering questions.

The compliance officer can do much to steady the ship. Employees can, for instance, be advised, in answering questions, to remember examination room techniques: listen to the question carefully; ask for the question to be repeated if necessary; answer the question that you have been asked; answer the question simply, directly and confidently; do not waffle; do not use unnecessarily colourful language; whilst you probably have a couple of points that you want to make, you will look weak in introducing them in answer to every question.

Throughout the process all will be seeking the compliance officer's reassurance that the bank will soon be back on an even keel.

External auditors

14.96   Capital adequacy, liquidity and financial reporting are rarely dealt with by banks' compliance officers, except perhaps in relation to non-banking subsidiaries engaged in financial services. Nevertheless, there are still significant points of contact with the auditors. The bank must instruct the auditors to conduct an annual review of and report to the FSA on compliance with the rules on clients' assets.[1]

These are important topics, and the compliance officer must ensure that his bank's systems and procedures are satisfactory to the auditors. More generally, the auditors in their overall scrutiny of the bank's controls are entitled, indeed under a duty, to consider the effectiveness of its compliance policies and procedures. It is, therefore, essential that they understand the aims and methods of the compliance officers.

1   SUP 3.10.

14.97   Compulsory matters apart, most large firms of accountants offer advisory services in relation to the FSA and compliance systems and procedures. Several of them have well-developed units specialising in this function. Undoubtedly, if there is a need to set up a compliance function swiftly and from scratch, they can be extremely helpful. Even an established compliance department may gain value from a review by experienced accountants of its procedures and methods of operation.

Chapter 15

Capital adequacy

INTRODUCTION

15.1 Capital adequacy is one of the core control components within any modern regulatory system although it is of only relatively recent origin.[1] Banking practice has always been concerned with monitoring the financial position of banks. This has historically tended to focus on liquidity requirements which are concerned with monitoring a bank's source of funds rather than its capital position. Concern with the imposition of formal capital adequacy requirements in the UK generally only dates from 1975.[2] Capital controls are a useful regulatory tool although their importance and value must not be overestimated.

1   See paras 15.6–15.10.
2   See para 15.11.

Objective

15.2 The objective of capital adequacy is to provide some level of cover against the risk of default on a bank's loan or other credit facilities. Capital adequacy is then concerned with credit or counterparty default which may affect both the payment of interest during the term of a facility and repayment of principal on maturity. This is clearly of importance as a bank's loan or banking book constitutes the main asset item on its balance sheet. Loans are assets to the extent that they generate income through the interest charged. The source of the funds are shown as liabilities on the balance sheet which will generally either be made up of retail or corporate deposits or inter-bank lending.

Market risk

15.3   The banking book is distinct from the trading book in which banks hold Government Gilts or other transferable securities as well currency or commodity positions. The main risk that arises with regard to securities is market or position risk. This is not concerned with credit default as such but with the rise and fall in the value of the security on any formal exchange or over-the-counter market. Banks holding foreign currency, interest rate or commodity positions must also monitor the changes in their asset values.

These financial related risks can then be distinguished from operational risk and legal risk.[1] Operational risk is concerned with losses arising as a result of inadequate internal decision taking and control procedures which will also include fraud (both internal and external) and more general systems failure. Legal risk is concerned with losses arising as a result of contract unenforceability. This is generally dependent upon documentation validity, capacity or authority and enforceability on bankruptcy or insolvency.[2]

Bank capital adequacy is generally only directly concerned with credit risk although separate requirements have been developed in respect of market risk as well as interest rate and currency risk. Recent proposals at the international level have also been made to include operational risk within modern capital adequacy frameworks.[3]

1   See generally, G Walker, *International Banking Regulation Law, Policy and Practice* (2001), Introduction, notes 11, 12, 14, 15, 16 and 17.
2   See Chapter 16, para 16.5.
3   See paras 15.129–15.136.

Common standards

15.4   Common standards in connection with capital adequacy were first agreed at the international level with the Basel Committee on Banking Supervision's Capital Accord in July 1988. This established a minimum 8% of defined capital as against the risk adjusted value of a bank's loan book. This quickly became the *de facto* global standard for capital control.

The Capital Accord was given effect at the European level through the Own Funds Directive and Solvency Ratio Directive in 1989. These were adopted with the Second Banking Directive to create a minimum common capital regime across European. The Own Funds Directive introduced a common definition of capital (which was generally based on the Basel requirements) with the Solvency Ratio Directive implementing the 8% minimum ratio requirement in Europe.

A separate Capital Adequacy Directive was then adopted in 1993 which introduced further capital requirements in respect of market risk for debt and equity instruments as well as new charges for currency risk and financial derivatives. This operated on the basis of a 'building block approach' which provided for separate charges for each of the main securities related risks to be aggregated to arrive at a total cover figure. This was followed at the international level with the Basel Committee Market Risk Amendment in

January 1996. This generally adopted the European building block approach to which it also added commodity related risks.

All of these provisions were implemented in the UK through Bank of England supervisory papers which were consolidated into its Guide to Banking Supervisory Policy. The Guide was then reissued by the Financial Services Authority (FSA). Most of these provisions have since been restated as rules and guidance in the Interim Prudential Sourcebook for banks (IPRU (BANK)) section of the FSA Handbook of Rules and Guidance.

Scope of the chapter

15.5　The purpose of this chapter is to consider the historical development and nature of modern capital adequacy. The operation of the Basel Committee's original Capital Accord rules are explained and their relative advantage and disadvantage noted. The background to the FSA's Handbook and, in particular, the interim prudential sourcebook for banks is considered. The content of the sourcebook is then examined in further detail. This is mainly concerned with the capital related sections of the sourcebook although the other chapters are referred to. The recent proposals for the replacement of the original 1988 Accord at the international level with a new more sophisticated and extended New Basel Accord are also assessed.

HISTORICAL DEVELOPMENT

15.6　Banking business is generally concerned with the management of deposited funds received from the general public. The deposits made by retail and business customers are pooled and on-lent to borrowers generally through term loans or overdraft facilities which are repayable on demand.

The traditional business of banking then involves both a savings and credit function. This was reflected in the definition of deposit-taking business as set out in the Banking Act 1987[1] and as restated in the new provisions adopted under the Financial Services and Markets Act (FSMA) 2000.[2]

The other main function of a bank is the provision of payment services. This can either be considered to constitute an independent or an ancillary function. Historically, this arose out of the right of the depositor either to require repayment of funds directly or to have them paid to a third party. The obligation of the bank to return the deposited funds would be discharged in either case.

1　See Ross Cranston, *Principles of Banking Law* (2000), Ch 1.
2　FSMA 2000, Sch 2, para 22; and The Financial Services and Markets Act 2000 (Regulated Activities) Order 2001 (SI 2001/544). See Chapter 6, paras 6.11–6.14.

15.7　In discharging these savings and credit functions, banks have to manage the source of funds as against their credit commitments. The risk that arises on the funding or liability side is that depositors may request repayment of funds in excess of the reserve maintained. To cover such demands, banks have traditionally held a reserve of cash or other liquid assets (equal to approximately one-third of their total deposit base). This has historically been referred to as fractional reverse banking.

15.8 On the asset side of the balance sheet, the main risk is credit or counterparty default on loans or credit commitments. Borrowers may not pay interest during term or repay principal on maturity. To the extent that banks hold a large liquid reserve, again few difficulties should arise in this regard as some losses can be easily absorbed. Under standard accounting practices, banks are also generally required to make provisions for known or expected losses.

15.9 With the development of the secondary money markets during the late 1950s and early-1960s, banks were able to borrow significant amounts of money from other banks. The new markets se up at this time included the Local Authority Market, the Certificate of Deposit Market and the Sterling Certificate of Deposit Market, the Corporate Debt Market and the Inter-Bank Market. These grew separately from the traditional primary or Discount House market through which the Bank of England controlled the volume and cost of funds in the UK financial system.

With these new secondary markets and, in particular, the Inter-Bank Market, banks were able to borrow significant new levels of funds on an overnight or short-term basis limited only by their credit standing in the market. The availability of these new sources of funds meant that banks were no longer constrained by their traditional deposit bases. It was for this reason that traditional liquidity practices became of less importance and were replaced by new liability and asset and liability management techniques. Rather than hold large liquid reserves, banks could manage their short-term liquidity and liability commitments directly with the effect that they could hold much less cash or other liquid assets. Banking then became asset (loan) driven rather than liability (deposit) based.

It was following these changes in traditional liquidity management practices that supervisory authorities began to focus on bank capital levels and the creation of new capital adequacy requirements for banks.

15.10 Capital examination began in the US during the 1950s although it was not until 1981 that any express joint guidelines emerged. The New York Federal Reserve District Bank had begun to develop a new reporting framework in 1952 which required banks to assign different risk weights to various asset classes. This was adopted by the Federal Reserve Board in 1956 and refined in 1972.[1]

A separate approach was being considered by the Comptroller of the Currency which was developed into the CAMEL management and financial system.[2] A Joint Policy Statement proposing Adequacy Guidelines was eventually issued by the Federal Reserve Board and the Comptroller in 1981 with a separate Statement of Policy on Capital Adequacy by the Federal Deposit Insurance Corporation (FDIC). The Joint Policy Statement set out a number of complex related ratios. The FDIC proposed a basic 6% ratio of adjusted equity capital to total assets as a minimum figure with a 5% level requiring corrective action.

Following adoption of the International Lending Supervision Act in November 1983 in response to the international debt crisis, the federal banking authorities were mandated to establish common capital standards and to consult with bank regulators in other countries with regard to the development of common international practices in this regard. Proposed uniform capital standards were issued in 1984 and formal guidelines in April 1985.

1   See JJ Norton, *Devising International Bank Supervisory Practices* (1995), Chapter 4.

2   This was used as the basis for the design of the new bank RATE system which was developed by the Bank of England as part of its review of bank supervision conducted after the collapse of Barings Bank in 1995. The new bank RATE was based on a revised CAMEL (Capital, Assets, Market risk, Earnings and Liquidity) and B (Business risk) assessment which was set against the individual bank's COM (Controls, Organisation and Management) capability. See Blair et al (2nd edn), Chapter 4. This is currently being reviewed and incorporated into the FSA's new integrated supervision by risk approach and larger operating framework. See Chapter 6, paras 6.84–6.100.

15.11   In the UK, a Joint Working Party of Scottish and London Clearing Banks considered the development of new capital standards to replace the earlier cash and liquidity ratios in 1975. This was considered as part of the new approach being developed by the Bank of England in response to the Fringe (or Secondary) Banking Crisis in 1972 and 1973.[1] The Bank then began to consider the relationship between capital and reserves and the possible development of new capital related ratios.

With the shift from the provision of credit facilities based on deposit volumes to wholesale market borrowings referred to, the Bank started to look at the possible construction of a new 'free resource' capital ratio (current liabilities to capital resources excluding infrastructure finance and other non-bank assets) and a separate 'risk asset' ratio (the risk of loss inherent in the asset groups of a bank against available capital).

With the enactment of the Banking Act 1979, the Bank of England was required to issue formal licences to banks for the first time taking into account, in particular, their overall financial soundness. The establishment of a formal licensing system had been required under the European First Banking Directive in 1977.

A number of consultative papers were subsequently issued by the Bank in connection with capital adequacy, foreign currency exposure and the regulation of discount market and liquidity adequacy.[2] The Bank's September 1980 consultative paper on the measurement of capital, in particular, proposed the calculation of total of risk adjusted assets by applying a system of risk asset gradations to specific assets within a bank's balance sheet.

1   See generally G Blunden, 'The Supervision of the UK Banking System', BEQB (June 1975), No 2, 190. See also J Revell, *Solvency and Regulation of Banks: Theoretical and Practical Implications* (1975).
2   See Bank of England, 'The Measurement of Capital', 20 BEQB 324; Bank of England, 'Foreign Currency Exposure', 21 BEQB 235; Banking of England, 'Prudential Arrangements for the Discount Market', 22 BEQB 209; and Bank of England, 'The Measurement of Liquidity', 22 BEQB 399. See also the Banking of England, 'The Capital and Liquidity Adequacy of Banks', 15 BEQB (1975).

15.12   At the international level, the Basel Committee on Banking Supervision had become concerned with the significant drop in capital levels of internationally active banks by the early 1980s. The Committee recommended in June 1982 that no further erosion of capital levels should be permitted.[1]

The Committee accepted in 1984 that it would be difficult to establish common constituent elements of capital although it might be possible to develop a system of functional equivalence of measurement to deal with national divergencies.[2] A basic six-tier definition of 'capital' was then produced with a 6% ratio with the assistance of the European Banking Advisory Committee.

1   See Basel Committee, *Report on International Developments in Banking Supervision* (1982), p 7.
2   See Basel Committee, *Report on International Developments in Banking Supervision 1984* (1985), pp 8–15.

15.13   In the light of the difficulties that arose in agreeing common international standards, representatives from the Federal Reserve Board in the US and the Bank of England entered into direct negotiations with a view to trying to produce some common agreement between themselves. It was realised that the two countries were not that far apart and an agreed proposal was produced on primary capital and capital adequacy conditions in January 1987.

The effect of issuing this bilateral Accord between the US and the UK placed significant pressure on the countries involved with the Basel Committee negotiations. Despite criticism of the tactic adopted, the Committee was able to produce a consultative paper on International Convergence of Capital Measurement and Capital Standards within eleven months.[1] After six months of further negotiations, the Committee produced its final Accord in July 1988.[2]

To deal with German and Swiss objections, it had been agreed that the 8% minimum standard would have to include, at least, 4% of fully paid share capital with a further 2% limit being placed on qualifying (five-year) subordinated debt. A short two-year transitional period was agreed although an interim standard of 7.25% was accepted. Further concessions had to be agreed on Japanese compliance.

1   See Basel Committee, *Proposal for International Convergence on Capital Measurement and Capital Standards* (1987).
2   See Basel Committee, *International Convergence of Capital Measurement and Capital Standards* (July 1988).

CAPITAL REGULATION

15.14   The main elements of modern capital regulation are still based on the Basel Committee's 1988 Accord requirements[1] pending the further revisions recently proposed.[2]

The stated objective is to provide a new framework of regulation to strength the soundness and stability of the international banking system and to ensure that the system is fair and generally consistent in its application to banks in different countries at the same time as ensure competitive equality among international banks insofar as possible. These objectives are accordingly stability and competition-based. While the stand-ards agreed have been of considerable assistance in ensuring that credit risk is more effectively managed, the standards have significantly failed in their underlying political objective of creating a level playing field.

One of the main concerns that had arisen was that Japanese banks were able to benefit from significantly lower (almost zero) capital costs which gave them a competitive advantage against the American and European banks. Although common standards were agreed in Basel, the concessions permitted to the Japanese as well as residual differences in other related areas such as loss provisioning and valuations meant that various competitive imbalances persisted.

1   See generally, Walker, *International Banking Regulation Law, Policy and Practice* (2001), Capital Postscript. See also Walker, 'Banks' in *Financial Services Regulation* (Butterworths loose leaf).
2   See paras 15.129–15.136.

15.15   The original Accord established a basic risk-adjusted asset and capital ratio calculation. This required that a total risk-adjusted asset figure be calculated for each bank which is set against its defined capital position.

The risk-adjusted asset figure is calculated by placing each of the loans of the bank into agreed risk categories or buckets (either 0% or 10%, 20%, 50% or

100%).[1] These are set having regard to the general creditworthiness of the borrowers within each category. OECD governments and central banks are, for example, assigned a 0% risk factor. Secured lending is rated at 50% (due to the possibility that the security may not be fully realised) with all other commercial debt being graded at a full 100%.

A risk-adjusted figure within each asset class or risk bucket is calculated by multiplying the total loans outstanding in that category with the applicable risk factors. The total risk-adjusted figure is then the aggregate of each of these separate calculations across all asset classes. By risk adjusting the loan or banking book of the bank, the effect is to remove low (or lower) risk debt and consequently produce a lower total amount of exposed lending against which capital has to be set.

1 See Table 15.1.

15.16 One of the reasons for adopting the risk-adjusted approach developed was that it allowed for off-balance sheet items to be included. Off-balance sheet items are again divided into various asset classes and assigned a conversion factor (either 0%, 20%, 50% or 100%).[1] The assets within each category are again totalled and then multiplied by the relevant conversion factor. This creates an on-balance sheet credit equivalent value.

The credit risk factor applicable to the borrower is then applied and totalled with the other asset figures to create the total (on- and off-balance sheet) risk-adjusted figure for the bank.

Special rules are adopted with regard to options and other derivative contracts which may either be dealt with on a current or original (Japan only) method.[2]

1 See Table 15.2.
2 See Table 15.3.

15.17 The Bank's capital is calculated by totalling all qualifying items available subject to certain restrictions and deductions.[1] Qualifying items may either fall within the tier 1 (primary) or tier 2 (secondary) classification.

Tier 1 capital is principally made up of paid-up share capital (common stock), general reserves and retained profit. Tier 1 must constitute, at least, 50% of the minimum 8% qualifying capital of the bank (that is 4%).

Tier 2 capital includes revaluation reserves, general provisions and subordinated debt as well as certain hybrid capital instruments. To qualify for credit risk cover purposes, the subordinated debt must be, at least, five years in duration. Qualifying capital for market risk purposes may include two-year subordinated debt. While tier 2 can only make up 50% of the total capital amount (4%), the five-year subordinated debt is restricted to 50% of the tier 2 amount (2%).[2] While subordinated debt will generally constitute the single largest item within a bank's balance sheet, this is then restricted to 2% of qualifying capital due to its non-equity nature (essentially related to permanence and ownership).

Goodwill and investments in unconsolidated banking and financial subsidiary companies as well as other banks and financial institutions are deducted from the capital base. National rules may also impose further specific deductions either from tier 1 or total capital.

1 See Table 15.4.
2 See Table 15.4.

Table 15.1: Original risk weights by category of on-balance sheet asset

0 %	(a)	Cash
	(b)	Claims on central governments and central banks denominated in national currency and funded in that currency
	(c)	Other claims on OECD central governments and central banks
	(d)	Claims collateralised by cash of OECD central government securities or guaranteed by OECD central governments
0, 10, 20 or 50 % (at national discretion)	(a)	Claims on domestic public-sector entities excluding central government and loans guaranteed by or collateralised by securities issued by such entities
20 %	(a)	Claims on multilateral development banks (including the IBRD, the IADB, ADB and EIB) and claims guaranteed or collateralised by securities issued by such banks
	(b)	Claims on banks incorporated in the OECD and loans guaranteed by OECD incorporated banks
	(c)	Claims on securities firms incorporated in the OECD subject to comparable supervisory and regulatory arrangements including in particular risk-based capital requirements and claims guaranteed by these securities firms
	(d)	Claims on banks incorporated in countries outside the OECD with a residual maturity of up to one year and loans with a residual maturity of up to one year guaranteed by banks incorporated in countries outside the OECD
	(e)	Claims on non-domestic OECD public-sector entities excluding central government and loans guaranteed or collateralised by securities issued by such entities
	(f)	Cash items in process of collection
50 %	(a)	Loans fully secured by mortgage and residential property that is or will be occupied by the borrower or that is rented
100 %	(a)	Claims on the private sector
	(b)	Claims on banks incorporated outside the OECD with a residual maturity of over one year
	(c)	Claims on central governments outside the OECD with a residual maturity of over one year
	(d)	Claims on central governments outside the OECD (unless denominated in national currency and funded in that currency)
	(e)	Claims on commercial companies owned by the public sector
	(f)	Premises, plant and equipment and other fixed assets
	(g)	Real estate and other investments (including non-consolidated investment participations in other companies)
	(h)	Capital instruments issued by other banks (unless deducted from capital)
	(i)	All other assets

Source: Besel, *Capital Accord* (1988).

Table 15.2: Original credit conversation factors for off-balance sheet items

1.	Direct credit substitutes, e.g. general guarantees of indebtedness (including standby letters of credit serving as financial guarantees for loans and securities) and acceptances (including endorsements with the character of acceptances).	100%
2.	Certain transaction-related contingent items (e.g. Performance bonds, bid bonds, warranties and standby to letters of credit related to particular transactions).	50%
3.	Short-term self-liquidating trade-related contingencies(such as documentary credits collateralised by the underlying shipments).	20%
4.	Sale and repurchase agreements and asset sales with recourse, where the credit risk remains with the bank.	100%
5.	Forward asset purchases, forward deposits and party-paid shares and securities, which represent commitments with certain drawdown.	100%

Table 15.3: Current and original exposure methods

1. Current Exposure Method

Residual Maturity	Interest Rate	Exchange Rate and Gold	Equity except Gold	Precious Metals Commodities	Other
One year or less	0.0%	1.0%	6.0%	7.0%	10.0%
One to five years	0.5%	5.0%	8.0%	7.0%	12.0%
Over five years	1.5%	7.5%	10.0%	8.0%	15.0%

2. Original Exposure Method

Maturity	Interest Rate Contracts	Exchange Rate Contracts and Gold
One year or less	0.5%	2.0%
One to five years	1.0%	5.0% (2% + 3%)
Over five years	1.0%	3.0%

Source: Besel, *Capital Accord* (1988).

Table 15.4: Constituents of capital

Definition of capital included in the capital base		
A.	**Capital Elements**	
Tier 1	(a)	Paid-up share capital/common stock
	(b)	Disclosed reserves
Tier 2	(a)	Undisclosed reserves
	(b)	Asset revaluation reserves
	(c)	General provisions/general loan-loss reserves
	(d)	Hybrid (debt/equity) capital instrument
	(e)	Subordinated debt
		The sum of Tier 1 and Tier 2 elements will be eligible for inclusion in the capital base subject to the following limits.
B.	**Limits and Restrictions**	
	(i)	The total of Tier 2 (supplementary) elementary elements will be limited to a maximum of 100% of the total of Tier 1 elements;
	(ii)	Subordinated term debt will be limited to a maximum of 50 % of Tier 1 elements;
	(iii)	Where general provisions/general loan-loss reserves include amounts reflecting lower valuations of asset or latent but unidentified losses present in the balance sheet, the amount of such provisions or reserves will be limited to a maximum of 1.25 percentage points;
	(iv)	Asset revaluation reserves, which take the form of latent gains on unrealised securities, will be subject to a discount of 55%.
C.	**Deductions from the Capital Base**	
	From Tier 1	Goodwill
	From Total Capital	(i) Investments in unconsolidated banking and financial subsidiary companies.
		(ii) Investments in the capital of other banks and financial institutions (at the discretion of national authorities).

Source: Basel, *Capital Accord* (1988).

15.18 The final capital or credit risk ratio is calculated on the basis of the sum of the qualifying capital elements (total capital) against the aggregated risk-adjusted position of the bank (total risk-adjusted assets). This ratio must be, at least, 8% under the Basel Capital Accord.

The 8% figure has become the *de facto* global standard although countries have a certain discretion in defining qualifying capital items and the specific assets falling within each risk bucket. While this only provides a minimum figure, many countries will in practice apply a higher ratio having regard to the individual position of the banks being examined.

In the UK average ratios have been set at between 11% and 14%. It is understood that the Basel 8% figure was arrived at as the Americans wanted to impose a 6% minimum and the British a 10% minimum figure. The medium was agreed and compared with industry practice and available data at the time.

15.19 The advantage of the Capital Accord was that it was simple to calculate and apply. This facilitated its quick operational adoption and application. The apparent market credibility that it generated also created a further incentive for a bank compliance.

The combination of operational simplicity and market credibility meant that a large number of countries decided to adopt it as a national measure. While the original 1988 Capital Accord was only designed for internationally active banks within the G10, it quickly became the global standard at the national and cross-border levels.

In terms of agency or institutional significance, it also provided the first model for technical co-operation in such a difficult and sensitive area at the international level.

15.20 Against these advantages, the Accord suffered from a number of internal and external deficiencies. The simplicity that had facilitated its adoption, had the necessary effect of undermining its measurement accuracy.

The simplicity of the risk bucket structure was, in particular, quickly criticised especially with regard to the treatment of all unsecured commercial borrowers on a flat 100% basis. This undermined the underlying credit assessment process that banks were meant to undertake.

Significant anomalies also arose between the perceived penal (100%) capital treatment of the best commercial borrowers as against the privileged (0%) credit rating for the less credible OECD member countries. This had the perverse effect of making it considerably more expensive to lend to a triple A commercial undertaking as against the lowest-rated OECD qualifying debt.

15.21 The imposition of the original capital charge only on loans rather than capital market instruments (gilts, bonds, euro notes and commercial paper) had the more general effect of promoting the use of securitised forms of debt as against bank credit (loans and overdrafts). It was not until the adoption of the Basel Committee Market Risk Amendment in 1996 (on the European model of the Capital Adequacy Directive), that this regulatory defect was, to some extent corrected.

Compliance incentives were also distorted and unnecessary arbitrage opportunities created.

Difficulties also arose as a result of continuing differences in other accounting or fiscal related practices especially with regard to loan loss provisioning. As noted, the underlying objective of creating a level playing field would become wholly discredited.

15.22 It was partly in response to these criticisms, but also the continuing changes that took place within market structure and market practice, that the Basel Committee announced that it would undertake a review of its original capital rules.

A large number of working parties were then set up involving participants from many national central banks and regulatory agencies to develop specific aspects of the new programme. The Committee issued a series of consultation documents in June 1999 which were subsequently taken forward in January 2001.

These new proposals operate through the adoption of a three-pillared approach based on a revised minimum capital requirement (one aspect of which retains the original 8% minimum ratio), a new supervisory review process and enhanced market discipline (through mandatory disclosure of internal capital related information and data).[1]

Of possibly more significance, the new framework draws together all of the other capital charges such as with regard to debt and equity instruments, foreign exchange, commodities and derivatives into a clearer and more integrated structure.

The most questionable aspect of the new regime is possibly the inclusion of a new charge in respect of operational risk. While measurement incentives will reward banks for developing more sophisticated and accurate internal systems, any financial advantage will then be removed through the imposition of the new operational charge. This is considered further below.[2]

1 See paras 15.129–15.136.
2 See para 15.132.

UK CAPITAL COMPLIANCE

15.23   The Bank of England has been one of the main agents in the initial development and revision of capital regulation at the international level and within the UK both before and since the transfer of its supervisory functions to the FSA.

The Bank's approach to the measurement of capital was initially set out in a consultation document in September 1980.[1] This general policy was subsequently developed through a number of Banking Supervision Divisions papers (including BSD/1986/4 and BSD/1986/2).[2]

With the adoption of the Second Banking Directive and the Own Funds Directive and Solvency Ratio Directive in 1989,[3] the earlier capital papers had to be revised to reflect the new implementation requirements imposed. This was generally effected under BSD/1990/2 with regard to own funds and BSD/1990/3 on solvency ratios.[4] The European banking directives would subsequently be consolidated in March 2000.[5]

The Bank of England had also developed provisional proposals with regard to the imposition of controls on large exposures at an early stage.[6] This imposed limits on the total amount of exposure to individual borrowers or connected borrowers. Equivalent provisions were subsequently adopted at the European level with the Large Exposures Directive in 1992 following an earlier recommendation in this area.[7]

The Bank had also adopted guidelines in connection with foreign currency exposures.[8] The 1988 Basel Capital Accord was implemented in the UK under BSD/1988/3.[9]

1 See Bank of England, 'The measurement of capital', BEQB (September 1980). See also Bank of England, 'Foreign currency exposure', BEQB (June 1981); Bank of England, 'The measurement of liquidity', BEQB (September 1982); and Bank of England, *Foreign Currency Options* (April 1984).
2 See Bank of England, *Measurement of Capital* (June 1986), BSD/1986/4; and Bank of England, *Subordinated Loan Capital Issued by Recognised Banks and Licensed Deposit-takers* (March 1986), BAD/1986/2. See also Bank of England, 'Off-balance sheet business of banks' (March 1986), Consultative paper. See also Bank of England, 'Agreed proposal of the United States Federal Banking Supervisory Authorities and the Bank of England on primary capital and capital adequacy assessment', BEQB (February 1987); Bank of England, 'Potential credit exposure on interest rate and foreign exchange rate related instruments' (March 1987); and Bank of England, 'Agreed proposal: credit equivalent amounts for interest rate and foreign exchange rate related instruments' (March 1987).
3 See Second Council Directive 89/646/EEC on the co-ordination of laws, regulations and administrative provisions relating to the taking up and pursuit of the business of credit institutions and amending Directive 77/780/EEC; Council Directive 89/299/EEC on the own funds of credit institutions; and Council Directive 89/647/EEC on a solvency ratio for credit institutions.
4 See Bank of England, *Implementation in the United Kingdom of the directive on own funds of credit institutions* (December 1990), BSD/1990/2; and Bank of England, *Implementation in the United Kingdom of the Solvency Ratio Directive* (December 1990), BSD/1990/3. BSD/1990/2 was amended by BSD/1992/1, BSD/1992/5 and S&S/1995/5.
5 See Council Directive 2000/12/EEC of the European Parliament and of the Council of 20 March 2000 relating to the taking up and pursuit of the business of credit institutions.

6 See Bank of England, *Large Exposures Undertaken by Institutions Authorised under the Banking Act 1979* (July 1986), Consultative Paper; Bank of England, *Large Exposures Undertaken by Institutions Authorised under the Banking Act 1979* (February 1987), Consultative Paper; Bank of England, *Large Exposures Undertaken by Institutions Authorised under the Bank Act 1987* (September 1987), BSD/1987/1; Bank of England, *Large Underwriting Exposures* (February 1988), BSD/1987/1.1.
7 See Council Directive 92/121/EEC on the monitoring and control of large exposures of credit institutions.
8 See Bank of England, 'Foreign currency exposures', BEQB (June 1981).
9 See Bank of England, *Implementation of the Basle Convergence Agreement in the United Kingdom* (October 1988), BSD/1988/3.

15.24 To supplement the banking measures already in place, the European Community adopted the Investment Services Directive in 1993.[1] This created a parallel passport regime for investment firms to that established for banks under the Second Banking Directive and then the Banking Consolidation Directive.[2]

The Investment Services Directive was followed by the Capital Adequacy Directive (CAD) in 1993 which created a separate capital regime for investment firms. This introduced the 'building block' approach which involved the aggregation of the separate charges imposed with regard to debt and equity instruments, foreign exchange and general risk (equal to three months' trading to allow securities firm to wind down its business).[3] The CAD was implemented in the UK under S&S/1995/2.[4]

While the Basel Committee had attempted to develop parallel capital standards for market risks during the early 1990s with International Organisation of Securities Commissions (IOSCO), it was impossible to arrive at any agreement. The Basel Committee then considered the creation of separate capital standards for the securities positions of banks on its own. The Committee produced a consultative paper in April 1995 which was later adopted as the January 1996 Market Risk Amendment.[5] The Basel Committee generally followed the structure established under the CAD with some amendment. Further provision was also included with regard to commodity related risk in connection with which a simplified (15% of net position in each commodity), maturity ladder or models based approach was introduced.

1 See Council Directive 93/622/EEC of 10 May 1993 on investment services in the security field.
2 See para 15.23, notes 3 and 5.
3 See Council Directive 93/6/EEC of 15 March 1993 on the capital adequacy of investment firms and credit institutions.
4 See Bank of England, S&S/1995/2 as amended by S&S/1995/4.
5 See Basel Committee, *Planned Supplement to the Capital Accord to Incorporate Market Risks: Consultative Proposal by the Basle Committee on Banking Supervision* (April 1995); and Basel Committee, *Amendment to the Capital Accord to Incorporate Market Risks* (January 1996).

15.25 The Bank of England's earlier Banking Supervision Division (BSD) and Supervision and Surveillance (S&S) papers were subsequently replaced by separate chapters in the Bank's Guide to Banking Supervisory Policy[1] (this was produced as part of its post-Barings review of bank supervision).[2]

This included chapters on capital adequacy overview (CO), the trading and banking book division (CB) and definition of capital (CA). Credit risk in the banking book was dealt with under chapter BC (credit risk in the banking book) with proxies for market risk in the banking book under BO (proxies for market risk in banking). Foreign exchange, commodity position and counterparty risk were treated separately (FX, CM and DU respectively).

A number of chapters then dealt with position risk (TI (interest rate position risk), TE (equity position risk), TC (counterparty risk in the trading book), TL (incremental for large exposure), TU (underwriting in the capital adequacy framework), TS (CAD 1 models) and TV (the use of internal models to measure market risk)); large exposures (LE); and credit derivatives (CD).

1 See Bank of England, *Guide to Banking Supervisory Policy* (2 vols).
2 See Chapter 6, para 6.4.

15.26 The Bank's Guide was re-issued by the FSA following its assumption of authority for banking supervision under the Bank of England Act 1998.[1] The FSA Guide was then revised to constitute the interim prudential sourcebook for banks (IPRU (BANK)) within the FSA Handbook of Rules and Guidance which came into effect on N2.[2] The interim sourcebook is to be replaced by a fully integrated final sourcebook (PSB) for all financial sectors.[3] Until then, IPRU (BANK) will govern the regulation for capital adequacy and internal control systems and related matters in the UK.

The integrated sourcebook will draw all of the provisions together set out in each of the existing interim sourcebooks. The proposed new arrangements will operate through the identification and measurement of credit, market, operational, insurance and group risks. The intention is to develop a more streamlined and transparent set of requirements to promote competition and ease of compliance, in particular, through the convergence of cross-sector prudential standards.

The final sourcebook will come into effect beginning 2004. Unfortunately, it will not be possible to confirm when it will be applied to banks until the revisions being considered at the Basel Committee level and associated European amendments have been finalised.[4] The interim arrangements set out in IPRU (BANK) will apply until that time.

1 See Chapter 2, paras 2.49–2.50.
2 See Chapter 2, paras 2.83–2.146.
3 FSA, *Integrated Prudential Sourcebook* (June 2001), Consultation Paper 97. See Chapter 6, paras 6.85–6.88.
4 See Chapter 6, para 6.86.

INTERIM PRUDENTIAL RULES[1]

15.27 The requirements governing the capital and related financial positions of UK banks are currently set out in the interim prudential sourcebook (IPRU (BANK)).[2] This was made by the FSA Board on 21 June 2001.

The FSA has designated para 4(4) of Sch 3 to the Banking Act 1987 which applies to liquidity requirements as a continued rule.[3] This then has continuing effect under the FSA's general rule-making power as set out in the Act subject to any minor modifications. The other requirements formerly set out in Sch 3 to the Act are re-issued as new rules. The sourcebook sets out the detailed prudential standards and related notification requirements to be applied to banks authorised under the Act. Although the sourcebook applies to all banks, most of the provisions only apply to UK banks with limited provisions being relevant to European Economic Area (EEA) banks.[4]

The objective of the sourcebook is to ensure that banks manage all relevant risks adequately to ensure that they can meet their liabilities as they fall due. For this purpose, banks have to maintain capital resources commensurate with their risks as well as appropriate systems and controls to enable them to manage those risks. The sourcebook gives effect to requirements contained in the Principles for Businesses (PRIN) and the Threshold Conditions (COND) set out in Sch 6 to the 1987 Act. The standards formerly applied to banks under the Banking Act 1987 are generally followed although these are now expressed as guidance to the equivalent standard imposed. The revised rules are now set out in section 3 of the sourcebook. The specific requirements imposed are developed in separate chapters to the sourcebook.

1   See also Walker, 'Interim Prudential Sourcebook: Banks' in *Financial Services Regulation* (Butterworths loose leaf), Division B.
2   See Table 15.5.
3   See Financial Services and Markets Act 2000 (Transitional Provisions and Savings) (Rules) Order 2001 (SI 2001/1534), art 4(1).
4   See, for example, Rule 3.3.15 and Chapter LM (on rules and guidance on liquidity) and Chapter FR (on fraud) 15.28.

15.28   The rules are generally divided into (a) prudential rules and (b) policy statement rules. The main rules imposed under section 3 of IPRU (BANK) may be summarised as follows:

Prudential rules

15.29   Banks are subject to six sets of express rules with regard to (i) direction, (ii) capital, (iii) liquidity, (iv) provisions, (v) large exposures and (vi) audit committee, with one further evidential provision on internal audit compliance.

Business to be directed by at least two individuals

15.30   A UK bank and an overseas bank must ensure that at least two individuals effectively direct its business.[1] This is referred to as the 'four eyes requirement' and was formerly imposed under para 2 of Sch 3 to the Banking Act 1987. The obligation was originally introduced under article 3 of the European First Banking Directive (and now under article 6(1) of the Banking Consolidation Directive 2000/12/EC). This will assist ensure that the banks comply with the 'Management and Control' requirement imposed under the Principles for Businesses and the 'Suitability' obligation under the Threshold Conditions. This is also relevant to the Senior Management Arrangements – Systems and Controls rules (SYSC).

In applying the provision, the FSA expects two independent minds to be applied both to the formulation and implementation of the policies of the bank. Each should play a part in both the decision-making process and all significant decisions. Both have to demonstrate the qualities and application to influence strategy, day-to-day policy and its implementation.[2]

1   3.3.1 R.
2   3.3.6 G.

Table 15.5: Interim Prudential Sourcebook for Banks (IPRU (BANK))

Interim Prudential Sourcebook	GN
Contents	section 1
The Prudential Sourcebook for banks: Introductions	section 2
The FSA's requirements (rules)	section 3
Presentation and conventions	section 4

Capital adequacy

CO	Capital adequacy overview
CB	Trading book/banking book division
CA	Definition of capital

Banking book
BC	Credit risk in the banking book
BO	Proxies for market risk in banking book

Banking and trading book
FX	Foreign exchange risk
CM	Commodities risk
DU	Common treatments for counterparty risk

Trading book
TI	Interest rate position risk
TE	Equity position risk
TC	Counterparty risk in the trading book
TL	Incremental capital for large exposures
TU	Underwriting in capital adequacy framework
TS	CAD1 models
TV	The use of internal models

Other financial provisions
LE	Large exposures
CD	Credit derivatives
SE	Securitisation and asset transfers

Adequate liquidity

LM	Mismatch liquidity
LS	Sterling stock liquidity

Adequate records, systems and controls

AR	Accounting and Other Records and Internal Control Systems
ST	Foreign exchange – risk-based supervision
FR	Fraud

Controllers: fit & proper requirement

CL	Comfort letters

Ancillary measures

VA	Valuation
NE	Collateral and netting
CS	Consolidated supervision
OS	Outsourcing
PN	Provisioning policy statements

Source: FSA, IPRU (BANK).

Capital requirements

15.31   A UK bank and an overseas bank must have initial capital amounting to not less than EUR 5 million at the time they obtains their Part IV permission to accept deposits.[1]

1   3.3.9 R.

15.32   A UK bank and an overseas bank must maintain own funds which amount to not less than EUR 5 million. This is subject to an exception with regard to UK banks authorised under the Banking Act 1987 immediately before 1 January 1993.[2] Such banks must maintain the relevant amount set.[3]

1   3.3.11 R.
2   3.3.12(1) R.
3   3.3.12(2) R.

15.33   A UK bank and an overseas bank must maintain capital resources that are commensurate with the nature and scale of its business and the risks inherent in their business.[1] In the case of a UK bank and an overseas bank which is a member of a group, those capital resources must also be commensurate with the risks inherent in the activities of the other members of the group insofar as those risks may affect the bank.

1   3.3.13(1) R.

15.34   These rules are developed in separate chapters of the sourcebook. The underlying policy is explained in chapter CO (Capital adequacy overview) and then developed in chapter CB (Trading book and banking book division), CA (definition of capital), BC (Credit risk in the banking book), BO (proxies for market risk in banking), FX (Foreign exchange risk), CM (commodities risk), DU (Common treatments for counterparty risk), TI (Interest rate position risk), TE (Equity position risk), TC (Counterparty risk in the trading book), TL (Incremental capital for large exposures), TU (Underwriting and capital adequacy framework), TS (CAD1 models) and TV (Use of internal models).

Liquidity requirement

15.35   A bank, except an EEA bank that does not have a UK branch, must maintain adequate liquidity taking into account the nature and scale of its business so that it is able to meet its obligations as they fall due.[1] In the case of an EEA bank with a UK branch, this only applies in relation to the branch. Further guidance is provided in chapters LM (Mismatch liquidity) and LS (Sterling stock liquidity).

1   3.3.15(1) R.

Adequate provisions

15.36   A UK bank and an overseas bank must maintain adequate provisions for the depreciation or diminution in the value of their assets (including provisions for bad and doubtful debts), for liabilities that will or may fall to be met by them and for losses that they will or may incur.[1] Guidance is developed in chapter PN (Provisioning policy statements).

1   3.3.17 R.

Large exposures

15.37   A UK bank and an overseas bank must have adequate systems and controls to enable them to monitor and control their large exposures in conformity with a large exposures policy statement adopted under the sourcebook and be able to calculate their large exposures accurately.[1] Guidance is developed in chapters LE (Large exposures) and TL (Incremental for large exposures).

1   3.3.19 R.

15.38   A UK bank must also notify the FSA if it proposes to enter into a transaction or transactions that would result in it having an exposure that exceeds 25% of capital.[1] A UK bank which consolidates one or more of the subsidiaries in its reports to the FSA for the purpose of the solo consolidated reporting of large exposures under the Supervision Manual[2] must for this purpose include the transactions and capital of those subsidiaries with those of the bank.[3] Guidance is developed in chapters LE (Large exposures) and TL (Incremental capital for large exposures).

1   3.3.21(1) R.
2   16.7.8 R.
3   3.3.21(2) R.

Internal audits

15.39   There are no separate rules imposed with regard to internal audits only evidential provisions. A UK bank and an overseas bank should have an internal audit function which may either be in-house or outsourced to a third party.[1] Breach of this requirement may be relied on to establish contravention of the Senior Management Arrangements, Systems and Control.[2] (SYSC) 2.1.1R requires a firm to take reasonable care to establish and maintain a clear and appropriate apportionment of significant responsibilities among its directors and senior managers. This is to ensure that the business and affairs of the firm can be adequately monitored and controlled by the senior managers and governing body of the firm. Further guidance is provided in chapter AR (Accounting and Other Records and Internal Control Systems).

1   3.3.23(1) E.
2   3.3.23(2) E.

Audit committee

15.40   A UK bank must have an audit committee which should either be chaired by a non-executive director of the bank or be an audit committee of non-executive directors of the bank's holding company where that committee fulfils the role of audit committee in respect of the bank itself.[1] Breach may be relied on to establish contravention of SYSC rule 3.1.1 which requires firms to take reasonable care to establish and maintain such systems and controls as are appropriate to their business. Further guidance is available under chapter AR (Accounting and Other Records and Internal Control Systems).

1   3.3.25(1) and (2) R.
2   3.3.25(4) R.

Policy statement rules

15.41   Banks are required to provide four main specific policy statements and comply with certain further requirements with regard to their preparation and reporting.

Types of policy statements

(I) LARGE EXPOSURES POLICY STATEMENT

15.42   A UK bank and an overseas bank must set out their policy on large exposures in a written statement.[1] This must be such that it details how the bank controls its exposures to ensure compliance with its large exposure limits and the reporting to the FSA of all relevant exposures.[2] Guidance is available under chapters LE (Large exposures) and TL (Incremental charge for large exposures).

1   3.4.1(1) R.
2   3.4.1(2) R.

(II) LIQUIDITY POLICY STATEMENT

15.43   A UK bank and an overseas bank must set out their policy on the management of liquidity in a written statement.[1] This must be such that compliance would enable the bank to maintain adequate liquidity under rule 3.3.1.[2] Guidance on liquidity is developed in chapters LM (Mismatch liquidity) and LS (Sterling stock liquidity).

1   3.4.3(1) R.
2   3.4.1(2) R.

(III) PROVISIONING POLICY STATEMENT

15.44   A UK bank and an overseas bank must set out their policy on provisions in a written statement.[1] This policy must allow the bank to comply with rule 3.3.17 except that an overseas bank only has to cover such provisions as are made in the accounts of its operations in the UK. Provisioning is developed in chapter PN (Provisioning policy statements).

1   3.4.5(1) R.
2   3.4.3(1) R.

(IV) TRADING BOOK POLICY STATEMENT

15.45   A UK bank must set out its trading book policy in a written statement.[1] This must confirm whether or not the UK bank splits its business between a banking and trading book for the purposes of its capital adequacy calculations. If its business is not split, the reasons for that must be provided.[2] If the business is split, the bank must explain the means and methodologies by which it identifies its trading book, assigns positions between the banking and trading books, controls transfers of positions between the banking and trading books, values its positions in the trading book and measure market risks in the trading books. Guidance is developed in chapters TB (Trading book and banking book division), DU (Common treatments for counterparty risk), TC (Counterparty risk in the trading book), TS (CAD1 models) and TV (The use of internal models).

1 3.4.7(1) R.
2 3.4.7(2)(a) and (b) R.
3 3.4.7(3) R.

Policy statement procedures

15.46 A bank's policy statements should be approved by its board or, where appropriate, by a person or body of persons to whom the board has delegated this function.[1] Such delegation should only take place if the bank's board is satisfied that the delegate is suitable for the purpose and any such delegation is effected formally and expressly by the board.[2] The bank must also review its policy statements and, where necessary, update them, at least, once a year and incorporate within the appropriate policy statement any change to its policies covered by the statement as soon as it has adopted the change.[3]

1 3.4.9(1) R.
2 3.4.9(2) R.
3 3.4.9(3) R.

15.47 Breach of any of these rules with regard to relevant procedures may be relied on to establish contravention of SYSC 2.1.1R.[1] This requires firms to take reasonable care to establish and maintain clear and appropriate apportionment of significant responsibilities between its directors and senior managers. This is to allow the business and affairs of the firm to be adequately monitored and controlled by the senior managers and governing body of the firm.[2] A bank should separately notify the FSA of its intention to make any significant changes in these policies before the bank adopts the changes.[3]

1 3.4.9(4) R.
2 3.4.10 G.
3 3.4.11 G.

15.48 A bank must send to the FSA a copy of its first policy statements adopted under these rules as soon as possible after adoption and a copy of the current version of the policy statement annually at the beginning of each calendar year.[1] If the policy statement is significantly amended during the year, the bank must send a copy of the amended statement to the FSA as soon as possible after adoption.[2] Even if the policy statement is not amended, a copy should be sent annually to the FSA.[3] Transitional provisions apply with regard to written statements provided in respect of large exposures, liquidity, provisioning or trading book policies in the year proceeding the coming into effect of this requirement.[4]

1 3.4.12(a) and (b) R.
2 3.4.12(b) R.
3 3.4.13 G.
4 3.4.14 G.

INTERIM PRUDENTIAL SOURCEBOOK FOR BANKS

Overview

15.49 The interim prudential sourcebook for banks (IPRU (BANK)) is divided into 30 chapters.[1] The application and purpose of the sourcebook is set out in the general provisions (chapter GN). Following that, the main chapters are concerned with financial requirements (including both capital adequacy and liquidity), systems and controls and controllers. The remainder of the sourcebook deals with some ancillary measures.

Banks will also have to comply with all of the other relevant sections of the Handbook in addition to IPRU (BANK). This will include the High Level Standards in Block 1 as well the Supervision and Enforcement Manuals in Block 3 and all other relevant provisions.[2]

1 See Table 15.5.
2 See Chapter 2, paras 2.93–2.131.

Capital

15.50 The sourcebook contains 18 chapters on capital. These distinguish between the treatment of the banking (loan) and trading (securities) books of banks.

The capital provisions provide an overview (CO), distinguish between the banking and the trading book (CB) and define capital for the purposes of the Handbook (CA).

The main chapter (BC) deals with credit risk in the banking book and generally applies the Basel Committee 8% minimum requirement as adjusted through the European Own Funds and Solvency Ratio Directives. There is also a separate short provision for market risk in the banking book (BO).

15.51 The following three chapters deal with foreign exchange risk (FX), commodities risk (CM) and counterparty risk (DU). Although these were developed as part of the 'building block' approach for market risks, they are still to apply with regard to both the banking and trading books.

The following seven chapters deal specifically with the trading book and include sections on interest rate and equity position risk (TI and TE), counterparty risk and large exposures in the trading book (TC and TL), underwriting (TU) and CAD1 and CAD2 models (TS and TV).

There are also three more specialist sections on large exposures (LE), credit derivatives (CD) and securitisation and asset transfers (SE).

Liquidity

15.52 General mismatch and more specific (essentially retail) sterling stock liquidity is dealt with separately (LM and LS).

Records, systems and controls

15.53 The sourcebook contains three revised provisions on records, systems and controls including record systems (AR), foreign exchange supervision (ST) and prevention of fraud (FR). The chapter on comfort letters (CL) has been retained from the earlier Guide although moved until later within the sourcebook.

There are also further more ancillary provisions with regard to valuation (VA), collateral and netting (NE), consolidated supervision (CS), outsourcing (OS) and provisioning policy statements (PN).

General provisions

15.54 The general provisions (chapter GN) are limited. These set out the structure and content of the sourcebook and confirm the application, purpose and general approach adopted. The rules applicable to banks are listed and presentation and conventions explained.

Capital adequacy: introductory chapters

15.55 The sourcebook contains three introductory chapters on capital adequacy. These provide an overview of the FSA's policy in this regard, the general distinction between the trading and banking books (including CAD and non-CAD banks) and the definition of 'capital'.[1]

1 See IPRU (BANK), chapters CO (Capital adequacy overview), CB (Trading book/banking book division) and CA (Definition of capital).

15.56 The general objective of the sourcebook is stated to be to ensure that banks maintain capital resources commensurate with their risks and appropriate systems and control to enable them to manage those risks.[1] For this purpose, the FSA requires that banks maintain adequate capital against risk, adequate liquidity and identify and control all relevant large credit exposures.

With regard to capital, it is stated that capital enables banks to absorb losses without endangering customer deposits.[2] While the meaning of this is questionable, it has to be accepted that banks should maintain adequate reserves against their lending and trading positions. Capital does not provide an active or available source of funds to absorb losses on an ongoing basis as such. Capital represents a proportionate share of the residual net value of the institution on a winding-up. (Ongoing commitments are dealt with through liquidity rather than capital requirements.) Capital does, nevertheless, act as a minimum source of value to avoid the bank falling into insolvency in the event that losses are incurred. Capital is accordingly more of a technical solvency rather than an active liquidity tool.

The need to comply with capital rules also focuses banks' management attention on the assessment of credit risk and, in turn, improves internal reporting and control systems within the institution. Capital adequacy accordingly remains a useful device although its importance should not be overestimated.

1 IPRU (BANK), chapter GN, section 2, para 4.
2 IPRU (BANK), chapter GN, section 2, para 4.

15.57 The statutory basis for capital control are the Threshold Conditions which require that firms must have adequate resources having regard to their regulated activities.[1] Principle 4 requires that a bank maintains adequate financial resources while the capital rule 3.3.13 specifically requires that the bank maintains adequate capital resources which are commensurate with the nature and scale of its activities and the risks inherent in those activities.[2]

A UK bank must also maintain minimum own funds of EUR 5 million subject to grandfathering.[3] These provisions implement the relevant requirements set out in the European Banking Consolidation Directive (formerly the Own Funds Directive 89/299/EEC and Solvency Ratio Directive 89/647/ EEC)[4] and the Capital Adequacy Directive 93/6/EC (as amended by 98/31/ EC).

The credit risk provisions provided for under the Banking Consolidation Directive generally follow the original credit risk requirements established by the Basel Committee on Banking Supervision under its 1988 Capital Accord which established the 8% minimum as a global standard. This generally operates by defining capital,[5] establishing a risk weighted framework for all loan (or asset) items[6] and sets a minimum capital ratio of 8% (of capital against the risk-adjusted asset figure).

1 See Banking Act 1987, Sch 6, para 4(1).
2 See chapter GN, rule 3.3.13.
3 See chapter GN, rule 3.3.9.
4 See Banking Consolidation Directive, Title V, Chapter 2, sections 1 and 2 which define capital resources for supervisory purposes and risk weightings for the banks' asset classes subject to a minimum risk asset ratio of 8%.
5 See Table 15.6.
6 See Table 15.7.

Asset books and ratios

15.58   The objective of the FSA's capital rules is to ensure that banks maintain sufficient capital, having regard to all of the main risks that arise from their activities. In considering these risks, the sourcebook distinguishes between those that arise in the bank's banking and its trading book.

The 'banking book' refers to the total number of loans or asset items held within the balance sheet. These are specific debt obligations entered into with individual borrowers. The 'trading book' consists of all securities of whatever form held by the bank either for trading or hedging purposes.

The chapters of the sourcebook are structured to deal with risks arising in the banking book, the banking and trading books and then only those in the trading book.[1]

1 See IPRU (BANK), chapter CB (Trading book/banking book division).

15.59   The other main distinction drawn in the sourcebook is between the trigger and target capital ratio to be imposed on individual banks. The 'trigger ratio' refers to the minimum ratio that the FSA considers a bank should maintain having regard to the nature of its activities. The 'target ratio' represents a slightly higher figure that banks should attempt to achieve. In the event that their capital levels fall below the target ratio, this acts as a warning that the bank's capital position should be examined to avoid any intentional or accidental breach of the trigger ratio. The difference between the trigger and target ratios depends upon the nature of the bank and its exposure to seasonal variations or changes in the business cycle.

Table 15.6: General constituents of capital

A. Definition of capital included in the capital base

Capital Elements

Tier 1

(a) Permanent Share Capital — **(Tier 1 – Externally Generated)** **(Perpetual and non-cumulative issued capital)**

    (i) **Allotted, called up and fully paid ordinary share capital/common stock**

    (ii) Perpetual non-cumulative preferred (or preference) shares

(Tier 1 – Internally Generated)

(b) General and other Reserves (from appropriations of earnings)

(c) Accrued Profit and Reserves

(d) Minority Interests (consolidation in permanent shareholder's equity)

Tier 2

(a) Revaluation reserves — **(Lower Tier 2 – Perpetual but cumulative (deferred))** (tangible fixed assets and fixed asset investments)

(b) Fully Paid Equity (from capitalisation of property reserves)

(c) General Provisions

(d) Minority Interests in Tier 2 Preferred Shares

(e) Hybrid (debt/equity) capital instruments

    (i) Perpetual cumulative preferred shares

    (ii) Perpetual subordinated debt

(f) Subordinated debt (5 year) — **(Lower Tier 2 – Generally dated)**

The sum of Tier 1 and Tier 2 elements will be eligible for inclusion in the capital base subject to the following limits.

Tier 3

(a) Short term (2 year) subordinated debt

(b) Minority Interests in Tier 3 capital

B. Limits and Restrictions

(i) The total of Tier 2 (supplementary) elementary elements will be limited to a maximum of 100% of the total of Tier 1 elements;

(ii) Subordinated term debt will be limited to a maximum of 50 % of Tier 1 elements;

(iii) Where general provisions/general loan-loss reserves include amounts reflecting lower valuations of asset or latent but unidentified losses present in the balance sheet, the amount of such provisions or reserves will be limited to a maximum of 1.25 percentage points;

(iv) Asset revaluation reserves, which take the form of latent gains on unrealised securities, will be subject to a discount of 55%.

C. Deductions from the Capital Base

From Tier 1

(i) All holdings of own shares

(ii) Goodwill

(iii) Current year's unpublished net losses on banking and trading books

(iv) Capitalisation of property revaluation reserves

From Total Capital

(i) Investments in unconsolidated banking and financial subsidiary companies

(ii) Connected lending of a capita nature

(iii) All holdings of capital instruments issued by other credit or financial institutions

(iv) Other deductions agreed on case by case basis

(v) Qualifying holdings in non-financial companies

Source: FSA, IPRU (BANK), chapter CA.

Table 15.7: General risk weights by category of on-balance sheet items

0 %	(a)	Cash and claims collateralised by cash deposits
	(b)	Gold and other bullion held in vaults or on unallocated basis
	(c)	Claims on Zone A (OECD) central governments and central banks
	(d)	Claims guaranteed by Zone A central governments and central banks
	(e)	Claims on Zone B (non-OECD) central governments and central banks denominated in national currency and funded in that currency
	(f)	Claims guaranteed by Zone B central governments and central banks
	(g)	Certificates of deposit
	(h)	Items in suspense where they represent position risk
10 %	(a)	Certain holdings of government securities
20 %	(a)	Claims on multilateral development banks (including the IBRD, the IADB, AsDB, AsDB and EIB) and claims guaranteed or collateralised by securities issued by such banks
	(b)	Claims on credit institutions incorporated in Zone A countries and loans guaranteed (or accepted or endorsed) by Zone A credit institutions and cash collateral in or of deposit with Zone A credit institution
	(c)	Claims on credit institutions incorporated in Zone B countries with a residual maturity of up to one year and loans with a residual maturity of up to one year guaranteed by such institutions
	(d)	Cash items in process of collection
	(e)	Claims on Zone A public sector entities and claims guaranteed by such entities
	(f)	Claims on investment firms (but not unregulated affiliates) subject to CAD or incorporated in a non-EEA state subject to an equivalent regime
	(g)	Claims on clearing houses and exchanges recognised under IPRU(BANK), chapter BC including initial cash margins and surplus variation margins at futures exchanges or clearing houses recognised under IPRU(BANK), chapter BC
	(h)	Claims that are directly, explicitly, unconditionally and irrevocably guaranteed by investment firms, exchanges of clearing houses recognised
	(i)	Certain holdings of government securities as a proxy for market risk
50 %	(a)	Loans to individuals fully and completely secured by a first priority charge on residential property that is (or is to be) occupied by the borrower or is rented
	(b)	Loans to housing associations, registered with the Housing Corporation or Scottish or Welsh Office fully secured by mortgage on residential property that is already let or under development and will be let on condition that the development attracts Housing Grant (HAG) or other public subsidy on equivalent terms of, at least, 50% of the approved scheme cost
	(c)	Mortgage sub-participations (where the risk to the sub-participating bank is fully and specifically secured against residential mortgage loans that would qualify for the 50% weight)
	(d)	Mortgage backed securities (MBS) issued by special purposes mortgage finance vehicles subject to certain conditions
	(e)	Loans to public universities fully secured by a mortgage residential property that is already let or under development and will be let on condition that the lender is in possession of a certificate showing that work to the value of 20% of the projected finished end value has been completed and can be readily sold or let in the on-student market
100 %	(a)	Claims on the non-bank sector
	(b)	Claims on banks incorporated in Zone B countries with a residual maturity of over one year
	(c)	Claims on Zone B central governments and central banks (unless denominated in the national currency and funded by liabilities in the same currency)
	(d)	Claims on Zone B regional governments or local authorities
	(e)	Claims guaranteed by Zone B central governments and central banks (not denominated and funded in the national currency common to the guarantor and borrower)
	(f)	Claims on commercial entities owned by the public sector
	(g)	Claims on Zone B public sector entities
	(f)	Premises, plant and equipment and other fixed assets
	(g)	Real estate, trade investments and other assets not otherwise specified

Source: FSA, IPRU (BANK), chapter BC, section 3.

Further provisions

15.60 In addition to the provisions concerning credit and market risk, IPRU (BANK) contains further provisions with regard to large exposures (LE), credit derivatives (CD) and securitisation and assets transfers (SE).[1]

The sourcebook also contains chapters on liquidity (LM (Mismatch liquidity) and LS (Sterling stock liquidity)), systems and controls (AR (Accounting and other records and internal control systems), ST (foreign exchange) and FR (Fraud)) and controllers (CL (comfort letters)).

Further provisions are also included with regard to valuations (VA), collateral and netting (NE), consolidated supervision (CS), outsourcing (OS) and provisioning policy statements (PN).

1 See Table 15.5.

Capital, liquidity and controls

15.61 After general provisions and the introductory capital chapters, the sourcebook develops the nature of the obligations imposed on banks in 25 chapters consisting generally of capital, liquidity and controls, as well as controllers (comfort letters) and certain other more ancillary provisions. Each of these is considered in further detail below.

Capital adequacy and the banking book

15.62 The capital rules set out in the sourcebook are structured having regard to those that apply to the banking book alone, the banking and trading books and the trading book alone.

CREDIT RISK (BC)

15.63 Credit risk relates to the risk of borrower or counterparty default on a loan. This may either involve the non-payment of interest during the term of the loan or repayment of principal on maturity. To the extent that loans comprise the main assets of a bank, credit risk is the most significant risk that has to be considered and managed.

15.64 Credit risk is generally dealt with by grouping the various categories of loans that a bank holds into particular asset classes and then assigning them a relevant risk weight.

The most common division is based on (a) OECD governments, central banks and banks, (b) non-OECD governments, central banks and banks, (c) secured items and (d) commercial loans. This reflects the general asset division developed by the Basel Committee and followed in the relevant European measures.[1] This was incorporated by the Bank of England into its supervisory papers in the area of capital and now into the sourcebook.[2] Off-balance sheet items are converted into on-balance credit equivalent values and then assigned the risk weighting applicable to the particular counterparty.[3]

The permitted capital items are then against the total risk-adjusted asset figure to produce the capital ratio which must not be less than 8% as an absolute minimum although all UK banks will have been assigned a higher trigger and target ratios.

1 See paras 15.12–15.13 and 15.14–15.26.
2 See IPRU (BANK), chapter BC (Credit risk in the banking book).
3 See Table 15.8.

Table 15.8: Credit conversation factors for off-balance sheet items

1.	(a) Direct credit substitutes, e.g. general guarantees of indebtedness (including standby letters of credit serving as financial guarantees for loans and securities) and acceptances (including endorsements with the character of acceptances).	100%
	(b) Sale and repurchase agreements and asset sales with recourse where the credit risk remains with the bank.	
	(c) Forward asset purchases, forward forward deposits placed and the unpaid part of partly-paid shares and securities and any other commitments with a certain draw-down.	
2.	(a) Certain transaction-related contingent items (e.g. performance bonds, bid bonds, warranties and standby letters of credit related to particular transactions).	50%
	(b) Note issuance facilities and revolving underwriting facilities.	
	(c) Other commitments (such as formal standby facilities and credit lines) with an original maturity of over 1 year.	
3.	Short-term self-liquidating trade-related contingencies (such as documentary credits collateralised by the underlying shipments).	20%
4.	(a) Endorsements of bills (including per aval endorsements) which have previously been accepted by the bank.	0%
	(b) Other commitments (such as standby facilities and credit lines) with an original maturity of up to 1 year or which can be unconditionally cancelled at any time.	

Source: FSA, IPRU (BANK), chapter BC, section 4.

15.65   In addition to credit or counterparty default risk in the banking book, there may also be an element of market risk to the extent that securities are held in the banking rather than trading book. This may include, for example, government securities such as US Treasury Bills or UK Gilts held for income (interest) and reserve purposes within the banking book.

The European Solvency Ratio Directive allowed Member States discretion as the manner in which this may be dealt with although no further guidance was provided. The 1988 Basel Accord provided that either a zero or low weight may be assigned to government securities to reflect market or investment risk.

The FSA deals with this by adopting a series of proxies for market risk in respect of the main types of government paper held. These are either signed a 10% or 20% weight.[1]

1   See IPRU (BANK), chapter PO (Proxies for market risk in the banking book).

15.66   Under the FSA proxy rules, the 10% weight is assigned to nil risk weighted holdings of Zone A central government fixed interest rate paper with a residual maturity of one year or less, floating rate or index linked paper of any maturity and Zone B central government nil risk weighted paper (with a residual maturity of one year or less) denominated and funded in the local currency. The 20% weight is assigned to Zone A central government fixed rate paper (with a remaining maturity of over one year) and holdings of Zone B nil risk weighted paper (with a residual maturity of over one year) denominated and funded in the local currency. Holdings of Zone B central government

securities not denominated or funded in the local currency are assigned a full
100% weight.[1]

1   See IPRU (BANK), chapter PO (Proxies for market risk in the banking book).

Banking and trading books

15.67   The banking and trading books are subject to three common charges
with regard to foreign exchange risk, commodities related risks and counterparty risk with regard to over-the-counter (OTC) derivatives, unsettled trades
and free deliveries.

FOREIGN EXCHANGE RISK (FX)

15.68   Foreign exchange risk is concerned with losses arising as a result of
adverse movements in a relevant exchange rate or rates. This may either relate
to net open positions held for trading purposes or exposures in a bank's total
assets and liabilities.[1] To the extent that foreign exchange risk arises in the
trading and banking groups, it is treated on a common basis.

The foreign exchange rules implement the relevant requirement set out in
Annex III of the CAD. Under the CAD, the FX charge is generally 8% of
overall net foreign exchange positions in excess of 2% of capital.

1   See IPRU (BANK), chapter FX (Foreign exchange risk), section 2.1.

15.69   Under the sourcebook, the charge is calculated by converting all of the
currencies held into a reporting currency. The net open position is calculated
(being the difference between the long and short positions held). The net open
currency position is aggregated with the net open position in gold (whether
long or short).

Under the basic method, the capital charge is set at 8% of the aggregate
figure. Currency options are then subject to a separate 'carve out' method or
recognised model (including scenario matrix). The total capital charge is the
basic charge plus the two option charges to the extent relevant.

COMMODITIES RISK (CM)

15.70   Commodity position risk is the risk of price movements in any
positions held in commodities (excluding gold). Commodity position risk is
generally more complex and volatile than currency or interest rates. The
exposure may also be more severe as the markets are less liquid.

A commodity position may, in particular, be effected by basis risk, interest
rate risk or forward gap risk. Basis risk is the risk that the relationship between
prices in similar commodities may change over time. Interest rate risk is the risk
of a change in the cost of financing for forward positions and options in
commodities. Forward gap risk is the risk that the forward price may change for
reasons other than a change in interest rates.

A bank must calculate capital charges in respect of its commodity contracts
held in either the banking or trading book to cover counterparty risk exposure.[1]

1   See IPRU (BANK), chapter CM (Commodities risk).

15.71   In calculating its capital charge in respect of commodities, a bank may
adopt either a simplified, a maturity ladder or an internal models based
approach.[1]

Under the simplified approach, the charge is 15% of the overall net open position (long or short) in respect of each commodity plus 3% of the gross position (long plus short) to cover basis, interest rate and forward gap risk.

Under the maturity ladder approach, each commodity position (spot plus forward) is expressed in terms of a standard unit of measurement (barrels, tonnes or kilos). Holdings are then assigned to one of seven maturity or time bands depending upon delivery dates. Any contracts maturing within 10 days of each other may be offset immediately (as part of a pre-processing, offsetting or optimisation process). All other contracts are offset within each time band and the matched long and short positions multiplied by the spot price for the commodity (expressed in the reporting currency) and then the spread rate for the band (always 1.5%). The final net long (or short) position in the relevant commodity is multiplied by 15% to produce the capital charge. Unmatched positions the time band should be carried forward to the next time band.

Banks may also use an internal models approach provided they satisfy certain qualitative and quantitative standards as set out in the Handbook.[2]

1   See IPRU (BANK), chapter CM (Commodities risk).
2   See IPRU (BANK), chapter CM (Commodities risk).

COUNTERPARTY RISK (DU)

15.72   Counterparty risk is the possibility of loss arising through the failure by the other party to perform its obligations under an agreement or transaction. Counterparty risk is concerned with the exposure created by the trading counterparty rather than the issuer of the securities as such. This can be regarded as a form of settlement risk.

Banks have to hold capital in respect of both market and counterparty risk. Counterparty risk is generally dealt with as part of the credit risk chapter (BC) although certain contracts require a common treatment including OTC derivatives, unsettled trades and free deliveries.

15.73   OTC derivatives include interest rate, foreign exchange rate, equities, precious metals (excluding gold) and other commodity contracts that are not exchange traded. This will not include options as there is (by definition) no counterparty on a written option.

The capital charge for these off-balance sheet items is calculated by multiplying the credit equivalent amount (the CEA) by the risk weight attaching to the counterparty. The credit equivalent amount is calculated using a replacement cost method. This is made up of the total replacement cost of all relevant contracts with a positive value (marked to market) with an additional amount to capture any future credit exposures on all contracts (referred to as the add-on). Add-ons are calculated having regard to their residual maturity (1, 1–5 and over 5 years).

A particular percentage is assigned (between 0% and 15%) to interest rate, foreign exchange, equities, metal and commodity positions.[1]

1   See IPRU (BANK), chapter DU, section 3, p 2.

15.74   Charges have also to be calculated in connection with unsettled transactions and free delivery. An unsettled transaction is one where delivery of the instrument is due to take place against the receipt of cash but which remains unsettled five business days after the due settlement date. The objective is to apply a capital charge where settlement is due but has not yet been completed. No capital charge is required in respect of spot and forward foreign exchange transactions.

The charge may either be calculated on a normal or alternative treatment basis. In both cases, the charge is based on the difference between the amount due and the current market value of the instrument. This is subject to a rate charge (of between 0% and 100%) depending upon the number of working days due after settlement (0, 4, 5–15, 16–30, 31–45 and 46 or more). The normal treatment will generally be applied (involving a 0%, 8%, 50%, 75% and 100% charging).

Express approval may be obtained from the FSA to use the alternative treatment (with a 0%, 0.5%, 4%, 9% and 100% rating applied). The charge for unsettled transactions is then calculated using the rates given rather than the counterparty risk weights in both cases.

15.75   Free deliveries arise where a bank has paid (or received) its side of the transaction but has not yet received (or paid) the securities or cash agreed. If the exposure is in the trading book, the capital requirement is the counterparty claim multiplied by the counterparty risk weight and a further 8%. If the exposure is in the banking book, the risk weighted amount should be the counterparty claim multiplied by the counterparty risk weight.

No charge is required with regard to spot and forward foreign exchange transactions. A one-day window is allowed with regard to cross-border trades. The charge will generally otherwise be applied to all exchange traded contracts involving physical delivery.

Trading book

15.76   CAD banks have to maintain addition capital in respect of their debt and equity positions as well as separate charges for counterparty risk and large exposures in the trading book. Although underwriting is also subject to a further charge, allowances are available.

Rather than calculate relevant charges on flat generally arithmetical bases, banks with more sophisticated internal control systems may use modelling either for limited risk aggregation (data collection and summary) or options pricing purposes (under CAD 1) or for more general risk management purposes (under CAD 2).

To qualify for model recognition, banks must satisfy a number of qualitative and quantitative criteria and be subject to an on-site review process.

DEBT SECURITIES – INTEREST RATE POSITION RISK (TI)

15.77   CAD must maintain separate capital against their debt securities and equity positions. These are aggregated with the foreign exchange, commodity and large exposure risk charges to create the total liability for the trading book. This totalling or aggregation is referred to as the building block approach. This was introduced under the Capital Adequacy Directive 93/6/EEC (as amended by 98/31/EC).

15.78   The two main elements within the trading book calculation are the charges for debt securities (government or corporate bonds) and equities. Debt securities are dealt with under chapter TI.[1] After an overview, this explains how interest rate risk may arise, divides the charge into a specific and general market risk element, explains how each is dealt with under a standard and simplified methods and how derivatives are dealt with within the calculations.

1 IPRU (BANK), chapter TI (Interest rate position risk).

15.79 Interest rate risk arises from exposure to loss through movements in interest rates. Any contract or transaction that affects a bank's position at a future date will give rise to an interest rate exposure as well as a position in the underlying instrument (unless it is fully hedged).[1] Interest rate risk accordingly arises as a natural result of any banking activity although excessive exposures may be created where interest rate sensitivity is not properly monitored and controlled. This may then affect net interest income and the level of other interest sensitive income and operating expenses as well as the underlying value of a bank's assets, liabilities and off-balance sheet instruments (due to the present value of future cashflows being adjusted to reflect interest rate changes). An affective interest rate management process is accordingly essential for all banks.

1 IPRU (BANK), chapter TI, section 2.1.

15.80 Various specific types of interest rates exposure may be identified. These include:

(a) repricing risk is the main form of interest rate risk that arises where there are timing differences in the maturity (for fixed rate) or repricing (for floating rate) of bank assets, liabilities or off-balance sheet items;

(b) yield curve risk arises where unanticipated shifts of the yield curve have adverse effect on the bank's income or underlying value with the yield affected by any repricing mismatches;

(c) basis risk arises where there is an imperfect correlation in the adjustment of the rates earned and paid on different instruments which otherwise have similar repricing characteristics;

(d) interest rate risk also arises with embedded options within bank assets, liabilities or off-balance sheet items;

(e) portfolios are also sensitive to risk changes especially where bonds and notes may include call or put options, loans have repayment rights attached or deposits allow funds withdrawal without penalty.

15.81 Under the CAD framework, interest rate risk is divided between general and specific (interest rate) risk. The calculation is generally based on a standard approach although a simplified variation is also available. Risk models may also be used where the institution concerned has satisfied certain qualitative and quantitative criteria.[1]

Specific risk is generally concerned with factors that affect risks that are particular to the instrument or issuer concerned. General risk is concerned with more general market factors.

1 See IPRU (BANK), chapter TV.

15.82 The general risk calculation for interest rate exposure is designed to measure the risk in future cashflows in the trading book currency by currency.[1] A separate calculation should be undertaken for each currency irrespective of where the individual instruments are physically traded or listed. Long and short positions are offset. Each of the separate currency requirements is then aggregated to produce the total charge. The calculation may either be carried out on a maturity band or duration based method.

Under the maturity band, individual net positions are allocated to one of thirty weighting categories depending upon residual maturity (of between 1 month and over 20 years) and coupon (either 3% or more or under 3%). Weighting factors of between 0% and 12.50% are then assigned to each band. Positions may be matched within a band, within a zone (1, 2 or 3) or between zones. Any residual unmatched weighted positions are aggregated. The total general interest rate risk capital is then calculated by applying a further risk weighting (10% to 150%) to the total matched position, each of the zones (1, 2 and 3) and between zones (1 and 2, 2 and 3 and 1 and 3).[2] The effect is to increase the charge as the spread across which the positions are matched increases. The higher charge for matched positions within Zone 1 reflects the greater volatility at the shorter end of the yield curve.

1   See IPRU (BANK), chapter TI, section 4.1.
2   See IPRU (BANK), chapter TI, section 4.2, paras 5 and 6.

15.83   Under the alternative method, banks may use a modified duration approach to determine their general interest rate capital requirement for traded debt instruments and other sources of interest rate exposure including derivatives. Modified duration is a measure of the price sensitivity of individual positions to changes in market yields taking into account the coupon of the instrument. It is based on duration and provides the percentage change in the value of a bond for a given percentage in its yield. This method is more complex to calculate although it produces a more accurate measurement.

The approach operates by calculating the yield to maturity (or redemption yield) at current market value that is used to calculate the modified duration. The weighted position is calculated by allocating each net position to one of 15 time bands (1 month to 20 years) to which is assigned a rate (the assumed move in rates of between 1% and 60%). Matched and unmatched positions are offset within and between time bands with any residual unmatched weighted positions being aggregated. The general interest rate charge is then calculated by totalling the weighted positions multiplied by a further factor either on a gross, individual or combined basis (as with the maturity based method) although using slightly different rates (5% to 100%).

Under the simplified method, fixed and floating rate instruments are allocated across the same 13 time bands as under the maturity based method although revised weighting factors are applied to the gross position within each band. The 13 weighted figures are then totalled to provide the general risk charge.[1]

1   See IPRU (BANK), chapter TI, section 4.4, para 13.

15.84   Specific risks may either be calculated on a standard or simplified method. Specific risk is the risk that the price of a security will change relative to prices of securities generally. This is usually attributable to changes in the perceived creditworthiness of the issuer although other factors may be relevant.

Instruments are weighted depending upon whether they are government instruments (0.00%) or otherwise according to maturity (qualifying items less than 6 months: 0.25%; 6–24 months: 1.00%, over 24 months: 1.60%; and non-qualifying items: 8.00%). Zone A central governments and central banks (including the European Communities) are nil weighted under band 1.

Qualifying items then include Zone B central governments and central banks, multilateral development banks, credit institutions with a Zone A country or Zone B country (provided the residual maturity is 1 year or less), issued or guaranteed by an investment firm subject to the CAD, issued or guaranteed by Zone A public sector entities, companies whose equity is eligible for a 4% equity specific risk weighting or it is assigned a 50% weighting under the FSA's implementation of the Solvency Ratio Directive.

The total charge is the sum of the weighted value within each band. Under the simplified method, the 6–24 month band is removed with only the four Zone A, less than 6 months, over 6 months and non-qualifying item ratings being used.

15.85   Special rules apply with regard to the interest rate position risk on derivatives.[1] A dual (or two-legged) approach is followed with the position being divided into the maturity of the future forward rate agreement and the position representing the underlying instrument (or an equivalent notional instrument where there is no underlying as with an interest rate swap).

Different rules then apply depending on whether the contract is an FX forward, deposit future or forward rate agreement, swap, option, index linked security or repo or reverse repo or similar transactions (generally sell-buy or stop lending).

1   See IPRU (BANK), chapter TI, section 6.

15.86   Option model recognition may be available where there is a significant options position which is actively managed. A 'carve out' is also available for purchased plain vanilla options or warrants in bonds, interest rates and futures and swaps and variants.[1]

1   See IPRU (BANK), chapter TI, section 7.

EQUITY POSITION RISK (TE)

15.87   A bank which holds equity positions (long or short) in its trading book will be exposed to movements in the instruments held. A position is the amount in the security that the bank owns (its long position) or owes to another party (its short position).

Specific equity position risk is the risk that the value of the equities held in individual companies relative to the market may move against the bank.

General equity position risk is concerned with movements in the market as a whole while specific risk is concerned with factors related to individual entities including issuer risk and liquidity risk.

15.88   The chapter on equity position risk (TE) implements the relevant requirements in the Capital Adequacy Directive. This again only applies to CAD banks. The risk is again divided between specific and general. The FSA provides a standard method for calculating both types of risk as well as a simplified method for specific market risk. The general elements of the FSA's approach are explained and standard and simplified methodologies developed. Derivatives are again treated separately.

15.89   Specific risk is calculated with regard to the instruments listed in the rules. These include shares, depository receipts, convertible preference securities, convertible debt securities and derivatives in any of these instruments.[1]

Both the standard and simplified methods are calculated on a country-by-country basis. Banks may net long and short positions in the same equity or underlying equity where derivatives (other than options) are involved to produce an individual net position in the instrument. Tranches in equity instruments may be netted provided that the tranches involved enjoy the same rights in all respects and become fungible (exchangeable) within 180 days.

1   See IPRU (BANK), chapter TE (Equity position risk), section 2.2.

15.90   In calculating general equity position risk, banks must deduct all holdings of capital instruments issued by other credit institutions or investment firms, net all holdings in the same stock to produce an individual net position and assign each individual net position to a country portfolio.[1] The capital charge is then 8% of the overall net position after totalling the net country figures.

A separate concentration adjustment has to be undertaken with regard to large exposures in any particular instrument. When an individual net position represents more than 20% of the overall gross equity position of the country, the amount of the individual net position above 20% must be removed from the calculation of the overall net equity position for the country and added back on a gross basis. This is then subject to a separate 8% charge to cover the additional exposure to the territory concerned.

1   See IPRU (BANK), chapter TE, section 3.1.

15.91   Specific risk is more concerned with factors relevant to the individual instrument and issuer. The objective of the specific risk requirement is to cover differences between general market index movements and those of particular equity portfolios. It accordingly covers a variety of factors including the perceived credit quality of the issuer, liquidity of individual stocks, event risk (such as the effect on prices of takeovers and mergers) and diversification within country portfolios.[1] Ether a standard or simplified methodology may be adopted.

The general effect of the standard method is to apply an 8% or 4% weighting to the net position depending upon whether the holding is liquid and well diversified. Individual net positions are calculated for each country. These are totalled to produce the bank's total specific equity position risk exposure. The 4% weight will then be applied provided the equities satisfy both a liquidity and a diversity test failing which the 8% will be applied. The purpose of the liquidity element is to determine whether highly liquid markets exist for specific equities to allow investors to move in and out of positions readily without incurring loses due to wide spreads.[2] An equity included on the list of highly liquid indices for markets in various countries is deemed to be highly liquid. Other non-index linked stock may also be included provided it has, at least, six registered market makers and its market size is 5,000 shares. The purpose of the diversity element is to ensure that the portfolio is not over-concentrated in particular stock. No individual position may comprise more than 10% of the gross value of the country portfolio and the total value of positions that comprise between 5% and 10% do not exceed 50% of the gross value of the country portfolio.

The simplified method involves applying a single weighting of 8% to all net positions through the removal of the liquidity and diversity tests.

1   See IPRU (BANK), chapter TE, section 4.1.
2   See IPRU (BANK), chapter TE, section 4.2.2, para 7.

15.92 Special rules again apply with regard to derivatives. Derivatives positions in equity futures, forwards and swaps related to equity positions or indices should be converted into notional underlying instruments. The rules applicable are set out in the chapter.[1]

1 See IPRU (BANK), chapter TE, section 5.

15.93 The effect of the equity related market risk rules is to allow a 4% charge on all net holdings in liquid and diversified stock. This portfolio approach to risk management can be contrasted with the flat capital charging adopted in the US. Under the Securities and Exchange Commission rules, shares are generally subject to a flat 15% charge with permitted haircuts (or deductions). The CAD has generally adopted the more sophisticated UK portfolio approach with the effect that European banks can generally hold significantly less capital against their US counterparts.

The differences between these two systems had been considered by the international securities organisation (IOSCO) in its attempt to develop common international standards in this regard. Unfortunately, IOSCO could not agree on any specific approach.

15.94 The Basel Committee had been discussing the development of a joint approach to capital for securities firms with IOSCO until the early 1990s. A number of meetings had been held and attempts made to develop a common position. With IOSCO's inability to agree any clear rules, the Basel Committee felt constrained to develop its own capital requirements in respect of the securities positions of banks separately. This resulted in the production of a draft Market Risk Amendment which was finally adopted in January 1996.

The Basel Market Risk Amendment now represents the minimum standards for the capital positions of banks globally. This generally adopts the same approach as set out in the European CAD although some additional discretion is conferred and separate requirements included with regard to commodity risk.

COUNTERPARTY RISK IN THE TRADING BOOK (TC)

15.95 Counterparty exposure is concerned with the risk that a party, other than the issuer of the underlying instrument, may at some future date fail to discharge its obligations under the contract resulting in loss to the bank. Counterparty (as opposed to credit) risk is only relevant where deals have not been finally settled. This can be considered as a form of settlement risk although the relevant charges for free deliveries and unsettled trades are dealt with separately.[1] The exposure arises with regard to the trading counterparty rather than the issuer of the underlying securities.

The trading book rules for counterparty risk apply in relation to contracts traded on exchanges subject to daily margining requirements, OTC foreign exchange contracts with an original maturity of 14 calendar days or less and overdue transactions involving the delivery of an instrument against the receipt of cash less than five days beyond their due date. Capital is to be assigned to the risk on any trade that is not due for final settlement or is overdue. All exposures should be marked to market, at least, daily.

The charge is calculated by applying the counterparty risk weights used for trading counterparties and the weights used in the banking book to the differences in value between the cash or instruments paid and to be received. Special rules apply with regard to collateral and repos.[2]

1 See IPRU (BANK), chapter DU (Common treatments for counterparty risk).
2 See IPRU (BANK), chapter TC (Counterparty risk in the trading book).

LARGE EXPOSURES (TL)

15.96 Separate additional (or incremental) capital has to be set aside for large exposures in trading book items.[1] This is distinct from the general regime that applies to large exposures.[2] Where an exposure exceeds 25% of a bank's large exposures capital base as a result of long securities positions in the trading book, a 'soft limits' regime may be agreed in writing with the FSA. In such a case, the large exposures capital base will be amended to include any tier 3 capital eligible to support the trading book. Where the exposure exceeds 25% of the amended large exposures capital base, incremental capital has to be included in the bank's capital adequacy calculation. This excess should only arise through holdings of tradable securities in the trading book.

The exposure is related to issuer risk on the security. The calculation is based on the identification of the 'head room' between the non-securities exposures and 25% of the amended capital base (the capital base (tier 1 and tier 2) with eligible tier 3 capital). The remaining net long securities positions are ranked according to specific risk weighting factors with the lowest weighted items being applied to the head room figures. The incremental capital is then calculated with regard to the remaining net long securities positions.

If the exposure has been outstanding for 10 days or less, the specific risk weighting for the remaining exposures is multiplied by 200%. If the exposure has been outstanding for more than 10 days, higher factors are applied (of between 200 and 900%).[3]

1 See IPRU (BANK), chapter TL (Incremental capital for large exposures).
2 See IPRU (BANK), chapter LE (Large exposures).
3 See IPRU (BANK), chapter TL (Incremental capital for large exposures), section 2.2, para 6.

UNDERWRITING (TU)

15.97 The capital framework includes concessionary treatment for the calculation of capital cover in respect of underwriting commitments.[1] All underwriting commitments should be included within the trading book although certain adjustments are permitted.

Underwriting is concerned with agreeing to purchase a specified quantity of securities in a new share or loan stock issue on a given date and at a given price in the event that they are not otherwise purchased following issue. This provides a guarantee or insurance that the issue will not be under-subscribed.

The underwriting regime operates by allowing reductions in requirements for the specific and general risk elements of bond and equity type issuer having regard to the number of days from the date of issue. Banks are required initially to place capital against their net underwriting commitments from the date that the initial commitment to underwrite the issue was given.

The net commitment (or net underwriting position) is calculated as the amount of gross commitment adjusted over the period the commitment remains on the bank's books. The rules refer to the working day on which the bank becomes unconditionally committed to accept the securities as Working Day 0. Until Working Day 0, the capital requirements on bond underwritings is the general market risk requirement. For equity underwritings, the capital requirement is the specific and general market risk requirements applied to the entire net commitment and the instrument reduced by 90%. From Working Day 0, further scaling factors are applied.

For bonds, the specific risk requirement is the net commitment reduced by the factor applicable for each day following Working Day 0 (100%, 90%, 75%, 75%, 50%, 25% and 0%). No reductions are allowed on the general risk applicable to bonds. For equities, the same reductions apply to both the specific and general market risk requirements (90%, 90%, 75%, 75%, 50%, 25% and 0%).

1   See IPRU (BANK), chapter TU (Underwriting in capital adequacy framework).

CAD 1 MODELS (TS)

15.98   CAD 1[1] models may be used to calculate capital requirements in respect of market risk. CAD 1 models may either consist of risk aggregation models or options pricing models. These are distinct from Value at Risk (VaR) models permitted under CAD 2[2] which was implemented on 30 September 1998 in the UK. Only limited use of VaR models was permitted under CAD 1. Some changes were then necessary to the CAD 1 rules following implementation of CAD 2.[3] The availability of VaR models under CAD 1 was withdrawn on 30 September 1998 due to the extended options available under CAD 2.

1   Capital Adequacy Directive 93/6/EEC. On relevant Basel Committee requirements, see para 15.131 and Table 15.14 below.
2   Directive amending the Capital Adequacy Directive 98/31/EC.
3   These included withdrawing the option to use back testing models to calculate FX risk capital charges and limiting the types of instruments that can be put through interest rate sensitivity models. See IPRU (BANK), chapter TS, section 1.2, note (a).

15.99   A 'model' is referred to as any formalised and systematic method of analysing risk and the programme used to carry out that analysis.[1] Models can be used to assess market and credit risks although the FSA notes that they can also act as a source of risk to the extent that they are based on unrealistic assumptions.

The objective of model recognition is to allow banks with developed risk management systems to benefit from more accurate capital measurement and charging. This accordingly creates an incentive for the development of more sophisticated internal risk management techniques.

Model recognition is permitted following a model review process that looks at the bank's specific model design and supporting systems. The review accordingly examines both the model and its more general operating environment within the bank.

1   IPRU (BANK), chapter TS (CAD 1 models), section 2.1.

15.100   CAD 1 model recognition is only available for risk aggregation and options pricing models. Risk aggregation may either involve options risk aggregation or interest rate sensitivity modelling.

Options risk aggregation models may be used for interest rate, equity, foreign currency and commodity options. These are used to examine and aggregate option risk for each underlying instrument and to calculate the capital charge directly or provide inputs or both depending upon the specific model used.

Interest rate sensitivity models may be used where a bank marks to market daily and manages its interest rate risk on derivative instruments on a discounted cash flow basis.[1]

Options pricing models are examined as part of risk aggregation and interest rate sensitivity recognition.[2]

1   IPRU (BANK), chapter TS, section 3.1.
2   IPRU (BANK), chapter TS, section 3.2.

15.101   The CAD 1 model review process involves the examination of the underlying model and systems through a series of model review visits.[1] A three-month notification period is generally required to allow banks to provide sufficient pre-visit information to the model review team.

Information requested is generally sent out six weeks before the visit with a deadline of two weeks before the visit for receipt of all relevant information requested. Pre-visit information may also be obtained through a standard questionnaire returned to the FSA with background information. The questionnaire is concerned with the bank's market position in relevant products, organisational structure and personnel profile and risk information, operational controls, supporting IT systems, models, VaR framework, model release and control procedures, risk management and control framework, market risk limit structures and possible future development relevant to model recognition. A minimum level of standards will have to be satisfied with regard to model mathematics and underlying assumptions as well as systems and controls. The relevant standards will vary depending upon firm size, nature of business and particular models used.

Following on-site visits, subsequent information may be requested before recognition is granted.

1   IPRU (BANK), chapter TS, section 4.

15.102   The general principle behind model recognition is to ensure that the model is appropriate to determine capital requirements for each product type. The ability of the model to satisfy various operational conditions will be examined and recognition only given if the FSA is satisfied that the model and its supporting control systems are of a sufficient standard.

The FSA will require the firm to issue a formal letter of acknowledgement confirming that it accepts its responsibilities under the CAD 1 model recognition process and its acceptance of the terms under which model recognition is granted. This must be signed by a senior member of staff. Model recognition will then be granted in a formal letter with a CAD 1 model recognition statement attached. This will, in particular, set out the products and locations covered and applicable conditions for recognition.

Provisional recognition may be granted with regard to the use of models in overseas branches or subsidiaries of UK authorised banks. Internal or external auditors will have to have confirmed that the necessary systems and controls are in place and that no additional matters of material concern arise with regard to risk management.

Full recognition may then be granted once the FSA has been able to conduct its own examination visit and is satisfied that the relevant mathematics are robust and comprehensive and satisfy the CAD requirements and that the necessary systems and controls are in place.

MARKET RISK MODELS (TV)

15.103   Market risk may either be calculated on a standard approach or internal model approach basis or using a combination of both methodologies. Capital must always be held to cover relevant market risk in respect of equities and debt instruments as well as off-balance sheet items in the trading book and foreign exchange and commodities risk cover in the trading and banking books.

Separate VaR model recognition is available for this purpose under CAD 2. Although CAD 2 was only implemented in the UK on 30 September 1998, the equivalent provisions had already been agreed under the Basel Committee Market Risk Amendment which was issued in January 1996. The January 1996 Basel paper was subsequently amended in September 1997 to allow specific risk modelling. The purpose of CAD 2 was to revise CAD 1 to allow for the extended use of model recognition permitted under the Market Risk Amendment.

15.104 Banks must obtain FSA approval before using an internal model to calculate capital requirements.[1] For this purpose, a model must be accurate and operated with integrity in a well-controlled environment. The bank must satisfy a number of qualitative and quantitative standards before it may use models to ensure a minimum degree of prudence, consistency and transparency.

To the extent that modelling is more sophisticated and accurate in its risk measurement, capital charges should be lower. Banks accordingly have an incentive to invest in risk management and systems construction. Risk management is understood to refer to the wider environment in which the model operates with risk measurement being related specifically to the internal model adopted.[2]

1 See IPRU (BANK), chapter TV (The use of internal models), section 1.1, para 2.
2 See IPRU (BANK), chapter TV, section 2, para 7.

15.105 The internal models approach adopted by the FSA is based on a Value at Risk (VaR) methodology. The VaR measure is stated to provide an estimate of the worst expected loss on a portfolio resulting from market movements over a specified period of time at a given confidence level.[1] It must be stressed that VaR is not a model or modelling technique as such but a measurement framework or objective. This provides a common framework for the measurement and expression of the exposure that the underlying model is designed to achieve.

A large number of separate management models are available. The most common include historical or Monte Carlo simulation or some form of variance-covariance model. There is no agreement as to the best model or the model that produces the most accurate results. In tests, it has also been shown that all of the models will produce substantial variations in results even when applied to a common portfolio.

The objective of model recognition is not to prescribe the specific model or approve the use of any particular model as such. Rather the purpose is to approve the use of the model selected within the larger control framework established within any particular bank. Unfortunately, the chapter is possibly not as clear as it might be on the distinction between VaR as a measurement technique and modelling as such.

1 See IPRU (BANK), chapter TV, section 2, para 5.

15.106 In considering applications for a model recognition, the FSA has stated that it is important that banks use the model selected for its own internal modelling purposes rather than develop a separate or parallel model for market risk calculations alone.[1]

Once a model has been recognised, the FSA will be concerned to confirm its continuing accuracy and integrity in operation and use. The FSA will also have to be satisfied that the impacts of material errors are properly taken into account either in the assumptions underlying the model or in predicted market moves. A full programme of stress testing and back testing will accordingly have to be established with the model also being subject to independent internal and external validation.

While the FSA aims to be consistent in its treatment of model recognition across banks, it will not be prescriptive as to the specific risks covered in each case. It will also not expect banks with the same portfolio composition to attract the same capital requirement in each case.

The quantitative standards adopted allow a reasonable range of difference to be acceptable in practice. Once a model has been approved, if any material inaccuracies arise, the FSA will expect remedial action to be taken in early course failing which it will withdraw recognition.

1 See IPRU (BANK), chapter TV, section 2, para 8.

15.107 The recognition process for CAD 2 models is similar to that set up for CAD 1 systems. This is generally based on a combination of on-site visits, interviews with relevant personnel supported by preparatory and follow-up correspondence.

The on-site visits will be conducted by the FSA's Traded Risk Department. The structure and number of visits will depend on the bank and systems involved. It is expected that several visits generally lasting two days each will be necessary. This may take a number of months.[1]

If model recognition is to be granted, the terms of the recognition will be set out in a model recognition letter attached to which will be a schedule of parameters that will define the extent and use of the model and any supporting conditions to the recognition.

1 See IPRU (BANK), chapter TV, section 3.

15.108 Banks have to satisfy a number of qualitative and quantitative standards as part of the recognition process. The qualitative standards deal with such matters as integrated use, existence of an independent risk control unit, management involvements, sufficient skilled staff, effective monitoring and compliance procedures, a reasonable history of model accuracy, a stress testing programme, regular risk measurement reviews and internal evaluation of model accuracy and performance.

The only surprise element is possibly the requirement of a proven track record of reasonable accuracy in risk measurement.[1] This would appear to be data based and quantitative rather than qualitative in nature. The guidance to the requirement, however, stresses the internal model validation and examination procedures rather than the model results as such. The FSA refers specifically to testing the validity of the assumptions and approximations underlying the model, investigation of the limitations of the model and testing of the accuracy of parts of the model as well as the model as a whole. The drafting of the specific requirement in terms of historic accuracy is possibly then misleading. The FSA will also examine the systems used to run the model and associated calculations to confirm its implementation integrity.

As part of this supporting information systems examination, the FSA will, in particular, consider feeder systems (for material risks), risk aggregation systems, the time series databases, supporting VaR system, the stress testing system and back testing systems, data quality, reconciliations and checks on completeness of capture. System development, change control and documentation as well as security and audit trails, systems availability and contingency procedures and network adequacy will also be assessed with operational statistics relating to the VaR production process.[2] While model accuracy and integrity is the responsibility of bank management, this is stated to include obtaining appropriate independent validation through an effective external audit function.[3]

1 See IPRU (BANK), chapter TV, section 4.2, para 4(f).
2 See IPRU (BANK), chapter TV, section 4.3.
3 See IPRU (BANK), chapter TV, section 4.4.

15.109 In addition to qualitative standards, the bank must also satisfy certain quantitative standards.[1] Although a number of common quantitative standards are set, the principle of equivalence adopted by the FSA allows banks to adopt other standards following agreement with the FSA. This will be provided on condition that the resulting capital requirement is not lower than that achieved under the general standards set.

The quantitative standards adopted by the FSA generally require that the VaR should be computed, at least, daily using a 99% one-tailed confidence limit. The bank must use a 10-working day holding period. The VaR measures should be based on an effective historical observation period of, at least, 150 days (unless a shorter observation period is justified by a significant change in price volatility). Data sets must be updated no less frequently than quarterly and more frequently whenever market prices are subject to material changes. Correlations within and between broad risk categories may be used provided that the measurement system is sound and implemented with integrity.

The model must accurately capture all material risks arising on options and option-like products. Any risks not captured must be covered by adequate own funds.

1 See IPRU (BANK), chapter TV, section 5.

15.110 Banks may combine the standard and internal model approach although where modelling is used for one risk, it is expected that it will be extended to cover all market risks over time.[1] The FSA is concerned to avoid 'cherry picking' with the standard approach being used to secure a lower capital requirement than would otherwise be available under modelling. A single approach will generally be required for all broad risk factor categories. A risk factor category means interest rates, exchange rates (including gold), equity prices and commodity prices as well as option volatilities within each to the extent relevant.

A combination of the two approaches for material risks within a risk factor category or across different entities or locations within the bank will not generally be permitted. One exception may be with regard to group units that are consolidated on an aggregation plus basis with their parent. Banks implementing or improving their models will be allowed some flexibility in omitting some particular product types. The bank will also not be required to capture immaterial risks on new products in an otherwise complete model. Where both approaches are used, the results of each must be totalled to provide the final capital figure.

Once a bank has adopted the internal model approach for a portfolio, it will not generally be allowed to revert to the standard approach other than in exceptional circumstances. Any changes in the combination used must also be discussed with the FSA. Modelling will only be permitted with regard to instruments within the trading book and foreign exchange and commodity positions.

1   See IPRU (BANK), chapter TV, section 8.

15.111   Modelling is subject to both stress testing and back testing. Stress testing is used to identify the exposure of the bank arising as a result of the breakdown of model assumptions or by low-probability events.

Modelling must be subject to rigorous and comprehensive stress testing with the results constituting a key part of the bank's assessment of its capital position.[1] The FSA will examine the bank's stress testing programme including its supporting procedures to assess and respond to the results obtained. The bank must periodically and actively identify the full spectrum of possible worst-case scenarios that are relevant to its portfolio. The results must be communicated to senior management on a regular basis and periodically to the board of directors. The FSA will, in particular, consider the appropriateness of the scenarios used to the test the effect of adverse movements in market volatilities and correlations and the effect of changing the assumptions underlying the internal model. Non-linear effects must also be adequately captured.

Specific scenarios will not be generally prescribed although the bank will be expected to discuss its stress testing programme and results with the FSA on a routine basis.

1   See IPRU (BANK), chapter TV, section 9.

15.112   Back testing is used to assess the effectiveness or quality of a model by comparing its output (the VaR forecast) with subsequent trading outcomes (referred as the 'P&L'). P&L means the day's profit and loss arising from trading activities within the scope of the model.[1] This is also referred to as actual P&L although this must be 'cleaned' by excluding all material non-market elements that might cause a loss including fees and commissions, reserves not directly related to market risk and one-off marketing profits from large new deals. The hypothetical P&L is the profit and loss that would have occurred had the portfolio remained unchanged. Model recognition will only be granted once the bank has, at least, three months' back testing results.

During the first 150 days after a bank begins to use its internal model, the P&L and the VaR measures must be compared although not on a formal basis. After the first 150 days, the bank must compare each of the P&L figures for these days with the corresponding one-day VaR measures. This comparison should be made daily using a rolling 250-day period. The VaR will be calibrated to a one-day holding period and a 99% one-tailed confidence level. Exceptions arise where a day's loss exceeds the corresponding VaR measure. The FSA must be notified orally by close of business within two working days of the loss being incurred (this is a referred to as close of business on day N +2). The FSA must also be provided with a written report on a monthly basis of each month's exceptions. The reason for the exceptions must be explained with the bank's response. Oral reporting is carried out on a provisional basis as the final data may confirm that an exception did not arise.

All of the information obtained by the FSA will be used as part of its ongoing qualitative assessment of the bank's internal model. All confirmed exceptions are referred to as recorded exceptions which will be taken into account in assigning plus factors by the FSA. Banks may request that exceptions are not recorded depending upon their nature, size and frequency and available model evidence. If appropriate corrective action has been taken, the exception may not have to be recorded.

1   See IPRU (BANK), chapter TV, section 10.5.

15.113   A number of plus factors and multiplication factors are applied depending upon how many exceptions are recorded. A bank with four or more exceptions is automatically placed in the Green Zone.[1] This attracts a basic multiplication factor of three with a zero plus factor.

Banks with between five and nine exceptions are placed in the Yellow Zone with additional plus factors being added to the multiplication factor in each case (0.40, 0.50, 0.65, 0.75 and 0.85). A bank with ten or more exceptions is placed in the Red Zone and the multiplication factor increased to four following the addition of a plus factor of one.

The effect of back testing is then to adjust the minimum multiplication factor that will be applied by the supervisory authorities. The multiplication factor will vary between 3 and 4 depending upon the number of exceptions that are confirmed by the back testing history.

1   See IPRU (BANK), chapter TV, section 10.3, para 13, table.

15.114   Even where a bank only has four or less exceptions it will still be subject to a minimum multiplication factor of three. This means that whatever the accuracy of its modelling results in terms of risk identification and measurement, the resultant capital figure will still have to be multiplied by three. The objective is to create a form of capital cushion against model inaccuracies or weakness. This may arise where price movements display patterns (such as fat tails) that differ from the statistical simplifications used.

The VaR estimates are typically based on end-of-day positions and generally do not take account of intra-day trading risk, models cannot adequately capture event risk arising from exceptional market circumstances and many models rely on simplifying assumptions to value the positions in the portfolio especially with regard to such complex instruments as options. The FSA also accepts that 'the past is not always a good approximation of the future'.[1]

The anomaly that arises is that while the lower charging that may result from the development of increasingly sophisticated models will act as an incentive for bank investment, the subsequent simple multiplication of this by a crude factor of three will act as a severe disincentive against process and practice development. The factor of three was agreed by the Basel Committee as part of its Market Risk Amendment in January 1996 although it accepted that this may be unnecessarily strict and reduced over time. Unfortunately, this has been accepted as an absolute minimum by the FSA at this stage with the plus factors only then being added on in the event of back testing difficulties.

The FSA will also apply a further surcharge for specific risk.[2] The objective would appear to be to capture event and default risk for traded debt and equity positions and related off-balance sheet exposures. The surcharge is calculated as either an amount equal to the specific risk portion of the VaR measure or the VaR measures of sub-portfolios that are subject to specific risk with the results being averaged over the previous 60 business days.

1   See IPRU (BANK), chapter TV, section 11.3, para 8.
2   See IPRU (BANK), chapter TV, section 11.4.

15.115   The purpose of the modelling allowances are to provide recognition of the extent to which a number of banks have already developed sophisticated internal risk management systems to measure their market risk exposures. These systems are clearly considerably more sophisticated than the standard and simplified approaches developed by the EU, the Basel Committee and the FSA.

To refuse to recognise the value of these internal processes would be economically and in supervisory terms inefficient at the same time as impose unnecessary burdens on banks to the extent that they would have to develop separate management systems for their own internal and external capital purposes. Model recognition has accordingly been developed in response to changes in developments within the markets and market risk practice more generally.

The lower capital charges available through modelling also create a natural incentive for banks to develop more sophisticated systems. This must be encouraged by the authorities. To that extent, modelling will act as both a recognition of past success as well as an incentive for future development.

15.116   In considering the value of modelling, however, a number of inherent disadvantages must not be ignored. Models are based on often simple statistical assumptions and generally attempt to predict future results from historic data. This is inherently flawed.

To the extent that models are based on analyses of historic information, their effectiveness will be limited irrespective of how sophisticated they become. It is for this reason, that the authorities had to agree some safety or multiplication factor to allow for a reasonable level of additional cover within the capital charges that resulted from the modelling processes.

In terms of initial model recognition, the factor of three may have seen reasonable although as modelling continues to develop this should be reduced. To the extent that back testing is also used to assess the historical effectiveness of a model, rather than simply add a further multiplication charge where exceptions arise, they should also be used to reward successes by lowering the minimum factor of three. This should be given early consideration.

Other financial provisions

LARGE EXPOSURES (LE)

15.117   The FSA policy with regard to large exposures is set out in chapter LE. This develops the detailed requirements set out in chapter GN (section 3) and in the reporting requirements section of the Supervision Manual.

A bank is generally subject to three obligations. The bank must establish a large exposures policy and provide the FSA with a copy statement. It must maintain adequate systems and controls to monitor and limit its large exposures and notify the FSA whenever it has entered into an exposure that exceeds 10% of capital or proposes to enter into an exposure that exceeds 25% of capital. A bank may only hold large exposures in excess of 10% of capital up to a total limit of 800% of capital.[1]

These requirements give effect to the European Large Exposures Directive (LED) 92/121/EEC as restated in the Banking Consolidation Directive. In addition to these 'hard' limits, 'soft' limits were also introduced under the Capital Adequacy Directive which that additional capital to be held where large exposures in the trading book exceed 25% of capital base.

---

1   See IPRU (BANK), chapter LE (Large exposures), section 1.1.

15.118 Large exposures are concerned with avoiding excessive concentrations within the loan book or trading book of a bank. These may arise where the bank becomes over-committed to any individual customer or particular sector or geographic area. The exposure created is concerned with the extent of the loss that will arise in the event of the particular borrower defaulting. Basic rules were accordingly agreed at the European level under the Large Exposures Directive to avoid banks becoming over-committed to any single borrower. These were then supplemented by the further soft limits introduced under the Capital Adequacy Directive and certain further policy positions adopted by the FSA.

15.119 A large exposure is any exposure to a counterparty or group of closely related counterparties which is greater than or equal to 10% of the bank's large exposures capital base (essentially own funds). The large exposures capital base (referred to as the LECB in the handbook) is the sum of allowable Tier 1 and Tier 2 capital less any deductions. The large exposures capital base may also include eligible Tier 3 capital where soft limits have been agreed with the FSA in respect of exposures in the trading book. The calculation is based on the bank's previous period's capital adequacy returns. The returns are made on Form LE2 quarterly.

An exposure is the maximum loss a bank will suffer if a counterparty or group of closely related counterparties fails to meet its obligations or the maximum loss that might be experienced as a result of the bank realising assets or off-balance sheet positions. A number of deductions are permitted under the rules.[1]

A counterparty is any party in which a bank has a claim on a direct or indirect basis. An exempt exposure is not subject to the 25% limit but should be reported. Exempt exposures include short-term (less than 1 year) exposures to banks, CAD investment firms, recognised exchanges and clearing houses, Zone A governments and central banks, Zone B governments dealing in the local currency, secured transactions (cash or Zone A securities), underwriting exposures and certain other connected exposure concessions.[2] Other key definitions are set out in chapter LE.[3]

1 See IPRU (BANK), chapter LE, section 4.3.
2 See IPRU (BANK), chapter LE, section 9.2.
3 See IPRU (BANK), chapter LE, sections 4, 5, 6 and 7.

15.120 A bank must notify the FSA if it proposes to enter into an exposure exceeding 25% of capital.[1] Banks must be able to monitor exposures on a daily basis and must not incur an exposure to any individual counterparty or group of closely related counterparties in excess of 25% of its large exposures capital base unless it is an exempt exposure. CAD banks may breach the 25% limit with regard to holdings in their trading books provided appropriate incremental capital is held. Short-term clearing book positions may also be held in subsidiaries or other subgroup exposures with written consent.

Banks must notify the FSA immediately of any breach of the 25% limit and 'post-notify' all exposures over 10% of the large exposures capital base. FSA approval is required where the total large exposures held by a bank exceed 300% of capital subject to a maximum limit of 800%.

Banks must comply with these limits and notification requirements on a solo (or solo consolidated) and on a consolidated basis. Where large exposures exceed 100% of capital, the FSA may increase the bank's capital ratios. This is referred to as clustering.[2] The Handbook contains additional provisions with regard to the content and examination of the bank's policy statement[3] and notification procedures.[4]

1 See IPRU (BANK), chapter GN, section 3.
2 See IPRU (BANK), chapter LE, section 8.2.
3 See IPRU (BANK), chapter LE, section 8.
4 See IPRU (BANK), chapter LE, section 10.

15.121 In addition to the provisions concerning credit and market risk, IPRU (BANK) contains further provision with regard to credit derivatives (CD) and securitisation and assets transfers (SE).[1]

1 See Walker, 'Interim Prudential Sourcebook: Banks' in *Financial Services Regulation* (Butterworths loose leaf), Division B, paras 820–835.

Further sections of the sourcebook

15.122 The remainder of the sourcebook contains chapters on liquidity (LM (Mismatch liquidity) and LS (Sterling stock liquidity)) and systems and controls AR (Accounting and other records and internal control systems), ST (foreign exchange) and FR (Fraud)) and controllers (CL (comfort letters)).

Further provisions are also included with regard to ancillary measures: valuations (VA), collateral and netting (NE), consolidated supervision (CS), outsourcing (OS) and provisioning policy statements (PN).[1]

1 See also Walker, 'Interim Prudential Sourcebook: Banks' in *Financial Services Regulation* (Butterworths loose leaf), Division B, paras 836–1036.

INDIVIDUAL CAPITAL ADEQUACY FRAMEWORK

15.123 To support the application of the capital requirements to be imposed on particular firms, the FSA has been developing an individual measurement framework for capital compliance. A consultation document on the establishment of a new capital framework was produced in May 2002.[1] The objective is to establish a new treatment for individual capital adequacy standards (referred to as ICAS) for all authorised firms. This will provide a common methodology for all firms and operate within the FSA's New Regulator framework[2] and will form part of the proposed Integrated Prudential Sourcebook (PSB) and the Supervision Manual (SUP).[3]

1 See FSA, *Individual Capital Adequacy Standards* (May 2002), Consultation Paper 136. See also FSA, *Individual Capital Ratios for Banks* (July 2001), Policy Statement.
2 See FSA, *A New Regulator for the New Millennium* (January 2000); FSA, *Building a New Regulator: Progress Report 1* (December 2000); and FSA, *Progress Report 2* (February 2002). See Chapter 6, paras 6.84–6.100.
3 See FSA, *Integrated Prudential Sourcebook* (June 2001), Consultation Paper 97.

15.124 The requirement for authorised firms to hold adequate resources under the Threshold Conditions for Authorisation set out in the Financial Services and Markets Act is given effect to under Principle 4 of the FSA Principles for Businesses[1] which is to be developed further under the proposed rules to be set out within Chapter 4 of the Application and General Requirements (PRAG) within the draft PSB.

The ICAS framework will assist determine whether individual institutions maintain adequate resources having regard to their risk and control ability. In so doing, it will be apply relevant international and European standards to individual firms at the same time as allow adjustments to be made in connection with their application to individual firms. The framework will then, in particular, assist implement the Supervisory Review set out in Pillar 2 of the proposed new Basel Capital Accord.[2]

1 See Chapter 2, paras 2.94–2.96.
2 See para 15.130.

15.125 The proposed ICAS framework will be made up of an Internal Capital Assessment (ICA) and a Supplementary Capital Assessment (SCA).

The ICA will address business and systems and control risks that are not adequately covered within the minimum capital requirements applicable to the particular firm. This will be determined on a firm-by-firm basis which will be set using an internal self-certification procedure that will, in turn, either be based on the firms' own assessment of its capital requirements or through the use of economic capital models (including add-ons) where certain pre-conditions are satisfied. This will apply to all PRU categories 1, 2 and 3 which covers deposit-takers as well as insurers and principal position takers. The prudential categories (PRU) are set under PRAG (which forms part of the PSB).[1]

The SCA will then be used as a separate supervisory tool by the FSA to impose additional capital requirements where it is considered that this is necessary to cover specific systems and controls related issues or exceptional business risks not dealt with within the ICA. This will form part of the regulatory toolkit included within the Supervision Manual. Whether additional capital is required will be determined on a discretionary basis within the FSA's larger risk-based framework set up within the New Approach.

1 See Consultation Paper 136, paras 2.11–2.14. See Chapter 6, paras 6.85–6.88.

15.126 In practice, the SCA will be used to adjust the internally set ICA having regard to any particular and more general risks or exposures that may arise. The final ICAS will be structured having regard to the particular risks included within the PSB (including credit risk, market risk, operational risk and insurance risk).

Firms are required to hold minimum capital under PRCA 1 and to hold adequate financial resources under PRAG 4. Firms will then assess their own requirements under the ICA guidance to be provided. Having established their minimum compliance levels, they will self-certify compliance with that amount. Aspects of this may be discussed or confirmed with FSA personnel as part of its baseline monitoring of the institution's functions.

The FSA will then formally review whether any further action is required under the SCA procedures. If it is considered that there is no need for the firm to maintain any additional capital, no further action will be taken. If concerns have arisen either with regard to internal systems and controls issues or other external factors, the SCA level will be set or weaknesses discussed with the firm with the SCA being confirmed following this further consultation process.

The SCA will be set either as individual guidance or as a variation on the firms' Part IV permission under s 45 of the Act. Failure to comply with the ICA guidance or the final SCA will constitute breach of Principle 4, PRAG 4, SYSC 3.2.6R (effective systems and controls) and the Threshold Conditions set under the Act.

15.127   The FSA has described the ICA as being a risk-focused process designed to address business and systems and control risks not adequately covered within the minimum capital requirements.[1] This then provides a framework within which to determine whether the firm's financial resources satisfy PRAG 4.

The international minimum 8% capital ratio will form the basis of the ICA for deposit-takers and investment firms. Numeric percentage add-ons will then be included within the ICA to reflect business risks not covered within the base model (referred to as model fit) and systems and control weaknesses. These add-ons may either be generated by qualitative or quantitative measures (such as through stress tests). The FSA will attempt to include some offsetting within this add-on process to avoid penal total or aggregate levels arising.

The ICA guidance will follow the structure of the PSB modules including high level systems and controls, capital, credit risk, market risk, operational risk, and operational risk.[2] In connection, for example, with regard to systems and controls, firms will required to self-certify that the guidance has been complied with in conducting the relevant test, senior management have approved the results and all relevant internal and external information on the firm's business and control environment have been taken into account. Relevant issues to be considered will include group structure, risk management, policies, procedures and controls, market information, information technology, compliance, internal audit, outsourcing and third-party providers, business continuity, corporate governance, allocation and definition of management responsibilities and human resources. A range of capital add-ons will be developed for each criterion and guidance set in the final ICA rules.

Separate guidance will be provided on the setting of an SCA within the PSB and the Supervision Manual. While this will attempt to be as complete as possible, it has to be expected that this will operate on a more discretionary and necessarily selective basis. The FSA has nevertheless confirmed that it will attempt to apply the ICAS framework in as fair and justifiable a manner as possible with decisions being taken on a timely basis with supporting reasoning being provided.[3]

1   See Consultation Paper, para 4.2.
2   See Chapter 6, para 6.87.
3   See Consultation Paper, para 5.12.

15.128   It was originally proposed that the ICAS would be implemented with the PSB in early 2004. In light of the delays that have arisen with regard to the conclusion of the Basel credit risk revision process and associated European measures, no firm implementation date has been confirmed for banks. Although this is now expected during 2006, it was intended that insurance firms should be required to comply with the new framework from 2004.

Once it is fully operational, the new framework will assist ensure that particular firms have adequate resources having regard to their specific exposures. It should then improve measurement accuracy and correct any problems with model fit. The extent to which this gives effect to the Basel recommended supervisory review process, this has to be welcomed although the need for additive capital charging as such has to be questioned.

The effect would appear to be that the FSA has combined the desire to include business and systems risks (as developed under the earlier bank RATE approach) and supervisory review within a single framework. This is to supported provided again that it is not simply used to impose unnecessary additional charges.

Whether this should be achieved through the use of a dual (internal) self-assessment and (external) supervisory review is less clear. Firms should be entitled to discuss appropriate compliance levels with the FSA although this would have been possible under a single supervisory review process. The need for the inclusion of a separate self-assessment stage is possibly then unnecessary. This may, to a large extent, simply increase management function and cost as well as potential liability.

CAPITAL REVISION[1]

15.129   The capital rules adopted by the FSA give effect to the main European and international standards adopted in this area subject to certain revisions to reflect local conditions and supervisory practices. A number of key aspects of capital policy, however, will have to be further revised following the coming into effect of the new proposals issued by the Basel Committee on capital adequacy.

The Committee issued an initial consultation document on capital revision in June 1999. This was followed by the publication of a number of framework documents in January 2001.[2] In the light of the industry comment received, it is now expected that final proposals will be issued during 2002, a New Accord coming into effect in 2005.[3]

1   See Walker, 'Interim Prudential Sourcebook: Banks' in *Financial Services Regulation* (Butterworths loose leaf), Division B, paras 1037–1144.
2   See Basel Committee, *The New Basel Capital Accord* (January 2001). See also Basel Committee, *The New Basel Capital Accord: an explanatory note* (2001); Basel Committee, *Overview of The New Basel Capital Accord* (2001); Basel Committee, *The Standardised Approach to Credit Risk* (2001); Basel Committee, *The Internal Ratings-Based Approach* (2001); Basel Committee, *Asset Securitisation* (2001); Basel Committee, *Operational Risk* (2001); Basel Committee, *Pillar 2 (Supervisory Review Process)* (2001), *Principles for the Management and Supervision of Interest Rate Risk* (2001); and Basel Committee, *Pillar 3 (Market Discipline)* (2001).
3   For comment, see GA Walker, 'New Accord', *FRI* (February 2001), p 1; and Walker, 'The New Capital Accord' (April 2001), p 1 and (May 2001), p 1. See also Walker, 'So close but so far', *FRR* (May 1999), p 1; Walker, 'Accord at Last', *FRR* (July/August 1999), p 1; and 'A New Capital Adequacy Framework', *FRR* (July/August 1999).

Pillars

15.130   The new Basel capital framework will be based on three parallel pillars.[1] These will comprise: (a) a revised minimum capital requirement (pillar 1), supplemented by (b) a new supervisory review process (pillar 2) and (c) enhanced market discipline (pillar 3).

The revised minimum requirement is to be based either on a standardised or internal ratings based (IRB) approach. The standardised approach consists of a revised minimum requirement in respect of credit risk, a slightly amended market risk charge and a new operational risk component. The earlier 8% minimum requirement has been retained although the calculation process has been made more sophisticated by including credit risk gradings within each of the original risk buckets of assets bands included within the 1988 Accord.[2] The original bands generally assign a risk weighted factor of 0% to OECD government and central bank debt (dominated in the local currency), 10%–20% factor to non-OECD debt, 50% factor to secured transactions and 100% factor to all other transactions. A series of gradings (0%, 20%, 50%, 100% and 150%) will now be included within each bands (or bucket) based on external credit rating figures. The use of external credit ratings will, in turn, be subject to a number of eligibility criteria.[3]

The objective is to make the rating or grading process more sensitive and accurate. Although some of the earlier anomalies have been removed (such as the preferred treatment of low grade OECD debt), the grading system will now allow banks in highly rated markets such as North America and London a significant competitive advantage over ungraded areas.

1   See Table 15.9.
2   See Table 15.10.
3   See Table 15.11.

Market risk

15.131   The market risk calculations will generally follow the original proposals set out in the Basel Committee January 1996 Market Risk Amendment.[1] This provided for the adoption of the European 'building block' approach at the international level which set separate requirements for the position or market risk of debt instruments and equities and for these to be aggregated with the separate charges imposed on foreign exchange, commodities and derivatives.[2]

Position risk is generally divided into general and specific risk factors with a series of duration or maturity band approaches being available. Equity position risk, in particular, allows for a highly liquid 2% concession on the basic 4% general risk requirement with specific risk exposures being netted. This allows the charge to fall to 2% for highly net positions.

Market risk may alternatively be calculated on a models basis subject to certain quantitative and qualitative criteria being satisfied as well as conditions in respect of stress testing and back testing.

The foreign exchange charge will generally remain at 8% of net foreign exchange exposure in the reporting currency over 2% of own funds. Commodities may either be assessed on a simplified, maturity ladder or models based approach. Special adjustments apply with regard to derivatives.

Sophisticated firms could also use various modelling techniques where they satisfied certain qualitative and quantitative conditions as well as other back testing and other validation requirements.[3]

1   See Table 15.12.
2   See Table 15.13.
3   See Table 15.14. See also paras 15.98–15.116.

Table 15.9: The new capital accord

1.	**Pillar 1**	**Minimum Capital Requirement**		
		(1) Standardised Approach		
			(a) Credit Risk	(i) Total Risk Adjusted Assets
				(ii) Qualifying Tier 1 and Tier 2 Capital
				(iii) 8% Minimum Ratio Requirement
			(b) Market Risk	
			(i) Standardised	(i) Debt Instruments
			(ii) Models	(ii) Equities
				(iii) Foreign Exchange
				(iv) Commodities
				(v) Derivatives
			(c) Operational Risk	
			(i) "Basic Indicator"	
			(ii) "Standardised"	
			(iii) "Internal Measurement"	
		(2) Internal ratings Based (IRB)		(i) Corporate Exposures
				(ii) Sovereign Exposures
			(a) "Foundation"	(iii) Bank Exposures
			(b) "Advanced"	(iv) Retail Exposures
				(v) Project Finance Exposures
				(vi) Equity Exposures
2.	**Pillar 2**	**Supervisory Review**	(a) Capital Assessment	
			(b) Capital Review and Intervention	
		Review Principles	(c) Supplementary Capital Ratio	
			(d) Supervisory Intervention	
3.	**Pillar 3**	**Market Discipline**	Core and Supplementary Disclosure	

Operational risk

15.132 The most regressive aspect of the new proposals is possibly the inclusion of an express operational risk charge. This is in respect of such operational exposures as fraud or other systems or records failures.

The charge may either be calculated on a basic indicator (a fixed percentage (the alpha) of the indicator selected (generally gross income)), a standardised (using distinct business units and lines and a beta factor) or an internal measurement based approach (using a separate exposure indicator (EI), probability event (PE), loss given event (LGE) and expected loss (EL)).

The basic charge was generally expected to amount to a 20% additional factor. This would mean that while banks are provided with incentives to invest in increasingly sophisticated risk management systems in respect of credit and market risk, any benefit would then be lost with the introduction of a new 20% operational risk charge. The definition of operational risk and the amount of the basic charge is currently being reconsidered by the Committee.

Table 15.10: Revised risk weights

	AAA to AA-	A+ to A-	BBB to BB-	BB+ to B-	Below B-	Unrated
Sovereigns	0%	20%	50%	100%	150%	100%
Banks Option 1	20%	50%	100%	100%	150%	100%
(Risk weighting based on that of sovereign in which bank incorporated)						
Option 2	20%	50%	50%	100%	150%	50%
(Risk weighting based on assessment of individual bank)						
Public Sector Entities (PSEs)	(Same as banks subject to exemption)					
Securities Firms	(Same as banks subject to compliance with IOSCO 30 Objectives and Principles of Securities Regulation)					
Corporates	20%	100%	100%	150%	100%	
Loans Secured by Property	50% (For mortgages on residential property occupied by borrower)					
('In principle')	100% (For mortgages on commercial real estate subject to national derogation)					
Higher Risk Items	150%					
Other Claims	100%					

Source: Basel Committee, *New Accord* (2001).

Table 15.11: Criteria for eligible external credit assessment institutions

1. Objectivity

The methodology used must be rigorous, systematic, continuous and subject to some form of validation based on historical experience while assessments must be subject to ongoing review and responsive to changes in financial conditions.

2. Independence

The methodology must be as free as possible from any external political influence or constraints or economic pressure from assessed entities.

3. International Access and Transparency

For validation purposes, the individual assessments should be publicly available. Results should also be available to non-domestic parties on the same basis as national users although non-domestic firms need not be assessed.

4. Disclosure

The ECAI must make certain disclosure such as with regard to definition of default, time horizon and meaning of each rating, actual default rates experienced in each assessment category and transitions of the assessments.

5. Resources

Institutions should have sufficient resources to allow substantial ongoing contact with senior and operational levels of assessed entity.

6. Credibility

Credibility should generally be assessed having regard to the above criteria with any new agencies being properly assessed.

Internal ratings

15.133 The alternative to the standardised approach with regard to credit risk is the new internal ratings based (IRB) framework. This is based on either a foundation or advanced approach. These both use a number of credit risk factors including the probability of default (PD), loss given default (LGD), exposure at default (EAD) and maturity (M) with expected loss (EL).

Under the foundation approach, banks will be allowed to use their own internal ratings to set the probability of default (the PD) with all other inputs being supplied. Under the advanced approach banks will be allowed to use their own PD, LGD and EAD (subject to a 90% floor on the foundation).

These are important initiatives in allowing banks to make increasing use of their own internal (rather than externally provided) figures. The Committee is currently considering the calibration of the various factors. The objective is to allow banks to obtain between a 2 and 3% reduction in their credit risk charges. This is of value in attempting to bring the capital calculation more into line with internal bank practice.

The Committee has rejected the use of internal risk models at this stage due to lack of historical data and inaccuracy. This may, however, be considered in the future.

Table 15.12: Market risk – outline

I.	**Standardised Methodology**				**'Building Block Approach'**
	(1)	**Interest Rate Risk**	(Part A)		
			(a)	Specific	
			(b)	General	
	(2)	**Equity Position**	(a)	Specific	
			(b)	General	
	(3)	**Foreign Exchange**			
	(4)	**Commodities**	(a)	Simplified	
			(b)	Maturity Ladder	
			(c)	Models	
II.	**Internal Risk Management Models**	(Part B)			
	(1)	General Criteria (on Adequacy of Risk Management System)			
	(2)	Qualitative Standards (on Internal Oversight of Use of Models)			
	(3)	Guidelines (for Appropriate Market Risk Factors)			
	(4)	Quantitative Standards (on Use of Common Minimum Statistical Parameters)			
	(5)	Guidelines for Stress Testing			
	(6)	Validation Procedures (on External Oversight of Use of Models)			
	(7)	Mixed Models and Standardised Rules			

Revised Capital Definition

(1)	Tier 1	(same as credit risk)
(2)	Tier 2	(same as credit risk)
(3)	Tier 3	Short term Subordinated Debt
		(Limited to 250% of tier 1 capital required to support market risks – that is approximately 28$\frac{1}{2}$% market risk)

Source: Basel Committee, *Market Risk Amendment* (1996).

Table 15.13: Market risk – standardised methodology

I. Standardised Methodology	(Part A)	"Building Block Approach"
(1) Interest Rate Risk		
(a) Specific	Net positions multiplied by -	
Government items		0%
"Qualifying items"		0.25% where residual maturity 6 months
		1.00% for 6 to 24 months
		1.60% for over 24 months
Other		8%
(b) General		
(i) Maturity Based Method		
10% to 150% of weighted matched positions		
plus 100% of weighted unmatched positions in accordance 13		
Zone/coupon maturity bands		
(ii) Duration Based Method		
2% to 150% of matched duration-weighted positions plus 100%		
unmatched duration-weighted position yield to maturity on basis 3		
Zone/modified duration/assumed interest bands		
(c) Interest Rate Derivatives		(i) Futures and Forwards
		(ii) Swaps (Summarised Table 4)
(2) Equity Position		
(a) Specific		4% of Gross Amount or 2% if Diversified
(b) General		8% of Net Position
(c) Equity Derivatives		(Summarised Table 5)
(3) Foreign Exchange	8% of "overall net foreign-exchange position" in excess of 2% capital	
(4) Commodities		
(i) Basis Risk		Price relationship over time
(ii) Interest Rate		Changes in cost of carry
(iii) Forward Gap		Forward price changes not (ii)
(a) Simplified	15% Net Position Each Commodity	
(b) Maturity Ladder		(Summarised Table 7)
(c) Models(Revised)		

Source: Basel Committee, *Market Risk Amendment* (1996).

Table 15.14: Market risk – models

II. Internal Risk Management Models   **(Part B)**

   (1)   **General Criteria**   **(Adequacy of Risk Management System)**

     (a)   Approval Authority
     (b)   Conditions Approval
     (c)   Initial Monitoring and Live Testing

   (2)   **Qualitative Standards (Internal Oversight of Use of Models)**

     (a)   Independent Risk Control
     (b)   Regular Backtesting
     (c)   Involvement Board Directors and Senior Management
     (d)   Integrated Internal Risk Measurement Model
     (e)   Internal Trading and Exposure Limits
     (f)   Routine and Rigorous Stress Testing
     (g)   Compliance Documented Set of Internal Policies
     (h)   Regular Independent Review

   (3)   **Specification of Market Risk Factors**   **(Guidelines)**

   (4)   **Quantitative Standards (on Use of Common Minimum Statistical Parameters)**

     (a)   Daily Value-at-Risk Calculation
     (b) 99th % (one-tailed) confidence interval
     (c)   10 Holding Day Period
     (d)   1 year Historical Observation Period
     (e)   Update data sets every 3 years
     (f)   No prescribed models
     (g)   Discretion in recognition empirical correlations
     (h)   Capture options risks
     (i)   Daily capital requirement higher previous day VAR or 60 day average multiplied by 3
     (j)   Supervisors to set multiplication factor (but not less than 3)
     (k)   Standardise charge for specific risk interest rate and equity securities

   (5)   **Stress Testing**   **(Guidelines)**

   (6)   **External Validation Procedures**

     (a)   Internal validation processes
     (b)   Formulae validation
     (c)   Adequate structure models
     (d)   Results backtesing
     (e)   Transparent and accessible data flows and processes

   (7)   **Mixed Models and Standardised Rules**

     (a)   Single approach each general risk factor
     (b)   All models criteria to be complied with
     (c)   Not alter combination without reason
     (d)   No element escape measurement
     (e)   Aggregate charges under two approaches

Source: Basel Committee, *Market Risk Amendment* (1996).

Capital comment

15.134 The most interesting elements of the new framework are possibly the supervisory review (pillar 2) and market discipline (pillar 3) proposals. The purpose of the supervisory review requirement is to ensure that banks maintain effective internal control systems and that supervisory agencies assess the quality and effective operation of these arrangements. This is essential to ensure that all relevant risk is properly identified and managed in practice.

The 'review principles' set out in pillar 2 also allow for the imposition of additional target and trigger ratios in addition to the 8% minimum with national agencies being required to monitor the possibility of pre-crisis loss dissipation through supervisory intervention for the first time.

It could be argued that the core function of supervisors should always have been to ensure that banks maintain effective internal risk management and control procedures. The importance of this development is that this will now create an absolute minimum requirement in this regard at the international level. The only danger that may arise is that supervisory review is restricted in practice to capital compliance and not extended to more general risk management within the operations of banks.

15.135 The market discipline proposals are also important to the extent that the objective is to increase market oversight and sanction through improved disclosure. Banks will be expected to make a number of new mandatory core and supplementary disclosures. Care will only have to be taken to ensure that the industry costs involved are not excessive and that confidential and proprietary information is not unnecessarily compromised.

Capital revision

15.136 The relevant sections within the FSA's sourcebook will have to be amended on adoption of the Basel Committee's new proposals. Consultation is currently taking place at the European level to ensure that appropriate revisions are adopted in parallel. Rather than amend the interim prudential sourcebook (IPRU (BANK)) as such, it has to be expected that the FSA will include the new elements especially with regard to supervisory review and market discipline in its integrated final sourcebook (PSB). Further consultation is expected.

Chapter 16

Financial derivatives

INTRODUCTION

16.1   The sale and management of financial derivatives remain core components within the business activities of many financial institutions. Despite the recent losses suffered by a number of operators and particular incidents of collapse as well as some reduction in growth in certain markets, significant income generation is still possible for financial intermediaries while derivatives continue to provide essential risk management functions for both intermediaries and end-users.

In terms of size, by June 2001 the total global notional amount outstanding of over-the-counter (OTC) derivatives was in excess of US$100 trillion.[1] This represented a 38% increase since April 1998. Global daily turnover in foreign exchange and interest rate derivative contracts had also increased over the last three years by an estimated 10% to US$1.4 trillion although this represented a significant decline in market expansion as against the period 1995–98 when daily business had grown by 44%. The bulk of this slowdown was in interest rate instruments especially following the introduction of the euro. London and New York nevertheless remained the most important centres for OTC derivatives although Frankfurt had grown significantly replacing Tokyo as the third most important trading centre. Despite this relative slowdown in growth over the triennial period covered, the markets then grew by a further 11% until end December 2001.

By the beginning of 2002, the total notional amount outstanding stood at $111 trillion with gross market values having grown by 24% to US$3.8 trillion.[2] The total notional or face value of all financial derivatives had earlier grown from US$11 trillion as at 31 December 1993 to US$15.6 trillion by the end of 1994 and to US$47.5 trillion by 1995/1996.[3]

1 See Bank for International Settlements (BIS), *Triennial Central Bank Survey of Foreign Exchange and Derivatives Market Activity 2001 – Final Results* (18 March 2002).
2 See BIS, *OTC Derivatives* (May 2002).
3 See G Walker 'Financial Derivatives – Global Regulatory Developments' [1996] JBL, January, 66 at 70.

16.2   Financial derivatives continue to be used to carry out a number of essential functions in modern markets, especially in terms of interest rate and currency risk management.

Derivatives have allowed end-users to lower funding costs through arbitrage opportunities and the issuance of customised debt. They have also resulted in increased returns on underlying investments through better management of existing portfolios or assets and participation adjustments in specific financial markets or countries.

Financial intermediaries have been able more effectively to manage their exposures as well as substantially increase earnings through the provision of tailor-structured or standard market-traded derivative products.[1]

New forms of contracts also continue to be developed, for example, with regard to credit derivatives[2] or Euro-related contracts while all types of derivatives are commonly used to manage risk or convert payment streams in other increasingly complex financial transactions.

1 See Global Derivatives Study Group, *Derivatives: Practices and Principles*, Group of 30 (July 1993) ('the G 30 Report'), pp 34–43.
2 See para 16.10.

16.3   The size and complexity of derivatives markets have, however, created significant new problems for regulators and market participants. With every new financial product, additional types and levels of risk are created which have to be properly identified and managed. The speed with which positions can change and the high levels of concentration within the market also create significant problems.[1]

Although concentration results in an increased level of interdependence which creates a higher risk of contagion or possible knock-on effects in the event of a crisis, this does allow the authorities to allocate their resources more efficiently by focusing on the main market players as well as any other high-risk institutions (or outliers) which are considered to require particular attention.[2]

1 See Walker, 'Financial Derivatives – Global Regulatory Developments' [1966] JBL, January, 70–71.
2 See note 1 above.

16.4   The general regulatory response developed to date to the explosive growth of financial derivatives has generally been to impose additional capital requirements on banks and other financial intermediaries within existing credit and market risk structures.

Such charges on their own, however, constitute an inadequate solution to the problems created. National and international authorities have accordingly focused on the importance of internal risk management and control systems, initially with regard to derivative activities specifically but then more generally. Most recently, they have looked at increased supervisory and larger market reporting and disclosure requirements.[1]

Apart from attempting to control particular types of financial risk, the additional difficulty that arises with regard to financial derivatives is the possibility of losses incurred in more volatile derivatives-related markets being transferred into other securities or banking and insurance sectors with the larger systemic damage which that could cause. This risk of intra-sector loss transfer remains a fundamental problem which has still not been fully resolved.[2]

1 See Chapter 21, paras 21.51–21.55.
2 See G Walker, *International Banking Regulation – Law, Policy and Practice* (2001), Ch 3.

16.5 With regard to market operators and end-users, apart from managing their financial exposures, the main risks that have to be controlled are operational risk and legal risk.[1]

Operational risk is the risk of loss arising as a result of inadequate internal systems and controls. While this is relevant with regard to the activities of all financial firms, the complexity of derivatives requires that additional care is taken to ensure that transactions and positions are properly monitored and controlled.

Legal risk is the risk of loss arising from the unenforceability of a contract. This includes documentation effectiveness, capacity or sufficiency of authority (*vires*) and uncertain legality and enforceability on bankruptcy or insolvency. In practice, legal risk with regard to exchange-traded derivatives is controlled through the use of standard term contracts and conditions supported by fixed settlement procedures. The exchange may also use a settlement agent to act as a central counterparty following the novation of the exchange contract.

The off-exchange or over-the-counter (OTC) market is, however, much larger and operates on a purely contractual basis with no central counterparty. The market is also of its nature inherently non-transparent, largely cross-border and consequently to a large extent unregulated. Contracts can be standardised through the use of model contracts prepared by such bodies as the British Bankers Association (BBA) or the International Swaps and Derivatives Association Inc (ISDA)[2] although difficulties continue to arise with regard to the effectiveness of some of these provisions such as close-out netting. Their general enforceability can also only be determined by the laws of the particular jurisdiction or jurisdictions involved with any transaction or series of connected transactions.

In addition to the more specific aspects of legal risk referred to in both the traded and OTC market, participants must also ensure that no separate contractual or tortious liabilities arise through their dealings with clients or other counterparties.[3]

1 See the G30 Global Derivatives Report, pp 50–52.
2 See paras 16.85–16.103.
3 See paras 16.104–123.

Scope of the chapter

16.6 The purpose of this chapter is to consider the nature of the main types of derivatives contracts involved. The earlier relevance of the Financial

Services Act 1986 and then the Financial Services and Markets Act (FSMA) 2000 to derivatives-related activity is explained. The general structure and content of the new Financial Services Authority (FSA) Handbook of Rules and Guidance, as well as the main provisions contained in the Conduct of Business (COB) section within Block 2 (Business Standards) are considered in further detail.

The nature and operation of exchange traded markets are then examined with reference to the London International Financial Futures Exchange (LIFFE) and to the particular control mechanisms that it operates. The more general standards applicable to the conduct of OTC derivatives-related activities on the wholesale markets within the UK are assessed and the most commonly used forms of standardised documentation in the OTC market outlined.

The potential private law liability issues that arise in practice in relation to the sale of OTC derivatives are then considered.

DERIVATIVE PRODUCTS

16.7 Derivatives are financial contracts the value of which depends upon a reference rate or the value of an underlying asset or index.[1] The basic purpose is to transfer risks associated with fluctuations in variable factors such as interest rates, exchange rates and the prices of equities or commodities.

Derivatives are a class of off-balance sheet contingencies or commitments, the traditional forms of which include acceptances, guarantees, letters of credit, forward asset purchase agreements and general commitments to lend.[2]

1 See the Basel Committee, *Prudential Supervision of Bank's Derivatives Activities* (December 1994), para 7. See Walker, 'Financial Derivatives – Global Regulatory Development', pp 70–71.
2 See Chapter 21, paras 21.51–21.55.

16.8 A large number of different types of contract fall within the general classification of financial derivatives although the common factor that determines their inclusion is their reference or derivative pricing.

The main categories of derivative contracts can be distinguished as being either forward- or option-based. Forward-based derivatives include forward contracts, swap transactions and futures contracts. Option-based derivatives include option transactions, caps, floors and collars as well as options on futures.[1]

1 See the G30 Global Derivatives Report, pp 28–34.

16.9 Each of these contracts is fundamentally different in terms of their nature, operation and commercial purpose despite their common generic classification. As a result of the differences that exist between distinct types of derivative contract, it is impossible to treat them all in identical legal or regulatory terms. A number of particular issues arise with regard to each and their regulatory and private law applications have to be considered separately.

It must be stressed that the simplicity of their collective classification as derivative contracts denies the incongruity of the various types of separate financial product involved and the distinct commercial and legal issues that arise.

16.10   The most commonly entered into types of derivative contract include swaps, debt and equity options and forwards and futures.[1] Warrants are also often used in practice, especially with regard to equities. Bonds with warrants may also be issued which are debt instruments that convert into equities once the strike price has reached a certain level. Although warrants fell within para 4 (Instruments entitling to shares or securities) of Sch 1 to the Financial Services Act 1986 and were not to be regarded as derivatives for the purposes of the Act under Note (2) of para 4, they were treated in the same way as derivatives by the market where they performed the same functions as options.[2]

Various hybrid derivative contracts may also be issued such as a swaption, which is an option to enter into a swap. Credit derivatives have also become of increasing importance in recent years.[3]

The commercial classifications of the instruments used in the market, however, was not fully reflected in the definitions adopted in the Financial Services Act 1986 nor in the FSMA 2000.

1   See paras 16.13–16.20 and 16.26–16.31 below. See generally Alastair Hudson, *The Law on Financial Derivatives* (2nd edn, 1998), Part 1.
2   See paras 16.11–16.13.
3   The total aggregate notional amount of credit derivatives outstanding as at end 2002 was estimated to be US$1.581 trillion. The most commonly used form of credit derivatives are credit (default) swaps which provide for the transfer of credit risk between the 'protection' buyer and seller. Other composite products include portfolio default swaps, basket default swaps, synthetic collateralised loan obligations (CLOs) while credit linked notes have also become of increasing importance. Other forms of credit spread options have not developed as substantially as expected. See generally Bank of England, *Developing a Supervisory Approach to Credit Derivatives*, November 1996; SFA, Board Notice 482 amending Board Notice 414 (April 1997); FSA, *Report of Consultation on Credit Derivatives* (July 1998); British Bankers' Association, *Credit Derivatives; Key Issues* (2nd edn, March 1999); and FSA, *Cross-sector risk transfers* (May 2002). For comment on related market and regulatory developments, see David Rule, 'the credit derivatives market: its development and possible implications for financial stability' Financial Stability Review (June 2001), 117; and Schuyler Henderson, 'Credit Derivatives at a Crossroads?' BJIBFL (May 2001), 211. See also Henderson, 'Credit Derivatives: Part 1: the Context' 8 JIBFL (1998), 332; Henderson, 'Credit Derivatives: Part 2: Selected Documentation Issues' 9 JIBFL (1998) 399; Henderson, 'Credit Derivatives: Part 3: Selected Legal Issues' 5 JIBFL (1999), 193.

FINANCIAL SERVICES ACT 1986

16.11   Under the Financial Services Act 1986, authorisation in the UK was required for derivatives-related activities to the extent that the particular instrument fell within the definition of investments as set out in Part I and the activity concerned fell within those set out in Part II of Sch 1 to the Financial Services Act 1986.[1]

Related activities included dealing in investments, arranging deals in investments, managing investments, giving investment advice, establishing a collective investment scheme as well as custody of investments and sending dematerialised instructions. This included almost all professional activities in derivatives.[2]

All activities and products should now be governed by the FSA Handbook of Rules and Guidance especially with the inclusion of the new definition of 'quasi-derivative contract'.[3]

1   See generally E Bettelheim, H Parry and W Rees, *Swaps and Off-Exchange Derivatives Trading: Law and Regulation* (1996).
2   See Blair et al (2nd edn), paras 14.11–14.13.
3   See para 16.31.

16.12   Insofar as derivatives constituted investments for the purposes of the Financial Services Act 1986 and authorisation was required, firms engaging in derivatives-related activities were subject to the provisions contained in the Rules of their relevant SRO. Pre-N2, only a small number of firms remained to be supervised directly by FSA. The day-to-day supervision of even these firms was generally dealt with through one of the other regulatory bodies and, in particular, SFA or IMRO.

A number of separate sets of requirements had then to be complied with including with regard to adequacy of internal systems and controls, conduct of business requirements and dealing rules, records and reporting provisions. The conduct of business rules, in particular, included dealing restrictions on OTC derivative contracts and enhanced rules on suitability and understanding risks with further risk warnings as well as other rules relating to advertising and customer agreements.[1]

All of these requirements have since been incorporated into the revised provisions set out in the FSA Handbook of Rules and Guidance[2] depending upon the nature of the client.[3]

1   See Blair et al (2nd edn), paras 14.14–14.41. For discussion of some of these provisions, see *Morgan Stanley UK Group v Puglisi* (29 January 1998, unreported), Commercial Court. See para 16.110.
2   See paras 16.21–16.57. See also Chapter 2, paras 2.83–2.146
3   See paras 16.30, 16.40–16.44 and 16.75–16.80.

FINANCIAL SERVICES AND MARKETS ACT 2000

16.13   Following the coming into effect of the FSMA 2000 on N2, any person carrying on a regulated activity in the UK must either be an authorised or exempt person[1] and act in accordance with the permission held.[2] An activity is a regulated activity for the purposes of the Act if it is of a specified kind listed in the Regulated Activities Order.[3]

1   FSMA 2000, s 19(1) and ss 33(1)–39.
2   FSMA 2000, s 20(1) and ss 40–55.
3   See Financial Services and Markets Act 2000 (Regulated Activities) Order 2001 (SI 2001/544) as amended by Financial Services and Markets Act 2000 (Regulated Activities) (Amendment) Order 2001 (SI 2001/3544).

16.14   Under s 22(1) of the Act, an activity is a regulated activity if it is of a specified kind carried on by way of business and relates to an investment of a specified kind or is an activity of a specified kind relating to property generally.

The main activities and investments covered are listed in Sch 2 to the Act. This includes dealing and arranging deals in investments as well as managing investments and the provision of investment advice.[1] Deposit-taking, safe keeping and the administration of assets, establishing collective investments schemes and using computer-based systems for providing investment instructions are also regulated activities.

Investments include options, futures and contracts for differences[2] in addition to securities, instruments creating or acknowledging indebtedness, government and public securities, instruments giving entitlement to investments, certificates representing securities, units in collective investment schemes, contracts of insurance, participation in Lloyd's syndicates, deposits, loans secured on land and rights in investments.[3]

The specific content and nature of these activities and investments are expanded in the Regulated Activities Order.[4] Schedule 2 to the Act only sets out the general scope of activities and investments covered. The scope of the Act is not limited by the Schedule but by its overall objective and purpose.[5] The general nature of the activities set out in Sch 2 only then informs and indirectly limits the extent of the Treasury's power to bring further activities within the scope of the Act.[6]

The main specified activities under the Order are dealing, arranging deals and managing investments and relevant investments options, futures and contracts for differences. The Regulated Activities Order was also issued with the Exemption Order, the Appointed Representatives Regulations, the Non-Exempt Activities Order and the Business Order.[7]

1   See FSMA 2000, Sch 2, Pt I, paras 2, 3, 6 and 7.
2   See FSMA 2000, Sch 2, Pt II, paras 17, 18 and 19. See Chapter 2, paras 2.54–2.60; and Chapter 3.
3   See FSMA 2000, Sch 2, Pt II, paras 11, 12, 13, 14, 15, 16, 20, 21, 22, 23 and 24.
4   Financial Services and Markets Act 2000 (Regulated Activities) Order 2001 (SI 2001/544) as amended.
5   See HM Treasury, *Financial Services and Markets Act 2000 – Explanatory Notes* (14 June 2000), para 777.
6   See note 5 above.
7   See Financial Services and Markets Act 2000 (Regulated Activities) Order 2001 (SI 2001/544) as amended by Financial Services and Markets Act 2000 (Regulated Activities) (Amendment) Order 2001 (SI 2001/3544). See Financial Services and Markets Act 2000 (Exemption) Order 2001 (SI 2001/1201) as amended by Financial Services and Markets Act 2000 (Exemption) (Amendment) Order 2001 (SI 2001/3623); Financial Services and Markets Act 2000 (Appointed Representatives) Regulations 2001 (SI 2001/1217) as amended by Financial Services and Markets Act 2000 (Appointed Representatives) (Amendment) Regulations 2001 (SI 2001/2508); Financial Services and Markets Act 2000 (Professions – Non-Exempt Activities) Order 2001 (SI 2001/1227); and Financial Services and Markets Act 2000 (Carrying on Regulated Activities by Way of Business) Order 2001 (SI 2001/1177). See Chapter 2, para 2.57; and Chapter 3.

16.15   The Order contains separate definitions for dealing in investments as principal (article 14) and dealing in investments as agent (article 21). Buying, selling, subscribing for or underwriting securities or contractually based investments (other than funeral plan contracts or rights to or interests in investments to the extent relevant) as principal is an activity of a specified kind.[1]

Excluded from dealing in investments as principal are activities not involving any holding out as willing to deal or engaging in the business of dealing, dealing in contractually based investments with an authorised or exempt person, accepting instruments creating or acknowledging indebtedness, the issue by a company of its own shares and non-investment business risk management including Treasury activities.[2]

Dealing as agent is also a specified activity[3] unless the deals are carried with or through an authorised person or for non-investment business risk management purposes.[4]

Also excluded are trustee activities,[5] the sale of goods and supply of services,[6] groups and joint enterprise activities,[7] sale of a body corporate,[8] employee share schemes[9] and overseas persons.[10]

1   Financial Services and Markets Act 2000 (Regulated Activities) Order 2001 (SI 2001/544), art 14. See Chapter 3.
2   SI 2001/544, arts 15, 16, 17, 18 and 19.
3   SI 2001/544, art 21.
4   SI 2001/544, arts 22 and 23.

5   SI 2001/544, art 66.
6   SI 2001/544, art 68.
7   SI 2001/544, art 69.
8   SI 2001/544, art 70.
9   SI 2001/544, art 71.
10 SI 2001/544, arts 20 and 24; art 72.

16.16   Arranging deals is an activity of a specified kind where a person makes arrangements for another person (whether as principal or agent) to buy, sell, subscribe for or underwrite a particular investment which is either a security or contractually based investment or rights to or interest in investments or Lloyd's syndicate related.[1] This also includes making arrangements with a view to a person who participates in the arrangements, buying, selling, subscribing for or underwriting the investments referred to.[2]

The Order excludes arrangements not causing a deal, enabling parties only to communicate, arranging transactions to which the arranger is a party, arranging deals with or through authorised persons, arranging transactions in connection with lending on the security of insurance policies, arranging the acceptance of debentures in connection with loans, provision of finance, introductions, arrangements for the issue of shares and other securities, international securities, self-regulatory organisations and the other exclusions referred to.[3]

1   Financial Services and Markets Act 2000 (Regulated Activities) Order 2001 (SI 2001/544), art 25(1)(a), (b) and (c).
2   SI 2001/544, art 25(2).
3   SI 2001/544, arts 26–36.

16.17   Managing assets belonging to another person is a specified activity if the assets consist of or include any investment which is a security or a contractually based investment or the arrangements for their management are such that the assets may consist of or include such investments and either the investments have been of such a nature since 29 April 1988 or the arrangements have at any time (whether before or after that date) been held out as arrangements under which the assets would be of such a nature.[1] This does not include persons acting under a power of attorney or trustee activities, sales of goods and supply of services and goods and joint enterprises.[2]

1   Financial Services and Markets Act 2000 (Regulated Activities) Order 2001 (SI 2001/544), art 37(a) and (b).
2   SI 2001/544, arts 38 and 39.

16.18   Advising a person is a specified activity if the advice is given to the person in the capacity as investor or potential investor or in the capacity as agent for investor or potential investor and the advice relates to the merits of buying, selling, subscribing for or underwriting a particular investment which is a security or a contractually based investment (whether as principal or agent) or exercising any right conferred by such an investment (whether as principal or agent).[1]

Investment advice does not include the giving of advice in writing or other legible form where this is contained in a newspaper, journal, magazine or other periodical publication or is given by way of a service comprising regularly updated news or information where the principal purpose of the publication or service taken as whole and including any advertisements or other promotional material is neither the giving of advice as defined nor the leading or enabling persons to buy, sell, subscribe for or underwrite securities or contractually based investments.[2] Also excluded is the giving of advice in any service consisting of the broadcast or transmission of television or radio programmes provided that the principal purpose of the service is again not to give investment advice as defined nor lead or enable persons to buy, sell, subscribe for or underwrite.[3]

The FSA may certify any such publication or service on application of the proprietor. Such certification is conclusive evidence of the matters covered subject to revocation.[4] The Order also excludes trustee committees, professional or non-investment business, the sale of goods and supply of services, groups and joint enterprises, the sale of a body corporate and overseas persons.[5]

1   Financial Services and Markets Act 2000 (Regulated Activities) Order 2001 (SI 2001/544), art 53(a) and (b).
2   SI 2001/544, art 54(1)(a) and (b).
3   SI 2001/544, art 54(2).
4   SI 2001/544, art 54(4).
5   SI 2001/544, art 55.

16.19   Specified investments include options to acquire or dispose of a security or contractually based investment in the UK or any other currency, palladium, platinum, gold or silver or an option to acquire or dispose of any such investment.[1] Futures are included as rights under a contract for the sale of a commodity or property of any other description under which delivery is to be made at a future date and at a price agreed on when the contract is made provided that the contract is not made for commercial rather than investment purposes.[2]

A contract is made for investment purposes if it is made or traded on a recognised investment exchange or is made otherwise than on a recognised investment exchange but is expressed to be as traded on such an exchange or on the same terms as those on which an equivalent contract would be made on the exchange. Any other contract is to be treated as being made for commercial purposes provided the terms of the contract delivery are to be made within seven days unless it can be shown that there existed an understanding that (notwithstanding the express terms) delivery would be made within seven days.[3]

Other indications that a contract is made for commercial purposes include where one or more of the parties is a producer of the commodity or other property or uses it in his business or the seller delivers or intends to deliver the property or the purchaser takes or intends to take delivery of it. This also includes where the prices, lot, delivery date or other terms are determined by the parties for the purposes of the particular contract and not by reference (or not solely by reference) to regular published prices, standard lots or delivery dates or standard terms.[4]

Indications that a contract is made for investment purposes include it being expressed to be as traded on an investment exchange, performance is ensured by an investment exchange or clearing house or arrangements are made for the payment or provision of margin.[5] The price is to be taken to be agreed on when the contract is made notwithstanding that it is to be determined by reference to market or exchange contracts and notwithstanding that provision is made for variation in the price calculated by reference to a standard lot or quality.[6]

1   Financial Services and Markets Act 2000 (Regulated Activities) Order 2001 (SI 2001/544), art 83. See Chapter 3.

2   SI 2001/544, art 84(1) and (2).
3   SI 2001/544, art 84(3) and (4).
4   SI 2001/544, art 84(5) and (6).
5   SI 2001/544, art 84(7).
6   SI 2001/544, art 84.

16.20   Rights under a contract for differences or any other contract the purpose or pretended purpose of which is to secure a profit or avoid a loss by reference to fluctuations in the value or price of property of any description or an index or other factor designated for that purpose in the contract is of a specified kind.[1]

This will not include rights under a contract if the parties intend that the profit is to be secured or loss avoided by one or more parties taking delivery of any property to which the contract relates, money is received by way of deposit on terms that any interest or other return is to be calculated by reference to fluctuations in an index, rights under a qualifying contract of insurance or the money is received by a National Savings Bank or raised under the National Loans Act 1968.[2]

A qualifying contract of insurance means a contract of long insurance which is not a re-insurance contract nor a contract in respect of which the benefits are only payable on death or in respect of incapacity due to injury, sickness or infirmity, the benefits are only payable on death within 10 years of the contract, the contract has no surrender value or the consideration only consists of a single premium with the surrender value not exceeding that premium or the contract makes no other provision for its conversion or extension.

1   Financial Services and Markets Act 2000 (Regulated Activities) Order 2001 (SI 2001/544), art 85(1)(a) and (b). It was held in *Larussa-Chigi v CS First Boston Ltd* [1998] CLC 277 that foreign exchange transactions constituted contracts for differences for the purposes of the Financial Services Act 1986 in that they required cash settlement and netting rather than physical delivery of the foreign exchange under Sch 1, para 9.
2   SI 2001/544, art 85(2)(a), (b), (d) and (c).

FSA HANDBOOK OF RULES AND GUIDANCE

16.21   The general functions of the FSA are principally defined in the FSMA 2000 in terms of its rule-making powers.[1] The general functions of the FSA are to make rules, prepare and issue codes, provide guidance and determine general policy and principles.

Under the Act, the FSA may issue general rules,[2] endorsing rules[3] and specific rules. Specific rules include insurance business rules,[4] price stabilising rules,[5] financial promotion rules,[6] money laundering rules,[7] control of information rules[8] and auditors and actuaries rules.[9] The issuance of rules is subject to the procedures set out in the Act.[10]

All of these rules are now set out in the FSA's Handbook of Rules and Guidance. The rules have the same effect as secondary legislation although the usual Parliamentary procedures are disapplied.[11]

1   FSMA 2000, s 2(4)(a). See Chapter 2, paras 2.61–2.63.
2   FSMA 2000, s 138(1) and (2).
3   FSMA 2000, s 143(1).
4   FSMA 2000, s 141.
5   FSMA 2000, s 144.
6   FSMA 2000, s 145.
7   FSMA 2000, s 146.

8   FSMA 2000, s 147.
9   FSMA 2000, s 340.
10 FSMA 2000, ss 152–156.
11 See Mark Threipland, 'Rules and Guidance', Chapter 12 of M Blair, L Mingella, M Taylor, M
    Threipland and G Walker, *Financial Services & Markets Act 2000* (Blackstone, 2001), at p 137.

16.22   The main principles that govern the design and structure of the Handbook were issued in 1998.[1] The general approach by the FSA to the discharge of its regulatory responsibilities had also been outlined at an early stage.[2] This committed the FSA to a flexible but differentiated approach to financial market regulation which required separate provision to be included in the Handbook for different types of business and markets and relevant counterparties.

To the extent possible, existing material was to be re-used with minimal amendment to allow firms to assimilate the new material and develop appropriate systems and procedures. A balance had to be struck between continuity and change in the construction of the new regime.

The general design objectives of the Handbook were stated to be based on communication, consistency and implementation each of which was divided into a number of sub-functions. Five design principles were also adopted. There should be a succinct authoritative statement of high level principles beginning with the fundamental obligations of regulated businesses. There should be a solid structure of further rules to facilitate enforceability and other requirements. There should be a major role for guidance. There should be a presumption against differentiation except on policy grounds. Regulatory standards should focus on firms' outputs and on the adequacy of internal systems and controls.

The basic architecture had also been agreed at an early stage with an initial six-block structure being adopted.[3]

1   See FSA, *Designing the FSA Handbook of Rules and Guidance* (April 1998). See Chapter 2, paras
    2.84–2.86.
2   See FSA, *Financial Services Authority: an outline* (October 1997).
3   See FSA, *Designing the FSA Handbook of Rules and Guidance* (April 1998). See Chapter 2, para
    2.85.

Blocks

16.23   The final Handbook is made up of a number of blocks, or modules (see Table 2.1).

Following the Prefatory material and the Readers' Guide, Block 1 sets out the High level standards. This includes the Principles for Business (PRIN), Senior management arrangements, systems and controls (SYSC), Threshold conditions (COND), the Statements of principle and code of practice for approved persons (APER) and the fit and proper tests for approved persons (FIT) as well as the General provisions (GEN).

Block 2 sets out the Business Standards which include the Interim prudential sourcebook: Investment businesses (IPRU (INV)), the Interim prudential sourcebook: Banks (IPRU (BANK)), the Interim prudential sourcebook: Building societies (IPRU (BSOC)), the Interim prudential sourcebook: Insurers (IPRU (INS)) and the Interim prudential sourcebook: Friendly societies (IPRU (FS)) as well as the Conduct of Business sourcebook (COB), the Market conduct sourcebook (MAR), the Training and competence sourcebook (TC) and the Money laundering sourcebook (ML).

Block 3 Regulatory processes consists of the Authorisation manual (AUTH), the Supervision manual (SUP), the Enforcement manual (ENF) and the Decision making manual (DEC).

Block 4 Redress contains new provisions concerning Dispute resolution: complaints (DISP), Compensation (COMP) and Complaints against the FSA (COAF).

A number of Specialist sourcebooks have also been issued as part of Block 5 including the Collective investment schemes sourcebook (CIS), the Professional firms sourcebook (PROF), the Lloyd's sourcebook (LLD), the Electronic Commerce Directive (ECD), Electronic Money (ELM) and the Recognised investment exchanges and recognised clearing houses sourcebook (RBC) with further provisions to follow on mortgages (MORT) and listing (UKLA).

A further Block 6 has also been added on Special guides which includes Energy market participants (EMPS), Small friendly societies (FREN), Oil market participants (OMPS) and Service companies (SERV).

16.24   Most of the Handbook modules were made by the Board of the FSA on 21 June 2001.[1] These consist of all of the main sections of the Handbook including the High Level Standards, the Business Standards, Regulatory Processes and most of the Specialist sourcebooks. Most of this was issued as 'final' text which refers to post-consultative text that had been approved by the Board which then came into effect on N2. The rest of the Handbook was made by the Board over the summer 2001.[2] Most of the Handbook came into effect on 1 December 2001 although some had been operational since either 21 June 2001 or 3 September 2001 to allow the FSA to undertake preparatory work.

1   See FSA, *Handbook Notice 1* (21 June 2001).
2   See Chapter 2, paras 2.89–2.146.

16.25   A regulated person carrying on any form of derivatives-related activity will have to comply with all of the relevant provisions set out in the Handbook depending upon the nature of the counterparty.[1] This will include all of the general provisions set out either in Block 1 or Block 2 including the relevant interim solvency (prudential) sourcebook and conduct of business (COB) provisions (except with regard to inter-professional dealings).[2]

The supporting measures set out in the Regulatory Processes Block 3 and Redress Block 4 will also apply as well as any of the provisions in the Specialist sourcebooks (Block 5) to the extent relevant. Some of the main provisions, in particular, contained in the COB are considered in the following subsections.

1   See paras 16.30 and 16.40–16.44.
2   See paras 16.75–16.80.

Definitions

16.26   The relevant definitions supporting the Handbook are set out in the separate Glossary which is attached before the Index. While the term 'derivative' is not defined in the FSMA 2000, it is defined in the Glossary to mean a contract for differences, a future or an option.

A number of related terms are also introduced including commodity future and option, spread bet, rolling spot forex contract, contingent liability investment, margined transaction and quasi-derivative contract.

Earlier more general definitions had been provided for in the SRO Rules including contingent liability transactions, margined transactions and limited liability transactions.[1]

1 See SFA Rules, Chapter 9; and IMRO Definitions Schedule. See Blair et al (2nd edn), paras 14.16–14.19.

16.27 Under the FSA Glossary, a 'derivative' is defined to mean a contract for differences, a future or an option.[1] A contract for differences is as specified in article 85 of the Regulated Activities Order which applies to rights under a contract for differences or any other contract the purpose or pretended purpose of which is to secure a profit or avoid a loss by reference to fluctuations in the value or price of property of any description or an index or other factor designated for that purpose in the relevant contract.[2]

A future is as set out in article 84 of the Regulated Activities Order which covers rights under a contract for the sale of a commodity or property of any other description under which delivery is to be made at a future date and at a price agreed on when the contract is made.

An option is as set out in article 77 of the Regulated Activities Order which is an option to acquire or dispose of a designated investment (other than an option), currency, palladium, platinum, gold or silver or an option to acquire or to dispose of an option in any of these rights.[3]

1 See paras 16.19–16.20
2 Para 16.20.
3 Para 16.19.

16.28 A 'designated investment' is defined to include a contract for differences, a future or an option. In this case, however, a contract for differences is subdivided into a contract for differences (excluding a spread bet and rolling spot forex contract) and a spread bet and rolling spot forex contract.

A spread bet is a contract for differences that is a gaming contract whether or not s 412 of the FSMA 2000 (gaming contracts) applies. Section 412 generally provides that gaming contacts are not void or unenforceable due to breach of the gaming laws. Under the Gaming Act 1968, gaming means the playing of a game of chance for winnings in money or money's worth whether any person playing the game is at risk of loss.

A rolling spot forex contract means either a future (other than a future traded or expressed to be as traded on a recognised investment exchange) where the property which is to be sold under the contract is foreign exchange or a contract for differences where the profit is to be secured or loss avoided by reference to fluctuations in foreign exchange and the contract is entered into for speculation in both cases.

A future is defined with regard to a designated investment to include a future (excluding a commodity future and a rolling spot forex contract) and a commodity future and a rolling spot forex contract.

A commodity future means a future relating to a commodity.

An option is defined as an option (excluding a commodity option and an option on a commodity future) and a commodity option and an option on a commodity future. A commodity option means an option relating to a commodity.

16.29 A 'contingent liability investment' is a derivative under the terms of which the client will or may be liable to make further payments (other than charges and whether or not secured by margin) when the transaction falls to be completed or upon the earlier closing out of the position. This would include most options and futures whether traded or not.

A margined transaction (other than under COB 9.3) is a transaction executed by a firm with or for a client relating to a future, option or contract for differences (or any right to or interest in such an investment) under the terms of which the client will or may be liable to provide cash or collateral to secure performance of obligations which he may have to perform when the transaction falls to be completed or upon the earlier closing out of the position. This would apply to the normal margin payments required in respect of exchange traded futures and options.[1]

This constitutes a revised version of the earlier definition of a contingent liability transaction but with only minor amendment. The earlier definition of a limited liability transaction has not been retained.

For the purposes of COB 9.3, a margined transaction will also include an option purchased by a client, the terms of which provide that the maximum liability of the client in respect of the transaction is to be limited to the amount payable as premium. This replaces the earlier definition of a limited liability transaction.[2]

1 See *Morgan Stanley UK Group v Puglisi* at para 16.110, n 1.
2 See Blair et al (2nd edn), para 14.17.

16.30 For the purposes of the Handbook, 'client' means any person with or for whom a firm conducts or intends to conduct designated investment business or any other regulated activity. This includes a potential client, a client of an appointed representative, a collective investment scheme and either an agent or principal.[1] A client does not include a trust beneficiary, a corporate finance contact and a venture capital contact.

Separate provisions apply with regard to money laundering (ML) and professional firms (PROF). Under the Handbook, every client is either a customer or a market counterparty. Inter-professional dealings are dealt with under a separate code.[2]

1 Under COB 4.1.5R.
2 See paras 16.75–16.80.

16.31 The Glossary also includes a new definition of 'quasi-derivative contract' which is a contract or asset having the effect of a derivative contract. This will act as a form of general 'catch all' provision with all contracts falling with the traditional definition or forms of derivative being covered as well as anything having the same effect whatever its designation or classification.

While this will extend the application of some of the rules set out in the Handbook, this does not of itself extend the scope of the Act and of the activities regulated under the Act as such.

The inclusion of the term had been considered in the proposed revisions to be made to the Rules of IMRO with regard to financial derivatives under its Consultation Document 33.[1] The IMRO Definitions Schedule was to be revised to include a new category of 'quasi-derivative instrument' to ensure that its Rules continued to apply to all new product types developed within the derivatives markets. IMRO had been concerned that new techniques in financial engineering and product innovation may have resulted in the creation of new instruments the value of which was derived from other assets such as debentures, instruments entitling to shares or securities, certificates representing securities or rights and interests in securities but outside the definitions of options, futures or contracts for differences.[2]

1 See IMRO *Derivatives*, Consultation Document 33, November 1996, paras 2.4–2.6.
2 See Blair et al (2nd edn), para 14.19.

Conduct of Business (COB)

16.32 The main provisions that apply with regard to the relationship between regulated firms and their customers are set out in the Conduct of Business (COB) module of the Handbook. This sets out a series of revised general provisions, financial promotion rules, client identification and conduct of business rules. The former requirements were set out in the SIB and separate SRO Rulebooks.[1] These included the separate provisions applied by the SFA and IMRO which differed in certain respects. All of these earlier provisions have since been drawn together within the COB. In so doing, the FSA has attempted to harmonise the relevant provisions insofar as possible.[2]

The COB is in 12 parts with six schedules in addition to the transitional rules for pre-N2 and ex-section 43 firms[3] and for ex-RPB firms.[4] The COB then includes application and general provisions,[5] general rules applying to all firms conducting designated investment business,[6] financial promotion,[7] accepting customers,[8] advising and selling,[9] product disclosure and customer's right to cancel or withdraw,[10] dealing and managing,[11] reporting to customers,[12] client assets,[13] collective investment scheme operators,[14] trustee and depositary activities[15] and Lloyd's.[16] Some of the main provisions relevant to the conduct of derivatives-related activities are considered below.

1 See Blair et al (2nd edn), paras 14.14–14.41.
2 See FSA, *Conduct of Business*, Consultation Paper.
3 COB TP 1.
4 COB TP 2.
5 COB 1.
6 COB 2.
7 COB 3.
8 COB 4.
9 COB 5.
10 COB 6.
11 COB 7.
12 COB 8.
13 COB 9.
14 COB 10.
15 COB 11.
16 COB 12.

General rules

16.33 COB imposes a number of general rules with which all firms conducting designated investment business must comply. These are generally concerned with communications, inducements and commission, reliance, Chinese walls and exclusion of liabilities.

CLEAR, FAIR AND NOT MISLEADING COMMUNICATION

16.34 When a firm communicates information to a customer, the firm must take reasonable steps to communicate it in a way that is clear, fair and not misleading.[1] This applies to all firms communicating information to customers in the course of or in connection with its designated investment business other than in the form of a financial promotion.[2] This restates as a separate rule part of Principle 7 (Communications with clients). Private customers may bring an action for damages under s 150 of the FSMA 2000 to recover loss resulting from a firm communicating information in the course of a designated investment business in a way that is not clear or fair or misleading.

1   COB 2.1.3R.
2   COB 2.1.1R.

INDUCEMENTS AND SOFT COMMISSION

16.35   A firm must take reasonable steps to ensure that it, and any person acting on its behalf, does not offer, give, solicit or accept an inducement or direct or refer any actual or potential item of designated investment business to another person on its own initiative or on the instructions of an associate if it is likely to conflict to a material extent with any duty that the firm owes to its customer in connection with the designated investment business or any duty that such a recipient firms owes to its customers.[1] Firms are required under Principles 1 and 6 to conduct their business with integrity, to pay due regard to the interests of its customers and to treat them fairly. These provisions ensure that the firm does not conduct business under arrangements that might give rise to a conflict with its duty to its customers. (Firms are, in particular, required not to enter into certain specific arrangements with independent intermediaries for the sale of packaged products including volume overrides, non-disclosed commission, indemnification payments and non-sales commission payments.) Indirect benefits are permissible including gifts, hospitality and promotional competition prizes of a reasonable value, business leads and past business reviews with regard to pension transfers and opt-outs. Other reasonable indirect benefits are listed in the table to COB 2.2.7G. Firms must not deal in investments as agent for a customer, either directly or indirectly, through any broker under a soft commission agreement unless certain conditions have been complied with including an appropriate written agreement has been entered into, best execution is provided and adequate disclosure is secured.[2] Further requirements are imposed with regard to allowable benefits,[3] prior disclosure,[4] period disclosure,[5] exceptions[6] and record-keeping.[7]

1   COB 2.2.3R.
2   COB 2.2.8R.
3   COB 2.2.12R.
4   COB 2.2.16R.
5   COB 2.2.18R.
6   COB 2.2.19R.
7   COB 2.2.20R.

RELIANCE ON OTHERS

16.36   A firm will comply with any COB rule that requires it to obtain information where it can show that it was reasonable for the firm to rely on information provided to it in writing by another person.[1] Principle 2 requires that firms conduct their business with due skill, care and diligence. This rule confirms the extent to which the firm can rely on information provided by others. Firms are generally entitled to rely on written information provided by unconnected authorised persons or other professional firms unless the firm is aware or ought reasonably to be aware of any fact that would give reasonable grounds to question the accuracy of the information supplied. Any information required to be sent to customers may be transferred to other persons on the instruction of the customer other than connected firms.[2] Firms are not required to send information to a customer where they have taken reasonable steps to establish that this has been or will be supplied by another person.[3]

1   COB 2.2.3R.
2   COB 2.3.6R.
3   COB 2.3.6(1)R.

CHINESE WALLS

16.37   Chinese walls are concerned with arrangements that require information held by a person in the course of carrying on part of its business to be withheld from or not to be used by any person with or for whom it acts in the course of carrying on another part of the business.[1] Principle 8 (conflicts of interest) requires a firm to manage a conflict of interest fairly both between itself and its customers and between a customer and another client. This may be effected through internal arrangements such as Chinese walls although this is subject to the requirements on the withholding of information set out in the COB. If a firm has established and maintains a Chinese wall, it may withhold or not use the information held and permit persons employed in the first part of the business to withhold the information held from those employed in the other part of the business but only to the extent that the business involves the carrying on of designated investment business or related ancillary activities. Information may also be withheld or not used by a firm when this is required by an established arrangement maintained between different parts of the business (of any kind) in the same group. With regard to the attribution of knowledge, or any COB rule which requires that a firm acts with knowledge, the firm will not be taken to act with the relevant knowledge if none of the individuals concerned acts with that knowledge as a result of the Chinese walls established.[2]

1   COB 2.4.4R.
2   COB 2.4.6R.

EXCLUSION OF LIABILITY

16.38   Principle 6 (customers' interests) requires that firms pay due regard to the interests of customers and treat them fairly. This means that firms may not exclude duties owed to customers under the Act or Handbook unless it is reasonable to do so. A firm must not in any written or oral communication seek to exclude or restrict or rely on any exclusion or restrictions of any duty or liability it may have to a customer under the regulatory system.[1] A firm must not seek to exclude or restrict in any written or oral communication with a private customer any such duty or liability unless it is reasonable for it to do so.[2]

1   COB 2.5.3R.
2   COB 2.5.4R.

Financial promotion

16.39   The financial promotion rules set out in COB 3 may apply with regard to any communications or promotions with regard to derivatives activities. The financial promotion rules are considered separately.[1]

1   See Chapter 8.

Accepting customers

16.40   Firms are subject to a general requirement of proper client classification. Before conducting designated investment business with or for any client, a firm must take reasonable steps to establish whether that client is either a private customer, intermediate customer or market counterparty.[1] Client includes any person with whom a firm is dealing or proposes to deal. Clients are generally divided into market counterparties and customers with customers being further split into either intermediate or private customer status. Intermediate customers generally include large businesses and experts while private customers include individuals and small businesses. The COB then provides for clients entitled to a higher degree of protection to opt-up to a lower protected status and for low protected clients to opt-down to a higher protected status.

1   COB 4.1.4R.

16.41   Private customers are persons not falling within the definition of a market counterparty or intermediate customer. This will generally include individuals and small businesses. A market counterparty is defined as a government agency, central bank, supranational agency, state investment body, another authorised firm or overseas financial services institution, an associate of an authorised firm or overseas financial services institution if the firm or institution consents and any intermediate customer who has opted up to market counterparty status. An intermediate customer includes any local authority or public authority, a listed company or one that has in the last two years had net assets or called-up share capital of £5 million or more (or any holding company or subsidiary), special purpose vehicles, partnerships with net assets of £5 million or more (within the last two years), trusts with aggregate assets of more than £10 million within the last two years), occupational pension scheme trustees with more than 50 members and £10 million of assets under management (within the last two years) and unregulated collective investment schemes.

16.42   Clients may also be classified as discretionary, advisory or execution only. Discretionary clients are customers that have granted firms authority to manage and deal on their behalf. Advisory customers request opinions and recommendations but take their own investment decisions. Execution only customers issue instructions for firms to trade or deal in accordance with the direction provided.

16.43   The COB provides for a number of automatic classification rules subject to certain adjustments. Firms that conduct designated investment business or related ancillary activities for another firm or an overseas financial services institution are to classify that other party as a market counterparty subject to certain exceptions.[1] The other party will be an intermediate customer if inter-professional business is involved unless it is decided that the underlying client should be reclassified as an intermediate customer or where inter-professional business is not involved and the other party is acting on its behalf or is a long-term insurer acting on behalf of a life fund. Unregulated collective investment schemes are classified as intermediates and regulated collective investment schemes as private customers. An expert private customer may be classified as an intermediate customer if reasonable care has been taken to determine that the client has sufficient experience and understanding and written notice has been given of the protections lost, sufficient time to consider the reclassification provided and written or other consent obtained.[2] Large intermediate customers may be classified as market counterparties where they satisfy the general asset tests referred to.[3] This includes a body corporate (with called-up shared capital of, at least, £10 million), local authorities and public authorities and relevant partnerships or trustees. The client may also be reclassified where notice has been given with a warning of the protections lost and sufficient time provided to consider whether the client should object.

1   COB 4.1.7R.
2   COB 4.1.9R.
3   COB 4.1.12R.

16.44   A client who would otherwise be a market counterparty or an intermediate customer (other than a firm or an overseas financial services institution) may be classified a private customer provided that appropriate notice is given.[1] Such clients should be notified that they may not necessarily have the rights available under the Financial Ombudsman Service or the compensation scheme. Intermediate and market counterparty classification should be reviewed, at least, annually unless no business has been conducted for the previous twelve months.[2] Appropriate records of customer classifications including sufficient information to support the allocation must be kept for, at least, three years and six years for life policies or pensions contracts and indefinitely for other pension transfers or opt-outs.[3]

1   COB 4.1.14R.
2   COB 4.1.15R.
3   COB 4.1.16R.

16.45   Firms must provide customers with appropriate terms of business which set out the basis on which the designated investment business is to be conducted.[1] Firms must enter into client agreements with private customers where the business includes managing investments on a discretionary basis, designated investment business relating to contingent liability investments, stock lending activity or underwriting.[2] In such cases, the firm must not enter into the client agreement unless it has taken reasonable care to ensure that the private customer has had a proper opportunity to consider the terms unless the customer is habitually resident outside the UK and the firm has taken reasonable steps to establish that the private customer does not wish to enter into the client agreement. The terms of business (including a client agreement) must set out in adequate detail the basis on which the designated investment business is to be conducted.[3] This may be provided in more than one document provided that they collectively constitute the terms of business[4] with no amendments being permitted on less than 10 days' notice.[5] Adequate records must be kept of the terms of business and any amendments which must generally be kept, at least, for three years.[6]

1   COB 4.2.5R.
2   COB 4.2.7R.
3   COB 4.2.10R.
4   COB 4.2.12R.
5   COB 4.2.13R.
6   COB 4.2.14R.

16.46   The general requirements to be set out in the terms of business (including the client agreement if appropriate) are set out in the Table to COB 4.2.15E. This includes commencement, relevant regulator, investment objectives and restrictions, services and payments. There must also be disclosure of polarisation status (pending review), investment manager arrangements, accounting, right to withdraw (with regard to certain products), any right to make unsolicited real-time financial promotions, right to act as principal, conflicts of interest and material interests, broker fund advisers and use of soft commission agreements. Appropriate risk warnings must be included where the firm has elected to provide these in the terms of business. These include with regard to warrants or derivatives, non-readily realisable investments, penny shares, securities subject to stabilisation and stock lending activity. Further requirements apply with regard to unregulated collective investment schemes, underwriting, stock lending, realisation of private customer's assets, complaints, compensation, termination, contracting out of best execution and authorised professional firms. Separate requirements apply in connection with the management of investments on a discretionary basis.[1]

1   COB 4.2.16E.

Advising and selling

16.47   COB imposes additional rules on advising and selling specific products. This includes the polarisation and status disclosure requirements that apply with regard to the provision of advice on packaged products and marketing groups.[1] Firms are then subject to the restated know your customer, suitability and understanding of risk requirements. Before a firm gives any personal recommendation concerning a designated investment to a private customer or acts as an investment manager for a private customer, it must take reasonable steps to ensure that it is in possession of sufficient personal and financial information about that customer relevant to the services that the firm has agreed to provide.[2] Adequate records must be kept of private customer's personal and financial circumstances which must be kept for, at least, three years.[3] Firms must also take reasonable steps to ensure that they do not make any personal recommendation to a private customer to buy or sell a designated investment or effect a discretionary transaction for a private customer unless it is suitable for the customer having regard to the facts disclosed by the customer and all other relevant facts about the customer of which the firm is or ought reasonably to have been aware.[4]

1   COB 5.1.
2   COB 5.2.5R.
3   COB 5.2.9R.
4   COB 5.3.5R.

16.48   Firms must not make any personal recommendation of a transaction, act as discretionary investment manager, arrange (bring about) a deal in a warrant or a derivative or engage in stock lending activity for a private customer unless it has taken reasonable steps to ensure that the customer understands the nature of the risks involved.[1] With regard to warrants or derivatives, the firm most provide the private customer with a notice in the appropriate form and require the customer to acknowledge receipt of the notice and confirm acceptance of its contents in writing.[2] This is not required where the private customer is ordinarily resident outside the UK and the firm has taken reasonable steps to determine that the client does not wish to receive the notice. This is also not required for warrants that are already held or warrants attached to other designated investments. The Warrants and derivatives risk warning notice is set out in COB 5 Annex 1. This contains further information with regard to warrants, off-exchange warrant transactions, futures, options, contracts for differences, off-exchange transactions in derivatives, foreign markets, contingent liability investment transactions, limited liability transactions, collateral, commissions, suspensions of trading, clearing house protections and insolvency. Firms are required to send out the notices with all of the prescribed information being provided. The name of the firm must also be added and the client and any joint account holder confirm in writing that they have read and understood the warning. This revised warning notice replaces the earlier separate notices contained in the SFA and IMRO rules.[3]

1   COB 5.4.3R.
2   COB 5.4.6E.
3   See Blair et al (2nd edn), paras 14.30–14.34.

16.49   Firms are required to provide general information about themselves and their activities (COB 5.5). Special rules apply with regard to excessive charges (COB 5.6) and general disclosure of charges, remuneration and commission (COB 5.7). Separate provisions apply with regard to customers introduced to clearing firms by brokers and overseas brokers (COB 5.8) and information about stakeholder pension schemes (COB 5.9).

Dealing and managing

16.50   Separate provisions apply with regard to dealing in and managing investments. These include conflicts of interest and material interests,[1] churning and switching,[2] dealing ahead[3] and customer order priority.[4] Where, in particular, a firm has any material interest in a transaction or a conflict of interest has arisen, they must not advise or deal unless it has taken reasonable steps to ensure fair treatment for the customer.[5] Material interests should generally be disclosed to customers. Firms are then required to provide best execution in carrying out a customer order in any designated investment.[6] In so doing, firms must take reasonable care to ascertain the price which is the best available for the customer order in the relevant market at the time for transactions of the kind and size concerned and execute the order at a price that is no less advantageous to the customer unless reasonable steps have been taken to ensure that it would otherwise be in the customer's best interests not to do so.[7] Further obligations then apply with regard to timely execution,[8] aggregation and allocation,[9] realisation of assets[10] and lending.[11]

1   COB 7.1.
2   COB 7.2.
3   COB 7.3.
4   COB 7.4.
5   COB 7.1.3R.
6   COB 7.5.3R.
7   COB 7.5.5R.
8   COB 7.6.
9   COB 7.7.
10 COB 7.8.
11 COB 7.9.

MARGIN REQUIREMENTS

16.51 Firms must obtain any margin payable from a private customer whether at the outset or subsequently in connection with any contingent liability investments.[1] The minimum margin to be obtained for an on-exchange transaction is the amount or value equal to the margin requirement on the relevant exchange or clearing house.[2] Customers should generally be notified of the circumstances in which they will be called to pay margins, the form in which the margin may be provided and the steps the firm may be entitled to take in the event that the margin is not paid. This includes the need to close out the customer's position. Any other circumstances that may lead the firm to close the customer's position without prior reference should also be disclosed.

1   COB 7.10.3(a)R.
2   COB 7.10.3(2)R.

16.52 A firm is required to close out a private customer's open position if the customer fails to meet a margin call made for the position for five business days following the date on which the obligation to make the call accrues.[1] This applies unless the firm has received confirmation from a relevant third party that the customer has given instructions to pay in full and the firm has taken reasonable care to establish that the delay in its receipt is owing to circumstances beyond the private customer's control. The firm may alternatively make a loan or grant credit to the customer to enable the payment of the margin in full although this is subject to the separate restrictions on lending to private customers set out in COB 7.9.3. These replace the equivalent provisions formerly set out in SFA Rule 5.28 and IMRO Rule 2.4.

1   COB 7.1.5R.

NON-EXCHANGE TRADED SECURITIES

16.53 Firms are required to deal fairly with private customers in relation to the sale and subsequent purchase of non-exchange traded (OTC) securities. This applies where the firm has sold the security to the customer and then holds itself out as market maker in that security. Security would include most derivatives contracts. In such circumstances, the firm must give written notice to the private customer, no later than the time of sale, that a reasonable price for repurchase will be available for a period specified in the notice (of not less than three months from the date of notice) and that sale after the end of that period may be difficult due to the nature and possible illiquidity of the security. The firm must ensure that a reasonable price is available to the private customer for the duration of the period specified (COB 7.11.3R).

16.54 COB contains further provision with regard to customer orders and execution records,[1] personal account dealing,[2] programme trading[3] and non-market price transactions.[4] Under COB 7.12, firms are required to establish and maintain appropriate procedures that allow it then to record adequate information promptly in connection with the execution of customers' orders and own account transactions.[5] The minimum contents of the customer order and execution orders are set out in the Table to COB 7.12.6E. The price at which Internet orders are automatically executed should also be recorded as well as the relevant price applicable if the transaction was not executed immediately on receipt. Records must be generally kept for, at least, three years.

1   COB 7.12.
2   COB 7.13.
3   COB 7.14.
4   COB 7.15.
5   COB 7.12.3R.

Reporting to customers

16.55   Firms must provide transaction confirmations and periodic state-ments to customers. Firms must, in particular, despatch to the customer a written confirmation recording the essential details of the transaction promptly.[1] The essential details to be included are listed in COB.[2] Additional information has to be provided with regard to derivatives-related transactions. This includes the maturity, delivery or expiry date of the derivative. In the case of an option, a reference must made to the last exercise date, whether it can be exercised before maturity and the strike price. If the transaction involved the purchase of one currency with another, the rate of exchange involved or a statement that the rate will be supplied when the currency has been purchased must be provided including the maturity or expiry of the currency hedge unless this is separately reportable. If the transaction closes out an open futures position, all essential details must be provided in respect of each contract comprised in the open position and each contract by which it was closed out and the profit or loss to the customer arising out of the closing out (the difference account).

1   COB 8.1.3R.
2   COB 8.1.5E and the Table set out in COB 8.1.15E.

16.56   Where a firm acts as investment manager or operates an account containing uncovered open positions in contingent liability investments, periodic statements must be provided. The firm must promptly and at suitable intervals provide the customer with a written statement containing adequate information on the value and composition of the customer's account or portfolio with the firm as at the end of the period covered by the statement.[1] This is not required where the private customer is habitually resident outside the UK and certain intermediate customers provided that the customer has so requested or the firm has taken reasonable steps to establish that he does not wish to receive the statement. A periodic statement is also not required where this would duplicate information provided by another party. Copies of the periodic statements provided must be retained for, at least, three years. Periodic statements should generally be provided to private customers within 25 business days after the end of the period to which the statement relates or 10 days if the portfolio includes undercovered open positions in contingent liability investments. The statement should be provided monthly if the customer's portfolio includes uncovered open positions in contingent liability investments or six monthly generally or, at least, annually otherwise.

The statement should contain certain general information with regard to contents and value and the basis for valuation. With regard to contingent liability investments, the statement should disclose all changes in value, open positions, closed positions, aggregate of contents (including cash, collateral value, management fees and commissions) and options information (including the share, future, index or other investment involved, the trade price and date of transaction, market price and exercise price of the contract).

1   COB 8.2.4R.

Further provisions

16.57   COB contains further provision with regard to client assets,[1] collective investment schemes,[2] trustee and depositary activities[3] and Lloyd's.[4] The client asset rules, in particular, include specific obligations with regard to custody,[5] mandate,[6] client money,[7] collateral[8] and client money distribution.[9]

Relevant record-keeping requirements under COB are summarised in Sch 1[10] with notification requirements in Sch 2.[11] The other schedules contain standard information with regard to fees, powers exercised, rights of action and rules that may waived.[12] All of these provisions will have to be complied with depending upon the nature of the client and the particular services to be provided.

1   COB 9.
2   COB 10.
3   COB 11.
4   COB 12.
5   COB 9.1.
6   COB 9.2.
7   COB 9.3.
8   COB 9.4.
9   COB 9.5.
10 COB Sch 1.
11 COB Sch 2.
12 COB Schs 3, 4, 5 and 6.

EXCHANGE TRADED CONTRACTS AND LIFFE

16.58   Different levels and types of risk arise with regard to exchange traded and OTC derivative contracts.[1] The main advantages of exchange traded dealings include price transparency and standardisation of terms and procedures with clearing and settlement being affected through a central agent or counterparty facility. The main disadvantages are that only a limited number of more simple contracts may be traded and then only on fixed terms. The main formal derivatives market in the UK is LIFFE[2] although derivatives trading is also undertaken on the other recognised investment exchanges such as the London Stock Exchange, the London Securities and Derivatives Exchange (OM London Exchange or OMLX) as well as the London Metal Exchange (LME) and the International Petroleum Exchange (IPE).[3]

1   See paras 16.5 and 16.59–16.69.
2   See para 16.6.
3   See M Blair, *Financial Services and Markets Act 2000* (2001), Ch 20.

Introduction to LIFFE

16.59   LIFFE was opened for trading at the Royal Exchange in September 1982. The initial contracts traded included a range of purely domestic and Eurodollar products such as options, Eurobond futures, short gilt futures and FT index futures.

Futures trading in the FTSE100 began in 1984 with options being introduced in 1985. Japanese or continental European financial instruments were not considered at first although other contracts such as gold futures, FT Index options, gilt options and FX options were discussed.[1] German

Government Bond (Bund) futures were introduced in 1988 and three month Euromark futures, ECU futures and Bund options in 1989.

New trading facilities were opened at Cannon Bridge in the City of London in December 1991. LIFFE merged with the London Commodities Exchange in September 1996 as a result of which it now trades a range of soft commodity and agricultural products including futures and options in cocoa, robusta, coffee, white sugar, grain, potatoes and the Baltic Freight Index.

Since opening contract volumes have grown year by year at a compound rate of over 40% with over 167 million contracts being traded in 1996. This represented an average daily volume of 660,000 contracts.[2] By 30 April 1997, the average daily volume of all options and futures contracts exceeded 800,000.

1   See generally D Kynaston, *LIFFE: A Market and its Makers* (1997).
2   See LIFFE, *An Introduction to LIFFE* (2001).

16.60   Historically, trading on LIFFE was generally conducted through open outcry. This meant that individual products were traded in separate pits on the exchange floor by teams of brokers who were members of LIFFE.

This was replaced by an electronic trading system LIFFE CONNECT (TM) in November 1998 with the closure of the LIFFE floor in London. Trading has subsequently been conducted through computer screens.[1] LIFFE CONNECT allows for orders to be submitted through a trading application (the front-end software) into the electronically maintained central order book. The Trading Host then matches orders in accordance with the input criteria set. Executed transactions are fed from the Trading Host to the Trade Registration System (TRS) on a real-time basis. TRS provides for post trade processing. Trades are then passed into the Clearing Processing System (CPS) with the London Clearing House (LCH) acting as the central counterparty.

LIFFE now trades an average of 550 billion pounds (euro 603) billion every day which includes 45% of all euro-denominated bond issues within the City of London, 32% of all foreign exchange turnover and 95% of all euro money market exchange traded derivatives business.[2]

1   See LIFFE, *Global Derivatives Trading on LIFFE – Gaining Access to the Market* (2001).
2   See LIFFE, *Summary of futures and options contracts* (2002). See also LIFFE – the Exchange on www.liffe.com/about/index.htm.

16.61   The LIFFE futures and options market is administered by LIFFE Administration and Management which is a subsidiary of LIFFE (Holdings) plc. LIFFE Administration and Management is referred to as the Exchange in the LIFFE Rules. This is the recognised body for the purposes of the Financial Services and Markets Act.

Firms applying for membership of LIFFE are generally also regulated by the FSA (formerly members of SFA). Although recognition is conditional upon maintaining and enforcing certain rules on members this does not authorise them to carry on investment business as such. To the extent that most members of LIFFE are regulated by the FSA, they will be subject to the terms of the FSA Handbook of Rules and Guidance.[1]

LIFFE is managed by a Board of Directors which are elected from market participants although the Board may delegate matters to various committees[2] such as the Membership, Rules & Committee.

1   See paras 16.21–16.57.

2 Rules 1.5.1 and 1.5.3 of the Rules of LIFFE (1 December 2001 (incorporating amendments issued on 27 November 2001)). See Blair et al (2nd edn), para 14.44.

16.62 LIFFE contracts are settled through the London Clearing House (LCH). The London Produce Clearing House Ltd was set up in 1888 to clear coffee and future trades. This was subsequently renamed the International Commodities Clearing House Ltd in 1973 which was again renamed The London Clearing House Ltd in 1991. LCH was formerly owned by six of the major UK banks although it was acquired in October 1996 by LIFFE, the International Petroleum Exchange (IPE) and the London Metal Exchange (LME).

LCH is a Recognised Clearing House under the Financial Services and Markets Act. As such it clears trades for LIFFE, IPE, LME and Tradepoint. Clearing members of LIFFE are also members of LCH. LCH maintains strict membership rules which include a liquid minimum financial resources requirement depending upon the type of business conducted.

LCH members are subject to periodic financial reporting requirements and must also comply with the initial and additional margin requirements imposed by the LCH and LIFFE.

The margin requirements are designed to ensure that all members are protected from default by another member. This is effected by requiring all open positions to be covered on a daily basis by either liquid funds or other collateral. Initial margins are calculated by LCH in consultation with LIFFE having regard to recent daily price moves, volatility and possible future events in particular contracts. A variation margin is also imposed equal to the difference between the settlement price and the previous day's settlement price.

Necessary payments are made through a Protected Payments System following calculation by LCH of shortfall or surplus cash and collateral positions per currency and per account having taken into account profits and losses and margin requirements.

Investor protection and market stability

16.63 The interests of investors and the integrity of the LIFFE market are protected through a number of overlapping mechanisms. These are partly concerned with the status of LIFFE as a regulatory institution but also with the supervisory arrangements adopted in respect of member firms. The standards set are reinforced through the dealing rules operated on the floor of the Exchange as well as specific provisions applicable to client money, other assets and collateral. LIFFE and LCH also maintain separate default procedures in the event of a member experiencing trading difficulties or its insolvency.

It is through these mechanisms that LIFFE is able to protect the efficiency and financial integrity of its market place as well as the interests of its members and their clients. As an exchange, however, it must be stressed that the interests of member clients would only be protected indirectly in the absence of specific provisions. Members dealing on LIFFE do so on a principal-to-principal basis and the contracts entered into are only between the member and LIFFE and LCH. The client is accordingly not party to the immediate contractual relationships created in a trade. It is for this reason that LIFFE imposes a number of specific obligations on its members in dealing with their clients.

These are considered necessary to ensure that members comply with all regulatory, contractual or fiduciary duties owed to their clients. These include informing the client that the member can only act as principal and not agent and complying with the LIFFE client agreement requirements before opening a client account which include notifying the client of the overriding effect of the LIFFE Rules on the client contract in the event of any conflict arising but also of the margin requirements and dispute resolution procedures available under the Arbitration Rules.

LIFFE as a recognised investment exchange

16.64   As a recognised investment exchange LIFFE is supervised by FSA. This means that is has and continues to satisfy the relevant requirements imposed in connection with financial resources, monitoring and enforcement rules, investigation of complaints and the promotion and maintenance of high standards of integrity and fair dealing.

The new rules with regard to recognised investment exchanges are set out in the Recognised Investment Exchange and Clearing House sourcebook (REC) in Block 5 of the FSA Handbook. The REC sets out guidance on the application of the revised provisions in Part XVIII of the Act concerning the recognition of investment exchanges and clearing houses. While this generally continues the earlier regime set up under the Financial Services Act 1986, the powers of the authorities with regard to exchanges and clearing houses are strengthened.

REC provides particular guidance on the recognition requirements set out in the Act and the application procedures for recognition as well as the FSA's approach to the supervision of these bodies. Further provisions are included with regard to notification rules and fees. Parts of the draft sourcebook (REC 1 to REC 6) were issued for consultation in January 2000 with the fees rules in June 2001.[1] The Final form REC 1 to REC 6 were issued in April 2001.[2]

1 See FSA, *RIE and RCH Sourcebook* (January 2000), CP 39; and FSA, *Third Consultation Paper on the FSA's post-N2 fee-raising arrangements*, CP 95. See Chapter 18, paras 18.116–18.142.
2 See FSA, *RIE and RCH Sourcebooks: Feedback on CP 39* (April 2001), Policy Statement.

Membership

16.65   The relevant provisions concerning the supervision of LIFFE members and their activities were set out in the LIFFE Rules, an ATS (automated trading system) user agreement as well as the terms of the contracts traded, other written or oral instructions from the Exchange and other prescribed agreements entered into for certain purposes such as clearing, market making or automated trading.

The membership criteria are set out in Rule 3.1.1 of the LIFFE Rules. Applicants must satisfy the Board that they are fit and proper, have a suitable financial and business standing, staff are fit and proper and adequate internal procedures and controls are maintained. Applicants must also be already authorised or otherwise licensed or permitted to conduct business on the market. This will include authorisation and permission to carry on investment business for the purposes of the Financial Services and Markets Act as well as membership of LCH if the applicant is to become a clearing member of LIFFE.

LIFFE members are either Pubic Order or Non-Public Order Members. Only public order members may deal for or advise clients who are not members of LIFFE under Rule 3.3.1. Members are also either Clearing (General Clearing or Individual Clearing) or Non-Clearing Members. Applications may also be made for affiliate member status which deal through full LIFFE members.

Market operations and supervision

16.66 Compliance with all the relevant Rules and other provisions is, in particular, secured through LIFFE's Market Supervision Department (MSD) which attempts to ensure that a fair and orderly market is maintained and that high standards of integrity and fair dealing are followed.[1] MSD is principally concerned with market supervision and regulation, membership and development and planning although is also generally responsible for with trade monitoring, complaints investigation, disciplinary enforcement, promotion of high standards and regulatory co-operation.

1 On earlier arrangements, see Blair et al (2nd edn), para 14.47–14.51.

Supervision

16.67 MSD is divided into a number of sections comprising Market Supervision, Market Regulation, Membership and Development and Planning. The Market Supervision section was divided into the Compliance and Audit, Financial Surveillance, Market Surveillance, Market Regulation and Administration units. The Compliance and Audit unit was responsible for ensuring that the internal control systems and procedures of member firms are adequate. Financial Surveillance was concerned with ensuring compliance with all relevant financial resources requirements especially through the examination of regular returns and liaison with other authorities. Market Surveillance was responsible for protecting market and contract integrity through routine maintenance functions and more event specific activities.

Investigations and discipline

16.68 MSD is also responsible for the investigation of alleged violations of any obligations imposed on LIFFE members under the Rules, relevant contracts or otherwise as well as for taking any appropriate disciplinary action required. Any alleged violation will be investigated by MSD which will then submit a preliminary report to the Membership, Rules & Trading Committee or the Chief Executive (Rule 5.2.1). If there is *prima facie* evidence of a violation, a hearing by a Disciplinary Panel will be arranged (Rule 5.2.2). The Panel will consider and determine whether the breach has occurred.

The Panel will be made up of a Chairman and two members and a further non-voting appointment to assist its work. The Panel will set its own procedures with hearings being in private and confidential (Rule 5.4.2). The complainant is given the opportunity to be heard under the Rules and be required to attend by the Panel (Rule 5.4.4).

If the complaint is upheld, the Panel may impose a fine up to 250,000, issue a warning or reprimand or recommend to the Board that the person be expelled or that some or all of their rights be suspended or other facilities terminated (Rule 5.5.1). A right of appeal is provided to the Board within 10 business days (Rule 5.7.1). Expulsion and suspension is dealt with under Section 7 and appeals under Section 8 with separate arbitration procedures being provided under Section 6.

Default rules

16.69   As a recognised investment exchange LIFFE must maintain appropriate default rules. There revised procedures are set out in Section 9 of the LIFFE Rules. These apply where an event of default has arisen as defined in Rule 9.3.1. These include situations in which a member has failed to satisfy its obligations under one or more market contracts or failed to make a margin payment. It is also an event of default where a member becomes unable to pay its debts within the meaning of s 123 of the Insolvency Act 1986 or comparable provisions under the law of any other jurisdiction.

If an event of default arises, LIFFE is required to take one of a number of steps under the Rules unless the FSA requires it not to take any action or some alternative action (Rule 9.4.1). The action provide for under the LIFFE rules is generally concerned the settling any unsettled contracts in the most efficient manner including making any necessary adjustments in books of the defaulter (Rule 9.4.3).

LIFFE must ensure that all relevant counterparties are properly notified (Rule 9.5) and may prescribe appropriate procedures under the Companies Act 1989 and the FSMA 2000 (Rule 9.6).

LIFFE's supervisory requirements

16.70   LIFFE is able to maintain high standards of integrity and fair dealing as well as secure a fair and orderly market through its various supervisory and regulatory mechanisms. Members have to satisfy its application procedures and criteria in addition to those of the FSA. A number of specific requirements are then imposed on the conduct of business including client disclosures, margin payments and compliance with relevant client money and other asset rules[1] as well as regular reporting requirements.[2]

The maintenance of adequate internal controls as well as compliance with all relevant rules is strengthened through the activities of MSD which are concerned with individual member compliance and with protecting the efficient and stable operation of the market as a whole.

Through of these mechanisms many of the legal and other regulatory risks that would otherwise arise in conducting derivative business are controlled. Although the range of products is limited despite LIFFE's expansion, the tightly controlled nature of the market safeguards the interests of both participants and wider investors. Considerably more serious difficulties arise with regard to the OTC market where comparable protections are not in place.

1   In connection with the application of the former Financial Services (Client Money) Regulations 1991 with regard to clearing arrangements, see *Re Griffin Trading Co* [2000] BPIR 256.
2   See paras 16.21–16.57.

LONDON CODE OF CONDUCT AND GREY PAPER

16.71   In contrast to derivatives dealt with on an exchange, the OTC market is subject to little direct regulation. The conduct of derivatives-related investment business is to some extent controlled through certain provisions contained in the FSA Handbook (formerly the SRO Rules) which effect dealings in both traded and OTC derivatives.[1] This is, however, distinct from the regulation of the market itself while the more onerous requirements imposed are directed at the protection of the interests of private as opposed to professional or business investors.

With regard to the OTC market at the wholesale level, general standards of conduct for principals and broking firms were set out in The London Code of Conduct which operated as part of the Bank of England's Grey Paper regime for the regulation of the wholesale cash and OTC derivative markets. The London Code has since been replaced by the FSA's code of Inter-Professional Conduct which forms part of the Market Conduct sourcebook (MAR) within Block 2 (Business Standards) of the new Handbook.[2]

The conduct of business on the OTC derivatives market is still otherwise left to private bargain although this has become standardised to a large extent through the use of pro forma documentation such as that produced by ISDA.[3]

1   See paras 16.21–16.57.
2   See paras 16.75–16.80.
3   See paras 16.81–16.102.

16.72   The regulation of the wholesale OTC derivatives markets was formerly dealt with under the Bank of England's The London Code of Conduct[1] and Grey Paper concerning the oversight of the wholesale cash and OTC derivatives markets. The London Code applied to the products set out in Chapter 6 which included Sterling, foreign currency and gold and silver wholesale deposits as well as spot and forward foreign exchange and gold and silver bullion.[3]

The Code was part of the larger regulatory regime set up under the Grey Paper which applied to listed institutions formerly exempt from the provisions contained in s 43 of the Financial Services Act 1986. This was managed by the Wholesale Markets Supervision Division of the Bank of England but was transferred to FSA under s 21(b)(i) of the Bank of England Act 1998. While the Grey Paper set out the basic structure and provisions applicable to the regulation of the wholesale markets, the Code contained general standards and controls with which firms were expected to comply.

The London Code of Conduct and the Grey Paper were reissued by the FSA in June 1999.[4] The restated London Code Conduct applied until N2 after which it was replaced by the revised provisions set out in the new Code for inter-professional conduct of business to be included within the Market Conduct sourcebook (MAR).[5]

1   See Bank of England, *The London Code of Conduct – For Principals and Broking Firms in the Wholesale Markets* (July 1995).
2   See Bank of England, *The Regulation of the Wholesale Cash and OTC Derivatives Markets (in Sterling, Foreign Currency and Bullion)* (December 1995).
3   This also included OTC options or futures on gold and silver as well as certificates of deposit (CDs), bank bills, commercial paper, other debentures (with a maturity of less than five years), UK local authority debt, other public sector debt, OTC options, interest rate and currency swaps and sale and repurchase agreements (repos). The foreign exchange contracts in *Larussa-Chigi v CS First Boston Ltd* [1998] CLC 277 were governed by the London Code of Conduct. See para 16.20 above.
4   See FSA, *The London Code Conduct; For principals and broking firms in the wholesale markets* (June 1999), Policy Statement; FSA, *The regulation of the wholesale cash and OTC derivative markets under section 43 of the Financial Services Act 1986* (June 1999) [Grey Paper].
5   See FSA, *The Inter-Professionals Code* (May 2000), Consultation paper. See also FSA, *Market Abuse: A Draft Code of Market Conduct* (July 2000), Consultation paper 59; FSA, *Supplement to the Draft Code of Market Conduct* (November 2000), Consultation paper 76; and FSA, *Code of Market Conduct – Feedback on CP59 and CP76* (April 2001). See paras 16.75–16.80.

London Code of Conduct

16.73   The earlier London Code applied to most wholesale market dealings which were not regulated by the rules of a recognised investment exchange.[1] This generally included the treasury operations of large banks. The objective of the Code was to sustain the efficient functioning of the London wholesale markets in which the products are traded and to avoid over-burdensome regulation.[2] The Code applied to 'core principals' which were the banks, buildings societies and other financial institutions authorised under s 43 of the Act as well as broking firms which dealt on behalf of other counterparties.

Compliance with the Code was considered necessary to ensure that high standards of integrity and fair dealing continued to be observed throughout the wholesale market. Breaches of the Code were considered to be treated as serious. This could be dealt with either by reprimands or restrictions on listed institutions' activities or possibly suspension or removal from the list. Compensation fund arrangements do not apply and so financial redress had to be agreed between parties. FSA could arbitrate in disputes as appropriate. The Code contained a number of specific provisions with regard to general standards, know your counterparty and dealing principles and procedures.[3]

1   See FSA, *The London Code Conduct*, Table, p 7.
2   See FSA, *The London Code Conduct*, paras 2 and 3.
3   See Blair et al (2nd edn), paras 14.56–14.59.

Grey Paper

16.74   The Grey Paper set out the manner in which the London wholesale cash and OTC derivatives markets in Sterling, foreign currency and bullion were regulated. The June 1999 restatement replaced the Bank of England's December 1995 Paper (which had superseded an earlier April 1988 version).

The conditions and arrangements for admission to the list maintained for the purposes of s 43 of the Financial Services Act were set out in Section B of the Grey Paper. Additional provisions concerning the supervision of listed institutions were contained in Section C with specific provision in connection with capital adequacy in Section E.

The application of the system of regulations set up under the Grey Paper to institutions authorised under the Investment Services Act was explained in Section D. Various Schedules were also attached.

FSA INTER-PROFESSIONAL CODE OF CONDUCT

16.75   The London Code and the Grey Paper have since been superseded by the FSA's Inter-Professional Code of Conduct. This is included as Chapter 3 of the Market conduct sourcebook (MAR) which is part of the Business Standards (Block 2) of the FSA Handbook.

Consultation

16.76   The FSA had originally consulted in October 1998 on the regulation of the relationship between professional market users.[1] This sought views on how the FSA should construct a new regulatory treatment for professional firms and their counterparties. This would apply immediately to the listed money market institutions or institutions still regulated by the SFA at that stage although its scope would be extended subsequently.

The paper set out certain provisional criteria to determine the institutions to be covered by the new regime. These were partly objective (involving authorised firms, net worth and transaction size) and subjective (essentially expertise and experience related). Such firms would be subject to the general principles set out in the High Level Standards of the Handbook[2] as well as the prudential requirements in Block 2. They would also have to comply with the new market abuse rules and code of practice covering such matters as dealing practices and market conventions.[3]

1   See FSA, *Differentiated regulatory approaches: future regulation of inter-professional business* (October 1998).
2   See Chapter 2, paras 2.93–2.107.
3   See Chapter 9.

16.77   Following the responses received, the FSA issued its outline proposals for the new regime in June 1999.[1] The FSA considered that it had received a clear mandate to create a new regulatory framework for inter-professional business that would build on the earlier successes achieved as well as benefit from the single institutional structure to be created under the Financial Services and Markets Act.

The new Code would follow the earlier Code of Conduct but cover a wide range of products traded off-exchange including bonds, equities and related derivatives as well as commodity derivatives and apply with regard to market counterparties and intermediate customers.

The draft Inter-Professional Code (IPC) was subsequently issued on 11 May 2000.[2] The draft IPC set out how the FSA's Principles for Businesses would apply with regard to bilateral inter-professional dealings. This would generally disapply most of the provisions set out in the conduct of business sourcebook (COB)[3] and create a new code of practice for such dealings. This would not, however, cover promotions or mediation and certain provisions set out in the earlier London Code would not be included such as with regard to brokerage payments, dealing mandates or the know your counterparty rules (which would be dealt with under the prudential sourcebooks).

1   See FSA, *FSA response to comments on discussion paper: The future regulation of inter-professional business* (June 1999).
2   See FSA, *The Inter-Professionals Code* (May 2000).
3   See Chapter 2, paras 2.114–2.115.

Inter-Professional Conduct

16.78   The final IPC provisions form chapter 3 of the Market conduct sourcebook (MAR 3). This is included within the Business Standards Block with the interim prudential sourcebooks (IPRUs), the conduct of business rules (COB), the training and competence sourcebook (TC) and the Money Laundering sourcebook (ML).[1]

The IPC rules apply to all firms (except service companies, non-directive friendly societies, non-directive insurers and UCITS qualifiers) and covers all regulated and ancillary activities involving dealing (as principal or agent), acting as arranger or giving transaction specific advice. This must, however, also be in respect of an inter-professional investment or be undertaken with or for a market counterparty (MAR 3.1.1 and 3.1.2).

The IPC provisions only apply with regard to a firm's activities carried on from an establishment maintained by the firm in the UK (MAR 3.1.4). Contravention of the rules set out in MAR 3 (IPC) will not give rise to a right of action by a private person under section 150 (MAR 3.1.5).

1 See Chapter 2, paras 2.108–2.119.

16.79 The IPC contains a number of provisions with regard to general standards (MAR 3.4). These include revised requirements concerning suitability and advice (MAR 3.4.3 and 3.4.4), communication and information (MAR 3.4.5–3.4.7), clarity of role (MAR 3.4.10–3.4.12) and marketing incentives, inducements and payments in kind (MAR 3.4.13 and 3.4.16).

With regard to suitability and advice specifically, the FSA Principles are stated not to require a firm to assess the suitability of a particular transaction for its client once it has established that it is dealing with a market counterparty (MAR 3.4.3 G). A market counterparty is generally a government agency, central bank, supranational agency, state investment body, another authorised firm or overseas financial services institution, an associate of an authorised firm or overseas financial services institution if the firm or institution consents and any intermediate customer who has opted up to market counterparty status.[1] The firm is then not obliged to ensure that the market counterparty understands the risks involved and is not under any duty to provide best execution or other dealing protection (MAR 3.4.3).

A firm is not obliged to give advice to a market counterparty and the mere passing of information will not mean that the firm has assumed responsibility for the provision of investment advice (MAR 3.4.4 G).[2]

1 See paras 16.30 and 16.40–16.44.
2 For further discussion, see paras 16.103–16.125.

16.80 Separate rules and guidance are provided with regard to transactions at non-market rates (MAR 3.5), taping (MAR 3.6), firms acting as wholesale market brokers or undertaking transactions through them (MAT 3.7) and codes of practice (MAR 3.8).

The FSA will not endorse any individual codes or practice (other than the Takeover Code) although it will take into account the differing standards and practices operating in distinct markets in interpreting the manner in which its Principles will apply. Breach of any such codes may also raise questions of integrity and competence (MAR 3.8.1 G).

A useful destination is provided[1] which lists the MAR rules with reference to the earlier provisions set out in the FSA's June 1999 London Code of Conduct.[2]

1 See MAR, separate attachment.
2 See paras 16.71–16.73.

STANDARD DOCUMENTATION IN THE OTC MARKET

16.81 In the absence of more direct controls, the interests of market participants and end-users in the OTC market are principally protected through the development of a range of specialist standard term contracts for use in connection with derivatives products.

Some of the earlier documentation was product specific, such as the BBA's recommended terms and conditions for interest rate swaps.[1] More recently, the market has developed increasingly comprehensive central documents referred to as master agreements with separate product specific sets of definitions which are incorporated through confirmation letters or telexes into a particular transaction.

The most commonly used of these are produced by ISDA.[2] The master agreements set out the general terms upon which the parties will transact with specific transactions being governed by the terms of the separate confirmations and relevant sets of product definitions.

Rather than treat all of the particular transactions as separate, the documentation attempts to have them considered as a single agreement with the master document. One of the main reasons for this is to allow close-out netting of all open positions in the event of the insolvency of one party. Although concerns had arisen with regard to the validity of close-out netting under English law a number of subsequent cases have supported its use.[3]

1　British Bankers' Association *Interest Rate Swaps ('BBAIRS' Terms)* (August 1985).
2　Other master documentation has been produced by the International Securities Market Association (ISMA), the Public Securities Association (PSA) and the Association of Futures Brokers (AFB). Other documents used include the Global Markets Repurchase Agreement (GMRA), the International Foreign Exchange Master Agreement (IFEMA), the Foreign Exchange and Options Master Agreement (FEOMA) and the International Currency Options Master Agreement (ICOM).
3　See *Stein v Blake* [1996] AC 243, HL; and the House of Lords in *Morris v Rayners Enterprises Inc* (1997) 141 Sol Jo LB 229. See also *MS Fashions Ltd v Bank of Credit and Commerce International SA (No 2)* [1993] Ch 425; and *Bank of Credit and Commerce International SA v Prince Fahd Bin Salaman Abdul Aziz Al-Saud* [1997] 1 BCLC 457, CA. See also R Goode, *Principles of Corporate Insolvency Law* (1997), Ch 8.

BBAIRS

16.82　The earliest sets of standard documentation produced in this area included the BBA's BBAIRS although this is now less commonly used.[1] BBAIRS sets out the recommended terms and conditions proposed by the Interest Rate Swaps Working Party of the BBA.

Three Working Parties had been set up by the Foreign Exchange Committee of the BBA in October 1984 to prepare recommended Terms and Conditions for Interest Rate Swaps, Foreign Currency Options and Forward Rate Agreements. By 1984 these had become the most important of the new instruments traded in London.

The objective was to attempt to create a measure of uniformity amongst the documentation that banks had been developing separately. The BBA was concerned not to inhibit further growth in the use of these products especially as they had brought significant business and a greater depth to the London inter-bank market. Each of the Working Parties prepared a series of standard terms and conditions for use in connection with the most common types of instruments used as well as more general clauses in all transactions.

In relation to swaps, for example, recommended terms were produced in connection with Single Currency Fixed/Floating Interest Rate Swaps, Cross-Currency Interest Rate Swaps and Cross-Currency Floating Rate Swaps. The product specific clauses included scope, definitions, exchanges, payments, deductions, default and termination and confirmation. The common clauses dealt with such matters as representations and warranties, deductions and withholdings, default interest, termination, events of default, currency of account, compensation and termination and governing law. Examples of standard form confirmations to be exchanged between the parties were provided in connection with each contract.

A number of other matters were also highlighted for special attention during negotiation of terms such as to whether the parties were dealing as principal or brokers.

1 The contracts in the *Westdeutsche Landesbank v Islington London Borough Council* and *Kleinwort Benson v Sandwell* cases were governed by the BBAIRS terms. See *Westdeutsche Landesbank Girozentrale v Islington* [1994] 4 All ER 890, [1994] 1 WLR 938; and *Kleinwort Benson Ltd v Sandwell Borough Council* [1994] 4 All ER 890.

ISDA

16.83   The most important work undertaken in connection with the development of standard documentation has been taken forward by ISDA.[1] ISDA is the largest global trade association for participants in what it refers to as the privately negotiated derivatives industry which constitutes the OTC market. This includes interest rate, currency, commodity and equity swaps and related products such as caps, collars, floors and swaptions.

ISDA was set up in 1985 and now has a membership of over 550 which includes Primary, Associate and Subscriber members. This represents institutions from 41 countries including the major financial firms, leading end-users and service providers and consultants. ISDA's main activities consist of the production and revision of its Master Agreement and related documentation, obtaining legal opinions on the enforceability of netting arrangements (for members only), developing sound risk management practices and promoting public understanding of financial derivatives and their use.

ISDA operates through a number of regional committees (including Asia-Pacific, Japan, Canadian Members, Eastern European and Latin America). There are also a number of more specific functional committees (dealing with such matters as Collateral, Credit Derivatives Market Practice, Documentation, Energy and Developing Products, Equity Derivatives, Euro, Operations, Regulatory, Risk Management, Tax and Trading Practice) and other working groups.[2]

1 See generally www.isda.org.
2 For a review of recent activities, see ISDA, *Year in Review* (March 2001) available on www.isda.org/wwa/fretro2000.hmtl.

ISDA documentation architecture

16.84   Prior to 1991, parties considering entering into contractual relationships using ISDA documentation for an interest rate or currency swap or related transaction could either use the 1987 Interest Rate and Currency Exchange (1987 Agreement) or the 1987 Interest Rate Swap Agreement. Special addenda in respect of caps, collars and floors and similar products were issued in May 1989 with further addenda being produced in July 1990.

The original 1987 Agreement contained detailed provisions concerning payment, representations, agreements, events of default, termination events, provisions for early termination, methods for calculating payments on early termination and other provisions. The schedule to the 1987 Agreement was used to make any modifications to the main text or exercise any options provided. Separate confirmations would then be entered into between the parties which would incorporate the 1987 Agreement, specify the economic terms of the particular transaction and any other particular modifications to the general terms to be applied to that contract.

The 1987 Interest Rate Swap Agreement was generally only used in respect of US Dollar denominated swaps and related products. This was based on an earlier Code of Standard Working Assumptions and Provisions for Swaps which had been published in 1985 and revised in 1986.[1]

1   ISDA, *User's Guide to the 1992 ISDA Master Agreements* (1993 edn), pp 8–9.

1991 ISDA definitions

16.85   In 1991, the 1987 ISDA Agreement was used as the sole master agreement with a number of the earlier additional documents being built into a single set of 1991 ISDA definitions which were incorporated into a particular transaction through the contract confirmation.[1]

The 1991 Definitions expanded the earlier 1987 Definitions, in particular, to include a larger number of currencies and rates and provisions for a wider range of transactions such as caps, collars and floors covered by the earlier Addenda as well as commodity and stock index-based products. A number of changes in the definitions were included, such as with regard to Termination Date, Day Count Fractions, Business Day Convention, Reset Dates, ECU and Rounding Conventions. New provisions were also included with regard to Currencies, IMM (International Money Market Section of the Chicago Mercantile Exchange), Flat Compounding, Rate Options, Price Options, Interpolation and Discounting. Draft letter agreements or telexes confirming transactions were set out in the Exhibits with additional provisions for confirmations for particular types of transactions.

The letter of agreement confirmed that relevant terms and conditions constituted a 'Confirmation' for the purposes of the master agreement and incorporated the terms of the 1991 Definitions. The letter of agreement then provided for the insertion of specific terms of confirmation depending upon the type of contract concerned. By 1991, the ISDA documentation had been updated and simplified generally only to include the 1987 Agreement and the 1991 Definitions which were incorporated through contract confirmations.

1   See ISDA, *1991 ISDA Definitions* (1991).

1992 ISDA Master Agreements

16.86   The 1987 Agreement was replaced in 1992 with two new master agreements for cross-border and local currency transactions with additional sets of definitions in respect of US Municipal counterparties, FX and currency options and commodity derivatives.[1] A further set of definitions in respect of commodity derivatives were published in 1993.[2] While two versions of the Master Agreement were issued in 1992, the multi-currency cross border document (the 1992 Master Agreement) is the most commonly used in practice even where a single currency and jurisdiction is involved.[3]

As with the 1987 Agreement, the 1992 Master Agreement provides for a master document structure to govern the relationship between the parties, incorporates the confirmations, includes specific provisions with regard to representations, events of default and termination events and covenants. It also sets out the early termination provisions and methods for calculating payments on early termination.

The schedule to the 1992 Master Agreement is again used to make changes to the standard provisions. The definitions relating to particular types of product transactions and forms of confirmation were set out in the various definition documents. To the extent that a particular transaction did not fall within any of the new sets of definitions, the 1991 Definitions were applied.

1 See ISDA, *US Municipal Counterparty Definitions* (1992); and ISDA, *FX and Currency Option Definitions* (1992).
2 ISDA, *Commodity Derivative Definitions* (1993).
3 See ISDA, *Master Agreement (Multi Currency – Cross-Border)* (1992); and ISDA *Master Agreement (Local Currency – Single Jurisdiction)*.

Structure and operation of 1992 Master Agreement

16.87 The most important standard document produced by ISDA remains the 1992 Master Agreement.[1] The 1992 Master Agreement is dated at the top and the parties identified.[2] ISDA recommends that the form and jurisdiction of each organisation should be set out on the first page and in the heading of the schedule. It is then provided that the parties have entered or anticipate entering into a number of 'Transactions' to be governed by the Master Agreement, including its 'Schedule' and the documents and other confirming evidence exchanged between the parties by way of 'Confirmation'.

The reference to other confirming evidence means that a written confirmation need not be exchanged. Section 9(e)(ii) provides that the parties may enter into some confirmation as soon as practicable although this may include an exchange of telexes or of electronic messages. It is, however, provided that the parties intend that they will be legally bound by the terms of each transaction from the moment they agree to the terms whether orally or otherwise. This was the same as under BBAIRS.

1 ISDA, *Master Agreement and Schedule to the Master Agreement.*
2 For comment, see A Hudson, *The Law on Financial Derivatives* (2nd edn, 1998), Ch 2.

16.88 In entering into Transactions, the parties expressly agree to be bound by the terms of the 1992 Master Agreement. These are set out in 14 sections.

INTERPRETATION

16.89 The definitions contained in Section 14 of the 1992 Master Agreement are incorporated and a provision introduced to ensure that if any inconsistencies arise between the Master Agreement and the Schedule and Transactions, the Schedule and separate Confirmations will prevail against the Master Agreement. The statement that the parties intend that all Confirmations are to form a single agreement with the Master Agreement is moved to the beginning of the document.

OBLIGATIONS

16.90 The parties undertake to comply with a number of specific obligations including general conditions concerning payment or delivery under Confirmations. Provisions are also included with regard to change of account, netting, deduction or withholding tax and default interest.

REPRESENTATIONS

16.91   A number of basic representations are made by each party to the other concerning status, powers, no violation or conflict, consents and obligations binding. These are repeated in the Form of Amendment. Additional representations are also incorporated with regard to the absence of certain events and litigation, accuracy of specified information and payer and payee tax representations. Options are provided in this regard in the Schedule. One of the difficulties which has arisen in practice is that in the event of the documentation being considered by the courts all of the provisions contained in the master agreements and related documentation are not considered where the contract has been held void *ab initio*.

AGREEMENTS

16.92   A number of further agreements are entered into with regard to furnishing documentation and information, authorisations, legal compliance, tax agreements and stamp tax. The specific forms to be provided are to be listed in Part 3 of the Schedule.

EVENTS OF DEFAULT AND TERMINATION EVENTS

16.93   The Events of Default provided for include failure to pay or deliver, breach of agreement, credit support default, misrepresentation, default under particular Transactions, cross default, bankruptcy and merger without assumption. Parties may also terminate in the event of illegality or a tax or credit event upon a merger. The operation of these provisions is expanded in Part 1 of the Schedule. Additional Termination Events may be provided for in Part 1, para (h) of the Schedule. This has caused problems in practice where firms have tried to make the clauses as extensive as absolutely possible.

EARLY TERMINATION

16.94   The 1992 Master Agreement contains revised provisions with regard to termination following Events of Default or Termination Events. These allow for the transfer of rights and obligations between offices or affiliates if termination could be avoided. Termination of all contracts is also provided for in certain cases with only termination of relevant transactions in others. Provision is included for calculating loss and making payments.

16.95   The operation of the termination provisions has been considered in some recent cases. It was held in *Australia and New Zealand Banking Group Ltd v Société Général*[1] that the loss in the value of a supporting hedging contract could not be offset as part of the 'Loss' under a currency swap. The case involved three NDFs (non-deliverable forward foreign exchange contracts) that had been entered into subject to separate Confirmations governed by an earlier Master Agreement. The objective was to provide for the mutual exchange of an agreed amount of separate currency payments (Russian roubles against US dollars) on the due settlement date. Such contracts are commonly entered into to eliminate delivery risk, for hedging purposes or simply to provide for the use of a freely convertible currency at settlement. In the particular case, SocGen had separately hedged its rouble exposure under the Confirmations with its Russian subsidiary, Societe General Vostok. On termination (following the introduction of a banking moratorium in Russia), SocGen sought to offset the loss on the hedging contracts against the amount

(US$16,719,459) due to ANZ under the Confirmation. It was held at first instance and on appeal[2] that SocGen had to pay the full amount due. The loss was not caused by the termination of the hedging contract but by the underlying moratorium. While this appears to have been correct, some concerns have been expressed with regard to the manner in which the court interpreted some of the standard ISDA documentation clauses.[3]

1   [1999] 2 All ER (Comm) 625, [2000] CLC 161.
2   [2000] 1 All ER (Comm) 682, [2000] Lloyd's Rep Bank 153, CA.
3   For comment, see Schuyler Henderson, 'English Cases Dealing with Settlement Provisions of the ISDA Master Agreement' (2000) 6 JIBFL 190.

16.96   The right of one party to specify Events of Default and then designate an Early Termination Date following failure to make payment as provided for under an Interest Rate and Currency Exchange Agreement (IRCEA) was confirmed in *Nuova Safim SpA v Sakura Bank Ltd*.[1] In that case, Sakura had entered into the IRCEA with Safim, a subsidiary of the Italian state holding company EFIM. Following the issuance of a series of temporary decrees in 1992 which suspended payments by Safim, Sakura sent a number of notices treating this and Safim's separate default on its syndicated debt as Events of Default. Safim was asked to make payment of the unpaid amounts due by 30 November 1992. Failing payment, Sakura designated 15 December as the Early Termination Date (as provided for under the contract documentation). After the Italian decrees had come fully into effect (which included provision preventing counterparties from terminating outstanding contracts), Safim sought payment of US$8 million from Sakura under the IRCEA on the basis that early termination had arisen as a result of a Termination Event rather than an Event of Default. It was claimed that a Termination Event arose following the liquidator's notice of termination after the laws had come into effect and the provision in the IRCEA that an event that was both an Event of Default and an Illegality constituted a Termination Event. While the events that had occurred may have constituted an Illegality, it was held that Safim had not treated them as such on the facts and had failed to serve proper notice on Sakura to that effect as provided for in the documentation. The IRCEA had accordingly been terminated by reason of an Event of Default which meant that Sakura did not owe anything to Safim.

1   [1998] Lloyd's Rep Bank 142; affd [1999] 2 All ER (Comm) 526, CA.

16.97   The strict interpretation of the terms of a credit default swap was also confirmed in *Deutsche Bank AG v ANZ Banking Group Ltd*[1] although the court was less formal and prepared to substitute the apparently clear and express terms of a valuation provision in a master agreement in *Peregrine Fixed Income Ltd (in liquidation) v Robinson Department Store plc*.[2] In *Peregrine*, a standard Market Quotation provision had provided that the middle of any three quotations would be used on termination although this only resulted in a figure that represented approximately 10% of the original contract value of the income stream concerned (US$87 million). The valuation had been effected by the subsequent restructuring of the respondent with quotations varying between US$25.5 million to US$750,000 and with US$9.5 million as the medium. In finding for Peregrine, the court substituted Loss (as provided for in a separate contact provision) for Market Quotation as defined. Although this interpretation was supported by certain other provisions in the Master Agreement, it was apparently contrary to general market intent and practice.

Some have accordingly questioned the use (but also the possible susceptibility) of the ISDA Master Agreement for such more creative commercial purpose.[3] In practice, it is necessary to ensure that all agreed terms are fully understood and expressed in the contract documentation (which may include amending the standard documentation and master agreements used appropriately) and that any possible confusion or ambiguity is eliminated.

1 (28 May 1999, unreported).
2 [2000] Lloyd's Rep Bank 304, [2000] CLC 1328; and 2000 WL 1027115.
3 For comment, see Henderson, para 16.95, note 3 above.

TRANSFER

16.98 Subject to the terms of the 1992 Master Agreement, all transfers whether by way of security or otherwise are declared void if not made with the consent of the other party. Consent is not required in the event of a consolidation or amalgamation or a merger subject to the rights of the other party in the event of a tax or credit event arising.

ADDITIONAL PROVISIONS

16.99 The 1992 Master Agreement also contains a number of further provisions with regard to contractual currency, miscellaneous provisions, multi-branch parties, expenses, notices, governing law and jurisdiction and definitions. Payments are to be made in the Contractual Currency as defined with any shortfalls being covered in the event of judgment being obtained in another currency. The obligations of each party are stated to be the same if a Transaction is effected through an office other than the head or home office with any changes requiring the prior consent of the other. A defaulting party is required to indemnify the other in respect of any losses arising. The Agreement may be governed by either English law or that of the State of New York.[1] A large amount of certainty and control is in this way created through the use of such standardised documentation in the OTC market.

1 If an arbitration agreement has been entered into, injunctive relief will be available to restrain the other party from proceeding to litigation. See *Bankers Trust Co v PT Jakarta International Hotels and Development* [1999] 1 All ER (Comm) 785; [1999] 1 Lloyd's Rep 910.

Subsequent ISDA documentation

16.100 In June 2000, a new set of ISDA Definitions was produced which consolidated and updated the 1991 Definitions, the 1998 Supplement and parts of the 1998 ISDA Euro Definitions. While specifically designed for use in interest rate and currency derivative documentation, these have also been used more generally in practice. ISDA produced an EMU Protocol in May 1998 to amend its master documentation to deal with the introduction of the Euro. A subsequent EMU Protocol (Greece) was released for signature in October 2001.

16.101 ISDA issued a separate set of Credit Derivatives Definitions in 1999 for use with Confirmations to be governed by the 1992 ISDA Master Agreement. ISDA has also worked with various authorities subsequently on the regulatory approach to be adopted with regard to credit derivatives.[1]

1 See para 16.10. See also ISDA, *Year in Review* (March 2001).

16.102   A 2000 Supplement to the 1993 ISDA Commodity Derivatives Definitions has been issued and a revised version of Annex A to the 1998 FX and Currency Option Definitions published. Most recently, the Termination, Valuation and Close-Out Working Group has prepared eight annexes to a proposed protocol to the 1992 Master Agreement. Revisions have also been considered by a Force Majeure and Impossibility Working Group and a Master Agreement Structural Issues Working Group.[1]

1   For a full list of ISDA documentation, see ISDA Publications on www.isda.org/publications/pubguide.html.

LIABILITY RISKS IN OTC DERIVATIVES SALES

16.103   This section[1] considers the nature of the obligations assumed by the seller of a derivatives product (dealer), typically a bank or other financial institution, to the purchaser (end-user) of the product concerned. The focus is on OTC derivatives rather than exchange-traded instruments. The reason for treating OTC derivatives differently in this context from exchange-traded instruments is that, 'There are some areas where OTC derivatives practitioners face substantially different risks to those involved with exchange-traded products. This is primarily because almost all of the parameters of an OTC derivative may be individually tailored and negotiated and agreed between the counterparties to the transaction (as an example, in the case of options, the maturity, strike and size may be negotiated). In addition, because many OTC derivatives may be tailored to meet the specific needs of the counterparties to the transaction, certain OTC derivatives may be more complicated and less standardised than those traded on regulated exchanges.'[2]

1   The section is based on W Blair, 'Derivatives Sales: Private Law and the Impact of Regulatory Standards', Ch 10 of *European Securities Markets: The Investment Services Directive and Beyond*, G Ferrarini (ed) (1998).
2   See M Taylor, *Mastering Derivative Markets* (1996), p 272. This section was written by compliance officers of Credit Suisse Financial Products.

16.104   The issue addressed is the extent to which (if at all) the seller undertakes to the purchaser that the product will be suitable for the purchaser's needs.[1] The conclusion reached is that there is generally no such undertaking given or expected, but that, applying ordinary legal principles, the facts of a particular transaction can give rise to liability on the part of the seller. Given that disputes are only likely to arise when the performance of the derivatives product concerned has failed to meet the customer's expectations, the resolution of disputes will depend on the facts of the particular case. Key issues are likely to be the complexity of the product concerned, the degree of risk entailed and the sophistication of the customer (and consequently its ability to understand the risk). For an overview of the issues from a US perspective, reference may be made to the October 1997 report of the GAO (General Accounting Office) on OTC Derivatives Sales Practices (referred to below as the 'GAO Report of October 1997').[2]

1   This is distinct from the issue of capacity and related questions of restitution and recovery. See generally *Hazell v Hammersmith and Fulham London Borough Council*, 1 All ER 545, [1991] 2 WLR 372. See also *Westdeutsche Landesbank Girozentrale v Islington London Borough Council* [1994] 4 All ER 890, [1994] 1 WLR 938; and *Kleinwort Benson v Sandwell Borough Council* [1994] 4 All ER 890, [1994] 1 WLR 938. The general right to the recovery of money paid against mistake of fact or law (subject to defences available in restitution) was confirmed by the

House of Lords in *Kleinwort Benson Ltd v Lincoln City Council, Kleinwort Benson Ltd v Birmingham City Council, Kleinwort Benson Ltd v Kensington and Chelsea Royal London Borough Council, and Kleinwort Benson Ltd v Southwark London Borough Council* [1999] 2 AC 349, [1998] 3 WLR 1095 and [1998] 4 All ER 513.
2   GAO, OTC Derivatives: Additional Oversight Could Reduce Costly Sales Practice Disputes (October 2, 1997) GGD-98-5.

Impact of regulatory standards

16.105   In considering the extent to which the seller of a derivatives product undertakes to his buyer that the product concerned will be suitable or appropriate for the buyer's needs, one looks for guidance primarily to conduct of business rules relating to 'know your customer', disclosure and suitability. These types of rules are capable of affecting private law obligations in a number of ways.

First, they may give rise to private law remedies. In practice, under English law (at least in the present context) such remedies are severely circumscribed. Section 62 of the Financial Services Act 1986 created a right of action for breach of regulatory rules at the suit of a person who suffered loss as a result although the right of action was only available to a 'private investor'.[1] This has now been replaced by s 150 of the FSMA 2000 which confers on a private person a right of action for damages where they suffer loss as a result of the contravention of a rule.[2] This will in practice generally exclude end-users in the OTC derivatives market.[3] Secondly, even where they do not give rise to specific remedies, conduct of business rules may influence courts of law in the formulation of legal duties. An example of this process in action is found in the well-known decision in *Bankers Trust International plc v PT Dharmala Sakti Sejahtra*.[4] The court cited the London Code of Conduct rules as to 'know your customer' to show that the market view corresponded with the court's legal analysis of the effect of alleged misrepresentations.[5]

1   Defined in SI 1991/489. The definition excludes public authorities.
2   'Private customers' are defined in the FSA Handbook as persons not falling within the definition of a market counterparty or intermediate customer. See para 16.41.
3   MAR 3.1.5 also expressly excludes any right of action in damages arising as a result of breach of the rules set out on MAR 3 (Inter-Professional Conduct). See para 16.77.
4   A decision of the English Commercial Court given on 29 November 1995 concerning derivatives. See below.
5   See note 4 above, transcript pp 18 and 19. On the London Code of Conduct, see paras 16.70–16.72.

16.106   The scope for regulatory rules to influence legal obligations in this way will obviously depend upon the content of the rules and the specificity with which they are drafted. The May 1992 version of the London Code of Conduct was considered in *Dharmala*.[1] This referred specifically to derivatives and the scope for confusion or misunderstanding where the deal was complicated and one of the counterparties is inexperienced. These points were not included in the 'know your counterparty' section of the 1995 version of the Code which was at a high level of generality. The Code established that the nature of the relationship for products in institutional markets involved transactions between principals, with end-users assumed to be capable of independently evaluating the transaction. In addition, the Code stated that if the end-user wished to retain the other party as an adviser, it should do so in writing. It also stated that participants shared an interest in maintaining high standards of business conduct and fair dealing. Compliance was mandatory. The Code indicated that the Bank of England would view breaches of its provisions seriously, investigate complaints and employ a range of sanctions against violators. These provisions are now substantially replicated in the FSA rules for Inter-Professional Conduct (IPC) set out in MAR 3 of the Handbook including, in particular, the new guidance on suitability and advice in MAR 3.4.3 and 3.4.4.[2]

1   See paras 16.70–16.72.
2   See paras 16.74–16.80.

16.107   The former SFA rules provided that a firm must not recommend a transaction to a 'private customer'[1] unless it has taken reasonable steps to enable him to understand the nature of the risks involved (Rule 5.30).[2] The requirement to send a Derivatives Risk Warning Notice also applied to private customers, so that these provisions were of limited effect in the OTC derivatives market. As regards suitability, SFA Rule 5.31 provided that a firm must take reasonable steps to ensure that it did not make any personal recommendation to a private customer of an investment or investment arrangement or effect or arrange a discretionary transaction with or for any customer unless the recommendation or transaction was suitable for him having regard to the facts disclosed by the customer and other relevant facts about the customer of which the firm was, or reasonably should have been, aware.

1   Defined to mean an individual or a small business investor (itself defined) who is not acting in the course of carrying on an investment business. See Blair et al (2nd edn), paras 14.20–14.21.3. See para 16.106, note 4, transcript pp 18 and 19.
2   See Blair et al (2nd edn), paras 14.14–14.41.

16.108   The SFA's guidance notes on this rule stated that in assessing the suitability of an OTC derivative transaction for a customer, the firm must have regard to the customer's understanding of the risks involved. Amongst other considerations, the suitability of an OTC transaction for a private customer would depend on the customer's financial standing. Firms should consider whether the net cost to the customer of the transaction, or the strategy of which it may form part, could materially impair the customer's financial standing. Other rules provided that certain derivatives transactions with private customers must be on exchange.[1] Again, the restriction of the rules to private customers meant that they were of limited application in the OTC market.

1   The SIB Core Conduct for Business Rules, Rule 27. See Blair et al (2nd edn), paras 14.23–14.26. On the revised provisions set out in the FSA Handbook, see paras 16.32–16.57.

16.109   The new Conduct of Business (COB) provisions set out in the FSA Handbook apply to private customers which are any clients other than a market counterparty or intermediate customer.[1] The revised rules and guidance set out in COB replace the former requirements in the SIB, SFA and other rulebooks. The COB includes a number of general rules applicable to all firms conducting designated investment business (COB 2). These generally relate to communications (which must be clear, fair and not misleading), inducements and commission, reliance, Chinese walls and exclusion of liabilities. The COB also contains revised provisions with regard to financial promotion (COB 3), accepting customers (COB 4), advising and selling (COB 5), product disclosure and customer's right to cancel or withdraw (COB 6), dealing and managing (COB 7), reporting to customers (COB 8) and client assets.[2] The restated know your customer, suitability and understanding of risk rules are set out in COB 4, 5 and 6.[3] The firm must, in particular, take reasonable steps to ensure that it is in possession of sufficient personal and financial information about the customer relevant to the services to be provided (COB 5.2.5 R). The firm must also take steps to ensure that it does not make any personal recommendation to a private customer to buy or sell a designated investment or effect a discretionary transaction for a private customer unless the recommendation or transaction is suitable for the customer having regard to the facts disclosed and other relevant facts the firm is or reasonably should be aware (COB 5.3.5 R). The nature and content of the general suitability obligation is then expanded in a number of further more specific provisions (COB 5.3.6–5.3.29). The new requirements with regard to risk warnings are set out in COB 5.4 which, in particular, includes a revised *Warrants and derivatives risk warning notice* (COB 5.4.6 E and COB 5 Annex 1).

1   See para 16.41.
2   See paras 16.32–16.57.
3   See paras 16.47, 16.48 and 16.49.

16.110   Article 11 of the Investment Services Directive (ISD)[1] requires Member States to draw up rules of conduct to implement the principles set out in the article. Significantly, the rules 'must be applied in such a way as to take account of the professional nature of the person for whom the service is provided'. This allows for a continuing distinction between private investors and business end-users. The principles themselves are formulated at an unspecific level. Investment firms are required to act 'honestly and fairly'. They must act with 'due skill, care and diligence, in the best interests of their clients'. They must seek from their clients information regarding their financial situation, investment experience and objectives as regards the services requested. This general approach is reflected in the proposed revisions currently being considered to the ISD although it is unclear what final terms may be agreed.[2]

1   Council Directive 93/22/EEC on investment services in the securities field of 10 May 1993 (OJ L 141, 11.6.1993, p 27); and Council Directive 93/6/EEC on the capital adequacy of investment firms and credit institutions of 15 March 1993 (OJ L 141, 11.6.1993, p 1).
2   See Communication from the Commission to the European Parliament and the Council, *Upgrading the Investment Services Directive (93/22/EC)* COM (2000) 729 final. See also IP/01/1055, IP/01/1266 and IP/02/464.

16.111   The result is that so far as the OTC derivatives market is concerned in which private investors do not typically participate, under UK law the impact of conduct of business rules on underlying legal obligations will be small. There will generally be no suitability requirement and as a general rule core principals will assume that their counterparties have the capability to make independent decisions and to act accordingly. The firm is not obliged to ensure that the market counterparty understands the risks involved nor is it under any duty to provide best execution or other dealing protections (IPC 3.4.3 G). However, the position is different in the case of a private investor. The *Dharmala*[1] case should be compared with *Morgan Stanley UK Group v Puglisi*[2] in which a private investor was sold risky and unsuitable derivatives contracts in breach of the (then) applicable rules. These were held to be unenforceable against him, though it is respectfully suggested that the result was surprising in the light of the risk warnings which were given and the investor's relevant experience and wealth.

1   Para 16.105.
2   [1998] CLC 481.

16.112   Two US initiatives may also be noted. These came in response to earlier political concerns over derivatives. In March 1995, the Derivatives Policy Group (with the co-operation of the SEC and the CFTC) released a 'Framework for Voluntary Oversight' which concerned with the relationship between professional intermediaries and non-professional end-users entering into OTC derivatives transactions. In another initiative, representatives from various financial trade groups (including ISDA) joined together under the co-ordination of the Federal Reserve Bank of New York to prepare 'Principles and Practices for Wholesale Financial Market Transactions'. The Principles were released in August 1995 and have particular authority because of the participation of the New York Fed. The Principles covered all wholesale financial market instruments, not solely derivatives transactions. It has been said authoritatively that:

> 'The Framework and Principles generally are sets of "best practices" that OTC derivatives market participants voluntarily may choose to follow and state upfront that they are not intended to create legally enforceable obligations. The Framework and Principles articulate the basic assumption in the OTC derivatives markets – participants transact on an arm's-length basis. As such, each participant is itself responsible for understanding the proposed derivative transaction and its attend-ant risks and obtaining the additional information or independent professional assistance required to do so. The Framework and Principles also emphasise, however, that participants should act honestly and in good faith in all dealings and should always seek to clarify the precise nature of their relationship with their counterparties in writing. The Framework and Principles further recommend actions that participants may take, for their own protection, when confronted with unsophisticated counterparties and other special situations.'[1]

The authors of the passage cited go on to say that:

> 'the "best practices", while not intended to create legally enforceable obligations, may be used by courts as standards to evaluate the nature of relationships between OTC derivatives counterparties and define their respective responsibilities under the common law'.

1   See Ernest T Patrikis and Diane L Virzera, 'Over-the-Counter Derivatives Sales Practices: Disclosure, Suitability, Appropriateness and "Best Practices" ', *Practising Law Institute*, 12 December 1995.

16.113   The Principles effectively exclude any suitability obligation and stipulate that an advisory role will only exist if it has been agreed in writing between the parties prior to entering into the transaction. It is stated explicitly that the Principles reflect principles and practices in the US and may not reflect those in other countries. In fact, the document has been influential internation-ally. Standard ISDA and other Master Agreement documentation is being, or has been, amended to reflect the principle that parties act at arm's-length and that one party is not relying on the other for advice in respect of the transaction.[1]

1   See paras 16.83–16.102.

16.114   The Framework imposes more obligations on dealers than does the Principles. This partially reflects the different orientation of the regulators involved. The first concern of the SEC in the Framework would be to protect investors, whereas the first concern of the New York Fed in the Principles would be to protect the safety and soundness of banks by limiting their liability.[1] Underlying the different emphasis between regulators is a more general point: plainly it is in the interest of banks to minimise the extent of any suitability obligation, whereas from the perspective of end-users, the interest may be the other way round. On the whole, banks have been more co-ordinated in their influence and so far their perspective has tended to prevail.

1   Hal S Scott, 'Liability of Derivatives Dealers', a chapter in *The Future for the Global Securities Market*, F Oditah (ed) (1996) p 280.

16.115   The 'arm's-length' principle should not obscure the fact that it is not in a bank's commercial interest to sell an unsuitable product to a customer. Banks are right to seek to protect themselves from legal liability by risk warnings and by expressly disclaiming an advisory role in respect of transactions. However, good business requires satisfied customers. Commercially, banks are likely to take a more sanguine view of their role than the limited regulatory requirements might suggest. This may, for example, be reflected in internal procedures encouraging staff to give clear explanations and requiring them to decline to enter into a transaction which they know is inappropriate for the proposed counterparty.

The nature of the obligation between bank and end-user

16.116   In a dispute concerning the suitability of an OTC derivatives transaction between a bank and an end-user, the parties will take different positions.[1] The end-user may claim that it entered into the transaction in reliance on advice from the bank. The bank may maintain that its role was wholly non-advisory and that the suitability and appropriateness of the transaction was solely a matter for the end-user. The court will have to determine the scope of the obligations each party assumed towards the other. In law:

> 'there is nothing about dealings in derivatives between a bank and its customer which marks it as an activity different in kind from other financial dealings. The developed rules of contract and tort law and the law relating to fiduciary duties [apply]'.[2]

1   See generally W Blair, 'Liability Risks in Derivatives Sales' [1996] 1 JIBL 18.
2   Financial Law Panel Transactions in Derivatives: Legal Obligations of Banks to Customers, A Discussion Paper (London, May 1995).

Contract

16.117   When determining the legal obligations between parties in any contractual relationship the starting-point is the contract itself. In the present context, the contract is likely to be contained in Master Agreements, confirmations or letters between the parties. ISDA has proposed standardised language that describes the nature of the relationship between counterparties to OTC derivative contracts. ISDA suggests that this language be added to the ISDA Master Agreement. If included as part of such contracts, each party would be representing that it was not relying on the other party and was making its own decisions about the transaction, it was capable on its own (or with independent professional advice) of understanding the terms of the transaction and its risks and it was not acting as a fiduciary or an adviser in the transaction.

16.118   According to the GAO Report of October 1997 (Chapter 4: 3.4), an official from a large US corporation indicated to the GAO that his firm refused to sign contracts with this provision. He said that, although his firm did not expect dealers to act as fiduciaries, it wanted to be able to rely on statements of fact made by the dealers about product performance under different market conditions.

16.119   If the contract is silent as to any advisory role on the part of the bank, in normal circumstances it is clear that the court will not imply such a role. In the *Dharmala* case, the court emphasised on a number of occasions that the relationship between a bank selling derivatives and its customer is not the conventional banker–customer relationship. It was said that the court should not be too ready to read duties of an advisory nature into this type of relationship. Sophisticated investors must make their own judgments. An important aspect of *Dharmala* was that the court accepted that the Bankers Trust personnel believed, as a result of previous contacts and what was generally known about the customer, that they were dealing with people who would be able and could be expected to undertake a close evaluation of the merits and risks of any proposal and to ask questions or seek further information if they felt they did not understand its workings or implications.

16.120   Of course, information which is given must be accurate and not misleading. In *Dharmala*, the court made it clear that on the facts of that case there was a duty on the derivatives seller presenting a proposed transaction to the potential buyer to present the downside and upside in a balanced fashion.[1] The difficult case is likely to be the one in which an inherently risky product is sold to an unsophisticated customer who is unaware of the implications of the transaction. Where such a customer is in fact relying on the bank for advice, it is an open question whether courts would observe non-reliance clauses in the documentation.[2]

1   Transcript p 86. See below as to disclosure duties.
2   See Patrikis and Virzera, 'Over-the-Counter Derivatives Sales Practices: Disclosure Suitability, Appropriateness and "Best Practices" ', *Practising Law Institute*, 12 December 1995.

Misrepresentation

16.121   A factual misrepresentation (as opposed to a statement of opinion which turns out to be wrong) is actionable if relied upon by a counterparty to its detriment. However tight the documentation it is difficult to avoid responsibility for a factual misrepresentation if it was reasonable for the other party to rely on it. Disclaimers may have to satisfy 'reasonableness' tests in unfair contract terms legislation (such as the English Act of 1977). Whether a particular statement is in law an actionable misrepresentation may depend on the sophistication of the party to whom it is made. This point was well brought out in *Dharmala*:

> 'The meaning and effect of words never falls to be viewed in a vacuum. It is shaped by the context of their communication, including the parties' respective positions, knowledge and experience. A description or commendation which may obviously be irrelevant or may even serve as a warning to one recipient, because of its

generality, superficiality or laudatory nature, or because of the recipient's own knowledge and experience, may constitute a material representation if made to another less informed or sophisticated receiver. Even in the case of a written description, there may be cases where a proposal or presentation misrepresents the nature or working of a transaction to a particular reader, although another sophisticated, more analytical or legally qualified reader would have been expected to appreciate the real nature or working of the transaction. What is fair and adequate presentation in one context between one set of negotiating parties may be unfair or inadequate in another context. Whether there was any and if so what particular representation must thus depend upon an objective assessment of the likely effect of the proposal or presentation on the recipient. In making such an assessment, it is necessary to consider the recipient's characteristics and know-ledge as they appeared, or ought to have appeared, to the maker of the proposal or presentation. A recipient holding himself out as able to understand and evaluate complicated proposals would be expected to be able to do so, whatever his actual abilities. These are problems on which it is commonly not necessary to focus in a commercial context. The assumption on which most business is conducted is that both parties understand, or avail themselves of advice about, the area in which they are operating and the documentation which they use. Business could not otherwise be carried on.'[1]

The court went on to say that the facts of that case might be different, because of the novelty and complexity of the products in question, and because of Bankers Trust's role in devising them and marketing them and the customer's lesser involvement with them. In the event, the customer's claim against Bankers Trust based on misrepresentation failed largely on the facts.

1   *Dharmala* transcript p 18.

Fiduciary duty

16.122   Fiduciary relationships are the antithesis of arm's-length relation-ships. They plainly will be rare in the commercial context.[1] The English courts have recently reaffirmed (in the agency context) that the scope of fiduciary duties can be defined by the terms of the contract and that fiduciary relationships should not be superimposed upon the contract in such a way as to alter the operation which the contract was intended to have.[2] The GAO Report of October 1997 summarises US law as follows:

'Determining whether a formal fiduciary relationship exists can be difficult. In some instances, fiduciary duties are clearly placed on a financial institution by law when the institution agrees to act as an agent in performing certain services. Such fiduciary duties arise, for example, when a bank's trust department manages the assets of an estate or when an investment advisor manages the assets of an estate or when an investment advisor manages the investments of a pension fund. In other instances, courts have found fiduciary duties applied to a financial institution that had not formally agreed to provide fiduciary services, but whose past relationship with a customer showed a pattern of reliance by the customer on the institution's advice. The factors that courts have considered to establish such a pattern of reliance include the extent to which a customer followed the institution's recommendations, statements by the customer indicating reliance or dependence on the institution, and the customer's general level of sophistication. Generally, courts have ruled that the larger and more sophisticated the customer, the greater its responsibility to independently assess the value and risks of a transaction and the lesser the dealer's responsibility to determine the suitability of a security and to fully disclose product risks and valuations. No specific standards distinguish between sophisticated and unsophisticated customers or degrees of sophistication (Chapter 4.1).'

1   Though not unknown: see *Ata v American Express Bank Ltd* (7 October 1996, unreported) in which it was held that a discretionary management agreement created a fiduciary relationship.
2   *Kelly v Cooper* [1993] AC 205, PC.

English and US case law

16.123   The English *Dharmala* decision (in which Bankers Trust obtained judgment in full against the customer) has already been noted. The facts of that case bear some similarity with the those of the famous P&G lawsuit in the US. In *Procter & Gamble Co v Bankers Trust Co*[1] the US federal district court for the Southern District of Ohio issued an opinion dismissing certain of the counts in P&G's complaint, by rendering summary judgment on several of the other counts. The court applied New York law in accordance with the choice of law clause in the applicable ISDA Master Agreement. The remaining counts would have gone forward to trial by jury but for the fact that a settlement was reached at the highest level of the two corporations shortly afterwards. The facts of the two cases were complex, but had a number of essential elements. *Dharmala* involved the sale of two interest rate swaps (fixed by reference to US$ LIBOR) by Bankers Trust's Singapore branch to an Indonesian buyer. *Procter & Gamble* involved the sale of two customised interest rate swaps by Bankers Trust to P&G (fixed, in the case of the first swap, by reference to 5-year US Treasury Notes and to 30-year Treasury Bonds and in the second swap by reference to the 4-year German DM rate). The swaps contained an element of leverage. In both cases, the end-users incurred heavy losses.

1   1996 US Dist Lexis 6435, 8 May 1996. For an excellent account of US litigation generally see S Henderson 'Derivatives Litigation in the United States', Ch 9 from *Swaps and Off-Exchange Derivatives Trading: Law and Regulation* (1996).

16.124   Although its ruling was by way of a preliminary opinion, there are a number of significant points in the *Procter & Gamble* decision. The district court rejected P&G's attempt to invoke several of the liability provisions of the federal and state securities laws and the federal commodities laws. With respect to the securities claims, the court found that these particular swaps were not 'securities' within the scope of the federal and state securities laws. The claims for misrepresentation and breach of fiduciary duty also failed. A significant part of the *Procter & Gamble* opinion relates to disclosure duties and duties of good faith. The district court concluded that Bankers Trust:

> 'had a duty to disclose material information to the plaintiff both before the parties entered into the swap transactions and in their performance and also a duty to deal fairly and in good faith during the performance of swap transactions'.

It is believed that (had the case gone forward to trial) the question of Bankers Trust's fulfilment of those duties would have been one of the primary points of contention.[1]

1   For a comparison of *Dharmala* and *Procter & Gamble* see W Blair and C Olive, 'Derivatives Sales Liability: Approach of the English and US Courts' [1996] 7 JIBL 263; see also DM Forster 'Derivatives: Procter & Gamble v Bankers Trust – An Analysis of the Holdings and their Potential Impact', BJIBFL, July–August 1996, 320.

16.125   By contrast, English law does not recognise generalised 'good faith' duties in the performance of contracts. Also, duties of disclosure are rarely applied by the courts outside specialised areas such as insurance contracts.

From that point of view, English law appears more favourable to banks than New York law. However, it does not follow that disclosure duties will *never* exist. For example, old English case law decided prior to the development of statutory requirements in respect of the sale of securities stresses the importance of full disclosure in a share prospectus.[1] It is obvious that in the context of OTC derivatives, proper disclosure should also be encouraged. So far as US law is concerned, the GAO Report of October 1997 states that:

'Even when no special relationship exists between a financial institution and an end-user, the institution may have an obligation to disclose to the end-user information regarding a transaction about which it has superior knowledge. Under principles defining common law fraud, superior knowledge or access to the means of knowledge can give rise to an affirmative duty to disclose material information, particularly when the information is not within reasonable reach of the other party. Applying this principle to the securities markets, federal courts have held that securities firms have a special duty not to take advantage of customers' lack of knowledge and, therefore, firms must disclose certain material information – such as the amount of the markup they are charging – even when executing a transaction on a principal-to-principal basis (Chapter 4.1).'

1 *New Brunswick Co v Muggeridge* (1860) 1 Drew & Sm 363; *Central Rly Co of Venezuela v Kisch* (1867) LR 2 HL 99.

Chapter 17

Global custody

INTRODUCTION

17.1   The provision of separate custodial and related services in relation to securities and other investments has become an increasingly important form of financial business since the 1970s at both the national and international levels.

These services involve the assumption of responsibility in connection with the safe-keeping and administration of a portfolio of assets (including securities and cash) by a financial intermediary on behalf of the beneficial owner. In practice, this core function of safe-keeping is usually extended to include settlement services in respect of the purchase and sale of securities.

Various other ancillary or supplementary services are also increasingly provided. These may include such closely related or associated services as dividend and income collection and corporate action or reporting as well as other value-added services such as cash management or foreign exchange.

17.2   While banks have traditionally provided some form of basic custodian and related administration services for clients, modern custody has emerged as a distinct service sector largely following regulatory intervention in the pension and mutual fund sector in the US. This provided for the statutory separation of the fund-management and custodial activities of US pension funds and required that only US service providers act as primary custodians.[1] A number of institutions accordingly began to develop the necessary systems and services for use in the US and abroad, out of which a new international service sector was created.

The term 'global custody' appears to have been first used by Chase Manhattan in late 1974. The subsequent history of the global custody industry has been characterised by major banks and other financial entities elsewhere attempting to follow the lead set by the US institutions to become global service operators at the same time as a large number of increasingly specialist niche service providers have emerged especially in the provision of local securities settlement and sub-custody facilities.

1 See J Essinger, *Global Custody* (1991) Ch 1; and S Thomas and M Beacham, *Global Custody* (1990) Ch 2.

17.3 Although the nature of the custody relationship involved appears to be simple in itself, complex legal issues arise. The main risk involved is generally referred to as custody risk, which is the potential loss of the underlying security or other asset as a result of the separation of its possession and beneficial ownership.

This is complicated by the large number of intervening interests that can be created in the security. These arise from the separate relationships created between the beneficiary and the principal custodian, its custodian and local sub-custodians, any other intermediaries to whom the securities may have been lent or otherwise provided as collateral as well as the various central depositories or settlement systems managers that may be involved. These separate levels or 'tiers' of custodians and sub-custodians and other intermediate parties may also increasingly hold the securities under various electronic systems that provide for their immobilisation or dematerialisation. This makes the application of traditional legal concepts and authorities difficult.

Many of the legal implications of these increasingly complex forms of computer-controlled holding, storage and clearing and settlement facilities have still not been fully resolved.

ORIGINS AND MARKET DEVELOPMENT

17.4 Banks have traditionally provided various basic custody services for their clients. The origins of banking itself can be attributed to the acceptance of specie or other valuables by jewellers, pawn-brokers or scriveners. The receipts that were issued in return for the deposited assets constituted the earliest form of promissory note and then bank note. The valuables accepted for deposit may also have included debt instruments such as other promissory notes or bills of exchange and all other forms of transferable security or stock.

By the early nineteenth century many institutions also provided various administrative support services for their overseas investors. This was common, for example, with regard to foreign railroad construction and other development.[1] In such cases, the overseas branches of English and Scottish banks would ensure that funds were properly invested and provide safe custody facilities for the storage of relevant share certificates and other documents.

1 The London Clearing Banks Evidence by the Committee of London Clearing Bankers Committee Review Functioning of Financial Institutions (The Wilson Committee), November 1997, paras 13.9–13.17.

17.5 By the early 1970s, it was common for banks to arrange for the purchase and sale of securities on behalf of customers. Banks may also arrange for customers to invest in national savings instruments, building societies and any other types of investment. Once acquired, interest and dividend payments would be credited directly to the customer's account or the bank would hold documents of title from which a schedule of investments and valuations could readily be produced as required.

Banks could also authorise deposits under exchange control regulations for the custody of foreign securities and were able to collect interest and deal with drawings and the redemption of bearer bonds.

17.6   In the UK, the demand for custody and, in particular, cross-border custody services had grown substantially by the early 1980s especially following the abolition of exchange controls in 1979. The distinction developed between the simple processing services provided by the clearing banks and the more complete valuation, performance analysis and reporting facilities provided by the new integrated global custodians especially from the US. A separate dedicated and specialist set of service providers accordingly emerged which has been followed by further consolidation and centralisation of activity within the new industry.

17.7   In the US, global custody became a profitable and separately identifiable service sector following the enactment of the Employee Retirement Income Securities Act (ERISA) in 1974. ERISA provided that US pension funds could no longer act as custodians in respect of their own assets. The immediate effect of this was to create a large demand for national custodian services by US banks although this was quickly extended to include the provision of overseas services to deal with foreign holdings and overseas client interests. It was significant that ERISA also provided that the custodian functions to be provided for pension funds could only be carried out by US banks.

In the mutual fund sector, the commercial need for funds to diversify their investment strategies by investing overseas lead to an increasing number of applications being made to the Securities and Exchange Commission (SEC) for exemption from the strict requirement that all assets be held with US service providers. The administrative burden placed on the SEC resulted in a general exemption being issued which permitted mutual fund trustees to consider using certain non-US institutions as sub-custodians that met certain minimum criteria and that were established in jurisdictions where the trustees were satisfied with regard to certain legal issues.

Although ERISA meant that only US service providers could act as the primary custodian for investments within the US and related overseas stock, the regime for sub-custodians was effectively harmonised with that for mutual funds.

17.8   Once established, the growth of global custody was affected by a number of other factors. These included various legislative or self-regulatory developments within countries which have included requiring institutional investors to hold funds through domestic or global custodians or which have prevented share certificates or other documents of debt being held outside the country, necessitating the use of a local custodian or sub-custodian.

The continuing global expansion of the portfolios held by institutional investors have also created an enormous demand for all types of custodial service. This has occurred during a period of global deregulation in many financial markets as a new single 24-hour global market in financial services has emerged.

SERVICE PROVIDERS AND SERVICES USERS

17.9   The main providers of custody services include the large global banking groups, security houses or investment banks and large pension and insurance companies as well as more specialist service providers, including dedicated trust companies and integrated investment management groups. There are also a number of depositories such as Euroclear and Clearstream which provide extensive clearing and settlement services.[1]

Large institutional funds such as pension funds, insurance companies and unit trusts are the most important users of custody services although a number of these institutions do manage their custody services directly through their own global networks of sub-custodians.

1   See para 17.18.

CUSTODY SERVICES

17.10   The types of services provided by custodians vary considerably across the market. These generally include the core services of custody or safe-keeping as well as settlement which comprises the receipt and delivery of security or cash to settle client trades.

Associated services have then traditionally included portfolio administration with dividend and income collection, corporate actions and tax reclamation.

In addition to these core and associated services, other more ancillary or value-added services may be provided depending upon the custodian.[1]

1   See Essinger, *Global Custody*, pp 5–7 and Ch 4; Thomas and Beacham, *Global Custody*, pp 48–79; and J Benjamin, *The Law of Global Custody* (1996), pp 1–2. See also J Benjamin, 'Global Custody: An Interview', BJIBFL December 1996, 510.

Core services

17.11   The core services provided generally comprise the safe-keeping or safeguarding of assets and clearance and settlement.

Safe-keeping

17.12   Custody has traditionally involved the physical custody of share certificates. Paper may still be important in particular situations. The modern practice, however, is for shares to be issued in a fungible paperless form, held through intermediaries and traded electronically by way of account entries. The custodian then 'holds' the stock or other instrument for its customer through the intermediaries or a central clearing system.

Settlement

17.13   Settlement is concerned with the completion of the relevant formalities to give effect to a transfer of securities. This will depend upon the operation of the particular market or separate clearance or settlement system concerned which may either operate on a paper or electronic basis. Settlement is distinct from clearing insofar as clearing is concerned with the determining of mutual positions prior to settlement.

17.14 In the UK, the most important paperless clearing and settlement systems were the Central Gilts Office (CGO), the Central Moneymarkets Office (CMO) and CREST. The CGO and CMO were operated through the Bank of England while CREST is managed by CRESTCo, which is a recognised clearing house for the purposes of the Financial Services and Markets Act (FSMA) 2000.

17.15 The CGO provided a computerised book entry transfer system for the settlement of transactions in gilt-edged and certain other securities. The CGO was developed jointly by the Bank of England and the London Stock Exchange and was set up in two phases during 1986.[1] All CGO members had CGO accounts which recorded available balances. Transfers were effected through dedicated terminals with payment being secured through an assured payments system.

The CGO was then updated using CREST software (the CGO II). Gilts settlement was transferred from the Bank of England to CREST on 24 May 1999. The migration of all British Government Stock was completed on 3 July 2000, after which the CGO ceased to continued to operate as a separate service.[2]

1 See, for example, Bank of England, *Central Gilts Office – Summary of the CGO Service*, Winter 1994 (revised); and the CGO Reference Manual.
2 See CREST, 'CREST absorbs Gilt Settlement,' Press Release, 3 July 2000. See also, J Benjamin, *Interests in Securities – A Proprietary Law Analysis of the International Securities Markets* (2000), paras 9.47 and 9.71–9.77.

17.16 The CMO was established on 1 October 1990 following the Bank of England's announcement in November 1988 that it would develop and operate a computerised settlement service in Sterling moneymarket bearer securities. This followed earlier attempts by the market to develop an appropriate system which had failed.

The CMO provides a central depository for physical moneymarket instruments and an electronic book entry transfer system for both physical and dematerialised instruments. The CMO applies to Treasury Bills, Local Authority Bills, Eligible Bank Bills, Ineligible Bank Bills, Trade Bills, Bank and Building Society Certificates of Deposit and Commercial Paper.[1]

The CMO was largely based on and was operated in parallel with the CGO. Following the integration of gilt settlement from the CGO within CREST,[2] the settlement of money market instruments was also to be consolidated into CEST during 2001.

1 See the CMO Reference Manual, Section A.3.
2 See para 17.15. See, Benjamin, *Interests in Securities*, paras 9.47 and 9.71–9.80.

17.17 CREST was set up following the establishment of a Task Force on Securities Settlement by the Bank of England in June 1993 to develop a new system for the electronic settlement of registered securities in London.[1] CREST operates on an optional basis in terms of which issuers can elect whether to make their securities CREST eligible while investors can either hold securities in a certificated or an uncertificated form within CREST.

The membership of CREST is now over 40,000 with 73.4 million transactions having been settled during 2001 (including a daily record volume of 480,000 contracts). The total amount of securities held within CREST is in excess of US$2.8 trillion. CREST is owned by 97 shareholders including a number of large international banks, securities firms, brokers, stock exchanges and registrars.

T+3 settlement was introduced on 5 February 2001 for London and Irish stock markets. A central counterparty service (CCP) was launched on 26 February in co-operation with the London Stock Exchange and London Clearing House (LCH).

Delivery versus Payment (DVP) and an Electronic Transfer of Title (ETT) service were also introduced on 26 November 2001.[2] ETT allows provides buyers with immediate and irrevocable legal title to dematerialised securities at point of transfer within CREST. The dematerialisation of CREST securities is facilitated under the Uncertificated Securities Regulations 1995.[3]

1 See, for example, Brian Smith, 'CREST: its Recognition and Approval', *Financial Stability Review*, Autumn 1996, 51. See also, M Evans, 'CREST: Payment, Security and other Related Issues for Banks', BJIBFL, June/July–August, 314. See, Benjamin, *Interests in Securities*, paras 9.46–9.100. See also CREST, 'History of CREST' available on www.crestco.co.uk/company/CRESTtim.htm.
2 See CREST, 'CREST settlement volumes soar in 2001', Press Release, 9 January 2002.
3 SI 1995/3272. See CREST, Reference Manual (November 2001).

17.18   At the international level, the two most important organisations involved with clearance and settlement are Euroclear and Clearstream. These act as international depositories and provide automated systems for the custody, clearance and settlement of bonds and other securities. Both were established to facilitate transfers in Eurobond markets following the difficulties experienced in attempting to deal with such instruments through traditional systems based on physical transfers and delivery.

Euroclear was originally set up in Brussels in 1968 and Cedel in Luxembourg in 1969. Euroclear was formerly operated by Morgan Guaranty Brussels although a separate Euroclear Bank (registered and licensed in Brussels) was set up in 2000 which was to assume responsibility for the system from 2001.[1]

Clearstream International was created in 1999 following the merger of Cedel and Deutsche Borse Clearing. Cedel International still owns 50% of Clearstream.[2] Although the two clearing systems are in direct competition for clearing, settlement and custody services, they maintain operating links including an automated electronic bridge which has been in operation since 1980.

1 See www.euroclear.com. The French securities depositary Sicovam merged with Euroclear in January 2001 (and was renamed Euroclear France). The pan-European stock exchange network EURONEXT was also to link Euroclear with the London Stock Exchange to develop trade settlement with Euroclear (settlement to be effected through the LCH).
2 See www.cedelinternational.com and www.cedel-bank.com.

17.19   In terms of global custody, the difficulty that arises in practice is that the sale or purchase of securities will often have to be effected in another country. From the custodians' perspective, while local settlement or settlement through an international depository can be carried out by the custodian directly, settlement of transactions in other countries may have to be carried out through a local sub-custodian.

Further problems will then arise in local custodian selection. For this reason, users of custodian services will generally consider the size of a particular custodian's proprietary and sub-custodian networks with reference to the number and location of the other countries in which they may wish transactions to be settled. Additional liability issues also arise which the parties will attempt to deal with through appropriate contractual provision.

17.20   In connection with the effectiveness and stability of clearing and settlement systems and the larger systemic risks which their failure or collapse could cause, a number of studies have been carried out. This became of a particular importance following the Stock Market Crash in 1987 when an enormous amount of pressure was placed on older national settlement systems. One of the most influential early papers in this regard was that produced by the G 30 on *Clearance and Settlement Systems in the World's Security Markets* in 1989. This examines different types of clearance and settlement systems and makes a number of recommendations in terms of their structure and operation. These recommendations have since been implemented through the revision of various national arrangements in many countries including the UK.

A significant amount of further work has also been carried out with regard to systems security and contingency planning since the tragic events of September 11, 2001. Despite the immediate closure of the financial markets in New York, almost all markets were able to re-open the following week with many businesses being able to transfer their operations to alternative or borrowed facilities elsewhere. Despite the resilience of the financial markets in the weeks following the attacks, a significant amount of further work has since been undertaken to insulate securities and money markets and their supporting clearing and settlement systems from external disruption. Firms have also tried to ensure that their contingency planning and back-up and safety systems are capable of dealing with such interference.

17.21   A number of more technical surveys and studies have also been produced in this area, especially by the Basel Committee on Payment and Settlement Systems (CPSS).[1]

In addition to resolving the more specific systems difficulties that arise in ensuring that these arrangements continue to operate in an effective manner, a number of legal issues must also be considered. These include choice and conflicts of law problems, the complications created by the involvement of a large number of intermediaries, the legal status of securities issues, finality of delivery and payment and cross-border bankruptcy complications.[2]

The CPSS has also been able to issue its own Core Principles for settlement systems on the model of the Basel Committee's Core Principles for Effective Banking Supervision and equivalent measures issued by the International Organisation of Securities Commissions (IOSCO) and the International Association of Insurance Supervisors (IAIS).[3]

1   See, for example, the CPSS, *Delivery Versus Payment in Securities Settlement Systems*, September 1992; the CPSS, *Cross-Border Securities Settlement*, March 1995. For more recent papers, see www.bis.org.
2   For discussion see, for example, M Fisher and H Yamaoka 'Legal Issues in Securities Settlements' App 3 to CPSS, *Cross-Border Securities Settlement*.
3   See Chapter 21, paras 21.59–21.64.

Associated services

17.22   Active custody management requires that a certain amount of action is carried out in connection with the securities held in safe-keeping. The most commonly provided associated functions include income and dividend collection, corporate actions, reporting and valuations and tax reclamation.

Income and dividend collection

17.23   The custodian will generally be responsible for the collection of all income and dividend payments and any other cash receipts. This will require proper identification, collection and allocation of all relevant payments. If sub-custodians are involved, the dividend payment made to the sub-custodian will have to be reconciled and allocated to the separate individual client accounts involved.

Corporate action

17.24   Clients will not wish to be concerned with the day-to-day administration of holdings in particular companies although they may be required to act in connection with various matters such as new issues, rights or bonus issues, reconstructions, takeovers or mergers and liquidation or other winding-up proceedings. In such cases, appropriate information reporting systems will have to be in place to ensure that clients are properly advised of their rights and their instructions carried out.

Reporting and valuations

17.25   In addition to taking instructions in connection with specific corporate matters, custodians may be expected to make a number of regular reports, such as with regard to valuation matters, cash analysis, performance and transaction reporting including trade reports, cash accruals income reports and transaction advices. The nature and content of the reports will depend upon the sophistication of the services provided by the custodian and demands of the particular client.

Tax reclamation

17.26   In addition to receiving payments, global custodians may be expected to make any relevant tax reclamations. This is usually concerned with the collection of withholding tax deducted at source. Other matters may include transfer tax, tax on capital income and local tax advice. Custodians will then have to maintain necessary procedures to monitor the tax positions of clients having regard to local fiscal requirements and relevant double taxation treaties.

Ancillary services

17.27   Other value added-services that may be cross-sold with basic custody facilities include cash management, stock lending, investment accounting, foreign exchange and other specific product services such as sale and repurchase agreements and derivatives.

The range of additional services that may be provided has expanded considerably since the early 1990s although there have been fewer new products in recent years.

Opinions also differ with regard to whether certain functions such as cash management and foreign exchange should be regarded as ancillary or value-added. This usually relates to the manner in which the particular custodian has historically developed its services.

Cash management

17.28   Cash management is concerned with the receipt and payment of funds in local and foreign currency accounts. A number of separate currency accounts may have to be maintained for each client depending upon the range of securities held. Local settlement will also require funds to be transferred to the sub-custodian. As many clients may not wish to have an unallocated cash balance in particular currencies, the client has to be provided with accurate balance sheet statements. This has also involved certain custodians providing clients with projected cash balances incorporating future payments and receipts.

Foreign exchange

17.29   Closely associated with cash management is the conduct of foreign exchange transactions. Sub-custodians will, in particular, require funds to be made available in local currencies to give effect to particular transactions. To the extent that custodians have to conduct a large amount of foreign exchange transactions on a daily basis, their own currency exposures have to be managed carefully. This may, however, also act as an important source of income for many custodians.

Stock lending

17.30   Stock lending has become an important source of income for institutions and for custodians, especially in the US. Stock lending operates by making particular classes of securities available to market makers to cover deficiencies in their trading as well as to maintain general market liquidity. The custodian will carry out the necessary administration including the matching of stock and effecting delivery.[1]

1   On the new rules that apply to stock lending in the UK, see para 17.70.

Investment accounting

17.31   More sophisticated global custodians will also provide investment accounting services which include performance-related analyses of the portfolio under control.

LEGAL NATURE OF CUSTODY RELATIONSHIPS

17.32   The legal relationships involved in the provision of custody services is said to be fraught with difficulties.[1] This is because of the complicated nature of the relationships themselves and also the different types of asset classes involved.

In the most simple case, a customer may deposit physical securities with his bank for safe-keeping. The relationship is then one of bailment and an action for conversion will lie for non-return.

At the other end of the factual spectrum, an investor may place a portfolio of securities with a bank custodian. The securities may include registered and bearer securities, equity and debt securities, securities of UK and non-UK issuers, securities existing only in dematerialised form and securities placed in a depository such as Euroclear or Clearstream. None of the securities may be held in the investor's own name. The contractual relationship is solely with the custodian.

The securities may also not be in the name of the custodian. They may be held in the name of sub-custodians, or in the name of a depository through which the securities can exclusively be transferred. The stocks held by all parties except for the ultimate holder may only consist in law of account entries in the books of intermediaries.

1   See Blair et al (2nd edn), para 15.32.

17.33   Equally difficult choice of law issues may also arise. Contractual disputes between the investor and the custodian will be governed by the choice of law clause in the custody agreement and so on up the line. A dispute as to competing entitlement to shares is, however, governed by the *lex situs* of the shares which will normally be the law of incorporation of the issuer.[1]

This rule will not necessarily apply, however, where the dispute relates to securities held by an investor through a custodian. Since the investor's rights may not subsist in the shares themselves, there are powerful arguments for applying the law of the place where the custodian's office is situated, because the subject matter of the dispute is not shares but the investor's rights against the custodian.[2]

1   See *Macmillan Inc v Bishopsgate Investment Trust plc (No 3)* [1996] 1 All ER 585, [1996] 1 WLR 387, CA.
2   See R Goode, 'The Nature and Transfer of Rights in Dematerialised and Immobilised Securities', Ch 7 of *The Future for the Global Securities Market*, F Oditah (ed) (1996) at p 124 and P Wood, *Comparative Law of Security and Guarantees* (1995) p 191. See also *Baker v Archer-Shee* [1927] AC 844, HL and *Archer-Shee v Garland* [1931] AC 212, HL. The issue of the private international law treatment of 'indirectly held securities' is currently being considered as part of the negotiations on the new Hague Convention on Private International Law (*Conference de la Haye de Droit International Prive*). This is generally based on the adoption of a 'place of the relevant intermediary' (PRIMA) approach although difficulties continue with regard *inter alia* to the operation of this rule and the securities to be covered. A preliminary draft Convention was produced on 17 January 2002. See Special Commission, *Preliminary draft Convention on the law applicable to certain rights in respect of securities held with an intermediary*, as adopted on 17 January 2002 (Prel Doc No 8 of 8 February 2002). For a review of the responses received to date see, 'Chart summarising comments received on the provisional version of the preliminary draft Convention on the law applicable to certain rights in respect of securities held with an intermediary' as adopted by the Special Commission on 17 January 2002 (available on www.hcch.net/e/workprog/securities.html). See also, J Benjamin, *Interests in Securities – A Proprietary Law Analysis of the International Securities Markets* (2000), Ch 7.

17.34   This raises the question of the nature of the investor's rights given that these rights have become decoupled from the securities. The starting-point is the contract between the investor and the custodian. The analysis of the relationship between them will depend on the terms of that contract. More generally, it is unlikely that the relationship is one of bailment.

In *MCC Proceeds Inc v Lehman Bros International (Europe)*[1] stock held by X was transferred into the name of Y as nominee. In breach of the terms of the agreement between them, Y later pledged the stock to a bank. The stock was in the form of certificates which were physically transferred. It was held that the relationship between Y and X was that of trustee and beneficiary, not bailee and bailor, and that because X's interest in the stock was merely equitable, it had no claim in conversion against the bank.

1   (1997) 142 Sol Jo LB 40, CA.

17.35   There was no authority until recently on the nature of the investor's rights, which in any case will vary according to the circumstances. Depending on the agreement between investor and custodian, his interest may be proprietary or non-proprietary. If proprietary, he will have rights in the nature of equitable co-ownership in the pool of securities held by the custodian. If non-proprietary, he will merely have a contractual right to the return of equivalent securities to those deposited.

The difference may be vitally important in the event of the custodian's insolvency. Unless the interest is proprietary, the stock held by the custodian will be available to satisfy all the custodian's creditors. That in turn affects the value as security for lending to the investor of his claim on the custodian. There are strong arguments under English law for treating the investor's interest as proprietary. This can be on the basis of a trust relationship, or by way of co-ownership of the pool of securities held by the custodian for its clients generally, or by way of an equitable tenancy in common of the pool of securities.[1]

Where the custodian is itself holding through sub-custodians, the nature of the rights of which the investor becomes co-owner depends on the nature of the custodian's rights against the sub-custodian. This again depends on the contract between them. Professor Goode points out that these rights should also be treated as proprietary and that the interest of the custodian should be treated as 'a derivative interest of the same character as the interest from which it derives'. If lower-tier interests are characterised as derivative in this way,

> 'then it follows that
>
> (a) their value cannot exceed a due proportion of the recoverable value of the issued securities;
>
> (b) transfers of all security rights over higher-tier interests which are effective under the law applicable to them are binding on holders of lower-tier interest; and
>
> (c) no holder of an interest can have rights to securities greater than those possessed by the holder of the higher-tier interest from which the former interest is derived'.[2]

The layering of 'custodians and interests thus produces a hierarchy of trusts, each lower-tier beneficial interest being an interest in a sub-fund derived from the fund or sub-fund above it'.[3]

1 See Goode (para 17.33, note 2 above), p 120; Wood (para 17.33, note 2 above), p 74; and Benjamin, *The Law of Global Custody*, p 46.
2 See Goode (para 17.33, note 2 above), p 122.
3 See Goode (para 17.33, note 2 above), p 126.

17.36 An objection which has been raised to the above analysis is that a trust requires certainty of subject matter. However, this principle does not invalidate the subsistence of a trust over a pool of fungible shares. In *Hunter v Moss*[1] a declaration of trust over shares was held valid although no segregation of specific securities took place.

In *Re Harvard Securities Ltd*[2] a dealer purchased shares on behalf of clients which were registered in the name of a nominee. On the dealer's liquidation, it was contended by the liquidator that the clients had no beneficial interest in the shares. Reliance was placed on cases holding that neither legal nor equitable title to goods can pass until the goods are appropriated to the transferee.[3] In rejecting this contention, the court held that the contractual documentation showed that:

> 'As between Harvard and its former clients, a particular number of unidentified

shares of a particular class in a particular company were being treated as the beneficial property of the client. Had the correspondence and internal records of Harvard gone one stage further, and identified the share numbers the subject of this arrangement, [counsel] accepts (quite rightly in my judgment) that the beneficial interest in the relevant shares would have been vested in the client. The only reason for contending that this is not the case is that the precise shares were not identified. In the light of the decision and reasoning in *Hunter*, and the above discussion, I do not consider that it is open to me to hold that that aspect prevents Harvard's former clients having a beneficial interest in the shares, so far as English law is concerned'.[4]

The court went on to hold that the liquidator should sell the shares and account to each former client out of the proceeds of sale of the relevant block of shares pro rata to that former client's holding.

1 [1994] 3 All ER 215, [1994] 1 WLR 452, CA.
2 [1997] 2 BCLC 369.
3 See, for example, *Re London Wine Co (Shippers) Ltd* [1986] PCC 121; *Re Goldcorp Exchange Ltd (In Receivership)* [1995] 1 AC 74, [1994] 2 All ER 806, PC.
4 At p 384.

17.37 The nature of the interest of the client in securities held a broker in a clearing system was considered in the Hong Kong case of *Re CA Pacific Finance*.[1]

The Central Clearing and Settlement System (CCASS) attached to the Hong Kong Stock Exchange operated a book-entry settlement system within which unnumbered share certificates were immobilised and deposited with a central securities depositary. CCASS was operated by Hong Kong Securities Co Ltd (HKSCC) with all brokers on the market being participants in CCASS. CCASS matched buying and selling orders and interposed itself in the settlement of the transaction by having the security sold to it and then on-sold to the purchaser. HKSCC acted as custodian with the securities being held in its name.

On the liquidation of one broker, CA Pacific Securities Ltd (CAPS), it was held on a preliminary issue that CAPS had acted as agent on behalf of its clients who held a beneficial interest in the securities. The fact that CAPS acted as principal within the relevant CCASS Rules did not refute that position. A trust relationship arose between CAPS and its clients from the fact that it was client money that was used to purchase the securities with no formal declaration of trust being required to vest proprietary interest in the clients. As the shares were fungibles (with each certificate held by HKSCC's depositary evidencing the same bundle of rights), there was no difficulty in finding certainty of subject matter. Each client had a beneficial interest in the securities held in CCASS with the shares not being held under a tenancy in common for all of the clients.

The decision was, however, made on the basis of the regulations setting up CCASS and HKSCC and the client agreement entered into between CAPS and its clients.

1 See *Re CA Pacific Finance Ltd (in liquidation)*, Court of First Instance, Hong Kong Special Administrative Region [2000] 1 BCLC 494.

17.38 The duties that may be owed by a custodian to its customers under the general law are considered in Benjamin.[1] The English courts have reaffirmed (in the agency context) that the scope of fiduciary duties (so far as these may exist in the custody context) can be defined by the terms of the contract.[2]

1   See Benjamin, *The Law of Global Custody*, Ch 8. See also, Benjamin, *Interests in Security* (2001), Ch 10.
2   See *Kelly v Cooper* [1993] AC 205, PC.

CONSULTATION ON THE REGULATION OF CUSTODY SERVICES

17.39   The provision of custody services is not generally considered to involve the creation of any major new exposure as such on the part of investors although a number of specific risks may arise in practice. These include the possible theft or loss of investors' assets as a result of management failure, unauthorised access or inadequate record-keeping. Assets may be misused or misapplied following co-mingling with the custodian's investments. Legal uncertainty may also arise as a result of inadequate documentation, especially with regard to the duties and responsibilities of the custodian.[1]

1   See L Murrall, 'Regulation of Custody in the UK', *Financial Stability Review*, Autumn 1997, p 69; and J Benjamin and A Holmes, 'The Evolving Legal Environment for Fund Management', BJIBFL, November 1996, p 480.

17.40   Custody services were not originally included as an investment business activity for the purposes of the Financial Services Act 1986. Certain practices were brought within the scope of review of the Securities and Futures Authority (SFA) and the Investment Management Regulatory Organisation (IMRO) on a discretionary basis although custody was not directly regulated as such.

This meant that other service providers not authorised by SFA or IMRO were not subject to any controls which latterly included those operating in the UK under the passport provided under the Investment Services Directive. A number of incidents such as the collapse of Barings and the losses suffered by the Maxwell Pension fund also raised further concerns in this area.

SIB Review

17.41   Following an announcement in July 1992, the Securities and Investments Board (SIB) conducted an initial review of custody services the results of which were published in a discussion document in August 1993.[1]

This was followed by a consultative paper in August 1995[2] which noted, in particular, that SIB had agreed with the regulatory authorities from 16 other countries to review the adequacy of existing arrangements for the protection of customer positions, funds and assets by financial intermediaries against the risks of loss through insolvency or misappropriation and to enhance such arrangements as appropriate.

While the 1993 discussion document was only concerned to attempt to identify and analyse a number of the issues that arose with regard to custody, the 1995 paper considered the possibility of making custody an authorised activity and the relevant standards to be applied.

1   See SIB, *Custody Review*, Discussion Paper, August 1993. See Blair et al (2nd edn), paras 15.38–15.41.
2   See SIB, *Custody*, Consultative Paper 90, August 1995.

17.42   The Government announced on 9 May 1996 that custody should, in principle, require authorisation under the Financial Services Act 1986. A consultation document was issued by the Treasury in June 1996 setting out the manner in which it proposed to amend the Act. The Treasury accepted that although custody was not considered to be inherently hazardous, the market was large with up to US$900 billion being held in domestic custody within the UK.

It also argued that although specific custody related activities were regulated, gaps did exist where stand-alone or third-party custody services were provided and investments were held other than in connection with an investment business. This had created an unlevel playing field especially in terms of the provision of third-party custody services.

A further gap in regulatory control also arose where the investor appointed the custodian rather than an authorised firm. Unless custody was regulated directly, investors would not be protected and, in particular, would not be able to make any claims under the Investors Compensation Scheme which was still in place at that stage.[1]

An Order[2] was made on 15 November 1996 inserting a new para 13A in Part II of Sch 1 to the Financial Services Act 1986. This was approved by Parliament on 12 December 1996 and came into effect on 1 June 1997.

1 See Chapter 2, para 2.82.
2 Financial Services (Extension of Scope Act) Order 1996 (SI 1996/2958).

Financial Services Amendment

17.43　Part II of Sch 1 to the Financial Services Act 1986 was amended by the Financial Services (Extension of Scope Act) Order 1996[1] by the insertion of the new para 13A. The Order also made incidental amendments to Part III and Part IV of Sch 1.

The Order applied to the safeguarding and administering or arranging for the safeguarding and administration of assets belonging to another. Offering or agreeing to safeguard and administer or to arrange for the safeguarding and administration of assets were also included.

1 SI 1996/2958. See para 17.42.

17.44　The inserted para 13A applied to safeguarding and administering or arranging for the safeguarding and administration of assets belonging to another where those assets consisted of or include investments or the arrangements for their safeguarding and administration were such that those assets may consist of or include investments and the arrangements had at any time been held out as being arrangements under which investments would be safeguarded and administered.

Offering or agreeing to safeguard and administer or arranging for the safeguarding and administration of assets belonging to another were also covered. The application of these provisions was then expanded in the notes to the paragraph.[1]

1 See Blair et al (2nd edn), paras 15.42–15.43.

Guidance Release

17.45　Following a consultation paper in March 1997 concerning the *Custody of Investments under the Financial Services Act 1986*,[1] the SIB published a

Guidance Release in June 1997.[2] The Guidance Release was issued to assist firms carrying on custody business or considering doing so by indicating the circumstances under which SIB considered that authorisation would be required.

1   See SIB, *Custody of Investments under the Financial Services Act 1986*, Consultative Paper 107, March 1997.
2   See SIB, *Custody of Investments under the Financial Services Act 1986*, Guidance Release 5/97, June 1997.

17.46   The Guidance Release noted that authorisation was only required if both safeguarding and administering were to be carried out in combination.

In introducing the Order, the Government had explained that the requirement for the activities to be conducted together would exclude, for example, small country solicitors who only held share certificates for their clients in a safe. Otherwise all multinational banks, fund managers, stockbrokers and trustees would be covered to the extent that they engaged in custody as defined. Authorisation would be required if the firm undertook contractual responsibility for the safeguarding and administering of assets even if either activity was subcontracted.

Safeguarding would include the physical possession of tangible assets such as gold, documents evidencing title to tangible assets such as share certificates and any other situation where the integrity of intangible assets not evidenced by a physical document was protected such as shares dealt within CREST.[1]

The administration of entitlements in a dematerialised system such as CREST was included under Note (3)(a) to para 13A. Administration was considered to retain its ordinary meaning and included maintaining accounts with clearing houses, settling transactions and investments, operating through depositories or sub-custodians in the UK or elsewhere, operating nominee accounts, cash processing, collecting and dealing with dividends or other income and carrying out such corporate actions as proxy voting. Only one activity had to be carried out in association with safeguarding although the list of activities included was stated not to be exhaustive.

The receipt of documents for onward transmission was excluded under Note 2 of para 13A along with basic financial information and foreign exchange activities.

1   See para 17.17.

17.47   The 1997 Guidance Release contained further information with regard to relevant assets, arranging, exemptions and additional provisions.[1]

1   See Blair et al (2nd edn), paras 15.45–15.48.

Custody standards

17.48   A separate set of standards for the regulation of custody was issued by SIB in August 1996.[1] This was addressed to the self-regulating organisations (SROs) and recognised professional bodies (RPBs) and set out the safeguards that they were expected to maintain so as to provide investors with a level of protection that was considered adequate for the purposes of their recognition requirements.

The standards did not apply directly to authorised persons but were to be given effect through the rules of each SRO and RPB. In so doing, they were expected to be applied in a flexible manner but without material dilution. They were not exhaustive and had to be implemented in accordance with their spirit and intent.

1 See SIB, 'Standards for the Custody of Customer's Investments', Guidance Release No 3/96, August 1996.

17.49 The standards were to be applied to firms which either provided or appointed a third party to provide custody services in respect of investments as defined in the Financial Services Act 1986.

The Guidance Release provided for four standards to be given effect to with regard to responsibilities, loss protection, separate identification and records and reconciliation. Under these requirements, custody arrangements had to be made with care and the responsibilities of all parties concerned clarified, customers' investments had to be capable of separate identification whether held by the custodian or an appointed third party, there had to be appropriate arrangements for the security and integrity of custody facilities and systems for the transfer of investments and individual investments had to be clearly recorded and frequently reconciled.

The content of the particular standards required were expanded in the Guidance Release.

SRO Rules

17.50 With the coming into effect on 6 June 1997 of the Financial Services Act 1986 (Extension of Scope of Act) Order,[1] the Financial Services Act 1986 became applicable to custody business. As a result this and the 1997 SIB Guidance provided, all of the SROs were required to amend their rules to cover custody activities.[2] Both the SFA and IMRO did so, following consultation papers in April 1997 with the new rules coming into force on 2 February 1998.[3]

1 SI 1997/2543.
2 See paras 17.43–17.46.
3 The SFA custody rules were set out in Board Notice 433, issued on 21 July 1997. IMRO's custody rules were set out in Rules Notice 37 issued on 4 August 1997. See Blair et al (2nd edn), paras 15.53–15.54.

17.51 The SRO rules contained a number of specific provisions dealing with such matters as use of assets, possession, custodian agreements, recording of assets and customer statements.[1] The revised rules issued under the Financial Services and Markets Act 2000 are considered below.[2]

1 See Blair et al (2nd edn), paras 15.55–15.77.
2 Paras 17.57–17.74.

FINANCIAL SERVICES AND MARKETS

17.52 Custody services now fall within the definition of the safekeeping and administration of assets as set out in Sch 2, para 5 of the Financial Services and

Markets Act (FSMA) 2000. As such, custody constitutes a regulated activity for the purposes of the Act which requires either authorisation or exemption[1] and permission.[2]

Under s 22(1), an activity is a regulated activity for the purposes of the Act if it is of a specified kind carried on by way of business and relates to an investment of a specified kind or is activity of a kind carried on with regard to property generally. 'Specified' means specified by order of the Treasury which was effected under the Regulated Activities Order on 26 February 2001.[3] The Regulated Activities Order followed a consultation document in February 1999 and a second consultation in October 2000.

The Regulated Activities Order was issued with the Exemption Order, the Appointed Representatives Regulations, the Non-Exempt Activities Order and the Business Order.[4]

1   Under FSMA 2000, s 19(1) and ss 31–39.
2   Under FSMA 2000, s 20(1) and ss 40–55. See Chapter 2, paras 2.54–2.60.
3   See Financial Services and Markets Act 2000 (Regulated Activities) Order 2001 (SI 2001/544) as amended by Financial Services and Markets Act 2000 (Regulated Activities) (Amendment) Order 2001 (SI 2001/3544).
4   See Financial Services and Markets Act 2000 (Exemption) Order 2001 (SI 2001/1201) as amended by Financial Services and Markets Act 2000 (Exemption) (Amendment) Order 2001 (SI 2001/3623); Financial Services and Markets Act 2000 (Appointed Representatives) Regulations 2001 (SI 2001/1217) as amended by Financial Services and Markets Act 2000 (Appointed Representatives) (Amendment) Regulations 2001 (SI 2001/2508); Financial Services and Markets Act 2000 (Professions – Non-Exempt Activities) Order 2001 (SI 2001/1227); and Financial Services and Markets Act 2000 (Carrying on Regulated Activities by Way of Business) Order 2001 (SI 2001/1177). See Chapter 2, paras 2.56–2.57; and Chapter 3.

17.53   The meaning of safeguarding and administering investments is set out in the Chapter VIII of Part II of the Regulated Activities Order. Article 40(1) applies to activities consisting of both the safeguarding of assets belonging to another and the administration of those assets as well as the arranging for one or more other persons to carry on those activities.

To constitute an activity of a specified kind for the purposes of s 19(1) of the FSMA 2000, two further alternative conditions must also be satisfied. The assets must consist of or include any investment which is a security or a contractually based investment or the arrangements for their safeguarding and administration must be such that the assets may consist of or include such investments and either the assets have been of such a nature since 1 June 1997 or the arrangements have at any time (whether before or after that date) been held as such investments.[1]

For the purposes of article 40, it is immaterial that title to the assets safeguarded and administered is held in uncertificated form and that the assets may be transferred to another person (subject to any commitment by the person safeguarding and administering them or arranging for their safeguard or administration that they will be replaced by equivalent assets at some future date or when requested by the person to whom they belong).[2]

For the purposes of the Regulated Activities Order, security means any investment of the kind specified in articles 76–82 or article 89 to the extent relevant.[3] This applies to shares, instruments creating or acknowledging indebtedness, government and public securities, instruments giving entitlement to investments, certificates representing certain securities, units in a collective investment scheme and rights under a stakeholder pension scheme (articles 76–82) as well as rights to or interests in an investment (article 89). Each of these classes of investment are further defined in the Order.

A contractually based investment means rights under a qualifying contract of insurance, any investment of the kind specified by articles 83, 84, 85 and 87 (options, futures, contracts for differences and funeral plan contracts) or rights to or interest in investments to the extent relevant (article 89).[4]

1   See Financial Services and Markets Act 2000 (Regulated Activities) Order 2001 (SI 2001/544), art 40(2)(a) and (b).
2   See SI 2001/544, art 40(3)(a) and (b).
3   See SI 2001/544, art 3(1).
4   See SI 2001/544, art 3(1).

17.54   Certain activities are excluded from constituting safeguarding and administering investments under the Order. These include acceptance of responsibility by a third party, introduction to qualifying custodians and activities not constituting administration.

Arrangements are excluded where a qualifying custodian undertakes responsibility for the assets as if it were conducting the safeguarding and administration directly and the arrangements are operated in the course of carrying on in the UK of the regulated activity of safeguarding and administering.[1] Certain other activities are also excluded including trustees (article 66), a profession or non-investment business (article 67), sales of goods and supply of services (article 68), groups and joint enterprises (article 69) and employee share schemes (article 71).

Introduction arrangements to a qualifying custodian are exempt provided the introducer is not a connected person.[2] Providing information on the number of units or value of any safeguarded assets, converting currency or receiving documents relating to an investment for transmission purposes do not constitute administration.[3]

1   See Financial Services and Markets Act 2000 (Regulated Activities) Order 2001 (SI 2001/544), art 41(1)(a) and (b).
2   See SI 2001/544, art 42(1).
3   See SI 2001/544, art 43(a), (b) and (c).

FSA HANDBOOK

17.55   Any person carrying on a regulated activity by way of business in the UK has to comply with all of the relevant requirements set out in the Financial Services Authority (FSA) Handbook of Rules and Guidance issued under ss 138 and 157.[1]

The High Level Standards (Block 1) include the Principles for Businesses (PRIN), Senior management arrangements, systems and controls (SYSC), Threshold Conditions (COND), Statements of Principle and Code of Practice for approved persons (APER), Statements of Principle and Fit and Proper Tests for Approved Persons (FIT) and General Provisions (GEN). The requirements set out in these chapters apply with regard to the carrying on of regulated activities generally.

To the extent that a bank provides custody services, it will have to comply with the Interim Prudential Sourcebook for Banks (IPRU (BANK)).[2] A securities firm will have to comply the prudential sourcebook for investment business (IPRU (INV)). The prudential sourcebooks generally set out the requirements applicable with regard to capital and financial adequacy, management and systems and controls.

In carrying on regulated activities, firms will also have to comply with the Conduct of Business sourcebook (COB) and other parts of Block 2 as well as relevant provisions within the Regulatory Processes (Block 3), Redress (Block 4) and any of the Specialist Sourcebooks to the extent relevant (Block 5).[3]

1   See Chapter 2, paras 2.83–2.146.
2   See Chapter 2, paras 2.109–2.110; and Chapter 15.
3   See Chapter 2, paras 2.114–2.141.

17.56   The main provisions regulating the day-to-day conduct of regulated business are set out in COB. COB applies to every firm except investment companies with variable capital (ICVCs).[1] COB contains a number of general provisions[2] and rules that apply to all firms conducting designated investment business.[3]

Further provision is included with regard to financial promotion,[4] accepting customers,[5] advising and selling,[6] product disclosure and cancellation or withdrawal rights,[7] dealing and managing[8] and reporting to customers.[9] COB 9 sets out further provisions with regard to client assets. These include custody,[10] mandate,[11] client money,[12] collateral[13] and client money distribution.[14] The COB contains separate provisions with regard to collective investment scheme operators,[15] trustees and depositary activities[16] and Lloyd's of London.[17]

The schedules contain additional requirements with regard to record-keeping, notification, fees and other required payments as well as powers, exercise, rights of action for damages and waived rules. The custody related sections are considered further below.[18]

1   COB 1.1.1G.
2   COB 1.
3   COB 2.
4   COB 3.
5   COB 4.
6   COB 5.
7   COB 6.
8   COB 7.
9   COB 8.
10 COB 9.1.
11 COB 9.2.
12 COB 9.3.
13 COB 9.4.
14 COB 9.5.
15 COB 10.
16 COB 11.
17 COB 12.
18 Paras 17.57–17.77.

Custody

17.57   The new custody rules are set out in COB 9.1. These are generally based on client consent and asset segregation or protection. The general purpose is to restrict the co-mingling of client and firm assets and minimise the risk of the client's safe custody investments being used by the firm without the client's agreement or contrary to the client's wishes. This will also insulate the assets from the firm's insolvency.

17.58 The custody rules apply to any firm that is safeguarding or administering investments subject to certain exceptions.[1] The custody rules apply where the firm safeguards and administers (without arranging) and arranges for the safeguarding and administration of either safe custody investments or custody assets.

Safe custody investments are designated investments that the firm receives or holds on behalf of the client. Custody assets include designated investments as well as any other assets that the firm holds or may hold in the same portfolio as a designated investment held for and on behalf of the client.

Under COB, client includes a market counterparty, intermediate customer or private customer. Customer does not include a market counterparty.[2]

1   COB 9.1.1R.
2   See Chapter 16, paras 16.30 and 16.40–16.44.

17.59 Firms are required to apply the custody rules to those custody assets that are not safe custody investments in a manner appropriate to the nature and value of those assets.[1] The custody rules do not apply to firms acting on behalf of affiliated companies unless the firm has been notified that the designated investment belongs to a client of the affiliated company or the affiliated company is a client dealt with at arms' length.

The operator of a regulated collective investment is not subject to the custody rules. Personal investment firms are also exempt where they hold non-bearer designated investments on behalf of clients provided that the client's ownership is recorded (for three years) and the asset is only held for as long as necessary to process and then passed on as soon as practicable thereafter either to the client or in accordance with the client's instructions.[2]

A firm must generally accept the same level of responsibility to its client for any nominee companies controlled by the firm in respect of any requirements of the custody rules.[3]

1   COB 9.1.3R.
2   COB 9.1.9R.
3   COB 9.1.11R.

17.60 Delivery versus payment transactions (DVP) are excluded unless the transaction fails to settle within three business days.[1] Until such transactions are settled, a firm may segregate money in accordance with the client money rules rather than the client's safe custody investment.[2]

A number of the custody obligations are also disapplied with regard to trustees and depositaries and arrangers.[3] It is not necessary to subject such firms to the full range of obligations imposed to the extent that they are already governed by equivalent requirements under the general law.

1   COB 9.1.13R.
2   COB 9.1.14R.
3   COB 9.1.16–19.26.

Segregation

17.61 The purpose of the segregation rules is to distinguish clearly between the safe custody investments held for clients and designated investments held on the firm's behalf. This is supported by the registration and recording requirements set out in the custody rules.

A firm is generally required to segregate safe custody investments from its own designated investments except to the extent required by law or permitted by the custody rules.[1] The firm must ensure that any safe custody investments recorded in its accounts are clearly stated to be held on behalf of a client and segregated from the firm's designated investments.[2]

Custodians are required to make it clear that the title of an account belongs to one or more clients of the firm.[3] Investments held on behalf of affiliated companies are to be held in a safe custody investment account unless the custody rules are applied to that investment under COB 9.1.9.

1 COB 9.1.28.
2 COB 9.1.30.
3 COB 9.1.32.

17.62 The basic segregation obligation is supported by the registration and recording rules imposed. These are designed to protect the entitlement of the client to the underlying assets.

To the extent practicable, firms are required to register or record legal title to safe custody investments in the name of the client or trustee firm unless the client is an authorised person acting on behalf of its client in which case the holding will be made in the name of the client of the authorised person.

Registration may be effected in the name of a nominee company, a custodian or the firm provided that the investment is subject to the law of another jurisdiction and it is in the client's best interest to do so or the client has been properly notified under the risk disclosure requirements[1] or written consent obtained from a private customer. Registration may be effected in the name of any other person in accordance with the client's written instruction provided that the appropriate risk disclosures are made[2] and the person is not an associate of the firm.[3]

A firm may only register or record legal title to its own designated investments in the same name as safe custody investments where the two sets of assets are separately identified or the client has been appropriately notified and written consent obtained where required.[4]

1 COB 9.1.57.
2 COB 9.1.58.
3 COB 9.1.35.
4 COB 9.1.38.

17.63 Further requirements are imposed with regard to the holding of documents of title by firms.

Firms are generally required to ensure that the arrangements made for the holding of any documents of title to a safe custody investment are appropriate to the value and risk of loss of the investment concerned and that adequate controls are in place to safeguard it from damage, misappropriation or other loss. Documents of title are either to be held in the physical possession of the firm or through a custodian for a private customer or a custodian or other appropriate person in respect of market counterparties or intermediate customers.[1]

Firms are required to ensure that any documents of title held in bearer form and which belong to the firm are clearly separated from safe custody investments.[2]

1 COB 9.1.40.
2 COB 9.1.42.

Custodians

17.64 Firms using or recommending custodians to private customers should ensure that appropriate systems are followed to assess the appropriateness of the custodian. This applies with regard to the continued use of existing custodians or a recommendation to use a custodian for the first time.

Firms are required to undertake an appropriate risk assessment of custodians where safe custody investments are to be held through the custodian or registration is to be arranged through the custodians.[1] An appropriate risk assessment must also be undertaken where a custodian is to be recommended to a private customer.[2]

Firms are expected to make and retain appropriate records of the grounds on which assessments have been made.[3] Various matters may be taken into account in making such an assessment. These include the expertise and market reputation of the custodian, arrangements in place to hold and safeguard investments, legal opinions provided with regard to the asset protection provided in the event of the custodian's insolvency, current industry standard reports available, regulation, financial standing, credit rating and other activities undertaken. All relevant circumstances including legal requirements and custodial practices in the relevant jurisdiction should be taken into account.

Firms are separately required to inform clients in writing where they intend to hold custody assets with a custodian which is in the same group as the firm.[4]

1 COB 9.1.43.
2 COB 9.1.44.
3 SYSC 3.2.20 (Records).
4 COB 9.1.48.

Client agreements

17.65 Firms are required to notify clients as to the appropriate terms and conditions that will apply to any safe custody services to be provided.[1] This includes those applicable where safe custody investments are not registered in the client's name, the extent of the firm's liability in the event of default by a custodian, realisation of collateral, claiming and receiving dividends, interest payments and other accrued entitlements, dealing with takeovers or other offers or capital reorganisations and exercising voting, conversion and subscription rights. This also applies to arrangements for the distribution of entitlements to shares and other benefits and arrangements for provision of information to the client on investments held by the firm or its nominee company.

The firm should separately advise the client as to how often a statement of custody assets will be sent and the basis on which the assets shown are valued, all relevant fees and costs for custody services and the use of any pooling arrangements. The meaning of pooling should be explained to private customers.

1 COB 9.1.49.

17.66 Firms should obtain written agreement from a private customer with regard to the arrangements for the giving and receiving of instructions and any lien or security interest to be taken over the investments by the firm or a third party (except for charges relating to the administration or safekeeping of the investments).

Written consent is not required where the service has been provided unintentionally or the client is ordinarily resident outside the UK, the firm has taken reasonable steps to determine that the client does not wish to execute the agreement and the firm makes and retains a record of the action taken.[1] Market counterparties or intermediate customers should be separately notified of these arrangements.

1   COB 9.1.52 and 9.1.53.

Risk disclosures

17.67   Certain risk disclosures must be made by firms under the custody rules. Before holding or arranging to hold a safe custody investment overseas, the customer must be notified in writing that different settlement, legal and regulatory provisions may apply and that distinct practices may operate with regard to the separate identification of relevant investments.[1]

The client must be notified and prior written consent obtained where the firm is to register or record legal title to a safe custody investment in its own name.[2] The client must also be notified of the risks involved in instructing the firm on the holding, registration or recording of safe custody investments as provided for under the custody rules.[3]

1   COB 9.1.54.
2   COB 9.1.57.
3   COB 9.1.58.

Client statements

17.68   Firms must provide each client or a nominated representative of the client with a written asset statement.[1] This statement must be provided as often as necessary or as often as agreed and, at least, annually. The statement should be provided within 25 business days of having been prepared although statements may be retained where the client is ordinarily resident outside the UK provided that prior written consent is provided.[2] The statement may either be retained electronically or in a hardcopy with responsibility for their management being dealt with by an employee or department not otherwise involved with the client.

Where a range of custody services are provided for a private customer and the statements are provided by more than one system, all statements should be produced as at the same date and despatched within one week of each other unless each statement makes it clear that it relates only to a particular service.[3]

Statements must list all custody assets held for the client and for which the firm is accountable. They should identify any safe custody investments registered in the client's own name separately from those registered in any other name. Custody assets used as collateral or pledged to third parties should be identified separately. The market value of any collateral held should be shown as at the date of the statement. Private customer statements should be based on either trade date or settlement date information for cash balances and investments with the basis being explained to the customer.

Relevant information may be set out in other periodic statements or documents provided that they are prepared with regard to the same date and delivered within a reasonable period of each other. Client money must also be included unless this has been separately notified within one month before or after the statement date.[5]

Statements are not required where investments have been obtained within the previous three months and no custody service is to be provided.[6]

1   COB 9.1.59.
2   COB 9.1.60 and 9.1.61.
3   COB 9.1.63.
4   COB 9.1.65.
5   COB 9.1.66.
6   COB 9.1.68.

Custodian agreements

17.69   Firms must agree in writing appropriate terms and conditions with custodians before any safe custody investments are transferred.[1] The custodian agreement should ensure that the title of the account shows that the investment does not belong to the firm or an affiliated company. The custodian should hold or record the investment belonging to the firm's client separately from designated investments belonging to the firm or the custodian. The custodian should be required to deliver to the firm a statement at an agreed date or dates setting out the description and amounts of all safe custody investments credited to the account.

Statements should generally be delivered within 20 business days of having been prepared. The custodian should not be entitled to claim any lien, right of retention or sale over any safe custody investment except where written consent has been provided by the client or in relation to administration or safekeeping charges.

Arrangements should be agreed for the registration or recording of safe custody investments where these are not to be registered in the name of the client. The custodian should not be permitted to withdraw any safe custody investments from the account except for delivery to the firm or on the firm's instructions.

The procedures and authorities for the passing of instructions to or by the firm should be clearly stated, as well as arrangements for the claiming and receiving of dividends, interest payments and other entitlements. The extent of the custodian's liability in the event of the loss of a safe custody investment caused by the fraud, wilful default or negligence of the custodian or its agent should also be clearly set out.

1   COB 9.1.69.

Use and stock lending

17.70   Firms are prohibited from using safe custody investments for their own account unless prior written consent has been obtained from a private customer or an intermediate customer or market counterparty appropriately notified.[1]

Firms must not use the safe custody investments of one customer for the account of another client unless prior written consent has been obtained or appropriate notification made.[2] A firm must not undertake or otherwise engage in stock lending activity with a third customer without consent or notification.[3]

Where stock lending is permitted, the firm must ensure that relevant collateral is provided by the borrower in favour of the customer, the current realisable value of the safe custody investment and relevant collateral are monitored daily and the firm provides relevant collateral to make up any difference where the current realisable value falls below that of the safe custody investment unless otherwise agreed in writing by the customer.[4] Stock lending is not permitted where safe custody investments of more than one customer are registered or held together unless all customers have consented and adequate systems and procedures are in place to ensure that the assets are only used where consent has been obtained.[5]

The requirements with regard stock lending apply to safe custody investments held collectively in any custody or settlement system. Appropriate systems must be maintained to distinguish between different investments. Any cash or custody assets held in favour of a customer or stock lending activity must be held in accordance with the client money rules or custody rules.[6] This will apply with regard to dividends (actual or payment in lieu), stock lending fees and other payments received for the benefit of a customer.

1   COB 9.1.72.
2   COB 9.1.73.
3   COB 9.1.74.
4   COB 9.1.78.
5   COB 9.1.79.
6   COB 9.1.80.

Reconciliation

17.71   Firms must conduct a reconciliation of their records of safe custody investments for which they are accountable but that are not physically held with the corresponding statements from relevant custodians. The statements should also be reconciled with the records of legal entitlement applicable to any dematerialised investments. The reconciliation must be effected, at least, every 25 business days.[1] Statements may be reconciled on longer intervals of up to 6 months where the information is provided by unit trust managers, ICVC operators or the administrators of off-shore mutual funds.[2]

1   COB 9.1.85.
2   COB 9.1.87.

17.72   Firms must separately carry out a count of all safe custody investments physically held on behalf of clients and reconcile their records of client holdings with the location of safe custody investments. This reconciliation must be conducted, at least, every six months or twice annually provided that they are, at least, five months apart.[1] These reconciliations should be conducted as soon as reasonably practicable after the date to which the reconciliation relates.[2] This should generally be effected within 25 business days of the date to which the statements relate. This reconciliation applies to all safe custody investments recorded in the firm's books and records and those of any nominee company used for the provision of safe custody services and controlled by the firm or an affiliated company.

Either a 'total count method' (which requires all safe custody investments to be counted and reconciled as at the same date) or an alternative reconciliation method (such as rolling stock) should be used. An alternative may only be used provided that all of a particular safe custody investment is counted and reconciled as at the same date, all investments are counted and reconciled during a period of six months and written confirmation is given to the FSA from the firm's auditor that appropriate systems and controls are in place to perform the reconciliation.[3]

Any discrepancies should be corrected and made good or the equivalent of any unreconciled shortfall should be provided. This applies whenever there are reasonable grounds for concluding that the firm is responsible for the shortfall.[4] This will include items recorded or held within a suspense or error account. Where the responsibility for the shortfall is in dispute, the firm is required to take reasonable steps to resolve the position with the other person.

1   COB 9.1.89.
2   COB 9.1.91.
3   COB 9.1.93.
4   COB 9.1.94.

17.73   Firms are required to notify the FSA in writing without delay if they have failed to comply with or are unable in any material respect to comply with any of the reconciliation requirements imposed under the custody rules. The FSA should also be notified where any discrepancy has not been corrected or made good as required under the rules.[1]

1   COB 9.1.97.

Records

17.74   Firms must ensure that proper records of all custody assets held or received are made and retained for a period of three years.[1] Safe custody investments available to be lent and which have been lent must be separately identified within the records.[2]

1   COB 9.1.98.
2   COB 9.1.99.

Additional obligations

17.75   COB 9 also contains a number of further provisions with regard to mandates,[1] client money,[2] collateral[3] and client money distribution.[4]

1   COB 9.2.
2   COB 9.3.
3   COB 9.4.
4   COB 9.5.

Mandates

17.76   The mandate rules apply to any firm in respect of which written authority has been provided by the client under which the client may control a client's assets or liabilities in the course of or in connection with the firm's designated investment business.[1] This includes stock lending activities, bank or building society account instructions such as direct debits and credit card details.

The mandate rules generally apply where firms control rather than hold assets or are able to create liabilities in the name of the client. The objective is to ensure that firms establish and maintain appropriate records and internal controls to prevent the misuse of the authority provided.

1   COB 9.2.1.

Client money

17.77   The client money rules apply to any firm that receives or holds money from, or on behalf of, a client in the course or in connection with its designated investment business.[1] The rules do not apply to the activities of life offices or friendly societies, coins held for the intrinsic value of the metal constituting the coin, money held with a firm that is an approved bank (with the customer being notified that the client money rules will not apply) or money held by regulated depositaries.[2]

The client money rules are designed to provide protection where cash or other financial claims are held by firms. Principle 10 (clients' assets) requires firms to maintain adequate protection for clients' assets which will include the proper accounting and handling of client money.

1   COB 9.3.1.
2   COB 9.3.2.

17.78   COB 9.3 contains a number of further provisions that clarify the scope of application of the client money rules. These include 'opt out' provisions, money received in connection with delivery versus payment transactions, affiliated company holdings, money due and payable and money held by solicitors or trustee firms.

COB 9.3 imposes a number of specific obligations with regard to segregation, mixed remittance, appointed or failed representatives and other agents, client entitlements, interest, third-party transfers, client bank accounts, bank selection, group banks, notifications, client money calculation, reconciliations and records.

Collateral

17.79   The provisions with regard to collateral apply to firms that receive or hold assets in connection with an arrangement to secure the obligation of a client in the course of, or in connection with its designated investment business.[1] The collateral requirements do not apply to firms that hold a bare security interest (without the right to hypothecate or realise the asset) in which case they must comply with the custody or client money rules.[2]

The purpose of the collateral rules is to provide client protection where certain security interests have been conferred. The rules distinguish between bare security interests and 'right to use arrangements' where legal title has been transferred subject to an obligation to re-convey or transfer.[3]

Where a firm receives or holds a client's asset or which exercises its rights over the asset, it must maintain adequate records to enable it to discharge any future obligations including return or equivalent return.[4]

1 COB 9.4.1.
2 COB 9.4.3.
3 COB 9.4.5–9.4.7G.
4 COB 9.4.8.

Client money distribution

17.80 The client money distribution rules apply to firms that hold client money subject to the client money rules at the time that a 'primary pooling event' or a 'secondary pooling event' occurs.[1] The objective is to facilitate the timely return of client money on the failure of a firm or third party with which the money is held.

Primary events generally relate to the failure of the firm while secondary events are concerned with the failure of third parties to which the client money has been transferred. Secondary pooling events include the failure of a bank. In such cases, additional protection is provided where clients have requested that funds be placed in a designated client bank account at a different bank.

The effect of these requirements is generally to protect the assets or interests of the client against any unforeseen loss.

1 COB 9.5.1.

Chapter 18

Listing and regulated exchanges and clearing houses

INTRODUCTION

18.1   Financial markets carry out a number of core functions within any economy. The main objective is to bring together sources of surplus capital which may then be used in deficit areas. Banks and other financial institutions generally act as financial intermediaries within this allocation process. In so doing, they discharge a number of essential savings, credit and payment functions which are essential to the operation of any modern market-based economy.

18.2   The two main markets within any financial system are the banking or money markets and the securities or capital markets. The *banking markets* operate through loans and similar forms of credit. These are essentially private debt instruments entered into between banks as creditors and their client borrowers.

The advantage of this personal debt relationship is that the creditor can exercise a considerable degree of control over the activities and consequent financial condition of the borrower. This is generally effected through a range of conditions precedent, warranties and undertakings as well as events of default set out in a term loan agreement.

The disadvantage is that as a personal obligation, the debt is inherently non-transferable (subject to adjusted modern assignment rules and other commercial or legal devices).

18.3   The *capital markets* are, in contrast, concerned with issuing and dealing in transferable securities of any form. These include the Government Gilt or Treasury Bill markets as well as other corporate bond markets and equity markets. These generally consist of the primary markets (of initial issuance) and secondary (dealing) markets.

The difference between a bond (government or corporate) and a share (equity or stock interest) is that a bond holder only holds the debt and receives an interest payment while the shareholder owns an interest in the company which entitles them to a dividend payment. These are still both forms of debt although the debt is in this case issued in a transferable paper or electronic form.

While loans and securities both constitute financial claims, the core difference is one of transferability and negotiability (the passing of perfect title with regard to such instruments as bills of exchange and cheques).

18.4   Banks and securities firms are both subject to financial regulation. The objective is to ensure that they are operated in an effective and stable manner at all times. Although the underlying financial risks involved are different, they are both subject to the same general suitability, systems and financial controls.

To the extent that securities are also offered to the general public, additional controls have to be imposed on their content and sale. The fundamental principle that applies is disclosure which may either operate on a pure information (UK) or merit (US) basis. As well as assist with the initial placement of a security on the market, firms advise or deal on behalf of clients in secondary trading.

Securities laws can accordingly be considered as being made up of underlying financial (prudential) provisions as well as public offer and private client rules.

Scope of the chapter

18.5   The purpose of this chapter is to consider the main rules that apply with regard to the content and sale of securities to the general public in the UK. This includes those to be placed on the official list maintained by the competent authority for listing, as well as the prospectus requirements applicable to non-listed issues.

The nature of listing is considered and the provisions with regard to listing set out in Part VI of the Financial Services and Markets Act (FSMA) 2000 examined in further detail. The general content of the current listing rules as well as the content of the United Kingdom Listing Authority (UKLA) Guidance Manual are considered.

Separate reference is made to the applicable corporate governance provisions set out in the Combined Code and to the requirements applicable to recognised investment exchanges (RIEs) and clearing houses (RCHs).

OFFICIAL LISTING

18.6   The relevant requirements concerning the operation of the official list and the powers and functions of the competent authority in the UK are now set out in Part VI of the FSMA 2000. These replicate the provisions contained in the Financial Services Act 1986. New powers to impose penalties for breaches of the listing rules are, however, included as well as power to allow the Treasury to transfer some or all of these functions to another body in certain circumstances.[1]

1 See G Walker, 'Official Listing' in M Blair, L Mingella, M Taylor, M Threipland and G Walker, *Financial Services & Markets Act 2000* (2001), Ch 8.

18.7 It was originally intended that the London Stock Exchange (LSE) would continue as the competent authority for listing within the UK. The Chancellor then announced on 4 October 1999 that responsibility for listing would be transferred to the Financial Services Authority (FSA). This followed the LSE's decision to demutualise and turn itself into a commercial company. It was thought that it would no longer be appropriate for the LSE to continue to act as the listing authority and the Treasury was asked to transfer authority and competence in this regard to the FSA. The transfer was effected in May 2000.

18.8 As the competent authority for listing, the FSA is responsible for the maintenance of the official list and the admission of qualifying securities to listing. The listing authority also approves documentation issued by listed companies, provides guidance on the application of listing rules and investigates rules breaches.

18.9 Although the FSA is now responsible for the admission of securities to listing, the LSE and the other exchanges in the UK continue to determine admission to trading.

Listing is accordingly concerned with the admission of securities to the approved list which means that they have satisfied the requirements set with regard to structure, content and presentation. Admission to trading is only concerned with allowing securities to be admitted to dealing on a particular exchange. This may or may not involve approved or listed securities.

Both of these functions were formerly undertaken by the LSE before demutualisation. Following their separation, certain consequential amendments had to be made to the terms of the relevant statutory provisions and listing rules.

18.10 The conditions with regard to listing (the Listing Rules) were formally set out in the LSE's 'Yellow Book'. These were largely continued through the FSA's reissued Listing Rules.

The Listing Rules gave effect to the requirements set out in the European 1979 Admission to Listing Directive, the 1980 Listings Particulars Directive and 1982 Interim Reports Directive[1] as well as the later 1989 Prospectus (Public Offers) Directive.[2]

The statutory provisions governing admission to listing were formally set out in the Companies Act 1985 and the Financial Services Act 1986. The European Directives were given effect, in particular, through the 1995 Public Offers of Securities Regulations and the Traded Securities (Disclosure) Regulations.

The Listing Rules will have to be amended further again in due course to give effect to the further European measures proposed under the Lamfalussy Committee and Financial Services Action Plan. This will, in particular, include the proposed new prospectuses directive which will create a single 'passport' for European issuers of securities.[3]

1 Council Directive 79/279/EEC of 5 March 1979 co-ordinating the conditions for the admission of securities to official stock exchange listing (OJ L 66, 16.3.1979, p 21) as amended by Directive 88/627/EEC (OJ L 348, 17.12.1988, p 62) ; Council Directive 80/390/EEC of 17 March 1980 co-ordinating the requirements for the drawing up, scrutiny and distribution of the listing particulars to be published for the admission of securities to listing (OJ L 100, 17.4.1980, p 1) as amended by Directive 94/18/EC (OJ: 135, 31.5.1994, p 1); Council Directive 82/121/EEC of 15 February 1982 on information to be published on a regular basis by companies the shares of which have been admitted to official stock exchange listing (OJ L 48, 20.2.1982, p 26). See also Council Directive 88/627/EEC of 12 December 1988 on the information to be published when a major holding in a listed company is acquired or disposed of (OJ L 348, 17.12.1988, p 62).
2 Council Directive 89/298/EEC of 17 April 1989 co-ordinating the requirements for the drawing up, scrutiny and distribution of the prospectus to be published when transferable securities are offered to the public (OJ L 124, 5.5.1989, p 8).
3 See para 18.15.

History of listing rules

18.11   The provisions contained in Part VI of the FSMA 2000 replace the earlier rules set out in the Financial Services Act 1986. The 1986 Act had been enacted to create a formal statutory framework for the regulation of all investment business within the UK but one based on an underlying system of self-regulation through a number of sector specific agencies and separate professional bodies. This followed the production of two reports by Professor Jim Gower in 1982 and 1985 and a Government White Paper on Financial Services in the UK in 1985.

18.12   Part IV of the 1986 Act introduced basic provisions concerning the admission to listing of defined securities. This included a prohibition on the admission of any security to the Official List of the Stock Exchange unless it complied with the listing rules of the competent authority under the Financial Services Act 1986, s 142.

The Council of the Stock Exchange (as it was then known) was designated as the competent authority. Persons responsible for the preparation of prospectuses had to ensure that they contained all such information as investors and their professional advisers would reasonably require irrespective of whether this complied with the terms of the LSE's Yellow Book.

The Financial Services Act 1986 also contained additional provisions in Part V which dealt with offers of securities that were not to be listed.

18.13   It was intended that Parts IV and V would replace the earlier prospectus provisions contained in Part III of the Companies Act 1985. While Part IV was implemented in 1987 (replacing the provisions relating to listed securities contained in the Companies Act 1985), Part V was never brought into force.

Difficulties had arisen with regard to the adoption of the Prospectus Directive (or Public Offers Directive) by the European Community in 1989. This set out the requirements for the issuance of prospectuses for the initial public offerings of securities which were not already listed on a stock exchange of any Member State and gave Member States the option to ensure that any offer of transferable securities to the public within their territories was subject to the publication by the issuer of pre-vetted or approved prospectuses.

With the adoption of the Prospectus Directive, Part V of the Financial Services Act 1986 had to be revised before it could be implemented. This was eventually secured on 19 June 1995 under the Public Offers of Securities Regulations 1995.[1] These provided for the repeal of Sch 3 to the Companies Act 1985 and Part V of the Financial Services Act 1986.

1   SI 1995/1537.

18.14   Three further directives were then adopted at the European level in connection with admission to listing, listing particulars and interim reports:[1]

—   The Admission to Listing Directive was adopted in 1979 which established minimum conditions for all securities to satisfy before admission to the official listing on any stock exchange within Member States. This included the legal status of the company and its shares, minimum size of the company and negotiability of shares. All Member States had to designate a national authority (or authorities) to determine decisions relating to the admission of securities to official listing.

—   The Listings Particulars Directive was adopted in 1980. This co-ordinated the requirements for the compilation, scrutiny and distribution of listing particulars. The admission of securities to official listing was made conditional on publication of an information sheet (referred to as the listing particulars) the contents of which had to enable investors and their investment advisers to make an informed assessment of the assets and liabilities, financial position, profits and losses and prospects of the issuer and of the rights attaching to such securities.

—   The Interim Reports Directive was adopted in 1982 requiring companies admitted to listing to publish specified information on a regular basis including half-yearly profit and loss statements. A separate Directive on the information to be published when major holding in a listed company was acquired or disposed of was issued in 1988.

The main Directives relating to listing were subsequently consolidated in May 2001.[2]

1   See para 18.10, note 1.
2   See Directive 2001/34/EC of 28 May 2001 on the admission of securities to official stock exchange listing and on information to be published on those securities (OJ L 184, 6.7.2001, p 1). This consolidates Directives 79/279, 80/390, 82/121 and 99/627 and related amending relevant measures.

18.15   A number of further European measures are currently proposed as part of the Financial Services Action Plan[1] and Lamfalussy Committee Report.[2] This includes a new single prospectuses directive based on full mutual recognition which will replace both Directive 80/390/EEC and Directive 89/298/EEC.[3]

The Commission has also been consulting on the transparency obligations of publicly traded companies.[4] This sets out a revised approach to the disclosure requirements for issuers of securities on regulated markets. This consolidates existing requirements and allows for electronic filings.

The Commission has presented a separate proposal for a new Directive on market abuse that will apply to both insider dealing and market manipulation.[5] This will update the earlier Insider Dealing Directive and add new offences with regard to misrepresentation and market distortion (as under s 118 of the FSMA 2000).

UK company and financial services law will have to be reviewed and revised accordingly on the adoption of each of these proposals.

1 The Financial Service Action Plan was adopted in 1988. See Commission Communication, *Financial Services: Building a Framework for Action*, COM (1998) 625 final of 28 October 1998. The Communication contained a number of comments with regard to regulatory apparatus, wholesale and retail financial markets and supervisory co-operation with a programme of directive adoption to achieve its objectives. A Financial Services Policy Group was set up to assist this process. The Action Plan is generally intended to be implemented by 2005 although the single market in securities is to be established by 2003.
2 A separate 'Committee of Wise Men' was also set up in July 2000 under Alexandre Lamfalussy which reported in February 2001. The Lamfalussy Report called for a four-level approach to be adopted for European securities regulation based on legislation, technical assistance (by a new European Securities Committee (ESC) and supported by a Committee of European Securities Regulators (CESR) which replaced the earlier FESCO), uniform implementation and strengthened enforcement. See IP/01/215.
3 See Commission Proposal for a Directive on the prospectus to be published when securities are offered to the public or admitted to trading (COM (2001) 280 final).
4 On the latest consultation, see IP/02/684 of 8.5.2002. An amended proposal was issued on 9 August 2002 following the original draft of 30 May 2001. See IP/01/759 and IP/02/1209.
5 IP/02/417 and IP/01/758 and MEMO/01/439.

Official listing provisions

18.16   The provisions with regard to official listing are now contained in Part VI of the FSMA 2000. This sets out the powers and functions of the competent authority and requirements with regard to the maintenance of the official list, applications for listing and the discontinuance and suspension of listings.[1]

The FSMA 2000 also contains separate provisions concerning the content and registration of listing particulars and prospectuses. The listing rules may require that listing particulars must be issued before securities can be admitted to the official list. A general duty of disclosure is imposed on those preparing the listing particulars.[2]

The FSMA 2000 also contains provision with regard to the issuance of supplementary listing particulars where there has been a significant change since admission of the particulars but before dealings have started.[3] Particulars must be registered with the Registrar of Companies on or before the date on which they are published.

1 FSMA 2000, ss 72–78. See paras 18.19–18.27.
2 FSMA 2000, ss 79–80. See paras 18.28–18.29.
3 FSMA 2000, ss 81–83. See paras 18.30–18.32.

18.17   The FSMA 2000 requires that a prospectus must be published before any securities are offered to the public in the UK for the first time before admission to the official list subject to certain exceptions.[1]

Persons may not offer new securities for which an application for listing has been made without publishing a prospectus. The requirements as to listing are to apply equally to prospectuses.[2]

Non-listing prospectuses may also be approved by the competent authority where securities are to be offered to the public although no application is to be made for listing.[3] This allows the prospectus to be used in other Member States where the relevant authorities are obliged to give it full effect on a mutual recognition basis.

1 FSMA 2000, ss 84–85. See para 18.33.
2 FSMA 2000, s 86. See para 18.34.
3 FSMA 2000, s 87. See para 18.35.

18.18 Persons responsible for the preparation of listing particulars, prospectuses and non-listing prospectuses are liable to pay compensation to those who suffer loss as a result of untrue or misleading statements or the omission of any information which is required to be contained in these documents.[1]

The competent authority is also given a new power to impose financial penalties on issuers who have breached their listing rules.[2]

Each of these main sets of provisions is considered further below.

1 FSMA 2000, s 90.
2 FSMA 2000, s 91.

The competent authority

18.19 Section 69(1) of the Financial Services and Markets Bill originally designated the LSE as the competent authority for official listing. It was then announced in October 1999 that this would be changed to the FSA. Section 72(1) of the FSMA 2000 accordingly now provides that the functions conferred on the competent authority under Part VI are to be exercised by the FSA.

18.20 A revised set of general functions with regard to listing are specified under s 73(2), although six of the general prudential principles set to in s 2(3) are re-applied under s 73(1) (with the exception of management responsibility in s 2(3)(b)). Certain amendments to other provisions contained in the FSMA 2000 are, however, set out in Sch 7 where the FSA acts as competent authority.

18.21 The Treasury is given further power under the 2000 Act to transfer these functions by order to another person in accordance with the provisions set out in Sch 8. Such a transfer of functions may be effected if the existing authority agrees in writing that the order should be made or it would otherwise be considered to be in the public interest that a transfer should be effected.[1]

Three specific possible public interest grounds were set out in paras 3, 4 and 5 of Sch 7 to the Bill, although these were subsequently deleted from the final Act. They related to improving competition having regard to the control of the official list, the rules and practices of the competent authority; restricting, distorting or preventing competition to a significant extent; and the performance of the transfer functions being significantly improved.

1 FSMA 2000, Sch 8, para 1(2).

18.22 A transfer order does not affect anything previously done by any person acting as competent authority for listing. The order may also include various other ancillary matters set out in FSMA 2000, Sch 8, para 2(2).

The official list

18.23 The competent authority is obliged to maintain the official list under s 74(1). The competent authority may only admit to the official list such securities or other instruments ('things') as it considers appropriate. For the purposes of the 2000 Act, 'security' means anything which has been, or may be, admitted to the official list.[1] 'Listing' means being included in the official list in accordance with Part VI of the Act. A security must comply with all relevant conditions set out in Part VI of the Act or rules issued under it and not otherwise fall within a description or category set out in a disqualification order issued by the Treasury.[2]

1   FSMA 2000, s 74(5).
2   See para 18.65.

Application for listing

18.24   Admission to the official list may only be granted on an application made in such manner as may be specified in the listing rules and the authority must be satisfied that the requirements of the listing rules and any other requirements imposed have been satisfied.[1] An application may be refused if the authority considers that granting it would be detrimental to the interests of investors but only having regard to factors relating to the issuer. Applications can only be made by or with the consent of the issuer of the securities.

Although securities may already be officially listed in another European Economic Area (EEA) state, an application may be refused if the issuer fails to comply with any relevant obligations relating to that listing.

1   FSMA 2000, s 75(1) and (4).

18.25   Applicants must be notified within six months of the original date of receipt of the application by the competent authority or the date on which any further information requested has been provided.[1] If due notice is not given, the application will be deemed to have been refused.[2] Once admitted, however, the admission may not be challenged on the ground that any relevant requirement or condition had not been satisfied.[3]

1   FSMA 2000, s 76(1).
2   FSMA 2000, s 76(2).
3   FSMA 2000, s 76(7).

Discontinuance and suspension of listing

18.26   The listing of any securities may be discontinued where there are special circumstances which preclude normal regular dealings as provided for in the listing rules.[1] Listing may also be suspended in accordance with the listing rules. This power applies irrespective of when the securities were admitted to the official list.

1   FSMA 2000, s 77(1).

18.27   Where securities are delisted, s 77(5) of the FSMA 2000 now allows the issuer to refer the matter to the Tribunal. A detailed procedure concerning the suspension or discontinuance of listing was added at the Bill stage. This is now set out in s 78 and generally provides for notice which must contain specified material including details and date of effectiveness, reasons for suspension or discontinuance, the right to make representations and relevant period and the right to refer the matter to the Tribunal. This is, however, without prejudice to the right of the FSA to delist with immediate effect.

Listing particulars

18.28   The listing rules may provide that securities (other than new securities) may not be admitted to the official list unless appropriate listing particulars have been submitted to and approved by the competent authority and published or such other document as may be required has been published.[1]

'Listing particulars' means a document in such form and containing such information as may be specified in the listing rules.[2] The persons responsible for listing particulars are to be determined in accordance with regulations issued by the Treasury.[3]

1 FSMA 2000, s 79(1).
2 FSMA 2000, s 79(2).
3 See para 18.65.

18.29 Section 80(1) of the FSMA 2000 imposes a general duty of disclosure in relation to listing particulars. Listing particulars are to contain all such information as investors and their professional advisers would reasonably require or expect to find there for the purpose of making informed assessments of the assets and liabilities, financial position, profits and losses and prospects of the issuer and of the rights attaching to the securities. This is without prejudice to any specific information required by the listing rules or by the competent authority. This only relates, however, to information within the knowledge of the person responsible for the listing particulars or which it would be reasonable for him to obtain by making enquires.

18.30 Supplementary listing particulars must be issued where there has been any significant changes to the matters set out in the original particulars.[1] This applies to any matters required to be set out in the listing particulars or to any significant new matters which subsequently arise which would otherwise have had to be included. The supplementary listing particulars are to be issued in accordance with the provisions set out in the listing rules. 'Significant' means significant for the purpose of making any informed assessment of the kind set out in s 80(1). There is no duty to issue supplementary particulars unless the issuer is notified of the change or new matter by a person responsible for the listing particulars. That person is, however, required to give appropriate notice.

1 FSMA 2000, s 81(1).

18.31 The competent authority may permit certain information to be omitted from the listing particulars where its disclosure would be contrary to the public interest, seriously detrimental to the issuer or otherwise considered unnecessary for the type of persons expected normally to buy or deal in the particular types of securities concerned.[1]

This may not, however, apply to essential information. 'Essential information' means information which a person considering acquiring securities of the kind in question would be likely to need in order not to be misled about any facts which it is essential for him to know in order to make an informed assessment.[2] The Secretary of State or the Treasury may issue a certificate confirming that the disclosure of certain information would be contrary to the public interest.

1 FSMA 2000, s 82(1).
2 FSMA 2000, s 82(6).

18.32 A copy of the listing particulars must be delivered to the Registrar of Companies on or before the date in which they are published under the listing rules.[1] A copy of the statement issued by the Registrar must be included within the listing particulars. Failure to provide the Registrar with a copy of the listing particulars is an offence under the FSMA 2000.[2]

1 FSMA 2000, s 83(1).
2 FSMA 2000, s 83(3).

Prospectuses

18.33 Listing rules must provide that no new securities for which an application for listing has been made may be admitted to the official list unless a prospectus has been submitted to and approved by the competent authority and published.[1] The prospectus must accordingly be published before the securities are offered to the public in the UK.

It is an offence for an unauthorised person to offer new securities for which an application for listing has been made without publishing a prospectus.[2] This is to be treated as a breach of the rules of the FSA if the offer is made by an authorised person. Any person who suffers loss may sue the person who made the offer of securities subject to the defences which are generally applied to breaches of statutory duty.[3]

1 FSMA 2000, s 84(1).
2 FSMA 2000, s 85(1) and (2).
3 FSMA 2000, s 85(5).

18.34 The provisions applicable to the issuance of listing rules and the obligations of issuers and other parties under Part VI of the FSMA 2000 are to apply equally to listing particulars and prospectuses and supplementary prospectuses.[1]

1 FSMA 2000, s 86(1).

18.35 The listing rules may require prospectuses to be submitted and approved by the competent authority where securities are to be issued to the public in the UK for the first time although no application for listing is to be made.[1] Such a 'non-listing prospectus' must be recognised by all competent authorities in other Member States once they have been approved under the Act. They are then entitled to benefit from mutual recognition throughout the EEA. Certain amendments are made to apply the listing provisions contained in the FSMA 2000 to non-listed prospectuses under Sch 9.

1 FSMA 2000, s 87(1).

Sponsors

18.36 Further provisions were added during the Bill stage with regard to sponsors. 'Sponsor' means any person approved by the competent authority for the purpose of the listing rules. The listing rules may require any person to make arrangements with a sponsor for the carrying out of certain specified services and for the maintenance of a list of relevant sponsors and conditions for listing.[1] The 2000 Act also now includes notice provisions and right to apply to the Tribunal where an application for approval as a sponsor is to be refused or an existing approval cancelled. The competent authority may alternatively issue a public censure of a sponsor again subject to notice and the right to apply to the Tribunal.[2]

1   FSMA 2000, s 88(3).
2   FSMA 2000, s 89.

Compensation

18.37   Any person responsible for listing particulars is liable to pay compensation to any person who has acquired securities to which the particulars apply and has suffered loss as a result of any untrue or misleading statement in the particulars or the omission of any matter which should otherwise have been set out in the particulars.[1] This is subject to certain exceptions set out in FSMA 2000, Sch 10.

Any person who fails to comply with the requirements with regard to the issuance of supplementary particulars is liable to a separate offence.[2] These offences are without prejudice to any other liability which may arise.

1   FSMA 2000, s 90(1).
2   FSMA 2000, s 90(4).

Penalties

18.38   Further penalties may be imposed by the competent authority on any person who has breached the listing rules.[1] This extends to include present and former directors who have been knowingly involved in a breach of the listing rules. Penalties are to be paid directly to the competent authority although no penalty may be imposed after two years from the date on which the authority knew of the contravention or of the circumstances from which the contravention could reasonably be inferred.

Alternatively again, a public censure may be used. These are an important new powers. Formerly, the competent authority could only issue private or public censures or suspend or cancel listing. This will accordingly allow the competent authority additional flexibility in dealing with listing breaches.

1   FSMA 2000, s 91(1).

18.39   Where a penalty is to be imposed, the authority must give the person concerned a warning notice stating the reasons for the proposed action, amount of fine or content of censure statement and right of appeal to the Tribunal. This must then be followed by a decision notice. Any other persons who may be materially prejudiced must also be notified.[1]

1   FSMA 2000, s 92.

18.40   A demand will be made in the form of a notice of payment which must be in writing and require payment within a specified period of not less than thirty days of service. The competent authority's policy with regard to the imposition of penalties and amount are to be set out in a published policy statement.[1] Arrangements are to be made and maintained allowing for appeal against the imposition of a penalty.

1   FSMA 2000, s 93.

Competition

18.41   The FSMA 2000 contains new provisions allowing the Treasury to order the regulating provisions and practices of the competent authority to be kept under review having regard to possible significant adverse effects on competition.[1]

1   FSMA 2000, s 95.

Further provisions

OBLIGATIONS OF ISSUERS

18.42   The listing rules may specify requirements to be complied with by issuers of listed securities and the action to be taken by the competent authority in the event of non-compliance.[1] This may include authorising the authority to publish the fact that an issuer has breached the rules or publish relevant information in the event that the issuer has failed to do so.

1   FSMA 2000, s 96.

INVESTIGATIONS

18.43   The competent authority may appoint one or more persons to conduct an investigation where it considers that there has been a breach of the listing rules or requirements of the FSMA 2000 with regard to registration or publication of prospectuses or the advertising rules.[1] This may include situations where a director of issuer or applicant company ha been involved with a breach of the rules.

1   FSMA 2000, s 97.

ADVERTISEMENTS

18.44   Advertisements in connection with applications for listing must either be approved or authorised by the competent authority in advance.[1] Reasonable belief that the advertisement or information had been approved or authorised is a defence. Once the information has been approved or authorised, no civil liability can arise with regard to any statement or omission in the information if taking the information and listing particulars together a person would not be likely to have been misled.[2]

1   FSMA 2000, s 98(1).
2   FSMA 2000, s 98(4).

FEES

18.45   Listing rules may require the payment of fees to the competent authority in respect of applications for listing and the continued inclusion of securities in the official lists.[1]

1   FSMA 2000, s 99.

PENALTIES

18.46   Additional provisions were added to the FSMA 2000 in connection with penalties. In determining its policy with regard to amount, the competent authority cannot have regard to anticipated costs in carrying out its functions under Part VI.[1] The penalty structure must be applied to benefit the issuers of securities admitted to the official list. Up-to-date information must also be set out in the scheme details issue by the authority.

1   FSMA 2000, s 100.

GENERAL PROVISIONS

18.47 The FSMA 2000 contains certain further general provisions in connection with the content of the listing rules.[1] The listing rules may make different provisions for different types of cases. Listing rules must be made by an instrument in writing. This must also be printed and made available to the public with or without payment. Listing rules may authorise the competent authority to dispense with or modify the application of the rules in particular cases and by reference to any particular circumstances.

1 FSMA 2000, s 101.

EXEMPTION FROM LIABILITY IN DAMAGES

18.48 The FSMA 2000 also contains a general exemption from liability and damages for the competent authority and its staff in connection with anything done or omitted in the discharge, or purported discharge, of the authority's functions under the Act.[1] This does not apply to acts of omissions shown to have been in bad faith or awards in connection with unlawful acts or omissions under s 6(1) of the Human Rights Act 1998.[2]

1 FSMA 2000, s 102(1).
2 FSMA 2000, s 102(2).

UKLA SOURCEBOOK

Background

LSE's Yellow Book

18.49 UK listing rules have traditionally been set out in the LSE's Yellow Book. The Council of the Stock Exchange had subsequently also sought to implement relevant European Directives through amendment to its own rules as set out in the Admission of Securities to Listing in 1984. These came into effect on 1 January 1985 under the 1984 Listing Regulations.[1]

The Yellow Book generally contains provisions concerning the conditions and applications for listing, content of listing particulars, rules as to publication and marketing, role of sponsors and listing agents and continuing obligations of issuers. The Yellow Book was re-issued in 1993 with effect from 1 December 1993. The Yellow Book was variously amended subsequently.

1 Stock Exchange (Listing) Regulations SI 1984/716.

18.50 Following the announcement that the FSA would assume responsibility for admission to listing, it was agreed that the LSE's Yellow Book would effectively also be transferred to the FSA. This would include those provisions not required under the European Directives or other UK legislative enactments.

The objective was to continue the operation of the existing standards, minimise duplication and ensure continuity insofar as possible, at least, in the short-term. Some minor consequential amendments were considered necessary.

These stand-alone FSA Listing Rules were to take effect from the date of transfer. Over time, it was intended that the Listing Rules would be integrated as a discrete sourcebook within the FSA Handbook.

18.51   Before the announcement of transfer of responsibility for admission to listing was made, the LSE had published, on 16 September 1999, a consultative document entitled 'Listing Rules 2000' setting out proposed amendments to its listing rules. These changes were subsequently finalised and came into effect in January 2000. Although the initial draft of the FSA Listing Rules did not contain these amendments, they were subsequently added.

18.52   As with earlier versions, the FSA Listing Rules apply to additional securities not set out in the European Directives or under the FSMA 2000.

Before the 1984 Listing Regulations[1] came into effect, the requirements of the Yellow Book applied to all securities listed. The listing also had no legislative basis although they still had some statutory effect with, for example, the then LSE being able to exempt certain companies from having to comply with the prospectus requirements set out in the Companies Act 1948.[2]

The November 1984 Yellow Book then contained separate provisions that gave effect to the requirements of the 1984 Listing Regulations and those that were simply imposed by the Council of the Stock Exchange without any statutory basis. When the 1984 Listing Regulations were replaced by the provisions set out in Part IV of the Financial Services Act 1986, they were only applied to the investments set out in Sch 1 to that Act.[3] This would then not include such other securities as those issued by overseas governments or local authorities admitted to listing in London. This was significant in that the Treasury could only issue directions to the LSE to the extent that it acted as competent authority under relevant EC provisions.[4]

1   SI 1984/716.
2   Companies Act 1948, ss 39 and 418.
3   Financial Services Act 1986, s 142(7).
4   Financial Services Act 1986, s 192.

18.53   While some confusion may also have arisen with regard to the extent of judicial review available in relation to securities which fell outside the scope of the Admissions Directive, it would appear that judicial review would apply generally in connection with any decisions taken by the competent authority for listing.

18.54   Although the listing rules are only defined as the requirements contained in the Yellow Book as from time to time amended by the UK Listing Authority (see definitions), they now give effect to:

(a)   requirements that are mandatory under the European Community Directive;
(b)   additional requirements of the UK Listing Authority under its powers as competent authority in relation to securities covered by Part VI of the FSMA 2000 (formerly Part IV of the Financial Services Act 1986); and
(c)   corresponding requirements in relation to other securities admitted to listing.

18.55   Applications for listing were processed through the LSE's Listing Department. This was transferred to the FSA with responsibility for admission to listing. This included the Listing Department's groups dealing with monitoring and enquiries, equity markets, capital markets and policy.

It was intended that the other advisory bodies to the UK Listing Authority (UKLA), the Listing Authority Advisory Committee (LAAC) and the Listing

Rules Committee (LRC) would continue in operation although they would subsequently report to the FSA.

18.56   The listing process now generally operates by the FSA considering applications for admission to listing with a view to determining whether all of the relevant conditions for listing (including any special conditions) have been complied with. Relevant listing particulars and other documents prescribed are examined and approved provided they satisfy all relevant requirements.

While further information may be requested in connection with matters set out in the particulars or supporting documents, the FSA is not responsible for the investigation or verification of the accuracy or completeness of the information provided. Primary responsibility for the accuracy of documents is stated to remain with the directors of an issuer.

FSA's UKLA Sourcebook

18.57   Listing is now regulated under the FSA's UKLA Sourcebook, which is included within Block 5 (Specialist soucebooks) of the FSA's Handbook of Rules and Guidance. The Sourcebook consists of (i) the revised edition of the Listing Rules[1] and (ii) the new UKLA Guidance Manual.[2]

The revised Listing Rules are amended to take into account changes required under the FSMA 2000 and came into effect on 1 December 2001. The Listing Rules consist of the chapters of the rules (1–21), the rules for approval of prospectuses where there is no application for listing and the schedules to the Listing Rules. The Combined Code is also attached as an appendix, although this is stated not to form part of the Listing Rules. Previous guidance issued in connection with listing has been incorporated into the UKLA Guidance Manual as well as the new guidance provided by the FSA as UKLA. Incorporated guidance includes the Price Sensitive Information (PSI) Guide which is now set out in Appendix 2 to the UKLA Guidance Manual.

1   See Table 18.1. See paras 18.61–18.102.
2   See Table 18.2. See paras 18.103–18.107.

18.58   The Listing Rules have to be complied with by issuers, sponsors, directors and former directors.[1] The UKLA Guidance also applies to persons whether or not they are subject to the Listing Rules.[2]

1   See Table 18.1.
2   UKLA Guidance Manual, para 1.1.1.

18.59   The revised Listing Rules contain 27 chapters (formerly 25) and 11 schedules (formerly 15). All market users are also subject to the Market Conduct sourcebook (MAR) of the Handbook which gives effect, in particular, to the market abuse provisions set out in Part XIII of the FSMA 2000.

18.60   Various statutory instruments have been adopted under the FSMA 2000. This includes prohibited securities under s 74(3),[1] persons responsible for listing particulars (s 79(3)), non-listing prospectuses (s 87(4)) and offers not to be treated as public offers (Sch 11). The Official Listing of Securities Transitional Provisions Order was made on 22 August 2001.[2] The provisions set out in the Public Offers of Securities Regulation 1995[3] are reapplied in

Table 18.1: Listing rules

Contents
Definitions
Chapters

1. Compliance with and enforcement of the Listing Rules
2. Sponsors
3. Conditions for listing
4. Methods of bringing securities to listing
5. Listing particulars
6. Contents of listing particulars
7. Listing application procedures
8. Publication and circulation of listing particulars
9. Continuing obligations
10. Transactions
11. Transactions with related parties
12. Financial information
13. Documents not requiring prior approval
14. Circulars
15. Purchase of own securities
16. Directors
17. Overseas companies
18. Property companies
19. Mineral companies
20. Scientific research based companies
21. Investment entities
22. Public sector issuers
23. Specialist securities (including eurobonds)
24. Miscellaneous securities
25. Innovative high growth companies
26. Venture capital trusts
27. Strategic investment companies

Rules for approval of prospectuses where no application for listing is made

Schedules

1A. Sponsor's confirmation of independence
2. Shareholder Statement
2A. Pricing Statement
3A. Application for admission of securities to the listing – shares and debts securities
3B. Application for admission of securities to the listing – specialist and miscellaneous securities
4A. Declaration by Sponsor
5. Block listing six monthly return
6. Declaration by Issuer
8. Specimen preamble for valuation report
9. Certificate from public sector issuer
10. Notification of major interests and shares
11. Notification of interests of directors and connected persons

The combined code

Source: FSA, UKLA Sourcebook (Re-issued Text).

Table 18.2: UK listing authority guidance manual

Contents
1.   Introduction
2.   Applications for listing
3.   Approval of non-routine circulars
4.   Sponsors
5.   Interpretation of listing rules and requests for individual guidance
6.   Dispensation or modification (variation) of the application of the listing rules, the Act or the POS Regs
7.   Information gathering and investigation powers
8.   Discipline of issuers, directors, former directors and sponsors for breaches of the listing rules
9.   Suspension and cancellation of the listing of securities
10.   Statutory notice decision-making : the RDC and executive procedures
11.   Interaction with the market abuse regime
12.   Fees
Appendices
1.   Mediation scheme for FSA disciplinary cases
2.   Price Sensitive Information Guide
3.   Continuing Obligations Guide
4.   UKLA Guidance Notes
Glossary of definitions applicable to UKLA guidance manual (excluding appendices)

Source: FSA, UKLA Sourcebook (Re-issued Text).

determining the timing and manner of publishing a non-listing prospectus for the purpose of s 87(3)(b) and (4) of the FSMA 2000.[4] Amendment regulations were also made to the Official Listing of Securities Regulations 2001.[5]

1   See Financial Services and Markets Act 2000 (Official Listing of Securities) Regulations 2001 (SI 2001/2956).
2   See Financial Services and Markets Act 2000 (Official Listing of Securities) (Transitional Provisions) Order 2001.
3   See Public Offers of Securities Regulations 1995 (SI 1995/1537).
4   See Financial Services and Markets Act 2000 (Offers of Securities) Order 2001, article 3.
5   See Financial Services and Markets Act 2000 (Official Listing of Securities) (amendment) Regulations 2001 (SI 2001/3439). For subsequent amendments see generally www.fsa.gov.uk/ ukla/.

UKLA LISTING RULES

18.61   The general provisions with regard to compliance and enforcement are set out in Chapter 1 to the Listing Rules. Information may be required in connection with applications, investor protector and compliance. Issuers must provide the UKLA without delay of all information and explanations reasonably required in deciding whether to grant an application for listing, all information considered appropriate to protect investors or ensure the smooth operation of the market and any other information or explanations necessary to confirm whether the listing rules have been complied with.[1]

The UKLA may refuse an application for listing where the applicant has not complied with the listing requirements or any special conditions imposed.[2] The application may also be refused where admission of the securities would be detrimental to the interests of investors.[3] Securities listed in other Member States may be refused listing where they have failed to comply with any relevant obligation in the home territory.[4]

Issuers may also be required to publish any such information as may be considered appropriate to protect investors or maintain the smooth operation of the market. If the issuer fails to comply, the information may be published by the UKLA directly after considering any representations made by the issuer.[5]

1 Listing Rules, rule 1.3.
2 Listing Rules, rule 1.4(c).
3 Listing Rules, rule 1.4(a).
4 Listing Rules, rule 1.4(b).
5 Listing Rules, rules 1.5 and 1.6.

18.62 The UKLA may appoint investigators into any breach of the listing rules or statutory offence and either impose a financial penalty or statement of censure. The penalty for censure may also be applied to any director knowingly concerned with the breach.[1] Behaviour in compliance with the listing rules will not amount to market abuse provided it is identified for this purpose.[2]

1 Listing Rules, rules 1.7, 1.8 and 1.9.
2 Listing Rules, rule 1.10.

18.63 The application of the Listing Rules may be dispensed with or modified as appropriate.[1] Issuers are required to notify the UKLA immediately of any matters material to the relevance or appropriateness of a variation and the UKLA may revoke or modify the variation as appropriate.[2] Guidance may be given in the form of information advice as considered appropriate in relation to the listing rules. The guidance may also be published.[3]

1 Listing Rules, rule 1.11.
2 Listing Rules, rules 1.12 and 1.13.
3 Listing Rules, rule 1.14.

18.64 Listing may be suspended where the smooth operation of the market is or may be temporarily jeopardised or where the protection of investors required the suspension.[1] This may be effected from such time as may be determined and in such circumstances as considered fit (whether or not at the request of the issuer or its agent). The issuer must still comply with all applicable listing rules unless otherwise agreed.[2] An issuer may request for its securities to be suspended with such request being confirmed in writing by it or its agent.[3] Conditions may be attached to the listing of the suspension.[4]

1 Listing Rules, rule 1.15.
2 Listing Rules, rule 1.16.
3 Listing Rules, rule 1.17.
4 Listing Rules, rule 1.18.

18.65 Listing may be cancelled where the UKLA is satisfied that there are special circumstances that preclude normal regular dealings.[1] The listing will also be cancelled where the security is no longer admitted to trading.[2] Where an issuer wishes a listing to be cancelled of its equity securities or preference shares, the Company Announcements Office must be notified and a circular sent to the holders of the securities providing, at least, 20 business days' notice of the cancellations.[3] Equivalent notification is required in connection with debt securities, securities granted a secondary listing or securities in respect of which application for admission to AIM will be made before the cancellation takes effect.[4] Notification is not required where equivalent notice has been provided in a takeover offer document or subsequent circular or equivalent circular has already been sent.[5]

1 Listing Rules, rule 1.19.
2 Listing Rules, rule 1.20.
3 Listing Rules, rule 1.21.
4 Listing Rules, rule 1.22.
5 Listing Rules, rule 1.23.

18.66 Documents may be sent, circulated or despatched in an electronic format or through the use of a designed website where this has been agreed between the issuer and holder.[1] Such documents must be made available during normal business hours for a period of not less than 21 days from the date of required communication on notification or until the conclusion of any general meeting to which the documents relate. The documents must also be provided in a printed form and free of charge in sufficient numbers to satisfy demand at the issuer's registered office and the offices of any paying agent.[2]

1 Listing Rules, rule 1.24.
2 Listing Rules, rule 1.25.

Sponsors

18.67 Provisions relating to the approval, function and appointment of sponsors are dealt with in Chapter 2 of the rules. A list of approved sponsors is to be maintained by the UKLA.[1] Sponsors must comply with a number of conditions set out in the Listing Rules. This includes being authorised under the FSMA 2000 or regulated by a designated professional body.

The sponsor must be a body corporate or partnership, have, at least, four eligible employees, satisfy the UKLA that it is competent to perform the services required and have paid the relevant fees.[2] Relevant employees must be employed at an appropriate level of seniority within the sponsor and have provided advice in connection with a significant transaction, at least, three times in the preceding 36 months and, at least, one in the preceding 12 months.[3]

1 Listing Rules, rule 2.2.
2 Listing Rules, rule 2.4.
3 Listing Rules, rule 2.5.

18.68 An issuer must have an appointed sponsor where it prepares a shelf document or makes an application for listing that requires the production of listing particulars or in relation to any transaction or matter a sponsor is required by the listing rules to report to the UKLA.[1]

Where the listing rules have been breached, the UKLA may require the issuer to appoint a sponsor to provide advice on application of the listing rules.[2] The resignation or dismissal of any sponsor must be notified to the UKLA in writing and copied to the sponsor. The reasons for any dismissal must also be provided.[3]

1 Listing Rules, rule 2.6.
2 Listing Rules, rule 2.7.
3 Listing Rules, rule 2.8.

18.69 The Listing Rules impose a number of obligations on sponsors. They must, in particular, satisfy themselves that to the best of their knowledge and belief, having made due and careful enquiry of the issuer and its advisers that the issue has satisfied all applicable conditions for listing and other relevant requirements of the listing rules where listing particulars are to be provided.[1]

With regard to any application for listing requiring the production of listing particulars, the sponsor must complete the required declaration[2] confirming that it has performed all relevant services to the best of its knowledge and belief. This applies with regard to all requirements imposed under Chapter 2 of the listing rules.[3]

A confirmation of independence must be submitted to the UKLA in connection with each transaction it acts as sponsor (in the forms set out in Sch 1A). Sponsors must not provide services or sponsor for any issuer with which it is not independent except with permission.[4] Directors must be advised of the nature of their responsibilities and obligations as directors of listed companies[5] which also applies to any new directors requested by the UKLA.[6] The sponsor must obtain written confirmation for the issuer that the directors have established appropriate procedures to provide a reasonable basis for them to make proper judgments as the financial position and prospects of the issuer and its group and be satisfied that this confirmation has been given after due and careful enquiry.[7] Similar provisions apply with regard to accountants' report, working capital, profit forecasts and financial information.[8]

The sponsor must also communicate and lodge all supporting documents with the Authority, seek approval of any shelf documents and listing particulars and discharge any of the other functions listed in the appendix to Chapter 2 to the extent relevant.[9]

1 Listing Rules, rule 2.9(a).
2 Listing Rules, Sch 4A.
3 Listing Rules, rule 2.12.
4 Listing Rules, rule 2.11.
5 Listing Rules, rule 2.13.
6 Listing Rules, rule 2.14.
7 Listing Rules, rule 2.15.
8 Listing Rules, rules 2.15–2.20.
9 Listing Rules, rule 2.21.

Conditions for listing

18.70 The main conditions for listing are set out in Chapter 3 of the rules. Additional conditions are set out in Chapters 17–26 with regard to overseas companies, property companies, mineral companies, scientific research based companies, investment entities, public sector issuers, issuers of specialist securities and miscellaneous securities, innovative high-grow companies and venture capital trusts.

18.71 The UKLA may make the admission of securities to listing subject to any special condition considered appropriate in the interests of protecting investors and of which the applicant is notified.[1] A number of general conditions are imposed on applicants. These relate to:[2]

(a) *Incorporation:* The applicant must be duly incorporated or otherwise validly established and operate in accordance with its memorandum and articles of association or equivalent constitutional document.
(b) *Accounts:* At least three years' consolidated accounts must be published.
(c) *Nature and duration of business activities.*
(d) *Directors:* Directors and senior management must have appropriate expertise and experience for the management of the group's businesses.
(e) *Working capital:* A working capital statement must be provided in appropriate cases.
(f) *Controlling shareholders:* Companies must be capable at all times of carrying on their businesses independently of any controlling shareholders.

1 Listing Rules, rule 3.1.
2 Listing Rules, rules 3.2–3.13.

18.72 Further conditions are applied with regard to the securities to be listed. These generally relate to validity, admission to trading, transferability, market capitalisation, public holding, whole class being listed, limits on warrants or options and convertible securities and be capable of settlement.[1]

Non-cash payments must be disclosed and not undermine the independence of any director, officer or adviser.[2] Applications to list certificates representing shares will be treated as applications for listing with the issuer being considered the applicant for the purposes of the Listing Rules.[3]

1 Listing Rules, rules 3.14–3.28.
2 Listing Rules, rule 3.29.
3 Listing Rules, rule 3.31.

Listing methods

18.73 Securities may be brought to listing in a number of ways. The options available are set out in Chapter 4 to the Listing Rules.

Where equity shares have not already been issued, securities may be brought to listing through either an offer for sale, an offer for subscription, a placing, an intermediaries offer, an introduction or any other method accepted by the UKLA.[1]

Where shares have already been listed, the applicant may also use a rights issue, an open offer, an acquisition or merger issue, a vendor consideration placing, a capitalisation or bonus issue (in lieu in dividend or otherwise), an issue for cash, conversion of securities into another class, an exercise of options or warrants to subscribe or any method as may be agreed.[2]

1 Listing Rules, rule 2.4.
2 Listing Rules, rule 4.1.

18.74 An *offer for sale* is an invitation to the public by or on behalf of a third party to purchase securities of the issuer already in issue or allotted.[1] An *offer for subscription* is an invitation to subscribe for securities not yet in issue or allotted.[2]

A *placing* is a marketing of securities already in issue but not listed or not yet in issue to specify persons or clients of the sponsor or any securities house assisting in the placing which does not involve an offer to the public or to existing holders of the issuer's securities generally.[3]

An *intermediaries offer* is a marketing of securities already or not yet in issue through and by or on behalf of the issuer to intermediaries for them to allocate to their own clients.[4]

An *introduction* involves bringing securities to listing without involving an issue of new securities or any marketing of existing securities as the securities are already widely held by the public.[5]

1 Listing Rules, rule 4.4.
2 Listing Rules, rule 4.5.
3 Listing Rules, rule 4.7.
4 Listing Rules, rule 4.10.
5 Listing Rules, rule 4.12.

18.75 A *rights issue* is an offer to existing holders of securities to subscribe or purchase further securities in proportion to their holdings made by means of the issue of a renounceable letter (or other negotiable document) which may be traded (as 'nil paid' rights) for a period before payment for the securities is due.[1]

An *open offer* is an invitation to existing holders of securities to subscribe or purchase in proportion to their holdings provided this is not made by means of a renounceable letter or other negotiable document.[2] Further rules apply with regard to the content, timetable and communication of the open offer.[3]

An *acquisition or merger issue* (or *vendor consideration issue*) is an issue of securities in consideration for an acquisition of assets or an acquisition of or merger with another company as consideration for the securities of that company.[4] No marketing of any securities is permitted during the offer period as defined in the City Code.[5]

1 Listing Rules, rule 4.16.
2 Listing Rules, rule 4.22.
3 Listing Rules, rules 4.23–4.26.
4 Listing Rules, rule 4.27.
5 Listing Rules, rule 4.18.

18.76 A *vendor consideration placing* is a marketing by or on behalf of vendors of securities that have been allotted as consideration for an acquisition.[1] A *capitalisation issue* (or *bonus issue*) in lieu of dividend or otherwise is an issue to existing holders of securities (in portion to their holdings) of further shares credited as fully paid out of the issuer's reserves.[2]

An *issue for cash* is an issue of securities to person who are specifically approved by shareholders in general meeting or an issue pursuant to a general disapplication of s 89 of the Companies Act 1985 approved by shareholders in general meeting.[3] Where the issue is to persons specifically approved by shareholders, it will not be regarded as a placing if the subscribers are limited in number and expressly named in the circular.

1 Listing Rules, rule 4.29.
2 Listing Rules, rule 4.31.
3 Listing Rules, rule 4.33.

18.77 Advisers and intermediaries are required to notify the Company Announcements Office where they become interested in 3% or more of any class of equity shares being marketed by a new applicant. This applies in any offer for sale, offer for subscription, placing or intermediaries offer. Notification must be made before admission of the securities is expected to become effective.

An adviser or intermediary is interested in equity shares held by market makers in the group of companies to which it belongs but is not interested in any securities held on behalf of *bona fide* clients by any company in the group to which it belongs. The shares marketed are to be treated as having already been issued in calculating the relevant percentages.[1]

1 Listing Rules, rule 4.38.

Listing particulars

18.78 The requirements with regard to listing particulars are set out in Chapter 5 of the Listing Rules. This applies to prospectuses, listing particulars, equivalent offering documents, exempt listing documents and certain other similar documents as well as shelf registration. The requirements are subject to the further general duty to disclose set out in s 80 of the FSMA 2000.

18.79 A prospectus prepared in accordance with Chapter 5 must be submitted for approval by the UKLA whenever an issuer applies for listing of its securities to be offered to the public in the UK.[1] Where the issuer applies for listing in any other cases, listing particular or a prospectus must be submitted.[2]

The requirements with regard to the content of a prospectus, submission and approval procedures and publication are the same as for listing particulars.[3] The prospectus or listing particulars is to be published in accordance with Chapter 8.[4]

1 Listing Rules, rule 5.1(a).
2 Listing Rules, rule 5.1(b).
3 Listing Rules, rule 5.1(d).
4 Listing Rules, rule 5.1(c).

18.80 The listing particulars and any supplementary listing particulars must include a responsibility statement.[1] (The form of the responsibility statement is set out in paras 6.A3 or 6.H3.) The listing particulars must contain the information specified in Chapter 6, any special issue information[2] and any additional information as the UKLA may require as appropriate in any particular case.[3]

1 Listing Rules, rule 5.2.
2 Listing Rules, Chapters 18–26.
3 Listing Rules, rule 5.6.

18.81 The procedures for the approval of listing particulars are set out in the Listing Rules.

Three copies of the documents listed are to be submitted in draft form, at least 10 business days in advance of any intended publication date. The documents include the listing particulars and any cover (although this is not part of the particulars), application forms to purchase or subscribe shares, formal notices or offer notices, mini-prospectuses, summary particulars, advertisement documents, accountants' reports, sponsor's working capital letter, directors' letter, non-applicable letter, omission of information letter, omission of material contract from display letter and any additional letters or statements provided for under the listing rules.[1] Original drafts must be annotated to indicate where paragraphs required by the chapter appendices have been included.[2]

All particulars must be formally approved by the UKLA before publication.[3] Approval will only be given where the information in the particulars is considered to be complete. This requires submission of many of the draft documents listed in a final form before approval will be given.

Supplementary listing particulars must be approved where there has been any significant change affecting any matter contained in the particulars or a significant new matter has arisen, the inclusion of information in respect of which would have been required in the original particulars.[4] 'Significant' means necessary to make an informed assessment of the assets and liabilities, financial position, profits and losses and prospects of the issuer of the securities and the rights attaching to the securities.[5] The UKLA may approve the omission of certain information from the particulars.[6]

1 Listing Rules, rule 5.9.
2 Listing Rules, rule 5.11.
3 Listing Rules, rule 5.12.
4 Listing Rules, rule 5.14.
5 Listing Rules, rule 5.16 and FSMA 2000, s 80(1).
6 Listing Rules, rules 5.17–5.22.

18.82 An abbreviated prospectus may be used where the issuer has already published a full prospectus in the UK in respect of different securities (whether or not of the same class) within the proceeding 23 months of the second offer date.[1]

Issuers may be exempt from the obligation to publish listing particulars in certain other cases. These include where the securities have already been subject to a public issue, are issued in connection with a takeover offer or merger. A 'relevant document' must also have been published in the UK within the previous 12 months containing equivalent information to that required to be included in the listing particulars.[2]

Securities may also have been listed in another Member State for not less than three months and the competent authorities of that territory have confirmed that the issuer complied with the requirements concerning information and admission to listing imposed by all relevant European Directives.[3]

The issuer's shares may also have been traded on the AIM for, at least, two years and equivalent information is already available to that required by the Consolidated Admission and Reporting Directive.[4]

Certain further issues will not require listing particulars.[5] Separate circulars are to be used in connection with warrants and options.[6] Separate summary particulars may also be used[7] with separate provisions applying to certificates representing shares[8] and shelf registrations.[9]

1 Listing Rules, rule 5.23.
2 Listing Rules, rule 5.23A(a).
3 Listing Rules, rule 5.23A(b).
4 Listing Rules, rule 5.23A(c).
5 Listing Rules, rules 5.27–5.30.
6 Listing Rules, rules 5.31–5.31A.
7 Listing Rules, rules 5.32 and 5.44.
8 Listing Rules, rule 5.34.
9 Listing Rules, rules 5.35–5.41.

CONTENTS OF LISTING PARTICULARS

18.83 Listing particulars are required to contain a number of specified items of information which will vary depending upon the nature and circumstances of the issuer and type of security concerned. Listing particulars for admission of shares to convertible debt securities to listing must contain the information set out in paras 6.A1 to 6.G2 (para 6.A). This concerns the persons responsible for listing particulars, auditors and other advisers, the shares for which application is made, the issue and its capital, group activities, issuer assets and liabilities, financial position and profits and losses, management and recent development and prospects of the group. A number of requirements are imposed under each of these subheadings.

18.84   Listing particulars for the admission of debt securities must contain the information set out in paras 6.H1 to 6.N2.[1] Paras 6.H to 6.N generally correspond with the requirements set out in paras 6.A to 6.G with certain amendments. The information required for the admission of securities representing shares to listing is set out 6.O (general information about the issuer) and 6.P (information about the certificates).

1   Para 6.H.

Listing application procedures

18.85   An issuer is required to comply with certain procedures in making an application for listing for securities.[1] Additional requirements are imposed with regard to public sector issuers and issuers of specialist securities and miscellaneous securities.[2] Applications for admission to listing are considered on business days between 9.00 and 17.30.

Admission of any securities only becomes effective when the decision of the UKLA to admit the securities has been announced either by electronic means or posted on a notice-board designated by the Authority where the relevant electronic systems are not available.[3]

Securities will generally not be admitted until each of the 48-hour documents have been submitted other than in exceptional circumstances.[4]

1   Listing Rules, Chapter 7.
2   Listing Rules, Chapters 22, 23 and 24.
3   Para 7.1.
4   Para 7.2.

18.86   The '48-hour' documents must be lodged in final form with the UKLA (marked for the attention of Listing Applications) no later than midday, at least two business days prior to the consideration of the application for admission.

The documents to be submitted include the application form, listing particulars (or equivalent document), copy advertisements, board resolution, additional documents for new applicants (including copy of certificate of incorporation or equivalent document and declaration of any corporate shareholding holding 5% or more of issued shares), trust deed letter of compliance, bearer securities (if relevant), sponsor's and authorised adviser's deferred settlement letter and application for admission to trading.[1]

Special dispensations may apply with regard to allotment resolutions. If the board resolution is not available for lodging, at least, two business days prior to the application, separate written confirmation may be provided (including by fax) that the securities have been allotted no later than one hour ahead of the admission to listing becoming effective.[2] The copy resolution must also be lodged in such cases no later than three business days after admission becomes effective. Other items may be lodged on the day of consideration of the application for admission. These relate to payment of listing fees, a letter of confirmation that securities will not be issued prior to admission and a shareholder or pricing statement in the appropriate form.[3]

1   Para 7.5.
2   Para 7.6.
3   Schs 2 and 2A.

18.87   Further documents are to be lodged as soon as practicable after the application and within, at least, five business days. These generally relate to additional information required in connection with special issues such as an intermediaries offer or an introduction. Confirmation is also required of the number of securities issued, a request for disbursement of listing fees or declaration from security printers with regard to bearer documents of title.[1]

Certain additional documents may also be required.[2] These include any agreement to acquire any assets, business or shares in consideration for which the securities are issued, any letter, report, valuation, contract or other documents referred to in the listing particulars, copy of the issuer's memorandum and articles of association, the annual report and accounts of the issuer and of any guarantor, any interim accounts, the executed the trust deed (with regard to debt securities), copy of temporary and definitive document or title, a copy of the scheme document (in relation to employee's share schemes) and copy of any relevant court order and certificate of registration issued by the Registrar of Companies (where court approval is required). Such documents are to be submitted not less than seven days.

Issuers may also apply to use a simplified application procedure (a formal application) or apply for a number of securities to be issued (a block listing). Simplified documentation and approval procedures apply in such cases.[3]

1   Para 7.8.
2   Para 7.9.
3   Paras 7.10–7.13.

Publication and circulation

18.88   Listing particulars and supplementary particulars must not be published, advertised or circulated until they have been formally approved.[1] They must also not be circulated or made publicly available unless published in accordance with the provisions set out in Chapter 8 of the Listing Rules.[2] Draft listing particulars may be circulated without approval to arrange a placing, a syndication or underwriting or to market an intermediaries offer where they are clearly marked as such.[3]

Listing particulars and shelf documents are generally to be published by making them available for public inspection at the Document Viewing Facility at the UKLA. They must also be made available in printed form, free of charge and in sufficient numbers to satisfy public demand at the issuer's registered office in the UK (if any) and the paying agent to the extent relevant.[4] Listing particulars must be available during normal business hours for, at least, 14 days from advertisement, despatch or listing became effective.[5]

A formal notice must be inserted in, at least, one national newspaper no later than the next business day following publication of the listing particulars unless the securities are of a class already listed.[6] An offer notice, mini-prospectus or full listing particulars may alternatively be published in a national newspaper in relation to an offer for sale or subscription.

Listing particulars must also be published, at least, two business days prior to the expected date of consideration of the application for admission to listing except in specified cases. Special provisions apply with regard to the definition of a formal notice, offer notice and mini-prospectus.[8] Further rules apply with regard to circulation,[9] supplementary listing particulars,[10] available documents[11] and approval and authorisation of advertisements.[12]

1   Para 8.1.
2   Para 8.2.
3   Para 8.3.
4   Para 8.4(a) and (b).
5   Para 8.5.
6   Para 8.7.
7   Para 8.8.
8   Paras 8.10–8.13.
9   Paras 8.14–8.19.
10 Para 8.20.
11 Paras 8.21 and 8.22.
12 Paras 8.23–8.27.

Continuing obligations

18.89   A number of continuing obligations are imposed under the Listing Rules. These are generally set out in Chapter 9 although further requirements apply with regard to transactions (Chapter 10), transactions with related parties (Chapter 11), financial information (Chapter 12), documents not requiring prior approval (Chapter 13), circulars (Chapter 14), purchase of own securities (Chapter 15) and directors (Chapter 16).

Compliance with these continuing obligations is considered essential to the maintenance of an orderly market in the securities and to ensure that all users of the market have simultaneous access to the same information. Failure to comply will result in action by the UKLA.

NOTIFICATION

18.90   Companies are subject to a number of general notification obligations. Companies must notify the Company Announcements Office without delay of any major new developments in its area of activity that are not public knowledge and which may lead to substantial movements in the price of its listed securities or effect its ability to meet its commitments.[1] Companies must notify of any relevant information that is not public knowledge concerning a change in its financial condition, performance of its business or expectation as to performance if this may lead to a substantial movement in the price of its securities.[2] These obligations are in addition to any specific requirements imposed under the listing rules.[3] The company must take all reasonable care to ensure that any statement or forecast or any other information notified to the Company Announcements Office or made available through the UKLA is not misleading, false or deceptive and does not omit anything likely to effect the import of such statement, forecast or information.[4]

Companies are not required to notify in connection with developments or matters in course of negotiation. Such information may also be released to advisers, counterparties, employees or trade unions and official bodies although any breach in such confidence must be notified immediately.[5]

Information that is required to be notified to the Company Announcements Office must not be given to anyone else before it has been properly notified except in connection with negotiation matters.[6] Information to be announced at a shareholders' meeting must be simultaneously published through the Company Announcements Office.[7] Companies may apply for dispensations from the general duties to notify where this is considered in the company's legitimate interests.[8] Where information is to be made available in the UK, equivalent information must also be provided in any overseas stock market where the securities are also listed.[9]

1 Para 9.1.
2 Para 9.2.
3 Para 9.3.
4 Para 9.3A.
5 Paras 9.4 and 9.5.
6 Para 9.6.
7 Para 9.7.
8 Para 9.8.
9 Para 9.9.

18.91   Further specific notification requirements apply with regard to capital arrangements. These include alterations to capital structure, new issues of debt securities, changes of rights attaching to securities, redemption or drawing, basis of allotment, temporary documents of title, issues affecting conversion rights and results of new securities.[1]

A company must also notify the Company Announcements Office of any information disclosed to it in accordance with ss 198–208 of the Companies Act 1985 (obligation to disclose certain major interests in the share capital of a company). Notification must also be made of any information obtained under s 212 of the Companies Act 1985 (persons interested in shares) or otherwise where it has become apparent that an interest exists or has been increased or reduced or has ceased to exist and this should have been disclosed under ss 198–208.[2]

Where information is to be notified to the Company Announcements Office when it is not open for business, the issuer must ensure that the information is disseminated through, at least, two national newspapers and two newswire services in the UK. The information must also be notified to the Company Announcements Office as soon as it re-opens.[3]

1 Para 9.10.
2 Paras 9.11 and 9.12.
3 Para 9.15.

HOLDERS OF SECURITIES AND SHAREHOLDERS

18.92   Separate obligations are imposed on companies with regard to holders of securities and shareholders. Companies are under a general duty to ensure equality of treatment between holders of shares and debt securities.[1]

Further provisions apply with regard to: pre-emption rights,[2] disapplication of pre-emption rights,[3] holding company participation[4] and issues by major subsidiary undertakings.[5]

Further rules apply with regard to communications with shareholders. These include making prescribed information available to all shareholders[6], registrar and paying agents,[7] proxy forms,[8] other classes of security,[9] holders or bearer securities,[10] use of airmail and first-class mail[11] and copies of circulars and resolutions.[12]

Certain further miscellaneous obligations are also imposed with regard to further issues,[13] controlling shareholders,[14] board decisions,[15] shares in public hands,[16] restriction on dealings,[17] settlement arrangements,[18] change of name,[19] sub-underwriting disclosure,[20] sanctions[21] and admission to trading.[22] An adjusted set of obligations are imposed on companies without listed equity securities or only listed debt securities.[23]

Equivalent adjustments also apply with regard to fixed income shares.[24] The issuer of the shares is also required to comply with the same continuing obligations in connection with certificates representing shares.[25]

1 Paras 9.16 and 9.17.
2 Paras 9.18 and 9.19.
3 Para 9.20.
4 Para 9.21.
5 Paras 9.22 and 9.23.
6 Para 9.24.
7 Para 9.25.
8 Para 9.26.
9 Para 9.27.
10 Para 9.28.
11 Paras 9.29 and 9.30.
12 Para 9.31.
13 Para 9.33.
14 Para 9.34.
15 Para 9.35.
16 Para 9.37.
17 Para 9.38.
18 Para 9.39.
19 Para 9.40.
20 Paras 9.41 and 9.42.
21 Para 9.43.
22 Paras 9.44 and 9.44A.
23 Paras 9.45 and 9.46.
24 Para 9.47.
25 Para 9.48.

Transactions

18.93 Transactions conducted by listed companies especially with regard to accusations and disposals are classified under the listing rules. The requirements are generally concerned with the imposition of additional notification obligations to the Company Announcements Office and circulars. Specific requirements are imposed in connection with announcements and circular and shareholder approval. Further specific requirements are then imposed with regard to takeovers and mergers.

Listed companies are required to consider the classification of any transactions conducted.[1] Classification is conducted by an assessment of its relative size. Transactions are generally classified as class 1 where the percentage ratio (as defined) is 25% or more, class 2 is 5% or more (but less than 25%) and class 3 of less than 5%.[2] The percentage ratios relate to assets, profits, turnover, market capitalisation and gross capital.[3] Separate requirements are then imposed depending upon the classification.[4]

Separate rules also apply in connection with reverse takeovers.[5] Further rules are imposed on the contents of Class 1 circulars[6] and in connection with takeovers and mergers.[7]

1 Para 10.2.
2 Para 10.4.
3 Paras 10.5–10.28.
4 Paras 10.29–10.38.
5 Para 10.39.
6 Para 10.40.
7 Paras 10.45–10.50.

TRANSACTIONS WITH RELATED PARTIES

18.94 A number of safeguards are provided for against current or recent directors or substantial shareholders (or associates) taking advantage of their positions. Where any transaction is proposed between a listed company (or any of its subsidiary undertakings) and a related party as defined, a circular and prior approval of the company in general meeting is generally required.[1] The related party will not be permitted to vote at such meetings.[2] Specific requirements are imposed on the contents of relevant circulars. The objective is to ensure that shareholders have sufficient information to enable them to evaluate the effects of the transaction.

Where a company is uncertain as to whether the transactions with related parties rules apply, it should consult with the UKLA.[4]

1 Para 11.4.
2 Para 11.5.
3 Para 10.10.
4 Para 11.3.

Financial information

18.95 Certain financial information is to be included in listing particulars and circulars. The nature of the information to be provided is developed in Chapter 12 of the Listing Rules. This also imposes certain continuing obligations with regard to certain financial matters. Chapter 12 is generally concerned with comparative table and accountants' reports,[1] profit forecasts and estimates,[2] pro-forma financial information,[3] financial information outside comparative tables or accountants' reports,[4] preliminary statements of annual results and dividends,[5] annual reports and accounts,[6] corporate governance and directors, remuneration,[7] summary financial statements,[8] half yearly reports[9] and change of accounting reference dates.[10]

1 Paras 12.1–12.20.
2 Paras 12.21–12.27.
3 Paras 12.28–12.26.
4 Paras 12.37–12.39.
5 Para 12.40.
6 Paras 12.41–12.43.
7 Paras 12.43A–12.44.
8 Para 12.45.
9 Paras 12.46–12.59.
10 Para 12.60.

Documents not requiring prior approval

18.96 Certain documents do not have to be submitted to the UKLA for approval. Such documents must comply with the requirements set out in Chapter 13 of the Listing Rules. A letter of compliance will generally be required for certain documents from the company's legal or other advisers. The company is generally otherwise required to ensure compliance. The UKLA should be consulted where any uncertainties arise or unusual features are involved.

18.97 Chapter 13 generally applies to memoranda and articles of association, trust deeds, employees' share schemes (as well as long-term incentive schemes and discounted option arrangements), temporary documents of title (including renounceable documents), definitive documents of title (including bearer securities), proxy forms and certain circulars.[1] Specific conditions apply with regard to the content of each.[2] The relevant conditions are developed in the appendices to the chapter.

1 Para 13.1.
2 Paras 13.8–13.32.

Circulars

18.98   The listing rules impose a number of general requirements with regard to all circulars sent by a company to holders of listed securities. Any circular must provide a clear and adequate explanation of its subject matter and allow an informed decision to be taken with regard to any rights to be exercised.[1]

Circulars must generally be approved by the UKLA before being circulated or made publicly available.[2] Approval will not normally be granted until a number of final documents have been submitted. Two copies of any circular in its final form must also be lodged at the same time as it is despatched to shareholders.[3]

Circulars of a routine nature will not require approval provided they comply with the general information and disclosure obligations imposed as well as further specific provisions depending upon the particular circular concerned.[4] These include:

— authority to allot shares (para 14.7);
— disapplication of pre-emption rights (para 14.8);
— increase in authorised share capital (para 14.9);
— reduction of capital (para 14.10);
— capitalisation issues (paras 14.11 and 14.11A);
— scrip dividends (paras 14.12 to 14.15A);
— purchase of own securities (para 14.16);
— notices of meetings (paras 14.17–14.19);
— chapter 13 circulars (para 14.21);
— early redemption (paras 14.22–14.24); and
— conversion rights reminders (paras 14.25–14.26).

1 Para 14.1(a) and (b).
2 Para 14.2.
3 Para 14.4.
4 Paras 14.5 and 14.7–14.26.

Purchase of own securities

18.99   Chapter 15 of the Listing Rules sets out the provisions that apply to a company wishing to purchase its own listed securities. This applies whether it is a market purchase or an off-market purchase (within s 163 of the Companies Act 1985). The requirements generally relate to the notification of proposed and actual purchases.

Directors

18.100   A number of obligations are imposed on issuers relating to directors (Chapter 16 of the Listing Rules). These include disclosure rules and dealings in securities by directors or connected persons. Directors may be personally responsible for information contained in listing particulars or supplementary listing particulars under the FSMA 2000 and the Financial Services and Markets Act 2000 (Official Listing of Securities) Regulations 2001.[1]

Directors are also required under the listing rules to accept responsibility for the information to be included in listing particulars[2] and to provide an assurance of compliance under para 5.5.[3] A listed company must ensure that its directors accept full responsibility, collectively and individually, for the company's compliance with the listing rules.[4]

Issuers must include the details about each of its directors and, where relevant, members of its senior management in any listing particulars published.[5] Information of all directorships held by each director must also be notified through the Company Announcements Office.[6] Any changes to the board must also be notified[7] and copies of each director's service contract being made available for inspection at the registered office and at the place of the annual general meeting for, at least, 15 minutes prior to and during the meeting.[8]

All interests of directors and connected persons must be notified to the Company Announcements Office[9] and the company require that its directors and any employees or directors of a connected company likely to be in the possession of unpublished price-sensitive information comply with the Model Code or an equivalent code.[10] The company must take all proper and reasonable steps to secure compliance with the Model Code.

Companies may also wish to impose more severe restrictions on dealings by directors and employees as required.[11]

1 SI 2001/2958. Para 16.1.
2 Para 5.2.
3 Para 16.1.
4 Para 16.2.
5 Para 16.3.
6 Para 16.4.
7 Para 16.7.
8 Para 16.9.
9 Paras 16.13–16.17.
10 Para 16.18.
11 Para 16.9.

18.101 The Model Code is attached as the appendix to Chapter 16. This notes that the freedom of directors and certain employees of listed companies to deal in their company's securities is restricted in a number of ways including by statute, common law and the listing rules. The Model Code imposes restrictions beyond those required by law. Its purpose is to ensure that directors, certain employees and connected persons do not abuse or place themselves under suspicion of abusing price-sensitive information that they have especially during periods leading up to results announcements.

Following the definitions section,[1] the Model Code imposes restrictions on dealings by directors and relevant employees. A director must not deal in any securities of the listed company on considerations of a short-term nature and take reasonable steps to prevent any dealings by or on behalf of any person connected with him in any securities of the listed company of a short-term nature.[2]

Directors must not deal in securities during a 'close period' as defined.[3] This includes the period of two months immediately preceding the preliminary announcement of the company's annual results or the period from the relevant financial year end up to and including the announcement.

A director must not deal in any securities of a listed company at any time when he is in possession of unpublished price-sensitive information in relation to those securities or otherwise where clearance to deal has not been provided under the Code.[4]

A director must not deal in any securities without advising the chairman (or one or more designated directors) in advance and without receiving clearance.[5]

Clearance must not be given for any director to deal during a 'prohibited period'.[6] A 'prohibited period' includes any close period and the period during which an announcement is to follow with regard to which the unpublished price-sensitive information relates or the dealing would otherwise be in breach of the Code. A written record must be maintained of any advice received from a director and of the clearance given.[7] Dealings may be permitted in exceptional circumstances.[8]

Separate provisions apply with regard to dealings by connected persons and investment managers.[9] Separate provision is included with regard to such special circumstances as awards of securities and options,[10] the exercise of options,[11] qualification shares[12] and savings schemes.[13] Certain other defined dealings are excluded.[14]

All relevant employees (as defined) must comply with the terms of the Model Code.[15]

1　Para 1.
2　Para 2.
3　Para 3.
4　Para 4.
5　Para 6.
6　Para 7.
7　Para 8.
8　Para 9.
9　Paras 11 and 12.
10　Paras 13, 13A and 13B.
11　Paras 14 and 15.
12　Para 16.
13　Paras 17–18.
14　Para 19.
15　Para 21.

Prospectuses where no application for listing is made

18.102　The listing rules may, under s 87 of the FSMA 2000, make provisions for the submission and approval by the UKLA of a prospectus where no application for listing is made. The relevant rules are set out as a pre-schedule appendix to the Listing Rules.

The rules apply where a prospectus is to be published in relation to securities which are to be offered to the public in the UK for the first time and in respect of which no application for admission to listing has been made and to securities to be offered to the public or admitted to listing in another Member State simultaneously or within a short period from the UK offer.[1]

Where the rules apply, the prospectus may be submitted by the issuer or by the offerer with the consent of the issuer for approval by the UKLA. The prospectus must comply with these rules with regard to the content and submission and approval procedures as well as requirements with regard to publication.[2]

The rules then revise the application of the listing rules with regard to such prospectuses. This includes submission and approval of prospectus requirements,[3] publication[4] and appeals.[5] A number of the specific amendments to be application of the listing rules are set out in the appendix.

1　Para 1(a) and (b).

2   Para 2.
3   Paras 4–11.
4   Paras 12–17.
5   Para 18.

UKLA GUIDANCE MANUAL

18.103   In addition to the Listing Rules, the UKLA Sourcebook includes the UKLA Guidance Manual.[1] This provides guidance on the exercise by the FSA of its functions with regard to listing under the FSMA 2000 and with regard to the application of the relevant provisions contained in the listing rules.

Where the FSA exercises its general functions in a capacity other than as competent authority for listing, it must have regard to the matters and objectives set out in s 2 of the FSMA 2000 (its general duties). These are disapplied with regard to its acting as UKLA but only in exercise of its general functions under Sch 7 to the FSMA 2000.

The FSA may seek to exercise its powers under the FSMA 2000 (outside Part VI) with regard to issuers, directors (former directors) or sponsors. Guidance on the application of non-listing powers are contained in the other sectors of the Handbook of Rules and Guidance.

1   See Table 18.2 above.

18.104   The functions of the UKLA are to make rules under Part VI of the FSMA 2000, to provide general guidance with regard to Part VI and to determine the general policy and principles by reference to which it will perform its functions under Part VI.[1]

In exercising its general functions as competent authority, the FSA has to have regard to the principles of good regulation other than management responsibility.[2] The FSA must also agree objectives with the Treasury each year in connection with its functions as UKLA. These are publicly available on the Treasury and FSA websites.

The regulatory objectives of the FSA as UKLA are to formulate and enforce listing rules that provide an appropriate level of protection for investors in listed securities, facilitate access to listed markets for a broad range of enterprises and seek to maintain the integrity and competitiveness of UK markets for listed securities.[3]

The FSA and Treasury will also agree operational objectives each year that are more task specific.[4]

1   FSMA 2000, s 73(2).
2   FSMA 2000, s 73(1) and 2(3).
3   Para 1.3.7.
4   Para 1.3.8.

18.105   The UKLA Guidance Manual also sets out a number of aims that the FSA has to comply with.[1] Issuers should be provided with ready access to the listed market for their securities while protecting investors. Investor confidence should be promoted in standards of disclosure, in the conduct of issuers' affairs and in the market as a whole under the listing rules and, in particular, the continuing obligations regime. Listed securities should be brought to the market in a way appropriate to the nature and number and which will facilitate an open and efficient market for trading in those securities. An issuer must make full and timely disclosure concerning itself and its listed securities at the time of listing and subsequently. Holders of listed equity securities must also be given adequate opportunity to consider in advance and vote upon major changes in the company's business operations and matters of importance concerning the company's management and constitution.

1   Para 1.3.9.

18.106   The functions of the FSA as UKLA under the FSMA 2000 are to consider applications for listing, cancel and suspend listing, approve listing particulars, prospectuses and other documents, approve sponsors and regulate sponsors with regard to the application of the listing rules, investigate breaches of the listing rules and certain offences under the 2000 Act, impose financial penalties and censure statements on issuers, directors and former directors as well as sponsors for breaches of the listing rules, make rules under Part VI and provide general guidance with regard to Part VI.[1]

1   Para 1.3.10.

18.107   The purpose of the UKLA Guidance Manual is to provide guidance relating to the FSA's discharge of these functions in its capacity as UKLA. The Guidance Manual deals with the following:

(1)   introduction, framework and structures (Chapter 1);
(2)   applications for listing including the timing and procedures governing the submission of listing particulars, prospectuses and other documents (Chapter 1);
(3)   procedures on the approval of non-routine circulars including the timing and submission of relevant documents for approval (Chapter 3);
(4)   procedures for applying to act as a sponsor and continuing requirements (Chapter 4);
(5)   interpretation of the listing rules and individual guidance procedures (Chapter 5);
(6)   approach to variations of the listing rules, the Act or the POS regulations including how applications for variation should be made (Chapter 6);
(7)   information gathering and investigation powers under the listing rules and the 2000 Act (Chapter 7);
(8)   private warnings and criteria used in deciding whether to take disciplinary action against issuers, directors or former directors and sponsors as well as power to impose public censures and impose financial penalties (Chapter 8);
(9)   suspension and cancellation of listing (Chapter 9);
(10)   decision-making procedures in cases involving Regulatory Decisions Committee and information concerning Committee operations (Chapter 10);
(11)   relationship between breach of listing rules and market abuse regime as well as safe harbour status under Code of Market Conduct (Chapter 11); and
(12)   fees charged under the listing rules (Chapter 12).

STABILISATION

18.108   The FSA's stabilisation rules provide a defence (or safe harbour) against the criminal offences of price or market manipulation and insider dealing. These were initially issued to create an exemption from the offence of market manipulation set out in s 47 of the Financial Services Act 1986. The purpose of stabilisation is to allow the price of equities and bonds to be supported by lead managers after issuance through dealings in the secondary market. This is considered essential to the effective operation of the issuing procedure, underwriting and the capital markets generally. The danger, however, is that stabilisation is potentially manipulative and open to abuse. It is for this reason that it is only permitted in certain circumstances.

18.109 The FSA has included the new stabilisation rules within the Market Conduct sourcebook in Block 2 of the Handbook of Rules and Guidance. The purpose of the chapter is to provide rules permitting but also regulating price support for new offers of equities and bonds. It sets out the circumstances in which lead stabilising managers and others acting with them (for the first time) are permitted to support the prices of new offers (including fresh offers of securities already traded in the market) for a limited period after offer. The purpose is to maintain an orderly initial market in the securities, facilitate new offers and reduce the issue costs to enterprises.

18.110 Managers are permitted to exert upward pressure on the price in the cash market by any means permitted by the price stabilising rules including the repurchase of securities previously sold short.

The stabilising manager of an offer of securities may go into the market to buy or agree to buy securities in order to support (but not suppress) the market price but only in certain conditions.

Before attempting to stabilise any price, the stabilising manager must take, or check that others have taken, proper steps to inform that market that stabilising action is possible and to confirm that the price is not already false. He must also be satisfied that proper systems have been set up for central recording of any stabilising action and not stabilised shares and certificates associated to bonds, loans, debentures or other securities if one is to be convertible into the other but the terms of conversion have not yet been announced.

The rules determine how the upper limit and the price at which securities may be stabilised. While this may be increased, it cannot be reduced.

The lead stabilising manager or managers must maintain a register which is available for inspection by the authorities in the UK. This must record every offer of securities made as part of the stabilising process.

18.111 The FSA is entitled to make further rules which confer safe harbour from market manipulation in connection with stabilisation undertaken pursuant to a foreign law.

The rules also contain further provisions concerning the accounting obligations of the manager to the issuer. The manager must allow the issuer access to the stabilisation register, the issuer must also be separately informed of action taken after the close of the stabilisation period.

Further information must be provided with regard to additional allotments.

18.112 These are useful provisions in allowing stabilisation to continue. Although a number of objections were made with regard to stabilisation and other non-transparent practices as part of the negotiation processes surrounding the adoption of the Investment Services Directive, the value of stabilisation is clearly recognised in such other jurisdictions as the US and Japan. In light of the possibility for abuse, it must only be carried on within specific guidelines with a requisite degree of transparency and accountability.

CORPORATE GOVERNANCE

18.113 Following the publication of the Cadbury and Greenbury Reports the London Stock Exchange's Committee on Corporate Governance produced its own report which, in particular, recommended that they should issue a set of principles and code which incorporated the proposals set out in the other papers. This became known as 'the Combined Code'.[1] In the light of its importance, this is now included as a separate attachment within the Listing Rules.[2]

1 See G Walker, 'Official Listing' in M Blair, L Mingella, M Taylor, M Threipland and G Walker, *Financial Services & Markets Act 2000* (2001), Ch 8.
2 See Table 18.1.

18.114 The Combined Code contains principles and detailed Code provisions. Listed companies are required to issue a disclosure statement in two parts. The first requires that the company will report on how it applies the principles contained in the Combined Code. In the second part, the company either confirms that it complies with the Code provisions or provides an explanation as to how and why certain provisions are not given full effect.

18.115 The basic policy adopted is to require companies to explain their governance policies including the circumstances which may justify any departure from best practice. This disclosure will then allow shareholders and others to evaluate the company's practice having regard to its particular circumstances. These are important rules and procedures especially as bank and firm governance have become increasingly significant parts of the general supervisory process.

RECOGNITION OF INVESTMENT EXCHANGES AND CLEARING HOUSES

Background

18.116 The main features of the former recognition and exemption regime for investment exchanges and clearing houses have been included in Part XVIII of the FSMA 2000. This provides for the recognition of all of the major exchanges and clearing houses in the UK. Although exempt from the need for authorisation as such, they have to comply with the recognition requirements set out in the 2000 Act and supporting orders issued by the Treasury under the Act. Draft regulations were issued in February 1999.

The FSMA 2000 also gives the FSA a new power to issue directions to recognised bodies to take steps to comply with the recognition requirements and also confers immunity on the bodies from civil action by their members in respect of anything done in the performance of their regulatory functions.

18.117 The recognition requirements formally set out in Sch 4 to the Financial Services Act 1986 in relation to exchanges and s 39 in relation to clearing houses were to be made more flexible by allowing the Treasury to set out and amend the relevant criteria by order.[1] These include the amendments, for example, to the Traded Securities (Disclosure) Regulations 1994.[2] Recognition will also be extended to include over-the-counter (OTC) trades which do not occur on a recognised investment exchange (RIE).

1   See G Walker, 'Official Listing' in M Blair, L Mingella, M Taylor, M Threipland and G Walker, *Financial Services & Markets Act 2000* (2001), Ch 8.
2   SI 1994/188.

18.118   The provisions set out in Sch 21 to the Companies Act 1989 in relation to market contracts (as defined in s 155) continue in effect. These prevent liquidators from attempting to unwind contracts made through exchanges or clearing houses. The Treasury was also to be empowered to extend this to include bodies clearing certain non-investment contracts in addition in ECHO.

18.119   Responsibility for determining whether overseas exchanges and clearing houses should be recognised has been transferred from the Treasury to FSA. As these bodies are already subject to extensive controls in their home territories, they are not subject to the full set out requirements imposed on domestic applicants. The test applied continues to be whether the degree of home state supervision secured together with the rules and practices of the particular body are such that the protection secured is, at least, equivalent to that provided under the recognition requirements imposed under the FSMA 2000.

Overview

Application

18.120   Any body corporate or unincorporated association may apply to the FSA for an order declaring it to be a recognised investment exchange (RIE) or clearing house (RCH) under ss 287(1) and 288(1) of the FSMA 2000.

Applications are to be in such manner as may be directed but must be accompanied by copies of the applicant's rules, a copy of any guidance issued, required particulars and such other information as may reasonably be requested. The required particulars refer to the proposed clearing arrangements to be entered into by an exchange applicant or clearing services to be provided by a clearing applicant. If clearing is to be provided in respect of transactions not effected on the exchange, the criteria to be applied in determining to whom these services will be provided must be specified. The FSA may also require the applicant to provide such further information as it reasonably considers necessary to determine the application.

Recognition orders are provided under FSMA 2000, s 290(1) where an application has been successful.

Revocation

18.121   Revocation is also provided for under s 298(1) where either a recognised body fails to satisfy the recognition requirements or any other obligation imposed under the 2000 Act. If an application is to be refused or recognition revoked, the FSA must give written notice of its intention to the recognised body concerned. It must also take such other steps as considered reasonably practicable to bring the notice to the attention of members and publish the notice in such manner as it considers appropriate. The notice must give reasons for the proposed decision and draw attention to the right of the recognised body, any member of the body or any other person whom is likely to be affected by the proposed order to make representations. Representations must generally be made within two months of the date in which the notice is served.

18.122   Instead of revoking recognition, the FSA may direct the body to take specified steps (including making alterations to its rules or suspending or discontinuing such of its operations as may be specified) where it has failed, or is likely to fail, to satisfy the recognition requirements or any other obligation imposed by the FSA or under the Act. Such directions are enforceable by injunction in England and Wales or an order for a specific performance in Scotland. The same notification and rights to make representations provided for in respect of refusals of applications and revocation decisions applies to the giving of directions.

Overseas bodies

18.123   An overseas investment exchange and clearing house may apply for recognition under FSMA 2000, s 292(1). The applicant must provide an address for service in the UK. In such cases, the FSA may (but is not required to) make a recognition order under s 292(2) where the application is subject in its home territory to requirements, at least, equivalent to the recognition requirements taking into account the supervision effected and the rules and practices of the applicant and that there are adequate procedures for dealing with persons who cannot complete market contracts. The FSA must also consider whether the overseas applicant and the home supervisory authorities are able and willing to co-operate in the sharing of information and otherwise.

Supervision

18.124   In addition to the recognition requirements, the FSA is also given new powers of supervision under FSMA 2000, s 293. The FSA may issue rules requiring notice of specific events or such other information as it may reasonably require to be provided by the recognised body. Written notice must also be provided where the recognised body alters or revokes any of its rules or guidance or makes new rules or guidance. Changes to clearing arrangements must also be notified in all cases. These supervision rules may be modified or disapplied in particular cases.

18.125   Overseas investment exchanges and clearing houses must provide an annual report which must include a statement as to whether any events have occurred which would affect the continuing validity of its recognition or have any effect in competition. A copy of the report must be sent to the Treasury and the Director General of Fair Trading.

18.126   The FSA must ensure that adequate arrangements are set up for the consideration of relevant complaints against a recognised body. This, however, only relates to matters which are relevant to whether the body's recognition should be maintained. The functions of the Tribunal may be extended by order to include recognised investment exchange or clearing house disciplinary proceedings. Such an order may be issued where the Treasury considers it necessary to ensure that disciplinary decisions are consistent with Tribunal decisions taken under Part VIII of the Act or otherwise or in accordance with the European Human Rights Convention.

Recognition requirements

18.127   Draft recognition regulations under FSMA 2000, s 286(1) were issued by the Treasury and the Secretary of State in February 1999. The regulations have to be approved by the Secretary of State where they include default rules (originally where they may have applied to market contracts as defined in s 155 of the Companies Act 1989). Default rules relate to the arrangements to be taken by the investment exchange or clearing house where a person appears to be unable or is likely to be unable to complete contracts with the exchange or clearing house.

18.128   The Government recognises that exchanges and clearing houses are necessarily expert in the operation of their markets and that they have strong incentives in ensuring that they function in a safe and proper manner. It was accordingly considered in the public interest to allow them a wide degree of flexibility in the determination and application of their own market rules.

On recognition, such bodies are accordingly exempt from the need for authorisation under the FSMA 2000, although they are still subject to the supervision and oversight of the FSA. While they do not have to comply with the FSA's conduct of business rules, their members will if separately authorised.

18.129   The requirements set out in the recognition regulations replace the earlier provisions contained in s 39 and Sch 4 to the Financial Services Act 1986. The further requirements with regard to default rules were set out in Sch 21 to the Companies Act 1989.

18.130   The earlier general rules with regard to financial resources, proper monitoring and the promotion and maintenance of standards are repeated. The new regulations, however, draw all of the relevant provisions together for the first time. They are also more explicit in their terms, provide for more delegation of function and allow clearing houses to be recognised on a stand-alone basis not tied to any particular investment exchange.

18.131   The new recognition requirements in respect of investment exchanges are set out in Part I of the Schedule to the regulations. An applicant investment exchange must accordingly now comply with the requirements set out in the Schedule. An applicant for recognition as a clearing house must comply with the requirements set out in Part II. These are almost identical to those imposed on an applicant exchange and correspond with the provisions set out in Part I.

18.132   Special rules apply in relation to exchanges or clearing houses which offer or propose to offer clearing services in respect of market contracts under s 155(2) or 155(3) of the Companies Act 1989. These are set out in Parts III (exchanges) and IV (clearing houses) of the Schedule respectively.

18.133 In such cases, appropriate default rules must also be in place which allow for appropriate action to be taken in respect of unsettled market contracts where a member is unable to meet its obligations in respect of one or more contracts. The default rules must enable action to be taken in respect of all unsettled market contracts other than those entered into by a recognised clearing house for the purposes of or in connection with the provision of clearing services for the exchange.

The effect of these additional rules is to ensure that all rights and liabilities between the parties to an unsettled market contract are discharged and for relevant net payments to be made in all cases.

RIE AND RCH SOURCEBOOK

18.134 The FSA issued Consultation Paper 39 on its *RIE and RCH Sourcebook* in January 2000. The objective was to note the key changes that would be introduced from existing rules and guidance and to attach full copies of the proposed sections. The new sourcebook now contains the FSA's guidance on the interpretation of the recognition requirements set out by the Treasury regulations issued under the FSMA 2000. The new notification rules for RIEs and RCHs replace the Financial Services (Notification by Recognised Bodies) Regulations 1995 and earlier guidance.

18.135 The Sourcebook incorporates the three main changes referred to in connection with the recognition regimes. The FSA includes the power to issue directions over RIEs and RCHs with guidance being provided in the sourcebook. A separate chapter of the Sourcebook deals with the assumption by the FSA of responsibility from the Treasury for the oversight of recognised overseas investment exchanges (ROIEs) and clearing houses (ROCHs). Provisions are also included to deal with the recognition of nominees which were inserted into the Bill during the Standing Committee stage. A recognised nominee is a body carrying out on behalf of a recognised body functions which would fall within the scope of the exemption available. Guidance in connection with these provisions was issued subsequently.

18.136 The Sourcebook contains the following specific provisions:

Applications

18.137 Chapter 1 explains the application of the Sourcebook and other more general introductory matters.

Recognition requirements

18.138 Chapter 2 sets out the FSA's draft guidance on the interpretation of the Recognition Requirement Regulations. This is important to the extent that the FSA will have no powers which apply to recognised bodies apart from the notification requirements. It is only otherwise able to provide guidance in connection with how these requirements will be interpreted in practice. The Sourcebook deals with definition of regulated activities, guidance on fitness and properness and related matters, financial resources, regulatory co-operation, standards of integrity, access to facilities, financial crime and market abuse, transaction reporting, monitoring and enforcing regulatory provisions, investigating complaints, proper markets and related matters and default rules.[1]

1   Sourcebook, ss 2.1–2.14.

Notification rules

18.139   Chapter 3 sets out the notification rules for UK recognised bodies issued under the Act. Recognised bodies will only be required to provide notice or information concerning events reasonably required by the FSA in connection with the exercise of its functions under the Act. These requirements generally continue the former rules set out in the earlier notification regulations issued under the Financial Services Act 1986. Chapter 3 includes specific provisions concerning timing and form of notification, modification and waiver, key individuals and internal organisation information, provision of organisation charts, changes to a recognised body's internal committee structure or amendments to its constitution, any disciplinary action taken against officers and employees, annual plan, and financial information.[1]

1   Sourcebook, ss 3.1–3.24.

Supervision

18.140   Chapter 4 sets out the revised risk-based supervisory approach to be adopted with regard to UK recognised bodies. This allows the FSA to make regular, comprehensive assessments of the risk that a UK recognised body will be able to discharge its specific obligations. Chapter 4 contains specific provisions concerning UK recognised body's internal review and control procedures, risk assessment components (including financial sources, supervision of members, business environment, operational infrastructure and governance), supervisory programme and feedback procedures. Recognised bodies will also be expected to issue an annual plan in accordance with the requirements set out in the Sourcebook. Chapter 4 also contains further provisions concerning complaints, default rules and directions and derecognition.

Applications for recognition

18.141   Chapter 5 sets out the procedures concerning applications and the information and documentation required.

Overseas investment exchanges and clearing houses

18.142   Chapter 6 sets out the new provisions required following the FSA's assumption of the responsibility for the supervision of ROIEs and ROCHs. This includes provisions concerning applications, relevant recognition requirements, competition scrutiny, supervision, notification rules and powers of direction and derecognition. These will ensure that the FSA is satisfied that the body concerns delivers a standard of investor protection equivalent to that delivered by UK recognised bodies as set out in s 267 of the Act. In carrying out its functions, the FSA will rely to a large extent on the supervision conducted by the home authorities. While the general approach adopted by the Treasury will be continued, Chapter 6, contains new provisions concerning notification requirements including annual reports and information concerning any serious disciplinary action taken.

Chapter 19

Investigations, discipline and enforcement

INVESTIGATIONS AND GATHERING INFORMATION

19.1   The Financial Services Authority (FSA) has the authority to conduct investigations and gather information. These powers are contained in Part XI of the Financial Services and Markets Act (FSMA) 2000, backed by chapter 2 of the Enforcement Manual (ENF) of the FSA Handbook.

The powers are broken down into a number of categories:

— requiring information from an authorised person;
— requiring a report from an authorised person;
— appointing an investigator to conduct an investigation on the FSA's behalf.

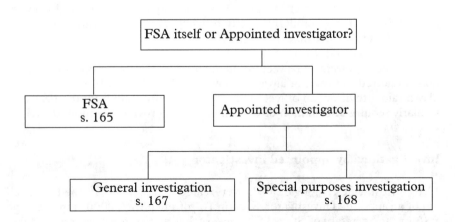

Investigations by the FSA

19.2   Section 165 of the FSMA 2000 contains the general power of the FSA directly to require information from an authorised person. Subsection (1) states that the FSA:

'may, by notice in writing given to an authorised person, require him–

(a)   to provide specified information or information of a specified description; or
(b)   to produce specified documents or documents of a specified description.'

Unlike certain of the powers of an appointed investigator, it does not extend to the population at large. The powers do, however, extend not only to the authorised person or firm itself but, by virtue of subsection (7), to any person connected with an authorised person; this covers officers, managers, employees or agents either of the authorised person itself or of any parent undertaking. Subsection (8) goes even further, extending to persons who were formerly authorised even though they are no longer so.

19.3   Apart from the powers only being exercisable in relation to authorised persons, past or present, and those connected with them, the only other limitation placed on them is in subsection (4):

'This section applies only to information and documents reasonably required in connection with the exercise by the Authority of functions conferred on it by or under this Act.'

The functions conferred on the FSA by or under the Act are, however, very wide. As discussed elsewhere in this book, they cover not only the regulation of the financial services industry in all its forms, but also the four regulatory objectives of promoting market confidence, promoting public awareness, protecting consumers and reducing financial crime. The heading of reducing financial crime includes, of course, the FSA's powers to prosecute any criminal offence contained in the FSMA 2000, ranging from engaging in a regulated activity without permission through breaching the rules on financial promotion to misleading the market, as well as the power to prosecute offences of insider dealing and money laundering.

19.4   In the furtherance of any of the above objectives or duties, therefore, the FSA may require any authorised person, past or present, or any person connected with that person, to provide it with any information or document that it wishes. It may similarly specify in what form the information is to be produced and by what time.

19.5   These powers are sweeping in themselves. Furthermore, the written notice referred to need not always be given. FSMA 2000, s 165(3) contains a 'dawn raid' provision: an officer with written authorisation from the FSA may similarly require information or documents to be provided 'without delay'.

Investigations by appointed investigator

19.6   Most wide-ranging of all, however, are the powers not of the FSA itself but of an appointed investigator. Section 167 of the FSMA 2000 empowers the FSA or the Secretary of State, 'if it appears that there is good reason for doing so', to appoint one or more competent persons to conduct an investigation on its behalf into:

(a)   the nature, conduct or state of the business of an authorised person or of an appointed representative;

(b)   a particular aspect of that business; or

(c)   the ownership or control of an authorised person.

'Business' explicitly covers 'any part of a business even if it does not consist of carrying on regulated activities'.

19.7   Such an investigator may, under s 171 of the FSMA 2000, summon the person under investigation, or any person connected with them, to appear before them at a specified time and place and answer questions or 'otherwise provide such information as the investigator may require'. In addition, they may 'require any person to produce at a specified time and place any specified document or documents of a specified description'.

19.8   The scope of the latter power is particularly worthy of note. First of all, it relates not just to the person under investigation or a person connected with them, but 'any person'. Secondly, and even more significantly, in sharp contrast to the FSA's own investigative powers, the powers of an appointed investigator extend beyond the authorised sector: 'any person' means precisely that. The only limitation is that the investigator must reasonably consider that the questions asked, the information sought or the documents required are relevant to the purposes of the investigation.

19.9   More specific provisions are contained in FSMA 2000, s 168, which provides for the appointment of investigators in specific circumstances, listed in subsections (1), (2) and (4). All of these relate to some specific form of wrongdoing and, in many cases, actual criminal offences. Under subsections (1) and (2), either the FSA or the Secretary of State may appoint an investigator where any of the following is suspected:

—   breaching the insurance regulations;
—   frustration of an investigation conducted by the FSA or on its behalf;
—   providing false or misleading information to the FSA or to an auditor;
—   engaging in a regulated activity by an unauthorised person[1] or, in the case of a European Economic Area (EEA) firm, exercising its rights under the Investment Services Directive, without first notifying the FSA;
—   falsely claiming to be authorised;
—   breaching the financial promotion rules;
—   misleading the market;
—   insider dealing;
—   market abuse.

1   Ie a person who has no authorisation whatsoever to engage in any regulated activity.

19.10   In addition to the above list, under subsection (4) the FSA may appoint an investigator where any of the following is suspected:

—   an authorised person acting without permission;[1]
—   a breach of the money laundering rules;
—   breach by an authorised person of an FSA rule;

— an individual may not be a fit and proper person to perform functions in relation to a regulated activity carried on by an authorised or exempt person;

— performing or agreeing to perform a function in breach of a prohibition order;

— an authorised or exempt person permitting a person covered by a prohibition order to exercise a function to which it relates;

— an authorised person permitting a controlled person or a contractor to engage in a regulated activity without FSA approval;

— a person whom the FSA has approved may not be a fit and proper person to perform the function to which that approval relates; or

— any case of misconduct.

It will be seen that the second list principally covers regulatory offences (the exception being breaches of the money laundering regulations, which are, of course, criminal) which are by their nature applicable to the authorised sector, while the first list may apply to the population at large.

1 Ie a person who is authorised to engage only in certain types of regulated activity engaging in others.

19.11   Where investigators are appointed under FSMA 2000, s 168, they have the same powers as under s 167, but their remit is wider. It is not only persons under investigation or persons connected with them who may be summoned to answer questions: FSMA 2000, s 172 makes clear that the summons may be issued to anyone, provided that the investigator is 'satisfied that the requirement (to attend an interview or provide information) is necessary or expedient for the purposes of the investigation'.

19.12   This is the most wide-ranging of all the powers. Unlike where the investigation is carried out under FSMA 2000, ss 167 and 171, the view of the investigator is not explicitly required to be reasonable; all that is required is that he or she is satisfied that the summons is necessary or expedient. Nor is any definition given of 'expedient'. In practice, therefore, an FSA investigator looking into, for example, suspected market abuse enjoys almost unlimited powers. The only real restriction on this is the power of the FSA (or Secretary of State as the case may be) under s 170 to limit the scope and conduct of the investigation; however, there is an equal power under the section to extend the scope. The investigator remains answerable throughout to the institution that appointed him, and to it alone.

19.13   Furthermore, where it appears to be the case that the documents or information sought are not in the hands of the person required to produce them but in those of a third party, the above powers may be exercised in relation to that third party. This applies equally to investigations by the FSA itself, the Secretary of State or an appointed investigator.

Similarly, if a person required to produce the information fails to do so, the person may be required to state where it is to be found. In the case of lawyers, FSMA 2000, s 175(4) explicitly states that they may be required to give the name and address of their client. This, of course, raises the question: what is meant by 'address'? What is the position of a lawyer who knows that his client is not at his usual address but at another location known to the lawyer, and furthermore has reason to believe that his client does not wish his whereabouts to be known either to the FSA or to anyone appointed by them? It is arguable that if he supplies his client's usual address, his duty under the Act is discharged. The FSA may, however, argue that a lawyer who furnishes the address of his client, knowing full well that he is not to be found there, will be guilty of providing misleading information to an investigator under s 177 or at least of the more general offence of misleading the FSA under s 398. As seen below, both of these carry serious penalties.

19.14 As regards banking confidentiality, under FSMA 2000, s 175(5), this may be overridden where the bank required to provide information or documents is itself the person under investigation or a member of its group. The same exception applies where the person to whom the obligation of confidentiality is owed is the person under investigation (or a member of its group).

Although this is certainly controversial, it is not a new departure. Provisions requiring banks to override the duty of confidentiality to clients in the context of an investigation of those clients have for some time now been a part of the anti-money laundering legislation.[1]

1 See for example Criminal Justice Act 1988 (as amended by the Criminal Justice Act 1993), Drug Trafficking Act 1994, Money Laundering Regulations 1993 and Proceeds of Crime Act 2002.

Informal investigative powers

19.15 It should not be overlooked that, in addition to the above powers provided for in statute, the FSA also has a number of informal powers under its own rules. These, of course, apply only to authorised persons; where the FSA wishes to obtain information from those outside the authorised sector, it will generally have to rely on the statutory powers. Nonetheless, because it is, for the most part, authorised persons who will be the subject of the FSA's scrutiny, these informal powers, which for banks reflect the approach taken by the Bank of England in the past, are worth noting.

Principle 11

19.16 Most of the informal powers are derived from Principle 11 of the Principles for Businesses. The Principles are rules set by the FSA and described by them as the fundamental obligations of authorised firms under the regulatory system. Principle 11 states:

'A firm must deal with its regulators in an open and co-operative way and must disclose to the FSA appropriately anything relating to the firm of which the FSA would reasonably expect notice.'

Dealing with the FSA in an open and co-operative way certainly includes co-operating with their investigations. In its guidance on compliance with Principle 11, the FSA has advised in its Supervision Manual[1] that a firm should:

(a)   make itself readily available for meetings with the FSA;
(b)   give the FSA reasonable access to any records, files, tapes or computer systems which are within the firm's possession or control and provide any facilities which the FSA may reasonably request;

(c) produce to the FSA specified documents, files, tapes, computer data or other material in the firm's possession or control as reasonably requested;

(d) print information in the firm's possession or control which is held on computer or on microfilm or otherwise convert it into a readily legible document or other record which the FSA may reasonably request;

(e) permit the FSA to copy documents or other material on the premises of the firm at the firm's reasonable expense and remove copies and hold them elsewhere or provide any copies as reasonably requested; and

(f) answer truthfully, fully and promptly all questions which are reasonably put to it by the FSA.

1 SUP 2.3.3.

19.17 The firm is also expected to ensure the same compliance on the part of its employees, agents and appointed representatives, as well as those of any other firm or company in its group.[1] Some of these are straightforward enough, for example being ready for meetings, while (d) and (e) are simply extensions of the requirements in (b) and (c).

It is requirements (b), (c) and (f) that are of particular note. Without resorting to any statutory power, the FSA is entitled to access to any documents, files or computer systems that the firm not only possesses but controls and, linked to this, a firm is required to produce to them any such documents (whether in electronic form or hard copy) that they may 'reasonably request'. Furthermore, the firm must answer truthfully and openly any questions that the FSA asks. Again, there is the qualifier that the request must be 'reasonable', but, given the wide range of the FSA's duties and responsibilities, it may be difficult to envisage many circumstances where the request would not be deemed reasonable. The principal ones would appear to be:

— where the request is made outside normal business hours;
— where the firm or its representative does not in fact possess the information requested.

As to the first of these, the FSA does, in fact, explicitly place this proviso on itself elsewhere in its rules. The second will not arise in the context of access to documents, since the rules refer to material 'in the firm's possession or control'. It may arise, however, in (f) above, the requirement to answer all questions put by the FSA; clearly, one cannot provide answers that one does not know.

1 SUP 2.3.4.

Further rules

19.18 In addition to Principle 11, the FSA's rulebook also contains two specific rules on the subject: SUP 2.3.5 and SUP 2.3.7. These oblige the firm to:

— permit the FSA or its representatives to have access, with or without notice, during reasonable business hours to any of the firm's business premises and to take reasonable steps to ensure that its agents, suppliers under material outsourcing arrangements and appointed representatives give that permission in relation to their premises; and
— take reasonable steps to ensure that each of its suppliers under material outsourcing arrangements deals in an open and co-operative way with the

FSA in the discharge of its functions under the FSMA 2000 in relation to the firm.

19.19   In fact, these are for the most part specific applications of what is already required under Principle 11; the exception being the requirement that 'suppliers under material outsourcing arrangements' (ie contractors or subcontractors who play a material part in the firm's operations) provide the same level of co-operation as the firm itself. It has been suggested that these rules have greater force because they have the status of Rules, rather than mere Principles, and as such, breach of them may lead directly to disciplinary sanctions. Nevertheless, were the FSA to consider a firm not to comply with one of the Principles, explicitly stated to be fundamental obligations, this would call into question whether it continued to regard the firm as 'fit and proper'. A withdrawal of permission on the basis that a firm was not fit and proper could be more devastating than formal disciplinary action.

REQUIRING OF REPORTS

19.20   In addition to its powers to investigate, the FSA is empowered under FSMA 2000, s 166 to require, by written notice, reports from what the Act calls 'skilled persons'. Such a requirement may be made to any person who either is at the requisite time or has in the past been:

(a)   an authorised person;
(b)   any other member of a group of which the authorised person forms part;
(c)   a partnership of which the authorised person is a member.

19.21   There are two other conditions:

(a)   the person to whom the notice is addressed must be carrying on a business, or at least have been doing so at the relevant time; and
(b)   the report required must concern matters in relation to which the FSA could require information under FSMA 2000, s 165, or indeed in relation to which it has already done so.

19.22   The FSMA 2000 also lays down requirements regarding the person who is appointed by the firm to write the report. Under subsection (4), it must:

(a)   be nominated or approved by the FSA; and
(b)   appear to the FSA to have the skills necessary to make the required report.

19.23   Supplementary to the FSMA 2000, the Supervision Handbook requires the firm to conclude a contract with the skilled person in relation to his or her appointment.[1] This emphasises an important point; although the FSA must approve the appointment and may even nominate the skilled person concerned, the actual appointment is by the firm.

This raises two issues. The first is that since it is the firm that appoints the skilled person, it is the firm, not the FSA, that pays. It has therefore been stated that the requiring of a skilled person's report is an effective way for the FSA to obtain information and insight while not expending its own resources. It is certainly an exception to the general principle that the cost of FSA enforcement measures is borne by the regulated community as a whole (through its financing of the FSA) rather than by the firm under investigation. On the other hand, this principle always applied to banks' investigating accountants appointed by the Bank of England.

The second issue raised is one of conflict of interest. The skilled person that the firm appoints – and pays – is placed in an uncomfortable position. It must write a report which will be handed over to the FSA and may lead to disciplinary, civil or, in extreme cases, criminal action against its client. That this is what the system requires is clear; what is equally clear is that because of this, the appointed skilled person must, although appointed and paid by the firm, explicitly retain its independence.

1   SUP 5.5.1.

19.24   A further question of conflict of interest may arise where the person appointed is a lawyer. Normally, of course, lawyers have a duty of confidentiality to the person who appoints them and legal professional privilege protects them from being forced to breach it.[1] It is clear, however, that the person compiling the report must be open and frank with the FSA and that no part of the report may be withheld. This duty will require the client to waive lawyer-client privilege, although only in respect of the lawyer-expert's dealings with the FSA, in relation to the report.[2] The question may thus fairly be asked, how such an appointment affects the lawyer/client relationship.

1   The only real exception to this principle is where the lawyer is asked to assist a client in the commission of a criminal offence, a notable example being money laundering.
2   For the skilled person's more general duties of confidentiality, see below.

19.25   The terms of the contract between the firm and the skilled person are specified by the FSA Handbook; it must:

'(1) require and permit the skilled person during and after the course of his employment:

> (a)   to cooperate with the FSA in the discharge of its functions under the Act in relation to the firm; and
>
> (b)   to communicate to the FSA information on, or his opinion on, matters of which he has, or had, become aware in his capacity as skilled person reporting on the firm in the following circumstances:
>
>> (i)   the skilled person reasonably believes that, as regards the firm concerned
>>
>>> (A) there is or has been, or may be or have been, a contravention of any relevant requirement that applies to the firm concerned; and
>>>
>>> (B) that the contravention may be of material significance to the FSA in determining whether to exercise, in relation to the firm concerned, any functions conferred on the FSA by or under any provision of the Act other than Part VI (Official Listing); or
>>
>> (ii) the skilled person reasonably believes that the information on, or his opinion on, those matters may be of material significance to the FSA in determining whether the firm concerned satisfies and will continue to satisfy the threshold conditions; or
>>
>> (iii) the skilled person reasonably believes that the firm is not, may not be or may cease to be a going concern;

(2) require the skilled person to prepare a report, as notified to the firm by the FSA, within the time specified by the FSA; and

(3) waive any duty of confidentiality owed by the skilled person to the firm which might limit the provision of information or opinion by that skilled person to the FSA in accordance with (1) or (2).'

The contract is also to be governed by the laws of a part of the UK and, crucially, is to be directly enforceable against the skilled person not only by the appointing firm but also by the FSA.

19.26 As regards the form which the report is to take, this is a matter for the FSA; subsection (3) states:

'The Authority may require the report to be in such form as may be specified in the notice.'

It is clear, however, that it will include any information which the skilled person discovers in the contexts referred to in the contract, set out above.

19.27 The obligation to provide assistance to a person required to write a report is similarly wide-ranging. Under subsection (5), anyone currently providing services to a person required to produce a report must give them 'all such assistance as the appointed person may reasonably require'. Equally, however, the duty to assist them applies not only to those currently providing services to them, but those who 'at any time' have done so.

The question, of course, arises as to what kind of 'services' are covered; the subsection does not elaborate. The guidance in the Supervision Manual states only that these include suppliers under material outsourcing arrangements. It would seem, therefore, that anyone providing any kind of professional services to the skilled person will be covered, save that lawyers in this context (in contrast to those appointed to write the report itself) are exempted from providing any information covered by legal professional privilege. Where such persons fail to provide the assistance requested, a court order may be sought, compelling them to provide it; failure to comply with this order, of course, will constitute contempt of court with the usual penalties of up to two years' imprisonment and/or an unlimited fine.

19.28 Not only are those providing services required to co-operate with and assist the skilled person, so too is the appointing firm. Failure to do so will constitute a breach of the FSA Rules as well as the general duty to co-operate under Principle 11. No criminal penalties or threat of injunction are provided for in these cases, but then, they are not needed. The persons providing services, who could be called upon for assistance, may not always be authorised persons; if they are not, they will not be subject to the FSA rulebook. Nor will they themselves be the subject of investigation, hence the powers of an investigator under s 167 or s 168 of the FSMA 2000 will not be applicable. Additional powers of compulsion are therefore needed. In contrast, an authorised person is subject to potentially Draconian disciplinary sanctions for failing to obey the FSA Rules. Furthermore, if the skilled person reports that the firm has hindered their enquiries, the FSA may respond by ordering a formal investigation with all the powers discussed above.

19.29 Criminal penalties are provided for, however, where the firm goes further than simply refusing to co-operate with the skilled person and engages in actual deception. Just as with an appointed investigator, knowingly or recklessly providing materially false or misleading information to a skilled person in purported compliance with the duty to assist that person in the compiling of a report is a criminal offence, carrying up to two years' imprisonment or an unlimited fine.[1] Where the skilled person, for his part, deliberately or recklessly misleads the FSA in his report, he too commits a criminal offence. However, this does not carry a prison sentence, merely an unlimited fine.[2]

1 FSMA 2000, s 177(4).
2 FSMA 2000, s 398(1).

19.30 A final point should be noted concerning the duties of confidentiality to which the skilled person is subject. As discussed, the skilled person has a wide duty of disclosure to the FSA. This is, however, not unlimited; other than in the contexts referred to in the contract, a skilled person is not required to disclose to the FSA information outside the scope of those areas on which he has been asked to report. Should the skilled person do so, this will arguably be a breach of duty of confidentiality to the firm.

19.31 Since the skilled person is a 'primary recipient' within the terms of the FSMA 2000, disclosure by that person to any person outside the FSA of any confidential information without the permission both of the FSA and the person to whom it relates (most likely the firm, but possibly one or more individuals within it) is also a criminal offence.[1] 'Confidential information' includes any information that has not been made public relating to the business or other affairs of any person and received for the purposes of carrying out any function of the FSA.[2] The offence carries up to two years' imprisonment and/or an unlimited fine. It should, incidentally, be noted that it covers not just disclosure by the skilled person but also any officer of the FSA; the FSA and its officers are also primary recipients.

1 FSMA 2000, s 348(1).
2 FSMA 2000, s 348(2).

WARRANTS

19.32 Although the above investigatory tools are supported by criminal sanctions, it is clear that these alone will not in every circumstance produce the required information. Indeed, the maximum sentence for the most serious types of non-cooperation is two years' imprisonment. This may be compared to, for example, a maximum seven years' imprisonment for insider dealing or 14 years for money laundering, both of which the FSA is empowered to investigate. Thus it might be worth a person's while to frustrate an investigation deliberately rather than risk exposure to the far greater sanctions to which discovery of information may lead.

19.33 Section 176 of the FSMA 2000 therefore empowers a magistrate to issue a warrant to enter premises where he is satisfied there are reasonable grounds to believe that certain circumstances apply. Essentially, these circumstances fall into one of two categories.

The first category is the more straightforward: a requirement to provide documents or information has been served on a person who has failed, wholly or in part, to comply with it. The second is at first glance equally simple: if such a requirement were made, it would either not be complied with or the requisite information or documents would be tampered with or even destroyed. This latter category is complicated, however, by an additional requirement: either the premises in question must be those of an authorised person or appointed representative or a criminal offence must have been committed, or must be in the course of commission, which is listed in s 168 of the FSMA 2000 and which carries a maximum sentence of at least two years' imprisonment. It is, of course, also a requirement in all cases that there are reasonable grounds to believe that information or documents, which are or could be the subject of an order under s 165, 167 or 168, are located on the premises!

19.34   An application for a warrant must be made by either the FSA itself, the Secretary of State or an appointed investigator, who must state in an information that there are reasonable grounds to believe that one (or more) of the above set of circumstances applies. The magistrate may then issue the warrant, which is enforced by a police officer. Refusal to co-operate with such a warrant is itself a criminal offence (see below).

FAILURE TO CO-OPERATE

19.35   Failure to co-operate with an investigation, launched by the FSA or the Secretary of State or by an appointed investigator, carries heavy penalties. Failure to comply with a requirement to provide information may result in the FSA (or the Secretary of State) certifying the failure to the High Court (or, in Scotland, to the Court of Session). The court, if it is satisfied that the person failed without reasonable excuse to comply, may deal with him as though he were in contempt of court, ie impose a sentence of up to two years' imprisonment or an unlimited fine.

19.36   What is meant by 'reasonable excuse' is, however, unclear, in particular the position regarding self-incrimination. Section 174 of the FSMA 2000 contains a protection against compelled self-incrimination in relation to criminal and market abuse proceedings[1] and it could therefore be argued that there is no need for a separate protection allowing a person in such cases to refuse to answer questions. But doubt remains over self-incrimination in relation to other proceedings, notably those in relation to restitution orders. Sections 382 and 383 of the FSMA 2000 permit the FSA, or the Secretary of State, to apply to the High Court for a restitution order where misconduct, including market abuse, has resulted either in a person suffering loss or the offender making a profit. This applies not just to the authorised sector but to any person.[2] It could be argued that where market abuse has resulted in a profit to the offender but no loss to anyone (for example, in cases of misuse of information), such a restitution order is merely a disguised form of confiscation. As such, it could be construed as criminal, rather than civil, in nature. If it is, a person will under the European Convention on Human Rights be protected from being compelled to give evidence that could be used in such proceedings.[3] Since, however, the Act does not preclude such evidence from being used in restitution order proceedings, it is at least arguable that a person could have a 'reasonable excuse' for refusing to supply it in the first place.

1 See paras 19.41ff below.
2 Under FSMA 2000, s 384, where the offender is an authorised person, the FSA may make the order itself without the need to refer the matter to the High Court.
3 A person convicted of a criminal offence may, under the Criminal Justice Act 1988 (as amended) be compelled to supply evidence of their financial assets in order to facilitate confiscation. But these procedures follow a criminal conviction, ie after the person's guilt has been established. A person may not be compelled to give evidence of guilt that may lead to such a hearing.

19.37   Where a person goes beyond mere failure to co-operate and actually frustrates an investigation (or attempts to do so), the person is guilty of a criminal offence. Such offences fall into two categories.

The first is providing false or misleading information to an investigator (including the FSA or the Secretary of State). This need not be deliberate – even providing such information recklessly will suffice. The second category is where a person, knowing or suspecting that an investigation is in progress, falsifies, conceals or destroys documents which that person knows or suspects to be relevant to the investigation. The same applies where the person knows or suspects that an investigation is likely to take place in the future. All of these are criminal offences, although the penalties are the same as for contempt of court: two years' imprisonment and/or an unlimited fine on indictment, six months' imprisonment and/or the statutory maximum fine (at the time of writing, £5,000) on summary conviction.

19.38   In this context, the general offence of misleading the FSA should not be overlooked. Section 398(1) of the FSMA 2000 states:

'A person who, in purported compliance with any requirement imposed by or under this Act, knowingly or recklessly gives the Authority information which is false or misleading in a material particular is guilty of an offence.'

This only applies, however, in cases where no other specific offence under the Act deals with the conduct in question. It is punishable by a fine only, unlimited on indictment, the statutory maximum summarily.

19.39   As regards skilled persons appointed to write a report under FSMA 2000, s 166, if a person providing services to the skilled person fails to provide the assistance required, that person may be compelled to do so by means of an injunction sought by the FSA. Failure to comply with such an injunction will constitute contempt of court and may be punished accordingly.

19.40   Obstruction of the exercise of a warrant issued under s 176 of the FSMA 2000 is also a criminal offence, although a rather less serious one. It is triable summarily only and is punishable with up to three months' imprisonment and/or a fine of up to the statutory maximum (at the time of writing, £5,000).

ADMISSIBILITY

19.41   There is little point in the FSA and the investigators that it uses having the powers listed above if the information they gain cannot be used. Section 174(1) of the FSMA 2000 therefore provides that:

'a statement made to an investigator by a person in compliance with an investigation requirement is admissible in evidence in any proceedings'.

This is qualified in two respects; but before looking at these, it is worth considering two issues raised by s 174(1) itself.

19.42   First, and perhaps most pertinently, the provision is limited to information gained by an appointed investigator; FSMA 2000, s 174(4) clearly states that 'investigator' means one appointed under s 167 or 168. Other than as regards admissibility, the purpose for which information, obtained by the FSA itself under s 165 or 166, may be used is not stated. Nor do the Explanatory Notes to these sections provide any further guidance or explanation. The rationale may, of course, be that the FSA's powers under these sections relate exclusively to the authorised sector and it is therefore to be understood that the information gained is to be used for the FSA disciplinary proceedings against authorised persons.

19.43   Secondly, the question arises, what is meant by a 'statement'? This, too, is not defined, either in the Act or in the Explanatory Notes. It would seem wrong, however, to suggest that answers to questions are admissible as evidence but documents and other material discovered in the course of a search are not.

Although the language is unhelpful, therefore, one must assume that, subject to the conditions that are laid down in the FSMA 2000, all material obtained by an appointed investigator in the course of an investigation is intended to be admissible. The first of these conditions is that the material must comply with the rules of evidence pertaining to the proceedings in question. This is perhaps obvious, but it emphasises that the provisions of the Act do not in any way override the normal rules of evidence.

The second condition, contained in s 174(2) of the Act, is that no evidence relating to a statement made following an investigator's requirement for information may be adduced in criminal proceedings. Nor, significantly, may it be adduced in proceedings relating to the imposition by the FSA of a financial penalty for market abuse under s 123 of the Act. This follows the human rights principle, enshrined in article 6 of the European Convention on Human Rights (and, since October 2000, the Human Rights Act 1998) that a person may not be compelled to incriminate himself in criminal proceedings. This protection was highlighted in the case of *Saunders*,[1] relating to the Department of Trade and Industry's powers to compel persons to answer questions asked in the course of its investigations. Its extension to market abuse provisions is illustrative of the debate surrounding penalties for market abuse while the Act was still in draft form. Although great effort was made to emphasise that the penalties are civil in nature, even to the point of abandoning the term 'civil fines' in favour of 'financial penalties', some continued to doubt whether the European Court of Human Rights might nonetheless view fines that could be imposed on the authorised and unauthorised alike as criminal in nature and the decision was therefore taken to extend the privilege against self-incrimination to market abuse proceedings.

1   (1996) 23 EHRR 313 ECtHR.

19.44   Subject to these provisos, however, statements are admissible in evidence 'in any proceedings'. This will include proceedings in relation to the making of a restitution order, either by the High Court under s 382 or 383 of the FSMA 2000 or directly by the FSA under s 384. In respect of offences under the money laundering regulations, it is quite conceivable that an application might be made to the FSA by victims of a crime who claimed that a breach of the money laundering regulations by an institution (for example inadequate identification of the client or failure to report suspicions) had led to them losing money. Such a claim might well be made, as an alternative to an action before the civil courts, by the government of a state whose assets had been appropriated by a former politician. Statements made under compulsion would also be admissible, of course, in civil proceedings.

19.45   Equally, such statements are admissible in disciplinary proceedings. This was emphasised in the case of *R on the application (Fleurose) v Securities and Futures Authority Ltd*.[1] In this case, Morison J held that the proceedings of a disciplinary tribunal were not criminal but civil proceedings and that article 6 of the Convention therefore does not apply to them.[2] Since the FSA has, since N2, been the successor to the SFA, the same is likely to apply in respect of the FSA's disciplinary system. Although failure to co-operate with an FSA investigation carries criminal penalties, the proceedings which follow such an investigation may, as seen above, only impose disciplinary sanctions. The nature of these sanctions is much the same as under the 1986 regime which governed the *Fleurose* case.

1   [2001] 2 All ER (Comm) 481. Although the FSMA 2000 was enacted in June 2000, the old system of the Financial Services Act 1986, including the SROs (self-regulating organisations), continued to operate until N2, ie December 2001.
2   Although the case went on to appeal, this point was upheld. See Chapter 20, paras 20.14ff.

MARKET ABUSE

19.46   A genuine innovation under the FSMA 2000, and one which has attracted particularly extensive discussion, is the creation of a new disciplinary offence of 'market abuse'. In essence, this consists of either insider dealing or market manipulation through misleading behaviour. A detailed discussion of 'market abuse' is contained in Chapter 9 above; in this chapter, it is proposed simply to deal with how it is punished.

19.47   Insider dealing and market manipulation were already criminal offences when the FSMA 2000 was drafted.[1] Indeed, they remain so; although the definitions of the relevant criminal offences are not identical to their market abuse counterparts, there is considerable overlap. Yet there was – and remains – a strong perception that the criminal law is ill-suited to dealing with offences against financial markets.[2] In particular, it was felt that to prove offences of insider dealing or market manipulation to a jury beyond reasonable doubt was very difficult, as evidenced by the low number of prosecutions and even lower number of convictions.

1   Insider dealing became a criminal offence in the UK through the Companies Act 1980; the current criminal provisions relating to it are found in the Criminal Justice Act 1993, Pt V, enacted in order to implement the EU Insider Dealing Directive. Criminal penalties for market manipulation were contained in the Financial Services Act 1986 and have been carried over into the FSMA 2000.
2   See, for example, BAK Rider and TM Ashe, 'The Fiduciary, the Insider and the Conflict' (1995).

19.48   A new disciplinary offence of market abuse is therefore created under s 118 of the FSMA 2000. This applies to the authorised and non-authorised alike but, in contrast to what went before, it is explicitly civil in nature. The penalty that it carries is a fine (albeit an unlimited one) and the standard of proof is unspecified and therefore falls below that required by the criminal justice system. It is the old regulatory standard, also applied in disciplinary proceedings for authorised persons: 'If the Authority is satisfied. . .'[1] This does not, however, mean that the FSA can make a finding on a whim: the basic standard is the civil one, although, as with the old SRO disciplinary system, the more serious the allegation, the higher the standard of proof the FSA may be expected to adopt. This matter is discussed further in Chapter 20, paragraphs 20.17ff.

1   FSMA 2000, s 123.

19.49   Although the FSMA 2000 sets out the main parameters for market abuse, the FSA is required, under s 119 of the FSMA 2000, to supplement this by preparing and publishing a code setting out the types of behaviour which in its view will constitute market abuse and also the types which will not. This it has done in the form of the Code of Market Conduct, which forms part of the FSA Handbook. This Code is important; the fact that a given type of behaviour is cited in it as not constituting market abuse is, under s 122, of itself sufficient to afford a defence. The FSA is entitled to amend the Code but the Act makes clear that, if it does, it must publish the new version.

19.50   As mentioned above, the penalty for market abuse is 'a financial penalty of such amount as the Authority sees fit'. This is essentially a fine, although the term 'financial penalty' was preferred in order to make clear that these are civil/administrative, not criminal, provisions. This was a major issue at the time when the Bill was in draft, not least because of the impact of the recently passed Human Rights Act 1998. It has always been the position of the Government, and subsequently the FSA, that the penalties for market abuse are civil. It was, however, feared in some quarters that the European Court of Human Rights might take a different view: fines imposed by a governmental authority are, after all, customarily criminal in nature.

To draw a comparison with the penalties imposed by the SROs under the 1986 regime (or indeed any other disciplinary regime) might have been unhelpful since such penalties could only be imposed on members of the relevant organisation. In contrast, the penalties for engaging in market abuse may be imposed on any person, authorised or not. As for civil measures, these are generally applied in order to compensate for some kind of loss, not for committing a wrong *per se*.[1]

Furthermore, such remedies are generally awarded by a court, (or at least backed by a threat of court action) not a regulatory authority; it is to be noted that restitution orders,[2] in contrast to financial penalties, unless the offender is an authorised person, are made on application to the court as with a normal civil action. Financial penalties are imposed directly by the FSA as a punishment for wrongdoing, not for causing a defined harm to a claimant. It is, of course, the position both of the Treasury and the FSA that market abuse causes harm: harm to general confidence in the financial markets and also to those who deal honestly on those markets. Nonetheless, it was feared that this might be viewed as too nebulous a cause of action.

1   Even where exemplary damages are awarded, for example where a newspaper has made a calculated increased profit through publishing a defamatory article, these merely increase the damages that would be awarded; they do not constitute a separate head of damage in their own right.
2   See paras 19.56 to 19.58 below.

19.51   These arguments are not conclusive; it may be pointed out that many other EU Member States also provide for civil penalties for insider dealing.[1] All of these states are of course also Member States of the Council of Europe and, as such, signatories to the European Convention on Human Rights. Rather than risk a test case, however, it was considered more prudent to incorporate safeguards whilst making it clear that these provisions were indeed civil in nature.

1   France, Greece, Ireland, Italy, Netherlands, Spain. Indeed, in Spain, insider dealing is almost exclusively a civil offence: criminal penalties are reserved for cases involving specified types of primary insider who make a profit (or avoid a loss) of €450,760.

19.52   As stated above, the financial penalties may be of 'such amount as the Authority sees fit'. This does not, however, mean that the level of the fine may be arbitrary; FSMA 2000, s 124 requires the FSA to publish a statement of policy, setting out what levels of penalties will be imposed in what kind of cases.

19.53   When imposing a financial penalty for market abuse, the FSA is required to go through the same process of warning notices and decision notices that it issues in respect of other disciplinary offences. This is set out at paragraphs 19.55ff below. In addition, the FSA may impose a restitution order, if the offender is an authorised person, or apply to the High Court[1] for one in other cases.[2] It may also apply to the court for an injunction to stop the abuse continuing. Where it makes such an application, it may also ask the court to impose the penalty rather than doing so itself.

1   Or, in Scotland, the Court of Session.
2   See paras 19.55ff.

19.54   A final point should perhaps be made concerning the overlap between the criminal offences of insider dealing and misleading the market and the civil/administrative offence of market abuse. It is clear that there will be cases which will fall within both regimes and while the Act was still in draft stage, there was considerable debate on the question of 'double jeopardy', especially as the FSA is entitled to prosecute both criminal offences. The Code of Conduct now states, however, that the same offence is not to be the subject of both a criminal prosecution and proceedings for market abuse; the FSA will choose one route or the other.

DISCIPLINARY PROCESS

19.55   The range of sanctions available to the FSA in relation to authorised persons are very similar to those of the SROs that preceded it under the 1986 regime, including fines, suspension or even termination of authorisation. The FSA may also amend the range of regulated activities which a person is permitted to engage in and/or provide that the person may only continue to engage in them under specified conditions, which the FSA lays down.

Restitution orders

19.56   An additional sanction has, however, been introduced in ss 382–384 of the FSMA 2000: restitution orders. Two conditions are required. First, a person must have committed a breach of a 'relevant requirement', ie an obligation imposed by the Act, or must have been knowingly concerned in such a breach. Alternatively, they may either themselves have engaged in market abuse or, through either action or failure to act, have encouraged or even required another person to do so. Secondly, the breach or market abuse must have resulted in a profit accruing to the offender or have caused loss or other detriment to one or more persons. Where both these conditions are met, the FSA may apply to the High Court for a restitution order, ie an order to pay the FSA such sum as the court considers just. Where however the misconduct or abuse is committed by an authorised person, the FSA may impose the restitution order itself rather than apply to the court.

19.57   The FSA may not, however, keep the funds, it must distribute them among such 'qualifying persons' as the court may direct. Where the order is made directly by the FSA, it orders the offender to pay the funds to the 'appropriate person(s)'; 'appropriate persons' are, however, defined in precisely the same way as 'qualifying persons'.

'Qualifying persons' are defined as either persons who have suffered loss or other detriment as a result of the misconduct or abuse or, where profits have accrued, those to whom those profits 'are attributable'. The first of these seems clear: victims are to be compensated for their loss. That said, there may be cases, particularly of misleading behaviour, where it is difficult to identify – or at least to choose – individual victims in certain cases.

Consider the following scenario, which in fact took place on the Madrid Stock Exchange but could equally have been perpetrated in the UK. Two banks in concert suddenly sell a very large number of securities on a market in the closing minutes of trade on 27 December, when trade is in any event slow. As a result, the price not just of the securities in question but of those across the market in general falls sharply. There are clearly persons who have been adversely affected. But which victims are to be chosen for restitution? Those who subsequently sold securities, possibly in performance of a pre-existing contract, at a price lower than they would otherwise have received? Everyone who was holding securities on that market when the manipulation took place? Or possibly everyone who would have dealt on that market had it not been destabilised (if one can identify them).

19.58   The question of profits is even thornier. To whom are they 'attributable'? It is to be recalled that the 'qualifying persons' are to be nominated not by the FSA but by the court; hence, one cannot necessarily look to the FSA for guidance. Where the profits have been made at the expense of others, it is arguable that the profits are attributable to the victims, subject to the points raised above. In some cases, however, notably those of misuse of information, there is a clear profit but the victims are less identifiable; indeed, it is the view of many that insider dealing or misuse of information may in some circumstances have no victims. It is then less than clear to whom profits in these cases are attributable.

There is also the opposite view that the victims are those who dealt in the relevant securities at the relevant time without the benefit of the inside information. This is the approach taken by the South African Financial Services Board. They impose financial penalties for insider dealing, provided for in legislation very similar to Part VIII of the FSMA 2000. These are treated, however, as restitution orders: the money is divided amongst all those who, within the qualifying period, concluded transactions in the relevant securities in the opposite direction to the offender.[1] The qualifying period is three days either side of the date on which the offender dealt.

Alternatively, it could be argued that the funds from a restitution order are attributable to the person from or through whom the insider obtained his information: the employer or possibly, in some cases, the client on the basis of a constructive trust. But this will not always be the case. Consider a waitress at a restaurant popularly frequented by those involved in confidential financial transactions or takeovers. If she uses the information that she overhears in the course of her work, are her profits to be attributable to the restaurant? Although this is clearly absurd, it is barely more appropriate to attribute them to the restaurant's careless customers.

1 Ie they sold where the offender bought, or vice versa.

Disciplinary procedure

19.59 Although the other sanctions which the FSA may impose are not new, the procedure that the FSA must go through when imposing sanctions is itself new. It was a criticism of the 1986 disciplinary regime that SROs acted as prosecutor, judge and jury; that there was no set procedure which they were required to adopt, they simply decided, following their own processes, that a given person or firm had committed a given type of misconduct and announced what 'sentence' they wished to impose. The perception within the financial services industry was that firms were not entitled to any meaningful form of defence; indeed, it was an indication of a firm's general co-operation with its regulator that it 'swallowed its medicine' when required to do so.

19.60 This perception was quite possibly unfair, but it led to the creation of a new, far more transparent disciplinary process. This is discussed further in Chapter 20. It is to be noted that this process applies not only to the FSA's disciplinary proceedings against authorised persons but also proceedings which it brings against any person in relation to market abuse. A Regulatory Decisions Committee (RDC) has been set up: a committee within the FSA, but explicitly kept separate from those who carried out the investigation. It is the RDC who then commence the disciplinary procedure.

19.61 The first stage of this procedure is a warning notice. The form that this must take is set out in s 387 of the FSMA 2000. The notice must state the allegation made against the person, the evidence supporting that allegation and also any secondary material that may undermine the FSA's case. There are exceptions to this access to material, notably where its release is not in the public interest, where it has been obtained under a warrant or where it concerns a third party and has only been used for comparative purposes. An example of the latter would be similar cases to which the FSA refers in deciding how to proceed. It must state what action the FSA proposes to take as a result. Finally, the notice must give the person on whom it is served 'a reasonable period', in any event not less than 28 days, to respond to it with representations to the FSA. Generally, see further Chapter 20.

19.62 The second stage is then a decision notice under s 388 of the FSMA 2000. This must, again, be served within 'a reasonable period' and sets out what action the FSA proposes to take. It may be a simple confirmation of the action proposed in the warning notice or some other form of action (for example a sanction less severe than that originally envisaged). Again, it must (with the same exceptions as for a warning notice) state the material on which the decision is based. Where, in contrast, the FSA has decided not to take any further action, a notice of discontinuance must be issued.

19.63 Clearly, if no further action is to be taken, this is the end of the matter. If, however, action is confirmed, the person on whom the sanction has been imposed may appeal. Under the 1986 regime, this was also possible, but to an Appeals Committee within the SRO that imposed the sanction in the first place. As stated above, there was a perception that appealing against an SRO sanction would be considered as *per se* unco-operative and that a firm which did so was not only wasting its time but risked harsher treatment in the future.

Appeals have therefore been placed completely outside the FSA structure in a newly created Financial Services and Markets Tribunal. This forms part of the Court Service of the Lord Chancellor's Department and any decision of the FSA may be appealed to it as of right. Should a party not be satisfied with the Tribunal's ruling, further appeal, on a matter of law only, may be made directly to the Court of Appeal.[1]

1 For details on the operation of the Tribunal, see Chapter 20.

Chapter 20

FSA decision-making and the Financial Services and Markets Tribunal

INTRODUCTION

20.1 Under the old system, there were various *ad hoc* bodies that exercised review and disciplinary functions. For example, there was provision under the Banking Act 1987 to constitute (where required) a Banking Appeal Tribunal, though it rarely sat. Much more frequently, the self-regulating organisations (SROs) constituted their own Disciplinary Tribunals and Disciplinary Appeal Tribunals when disciplinary matters arose as regards their members.

20.2 In the course of discussion and debate on the Financial Services and Markets Bill, considerable attention was paid to the decision-making process of the new regulator, and to the provision of adequate safeguards for persons affected. It has emerged as a distinctive feature of the new regime.

There are a number of reasons why this happened. At the time the Bill was going through Parliament, the Human Rights Act 1998 had recently been enacted. The debate frequently focused on the requirements of the European Convention of Human Rights as they might apply to financial institutions subject to action by the regulator. Convention articles considered potentially applicable include article 6 (right to a fair trial). This in turn raised issues as to the nature of regulatory action, for example whether parts of the process might be classified as criminal rather than civil, and the consequential implications, such as the use of compelled testimony, and the presumption of innocence. This was a particularly live issue because the new single regulator was perceived to be more powerful than anything that had preceded it. It was also tied in with the debate over the new market abuse regime. Critics believed that the new provisions were open-ended, and potentially oppressive, and this also caused focus on safeguards. The debate can be followed by reading the two reports of the Joint Committee of both Houses of Parliament chaired by Lord Burns, and the evidence given to it, and the Treasury response (all available on the Internet, including the Financial Services Authority (FSA) website[1]).

The Joint Committee examined these issues in considerable depth. Their examination resulted in changes to the statute, and also in changes to the FSA's own proposals.

1   See www.fsa.gov.uk.

20.3   The process of decision-making is consequently much more elaborate and structured than existed previously, or indeed than is the case in regulatory systems in other countries. It remains to be seen whether this fact, together with the right of recourse to an independent tribunal, will tend to militate against the judicial review of regulatory decisions. This was in any case not common under the old system, perhaps because judges perceived that financial regulation involves a considerable degree of regulatory expertise and discretion.

20.4   In this chapter, a description is given of the decision-making process within the FSA. (This is also dealt with elsewhere in this book: as regards discipline and enforcement, see Chapter 19, and as regards supervision, see Chapter 2.) Following that is an explanation of the working of the Financial Services and Markets Tribunal.

A. FSA DECISION-MAKING

NOTICES

20.5   The decision-making process has been formalised in various statutory provisions which require the giving of notices by the FSA to parties affected by particular types of decision. These notices then give rise to certain rights, including the right to make representations, and ultimately the right to refer the matter to the Tribunal.

20.6   The primary distinction drawn in the statute is between supervisory notices, and warning and decision notices.[1] This is intended to reflect a functional distinction. Broadly speaking, supervisory notices are concerned with regulatory issues, whereas the warning and decision notice procedure is used in the case of disciplinary matters.

However, the distinction is not very clearly drawn in the Financial Services and Markets Act (FSMA) 2000. For example, the supervisory notice procedure applies where the FSA uses its power to intervene in a firm's business, which (so far as UK authorised institutions are concerned) is now called the FSA's 'own initiative' power to vary a Part IV permission. But the warning and decision notice procedure applies to the refusal to grant, or the cancellation of, Part IV permission. Another example of the supervisory notice procedure is the power to suspend or cancel a stock exchange listing under s 77.[2] The relevant sections specify the required contents of the notices. Those provisions of the Act which call for supervisory notices are identified in s 395(13) of the FSMA 2000.

1   See FSMA 2000, s 395(1).
2   See FSMA 2000, s 78(3) and (5).

20.7   The warning and decision notice procedure is much more commonly stipulated for in the 2000 Act. It applies for instance as regards the FSA's enforcement powers in respect of approved persons, to disciplinary matters, and also in the case of the FSA's market abuse powers. There are various other heads, such as in respect of change in control of firms, and collective investment schemes. Where the procedures apply, if the FSA proposes to take action, it must first issue a warning notice.[1] If it goes on to decide to take action, it must then issue a decision notice.[2] There are various statutory requirements as to the contents of these notices which are set out in Part XXVI. These include the giving of reasons.

1   FSMA 2000, ss 207 and 126.
2   FSMA 2000, ss 208 and 127.

20.8   There are distinctions between the statutory provisions referable to the two different kinds of notices. For example, in disciplinary and market abuse matters, a measure introduced by the FSMA 2000, is that the party concerned has certain defined rights of access to FSA material under s 394. This applies not only to material on which the FSA relies in taking the decision, but to secondary material which might undermine it. Further, third parties who are implicated are given certain rights, including the right to refer the matter to the Tribunal.[1] These rights are inapplicable in the case of the supervisory notice procedure. Also as regards references to the Tribunal, the right generally arises on the first supervisory notice, whereas in the case of the warning and decision notice procedure, it arises on the giving of the decision notice. There are certain other notices specified in the 2000 Act, including final notices which essentially come at the end of the process, after the time for reference to the Tribunal has passed, or after the Tribunal's decision if there is a reference.[2]

1   FSMA 2000, s 393.
2   See the FSA Handbook, DEC 1.2.3.

20.9   Naturally, not all regulatory decisions have to be made using the formalised statutory notice procedure. That would be unnecessary and unworkable. It depends on whether the statute requires the procedure to be used. DEC T2 contains a table listing circumstances in which warning and decision notices must be given, and DEC T6 contains a similar table as regards supervisory notices. Notices are not required where applications (eg for permission) are granted, as regards decisions on applications for waivers or to give individual guidance, and 'decisions generally in the course of the FSA's oversight of regulated institutions' (DEC 1.2.8). Finally, it is important to put these procedures into context. Financial regulation in the UK has traditionally been consensual. There is every desire, and indeed every likelihood, that this approach will continue under the new regime.

FSA DECISION-MAKING PROCEDURES

20.10 How are decisions taken within the FSA, and who is responsible for giving the various notices described above? The FSA's decision-making procedures are contained within the block of the Handbook dealing with Regulatory Processes. The procedures are set out in the Decision Making Manual with the code reference 'DEC'.

The manual serves a number of purposes. It describes the statutory notice procedure, including (in the case of the warning and decision notice procedure) third-party rights and the right to access to FSA material. It specifies whether the relevant decision is to be taken within the FSA by the Regulatory Decisions Committee (RDC) or by executive procedures. The allocation of decision-making is specified in Chapter 4.

It is noteworthy that executive procedures continue to apply in the case of many prudential matters, whilst disciplinary matters are now always allocated to the RDC. The manual describes the constitution and procedures of the RDC. It summarises the right to refer matters to the Tribunal. And it describes the pilot mediation scheme available in certain disciplinary cases.

20.11 The RDC is not itself a creature of statute, rather it emerged during the passage of the Financial Services and Markets Bill through Parliament. Its origin is in the debate over disciplinary measures described above. Various models were proposed to meet what was seen as the required separation between the prosecution and adjudication of such matters.

The 'elegant hybrid'[1] that emerged was a non-judicial committee with a purely administrative role, which was nevertheless clearly separate from the operational divisions of the FSA. In the event, the FSA set up the RDC, which (unlike the Tribunal) is not a body prescribed by FSMA 2000. However, its establishment gives effect to s 395(2) by which the FSA's 'procedure must be designed to secure, among other things, that the decision which gives rise to the obligation to give [supervisory, warning and decision notices] is taken by a person not directly involved in establishing the evidence on which that decision is based'. Thus it can be seen immediately that the scope of the RDC's procedure in fact goes beyond disciplinary matters, since it also applies to supervisory notices.

The process of hybridisation, however, was not taken too far. The Treasury rejected a suggestion that the Chairman of the RDC should be appointed by the Lord Chancellor. It was said that this:

> 'would parallel and duplicate the existing requirements in relation to the Tribunal and could blur the distinction between the two stages. We therefore do not consider that putting such a requirement in the Bill is necessary or appropriate, given the distinction between the FSA's administrative and the Tribunal's adjudicative processes, although it may well be that the FSA would consider it appropriate . . . to give a key role to a person who was a distinguished lawyer and/or a practitioner'.

This last point was reflected in the appointment of the RDC's first Chairman.[2]

1 Joint Committee, First Report, para 198.
2 Mr Christopher Fitzgerald.

20.12   The RDC of the FSA comprises a Chairman, and a panel of practitioner members with financial services industry skills and knowledge, and others representing the public interest. It is outside the FSA management structure, and has a separate secretariat. In the FSA's words, it is 'responsible for all our more fundamental regulatory decisions'.

To take the example of enforcement procedures, first the matter will be referred to the RDC by the relevant FSA staff with a recommendation. In the light of the recommendation, the RDC has to consider whether to take the matter further by issuing a warning notice. Except in certain urgent cases, meetings include the Chairman and at least two members. The meetings are in private, and are conducted in such manner as the RDC considers suitable to determine the relevant matter.[1]

If a warning notice is issued, the provisions as to access to FSA material come into operation, as well as the provisions as to the making of representations by persons concerned (these also apply where the decision is made under the executive procedures). Subject to time limits, such persons are entitled to make written or oral representations in response to the warning (or first supervisory) notice. In the case of oral representations, a person may choose to be represented at the meeting by a lawyer.

The decision once taken by the RDC is communicated to the persons concerned by way of a further notice. If no action is to be taken, a notice of discontinuance is issued. If action is to be taken, a decision notice (or supervisory notice where that procedure applies) is issued. At that point, the right to refer the matter to the Tribunal arises. If the matter is not referred within 28 days, a final notice is issued, and the matter is effectively closed. (In the case of the supervisory notice procedure, the right of reference arises at the issue of both the first and second notices).

1   DEC 4.4.12.

20.13   As has been mentioned, the insulation of the decision-making process in a separate committee is a novelty in the field of financial regulation. The process should work well for most matters, particularly disciplinary matters. The informal, private nature of the process is likely to suit many financial institutions. It remains to be seen how it will function in the admittedly rare but usually high-profile cases where regulatory action raises basic policy issues, and requires co-ordination with the Bank of England and the Treasury, and their counterparts abroad. There is in fact provision made for special procedures in urgent cases. Where it is necessary to protect consumers, the decision to issue a supervisory notice can be taken at director of division level.[1]

1   FSMA 2000, s 395(3) and (4), and DEC 4.5.7.

B. FINANCIAL SERVICES AND MARKETS TRIBUNAL

THE TRIBUNAL AND THE LEGISLATIVE PROCESS

20.14   The debate in the course of the Parliamentary process which has been described above also included debate as to the nature of the Tribunal. The following passages from the First Report of the Joint Committee succinctly make the point.

'182. The Treasury have also announced changes to their plans for the Tribunal. The Tribunal is to be "a tribunal of first instance, fully able to consider the merits and facts of each case and with the authority to substitute its own conclusions for those of the FSA"; its name will be changed to reflect its role more accurately. The power in the draft Bill, for the Lord Chancellor to rule certain kinds of new evidence to be inadmissible before the Tribunal, is to be dropped; and the Government propose to "enhance [its] status and shorten the path to justice" by providing for appeal (on a point of law) direct to the relevant appeal court rather than via the High Court.

183. In Lord Lester's opinion,[1] the proposals for the Tribunal now meet the requirement of Article 6.1 of the ECHR for an entitlement to be heard by an "independent, impartial tribunal".'

So it was to be a first instance not an appeal tribunal, and matters were to be placed before it by way of 'reference' rather than 'appeal'. These provisions are now found in Part IX of FSMA. As an independent and impartial tribunal, the Financial Services and Markets Tribunal thus plays an important part in assuring that the regulatory decision-making process as a whole is compatible with the ECHR. For the same reason, it is set up, run and funded by the Lord Chancellor's department, not the FSA.

1 Lord Lester QC who advised various city institutions on the human rights aspects of the legislation.

ESTABLISHMENT AND COMPOSITION OF THE TRIBUNAL

20.15 The Financial Services and Markets Tribunal is established by FSMA 2000, s 132(1). The provisions as regards the Tribunal are found in FSMA 2000, Part IX and Sch 13, and in the Financial Services and Markets Tribunal Rules 2001[1] (referred to here as the 'Tribunal Rules') made by the Lord Chancellor under FSMA 2000, s 132(3). The main provisions are summarised in the remainder of this chapter.

As a creature of statute, the Tribunal, unlike a court, has no inherent jurisdiction. Its powers derive from the statute and the relevant rules. The Tribunal is composed of two panels appointed by the Lord Chancellor, a panel of legally qualified chairmen and a lay panel made up of people 'qualified by experience or otherwise to deal with matters of the kind that may be referred to the Tribunal'.[2] The lay panel consists of people with special experience of the financial sector. At the time of writing the President of the Tribunal is Mr Stephen Oliver QC. The President may give directions as to the practice and procedure to be followed by the Tribunal in relation to references to it.[3] It sits at 45 Bedford Square, London WC1.[4] For individual references, the President selects one of the members of the legal panel to chair the tribunal, and generally two members of the lay panel to sit on it (though it may consist of more than one legal chairmen and any number of lay members at the discretion of the President). The lay members are chosen with regard to their particular experience in accordance with the standing arrangements.[5]

1 SI 2001/2476.
2 FSMA 2000, Sch 13, para 3(4).
3 FSMA 2000, Sch 13, para 10.
4 The address is 15–19 Bedford Square, London WC1B 3AS. The Secretary has various duties under the rules.
5 FSMA 2000, Sch 13, para 7.

RIGHTS OF REFERENCE TO THE TRIBUNAL

20.16   There are wide-ranging rights of reference to the Tribunal in respect of decisions taken by the FSA given to parties affected by them. These are mainly (but not exclusively) set out in the FSMA 2000, and relate to discipline and enforcement in its various forms. They may be conveniently considered under the following headings.

Disciplinary measures

20.17   The right of reference applies to disciplinary measures in respect of authorised persons, that is to say, a public censure or a financial penalty imposed on a firm where the FSA considers that it has contravened a requirement imposed by or under the Act: see FSMA 2000, Part XIV. The authorised person may refer the matter to the Tribunal under FSMA 2000, s 208. The right also applies to disciplinary measures in respect of approved persons, that is to say, a penalty imposed on, or statement of misconduct published in respect of, an approved person under s 66. The person concerned may refer the matter to the Tribunal under s 67.

Permission to carry on regulated activities

20.18   An applicant who is aggrieved by the determination of an application for permission[1] made under Part IV may refer the matter to the Tribunal.[2] The right of reference also applies in the case of the variation of a firm's permission under the FSA's own initiative power under the FSMA 2000, s 53 procedures, and the cancellation of permission.[3] The right of reference also applies where the FSA exercises its analogous powers of intervention in respect of incoming firms under the s 197 procedures.

1   FSMA 2000, s 55.
2   The right applies to any applications made under FSMA 2000, Pt IV.
3   FSMA 2000, s 54. Cancellation takes place under the warning and decision notice procedure.

Matters relating to approval, and prohibition orders

20.19   The refusal of an application for approval in respect of a person performing controlled functions gives 'interested parties' the right to refer the matter to the Tribunal,[1] as does the withdrawal of approval.[2] A person the subject of a prohibition order has the right to refer the matter to the Tribunal,[3] and a further right if a subsequent application to vary or revoke the order is refused by the FSA.[4]

1   FSMA 2000, s 62.
2   FSMA 2000, s 63.
3   FSMA 2000, s 57.
4   FSMA 2000, s 58

Market abuse

20.20   If the FSA decides to take action against a person under the market abuse rules (under FSMA 2000, s 123 it is empowered to impose a penalty, or publish a statement), the person has the right to refer the matter to the Tribunal.[1]

1   FSMA 2000, s 127(4).

Restitution orders

20.21   In addition to its power to apply to the court for an order under FSMA 2000, ss 382 and 383, the FSA may itself require restitution under s 384(5). In that case, the person concerned has the right to refer the matter to the Tribunal.[1]

1   FSMA 2000, s 386(3).

Collective investment schemes

20.22   There are various rights of reference to the Tribunal in respect of the FSA's enforcement powers as regards unit trusts and other regulated collective investment schemes.[1] Rights of reference in respect of the FSA's powers as regards open-ended investment companies (OEICs) are given by the Open-Ended Investment Companies Regulations 2001.[2]

1   See FSMA 2000, Pt XVII.
2   SI 2001/1228 (rr 16, 22, 24, 27 and 28).

Listed companies

20.23   The refusal, suspension or discontinuance of a stock exchange listing by UKLA gives the applicant or issuer as the case may be the right to refer the matter to the Tribunal.[1] There are also rights of reference in relation to sponsors[2] and penalties.[3]

1   See FSMA 2000, ss 76(6) and 78(3) and (5).
2   FSMA 2000, s 88.
3   FSMA 2000, s 92(7).

Others

20.24   There are additional rights to refer matters to the Tribunal in FSMA 2000, ss 320 and 321 (Lloyd's), s 331 (provision of financial services by members of the professions), and s 345 (auditors and actuaries).

THE FUNCTION OF THE TRIBUNAL

20.25   In practice, most disputes will continue to be settled informally between regulator and regulated as has always been the case in respect of financial regulation in the UK. Of the rest, most will probably go no further than the RDC. But some will proceed to the Tribunal, and:

'as Tribunal decisions are published, a body of precedent will build up which should help to define the parameters within which the FSA can operate and thereby effect the FSA's approach in cases more generally. The Tribunal therefore forms a key part of the checks and balances on the FSA's actions under the FSMA 2000'.[1]

1   Freshfields Bruckhaus Deringer on Financial Services: Investigations & Enforcement (2001) para 6.1.

20.26   As already noted, the Tribunal is a first instance tribunal, rather than a body exercising a more narrow appellate function. As stated in the FSA's Legal Framework document, it 'can hear any disputed enforcement case from scratch'. Specifically, s 133(4) of the FSMA 2000 provides that 'on a reference the Tribunal must determine what (if any) is the appropriate action for the Authority to take in relation to the matter referred to it'. Its task therefore in the case of all references is to consider the evidence (whether or not available to the FSA when the decision was taken), and reach its own decision accordingly.[1] Hence it is not fettered by the decision-making process within the FSA which gave rise to the reference.

It does not follow from this, however, that the Tribunal will not have appropriate regard to the expertise and experience of the FSA as the body charged with the regulatory function, depending on the particular circumstances of the case. Nor does it follow that the Tribunal will substitute its own view for that of the FSA on broader policy issues. Generally speaking, the Tribunal's work takes place within the context of finance and the markets, and reflecting their needs, its procedures are intended to be as speedy and cost effective as the justice of the particular case requires.

1   *Eurolife Assurance Co Ltd v FSA*, decision published 26 July 2002, para 29.

Civil or criminal

20.27   The classification of enforcement action by regulatory bodies as civil or criminal for the purposes of article 6 of the ECHR was a matter debated at considerable length before the Joint Committee. A number of consequences may follow from the distinction.

20.28   The issue has subsequently been the subject of decision by the Court of Appeal in *Fleurose v Securities and Futures Authority*.[1] That case was a judicial review of disciplinary proceedings against the appellant by the Securities and Futures Authority (SFA) under the procedures then in force. But the decision is directly in point under the FSMA 2000 as well. The appellant had been found guilty of improper conduct as a securities trader, and his approved status had been suspended for two years, and he was ordered to pay £175,000 towards the costs of the SFA. The appellant submitted that the proceedings should be classified as criminal. It was argued that his privilege against self-incrimination was breached by the use against him in the tribunal of evidence which had been compelled from him during the investigation. He also submitted that, in breach of article 6, he was not afforded legal representation before the appeal tribunal. There were also issues as to the alleged vagueness of the charges against him. Upholding the decision of Morison J, all these arguments were rejected. It was said:

'We accept of course that to be debarred from gaining one's livelihood in an activity in which one has done so for much of one's life is a serious matter. However, applying the principles recently set out in *Han &Yau* quoted above[2] we are not persuaded by any of these submissions that the proceedings instituted by the SFA against M Fleurose are properly to be regarded as involving a criminal charge or offence'.[3]

1   [2001] EWCA Civ 2015.
2   *Han &Yau v Commissioners of Customs and Excise* [2001] EWCA Civ 1048, paras 65 and 66.
3   Para 13.

20.29   Though it is now clear that disciplinary proceedings will be classified as civil, in a number of important respects (eg, access to FSA material) criminal safeguards have been imported by the statute into the process.

20.30   In any case, whatever the classification, the party subject to the charges is equally entitled to a fair hearing. In this context, it is relevant to see the Court's treatment of the individual arguments in the *Fleurose* case. As regards the use of compelled evidence, Morison J said:

'Of their very nature, regulatory processes in the financial field can only work if a full investigation can be carried out. There are, by definition, no laws which compel cooperation with the regulatory authorities: only the powers that come through the threat of disciplinary sanction. In pursuance of the need to protect the investing public, it is justifiable to require traders to cooperate with proper investigations. Indeed, the investigatory process itself is dependent upon answers given, and if answers could be refused on grounds of self-incrimination, or if given those answers could not be used in a disciplinary case, then the regulatory authority would be hampered in its function of protecting the public and, effectively forced to continue to accept as a registered person[1] someone who it knew was unfit to be so. That cannot be the rule. For the individual, the loss of the right to silence in the context of discipline is a small price to pay for the privilege of being able to trade, and is simply part of the obligations undertaken on registration.'[2]

The charges in that case were based on breaches of the equivalent of the FSA's current Statements of Principle for Approved Persons. These are expressed at a high degree of generality. The question was whether they were at such a high degree of generality to make them unsuitable as the basis for disciplinary charges. Morison J accepted 'as a basic principle of fairness in a disciplinary context that the person should know what charge or case he has to meet; and that he should only be found guilty of misconduct if at the time he committed the alleged offence he knew or ought reasonably to have known that what he did was an offence. For this purpose, the Convention adds nothing to what must be a basic understanding of natural justice (or the rules of natural justice).'

On the facts, it was held that the appellant knew that if he was manipulating the market as alleged, then he was guilty of an offence. And in rejecting the allegation that the charges against him were too vague, it was held that having received a detailed summary of the facts, the appellant both knew what were the specific acts alleged and what was the state of mind alleged. So in the event, both requirements of natural justice were satisfied.

1   Equivalent to 'approved person' under FSMA 2000.
2   [2001] EWHC Admin 292. And see paras 24–25 of the Court of Appeal's judgment in [2001] EWCA Civ 2015.

20.31   Finally in this context, it may be noted that during the passage of FSMA 2000 through Parliament, the Government, whilst maintaining that the market abuse regime like the disciplinary regime is civil not criminal, introduced various changes to meet the possibility that this view was incorrect.[1] These include a provision that statements made to investigators under compulsion may not be adduced in market abuse proceedings under FSMA 2000, s 123.[2] Further, ss 134–136 stipulate a legal assistance scheme in respect of references to the Tribunal in respect of decisions taken under s 123. This has been established under the Financial Services and Markets Tribunal (Legal Assistance) Regulations 2001[3] (see below).

There is no provision for free legal representation before the Tribunal in any other type of case. In view of the comments of Morison J in *Fleurose*, it seems unlikely that the fact that a party is unrepresented will in itself give rise to any infringement of article 6 of the European Convention on Human Rights (ECHR).[4] The Tribunal, however, will have to be careful to ensure that the person concerned is not prejudiced by the lack of legal representation, and see that points in his favour receive proper consideration.

1 One distinction is that the market abuse regime unlike the disciplinary regime is not restricted to authorised persons, but applies generally.
2 FSMA 2000, s 174.
3 SI 2001/3632.
4 The point was not considered by the Court of Appeal: see paragraph 23 of their judgment in [2001] EWCA Civ 2015. See also *Pine v Solicitors' Disciplinary Tribunal*, Court of Appeal (Civil Division), 25 October 2001.

Burden and standard of proof

20.32 It is for the FSA to prove its case,[1] though in relation to particular issues the evidential burden may be on the party raising them. There was discussion during the passage of the Bill through Parliament about the standard of proof, though this now needs to be read in the light of the decision in the *Fleurose* case discussed above that disciplinary charges are classified as civil rather than criminal. In its First Report, the Joint Committee said that:

'175. As a matter of English law, criminal charges must be proved beyond reasonable doubt; civil actions are decided on the balance of probabilities. On the face of it, therefore, designating a regime as "civil" rather than "criminal" advantages the prosecutor by making it easier for him to get a favourable result. This raises the question whether using the civil burden of proof would fall foul of the ECHR in relation to provisions which are criminal for that purpose.

176. We have been told that this concern may be misplaced, since it is well-established that the court or tribunal in a civil action can apply a "sliding scale" of proof, applying more or less the criminal standard where criminal-type penalties are at stake. The FSA confirmed that this was its understanding; and we understand that this would be sufficient to satisfy the ECHR.'

1 *Fleurose v Securities and Futures Authority* [2001] EWCA Civ 2015, para 14. This was a disciplinary case, but the burden of proof is on the FSA in all references.

20.33 This approach was in effect adopted in *Fleurose* by Morison J, who said that 'the standard of proof will vary according to the circumstances and little, if any, practical difference is likely to be detectable in practice between the civil and criminal discipline'. (There is no discussion of the matter by the Court of Appeal.)

It is also consistent with the decision of the Competition Commission Appeal Tribunal in *Napp Pharmaceutical Holdings Ltd v Director General of Fair*

Trading.[1] In the context of penalties imposed by the Director General of Fair Trading (DGFT) for abuse of dominant position, it was held that the burden of proof under article 6(2)[2] of the ECHR lay on the Director throughout. Article 6 did not, however, require that the standard be proof beyond all reasonable doubt. The standard of proof in proceedings under the FSMA 2000 involving penalties is the civil standard of proof but that standard was to be applied bearing in mind that the infringements of the 2000 Act are serious matters attracting severe financial penalties.

1   64 BMLR 165.
2   Both parties had accepted that proceedings under the prohibitions imposed by the Competition Act 1998 which may lead to the imposition of a penalty under s 36 involve a 'criminal charge' or a 'criminal offence' for the purposes of art 6 of the ECHR.

REFERRING A MATTER TO THE TRIBUNAL

20.34   In many cases of regulatory action referred to the Tribunal, the action in question will not take effect until the reference has been determined. In the case of the warning and decision notice procedure, FSMA 2000, s 133(9) expressly provides that the FSA must not take the action specified in a decision notice during the period within which the matter to which the decision notice relates may be referred to the Tribunal, and if the matter is so referred, until the reference, and any appeal against the Tribunal's determination, has been finally disposed of. The Tribunal Rules also give the Tribunal specific power to suspend the effect of an FSA notice.[1] This power also applies to supervisory notices, but may only be exercised in certain circumstances (see below).

1   Tribunal Rules, rule 10(1)(e).

Legal assistance in market abuse cases

20.35   Legal aid is not normally available in proceedings before the Tribunal. The exception is in respect of market abuse cases against an individual. FSMA 2000, ss 134–136 accordingly stipulate a legal assistance scheme in respect of references to the Tribunal in respect of decisions taken under s 123. This has been established under the Financial Services and Markets Tribunal (Legal Assistance) Regulations 2001.[1] The Regulations are detailed, and this is only a brief summary.

Applications for a legal assistance order are made in writing to the Tribunal. The Tribunal grants legal assistance to an individual if it is satisfied that it is in the interest of justice to do so, and that his financial resources are such that he requires assistance in meeting legal costs.[2] The powers can be exercised by the Chairman alone, or by the Secretary.[3] Regulation 9 sets out the factors that are to be taken into account as regards the interests of justice test. It is also for the Tribunal to determine the financial eligibility of the applicant, and any contribution which he should pay, in accordance with the rules. Again, there are detailed provisions in that respect. A legal assistance order granted by the Tribunal may provide for solicitor alone or solicitor and advocate. There is also provision for legal assistance to be withdrawn.

1   SI 2001/3632.
2   SI 2001/3632, reg 8.
3   As a person authorised by the Tribunal: SI 2001/3632, reg 43.

The reference notice

20.36   A reference is made by filing a reference notice (the form is available from the Tribunal office). Filing takes place when the reference is sent to the Tribunal office[1] though in view of the time limits parties will wish to ensure that it has in fact been received. A reference must be made before the end of the period of 28 days beginning with the date on which the decision notice or supervisory notice in question is given.[2]

The Tribunal is empowered to extend any time limit for making a reference under the FSMA 2000 or the rules,[3] however the power is not unfettered. Rule 10(2) provides that Tribunal must be satisfied that an extension would be in the interests of justice. Further, it must not determine the application without considering whether the notice was such as to notify the applicant properly and effectively of the referred action, and also whether the existence of the right to make the reference and the time limit had been notified to the applicant, whether in the notice or otherwise. In fact, the notices are required to contain the latter information, and applicants are likely to have to produce good reasons for failing to make a reference in time. The time limit may be further extended by directions of the Tribunal, but only if the Tribunal is satisfied that the further extension would be in the interests of justice.[4]

1   Tribunal Rules, rules 2, 4(1), and 31(2).
2   FSMA 2000, s 133(1). See DEC 5.3.
3   Tribunal Rules, rule 10(1)(d).
4   Tribunal Rules, rule 10(3).

20.37   In the reference notice, the applicant includes reasons for making the reference, but these are likely to be brief. A copy of the relevant FSA notice must be attached.

Upon receipt, particulars of the reference are entered in the Tribunal register.[1] The register is open to inspection by the public.[2] A party is entitled to apply for a direction under rule 10(1)(p) that the register should include no particulars about the reference, in other words that it should remain confidential.[3] Such applications are unlikely to be common in practice, since the reference notice is not intended to set out the applicant's full case, and the particulars will be commensurately brief (no provision in this regard is made in the rules). However a party intending to apply for a hearing in private, might decide to make an application at this stage.

As to hearings, see paras 20.60ff below.

1   Tribunal Rules, rule 4(9).
2   Tribunal Rules, rule 2(1).
3   The Tribunal may give such a direction if it is satisfied that this is necessary, having regard to the interests of morals, public order, national security or the protection of the private lives of the parties; or any unfairness to the applicant or prejudice to the interests of consumers that might result from the register including particulars about the reference (Tribunal Rules, rule 10(9)). This mirrors the part of the rule relating to hearings in public contained in rule 17(3)(b), except that this sub-rule does not include reference to the interests of justice.

20.38   Rule 15 of the Tribunal Rules deals with references by third parties. It provides that in the case of any reference made by an applicant under FSMA 2000, s 393 (which is the section of FSMA 2000 dealing with third-party rights in the context of the warning and decision notice procedure) the rules apply subject to the modifications set out in rule 15.

Statement of case and reply

Statement of case and initial disclosure

20.39   The burden of proof being on the FSA, it files a statement of case within 28 days of being informed by the Tribunal that the reference has been received. The length of this document will vary according to the particular case. In essence, it contains the FSA's justification for the particular decision being referred.

There are a number of formal requirements contained in rule 5. The statement of case must specify the statutory provisions providing for the referred action, the reasons for the referred action, and must set out all the matters and facts upon which the Authority relies to support the referred action. This may be expected to include, for example, previous compliance history, where relevant.[1]

1   DEC 4.2.15 and 16.

20.40   To what extent is the FSA entitled to depart from the reasons given for the action concerned in the decision notice or the supervisory notice? The point is unlikely to arise frequently, but it might arise because of the emergence of new material (or because the FSA enforcement staff conducting the reference before the Tribunal wished to argue the case differently from the reasoning in the RDC decision).

The usual rule in judicial review or statutory appeals is that the relevant decision must be considered on the basis of the evidence available to the decision-maker.[1] This is subject to qualifications, so that (for example) the Court will not quash a flawed decision if new evidence makes the same result inevitable. However as has already been pointed out, under the FSMA 2000 the Tribunal is exercising a first instance not an appellate or review jurisdiction. This is emphasised by the fact that a decision notice does not result in a final notice until either the time for a reference has expired, or the Tribunal has given directions.[2] It follows from the *de novo* nature of the process that the matter is not necessarily dealt with on the basis of the same arguments that were deployed at the RDC stage.

As regards evidence, FSMA 2000, s 133(3) provides that the Tribunal may consider any evidence relating to the subject matter of the reference, whether or not it was available to the FSA at the material time.

1   In the regulatory context, see *Mount Banking Corp v Bank of England* [1994] 3 Bank LR 5 at 6–7 (the further appeal is reported at p 205). The appeal in that case was under provisions of the Banking Act 1987 which defined the question as being whether the decision in question was or was not justified by the evidence on which it was based.
2   FSMA 2000, s 390.

20.41   Rule 5(3) provides that the statement of case shall be accompanied by a list of the documents on which the FSA relies in support of the referred action, and the further material[1] which in the opinion of the FSA might undermine the decision to take that action. This will be referred to as 'initial disclosure'. The applicant may request copies of listed documents, and there is a right of inspection.[2] Disclosure by one party might seem somewhat unusual at this early stage, but it will be recalled that the applicant will already most likely have had access to this material at the time of the warning notice under the provisions of FSMA 2000, s 394. On the other hand, if the notice was a supervisory notice, this will be the first time the FSA has disclosed its material.

There is a further discussion of disclosure at paras 20.46–20.48 below.

1 The definition of 'further material' in rule 2(1) makes it clear that the term includes documents which are obtained by the FSA after giving the notice.
2 Tribunal Rules, rule 8(7).

Applicant's reply

20.42 The applicant files a reply 28 days after receiving the statement of case. In essence, the reply contains the applicant's case, as well as responding specifically to the points made in the statement of case.

There are a number of formal requirements contained in rule 6. The reply must state the grounds on which the applicant relies in the reference, identify all matters contained in the statement of case which are disputed by the applicant, and state the applicant's reasons for disputing them. The reply must be accompanied by a list of all the documents on which the applicant relies in support of his case.[1] Copying and inspection of documents listed is governed by rule 8(7). It will be seen that whereas the FSA's disclosure obligation includes documents that undermine its case, this obligation is not placed on the applicant.[2] However, the FSA may well already have had access to the applicant's records under its formal and informal information gathering and investigation powers.

1 Tribunal Rules, rule 6(3).
2 Compare standard disclosure in civil litigation under the Civil Procedure Rules (CPR) 1998, Pt 31, r 31.6.

20.43 Following the filing of the reply, the FSA is under a secondary disclosure obligation. Rule 7(1) provides that if in the light of the reply there is any further material which might be reasonably expected to assist the applicant's case and which has not already been disclosed in the rule 5(3) list, the FSA must file a list of such further material. This must be done within 14 days of the filing of the reply. Copying and inspection of documents listed is governed by rule 8(7).

By referring to documents that assist the applicant rather than undermining the decision (as does rule 5(3)), this rule has the effect of broadening the statutory obligation to give access to material which arises in respect of warning and decision notices under s 394 of the FSMA 2000.

20.44 There is provision in the rules for the Tribunal to permit or require supplementary statements,[1] and in some cases it may be convenient for the FSA to file a further statement, responding to the reply. There is power to order a statement or reply (or supplementary statement or written representation) to be struck out at any stage of the proceedings on the ground that it is scandalous, frivolous or vexatious.[2]

1 Tribunal Rules, rule 10(f).
2 Tribunal Rules, rule 26(3).

Time limits

20.45 One final point relates to the time limits for the statement of case and reply. In the nature of the Tribunal's work, it is important that these are adhered to. This is emphasised by rule 10(4) which provides that where a party files such a document or list later than any time limit without applying for a direction extending the time limit, that party shall be treated as applying for such a direction. However no such direction shall be given unless the Tribunal is satisfied that such an extension would be in the interests of justice.

Also, if no statement of case or reply is filed within the time limit, the Tribunal has power to determine the reference without an oral hearing under rule 14(3). Indeed, there is a more general power to order a reference to be struck out for want of prosecution.[1]

1 Tribunal Rules, rule 26(3).

Disclosure

Exceptions to the disclosure obligations

20.46   Rule 8 contains a number of exceptions to the disclosure obligations. These partly track the exceptions in s 394 of the FSMA 2000 to the FSA's obligation to give access to its material on giving a warning or decision notice. In some instances, they have been extended to cover the applicant's limited disclosure obligation under rule 6(3). In summary, the FSA need not include in its lists any document that relates to a case involving a person other than the applicant which was taken into account in the applicant's case only for the purposes of comparison with other cases. Neither party need include in its list any document the disclosure of which is prohibited by s 17 of the Regulation of Investigatory Powers Act 2000 (which is to do with intercepted communications). In the normal way, documents protected by legal privilege are included in the list, but copies are not disclosed.

There is a particular statutory provision defining documents protected by legal privilege. This is the definition of 'protected items' in s 413 of the FSMA 2000.

20.47   Rule 8(4) provides that a party may apply to the Tribunal (without giving notice to the other party) for a direction authorising the exclusion of a document from the relevant list on the ground that disclosure would not be in the public interest, or would not be fair. The fairness issue is determined having regard to:

(i)   the likely significance of the document to the applicant in relation to the matter referred to the Tribunal, and
(ii)   the potential prejudice to the commercial interests of a person other than the applicant which would be caused by disclosure of the document.

This is broadly the same language as is used in s 394 of the FSMA 2000, except that the provision is extended to cover the applicant's disclosure obligation.[1] In deciding the matter the Tribunal may require that the document be produced to it, and may give the other party the chance to make representations.

1 It is hard to see its relevance in that regard, since the applicant is only obliged to disclose documents on which it relies, and could hardly rely on documents which it did not disclose.

Further disclosure

20.48   The Tribunal may direct further disclosure under rule 10(g). This may be made in respect of documents in the custody or under the control of any party, in other words the applicant's documents are included within this provision. The test is whether the Tribunal considers that the document is or may be relevant to the determination of the reference. The general test in respect of directions will doubtless provide a reference point, namely whether the disclosure sought would help to ensure the just, expeditious and economical determination of the reference.[1]

The same exceptions apply as have already been noted in the discussion of rule 8 above.[2]

1 See Tribunal Rules, rule 9(1), and compare CPR 1998, r 31.12 and the overriding objective in CPR 1998, r 1.1 to similar effect.
2 See Tribunal Rules, rule 10(8).

DIRECTIONS AND PRE-HEARING REVIEW

20.49 Rule 9 of the Tribunal Rules contains the procedure for applying to the Tribunal for directions. The Tribunal also has power to give directions of its own initiative. Directions may be given to enable the parties to prepare for the hearing of the reference, to assist the Tribunal to determine the issues and generally to ensure the just, expeditious and economical determination of the reference.[1] Directions will usually be dealt with by the Chairman alone.[2] The application will normally be determined without an oral hearing,[3] and representations by a party objecting to a proposed direction will normally be in writing.[4] Notice of the Chairman's determination is given to the parties.[5] There is provision for objection after a direction has been made, in that the person to whom it is given may apply to the Tribunal showing good cause why it should be varied or set aside.[6] However, such an application is not to be granted without first notifying any person who applied for the direction and giving that party an opportunity to make representations.

1 Tribunal Rules, rule 9(1).
2 Tribunal Rules, rule 29, and FSMA 2000, Sch 13, para 9(d).
3 Tribunal Rules, rule 16(1)(b).
4 See the definition in Tribunal Rules, rule 2.
5 Tribunal Rules, rule 9(6).
6 Tribunal Rules, rule 9(8).

20.50 The Chairman may also direct a pre-hearing review (which again is held before the Chairman alone), and is likely to do so in complex cases. This is an oral hearing. Rule 9(11) enjoins the Chairman to give all directions appearing necessary or desirable for securing the just, expeditious and economical conduct of the reference, and to endeavour to secure that the parties make all admissions and agreements as they ought reasonably to have made in relation to the proceedings.

20.51 Subject to the provisions of FSMA 2000 and the Tribunal Rules, the Tribunal may regulate its own procedure,[1] which appears to give considerable latitude in the directions that may be given. In fact, rule 10 contains a long list of particular types of direction which covers most if not all of the matters which are likely to arise. A number of these directions are considered elsewhere in this chapter, and some others also merit individual mention.

1 Tribunal Rules, rule 26(2).

List of issues and skeleton arguments

20.52 Directions may be given to require any party to provide a statement of relevant issues and facts, identifying those which are, and are not, agreed by the other party.[1] This is standard practice in (for example) the Commercial Court, and can be useful in complicated cases in narrowing the areas of dispute. For the same reason, although the rules do not explicitly refer to skeleton arguments, it is likely in such cases that these will also be the subject of a direction.

1   Tribunal Rules, rule 10(1)(h).

Witnesses

20.53 Directions may be given requiring any party to file a list of the witnesses whom the party wishes to call to give evidence at the hearing of the reference, and statements of the evidence which those witnesses intend to give, if called.[1] Taken together with rule 10(1)(n) by which directions may be given providing for the manner in which any evidence may be given, the Tribunal is able to follow the modern practice of permitting witness statements exchanged between the parties in advance of the hearing to stand as evidence in chief.[2] It is, however, very 'possible that the Tribunal would try to limit the extent of the witness statements, to prevent their production becoming over-elaborate and costly and to keep the ambit of the case within appropriate bounds'.[3]

Under rule 12, the Tribunal can compel the attendance of witnesses, by issuing a witness summons requiring a person to attend before it to give evidence as a witness and/or to produce a document in his custody or under his control which the Tribunal considers it necessary to examine. Under FSMA 2000, Sch 13, para 11, failure to comply without reasonable excuse is a criminal offence.

1   Tribunal Rules, rule 10(1)(k).
2   CPR 1998, rr 32.4 and 32.5.
3   *Freshfields Bruckhaus Deringer on Financial Services: Investigations & Enforcement*, para 6.93.

Experts

20.54 A tribunal will include lay members with experience in the financial sector. Nonetheless, there is a wide perception that expert evidence is likely to play a considerable role in hearings. A potential example is the 'regular user of the market' test in the market abuse provisions. In the civil courts the use (and misuse) of experts has been the subject of thorough examination in the 1999 reform of civil procedure, and the Tribunal will seek to adhere to best current practice in this regard. The provisions in the rules are fairly brief. Under rule 10(l), directions may be given to make provision as to any expert witnesses to be called including the number of such witnesses and the evidence to be given by them. This issue is one that may fall to be dealt with at the pre-hearing review, if there is one. Under FSMA 2000, Sch 13, para 7(4) there is even provision for the Tribunal to appoint its own expert to provide assistance 'if it appears to the Tribunal that a matter before it involves a question of fact of special difficulty'. Under rule 10(m) directions may be given to provide for the appointment of such an expert and for the parties to be sent copies of any report that he produces.[1]

1 There are a number of issues in this respect which are presently unclear at this point, including responsibility for payment of such an expert, and his precise status at the hearing. The enabling power in para 7(4) is in the section of Sch 13 to FSMA 2000 headed 'Constitution of the Tribunal'.

Consolidation

20.55 Where two or more reference notices have been filed in respect of the same matter, directions may be given providing that the references or any particular issue or matter raised in the references be consolidated or heard together.[1]

1 Tribunal Rules, rule 10(q).

Preliminary issues

20.56 This is dealt with in rule 13, which provides that the Tribunal may direct that any question of fact or law which in relation to the reference be determined at a preliminary hearing. If the determination of the question substantially disposes of the reference, the Tribunal may treat the preliminary hearing as the hearing of the reference and may make such order by way of disposing of the reference as it thinks fit.

Suspending the FSA's action

20.57 Rule 10(1)(e) provides that directions given by the Tribunal may suspend the effect of an FSA notice (or prevent it taking effect) until the reference has been finally disposed of, or until any appeal against the Tribunal's determination of the reference has been finally disposed of, or both. In the case of the warning and decision notice procedure, this power will be academic, since the decision concerned will not take effect until after the Tribunal's determination. However there are some FSA decisions, for example a decision to take urgent action to vary a firm's Part IV permission by supervisory notice which may take effect immediately. This includes the withdrawal of a bank's permission to accept deposits where the FSA decides that such action is necessary to protect consumers. Such cases may be rare, but are of great importance to the institution concerned, to the regulator, and indeed often to the wider community. In practice, the notice may be combined with other steps taken under the regulatory powers, such as an application to the Court for the appointment of administrators. The question is when the Tribunal (on what are likely to be urgent applications at short notice) might exercise its power to suspend the effect of the notice.

In this regard, it is important to note the proviso contained in rule 10(6). This provides that the Tribunal may give such a direction only if it is satisfied that to do so would not prejudice:

(a) the interests of any persons (whether consumers, investors or otherwise) intended to be protected by the notice, or

(b) the smooth operation or integrity of any market intended to be protected by that notice.

Withdrawal of references and unopposed references

20.58 Rule 14 deals with withdrawal of references and unopposed references. The applicant may withdraw the reference, or the FSA may state that it does not oppose the reference or that it is withdrawing its opposition to it:

(a) at any time before the hearing of the reference, without permission, by filing a notice to that effect, or

(b) at the hearing of the reference, with the Tribunal's permission.

In either case, the Tribunal has power to determine the reference. Though there is no specific limitation on the power to determine the reference in these circumstances, it has been suggested that the rules are drafted flexibly in this respect to allow the Tribunal to give effect to a settlement between the FSA and the applicant by making a determination in accordance with the agreed terms.[1] When determining proceedings under rule 14, the Tribunal may make a costs order under rule 21.

1 *Freshfields Bruckhaus Deringer on Financial Services: Investigations & Enforcement*, paras 6.111 and 6.113.

Failure to comply

20.59 A number of specific sanctions have already been noted. There is a more general provision in rule 27 which provides that where a party has, without reasonable excuse, failed to comply with a direction or with a provision of the rules, the Tribunal may:

(i) make a costs order under rule 21 against that party;

(ii) where that party is the applicant, dismiss the whole or part of the reference (or, if there is more than one applicant, that applicant's reference);

(iii) where that party is the FSA, strike out the whole or part of the statement of case and, where appropriate, direct that the FSA be debarred from contesting the reference altogether.

These steps cannot be taken unless the Tribunal has given the party concerned notice and an opportunity to make representations.

THE HEARING

20.60 References do not have to be determined at an oral hearing. Rule 16 provides that the Tribunal may determine a reference, or any particular issue, without an oral hearing if the parties agree in writing. In such a case, the parties will make their representations to the Tribunal in writing. In practice most references will be determined at an oral hearing.

Rule 16 makes provision for the position as regards publicising the decision, which are effectively the same as apply where a reference is heard in whole or in part in private (see rule 20 below). The Tribunal must consider whether there are circumstances making it undesirable to make a public pronouncement of the whole or part of its decision. To that end, it may take steps anonymising the decision, editing the text of the decision, and/or declining to publish the whole or part of the decision. However, the rule goes on to stipulate that any such step shall be taken with a view to ensuring the minimum restriction on public pronouncement that is consistent with the need for the restriction.

Public or private hearings

20.61   During the passage of the Financial Services and Markets Bill, some commentators argued that the proceedings should be in private, as was the case with disciplinary tribunals set up by the SROs under the old system. It was argued that public hearings would deter financial institutions from exercising their right of reference. As regards article 6(1) of the ECHR, such comment-ators pointed out that a public hearing is an entitlement of a party subject to a charge, rather than a requirement. Also, as explained above, the RDC proceeds in private. On the other hand, its process is administrative, whereas the process of the Tribunal is adjudicative.

A countervailing point is that open justice is an important principle in itself.[1] In a written Parliamentary answer on 24 July 2001, the Lord Chancellor said that:

> 'during the passage of the Financial Services and Markets Bill, Ministers stated that the Rules for the Financial Services and Markets Tribunal would cover the circumstances in which tribunal hearings were not held in public. They also gave commitments that the tribunal would comply with best practice as laid down by the Council on Tribunals. The council's Model Rules favour, for tribunal proceedings, a presumption of publicity with provision for private hearings. This approach is followed in the procedure rules for the Financial Services and Markets Tribunal.'

An Opposition motion calling for the Tribunal rules to be replaced with rules that preserve the confidentiality of proceedings in the Tribunal was rejected in the House of Lords.[2] In the event, therefore, the debate has been resolved in favour of public hearings as the norm, with a power to sit in private.

1 *Hodgson v Imperial Tobacco Ltd* [1998] 1 WLR 1056; *Barings plc (in liquidation) v Coopers & Lybrand and others* [2000] 3 All ER 910; *Storer v British Gas plc* [2000] 1 WLR 1237.
2 See Hansard for 23 October 2001.

20.62   Rule 17 provides that 'subject to the following paragraphs of this rule, all hearings shall be in public'. The following paragraphs go on to stipulate when the Tribunal may direct that all or part of a hearing shall be in private. It may do so in two circumstances. The first is upon the application of all the parties. The second contains a similar though not identical provision to article 6(1) of the ECHR. The Tribunal may sit in private upon the application of any party, if it is satisfied that a hearing in private is necessary,[1] having regard to:

(i)   the interests of morals, public order, national security or the protection of the private lives of the parties, or

(ii) any unfairness to the applicant or prejudice to the interests of consumers that might result from a hearing in public.

In either case, the Tribunal must be satisfied that a hearing in private would not prejudice the interests of justice. And before giving a direction that the entire hearing should be in private, the Tribunal has to consider whether only part of the hearing should be heard in private. In practice it is likely to be limb (ii) which is relevant to applications under this rule. Unfairness to the applicant might result for example from publicity given to trade sensitive information, or information confidential to the applicant, or to its customers, or where publicity might prejudice other proceedings. It will depend on the circumstances of the particular case, and the power is likely to be exercised flexibly and responsively to the needs of the markets, and individual applicants.[2] The Tribunal has held that it 'must weigh both the likelihood and the seriousness of possible unfairness or prejudice, and consider whether, in the circumstances, a private hearing is really needed'.[3]

1 See eg *In re an Inquiry under the Company Securities (Insider Dealing) Act 1985* [1988] AC 660 at 704.
2 In the House of Lords debate, the Parliamentary Secretary to the Lord Chancellor's Department (Baroness Scotland) described the power as a very flexible tool.
3 *Eurolife Assurance Co Ltd v FSA*, decision published 26 July 2002, para 38. This decision contains a full discussion of the relevant issues.

20.63 Sometimes the type of reference involved may be relevant. For example, the Tribunal may be more inclined to sit in private if the issue relates to consideration of a firm's prudential arrangements and there is no wider public interest, than in the case of disciplinary proceedings where the sole reason for the application is to avoid embarrassment.

It may be noted in the context of 'prejudice to the interests of consumers' that the term 'consumer' is given an extended meaning in FSMA 2000, s 138(7), including anyone using financial services. Even if the whole hearing is not heard in private, there is power to hold part of it in private, and otherwise to protect confidential information. Rule 17(11) provides that where all or part of a hearing is held or is to be held in private, the Tribunal may direct that information about the whole or part of the proceedings (including information that might help to identify any person) shall not be made public.[1] Under rule 20, there are special provisions as regards the publication of the Tribunal's decisions if the hearing or part of it is in private (see below) which can be used where appropriate to protect evidence received in private.

1 Such a direction may provide for the information that is to be entered in the register or removed from it.

Procedure at hearings

20.64 Rule 19(1) provides that subject to the Act and the rules, the Tribunal shall conduct all hearings in such manner as it considers most suitable to the clarification of the issues before it and generally to the just, expeditious and economical determination of the proceedings. This rule reflects not only the overriding objective of the CPR, but also the special need in the financial context for justice to be done in an expeditious and cost-effective manner.

There are some other more specific provisions in rule 19(2). As regards representation, in practice, the FSA will be legally represented,[1] and the same will usually apply to applicants. However there are broader rights of representation and assistance. Under rule 18 the parties may appear at the hearing with assistance from any person if desired, and may be represented by any person, whether or not that person is legally qualified. Rule 18(2) qualifies this to the extent that if in any particular case the Tribunal is satisfied that there are good and sufficient reasons for doing so, it may refuse to permit a person to assist or represent a party at the hearing (though in practice a refusal is likely to be rare).

1   In 2001, Mr David Mayhew was appointed as the FSA's Leading Advocate to appear for it 'in high profile cases before the Tribunal, and in High Court civil actions and criminal court prosecutions'.

20.65   Generally, the procedure will follow that used in other tribunals and in the courts. Since the burden of proof is on the FSA, it will generally open the case, the applicant or applicants will follow, and the FSA will have the right of reply. Rule 19 specifically entitles parties to give evidence (and, with the consent of the Tribunal, to bring expert evidence), to call witnesses, to question any witnesses, and to address the Tribunal on the evidence, and generally on the subject matter of the reference. Significantly, rule 19(3) provides that evidence may be admitted by the Tribunal whether or not it would be admissible in a court of law, and whether or not it was available to the FSA when taking the referred action. This latter point reflects the express provision in FSMA 2000, s 133(3). If a party fails to attend without good and sufficient reason, the reference may be determined in his absence.[1]

1   Rule 19(4).

THE DECISION

20.66   FSMA 2000 sets out the parameters of decision-making by the Tribunal. The basic provision is s 133(4), by which 'on a reference the Tribunal must determine what (if any) is the appropriate action for the Authority to take in relation to the matter referred to it'. On determination, the Tribunal remits the matter to the FSA with such directions (if any) as it considers appropriate for giving effect to its determination.

There is an important limitation. In the case of the warning and decision notice procedure, the FSA may only issue a decision notice under the same part of the Act as the warning notice was issued.[1] Thus, the FSA cannot take action under Part VIII (market abuse) if the warning notice was issued under Part XIV in respect of a breach of the rules by an authorised person. The same limitation applies on a reference to the Tribunal. Section 133(6) provides that in determining a reference made as a result of a decision notice, the Tribunal may not direct the FSA to take action which it would not, as a result of s 388(2), have had power to take when giving the decision notice. Thus in deciding a reference about a disciplinary penalty, the Tribunal cannot substitute a market abuse penalty. Or if the FSA proposes to fine a firm for its regulatory breaches under Part XIV, the Tribunal may direct that the FSA impose a different fine or a public censure, but cannot impose a restitution order (under Part XXV), or a variation of the firm's permission (under Part IV). Similarly, in determining a reference made as a result of a supervisory notice, the Tribunal may not direct the FSA to take action which would have otherwise required the giving of a decision notice.[2] Within those parameters, the Tribunal must reach its own decision. It follows for example, that it may increase as well as decrease the penalty designated in a decision notice.

The statute also provides that the Tribunal may, on determining a reference, make recommendations as to the Authority's regulating provisions or its procedures.[3]

1   FSMA 2000, s 388(2).
2   FSMA 2000, s 133(7).
3   FSMA 2000, s 133(8).

20.67   A decision of the Tribunal may be taken by a majority, and the decision must state whether it was unanimous or taken by a majority. It must be recorded in a document which contains a statement of the reasons for the decision, and is signed and dated by the member of the panel of chairmen dealing with the reference. The Tribunal must send a copy to each party, and any authorised person concerned with the reference. A copy must also be sent to the Treasury.[1] The FSA must act in accordance with the determination of, and any direction given by, the Tribunal.[2] In the case of references under the warning and decision notice procedure, a final notice is issued accordingly.[3]

1   FSMA 2000, Sch 13, para 12.
2   FSMA 2000, s 133(10).
3   FSMA 2000, s 390(2).

20.68   There are special provisions in rule 20 of the Tribunal Rules that apply if the whole or any part of any hearing was in private. The Tribunal has to consider whether, having regard to the reason for the hearing or any part of it being in private, and the outcome of the hearing, it would be undesirable to make a public pronouncement of the whole or part of its decision. If it does, it may take appropriate steps. These include anonymising the decision, editing the text of the decision, and declining to publish the whole or part of the decision. However any such step shall be taken with a view to ensuring the minimum restriction on public pronouncement that is consistent with the need for the restriction.

Costs

20.69   In civil cases, the losing party generally pays the legal costs of the successful party, but again this was the subject of debate during the legislative process.[1] In the result, the Tribunal only has limited power to order costs. The two exceptional cases are both set out in FSMA 2000, Sch 13, para 13:

(1)   If the Tribunal considers that a party to a reference has acted vexatiously, frivolously or unreasonably it may order that party to pay to another party the whole or part of the costs or expenses incurred by the other party in connection with the proceedings.

(2)   The second exception applies specifically to the FSA. If the Tribunal considers that a decision of the FSA which is the subject of the reference was unreasonable it may order the FSA to pay to another party the whole or part of the costs or expenses incurred by the other party in connection with the proceedings.[2]

There is provision in rule 21 for the Tribunal to fix the costs, or order their assessment. An order of the Tribunal as to costs may be enforced as if it were an order of a county court, or in Scotland, as if it were an order of the Court of Session.[3]

1   See the First Report of the Joint Committee, paras 217–218.
2   According to one author, the FSA is not to be considered unreasonable 'just because its decision is overturned by the Tribunal': Alcock, *The Financial Services and Markets Act 2000, A Guide to the New Law* (2000), p 50.
3   FSMA 2000, s 133(11).

Review

20.70   Clerical mistakes in any document recording a direction or decision of the Chairman or the Tribunal, or errors arising in such a document from an accidental slip or omission, may be corrected by a certificate signed by the Chairman.[1] There is also a more general, though very limited, power under rule 22 to review a decision on the application of a party or of the Tribunal's own initiative. The power arises in two circumstances:

(1)   First, if the Tribunal is satisfied that its decision determining a reference was wrongly made as a result of an error on the part of the Tribunal staff.
(2)   Second, if new evidence has become available since the conclusion of the hearing to which that decision relates, the existence of which could not have been reasonably known of or foreseen.

Unless the application is made immediately following the decision at the hearing of the reference, it has to be filed not later than 14 days after the date on which notification of the decision was sent to the parties. The same time limit applies to an own initiative review. The parties have an opportunity to make representations, and if on review the decision is set aside, the Tribunal substitutes a new decision, or orders a re-hearing before either the same or a differently constituted Tribunal.

1   Rule 28(3).

APPEALS

20.71   Unusually, appeals from the Tribunal lie directly to the Court of Appeal. This was provided for in the statute so as to enhance the status of the Tribunal, and shorten the path to justice (see para 182 of First Report of the Joint Committee). In his Report of the Review of Tribunals[1] (March 2001), Sir Andrew Leggatt recommended that the position in this respect should be maintained. He said:

'6.14   There are a few tribunals where we think it desirable to preserve existing and specific provision for appeals. . . . There are . . . appeals direct to the Court of Appeal from a small number of first-tier tribunals: the Aircraft and Shipbuilding Industries Arbitration Tribunal, the Competition Commission Appeal Tribunal, the Financial Services and Markets Tribunal, the Foreign Compensation Commission, and the Special Immigration Appeal Commission. Each of these is a particularly expert tribunal, dealing with exceptionally complex cases. We consider that an appeal direct to the Court of Appeal would continue to be appropriate in each of these instances.'

1   This important Report proposed general reforms of the tribunal system.

20.72 The statutory provisions are contained in FSMA 2000, s 137. An appeal lies only on points of law. The section provides that a party to a reference to the Tribunal may with permission appeal to the Court of Appeal, or in Scotland, to the Court of Session, on a point of law arising from a decision of the Tribunal disposing of the reference. Thus there is no appeal against an interlocutory order, unless it disposes of the reference. 'Permission' means permission given by the Tribunal or by the Court of Appeal or (in Scotland) the Court of Session.

If, on an appeal the court considers that the decision of the Tribunal was wrong in law, it may remit the matter to the Tribunal for rehearing and determination by it, or itself make a determination. Rules 23 and 24 deal with applications for permission to appeal. The application is made orally when the decision is announced, or in writing not later than 14 days after the decision was sent to the parties. The rule in civil cases as regards permission, is that it will only be given where the appeal appears to have a real prospect of success, or there is some other compelling reason why the appeal should be heard.[1]

1   See CPR 1998, r 52.3.

Chapter 21

International supervisory co-operation

INTRODUCTION

21.1 A number of difficult issues arise with regard to the supervision of banks and securities firms in the new global markets of the new millennium. Although a single global market in financial services has been created supervision is still conducted on an essentially local and national basis. This creates what might be referred to as a fundamental global market and local control conflict.[1] Various forms of co-operation have been developed at the international level to attempt to correct the deficiencies that would otherwise arise in securing the complete and effective supervision of global financial markets.[2] Continuing instances of collapse and significant financial loss in the markets nevertheless confirm that this work is still far from complete.

1 See G Walker, 'Conglomerate Law and International Financial Market Supervision', Boston Annual Review of Banking Law, Vol 17 (1998). See also Walker, *International Banking Regulation – Law, Policy and Practice* (2001), Introduction.
2 See, for example, International Monetary Fund (IMF), *Towards a Framework for Financial Stability* (January 1988), Ch VIII.

Supervisory issues

21.2 In constructing an appropriate response to the challenges created by the new global markets in financial services, two principal sets of supervisory issues have to be distinguished.

644

Operational problems

21.3 In the first place, a number of basic operational problems have to be overcome in supervising the activities of an institution or group of institutions with offices in more than one country. Two ancillary issues arise in this regard with regard to supervisory co-operation and the proper scope of supervision:

(i)   *Supervisory co-operation:* Effective mechanisms must initially be established between the separate supervisors involved in each country.[1] These must, in particular, provide for the full exchange of all appropriate information in relation to the activities of the institution or group and allow all necessary action to be taken on a co-ordinated basis. In practice, this will be constrained by local restrictions on the exchange of confidential information and the jurisdictional problems that necessarily arise in attempting to conduct enquiries or investigations, enforcing sanctions or in exercising any rights of recovery on a cross-border basis. It is to facilitate such co-operation and co-ordination of activity that various types of Memoranda of Understanding (MoUs) or more specific Financial Information Sharing Agreements (FISMoUs) have been entered to between national authorities.[2]

(ii) *Proper scope of supervision:* The second problem that arises at the operational level is that the activities of an institution or group must not be considered in isolation or on a purely local basis. To ensure that proper supervision is effected, it is necessary to attempt to construct a larger, more complete perspective of all of its operations as a whole. It was for this reason that early concepts of consolidated supervision were developed from the late 1970s onwards.[3] Consolidated supervision was given effect to in the European Union under the first Consolidated Supervision Directive in 1983 which was extended in 1992.[4] Under the further Prudential Supervision Directive which was adopted in 1995[5] national authorities were required to refuse applications for authorisation in such cases as BCCI where the structure of the group was so opaque that it prevented effective supervision being conducted. Consolidated supervision as such is, however, only concerned with legal as opposed to business or management structures within a group and accordingly remains a limited, although still valuable, supervisory tool. Of more significant recent interest in this regard within the UK are the changes introduced under the new RATE[6] framework which consider all significant business as well as legal units of the supervised entity.[7] This assists, in particular, in allowing supervisors to respond more effectively to new management structures or techniques such as with the use of matrix management models on both a national and global basis.

---

1   See Walker, *International Banking Regulation – Law, Policy and Practice* (2001), Ch 4.
2   See paras 21.7–21.16.
3   See Chapter 6, para 6.3. See also Walker, 'Consolidated Supervision', BJIBFL (February/March 1996), 74 and 131.
4   See Council Directive 83/350/EEC of 13 June 1983 on the supervision of credit institutions on a consolidated basis; and Council Directive 92/30/EEC on the supervision of credit institutions on a consolidated basis.
5   See Council Directive 95/26/EEC of 29 June 1995 amending the First and Second Banking Directives 77/780/EEC and 89/646/EEC in the field of credit institutions, Council Directive 73/239/EEC in the field of non-life insurance, Council Directives 79/267/EEC and 92/96/EEC in the field of life insurance and Council Directive 93/22/EEC in the field of investment firms.
6   Risk Assessment, Tools of Supervision, Evaluation.
7   See Blair et al (2nd edn), Chapter 4, paras 4.43–4.92.

Common standards

21.4   The other major set of issues that arises at the international level is concerned with the absence of any common or harmonised standards in respect of the supervision and regulation of financial activities. In the absence of any single set of common measures, the activities of an institution or group will be subject to a number of distinct and possibly conflicting local provisions. This will result in increased costs and administration for the institution but may also create supervisory gaps where the local provisions are different in terms of the scope and content of the supervision effected.

It was partly to attempt to ensure that such supervisory gaps did not arise that the Basel Committee on Banking Supervision (Basel Committee) was originally set up in 1974.[1] The Basel Committee has subsequently been involved with both the development of co-operative practices between supervisors in respect of the cross-border supervision of banks and banking groups and the construction of appropriate common prudential standards such as with regard to capital adequacy, market risk and interest rate risks and most recently internal controls systems.[2] The International Organisation of Securities Commissions (IOSCO) has also been developing similar sets of standards in the securities area.

1 See Walker, *International Banking Regulation – Law, Policy an Practice* (2001), Ch 1.
2 See Walker, *International Banking Regulation – Law, Policy an Practice* (2001), Ch 2.

Financial conglomerates

21.5   The above issues that arise in supervising banks on a cross-border basis are further compounded by the recent growth of financial conglomerates which comprise institutions or groups of institutions active in more than one principal financial services area.[1] In such cases, even more distinct sets of provisions will apply to the various activities undertaken both within the same country and between countries as authorities from more than one financial sector are involved. This raises many complex issues which the authorities have only recently begun to attempt to resolve.

Early work in this area was undertaken by the Basel Committee and the International Organisation of Securities Commissions (IOSCO) separately in the early 1990s although a multidisciplinary Tripartite Group of Banking, Insurance and Securities Regulators was set up in 1992 at the instigation of the Basel Committee. Its purpose was to examine the feasibility of developing general principles for the supervision of financial conglomerates. This essentially *ad hoc* Tripartite Group was subsequently superseded by a more formal Joint Forum which continues to work in this area as a more permanent group of supervisors from the same three financial sectors. The Joint Forum has since published a number of consultative papers on the supervision of financial conglomerates.[2] Much of this work has also been taken forward more generally following the establishment of the Financial Stability Forum (FSF) by the G7 in 1999.[3]

1 See Walker, 'The Law of Financial Conglomerates: The Next Generation', *The International Lawyer* (Spring 1996), 57; and Walker, *International Banking Regulation – Law, Policy and Practice* (2001), Ch 3.
2 See paras 21.56–21.58.
3 See paras 21.72–21.80.

Scope of the chapter

21.6   The purpose of this chapter is to consider the content of the work undertaken to date at the international level in the construction of effective mechanisms for the cross-border supervision of financial markets.

The nature and operation of the Basel Committee and its work in the area of international bank supervision and regulation are considered. The structure and method of operation of IOSCO are examined and the important joint initiative launched between the Basel Committee and IOSCO noted.

The work undertaken by these organisations on either a joint or individual basis in the areas of financial derivatives, financial conglomerates, core principles of financial supervision and internal controls are then examined. The more recent work of the FSF is also referred to.

INTERNATIONAL SUPERVISORY CO-OPERATION

21.7   A number of mechanisms have been developed to facilitate co-operation between the authorities involved with the supervision of a particular institution or group of institutions. These include the conclusion of various types of informal and formal bilateral and multilateral agreements.[1] A College mechanism was also used in relation to BCCI[2] with more recent discussion focusing on the appointment of a lead supervisor or regulator at the international level, although only qualified progress has been made in this regard.[3]

1   See G Walker, 'Conglomerate Law and International Financial Market Supervision', para 17.1, n 1, Section A.
2   See Lord Justice Bingham, 'Inquiry into the Supervision of the Bank of Credit and Commerce International', 22 October 1992.
3   See Walker (note 1 above), Section A.5.

MoUs and FISMoUs

21.8   The most commonly used mechanisms to secure day-to-day co-operation between authorities are MoUs or FISMoUs.[1]

An MoU is an agreement between two or more supervisory agencies which sets out the terms on which they will co-operate with one another. This will usually include provisions with regard to the exchange of information in relation to the supervision of particular institutions or groups and possibly access to other documentation or information such as with regard to investigatory or enforcement actions. Some affirmative action may also be provided for under an MoU in certain cases such as with regard to the mandatory reporting of firms experiencing financial difficulties. Other agreements, although referred to as MoUs, may only provide for more general co-operation and assistance.

A FISMoU is a more limited type of MoU which provides for access to more specific information or for regular reporting in relation to, for example, risk assessment determinations of firms operating in more than one jurisdiction.[2]

Although MoUs and FISMoUs are usually entered into on a bilateral basis it is increasingly common for them to be used to secure multilateral co-operation.

1 See Walker, *International Banking Regulation – Law, Policy and Practice* (2001), Ch 4.
2 See IMF, *International Capital Markets: Developments, Prospects, and Policy Issues* (August 1995), Annex III, 'Mechanics for International Co-operation in Regulation', p 161.

Responsibility

21.9 In the UK, the Bank of England traditionally held routine and *ad hoc* meetings with its counterparts in other European Economic Area (EEA)[1] Member States under the terms of bilateral MoUs on supervisory co-operation. These included provisions concerning the exchange of information on credit institutions with presences in both countries, addressing common concerns or supervisory issues arising from the administration of European Union Directives in the banking and financial area or to exchange more general views on supervisory developments and other issues of mutual interest.[2]

The Bank also concluded a number of MoUs or exchange of letters concerning supervisory arrangements with other non-EEA authorities and developed a programme of formal and informal contacts with many non-EEA supervisory authorities to improve its understanding of the nature and scope of their supervision and to exchange information about UK banks' operations within their jurisdictions and about banks from their countries that have operations in the UK. The Bank had been advised by the Board of Banking Supervision following the Collapse of Barings to review its MoUs with other regulators and to extend international co-ordination through the conclusion of more MoUs, especially with non-banking authorities.[3] The Bank had accordingly developed a programme of appropriate initiatives in this area.[4]

While this work continues, many of these activities are now undertaken by FSA following transfer to it of responsibility in respect of banking supervision under the Bank of England Act 1998. Rather than provide for the full transfer of all of these functions from the Bank to the FSA, the Bank and FSA will often work together in many areas including maintaining joint attendance at meetings such as those of the Basel Committee. The Bank remains responsible for financial stability more generally under the new regulatory arrangements set up in the UK.[5]

1 The EEA consists of Norway, Iceland and Liechtenstein and the Member States of the European Union (EU).
2 See Bank of England Banking Act Report 1996/97, p 36; and Banking Act Report 1997/98, pp 27–28.
3 See Board of Banking Supervision, *Inquiry into the Circumstances Surrounding the Collapse of Barings*, HC (1994–95), 673, recos 9 and 10.
4 See Bank of England, 'The Board of Banking Supervision's Report on Barings', Press Notice, 11 January 1996, paras 12–14.
5 See Chapter 2, paras 2.40–2.47 on the FSA, Bank and Treasury MoU.

Bilateral agreements

21.10 An increasingly complex network of bilateral channels has subsequently been created between banking authorities and between banking and securities and other supervisors in recent years.[1] The authorities in the UK and US have, for example, entered into a large number of MoUs with counterparties within their own sectors at home and abroad and in other financial sectors.[2]

The Securities and Exchange Commission (SEC) in the US has been particularly influential in promoting the use of MoUs internationally.[3]

The Basel Committee has also formally endorsed the use of such arrangements in the banking area[4] while historically they were more commonly entered into between securities authorities.[5]

1 For a note of all of the various MoUs concluded between 1982 and 1994 see IMF, *International Capital Markets: Developments, Prospects, and Key Issues* (September 1996), Annex IV, 'International Co-operation of Supervision and Regulation of Financial Institutions', Box.
2 A list of the main MoUs currently in place between financial authorities in many countries is set out on the IOSCO website (www.iosco.org).
3 See Chapter 2, para 2.48. See generally M Mann, *The SEC's International Enforcement Program and Bilateral and Multilateral Initiatives*, 961 PLI Corp 7, 24 (1996).
4 See Basel Committee, *Essential Elements of a Statement of Cooperation between Banking Supervisors* (May 2001).
5 See Walker, *International Banking Regulation – Law, Policy and Practice* (2001), Ch 4.

Multilateral arrangements

21.11   The entering into of these bilateral agreements has been supplemented by the more recent conclusion of formal multilateral arrangements especially between securities exchanges in respect of information-sharing arrangements. The signing in May 1995 of the Windsor Declaration following a meeting of the regulatory authorities from 16 countries responsible for the supervision of the world's leading futures exchanges[1] and the work of the Futures Industry Association's Global Task Force on the Financial Integrity of Futures and Options Markets were particularly significant in this respect.[2]

1 See para 21.37.
2 See, for example, Futures Industry Association Global Task Force on Financial Integrity, *Financial Integrity Recommendations for Futures and Options Markets and Market Participants* (June 1995).

Standards

21.12   In light of their importance, a number of standards have been developed by IOSCO concerning the content and operation of MoUs in the securities area.[1]

These contain provisions with regard to their scope of subject matter, confidentiality obligations, implementation procedures, the rights of persons subject to MoU requests, regular consultation, public policy exceptions, types of assistance, participation by requesting authorities and cost-sharing. These would apply to MoUs entered into between securities authorities and between securities and other authorities. Similar principles are followed in other areas. Similar guidance has also been issued by the Basel Committee.[2]

1 See, for example, Working Party No 4 of the Technical Committee of IOSCO, *Principles for Memorandum of Understanding*, Documents of the XVI Annual Conference IOSCO, No 5, September 1991 (IOSCO Principles). In connection with information sharing see J Michau, Workshop No 4, *Information Sharing Between Securities Regulators (Market Surveillance and Insider Trading)*, XVth Annual Conference, November 1990.
2 See Basel Committee, *Essential Elements of a Statement of Cooperation between Banking Supervisors* (May 2001).

Potential problems

Informality

21.13   Despite the value of these standards it must be stressed that MoUs are not formal international documents such as treaties or conventions. They can therefore easily be negotiated, assuming, of course, that the relevant authorities have proper authority to do so, and can come into effect immediately without the need for any formal ratification. They are, however, essentially informal and unenforceable in themselves. They also require regular review and updating as circumstances change.

Operation

21.14   A number of difficulties also arise in terms of their operation. The MoU will provide for the exchange of certain information or possibly for co-ordinated action in certain defined circumstances. Whether the information can actually be transferred or action taken, however, will depend upon local law. It has to be expected that the supervisory authorities will attempt to have the local laws amended as appropriate to facilitate the effective operation of the MoU[1] although this may not always be possible. This will, in particular, depend upon the scope of the confidentiality laws in place in both countries and possibly on other procedural considerations.

Within the EU, difficult questions arise with regard to the scope of the permitted 'gateways' under which information may be exchanged between authorities.[2] Relevant provisions in the banking area were set out in article 12 of the First Banking Directive which were replaced under article 16 of the Second Banking Directive and then article 30 of the Banking Consolidated Directive.[3] In negotiating the Second Banking Directive one of the most difficult issues which arose was in agreeing the gateways to be provided for in respect of the exchange of supervisory information. Following the collapse of BCCI, these were extended further under the Prudential Supervision Directive.[4]

Potential conflicts also arise between European and national laws where EEA member countries try to negotiate MoUs with non-EEA countries. These difficulties have been substantially reduced where the Commission has concluded the relevant MoUs.[5] Following receipt of relevant MoUs, additional confidentiality obligations will also have to be placed on its use and restrictions or conditions attached to its further transmission.[6]

1   See IOSCO Principle 1.
2   See, for example, Banking Act 1987, Pt V.
3   See Council Directive 77/780/EEC of 12 December 1977 on the co-ordination of the laws, regulations and administrative provisions relating to the taking-up and pursuit of the business of credit institutions; and Council Directive 89/646/EEC of 15 December 1989 on the co-ordination of the laws, regulations and administrative provisions relating to the taking-up and pursuit of the business of credit institutions and amending Directive 77/780/EEC. These have both since been replaced by Directive 2000/12/EC of the European Parliament and the Council of 20 March 2000 relating to the taking up and pursuit of the business of credit institutions which was adopted under the SLIM (Simpler Legislation for the Internal Market) programme.
4   See para 21.3.
5   See Bank of England, Press Notice, January 1996, para 13.
6   See IOSCO Principle 2. See also Banking Act 1987, s 82(1).

Public policy

21.15   Separate public policy problems may also arise. Under IOSCO Principle 6, all MoUs should provide that the authority to whom a request is made maintains the right to refuse to provide assistance where it would violate the public policy of the particular state. This would include issues affecting sovereignty, national security or other essential interests. Although MoUs will generally try to be as broad as possible in their scope of application and operation many will include a public policy safeguard which may limit the assistance that could otherwise have been provided in practice, depending upon how widely the exception is interpreted and applied.

Summary

21.16   MoUs are accordingly of considerable value in facilitating co-operation in the supervision of an institution which operates in more than one jurisdiction, especially insofar as they set out agreed procedures and channels of communication and the terms upon which co-operation will be secured. Their effectiveness is, however, dependent upon relevant local law, especially with regard to confidentiality and public policy provisions as well as the continued goodwill and support of the authorities concerned.

THE BASEL COMMITTEE

21.17   In addition to constructing appropriate mechanisms to allow national authorities to co-operate on a bilateral or multilateral basis in relation to the supervision of a particular institution or group, it is necessary to develop more general rules to ensure that no gaps arise in the scope of supervision and that common or, at least, acceptable minimum levels or standards of financial regulation are in place in all countries.

The most important work in this regard in the banking area has been conducted by the Basel Committee. The Committee has issued a large number of papers designed at improving co-operation between national supervisory authorities at the same time as constructing minimum regulatory standards, especially with regard to capital adequacy in respect of both the loan and trading book activities of banks.

History

21.18   The Basel Committee was set up in 1974 following the collapse of Bankhaus Herstatt in June 1974 in West Germany after suffering heavy foreign exchange losses.[1]

A number of banks had also suffered significant losses following the collapse of the Bretton Woods system of managed exchange rates. This included Franklin National in the US which suffered a series of deposit runs following substantial losses in forex trading in May 1974. It was subsequently closed in September 1974. With the closure of Bankhaus Herstatt in June 1974, its co-respondent bank in New York, Chase Manhattan, refused to honour US$620 million in payment orders and cheques which almost resulted in the collapse of the American and the international banking systems.

This problem of currency exchange or settlement risk is now even more important with over US$1.4 trillion of foreign currency being traded daily.[2]

1 See, for example, J Norton, *Devising International Bank Supervisory Standards* (1995), Ch 4. See generally Walker, *International Banking Regulation – Law, Policy and Practice* (2001), Ch 1.
2 See Bank for International Settlement (BIS), *Settlement Risk in Foreign Exchange Transactions*, Report prepared by the Committee on Payment and Settlement Systems (March 1996).

21.19   In response to the crisis, the central bank governors of the Group of 10 industrialised countries (G10) (including Luxembourg and Switzerland and now Spain) issued a Support Communiqué in September 1974 to attempt to stabilise the markets. It was also decided, in December 1974, to set up the Basel Committee as a standing committee on bank regulations and supervisory practices. It was agreed that the Committee would operate out of the offices of the BIS in Basel with a secretariat being provided by the Bank of England.

International bank supervision

21.20   In the area of international bank supervision, the Committee has issued a number of papers since its first meeting in February 1975. The objective of these documents has been to set out rules in accordance with which international financial institutions or groups are to be supervised and to define the responsibilities of the authorities involved in the conduct of the supervision. They accordingly attempt to establish a more general framework within which supervision is to be conducted. (MoUs and FISMoUs, in contrast, set out the more specific procedures in accordance with which co-operation is to be secured between particular sets of authorities in particular cases.)

The 1975 First Concordat

21.21   The Basel Committee's earliest recommendations with regard to the development of effective supervisory techniques in connection with the overseas activities of international banks were set out in its first Concordat in September 1975.[1] This was principally concerned with the allocation of supervisory responsibility between the separate authorities involved with the oversight of the cross-border operations of a particular bank. Four basic principles were set out in the original Concordat:

(1) The supervision of foreign banking establishments was to be the joint responsibility of the host and parent authorities.
(2) The supervision of liquidity was to be the primary responsibility of the host authorities since foreign establishments generally had to conform with local practices in connection with their liquidity management.
(3) The supervision of the solvency of foreign branches should primarily be a matter for the parent authorities (although the host should be responsible for the solvency of subsidiaries, at least, at that stage).
(4) Practical co-operation should also be facilitated by transfers of information between the host and parent authorities and by the granting of permission for inspections by or on behalf of parent authorities on the territory of the host authority. Every effort should be made in this regard to remove any legal constraints especially with regard to professional secrecy that might hinder such co-operation.

The First Concordat was not initially published, as it was considered only to affect the relations between national authorities and not the banks concerned.[2]

1 See Basel Committee, *Report to the Governors on the Supervision of Bank's Foreign Establishments* (September 1975).
2 See generally, Walker, *International Banking Regulation – Law, Policy and Practice* (2001), Ch 2, Section 1.1.

The 1983 Revised Concordat

21.22   The First Concordat was replaced by a Revised Concordat in 1983.[1] The Revised Concordat was issued following the collapse of Banco Ambrosiano Holdings 1982. Banco Ambrosiano was the holding company for an Italian Banking group established in Luxembourg which was not fully regulated as the Luxembourg authorities did not consider it to be a bank. Following its collapse, a dispute arose between the Luxembourg and Italian authorities with regards to responsibility for the supervision of the activities of the holding company.

Structural features of international banking groups including holding companies and mixed activities groups were accordingly brought within the terms of the revised Concordat. The revised Concordat also incorporated the principle that banking supervisory authorities should not be fully satisfied about the soundness of individual banks unless they can examine the totality of each banks' business worldwide through the technique of consolidation. The principle of consolidated supervision had been first recommended by the Committee in an earlier paper in October 1978.[2] The revised Concordat restated the principle that no bank should escape supervision and that that supervision should be adequate.

A dual key principle was also introduced which required authorities to monitor the effectiveness of the supervision exercised by the others. This accordingly introduced an element of mutual review to ensure that supervisory standards were sufficient. The mechanism operated by requiring that if one authority was concerned with the extent or quality of the supervision carried out by the other, the supervision effected should either be increased or the operations of the bank in question prohibited in the local territory or made subject to additional conditions.

More sophisticated rules with regard to the monitoring of the solvency, liquidity and foreign exchange of branches, subsidiaries and joint ventures were included.

The revised Concordat also confirmed that responsibility for lender of last resort support was not to be confused with the allocation of supervisory responsibility of a bank's foreign establishments. The issue had remained unclear since the Committee had been established in 1975. Lender-of-last-resort issues would be dealt with by the Governors of the G10 directly.

1 See Basel Committee, *Principles for the Supervision of Banks' Foreign Establishments* (May 1983). See generally, Walker, International Banking Regulation – Law, Policy and Practice (2001), Chapter 2, Section 1.2.
2 See Basel Committee, *Consolidation of Banks' Balance Sheets: Aggregation of Risk-Bearing Assets as a Method of Supervisory Bank Solvency* (October 1978.)

The 1990 Information Supplement

21.23   An information and procedural supplement to the Revised Concordat was issued in 1990.[1] This was largely based on the results of a joint working party report prepared by the Basel Committee and the Off-Shore Group of

Banking Supervisors on the difficulties that had arisen in implementing the 1983 Revised Concordat. The Supplement contains a number of specific provisions with regard to authorisation, the information needs of the parent and host authorities, the removal of secrecy constraints and the importance of external audit.[2]

1   See Basel Committee, *Report on International Developments in Banking Supervision* (September 1990), Ch VI.
2   See Walker, *International Banking Regulation – Law, Policy and Practice* (2001), Ch 2, Section 1.3.

The 1992 Statement of Minimum Standards

21.24   The 1990 supplement was followed by a re-statement of Minimum Standards for Supervision in 1992.[1] A further review of International Supervisory Co-ordination had been undertaken in the summer of 1992 following the collapse of BCCI in July 1991 and other developments such as the events at the Atlanta Branch of the Banca Nazionale del Levoro.

Although the Committee had concluded that the Revised Concordat and 1990 Supplement were soundly based, supervisory authorities had to strengthen their commitment to implement the best efforts character of the principles set out. It was accordingly recommended that a number of absolute minimum standards for supervision were to be established which the authorities of all G10 countries would be expected to observe.[2]

1   See Basel Committee, *Report on International Developments in Banking Supervision* (September 1992), Ch VI.
2   See generally, Walker, *International Banking Regulation – Law, Policy and Practice* (2001), Ch 2, Section 1.4.

21.25   The minimum standards established in respect of the supervision of international banking groups and their cross-border establishments included the following:

(1)   All international banking groups and international banks should be supervised by a home country authority that capably performs consolidated supervision.
(2)   The creation of a cross-border banking establishment should receive the prior consent of both the host country supervisory authority and the bank's and, if different, the banking group's home country supervisory authority.
(3)   Supervisory authorities should possess the right to gather information from the cross-border banking establishments of the banks or banking groups for which they were the home country supervisor.
(4)   If a host country authority determines that any one of the foregoing minimum standards is not met to its satisfaction, that authority should impose measures necessary to satisfy its prudential concerns consistent with these minimum standards including the prohibition of the creation of banking establishments.

21.26   The specific requirements applicable to each principle are then developed in the text. A number of sub-rules are accordingly created in addition to the four minimum principles set:

The first principle restates the basic provisions of the 1975 Concordat and 1983 Revised Concordat including the 1978 recommendation concerning consolidated supervision.

The requirement of consent in the second principle reflects the authorisation rules set out in the 1990 Supplement. This, in particular, requires that initial contact should be made between authorities concerning an individual application with the host authority, in particular, ensuring that the parent authority has no objection before the licence is granted.

The third principle concerning information is designed to ensure that appropriate mechanisms are in place to allow the authorities to obtain all necessary information including through the conduct of on-side examinations. This reflects the information concerns set out in the 1990 Supplement and the general terms of the earlier papers produced.

Of most significance is the fourth principle which creates a host authority corrective action mechanism in place of the earlier dual key principle. This reflects the particular circumstances of BCCI and would now authorise the UK and US authorities to take all necessary remedial action against a banking group in respect of which serious concerns had arisen.

The 1996 Supervision of Cross-Border Banking

21.27 A Second Joint Working group report was prepared by the Basel Committee and the Off-Shore Group of Banking Supervisors in 1996.[1] As with the earlier 1986 investigation into the implementation of the 1983 Revised Concordat, the purpose of the 1996 enquiry was to examine the operational effectiveness of the new 1992 Minimum Standards set.

In the four years following the issuance of the Minimum Standards, the Committee had monitored the steps taken by national authorities to implement the standards in their own supervisory arrangements. Although a significant amount of progress had been achieved, a number of difficulties remained. The Working Group accordingly examined the impediments that arose concerning the operation of the Minimum Standards and practical arrangements to enable supervisors to ensure the compliance through their own regular supervisory techniques.[2]

1 See Basel Committee, *Report on International Developments in Banking Supervision* (September 1996), Ch V.
1 See Walker, *International Banking Regulation – Law, Policy and Practice* (2001), Ch 2, Section 1.5.

21.28 In an attempt to secure effective compliance, 29 recommendations were made. These are generally concerned with information access and effective consolidated supervision as well as proper home and host country supervision. Recommendations are, in particular, made with regard to information flows, ongoing supervision, home country inspections, serious criminal activities and information flows between home and host supervisors.

In securing effective home and host supervision, additional recommendations are made with regard to determining the effectiveness of home country supervision, monitoring host supervisory standards and other cross-border banking concerns. A set of standard procedures is also developed for Cross-Border Inspections and an Effective Consolidated Supervision and Off-Shore Group On-Site Examinations checklist issued.

With these recommendations, the Basel Committee has moved from solely developing appropriate general principles to ensuring that they are operationally effective in practice. Although the focus of the Working Group was on the supervision of off-shore banking (due to the composition of the group), the conclusions are capable of application to all home and host supervisory relationships.

21.29   Of particular value are the practical recommendations made with regard to conducting inspections and the checklist of matters to be considered in assessing the effectiveness of the consolidated supervision conducted by another authority. To secure continued effective compliance with the Minimum Standards, the Working Group also requested that a commitment to ensure compliance be re-affirmed at the following International Conference of Banking Supervisors in Stockholm in 1986 and that an implementation survey be conducted in advance of the next Conference in 1988. It was intended in this way that enhanced peer group review would assist in securing compliance over time.

International bank capital standards

The 1988 Capital Accord

21.30   Although the Basel Committee was established to develop common international prudential and supervisory standards and practices, the Committee became involved in the early 1980s with the need to attempt to establish a set of basic rules on the harmonisation of international capital adequacy standards. This was, in particular, necessary in the light of the continuing erosion of bank capital that was occurring on a global basis.

The Committee had been concerned since June 1982 that supervisors should not allow the capital resources of their major banks to deteriorate from present levels. While the Basel Committee was discussing the adoption of possible standards in respect of bank capital, the US and UK authorities entered into direct bilateral negotiations and issued an agreed proposal on primary capital and capital adequacy assessment in January 1987.[1] The purpose of issuing the bilateral accord was partly to place pressure on the countries negotiating within the Basel Committee arrangements to arrive at some form of early result.

Despite criticism of the tactic adopted, the members of the Basel Committee were able to agree on the terms of a draft capital accord within a year with the final document being published in July 1988 ('the 1988 Capital Accord').[2] The 1988 Capital Accord provides for the introduction of a minimum bank capital ratio of 8%. The same rules (with some minor amendments) were adopted in drafting the provisions of the European Own Funds Directive and Solvency Ratio Directive which were subsequently restated in the Banking Consolidated Directive.[3]

1   See Agreed Proposal of the United States Federal Banking Supervisory Authorities and the Bank of England on Primary Capital and Capital Adequacy Assessment, 8 January 1987.
2   See Basel Committee on Banking Regulations and Supervisory Practices *International Convergence of Capital Measurement and Capital Standards*, July 1988. See Chapter 15, paras 15.12–15.13 and 15.16–15.22.
3   See Chapter 15, paras 15.23–15.24.

1996 Market Risk Amendment Paper

21.31   Following a number of earlier consultative documents[1] the Basel Committee issued a further paper in January 1996 with a view to amending the 1988 Capital Accord to include market risks.[2]

While the 1988 Capital Accord had provided for capital cover in respect of credit risk, the January 1996 paper would amend the basic Accord to include risk calculation and cover requirements in respect of market risks which were defined as the risk of losses in or on off-balance sheet positions arising from movements in market prices. These risks would specifically include the risks in the trading book of debt and equity instruments and related off-balance sheet contracts and foreign exchange and commodity related risks. The trading book was defined as the bank's proprietary positions in financial instruments, including derivative products and off-balance sheet instruments, intentionally held for short-term resale, matched brokering and market making and hedge positions. This corresponds with the definition of the trading book contained in the European Capital Adequacy Directive.

The Committee's original 1988 Capital Standards are currently under review with a view to producing a New Accord by 2004/2005.[3]

1   See Basel Committee, *The Supervisory Recognition of Netting for Capital Adequacy Purposes*, April 1993; Basel Committee, *The Supervisory Treatment of Market Risks*, April 1993; and Basel Committee, *Measurement of Banks' Exposure to Interest Rate Risk*, April 1993.
2   Basel Committee, *Amendment to the Capital Accord to Incorporate Market Risks*, January 1996.
3   See paras 21.67–21.71 below; and Chapter 15, paras 15.129–15.136. See also Walker, *International Banking Regulation – Law, Policy and Practice* (2001), Pt V 'Capital Supplement'.

IOSCO

Background

21.32   The development of co-operation and common standards between securities authorities was initially much slower than in the banking area. This was due largely to the lack of perceived need. The expansion of international financial markets since the late 1950s had been led by banks mainly through the creation of overseas branch operations but also wholly owned subsidiaries or joint consortia. Until the early 1980s, the conduct of securities business had remained a largely nationally based activity often tied to local stock exchanges and related financial markets.

Substantial growth in all forms of securities related business was, however, possible during the 1980s, especially as a result of various deregulatory initiatives adopted in a number of countries but also through the technological improvements in telecommunications and computer-related support which occurred and the substantial cost savings which they created. This was assisted by increasingly liberal capital flows, especially following the removal of exchange control restrictions in many countries.

All of these developments resulted in the creation of a new 24-hour global securities and financial services market to which the supervisors had to respond.

Establishment

21.33   The International Organisation of Securities Commissions (IOSCO) had initially been set up in 1974 as the Inter-American Association of Securities Commissions, although it was subsequently reconstituted as an international body with 24 charter members in 1983 and its General

Secretariat and head office established in Montreal in 1986. The Secretariat is now based in Madrid.

Membership

21.34   The membership of IOSCO is made up of regular, associate and affiliate members:

(a)   *Regular members* include the statutory or governmental regulatory authorities responsible for the oversight of securities, futures and options markets. The membership is from over 70 countries and covers more than 90% of the world's capital markets.

(b)   *Associate members* comprise additional statutory authorities from specific jurisdictions where responsibility for the regulation of the markets is divided.

(c)   *Affiliate members* included former self-regulatory organisations (SROs) in the UK which did not have statutory authority in respect of the oversight of markets as well as other international bodies with an interest in securities market regulation. As a statutory agency, the FSA can now participate as a full member.

Objectives

21.35   The general purpose of IOSCO is to provide a vehicle through which securities regulators can communicate and co-operate with each other on an international basis. Discussions and bilateral or other arrangements between members are encouraged to the extent that they facilitate its objectives.

21.36   The stated objectives of IOSCO are as follows:

—   to co-operate with the aim of ensuring better regulation, on the domestic and international level, in order to maintain just and efficient securities markets;

—   to exchange information on their respective experiences in order to promote the development of domestic markets;

—   to unite their efforts to establish standards and the effective surveillance of international securities transactions; and

—   to provide mutual assistance to ensure the integrity of markets by rigorous application of the standards and by effective enforcement against offences.

Committee structure

21.37   The organisational structure of IOSCO is generally made up of five sets of committees consisting of the President's Committee, the Executive Committee, four Regional Standing Committees, two specialised functional Committees and Consultative Committee. The functional committees comprise the Technical Committee and the Emerging Markets Committee.

President's Committee

21.38   The President's Committee consists of the Presidents of all of the regular and associate member agencies of IOSCO. The President's Committee has all the powers necessary to achieve the objectives of IOSCO and meets once a year during the Annual Conference.

Executive Committee

21.39   The Executive Committee is made up of 18 members with 12 being elected by the President's Committee and the other six representing the four Regional Standing Committees and the two specialist functional Committees. The Executive Committee deals with all management and strategic planning issues necessary to achieve the objectives of IOSCO. The Committee meets periodically during the year.

Regional Committees

21.40   IOSCO has four Regional Standing Committees representing the Inter-American Region, the European Region, the Asia-Pacific Region and the Africa-Middle East Region. The Committees consider issues specific to the particular regions and meet as required.

Technical Committee

21.41   The functional committees of IOSCO comprise the Technical Committee and the Emerging Markets Committee. The Technical Committee is made up of representatives from the 16 larger and more developed securities markets. Its objectives are to review major regulatory issues concerning international securities transactions, to promote the adoption of common or equivalent rules worldwide and to co-ordinate practical responses to these concerns. The work of the Technical Committee is carried on through a series of specific issue working groups.

21.42   Since 1990, the Technical Committee has been divided into five major subject areas to deal with the particular issues that arise in connection with each. Each Working Group is instructed by way of mandates by the Technical Committee to deal with a particular issue or series of issues.[1] The Working Groups meet several times a year to pursue the specific areas of activity set out in their mandate from the Technical Committee. There are presently five Working Groups:

(a)   Multinational Disclosure and Accounting (WG1);
(b)   Regulation of Secondary Markets (WG2);
(c)   Regulation of Market Intermediaries (WG3);
(d)   Enforcement and Exchange of Information (WG4); and
(e)   Investment Management (WG5).

A large amount of work is produced by each Working Group each year.

1   The progress achieved by each Working Group is summarised in the Final Communiqué of each Annual Conference and expanded in a separate report prepared by the chairman of each Working Group for the Annual Conference.

21.43   Apart from continuing to develop closer relationships with the Basel Committee (especially through WG3 and the Financial Action Task Force

(FATF) through WG4), the Technical Committee has conducted a considerable amount of work in connection with the implementation of the Windsor Declaration.

Following the identification of how the principal recommendations of Windsor could be built into the specific mandates of the various Working Groups,[1] the Co-Chairmen of the Windsor Meeting reported on interim progress in implementing these arrangements at the Technical Committee meeting in July 1995.

The Report and recommendations of the meeting with regard to how IOSCO could co-ordinate its future work programme in the area with the Basel Committee and the Futures Industry Association[2] were subsequently approved by the Technical Committee.

1   The four principal areas concerned co-operation between market authorities, protection of consumer positions, funds and assets, default procedures and regulatory co-operation in emergencies.
2   See para 17.11.

Emerging Markets Committee

21.44   The objectives of the Emerging Markets Committee are to develop and improve the efficiency of the emerging markets by establishing principles or minimum standards, preparing training programmes for personnel of Committee members and by facilitating the exchange of information and transfer of technology and expertise.

The Emerging Markets Committee was set up in 1994 to replace the earlier Development Committee. The Committee followed the earlier working group structure of the Development Committee which uses separate groups on Disclosure, Institutional Investors, Derivatives, Clearing and Settlements and Market Incentives.

The Technical Committee and Emerging Markets Committee have subsequently agreed to exchange observers on Working Groups to facilitate practical co-operation in their activities.

Consultative Committee

21.45   The Consultative Committee is made up of the affiliate members which aim to facilitate close dialogue between statutory regulatory authorities, other SROs and international bodies. The objective is to provide for the injection of practitioner and other expertise into the considerations of IOSCO and, in particular, into the work of the technical and Emerging Markets Committee Working Groups.

THE G7 HALIFAX SUMMIT AND BASEL AND IOSCO RESPONSE

1995 G7 Halifax Summit

21.46   Attempts were made in the late 1980s to develop co-operative initiatives between the Basel Committee and IOSCO. These were, however, limited in their success especially with regard to common capital standards. The Basel Committee and IOSCO were then called upon to continue their collaborative efforts in the area of banking and securities supervision by the

Heads of State and Government of the seven major industrialised nations (G7) at their summit in June 1995 in Halifax, Nova Scotia.[1]

1 Heads of State and Government of the G7 and the President of the European Commission, Halifax, Nova Scotia Summit (15–17 June 1995), Communiqué.

21.47 With regard to strengthening the global economy, the G7 noted that closer international co-operation in the regulation and supervision of financial institutions and markets was essential to safeguard the financial system and prevent an erosion of prudential standards. For that reason, the G7 recommended that co-operation between regulators and supervisory agencies should be strengthened to ensure that an effective and integrated global approach was adopted to the development and enhancement of the safeguards, standards, transparency and systems necessary to monitor and contain financial risks in financial markets. Finance Ministers should, *inter alia*, commission reports from the Basel Committee and IOSCO and, in particular, on the adequacy of current arrangements with proposals for improvements where necessary.

Joint Basel–IOSCO Statement

21.48 Following the direction set out in the Halifax Summit, preliminary responses were issued by the Basel Committee and the Technical Committee of IOSCO in September and October 1995 with a Joint Statement being published on 20 May 1996.[1] The Joint Statement by the Basel Committee and IOSCO was sent to the G7 on 16 April 1996. The Statement was accompanied by two documents which outlined the past activities and future work programmes of each of the organisations. These were prepared separately in recognition of the differences in the historical background and traditional perspectives and responsibilities of bank and securities regulators.[2]

1 See Response of the Basel Committee on Banking Supervision and of the International Organisation of Securities Commissions to the Request of the G7 Heads of Government at the June 1995 Halifax Summit, Montreal, May 1996 ('the 1995 Joint Response').
2 See Tommaso Padoa-Schioppa, Chairman of the Basel Committee on Banking Supervision, and Edward J Waitzer, Chairman of the Technical Committee of IOSCO, letter addressed to Mr Jean Arthuis, Ministre de l'Economique et des Finances, 16 April 1996.

21.49 In pursuit of their common goals, however, the Basel Committee and IOSCO identified eight major principles that would guide their efforts and which their members had agreed to promote:

(1) co-operation and information flows among supervisory authorities should be as free as possible from both national and international impediments;
(2) all banks and securities firms should be subject to effective supervision, including capital supervision;
(3) diversified financial groups required special supervisory arrangements, both geographically and functionally;
(4) all banks and securities firms should have adequate capital;
(5) proper risk management by firms was a prerequisite for financial stability;
(6) the transparency and integrity of markets and supervision relied on adequate reporting and disclosure of operations;
(7) the resilience of markets to the failure of individual firms must be maintained; and
(8) the supervisory process must be constantly maintained and improved.

Joint work

21.50   A Co-ordinating Committee was established in 1995 to review regularly the joint work carried out by the two organisations as well as to exchange information on agendas and projects.

With regard to completed and ongoing initiatives, the work programme of the Basel Committee and IOSCO has been adjusted to establish concrete international understandings on safeguards, standards and transparency which are fully in line with the major principles referred to above.

The results generated have subsequently included initiatives in the areas of Internal Management Control Systems, Capital Adequacy, Reporting, Disclosure and Accounting, Financial Conglomerates, Operational and Settlement Systems, Worldwide Supervision and Market Emergencies.

FINANCIAL DERIVATIVES

21.51   The Basel Committee and IOSCO have undertaken a significant amount of work in connection with the development of recommendations for banks and securities firms concerning the management of derivative products.[1]

The Basel Committee had set out a number of detailed recommendations in response to the difficulties that arose in connection with financial derivatives through various papers which dated back to the early 1980s.[2] These included a study into the risks for banks associated with various types of off-balance sheet transactions which included recommendations as to how such risks should be reflected in capital adequacy measures[3] and discussion of the issues that arose in terms of the management and control of derivatives risks, payments and settlement systems and reporting, accounting and disclosure rules.

A separate paper was produced in July 1994 on the management of derivatives-related activities which set out the main elements of sound risk management for supervisors' guidance.[4] These elements included appropriate oversight by boards of directors and senior management, adequate risk management processes that integrated prudent risk limits, sound measurement procedures and information systems, continuous risk monitoring and frequent management reporting as well as comprehensive internal controls and audit procedures.

1   See G Walker, 'Financial Derivatives' [1996] JBL, 66.
2   For a general discussion of the activities of the Basel Committee in this area see, Basel Committee, *Prudential Supervision of Banks' Derivatives Activities*, December 1994.
3   Basel Committee, *The Management of Banks' Off-Balance-Sheet Exposures: A Supervisory Perspective*, March 1986.
4   See Basel Committee, *Strengthening Banks' Management of Derivatives Activity*, July 1994.

The Basel Committee and IOSCO

21.52   The most important recent work in the area of financial derivatives was carried out by the Basel Committee in association with the Technical Committee of IOSCO. Three joint papers have been produced to date as a result of this collaborative work.

Framework for supervisory information

21.53   In the first joint report which was produced in July 1995,[1] the Basel Committee and IOSCO examined the nature and content of the information which should be provided by banks and securities firms for supervisors in relation to OTC derivatives activities.

Given the rapid growth of derivatives activities in recent years, it was recognised as essential that supervisors continuously improve their understanding of how derivative instruments affect the overall risk profile and profitability of banks and securities firms. A framework of the types of information which regulated firms and material affiliates should produce internally and be accessible to supervisors was accordingly provided. This included both a comprehensive catalogue of information for supervisory purposes and a common minimum information framework. The areas of interest covered in the comprehensive framework included credit risk, liquidity risk, market risk and earnings. The minimum framework was concerned with credit risk, market liquidity risk and overall market activity but not specifically with market risk which is to be considered in the future.

The common minimum framework was also to be revised periodically while duplication in reporting obligations would be limited as a result of co-ordination of activities following the Euro-currency Standing Committee's[2] proposal to collect aggregate market data on a regular basis.

1   Basel Committee and Technical Committee of IOSCO, *Framework for Supervisory Information* (July 1995).
2   This was subsequently renamed the Committee on the Global Financial System.

Public Disclosure of the Trading Activities of Banks and Securities Firms

21.54   A survey of annual report disclosures from a sample of large internationally active banks or securities firms within the G10 was subsequently prepared in November 1995.[1] The survey concerned the trading (on-balance sheet instruments and off-balance sheet derivatives) and non-trading derivatives activities of the institutions involved.

The purpose of the survey was to provide the institutions concerned with a picture of the type of information currently disclosed by similar firms at the international level and to make recommendations for further improvements in the public disclosure of trading and derivatives activities.

The paper has to be regarded as part of larger attempts to improve public disclosures since 1993, especially with regard to derivatives activities. While there had been improvements in the disclosure of trading and derivatives activities during 1994, there remained a number of significant differences between the large internationally active banks and securities firms involved with respect, in particular, to the type and usefulness of the information disclosed.

Banks and securities firms were accordingly encouraged to continue their efforts to provide enhanced and quantitatively and qualitatively meaningful disclosures about how their trading activities contributed to their overall risk profile and profitability together with information on risk management practices and actual management performance.

While the recommendations made may improve the adequacy of disclosures generally with regard to on-balance sheet activities, the Committees were particularly concerned with trading and derivatives activities due to their rapid growth and complexity and the speed with which exposures can change.

1   Basel Committee and Technical Committee of IOSCO, *Public Disclosure of the Trading and Derivatives Activities of Banks and Securities Firms*, November 1995.

Survey of Disclosures of the Trading and Derivatives Activities of Banks and Securities Firms

21.55   The initial results of the survey conducted concerning the public disclosure of the trading activities of banks and securities firms was produced in November 1996.[1] The paper analysed the disclosures made over a more extended period of time. It confirmed, in particular, that although further improvements had been made with regard to the quality and breadth of disclosure made by certain firms, further work had to be carried out in this regard. As meaningful public disclosure is necessary to reinforce supervisory efforts to protect the stability of financial markets the paper is important in continuing the work of the Basel Committee and IOSCO in this regard.[2]

1   Basel Committee and Technical Committee of IOSCO, *Survey of Disclosures of the Trading and Derivatives Activities of Banks and Securities Firms*, November 1996.
2   See www.bis.org for more recent disclosures in this regard.

FINANCIAL CONGLOMERATES

21.56   A number of papers have been produced at the international level in connection with the regulatory response to be developed to financial conglomerates.[1] The main work produced, to date, in connection with the development of global responses to the difficulties created by the supervision and regulation of conglomerates was undertaken by the Basel Committee and IOSCO as well as the Tripartite Group of Banking, Insurance and Securities Regulators and Joint Forum.[2]

1   See Walker 'The Law of Financial Conglomerates: The Next Generation', para 17.5, n 1.
2   See Walker, *International Banking Regulation – Law, Policy and Practice* (2001), Ch 3.

The Basel Committee, IOSCO, IAIS and the Tripartite Group

21.57   The Basel Committee had been concerned from an early stage with the problems created by the development of financial and mixed-activity conglomerates. In the light of the difficulties that arose, the Committee decided to set up a multidisciplinary working group, made up of regulators from each of the three principal supervisory areas involved, to examine the feasibility of developing general principles for the supervision of financial conglomerates. This working group became known as the Tripartite Group of Banking, Securities and Insurance Regulators.

In connection with this work, the Basel Committee set out a series of general principles for the supervision of financial conglomerates for examination by the working group, which were reprinted in its 1992 Report on International Developments in Banking Supervision.[1] The Tripartite Group subsequently issued a progress report in 1994[2] and a final Report was published in July 1995. One month after the Basel Committee published its general principles in September 1992, IOSCO issued its Report on the Supervision of Conglomerates.[3]

1   Basel Committee, *Report on International Banking Supervision* (September 1992), Ch III.

2   The interim Report is reprinted in the Basel Committee, *Report on International Banking Supervision* (September 1992).
3   IOSCO Technical Committee, *Principles for the Supervision of Financial Conglomerates* (November 1992).

The Joint Forum on Financial Conglomerates

21.58   In February 1996, the Tripartite Group was formally re-established on a more permanent basis as the Joint Forum. Since its creation, the Joint Forum has produced a confidential Interim Report for the G10 Governors while a separate Progress Report was issued in April 1997, in advance of the Denver G7 Summit.[1]

The Joint Forum then issued a series of consultation documents on the *Supervision of Financial Conglomerates* in February 1998. The Joint Forum had reviewed the various means to facilitate the exchange of information between supervisors within their own sectors and between supervisors in different sectors. The means of enhancing supervisory co-ordination had also been examined and work carried out in the development of principles for the more effective supervision of regulated firms within financial conglomerates.

Seven consultative papers were produced for industry and supervisory comment on *Capital Adequacy Principles, Supplement to the Capital Adequacy Principles, Fit and Proper Principles, Framework for Supervisory Information Sharing, Principles for Supervisory Information Sharing, Co-Ordinator* and a *Supervisory Questionnaire*. Two further papers were then released in July 1999 on intra-group transactions and exposures (ITEs) and risk concentrations (RCs).[2] A final set of documents was issued in December 1999.[3]

1   See Progress Report by the Joint Forum on Financial Conglomerates (9 April 1997). See also correspondence from Dr T Padoa-Schioppa, Chairman of the Basel Committee, A Neoh, Chairman of the Technical Committee of IOSCO and Mr G Pooley, Chairman of the International Association of Insurance Supervisors (IAIS) to Mr Robert E Rubin, Secretary of the United States Treasury, April 1997.
2   See The Joint Forum, *Press Release* (8 July 1999).
3   See Joint Forum, *Press Release* (15 December 1999). See Walker, *International Banking Regulation – Law, Policy and Practice* (2001), Ch 3, Section 6.6.

CORE PRINCIPLES FOR EFFECTIVE BANKING SUPERVISION

21.59   In addition to developing principles for the supervision of institutions operating on a cross-border basis in each of the principal banking, securities and insurance sectors, the authorities concerned have more recently considered the possibility of agreeing more general core principles for the supervision of entities within each sector to be applied on a national and international basis. In addition to considering the cross-border implications of the provision of financial services, the core principles accordingly consider such other matters as authorisation, basic prudential requirements and ongoing supervisory techniques.

The Basel Committee initially issued a draft set of *Core Principles for Effective Banking Supervision* in April 1997 and a final in September 1997. The International Association of Insurance Supervisors (IAIS) issued an equivalent set of *Insurance Supervisory Principles* and *Principles Applicable to the Supervision of International Insurers and Insurance Groups and their Cross-Border Establishments* in September 1997.

IOSCO had also prepared a set of draft of Standards and Objectives for Securities Regulation in summer 1997 which were finalised in September 1998.

Core principles

21.60   The Basel Core Principles were issued in advance of the International Monetary Fund (IMF) and World Bank meetings in Hong Kong in late September 1997. In preparing the Core Principles, the Basel Committee worked closely with a number of non-G10 supervisory countries including Chile, China, the Czech Republic, Hong Kong, Mexico, Russia and Thailand. Eight other countries were also closely involved: Brazil, Hungary, India, Indonesia, Korea, Malaysia, Poland and Singapore.

The Core Principles lay down a minimum set of requirements in respect of the licensing and continuing supervision of banks. They are the first comprehensive set of standards to be developed and applied in respect of national banks as well as institutions operating on a cross-border basis. They deal with all aspects of pre-conditions for effective banking supervision, licensing and structure, arrangements for ongoing banking supervision, formal powers of supervisors as well as cross-border banking.

Specific issues relating to Government-owned banks are also identified as well as some more general guidance provided with regard to the use and operation of deposit protection schemes.

Core Principles Methodology

21.61   In connection with the implementation of the Core Principles, the Basel Committee has also issued a Core Principles Methodology which is designed to assist in the conduct of compliance assessments in particular countries.[1] This was prepared in association with the IMF.

The Methodology restates the objectives of the Core Principles and sets out certain considerations in conducting assessments. It then contains a large amount of detailed guidance on the assessment of compliance with each of the principles issued by the Committee.

1   See Basel Committee, 'Core Principles Methodology' (1999).

21.62   The Core Principles Methodology had been developed out of the early work conducted by the Fund and the World Bank in assessing country compliance with the underlying Core Principles. The first Core Principles Assessment (CPA) was conducted by Fund staff in February 1998 which was based on a series of short explanatory notes on each Core Principle.

The generality of many of the Principles meant that a number of interpretations could be adopted for each. The use of early self-assessment also meant that countries could take advantage of any uncertainties or inconsistencies to establish compliance.[1]

The Basel Committee then set up a working group in October 1998 to attempt to develop a Core Principles Methodology with senior Basel Committee members and Fund and World Bank staff. Regular contact was also maintained with both the full Committee and the Basel Core Principles Liaison

Group (which contains representatives from a number of emerging market as well as developed countries). Following circulation of a draft for comment, the final Methodology was produced in October 1999.

1   See IMF, *Experience with Basel Core Principles Assessments* (12 April 2000).

21.63   The Methodology is important in making consideration of general pre-conditions more explicit, clarifying the interpretation of each principle, providing a set format for the conduct, evaluation and presentation of assessments and include a scheme for assessing compliance with individual principles. The assessments rules, in particular, use four grades of:

(a)   compliant (full compliance or only insignificant deficiencies);
(b)   largely compliant (only minor deficiencies are observed but where no doubts are raised with regard to the ability of the authorities to secure compliance);
(c)   materially non-compliant (deficiencies raise doubts as to the ability of the authorities to secure compliance but substantial progress has already been made); and
(d)   non-compliant (no substantial progress has been achieved in securing compliance).

21.64   The Methodology requires each principle to be based on certain 'essential criteria' which are derived from the internationally accepted standards of best practice set out in the Basel Committee other papers or elsewhere.

Where appropriate, countries would also be assessed having regard to 'additional criteria' which require a higher level of compliance. Depending upon the particular circumstances, compliance with the essential criteria may still mean that the financial system is not stable in which case a satisfactory overall degree of adherence would not be achieved.

This is a useful paper especially for expert teams conducting on-site visits to determine material compliance with the Core Principles in any particular case. It accordingly adds further substance to the core rules as well as assists in their national adoption and implementation.

INTERNAL CONTROL SYSTEMS

21.65   The Basel Committee issued a paper on the *Framework for the Evaluation of Internal Control Systems* in January 1998. IOSCO issued a comparable report on *Risk Management and Control Guidance for Securities Firms and Their Supervisors* in March 1988.

These documents were significant in light of the increased importance of internal control systems, especially in larger complex institutions and groups which operated in more than one jurisdiction. These dangers were clearly illustrated by the Barings crisis and the losses suffered by Daiwa, Sumitomo, Morgan Asset Grenfell and others.

In the light of this, more recent papers have also been produced on operational risk and internal bank controls[1] including as part of the proposed capital revision.[2]

1   See, for example, Basel Committee, *Operational Risk Management* (September 1998); *Basel Committee, Enhancing Corporate Governance in Banking Organisations* (September 1999); Basel Committee, *Sound Practices for the Management and Supervision of Operational Risk* (December 2001).

2 See Basel Committee, *Operational Risk – Supporting Document to the New Basel Capital Accord* (January 2001).

21.66   The 1998 Basel paper was prepared as part of its ongoing efforts to encourage sound risk management practices within banks. A system of effective internal controls was considered to be a critical component of bank management and the foundation for the safe and sound operation of banking organisations. The framework paper accordingly describes possible problems and elements of a sound internal control system. Fourteen principles were issued for use by supervisory authorities in evaluating individual bank's internal control systems.

The Committee has issued similar papers in specific areas, such as with regard to derivatives, but has never attempted to be as comprehensive before. The model for this new development may have been the work conducted in connection with the preparation of the Core Principles for Effective Banking Supervision.

Although arguably overdue this most recent effort is particularly welcome. The issue of internal operational risk is a complex issue. It is also particularly difficult to review and assess in particular cases, especially in larger institutions or groups.

One omission may have been not extending the control systems discussed to deal with more complex group situations. Of possibly more importance than the particular rules themselves, is the contribution made by the Committee in drawing further attention to this core important aspect of internal bank management and larger supervisory practice which has since been taken further forward in the more recent papers produced.

NEW CAPITAL ACCORD

21.67   The Basel Committee has since 1999 been working on the production of a New Capital Accord to replace its original 1988 Capital Accord and 1996 Market Risk Amendment as well as subsequent papers on financial related matters.[1]

The objective of the revision is to replace the original Accord with a new more sophisticated, coherent and complete capital framework that covers all aspects of financial risk measurement and management.

The 1988 Capital Accord was important in being the first significant agreement in the regulatory area at the international level. Its simplicity also promoted global adoption and compliance while its market acceptance resulted in it quickly becoming the *de facto* global standard for all banks including national and internationally active firms.[2]

The inherent simplicity of the original measurement framework, however, meant that it only provided a crude measure of credit risk. The system adopted lacked proper compliance incentives, created unnecessary arbitrage opportunities and resulted in very distinct compliance effects (in particular, as a result of the concessions left in the outline rules and the failure to take into account differences in local provisioning practices).

The 1988 Capital Accord also failed to create the more general level playing field between international banks that was one of the more political underlying objectives involved.

1 See Basel Committee, *The New Basel Capital Accord* (January 2001). See Chapter 15, paras 15.12–15.13 and 15.14–15.22; and paras 15.129–15.136. See also paras 21.30–21.31.

2   For comment, see Walker, 'New Accord,' FRI (February 2001), p 1; and Walker, 'The New Capital Accord' (April 2001), p 1 and (May 2001), p 1. See also Walker, 'So close but so far,' FRR (May 1999), p 1; Walker, 'Accord at Last' FRR (July/August 1999), p 1; and 'A New Capital Adequacy Framework' FRR (July/August 1999).

Design principles

21.68   The Basel Committee has since attempted to construct a New Accord on the basis of five basic design objectives. These consist of:

(a)   the promotion of safety and soundness;
(b)   enhancing competitive equality;
(c)   creating a more comprehensive approach to risk;
(d)   continued common application to international and national banks; and
(e)   adherence by all countries.

Pillars

21.69   The new framework is to be constructed on three parallel pillars consisting of:

(1)   a revised minimum capital requirement;
(2)   a new supervisory review process; and
(3)   enhanced market discipline (secured through the introduction of new mandatory disclosure requirements on banks).

The first pillar (revised minimum requirement) will operate on either a standardised or 'internal ratings based' (IRB) approach. The standardised approach essentially consists of the original 8% minimum capital ratio of total risk adjusted assets.[1] The revised minimum requirement is, however, more accurate due to the inclusion of external risk grading figures. The alternative IRB approach will make increased use of bank's own internal estimates either on a foundation or advance basis. The revised minimum capital requirement will also include a new operational risk charge. This will either take the form of a basic indicator, standardised or internal measurement approach. It is expected that the general effect will be to impose a further 20% capital charge on operational risk failures including internal systems design and operational difficulties and internal and external fraud.

The second pillar (proposed supervisory review process) consists of a mandatory compliance requirement to be imposed on all national bank regulators to ensure that supervised institutions have all necessary internal control systems in place. While this should have been the main traditional objective of all national authorities, this has not been set out as an express requirement until now. The objective is to ensure that national banks have effective systems to identify and manage risk at the same time as supervisors maintain proper practices to ensure that such systems are in place and adhered to.

1   See Chapter 15, paras 15.12–15.13 and 15.16–15.22.

21.70   The first two pillars will be supported by the third pillar (enhanced market discipline) which is to be effected through mandatory disclosure of capital related data by banks. A list of core and supplementary disclosure requirements has been set out in the documentation. Banks will be expected to make all relevant information available to supervisory authorities and to the markets. The intention is to allow the markets to self-monitor and discipline poor practice and malpractice. The reflects the two staged (supervisory and market) approach originally developed with regard to derivatives.[1]

1   See paras 21.51–21.55.

Capital comment

21.71   The New Accord proposals contain a number of important initiatives especially with regard to the increased sensitivity of the standardised approach and new use of internal measures as part of the IRB options.

Supervisory review should ensure that capital compliance is more effective within individual institutions and that national authorities secure that all banks have necessary systems and controls in place. The only danger is that it may be interpreted as being capital specific rather than more general in scope and effect. Enhanced disclosure is also to be welcomed provided that proper allowance is made for sensitive or proprietary information resources. Subject to these reservations, this should generally improve transparency within supervisory and market practice.[1]

Market discipline should also be improved although the extent of this may be more limited than many expect, at least, initially in light of the complex and specialist nature of the disclosures to be made.[2]

1   For further comment, see Chapter 15, paras 15.128–15.135.
2   For the most recent progress on this work, see www.bis.org.

FINANCIAL STABILITY FORUM

Asian crisis

21.72   A number of related regulatory initiatives have been adopted in response to the Asian Financial Crisis which began with the collapse of the Thai baht on 2 July 1997.

While the crisis arose as a result of a combination of complex national and international circumstances, two of the common underlying aggravating factors were (i) exceptionally high levels of bank credit in a number of the new Asian economies, as well as (ii) underlying poor loan practices and weak bank supervision.[1] There had also been a massive inflow of investment from Western financial institutions but only of a short-term nature.

Following the trigger of currency crisis, a number of economies suffered significant damage with the removal of vast amounts of foreign capital and with the absence of any alternative short-term liquidity sources. Significant loss was consequently suffered in such countries as the Republic of Korea, Singapore and Taiwan as well as the newly industrialised countries of Indonesia, Malaysia and Thailand.

1   See Walker, *International Banking Regulation – Law, Policy and Practice* (2001), Ch 5.

21.73 Apart from the local damage inflicted, the significance of the Asian Crisis was that the contagion spread regionally and then globally with stock market prices in Hong Kong, London and New York being effected. The overall result was an increased realisation by all countries of the strength of the inherent interconnections and interdependence that had been created in the new global economy. This clear threat of global contagion meant that a new global response had to be constructed.

While this has variously been referred to as a new architecture or new international framework, the institutional nature of this reform has been limited. The earlier Interim Committee of the International Monetary Fund was reconstituted as the Monetary and Financial Committee. A separate G22 (originally G20 and then GX) was set up to provide representation for the emerging and newly industrialised countries.

The Financial Stability Forum has also most recently been set up although this is again more of an investigative and advisory body which draws together existing fora rather than creates any new formal institutional governance framework for the new global economy.

Establishment

21.74 The Financial Stability Forum (FSF) was set up by the G7 countries in February 1999. This followed a Report by Hans Teietmeyer on International Financial Markets Supervision.[1]

The objectives of the FSF are to assess vulnerabilities affecting the international financial system, to identify and oversee action needed to address these dangers and to improve co-ordination and information exchange between all of the authorities responsible for financial stability. Early meetings were held in Washington in April during 1999 with subsequent meetings being held in a number of other financial centres since.

The FSF generally meets twice a year although separate meetings are held through its subsidiary groups.[2]

1 See Teietmeyer, *International Cooperation and Coordination in the Area of Financial Market Supervision and Surveillance* (11 February 1999). For Comment, see Walker, 'Working Groups and Global Standards' FT-FRR (October 1999), p 1.
2 See Walker, 'A New Beginning,' FRR (April 1999), p 1; Walker, 'Working Groups and Global Standards' FRR (October 1999), p 1; and Walker, 'The New Global Rule Book' FRR (November 1999), p 1. See also Walker, *International Banking Regulation – Law, Policy and Practice* (2001), Ch 5, Sections 3, 4 and 5.

Membership

21.75 The membership of the FSF is principally made up of three representatives from each of the G7 countries. These generally include the head of the Treasury or Finance Ministry, the Central Bank Governor and head of the supervisory agency (if separate).

Two representatives attend from the Basel Committee, IOSCO and the IAIS. One representative is sent by the Basel Committee on Payment and Settlement Systems (CPSS), the Committee on the Financial System (CGFS) and one again from the IMF, the World Bank and the Organization for Economic Cooperation & Development (OECD).

Membership is accordingly structured to provide expert contribution by senior finance, central bank and national supervisory personnel as well as additional technical input from all of the main international sector as well as the International Financial Institutions.

Although the core membership is limited in terms of geographic spread, the FSF has deliberately extended this through its working and other subgroups.

Working groups

21.76 The FSA had originally set up three working groups on Highly Leveraged Institutions (HLIs), Capital Flows (CFs) and Offshore Financial Centres (OFCs). Each of these has since reported with further follow-up work having been conducted by the OFC group.[1]

The FSF has also set up two task forces on deposit protection and standards implementation which have produced further interim and final reports.

Follow-up work has also been conducted by the task force on implementation. This has, in particular, developed a number of recommendations on the promotion of standards adoption through a range of official and market incentives.[2]

1 See www.fsforum.org. For comment, see GA Walker, 'Hedge Funds' FRR (May 1999), p 1; Walker, 'Offshore Financial Centres,' FRR (July 2000), p 1; and Walker, 'Global Capital Flows' FRR (June 2000).
2 For comment, see Walker, 'Standards Implementation' FRR (June 2000), p 1; and Walker, 'Implementation Review' FRR (Nov 2000), pp 3–10 .

Compendium of Standards

21.77 The work of the FSF has generally been based on disclosure, standards and training. While this has generally involved the FSF supporting other initiatives in connection with disclosure and training, its main contribution has been in drawing together a number of the key papers in a wide range of financial areas.[1] This has resulted in the production of a Compendium of Standards which effectively constitutes a global financial rulebook. The Compendium consists of a number of the main standards papers produced by each of the principle sector and other international forums.

The Compendium is divided into a number of areas including policy transparency, sector supervision and regulation, disclosure, corporate governance, audit and accounting practices as well as payment and settlement. Each of the main technical sector committees and the IMF, the OECD and the audit and accounting associations were invited to submit the most relevant standards in each of these areas. The result was the production of a single set of requirements consisting of more than 42 separate standards papers.[2] While this originally only existed in an online or virtual (hypertext mark-up language (html)) format, the FSF has since produced a print volume.

Within these main global standards, the FSF has also identified 12 key standards for priority implementation. Implementation is again to be effected in accordance with the recommendations of the Task Force on implementation.

1 See Walker, 'The New Global Rule Book', FRR (November 1999), p 1.

2 See also Walker, *International Banking Regulation – Law, Policy and Practice* (2001), Ch 5, Section 6. See www.fsforum.org for the most recent full listing.

Institutional and regulatory comment

21.78 The establishment of the FSF has been significant in creating a new cross-interest (political, central bank and supervisory) as well as cross-sector (banking, securities and insurance) and cross-issue discussion device. This has allowed all of the potential difficulties that effect the stability and effective operation of international financial markets to be drawn together into a single framework and response. The FSF has also been of value in producing three (and then five) papers in such key areas of concern as hedge funds (highly leveraged institutions or HLIs), capital flows and off-shore financial centres (OFCs) as well as deposit protection and standards implementation. It has also assisted in the development of more effective general disclosure and training programmes and similar arrangements at the international level.

21.79 The most significant contribution of the FSF has probably been the production of the Compendium of Standards. This effectively creates a new global rulebook for financial market control. In developing this, the FSF has been able to identify many potential sources of instability and crisis and to draw together the main recommendations of all of the relevant committees, agencies and other bodies to try to develop a more integrated and effective response. In this way, rather than create a new formal institutional structure at the international level, the FSF has been able to draw together all of the existing participants into a new more co-operative and integrated framework. The quantity and quality of the work produced has then been significantly improved while the underlying G7 political base has added further impetus to the reception and application of the standards developed.

21.80 It would probably be an exaggeration to claim that a new formal international architecture has been constructed post-Asia. A revised set of closer and more effective operational relations has been set up between all relevant international agencies and important work carried out in the identification of potential sources of crisis and the construction of appropriate new regulatory responses. The treatment of previously disparate issues together for the first time has also allowed the construction of a more complete and coherent substantive body of regulatory provisions than has ever been possible before. The basis for a new global control programme has accordingly been produced. The main operational omission that remains is securing full and effective implementation of all of the relevant standards developed in all countries. It is in this area, that work must continue.

Appendix

Secondary legislation related to the Financial Services and Markets Act 2000

The following is a list of statutory instruments related to the regulation of financial services through the Financial Services and Markets Act 2000. The documents are ordered by the date of laying.

STATUTORY INSTRUMENTS

Orders 2002

SI 2002/2015: Electronic Commerce Directive (Financial Services and Markets) (Amendment) Regulations 2002

SI 2002/2157: Financial Services and Markets Act 2000 (Financial Promotion) (Amendment) (Electronic Commerce Directive) Order 2002

SI 2002/2013: Electronic Commerce (EC Directive) Regulations 2002

SI 2002/1777: Financial Services and Markets Act 2000 (Commencement of Mortgage Regulation) (Amendment) Order 2002

SI 2002/1776: Financial Services and Markets Act 2000 (Regulated Activities) (Amendment) (No 2) Order 2002

SI 2002/1775: Electronic Commerce Directive (Financial Services and Markets) Regulations 2002

SI 2002/1555: Financial Services and Markets Act 2000 (Consequential Amendments) Order 2002

SI 2002/1501: Financial Services and Markets Act 2000 (Consequential Amendments and Transitional Provisions) (Credit Unions) Order 2002

SI 2002/1409: Financial Services and Markets Act 2000 (Consequential Amendments) (Taxes) Order 2002

SI 2002/1310: Financial Services and Markets Act 2000 (Financial Promotion and Miscellaneous Amendments) Order 2002

SI 2002/1242: Financial Services and Markets Act 2000 (Administration Orders Relating to Insurers) Order 2002

SI 2002/765: Financial Services and Markets Act 2000, Banks and Banking, Electronic Money (Miscellaneous Amendments) Regulations 2002

SI 2002/704: Financial Services and Markets Act 2000 (Permission and Applications) (Credit Unions etc) Order 2002

SI 2002/682: Financial Services and Markets Act 2000 (Regulated Activities) (Amendment) Order 2002

Orders 2001

SI 2001/3816: Rehabilitation of Offenders Act 1974 (Exceptions) (Amendment) (No 2) Order 2001

SI 2001/3801: Financial Services and Markets Act 2000 (Consequential Amendments) (No 2) Order 2001

SI 2001/3800: Financial Services and Markets Act 2000 (Financial Promotion) (Amendment No 2) Order 2001

SI 2001/3771: Financial Services and Markets Act 2000 (Scope of Permission Notices) Order 2001

SI 2001/3729: Friendly Societies Act 1974 (Seal of the Financial Services Authority) Regulations 2001

SI 2001/3681: Financial Services and Markets Act 2000 (Prescribed Markets and Qualifying Investments) (Amendment) Order 2001

SI 2001/3650: Financial Services and Markets Act 2000 (Miscellaneous Provisions) Order 2001

SI 2001/3649: Financial Services and Markets Act 2000 (Consequential Amendments and Repeals) Order 2001

SI 2001/3648: Financial Services and Markets Act 2000 (Confidential Information) (Bank of England) (Consequential Provisions) Order 2001

SI 2001/3647: Financial Services and Markets Act 2000 (Consequential Amendments and Savings) (Industrial Assurance) Order 2001

SI 2001/3646: Financial Services and Markets Act 2000 (Transitional Provisions and Savings) (Information Requirements and Investigations) Order 2001

SI 2001/3645: Financial Services and Markets Act 2000 (Misleading Statements and Practices) Order 2001

SI 2001/3640: Financial Services and Markets Act 2000 (Savings, Modifications and Consequential Provisions) (Rehabilitation of Offenders) (Scotland) Order 2001

SI 2001/3639: Financial Services and Markets Act 2000 (Transitional Provisions and Savings) (Business Transfers) Order 2001

SI 2001/3635: Insurers (Winding Up) Rules 2001

SI 2001/3634: Bankruptcy (Financial Services and Markets Act 2000) Rules 2001

SI 2001/3633: Financial Services and Markets Tribunal (Legal Assistance Scheme – Costs) Regulations 2001

SI 2001/3632: Financial Services and Markets Tribunal (Legal Assistance) Regulations 2001

SR 2001/400 Rehabilitation of Offenders (Exceptions) (Amendment) (No 2) Order (Northern Ireland) 2001

SI 2001/3626: Financial Services and Markets Act 2000 (Control of Transfers of Business Done at Lloyd's) Order 2001

SI 2001/3625: Financial Services and Markets Act 2000 (Control of Business Transfers) (Requirements on Applicants) Regulations 2001

SI 2001/3624: Financial Services and Markets Act 2000 (Disclosure of Confidential Information) (Amendment) (No 2) Regulations 2001

SI 2001/3623: Financial Services and Markets Act 2000 (Exemption) (Amendment) Order 2001

SI 2001/3592: Financial Services and Markets Act 2000 (Transitional Provisions) (Partly Completed Procedures) Order 2001

SI 2001/3591: Bankruptcy (Financial Services and Markets Act 2000) (Scotland) Rules 2001

SI 2001/3582: Financial Services and Markets Act 2000 (Dissolution of the Board of Banking Supervision) (Transitional Provisions) Order 2001

SI 2001/3544: Financial Services and Markets Act 2000 (Regulated Activities) (Amendment) Order 2001

SI 2001/3542: Financial Services and Markets Act 2000 (Law Applicable to Contracts of Insurance) (Amendment) Regulations 2001

SI 2001/3439: Financial Services and Markets Act 2000 (Official Listing of Securities) (Amendment) Regulations 2001

SI 2001/3538: Financial Services and Markets Act 2000 (Commencement No 7) Order 2001

SI 2001/3437: Financial Services and Markets Act 2000 (Disclosure of Confidential Information) (Amendment) Regulations 2001

SI 2001/3436: Financial Services and Markets Act 2000 (Commencement No 6) Order 2001

SI 2001/3374: Financial Services and Markets Act 2000 (Interim Permissions) Order 2001

SI 2001/3338: Financial Services and Markets Act 2000 (Controllers) (Exemption) (No 2) Order 2001

SI 2001/3084: Financial Services and Markets Act 2000 (Gibraltar) Order 2001

SI 2001/3083: Financial Services and Markets Act 2000 (Transitional Provisions and Savings) (Civil Remedies, Discipline, Criminal Offences etc) (No 2) Order 2001

SI 2001/2968: Financial Services and Markets Act 2000 (Treatment of Assets of Insurers on Winding Up) Regulations 2001

SI 2001/2967: Financial Services and Markets Act 2000 (Transitional Provisions, Repeals and Savings) (Financial Services Compensation Scheme) Order 2001

SI 2001/2966: Financial Services and Markets Act 2000 (Consequential Amendments) (Pre-Commencement Modifications) Order 2001

SI 2001/2958: Financial Services and Markets Act 2000 (Offers of Securities) Order 2001

SI 2001/2957: Financial Services and Markets Act 2000 (Official Listing of Securities) (Transitional Provisions) Order 2001

SI 2001/2956: Financial Services and Markets Act 2000 (Official Listing of Securities) Regulations 2001

SI 2001/2955: Public Offers of Securities (Exemptions) Regulations 2001

SI 2001/2659: Financial Services and Markets Act 2000 (Consequential and Transitional Provisions) (Miscellaneous) (No 2) Order 2001

SI 2001/2657: Financial Services and Markets Act 2000 (Transitional Provisions and Savings) (Civil Remedies, Discipline, Criminal Offences etc) Order 2001

SI 2001/2639: Financial Services and Markets Act 2000 (Own-initiative Power) (Overseas Regulators) Regulations 2001

SI 2001/2638: Financial Services and Markets Act 2000 (Controllers) (Exemption) Order 2001

SI 2001/2637: Financial Services and Markets Act 2000 (Transitional Provisions) (Controllers) Order 2001

SI 2001/2636: Financial Services and Markets Act 2000 (Transitional Provisions) (Authorised Persons etc) Order 2001

SI 2001/2635: Financial Services and Markets Act 2000 (Law Applicable to Contracts of Insurance) Regulations 2001

SI 2001/2634: Financial Services and Markets Act 2000 (Insolvency) (Definition of Insurer) Order 2001

SI 2001/2633: Financial Services and Markets Act 2000 (Financial Promotion) (Amendment) Order 2001

SI 2001/2632: Financial Services and Markets Act 2000 (Commencement No 5) Order 2001

SI 2001/2617: Financial Services and Markets Act 2000 (Mutual Societies) Order 2001

SI 2001/2587: Financial Services and Markets Act 2000 (Communications by Auditors) Regulations 2001

SI 2001/2512: Financial Services and Markets Act 2000 (Transitional Provisions) (Reviews of Pensions Business) Order 2001

SI 2001/2511: Financial Services and Markets Act 2000 (EEA Passport Rights) Regulations 2001

SI 2001/2510: Financial Services and Markets Act 2000 (Gaming Contracts) Order 2001

SI 2001/2509: Financial Services and Markets Act 2000 (Consultation with Competent Authorities) Regulations 2001

SI 2001/2508: Financial Services and Markets Act 2000 (Appointed Representatives) (Amendment) Regulations 2001

SI 2001/2507: Financial Services and Markets Act 2000 (Variation of Threshold Conditions) Order 2001

SI 2001/2476: Financial Services and Markets Tribunal Rules 2001

SI 2001/2383: Financial Services and Markets Act 2000 (Collective Investment Schemes Constituted in Other EEA States) Regulations 2001

SI 2001/2364: Financial Services and Markets Act 2000 (Commencement No 4 and Transitional Provision) Order 2001

SI 2001/2361: Financial Services and Markets Act 2000 (Meaning of Policy and Policyholder) Order 2001

SI 2001/2326: Financial Services and Markets Act 2000 (Transitional Provisions) (Ombudsman Scheme and Complaints Scheme) Order 2001

SI 2001/2256: Financial Services and Markets Act 2000 (Rights of Action) Regulations 2001

SI 2001/2255: Financial Services and Markets Act 2000 (Transitional Provisions) (Designated Date for The Securities and Futures Authority) Order 2001

SI 2001/2188: Financial Services and Markets Act 2000 (Disclosure of Confidential Information) Regulations 2001

SI 2001/1858: Financial Services and Markets Act 2000 (Competition Information) (Specification of Enactment etc) Order 2001

SI 2001/1857: Financial Services and Markets Act 2001 (Disclosure of Information by Prescribed Persons) Regulations 2001

SI 2001/1821: Financial Services and Markets Act 2000 (Consequential and Transitional Provisions) (Miscellaneous) Order 2001

SI 2001/1820/c.62: Financial Services and Markets Act 2000 (Commencement No 3) Order 2001

SI 2001/1819: Financial Services and Markets Act 2000 (Regulations Relating to Money Laundering) Regulations 2001

SI 2001/1783: Financial Services and Markets Act 2000 (Compensation Scheme: Electing Participants) Regulations 2001

SI 2001/1534: Financial Services and Markets Act 2000 (Transitional Provisions and Savings) (Rules) Order 2001

SI 2001/1420: Financial Services and Markets Act 2000 (Service of Notices) Regulations 2001

SI 2001/1376: Financial Services (EEA Passport Rights) Regulations 2001

SI 2001/1335: Financial Services and Markets Act 2000 (Financial Promotion) Order 2001

SI 2001/1283: Financial Services and Markets Act 2000 (Dissolution of the Insurance Brokers Registration Council) (Consequential Provisions) Order 2001

SI 2001/1282: Financial Services and Markets Act 2000 (Commencement No 2) Order 2001

SI 2001/1228: Open-Ended Investment Companies Regulations 2001

SI 2001/1227: Financial Services and Markets Act 2000 (Professions – Non-Exempt Activities) Order 2001

SI 2001/1226: Financial Services and Markets Act 2000 (Designated Professional Bodies) Order 2001

SI 2001/1217: Financial Services and Markets Act 2000 (Appointed Representatives) Regulations 2001

SI 2001/1201: Financial Services and Markets Act 2000 (Exemption) Order 2001

SI 2001/1177: Financial Services and Markets Act 2000 (Carrying on Regulated Activities by Way of Business) Order 2001

SI 2001/1062: Financial Services and Markets Act 2000 (Collective Investment Schemes) Order 2001

SI 2001/1060: Financial Services and Markets Act 2000 (Promotion of Collective Investment Schemes) Exemptions Order 2001

SI 2001/996: Financial Services and Markets Act 2000 (Prescribed Markets and Qualifying Investments) Order 2001

SI 2001/995: Financial Services and Markets Act 2000 (Recognition Requirements for Investment Exchanges and Clearing Houses) Regulations 2001

SI 2001/544: Financial Services and Markets Act 2000 (Regulated Activities) Order 2001

SI 2001/516: Financial Services and Markets Act 2000 (Commencement No 1) Order 2001

Orders 2000

SI 2000/2952: Banking Consolidation Directive (Consequential Amendments) Regulations 2000

SI 2000/1734: Financial Services and Markets (Transitional Provisions) (Designated Date for Certain Self-Regulating Organisations) Order 2000

Index